# Exploring C++

## The Programmer's Introduction to C++

Ray Lischner

Apress®

**Exploring C++: The Programmer's Introduction to C++**

**Copyright © 2009 by Ray Lischner**

ISBN-13 (pbk): 978-1-59059-749-1

ISBN-10 (pbk): 1-59059-749-4

ISBN-13 (electronic): 978-1-4302-1895-1

Printed and bound in the United States of America 9 8 7 6 5 4 3 2 1

Trademarked names may appear in this book. Rather than use a trademark symbol with every occurrence of a trademarked name, we use the names only in an editorial fashion and to the benefit of the trademark owner, with no intention of infringement of the trademark.

Lead Editor: Matthew Moodie
Technical Reviewer: Francis Glassborow
Editorial Board: Clay Andres, Steve Anglin, Mark Beckner, Ewan Buckingham, Tony Campbell,
    Gary Cornell, Jonathan Gennick, Michelle Lowman, Matthew Moodie, Jeffrey Pepper,
    Frank Pohlmann, Ben Renow-Clarke, Dominic Shakeshaft, Matt Wade, Tom Welsh
Project Manager: Richard Dal Porto
Copy Editor: Octal Publishing, Inc.
Associate Production Director: Kari Brooks-Copony
Production Editor: Ellie Fountain
Compositor: Dina Quan
Proofreaders: Lisa Hamilton and Linda Seifert
Indexer: John Collin
Cover Designer: Kurt Krames
Manufacturing Director: Tom Debolski

Distributed to the book trade worldwide by Springer-Verlag New York, Inc., 233 Spring Street, 6th Floor, New York, NY 10013. Phone 1-800-SPRINGER, fax 201-348-4505, e-mail orders-ny@springer-sbm.com, or visit http://www.springeronline.com.

For information on translations, please contact Apress directly at 2855 Telegraph Avenue, Suite 600, Berkeley, CA 94705. Phone 510-549-5930, fax 510-549-5939, e-mail info@apress.com, or visit http://www.apress.com.

Apress and friends of ED books may be purchased in bulk for academic, corporate, or promotional use. eBook versions and licenses are also available for most titles. For more information, reference our Special Bulk Sales–eBook Licensing web page at http://www.apress.com/info/bulksales.

The source code for this book is available to readers at http://www.apress.com. You may need to answer questions pertaining to this book in order to successfully download the code.

# Contents at a Glance

# PART 2 ▪▪▪ Custom Types

# PART 3 ▪▪▪ Generic Programming

# PART 4 ■■■ Real Programming

# Contents

## PART 1 ■■■ The Basics

# PART 2 ■ ■ ■ Custom Types

# PART 3 ■■■ Generic Programming

# PART 4 ■■■ Real Programming

# About the Author

**RAY LISCHNER** is the author of *C++ in a Nutshell* and other books. He has been programming for over three decades, using languages as diverse as Algol, APL, Bash, C, C++, COBOL, csh, DCL, Delphi, Eiffel, Fortran, Haskell, Icon, Java, LISP, Pascal, Perl, PHP, PL/I, Python, Ruby, Scheme, Smalltalk, and a variety of assemblers.

In the years after he graduated from Caltech (in the mid-1980s), Ray worked as a software developer on both coasts of the United States, with stops in between. He has worked at companies big and small: from start-ups to Fortune 500. Not so very long ago, he decided to escape from the corporate rat race. Due to a minor error in timing, he quit before he figured out how to pay for such trivialities as food and shelter. Undaunted, he persevered and soon discovered writing as a means to keep the creditors at bay.

Ray has always enjoyed teaching. While his wife completed her Ph.D. in physics, he occupied his time teaching computer science at Oregon State University. Dissatisfied with the traditional introductory computer science curriculum, he revamped the first programming course and introduced novel lecture and teaching techniques. He pioneered interactive teaching labs—the genesis of this book.

Today, Ray lives in Maryland with his wife and two children. Ray has returned to full-time work as a software developer at Proteus Technologies, where he is the resident C++ expert. Writing has become a part-time endeavor. When he isn't working, Ray has a variety of other part-time, unpaid jobs: chef, taxi driver, house cleaner, arbitrator, soccer coach, banker, tooth fairy, story reader, and chief enforcer of the domestic nocturnal preparation procedure, just to name a few.

The best way to contact Ray is via email to `exploring@cpphelp.com`.

# About the Technical Reviewer

**FRANCIS GLASSBOROW** read Mathematics at Merton College, Oxford. He spent 25 years teaching mathematics and computing studies to teenagers. Ill health forced him to retire from teaching. In 1989 he became editor of C Vu (ACCU's principal journal) which job/office he held until 2002. He was chair of ACCU throughout the 1990s. He was a regular columnist for .EXE magazine (a UK developers magazine) from 1991 until it ceased publication in August 2000. He was chair of the annual ACCU conference for seven years. He has been an active member of the BSI panels for C and C++ since 1991 and is a regular member of the BSI delegations to SC22/WG21 (ISO C++) and SC22/WG14 (ISO C) and is frequently HoD for these meetings. He is the author of *You Can Do It!*, an introduction for novice programmers, and *You Can Program in C++*, an introduction to C++ for those who can already program.

# Acknowledgments

This book has been more difficult and time consuming than any of my previous books. I appreciate beyond words the patience of Apress and the staff who helped bring this project to fruition: particularly Matthew Moodie and Richard Dal Porto.

I am especially grateful to my Technical Reviewer, Francis Glassborow, whose deep knowledge of C++ has saved me from mistakes big and small. If any technical errors remain, no doubt I introduced them too late in the editing cycle for Francis to spot them.

Most of all, I thank my wife, Cheryl, whose support and encouragement sustained me when I lacked the strength to carry on. I also thank my children who put up with days and evenings without me while I finished this book. I love you all.

Finally, I thank the scientists and doctors who have worked miracles in the treatment of rheumatoid arthritis, permitting me to continue to work, write, and play.

# Introduction

**H**i, there. Thank you for reading my book, *Exploring C++*. My name is Ray, and I'll be your author today. And tomorrow. And the day after that. We'll be together for quite a while, so why don't you pull up a chair and get comfortable. My job is to help you learn C++. To do that, I have written a series of lessons, called *explorations*. Each exploration is an interactive exercise that helps you learn C++ one step at a time. Your job is to complete the explorations, and in so doing, learn C++.

No doubt you have already leafed through the book a little bit. If not, do so now. Notice that this book is different from most books. Most programming books are little more than written lectures. The author tells you stuff and expects you to read the stuff, learn it, and understand it.

This book is different. I don't see much point in lecturing at you. That's not how people learn best. You learn programming by reading, modifying, and writing programs. To that end, I've organized this book so that you spend as much time as possible reading, modifying, and writing programs.

## How to Use This Book

Each exploration in this book is a mixture of text and interactive exercises. The exercises are unlike anything you've seen in other books. Instead of multiple choice, fill-in-the-blank, or simple Q&A exercises, my lessons are interactive explorations of key C++ features. Early in the book, I will give you complete programs to work with. As you learn more C++, you will modify and extend programs. Pretty soon, you will write entire programs on your own.

By "interactive," I mean that I ask questions and you answer them. I do my best to respond to your answers throughout the lesson text. It sounds crazy, but by answering the questions, you will be learning C++. To help ensure you answer the questions, I leave space in this book for you to write your answers. I'm giving you permission to write in this book (unless you are borrowing the book from a library or friend). In fact, I encourage you to write all your answers in the book. Only by answering the questions will you learn the material properly.

Sometimes, the questions have no right answer. I pose the question to make you ponder it, perhaps to look at a familiar topic from a new perspective. Other times, the question has an unambiguous, correct answer. I always give the answer in the subsequent text, so don't skip ahead! Write your answer before you continue reading. Then and only then can you check your answer. Some questions are tricky or require information that I have not yet presented. In such cases, I expect your answer to be wrong, but that's okay. Don't worry. I won't be grading you. (If you are using this book as part of a formal class, your teacher should grade this book's exercises solely on whether you complete them, and never on whether your answer was correct. The teacher will have other exercises, quizzes, and tests to assess your progress in the class.) And no fair looking ahead and writing down the "correct" answer. You don't learn anything that way.

Ready? Let's practice.

**What is your most important task when reading this book?**

_____

_____

_____

This question does not have a single correct answer, but it does have a number of demonstrably wrong answers. I hope you wrote something similar to, "Completing every exercise" or "Understanding all the material." Another good answer is, "Having fun."

# The Book's Organization

C++ is a complicated language. To write even the most trivial program requires an understanding of many disparate aspects of the language. The language does not lend itself to neat compartmentalization into broad topics, such as functions, classes, statements, or expressions. This book, therefore, does not attempt such an organization. Instead, you learn C++ in small increments: a little bit of this, a little bit of that, some more of this, and pretty soon you will have accumulated enough knowledge to start writing nontrivial programs.

Roughly speaking, the book starts with basic expressions, declarations, and statements that are sufficient to work with simple programs. You learn how to use the standard library early in the book. Next, you learn to write your own functions, to write your own classes, to write your own templates, and then to write fairly sophisticated programs.

You won't be an expert, however, when you finish this book. You will need much more practice, more exposure to the breadth and depth of the language and library, and more practice. You will also need more practice. And some more. You get the idea.

# Who Should Read This Book

Read this book if you want to learn C++ and you already know at least one other programming language. You don't need to know a specific language or technology, however. In particular, you don't need to know C, nor do you need to know anything about object-oriented programming.

The C programming language influenced the design of many other languages, from PHP to Perl to AWK to C#, not to mention C++. As a result, many programmers who do not know C or C++ nonetheless find many language constructs hauntingly familiar. You might even feel confident enough to skip sections of this book that seem to cover old ground. Don't do that! From the start, the lessons present language features that are unique to C++. In a few, isolated cases, I will tell you when it is safe to skip a section, and only that section. Even when a language feature is familiar, it might have subtle issues that are unique to C++.

The trap is most perilous for C programmers because C++ bears the greatest superficial similarity with C. C programmers, therefore, have the most to overcome. By design, many C programs are also valid C++ programs, leading the unwary C programmer into the trap of thinking that good C programs are also good C++ programs. In fact, C and C++ are distinct languages, each with their own idioms and idiosyncrasies. To become an effective C++ programmer, you must learn the C++ way of programming. C programmers need to break some of their established habits and learn to avoid certain C features (such as arrays) in favor of better C++ idioms. The structure of this book helps you get started thinking in terms of C++, not C.

# Projects

This book also contains four projects. The projects are opportunities to apply what you have learned. Each project is a realistic endeavor, based on the amount of C++ covered up to that point. I encourage you to try every project. Design your project using your favorite software design techniques. Remember to write test cases in addition to the source code. Do your best to make the code clean and readable, in addition to correct. After you are confident that your solution is finished, download the files from the book's web site, and compare your solution with mine.

# Work Together

You can use this book alone, teaching yourself C++, or a teacher might adopt this book as a textbook for a formal course. You can also work with a partner. It's more fun to work with friends, and you'll learn more and faster by working together. Each of you needs your own copy of the book. Read the lessons and do the work on your own. If you have questions, discuss them with your partner, but answer the exercises on your own. Then compare answers with your partner. If your answers are different, discuss your reasoning. See if you can agree on a single answer before proceeding.

Work on the projects together. Maybe you can divide the work into two (or more) modules. Maybe one person codes and the other person checks. Maybe you'll practice some form of pair programming. Do whatever works best for you, but make sure you understand every line of code in the project. If you have asymmetric roles, be sure to swap roles for each project. Give everyone a chance to do everything.

# For More Information

This book cannot teach you everything you need to know about C++. No single book can. After you finish this book, I encourage you to continue to read and write C++ programs, and to seek out other sources of information. To help guide you, this book has a dedicated web site, `http://cpphelp.com/exploring/`. The web site has links to other books, other web sites, mailing lists, newsgroups, FAQs, compilers, other tools, and more. You can also download all the source code for this book, so you can save yourself some typing.

# Why Explorations?

In case you were wondering about the unusual nature of this book, rest assured that, "though this be madness, yet there is method in't."

The method is an approach to teaching and writing that I developed while I was teaching computer science at Oregon State University. I wanted to improve the quality of my teaching, so I investigated research into learning and knowledge, especially scientific knowledge, and in particular, computer programming.

To summarize several decades of research: everyone constructs mental models of the world. We acquire knowledge by adding information to our models. The new information must always be in concert with the model. Sometimes, however, new information contradicts the model. In that case, we must adjust our models to accommodate the new information. Our brains are always at work, always taking in new information, always adjusting our mental models to fit.

As a result of this research, the emphasis in the classroom has shifted from teachers to students. In the past, teachers considered students to be empty vessels, waiting to be filled from the fount of the teacher's knowledge and wisdom. Students were passive recipients of information. Now we know better. Students are not passive, but active. Even when their outward appearance suggests otherwise, their brains are always at work, always absorbing new information and fitting that information into their mental models. The teacher's responsibility has changed from being the source of all wisdom to being an indirect manager of mental models. The teacher cannot manage those models directly, but can only create classroom situations in which students have the opportunity to adjust their own models.

Although the research has focused on teachers, the same applies to authors.

In other words, I cannot teach you C++, but I can create explorations that enable you to learn C++. Explorations are not the only way to apply research to learning and writing, but they are a technique that I have refined over several years of teaching and have found successful. Explorations work because

- They force you to participate actively in the learning process. It's too easy to read a book passively. The questions force you to confront new ideas and to fit them into your mental model. If you skip the questions, you might also skip a crucial addition to your model.

- They are small, so your model grows in easy steps. If you try to grasp too much new information at once, you are likely to incorporate incorrect information into your model. The longer that misinformation festers, the harder it will be to correct. I want to make sure your model is as accurate as possible at all times.

- They build on what you know. I don't toss out new concepts with the vain hope that you will automatically grasp them. Instead, I tie new concepts to old ones. I do my best to ensure that every concept has a strong anchor in your existing mental model.

- They help you learn by doing. Instead of spending the better part of a chapter reading how someone else solves a problem, you spend as much time as possible working hands-on with a program: modifying existing programs and writing new programs.

C++ is a complicated language, and learning C++ is not easy. In any group of C++ programmers, even simple questions can often provoke varied responses. Most C++ programmers' mental models of the language are not merely incomplete, but are flawed, sometimes in fundamental ways. My hope is that I can provide you with a solid foundation in C++, so that you can write interesting and correct programs, and most importantly, so that you can continue to learn and enjoy C++ for many years to come.

# The C++ Standard

This book covers the current standard, namely, ISO/IEC 14882:2003 (E), *Programming languages — C++*. The 2003 edition of the standard is a bug-fix edition, containing corrections to and clarifications of the original 1998 edition. Most modern compilers do a decent job of conforming to the standard.

The standardization committee has also issued an addendum to the standard, adding regular expressions, mathematical functions, and a lot more. This addendum is an optional extension to the standard library called Technical Report 1, or TR1. Because it is optional, vendors are not required to implement it. Most vendors provide at least part of the library. A few implement TR1 in its entirety. You do not need TR1 support to use this book, but I point out a few cases where TR1 makes your life a little easier.

By issuing TR1 and having thousands of C++ developers use it, the standardization committee gained valuable practical experience to feed back into the next major revision of the C++ standard. Work on the next revision is underway as I write this. Depending on when you read this, their work may be complete. You may even have a compiler and library that conforms to the new release of the standard, which will likely be labeled ISO/IEC 14882:2010 (E).

Even if you have a brand new compiler, this book still has value. Many of the new features are advanced so they don't affect this book. Other planned features impact C++ programmers of all levels and abilities. I point out the proposed changes throughout this book, but keep my focus on the tools that are available and in widespread use today.

# PART 1

■ ■ ■

# The Basics

# EXPLORATION 1

■■■

# Honing Your Tools

**B**efore you begin your exploration of the C++ landscape, you need to gather some basic supplies: a text editor, a C++ compiler, a linker, and a debugger. You can acquire these tools separately or bundled, possibly as a package deal with an integrated development environment (IDE). Options abound regardless of your platform, operating system, and budget.

If you are taking a class, the teacher will provide the tools or dictate which tools to use. If you are working at an organization that already uses C++, you probably want to use their tools, so you can become familiar with them and their proper use. If you need to acquire your own tools, check out this book's web site, http://cpphelp.com/exploring/. Tool versions and quality change too rapidly to provide details in print form, so you can find up-to-date suggestions on the web site. The following section gives some general advice.

## Ray's Recommendations

C++ is one of the most widely used programming languages in the world: it is second only to C (depending on how you measure "widely used"). Therefore, C++ tools abound for many hardware and software environments and at a wide variety of price points.

You can choose command-line tools, which are especially popular in UNIX and UNIX-like environments, or you can opt for an IDE, which bundles all the tools into a single graphical user interface (GUI). Choose whichever style you find most comfortable. Your programs won't care what tools you use to edit, compile, and link them.

### Microsoft Windows

If you are working with Microsoft Windows, I recommend Microsoft's Visual Studio (be sure that you have a current release). In particular, the venerable Visual C++ 6.0 is obsolete and out-of-date. As I write this, the current release is Visual Studio 2008. If you want a no-cost option, download Visual C++ Express from Microsoft's web site (find a current link at http://cpphelp.com), or for an open source solution, download MinGW, which is a port of the popular GNU compiler to Windows.

Note that C++/CLI is not the same as C++. It is a new language that Microsoft invented to help integrate C++ into the .NET environment. That's why it chose a name that incorporates C++, just as the name C++ derives from the name C. It is, however, a distinct language from C. This book covers standard C++ and nothing else. If you decide to use Visual Studio, take care that you work with C++, not C++/CLI or Managed C++ (the predecessor to C++/CLI).

Visual Studio includes a number of doodads, froufrous, and whatnots that are unimportant for your core task of learning C++. Perhaps you will need to use ATL, MFC, or .NET for your job, but for now, you can ignore all that. All you need is the C++ compiler and standard library.

If you prefer a free (as in speech) solution, the GNU compiler collection is available on Windows. Choose the Cygwin distribution, which includes a nearly complete UNIX-like environment, or MinGW, which is much smaller and might be easier to manage. In both cases, you get a good C++ compiler and library. This book's web site has links with helpful hints on installing and using these tools.

## Macintosh OS 9 and Earlier

If you are stuck using an old Macintosh, download the no-cost Macintosh Programmer's Workbench from Apple's web site (link at `http://cpphelp.com`).

## Everyone Else

I recommend the GNU compiler collection (GCC). The C++ compiler is called g++. Linux and BSD distributions typically come with GCC, but you might need to install the necessary developer packages. Be sure you have a recent release (version 3.4 or later) of GCC.

Mac OS X also uses GCC. For a no-cost IDE, download Xcode from Apple's web site (link at `http://cpphelp.com`).

Some hardware vendors (Sun, HP, etc.) offer a commercial compiler specifically for their hardware. This compiler might offer better optimization than GCC, but might not conform to the C++ standard as well as GCC. At least while you work through the exercises in this book, I recommend GCC. If you already have the vendor's compiler installed and you don't want to bother installing yet another compiler, go ahead and use the vendor's compiler. However, if it ever trips over an example in this book, be prepared to install GCC.

If you are using an Intel hardware platform, Intel's compiler is excellent and available at no cost for noncommercial use. Visit the book's web site for a current link.

If you want to use an IDE, choose from Eclipse, KDevelop, Anjuta, and others (go to `http://cpphelp.com` for an up-to-date list).

# Read the Documentation

Now that you have your tools, take some time to read the product documentation—especially the Getting Started section. Really, I mean it. Look for tutorials and other quick introductions that will help you get up to speed with your tools. If you are using an IDE, you especially need to know how to create simple command-line projects.

IDEs typically require you to create a project, workspace, or some other envelope, or wrapper, before you can actually write a C++ program. You need to know how to do this, and I can't help you because every IDE is different. If you have a choice of project templates, choose "console," "command-line," "terminal," "C++ Tool," or some project with a similar name.

**How long did it take you to read the documentation for your compiler and other tools?**
_____

**Was that too much time, too little time, or just right?** _____

The C++ language is subject to an international standard. Every compiler (more or less) adheres to that standard, but also throws in some nonstandard extras. These extras can be useful—even necessary—for certain projects, but for this book, you need to make sure you use only standard C++. Most compilers can turn off their extensions. Even if you didn't read the documentation before, do so now to find out which options you need to enable to compile standard C++ and only standard C++.

**Write down the options, for future reference.**

_____

_____

_____

You may have missed some of the options; they can be obscure. To help you, Table 1-1 lists the command-line compiler options you need for Microsoft Visual C++ and for g++. This book's web site has suggestions for some other popular compilers. If you are using an IDE, look through the project options or properties to find the equivalents.

**Table 1-1.** *Compiler Options for Standard C++*

| Compiler | Options |
| --- | --- |
| Visual C++ command line | `/EHsc /Za` |
| Visual C++ IDE | Enable C++ exceptions, disable language extensions |
| g++ | `-pedantic -ansi` |

# Your First Program

Now that you have your tools, it's time to start. Fire up your favorite text editor or your C++ IDE and start your first project or create a new file. Name this file `list0101.cpp`, which is short for Listing 1-1. Several different file name extensions are popular for C++ programs. I like to use `.cpp`, where the "p" means "plus." Other common extensions are `.cxx` and `.cc`. Some compilers recognize `.C` (uppercase C) as a C++ file extension, but I don't recommend using it because it is too easy to confuse with `.c` (lowercase c), the default extension for C programs. Many desktop environments do not distinguish between uppercase and lowercase file names, further compounding the problem. Pick your favorite and stick with it. Type in the text contained within Listing 1-1. (With one exception, you can download all the code listings from this book's web site. Listing 1-1 is that exception. I want you to get used to typing C++ code in your text editor.)

**Listing 1-1.** *Your First C++ Program*

```
/// Sort the standard input alphabetically.
/// Read lines of text, sort them, and print the results to the standard output.
/// If the command line names a file, read from that file. Otherwise, read from
/// the standard input. The entire input is stored in memory, so don't try
/// this with input files that exceed available RAM.
```

```cpp
#include <algorithm>
#include <fstream>
#include <iostream>
#include <iterator>
#include <ostream>
#include <string>
#include <vector>

void read(std::istream& in, std::vector<std::string>& text)
{
   std::string line;
   while (std::getline(in, line))
       text.push_back(line);
}

int main(int argc, char* argv[])
{
   // Part 1. Read the entire input into text. If the command line names a file,
   // read that file. Otherwise, read the standard input.
   std::vector<std::string> text; ///< Store the lines of text here
   if (argc < 2)
     read(std::cin, text);
   else
   {
      std::ifstream in(argv[1]);
      if (not in)
      {
         std::perror(argv[1]);
         return EXIT_FAILURE;
      }
      read(in, text);
   }

   // Part 2. Sort the text.
   std::sort(text.begin(), text.end());

   // Part 3. Print the sorted text.
   std::copy(text.begin(), text.end(),
             std::ostream_iterator<std::string>(std::cout, "\n"));
}
```

No doubt, some of this code is gibberish to you. That's okay. The point of this exercise is not to understand C++, but to make sure you can use your tools properly. The comments describe the program, which is a simple sort utility. I could have started with a trivial, "Hello, world" type of program, but that touches only a tiny fraction of the language and library. This program, being slightly more complex, does a better job at revealing possible installation or other problems with your tools.

Now go back and double-check your source code. Make sure you entered everything correctly.

**Did you actually double-check the program?** _____

**Did you find any typos that needed correcting?** _____

To err is human, and there is no shame in typographical errors. We all make them. Go back and recheck your program.

Now compile your program. If you are using an IDE, find the Compile or Build button or menu item. If you are using command-line tools, be sure to link the program, too. For historical (or hysterical) reasons, UNIX tools such as g++ typically produce an executable program named a.out. You should rename it to something more useful, or use the -o option to name an output file. Table 1-2 shows sample command lines to use for Visual C++ and g++.

**Table 1-2.** *Sample Command Lines to Compiler* `list0101.cpp`

| Compiler | Command Line |
| --- | --- |
| Visual C++ | `cl /EHsc /Za list0101.cpp` |
| g++ | `g++ -o list0101 -pedantic -ansi list0101.cpp` |

If you get any errors from the compiler, it means you made a mistake entering the source code; the compiler, linker, or C++ library has not been installed correctly; or the compiler, linker, or library does not conform to the C++ standard and so are unsuitable for use with this book. Triple-check you entered the text correctly. If you are confident that the error lies with the tools and not with you, check the date of publication. If the tools predate 1998, discard them immediately. They predate the standard and therefore, by definition, they cannot conform to the standard. In fact, the quality of C++ tools has improved tremendously in the last few years; so much so that I recommend discarding any tools that predate 2005. If the tools are recent, you might try the old trick of reinstalling them.

If all else fails, try a different set of tools. Download the current release of GCC or Visual Studio Express. You may need to use these tools for this book, even if you must revert to some crusty, rusty, old tools for your job.

Successful compilation is one thing, but successful execution is another. How you invoke the program depends on the operating system. In a GUI environment, you will need a console or terminal window where you can type a command line. You may need to type the complete path to the executable file, or just the program name—again, this depends on your operating system. When you run the program, it reads numbers from the standard input stream, which means whatever you type, the program reads. You then need to notify the program you are done by pressing the magic keystrokes that signal end-of-file. On most UNIX-like operating systems, press Control+D. On Windows, press Control+Z.

Running a console application from an IDE is sometimes tricky. If you aren't careful, the IDE might close the program's window before you have a chance to see any of its output. You need to ensure that the window remains visible. Some IDEs (such as Visual Studio and KDevelop) do this for you automatically, asking you to press a final Enter key before it closes the window.

If the IDE doesn't keep the window open automatically, and you can't find any option or setting to keep the window open, you can force the issue by setting a breakpoint on the program's closing curly brace or the nearest statement where the debugger will let you set a breakpoint.

Knowing how to run the program is one thing; another is to know what numbers to type so you can test the program effectively. **How would you test list0101 to ensure it is running correctly?**

_____

_____

_____

_____

_____

Okay, do it. **Does the program run correctly?** _____

There, that was easy, wasn't it? You should try several different sequences. Run the program with no input at all. Try it with one number. Try it with two that are already in order and two numbers that are in reverse order. Try a lot of numbers, in order. Try a lot of numbers in random order. Try a lot of numbers in reverse order.

Before you finish this Exploration, I have one more exercise. This time, the source file is more complicated. It was written by a professional stunt programmer. Do not attempt to read this program, even with adult supervision. Don't try to make any sense of the program. Above all, don't emulate the programming style used in this program. This exercise is not for you, but for your tools. Its purpose is to see whether your compiler can correctly compile this program and that your library implementation has the necessary parts of the standard library. It's not a severe torture test for a compiler, but it does touch on a few advanced C++ features.

So don't even bother trying to read the code. Just download the file list0102.cpp from the book's web site and try to compile and link it with your tools. (I include the full text of the program only for readers who lack convenient Internet access.) If your compiler cannot compile and run Listing 1-2 correctly, you need to replace it (your compiler, not the program). You may be able to squeak by in the early lessons, but by the end of the book, you will be writing some fairly complicated programs, and you need a compiler that is up to the task. (By the way, Listing 1-2 pretty much does the same thing as Listing 1-1.)

**Listing 1-2.** *Testing Your Compiler*

```
/// Sort the standard input alphabetically.
/// Read lines of text, sort them, and print the results to the standard output.
/// If the command line names a file, read from that file. Otherwise, read from
/// the standard input. The entire input is stored in memory, so don't try
/// this with input files that exceed available RAM.
///
/// Comparison uses a locale named on the command line, or the default, unnamed
/// locale if no locale is named on the command line.

#include <algorithm>
#include <cstdlib>
#include <fstream>
#include <iostream>
```

```
#include <iterator>
#include <locale>
#include <ostream>
#include <string>
#include <vector>

/// Read lines of text from @p in to @p iter. Lines are appended to @p iter.
/// @param in the input stream
/// @param iter an output iterator
template<class Ch, class Tr, class OutIter>
void read(std::basic_istream<Ch,Tr>& in, OutIter iter)
{
    std::basic_string<Ch,Tr> line;
    while (std::getline(in, line))
    {
        *iter = line;
        ++iter;
    }
}

/// Sorter function object.
/// Parameterize the class with the character type used for strings.
/// The sorter object caches a locale and its @c collate facet, to use for
/// comparing strings.
template<typename Ch>
class sorter
{
public:
    /// Construct the sorter object, caching the locale that has the given name.
    /// @param locname The name of the locale to cache.
    sorter(Ch const* locname) :
        loc_(std::locale(locname)),
        collate_(std::use_facet<std::collate<Ch> >(loc_))
    {}
    /// Construct a default sorter object, using the global locale.
    sorter() :
        loc_(std::locale()),
        collate_(std::use_facet<std::collate<Ch> >(loc_))
    {}
    /// Compare for less-than, for use as a comparison predicate with any
    /// standard algorithm.
    /// @param lhs left-hand side operand
    /// @param rhs right-hand side operand
    /// @return true if @p lhs < @p rhs in the given locale, false otherwise
    template<typename Tr>
    bool operator()(const std::basic_string<Ch,Tr>& lhs,
                    const std::basic_string<Ch,Tr>& rhs)
```

```
        {
            return collate_.compare(lhs.data(), lhs.data()+lhs.size(),
                                    rhs.data(), rhs.data()+rhs.size()) < 0;
        }
private:
    std::locale loc_;                    ///< cached locale
    const std::collate<Ch>& collate_;    ///< cached @c collate facet
};


/// Make a sorter object by deducing the template parameter.
/// @param name the locale name to pass to the sorter constructor
/// @return a new sorter object
template<typename Ch>
sorter<Ch> make_sorter(Ch const * name)
{
    return sorter<Ch>(name);
}


/// Main program.
int main(int argc, char* argv[])
try
{
    // Throw an exception if an unrecoverable input error occurs, e.g.,
    // disk failure.
    std::cin.exceptions(std::ios_base::badbit);

    // Part 1. Read the entire input into text. If the command line names a file,
    // read that file. Otherwise, read the standard input.
    std::vector<std::string> text; ///< Store the lines of text here
    if (argc < 2)
        read(std::cin, std::back_inserter(text));
    else
    {
        std::ifstream in(argv[1]);
        if (not in)
        {
            std::perror(argv[1]);              return EXIT_FAILURE;
        }
        read(in, std::back_inserter(text));
    }

    // Part 2. Sort the text. The second command line argument, if present,
    // names a locale, to control the sort order. Without a command line
    // argument, use the default locale (which is obtained from the OS).
    std::sort(text.begin(), text.end(), make_sorter(argc >= 3 ? argv[2] : "" ));
```

```
    // Part 3. Print the sorted text.
    std::copy(text.begin(), text.end(),
              std::ostream_iterator<std::string>(std::cout, "\n"));
}
catch (std::exception& ex)
{
    std::cerr << "Caught exception: " << ex.what() << '\n';
    std::cerr << "Terminating program.\n";
    std::exit(EXIT_FAILURE);
}
catch (...)
{
    std::cerr << "Caught unknown exception type.\nTerminating program.\n";
    std::exit(EXIT_FAILURE);
}
```

I caught you peeking. In spite of my warning, you tried to read the source code, didn't you? Just remember that I deliberately wrote this program in a complicated fashion to test your tools. By the time you finish this book, you will be able to read and understand this program. Even more important, you will be able to write it more simply and more cleanly. Before you can run, however, you must learn to walk. Once you are comfortable working with your tools, it's time to start learning C++. The next Exploration begins your journey with a reading lesson.

■ ■ ■

# Reading C++ Code

I suspect you already have some knowledge of C++. Maybe you already know C, Java, Perl, or other C-like languages. Maybe you know so many languages that you can readily identify common elements. Let's test my hypothesis. Take a few minutes to read Listing 2-1 then answer the questions that follow it.

**Listing 2-1.** *Reading Test*

```
1 /// Read the program and determine what the program does.
2
3 #include <iostream>
4 #include <istream>
5 #include <limits>
6 #include <ostream>
7
8 int main()
9 {
10     int min(std::numeric_limits<int>::max());
11     int max(std::numeric_limits<int>::min());
12     bool any(false);
13     int x;
14     while (std::cin >> x)
15     {
16         any = true;
17         if (x < min)
18             min = x;
19         if (x > max)
20             max = x;
21     }
22
23     if (any)
24         std::cout << "min = " << min << "\nmax = " << max << '\n';
25 }
```

**What does Listing 2-1 do?**

_____

_____

_____

_____

Listing 2-1 reads integers from the standard input and keeps track of the largest and smallest values entered. After exhausting the input, it then prints those values. If the input contains no numbers, the program prints nothing.

Let's take a closer look at the various parts of the program.

# Comments

Line 1 begins with three consecutive slashes to start a comment. The comment ends at the end of the line. Actually, you need only two slashes to signal the start of a comment (//), but as you will learn later in the book, three has a special meaning. For now though, use three.

Note that you cannot put a space between the slashes. That's true in general for all the multicharacter symbols in C++. It's an important rule, and one you must internalize early. A corollary of the "no spaces in a symbol" rule is that when C++ sees adjacent characters, it always tries to construct the longest possible symbol, even if you can see that doing so would produce meaningless results. I predict that this rule will surprise you several Explorations down the road.

The other method you can use to write a comment in C++ is to begin the comment with /* and end it with */. The difference between this style and the style demonstrated in Listing 2-1 is with this method, your comment can span multiple lines. You may notice that some programs in this book use /** to start a comment. Much like the third slash in Listing 2-1, this second asterisk (*) is magic, but unimportant at this time. A comment cannot nest within a comment of the same style, but you can nest one style of comment in comments of the other style, as illustrated in Listing 2-2.

**Listing 2-2.** _Demonstrating Comment Styles and Nesting_

```
/* Start of a comment /* start of comment characters are not special in a comment
 // still in a comment
 Still in a comment
*/
no_longer_in_a_comment();
// Start of a comment /* start of comment characters are not special in a comment
no_longer_in_a_comment();
```

The C++ community uses both styles widely. Get used to seeing and using both styles.

Modify Listing 2-1 to change the /// comment to use the /** ... */ style then try to recompile the program. **What happens?**

_____

If you made the change correctly, the program should still compile and run normally. The compiler eliminates comments entirely, so nothing about the final program should be different. (With one exception being that some binary formats include a timestamp, which would necessarily differ from one compilation run to another.)

# Headers

Lines 3 through 6 import declarations and definitions from parts of the standard library. C++, like C and many other languages, distinguishes between the core language and the standard library. Both are part of the standard language, and a tool suite is incomplete without both parts. The difference is that the core language is self-contained. For example, certain types are built in, and the compiler inherently knows about them. Other types are defined in terms of the built-in types, so they are declared in the standard library, and you need to instruct the compiler that you want to use them. That's what lines 3 through 6 are all about.

In particular, line 3 informs the compiler about the names of the standard I/O streams (cin for the standard input and cout for the standard output). Line 4 fetches the input operator (>>), line 5 brings in the name numeric_limits, and line 6 brings in the output operator (<<). Note that names from the standard library generally begin with std:: (short for "standard").

In C++ parlance, the #include keyword is also a verb, as in "line 3 *includes* the iostream header," "line 5 includes the limits header," and so on. A *header* is typically a file that contains a series of declarations and definitions. (A declaration is a kind of definition. A definition tells the compiler more about a name than a declaration. Don't worry about the difference yet, but notice when I use declaration and when I use definition.) The compiler needs these declarations and definitions so it knows what to do with names such as std::cin. Somewhere in the documentation for your C++ compiler and standard library is the location for its standard headers. If you are curious, visit that folder or directory and see what you can find there, but don't be disappointed that you can't read the headers. The C++ standard library makes full use of the entire range of C++ language features. It's likely you won't be able to decipher most of the library until after you've made it through a large part of this book.

Another important C++ rule: the compiler needs to know what every name means. A human can often infer meaning or at least a part of speech from context. For instance, if I were to say, "I furbled my drink all over my shirt," you may not know exactly what "furbled" means, but you can deduce that it is the past tense of a verb, and that it probably is something undesirable and somewhat messy.

C++ compilers are a lot dumber than you. When the compiler reads a symbol or identifier, it must know exactly what the symbol or identifier means and what part of "speech" it is. Is the symbol a punctuator (such as the statement-ending semicolon) or an operator (such as plus sign for addition)? Is the identifier a type? A function? A variable? The compiler also needs to know everything you can do with that symbol or name, so it can correctly compile the code. The only way it can know is for you to tell it, and the way you tell it is by writing a declaration or by importing a declaration from a header. And that's what #include statements are all about.

Any line that begins with #, ends at the end of the line. C++ has several different # statements, but only #include concerns us at this time. Inside the angle brackets must be a header name, which is typically a standard library header, but it might also be a header from a third-party library.

Later in the book, you'll even learn to write your own headers.

Modify line 5 to misspell `limits` as `stimil`. Try to compile the program. **What happens?**

_____

_____

_____

The compiler cannot find any header named `stimil`, so it issues a message. Then it may try to compile the program, but it doesn't know what `std::numeric_limits` is, so it issues one or more messages. Some compilers cascade messages, which means every use of `std::numeric_limits` produces additional messages. The actual error becomes lost in the noise. Focus on the first one or few messages the compiler issues. Fix them then try again. As you gain experience with C++, you will learn which messages are mere noise and which are important. Unfortunately, most compilers will not tell you, for example, that you can't use `std::numeric_limits` until you include the `<limits>` header. Instead, you need a good C++ language reference, so you can look up the correct header on your own. The first place to check is the documentation that accompanies your compiler and library. If you want an additional reference, I recommend my book, _C++ in a Nutshell_ (O'Reilly, 2003), but feel free to choose any reference (this book's web site contains some recommendations and book reviews).

Most programmers don't use `<limits>` much; Listing 2-1 included it only to obtain the definition of `std::numeric_limits`. On the other hand, almost every program in this book uses `<iostream>` because it declares the names of the I/O stream objects, `std::cin` and `std::cout`. The `<istream>` header declares input operators, and `<ostream>` declares output operators. You will meet quite a few more headers in coming Explorations.

# Main Program

Every C++ program must have `int main()`, as shown on line 8. You are permitted a few variations on a theme, but the name `main` is crucial. A program can have only one `main`, and the name must be spelled using all lowercase characters. The definition must start with `int`.

---

■**Note**  Some books tell you to use `void`. Those books are wrong. If you need to convince someone `void` is wrong and `int` is right, refer the skeptic to section 3.6.1 of the C++ Standard.

---

For now, use empty parentheses after the name `main`.

The next line starts the main program. Notice how the statements are grouped inside curly braces ({ and }). That's how C++ groups statements. A common error for novices is to omit a curly brace, or miss seeing them when reading a program. If you are used to more verbose languages, such as Pascal, Ada, or Visual Basic, you might need some time acquainting yourself with the more terse C++ syntax. This book will give you plenty of opportunities to practice.

Modify line 8 to spell main in capital letters (MAIN). Try to compile the program. **What happens?**

_____

_____

_____

The compiler accepts the program, but the linker complains. Whether you can see the difference between the compiler and the linker depends on your particular tools. Nonetheless, you failed to create a valid program because you must have a main. Only the name main is special. As far as the compiler is concerned, MAIN is just another name, like min or max. Thus, you don't get an error message saying that you misspelled main, only that main is missing. There's nothing wrong with having a program that has a function named MAIN, but to be a complete program, you must be sure to include the definition main.

# Variable Definitions

Lines 10 through 13 define some variables. The first word on each line is the variable's type. The next word is the variable name. The name is followed optionally by an initial value in parentheses. The type int is short for integer, and bool is short for Boolean.

---

■**Note**  Boolean is named after George Boole, the inventor of mathematical logic. As such, some languages use the name logical for this type.

---

The name std::numeric_limits is part of the C++ standard library and lets you query the attributes of the built-in arithmetic types. You can determine the number of bits a type requires, the number of decimal digits, the minimum and maximum values, and more. Put the type that you are curious about in angle brackets. (You'll see this approach to using types quite often in C++.) Thus, you could also query std::numeric_limits<bool>::min() and get false as the result.

**If you were to query the number of bits in bool, what would you expect as a result?**

_____

Try compiling and running Listing 2-3, and find out if you are correct.

**Listing 2-3.** _Determining the Number of Bits in a bool_

```
#include <iostream>
#include <limits>
#include <ostream>

int main()
{
```

```
    // Note that "digits" means binary digits, i.e., bits.
    std::cout << "bits per bool: " << std::numeric_limits<bool>::digits << '\n';
}
```

Did you get the value you expected? If not, do you understand why you got 1 as a result?

# Statements

Line 14 of Listing 2-1 contains a while statement. Lines 17, 19, and 23 start if statements. They have similar syntax: both statements begin with a keyword, followed by a Boolean condition in parentheses, followed by a statement. The statement can be a simple statement, such as the assignment on line 18, or it can be a list of statements within curly braces. Notice that a simple statement ends with a semicolon.

Assignment (lines 16, 18, and 20) uses a single equal sign. For clarity, when I read a program out loud or to myself, I like to read the equal sign as "gets." For example, "x gets min."

A while loop performs its associated statement while the condition is true. The condition is tested prior to executing the statement, so if the condition is false the first time around, the statement never executes.

On line 14, the condition is an input operation. It reads an integer from the standard input (std::cin) and stores that integer in the variable x. The condition is true as long as a value is successfully stored in x. If the input is malformed, or if the program reaches the end of the input stream, the logical condition becomes false, and the loop terminates.

The if statement can be followed by an else branch; you'll see examples in future Explorations.

Line 23's condition consists of a single name: any. Because it has type bool, you can use it directly as a condition.

Modify line 17 to change the statement to just "if (x)". This kind of mistake sometimes happens when you get careless (and we all get careless from time to time). **What do you expect to happen when you compile the program?**

_____

_____

Were you surprised that the compiler did not complain? **What do you expect to happen when you run the program?**

_____

_____

_____

**If you supply the following input to the program, what do you expect as output?**

0   1   2   3

_____

_____

**If you supply the following input to the program, what do you expect as output?**

3    2    1    0

_____

_____

**Explain what is happening:**

_____

_____

_____

_____

_____

C++ is permissive about what it allows as a condition. Any numerical type can be a condition, and the compiler treats non-zero values as true and zero as false. In other words, it supplies an implicit ≠ 0 to test the numeric value.

Many C and C++ programmers take advantage of the brevity these languages offer, but I find it a sloppy programming practice. Always make sure your conditions are logical in nature, even if that means using an explicit comparison to zero. The C++ syntax for comparing ≠ is !=, as in x != 0.

# Output

The output operator is >>. You can print a variable's value, a character string, a single character, or a computed expression. The standard library places output operators in the <ostream> header, and <iostream> declares the name std::cout.

Enclose a single character in single quotes, such as 'X'. Of course, there may be times when you need to include a single quote in your output. To print a single quote, you will need to escape the quote character with a backslash (\'). Escaping a character instructs the compiler to process it as a standard character, not as a part of the program syntax. Other escape characters can follow a backslash, such as \n for a newline (that is, a magic character sequence to start a new line of text; the actual characters in the output depend on the host operating system). To print a backslash character, escape it: '\\'. Some examples of characters include the following: 'x', '#', '7', '\\', '\n'.

If you want to print more than one character at a time, use a character string, which is enclosed in double quotes. To include a double quote in a string, use a backslash escape:

```
std::cout << "not quoted; \"in quotes\", not quoted";
```

A single output statement can use multiple occurrences of <<, as shown in line 24, or you can use multiple output statements. The only difference is readability.

**Modify Listing 2-3 to experiment with different styles of output. Try using multiple output statements.**

Remember to use curly braces when the body of an if statement contains more than one statement.

See! I told you that you could read a C++ program. Now all you need to do is fill in some of your knowledge gaps about the details. The next Exploration starts doing that with the basic arithmetic operators.

■ ■ ■

# Integer Expressions

In Exploration 2, you examined a program that defined a few variables and performed some simple operations on them. This Exploration introduces the basic arithmetic operators. Read Listing 3-1 then answer the questions that follow it.

**Listing 3-1.** *Integer Arithmetic*

```
1 /// Read the program and determine what the program does.
2
3 #include <iostream>
4 #include <ostream>
5
6 int main()
7 {
8     int sum(0);
9     int count(0);
10    int x;
11    while (std::cin >> x)
12    {
13        sum = sum + x;
14        count = count + 1;
15    }
16
17    std::cout << "average = " << sum / count << '\n';
18 }
```

**What does the program in Listing 3-1 do?**

_____

_____

Test the program with the following input:

10   50   20   40   30

Lines 8 and 9 initialize the variables sum and count to zero. You can enter any integer value in the parentheses to initialize a variable; the value does not have to be constant. You must supply something in the parentheses, however, so if you want to leave a variable uninitialized, omit the parentheses entirely, as shown in line 10. Ordinarily, it's a bad idea not to initialize your variables, but in this case x is safe because line 11 immediately stuffs a value into it by reading from the standard input.

Lines 13 and 14 show examples of addition (+) and assignment (=). Addition follows the normal rules of computer arithmetic (we'll worry about overflow later). Assignment works the way it does in any procedural language.

Thus, you can see that Listing 3-1 reads integers from the standard input, adds them up, and prints the average (mean) value, as computed by the division (/) operator. Or does it? **What is wrong with Listing 3-1?**

_____

_____

_____

Try running the program with no input—that is, press the end-of-file keystroke immediately after starting the program. Some operating systems have a "null" file that you can supply as the input stream. When a program reads from the null file, the input stream always sees an end-of-file condition. On UNIX-like operating systems, run the following command line:

```
list0301 < /dev/null
```

On Windows, the null file is called NUL, so type:

```
list0301 < NUL
```

**What happens?**

_____

C++ doesn't like division by zero, does it? Each platform reacts differently. Most systems indicate an error condition one way or another. A few quietly give you garbage results. Either way, you get don't get anything meaningful.

Fix the program by introducing an if statement. Don't worry that the book hasn't covered if statements yet. I'm confident you can figure out how to ensure this program avoids dividing by zero. **Write the corrected program below:**

_____

_____

_____

_____

_____

_____

_____

_____

_____

_____
_____
_____
_____
_____
_____
_____
_____
_____
_____
_____
_____
_____

Now try your new program. **Was your fix successful?**

_____

Compare your solution with Listing 3-2.

**Listing 3-2.** *Print Average, Testing for a Zero Count*

```
 1 /// Read integers and print their average.
 2 /// Print nothing if the input is empty.
 3
 4 #include <iostream>
 5 #include <ostream>
 6
 7 int main()
 8 {
 9    int sum(0);
10    int count(0);
11    int x;
12    while (std::cin >> x)
13    {
14        sum = sum + x;
15        count = count + 1;
16    }
17
18    if (count != 0)
19        std::cout << "average = " << sum / count << '\n';
20 }
```

Remember that != is the C++ syntax for the ≠ operator. Thus count != 0 is true when count is not zero, which means the program has read at least one number from its input.

Suppose you were to run the program with the following input:

```
2   5   3
```

**What do you expect as the output?**

---

Try it. **What is the actual output?**

---

Did you get what you expected? Some languages use different operators for integer division and floating-point division. C++ (like C) uses the same operator symbol, and depends on the context to decide what kind of division to perform. If both operands are integers, the result is an integer.

**What do you expect if the input is**

```
2   5   4
```

---

Try it. **What is the actual output?**

---

Integer division truncates the result toward zero, so 5 / 3 equals 4 / 3 equals 1.

The other arithmetic operators are - for subtraction, * for multiplication, and % for remainder. C++ does not have an operator for exponentiation.

Listing 3-3 asks for integers from the user and tells the user whether the number is even or odd. (Don't worry about how input works in detail; Exploration 5 will cover that.) **Complete line 12:**

**Listing 3-3.** *Testing for Even or Odd Integers*

```
 1 /// Read integers and print a message that tells the user
 2 /// whether the number is even or odd.
 3
 4 #include <iostream>
 5 #include <istream>
 6 #include <ostream>
 7
 8 int main()
 9 {
10     int x;
11     while (std::cin >> x)
12         if (                    )            // Fill in the condition.
13             std::cout << x << " is odd.\n";
14         else
15             std::cout << x << " is even.\n";
16 }
```

Test your program. **Did you get it right?**

I hope you used a line that looks something like this:

```
if (x % 2 != 0)
```

In other words, a number is odd if it has a non-zero remainder after dividing it by 2.

You know that != compares for inequality. How do you think you should write an equality comparison? Try reversing the order of the odd and even messages, as shown in Listing 3-4. **Complete the condition on line 12:**

**Listing 3-4.** *Testing for Even or Odd Integers*

```
 1 /// Read integers and print a message that tells the user
 2 /// whether the number is even or odd.
 3
 4 #include <iostream>
 5 #include <istream>
 6 #include <ostream>
 7
 8 int main()
 9 {
10     int x;
11     while (std::cin >> x)
12         if (              )            // Fill in the condition.
13             std::cout << x << " is even.\n";
14         else
15             std::cout << x << " is odd.\n";
16 }
```

To test for equality, use two equal signs (==). In this case:

```
if (x % 2 == 0)
```

A common mistake that new C++ programmers make, especially those who are accustomed to Pascal and similar languages, is to use a single equal sign for comparison. In this case, the compiler usually alerts you to the mistake. Go ahead and try it, to see what the compiler does. **What message does the compiler issue when you use a single equal sign in line 12?**

_____

_____

_____

_____

A single equal sign is the assignment operator. Thus, the C++ compiler thinks you are trying to assign the value 0 to the expression x % 2, which is nonsense, and the compiler rightly tells you so.

What if you want to test whether x is zero? **Modify Listing 3-1 to print a message when count is zero.** Once you get the program right, it should look something like Listing 3-5.

**Listing 3-5.** *Print Average, Testing for a Zero Count*

```
 1 /// Read integers and print their average.
 2 /// Print nothing if the input is empty.
 3
 4 #include <iostream>
 5 #include <ostream>
 6
 7 int main()
 8 {
 9     int sum(0);
10     int count(0);
11     int x;
12     while (std::cin >> x)
13     {
14         sum = sum + x;
15         count = count + 1;
16     }
17
18     if (count == 0)
19         std::cout << "No data.\n";
20     else
21         std::cout << "average = " << sum / count << '\n';
22 }
```

Now modify Listing 3-5 to use a single equal sign on line 18. **What message does your compiler issue?**

_____

_____

_____

_____

Most modern compilers recognize this common error and issue a warning. Strictly speaking, the code is correct: the condition assigns zero to count. Recall that a condition of zero means false, so the program always prints No data., regardless of how much data it actually reads.

If your compiler does not issue a warning, read the compiler's documentation. You might need to enable a switch to turn on extra warnings, such as "possible use of assignment instead of comparison" or "condition is always false."

As you can see, working with integers is easy and unsurprising. Text, however, is a little trickier, as you will see in the next Exploration.

# EXPLORATION 4

■ ■ ■

# Strings

In earlier Explorations, you used quoted character strings as part of each output operation. In this Exploration, you will begin to learn how to make your output a little fancier by doing more with strings. Start by reading Listing 4-1.

**Listing 4-1.** *Different Styles of String Output*

```
#include <iostream>
#include <ostream>

int main()
{
    std::cout << "Shape\tSides\n" << "-----\t-----\n";
    std::cout << "Square\t" << 4 << '\n' <<
                 "Circle\t?\n";
}
```

**Predict the output from the program in Listing 4-1.** You may already know what \t means. If so, this prediction is easy to make. If you don't know, take a guess.

_____

Now check your answer. Were you correct? **So what does \t mean?**

_____

Inside a string, the backslash (\) is a special, even magical, character. It changes the meaning of the character that follows it. You have already seen how \n starts a new line. Now you know that \t is a horizontal tab: that is, it aligns the subsequent output at a tab position. In a typical console, tab stops are set every eight character positions.

**How should you print a double-quote character in a string?**

_____

Write a program to test your hypothesis then run the program. **Were you correct?**

_____

Compare your program with Listing 4-2.

**Listing 4-2.** *Printing a Double-Quote Character*

```
#include <iostream>
#include <ostream>

int main()
{
   std::cout << "\"\n";
}
```

In this case, the backslash turns a special character into a normal character. C++ recognizes a few other backslash character sequences, but these three are the most commonly used. (You'll learn a few more when you read about characters in Exploration 16.)

**Now modify Listing 4-1 to add Triangle to the list of shapes.**

What does the output look like? Tabs do not automatically align columns, but merely position the output at a tab position. To align columns, you need to take control of the output. One easy way to do this is to use multiple tab characters, as shown in Listing 4-3.

**Listing 4-3.** *Adding a Triangle and Keeping the Columns Aligned*

```
 1 #include <iostream>
 2 #include <ostream>
 3
 4 int main()
 5 {
 6    std::cout << "Shape\t\tSides\n" <<
 7              "-----\t\t-----\n";
 8    std::cout << "Square\t\t" << 4 << '\n' <<
 9              "Circle\t\t?\n"
10              "Triangle\t" << 3 << '\n';
11 }
```

I played a trick on you in Listing 4-3. Look closely at the end of line 9 and the start of line 10. Notice that the program lacks an output operator (<<) that ordinarily separates all output items. Anytime you have two (or more) adjacent character strings, the compiler automatically combines them into a single string. This trick applies only to strings, not to characters. Thus, you can write lines 9 and 10 in many different ways, all meaning exactly the same thing:

```
std::cout << "\nCircle\t\t?\n" "Triangle\t" << 3 << '\n';
std::cout << "\nCircle\t\t?\nTriangle\t" << 3 << '\n';
std::cout << "\n" "Circle" "\t\t?\n" "Triangle" "\t" << 3 << '\n';
```

Choose the style you like best, and stick with it. I like to make a clear break after each newline, so the human who reads my programs can clearly distinguish where each line ends and a new line begins.

You may be asking yourself why I bothered to print the numbers separately, instead of printing one big string. That's a good question. In a real program, printing a single string would be best, but in this book, I want to keep reminding you about the various ways you can write an output statement. Imagine, for example, what you would do if you didn't know beforehand the name of a shape and its number of sides. Perhaps that information is stored in variables, as shown in Listing 4-4.

**Listing 4-4.** *Printing Information That Is Stored in Variables*

```
1 #include <iostream>
2 #include <ostream>
3 #include <string>
4
5 int main()
6 {
7    std::string shape("Triangle");
8    int sides(3);
9
10   std::cout << "Shape\t\tSides\n" <<
11                "-----\t\t-----\n";
12   std::cout << "Square\t\t" << 4 << '\n' <<
13                "Circle\t\t?\n";
14   std::cout << shape << '\t' << sides << '\n';
15 }
```

The type of a string is std::string. You must have #include <string> near the top of your program to inform the compiler that you are using the std::string type. Line 7 shows how to give an initial value to a string variable. Sometimes, you want the variable to start out empty. **How do you think you would define an empty string variable?**

_____

_____

**Write a program to test your hypothesis.**

If you have trouble verifying that the string is truly empty, try printing the string between two other, nonempty strings. Listing 4-5 shows an example.

**Listing 4-5.** *Defining and Printing an Empty String*

```
1 #include <iostream>
2 #include <ostream>
3 #include <string>
4
5 int main()
6 {
7    std::string empty;
8    std::cout << "|" << empty << "|\n";
9 }
```

Compare your program with Listing 4-5. **Which do you prefer?** _____

**Why?**

_____

_____

You may have tried to define an empty string with empty parentheses, extrapolating from the definitions of shape and sides in Listing 4-4. Your reasoning is completely logical, but in this case, C++ works differently. To define a variable with no initial value, omit the parentheses entirely.

When you define a string variable with no initial value, C++ guarantees that the string is initially empty. **Modify Listing 4-4 so the shape and sides variables are uninitialized. Predict the output of the program:**

_____

_____

**What happened? Explain.**

_____

_____

_____

Your program should look like Listing 4-6.

**Listing 4-6.** *Demonstrating Uninitialized Variables*

```
 1 #include <iostream>
 2 #include <ostream>
 3 #include <string>
 4
 5 int main()
 6 {
 7    std::string shape;
 8    int sides;
 9
10    std::cout << "Shape\t\tSides\n" <<
11                 "-----\t\t-----\n";
12    std::cout << "Square\t\t" << 4 << '\n' <<
13                 "Circle\t\t?\n";
14    std::cout << shape << '\t' << sides << '\n';
15 }
```

When I run Listing 4-6, I get different answers depending on which compilers and platforms I use. One of the answers I get is the following:

```
Shape           Sides

-----           -----

Square          4
Circle          ?
        4226851
```

With another compiler on another platform, the final number is 0. Yet another compiler's program prints -858993460 as the final number. Some systems may even crash instead of printing the value of shape or sides.

Isn't that curious? If you do not supply an initial value for a variable of type std::string, C++ makes sure the variable starts out with an initial value—namely, an empty string. On the other hand, if the variable has type int, you cannot tell what the initial value will actually be, and in fact, you cannot even tell whether the program will run. This is known as *undefined behavior*. The standard permits the C++ compiler and runtime environment to do anything, absolutely anything, when confronted with certain erroneous situations, such as accessing an uninitialized variable. A design goal of C++ is that the compiler and library should not do any extra work if they can avoid it. Only the programmer knows what value makes sense as a variable's initial value, so assigning that initial value must be the programmer's responsibility. After all, when you are putting the finishing touches on your weather simulator (the one that will finally explain why it always rains when I plan ahead for a trip to the beach), you don't want the inner loop burdened by even one wasteful instruction. The flip side of that performance guarantee is an added burden on the programmer to avoid situations that give rise to undefined behavior. Some languages help the programmer avoid problem situations, but that help invariably comes with a performance cost.

So what's the deal with std::string? The short answer is that complicated types, such as strings, are different from the simple, built-in types. For types such as std::string, it is actually simpler for the C++ library to provide a well-defined initial value. Most of the interesting types in the standard library behave the same way.

If you have trouble remembering when it is safe to define a variable without an initial value, play it safe and provide one:

```
std::string empty("");
int zero(0);
```

I recommend initializing every variable, even if you know the program will overwrite it soon, such as the input loops we used earlier. The next Exploration demonstrates the importance of initializing every variable.

# EXPLORATION 5

■■■

# Simple Input

**S**o far, the Explorations have focused on output. Now it's time to turn your attention to input. Given that the output operator is <<, **what do you expect the input operator to be?**

_____

That didn't take a rocket scientist to deduce, did it? The input operator is >>, the opposite direction of the output operator. Think of the operators as arrows pointing in the direction that information flows: from the stream to variables for input, or from variables to the stream for output. The standard library declares input operators in the <istream> header.

Listing 5-1 shows a simple program that performs input and output.

**Listing 5-1.** *Demonstrating Input and Output*

```
#include <iostream>
#include <istream>
#include <ostream>

int main()
{
   std::cout << "Enter a number: ";
   int x;
   std::cin >> x;
   std::cout << "Enter another number: ";
   int y;
   std::cin >> y;

   int z(x + y);
   std::cout << "The sum of " << x << " and " << y << " is " << z << "\n";
}
```

**How many numbers does Listing 5-1 read from the standard input?** _____

Suppose you enter 42 and 21 as the two input values. **What do you expect for the output?**

_____

Now run the program, and check your prediction. I hope you got 63. Suppose you type the following as input?

42*21

**What do you predict will be the output?**

_____

Test your hypothesis. **What is the actual output?**

_____

Do you see what happened? If not, try xyz as the input to the program. Try 42-21. Try 42.21.

The program exhibits two distinct behaviors that you need to understand. First, to read an int, the input stream must contain a valid integer. The integer can start with a sign (- or +) but must be all digits after that; no intervening whitespace is allowed. The input operation stops when it reaches the first character that cannot be part of a valid integer (such as *). If at least one digit is read from the input stream, the read succeeds, and the input text is converted to an integer. The read fails if the input stream does not start with a valid integer. If the read fails, the input variable is not modified.

The second behavior is what you discovered in the previous Exploration; uninitialized int variables result in undefined behavior. In other words, if a read fails, the variable contains junk, or worse. When you learn about floating point numbers, for example, you will learn that some bit patterns in an uninitialized floating-point variable can cause a program to terminate. On some specialized hardware, an uninitialized integer can do the same. The moral of the story is that using an uninitialized variable results in undefined behavior. That's bad. So don't do it.

Thus, when the input is xyz, both reads fail, and undefined behavior results. You probably see junk values for both numbers. When the input is 42-21, the first number is 42 and the second number is -21, so the result is correct. However, when the input is 42.21, the first number is 42, and the second number is junk because an integer cannot start with a dot (.).

Once an input operation fails, all subsequent input attempts will also fail unless you take remedial action. That's why the program doesn't wait for you to type a second number if the first one is invalid. C++ can tell you when an input operation fails, so your program can avoid using junk values. Also, you can reset a stream's error state, so you can resume reading after handling an error. I will cover these techniques in future Explorations. For now, make sure your input is valid and correct.

Some compilers warn you when your program leaves variables uninitialized, but it is best to be safe and initialize every variable, all the time. As you can see, even if the program immediately attempts to store a value in the variable, it may not succeed, which can give rise to unexpected behavior.

Whenever possible, use initializers when defining a variable, so you can assure yourself that the variable holds the value you want it to hold. You can see this clearly in the definition of z, which has an initial value of x + y.

Did you think that integers could be so complicated? Surely strings are simpler because there is no need to interpret them or convert their values. Let's see if they truly are simpler than integers. Listing 5-2 is similar to Listing 5-1, but it reads text into std::string variables.

**Listing 5-2.** *Reading Strings*

```cpp
#include <iostream>
#include <istream>
#include <ostream>
#include <string>

int main()
{
   std::cout << "What is your name? ";
   std::string name;
   std::cin >> name;
   std::cout << "Hello, " << name << ", how are you? ";
   std::string response;
   std::cin >> response;
   std::cout << "Good-bye, " << name << ". I'm glad you feel " << response << "\n";
}
```

Listing 5-2 is clearly not a model of artificial intelligence, but it demonstrates one thing well. Suppose the input is as follows:

```
Ray Lischner
Fine
```

**What do you expect as the output?**

_____

_____

_____

Run the program and test your hypothesis. **Were you correct?** _____
Explain.

_____

_____

Experiment with different input and try to discern the rules that C++ uses to delimit a string in the input stream. Ready? Go ahead. I'll wait until you're done.

Back so soon? **How does C++ delimit strings in an input stream?**

_____

_____

_____

Any whitespace character (the exact list of whitespace characters depends on your implementation, but typically includes blanks, tabs, newlines, and the like) ends a string, at least as far as the input operation is concerned. Specifically, C++ skips leading whitespace characters. Then it accumulates nonspace characters to form the string. The string ends at the next whitespace character.

So what happens when you mix integers and strings? **Write a program that asks for a person's name (first name only) and age (in years) and then echoes the input to the standard output.** Which do you want to ask for first? Print the information after reading it.

Table 5-1 shows some sample inputs for your program. Next to each one, **write your prediction for the program's output.** Then run the program, and **write the actual output.**

**Table 5-1.** *Sample Inputs for Name and Age*

| Input | Predicted Output | Actual Output |
|---|---|---|
| Ray44 | | |
| 44Ray | | |
| Ray  44 | | |
| 44  Ray | | |
| Ray<br>44 | | |
| 44<br>Ray | | |
| 44-Ray | | |
| Ray-44 | | |

Think of the standard input as a stream of characters. Regardless of how the user types those characters, the program sees them arrive one by one. (Okay, they arrive in big chunks, by the buffer-load, but that's a minor implementation detail. As far as you are concerned, your program reads one character at a time, and it doesn't matter that the character comes from the buffer, not the actual input device.) Thus, the program always maintains the notion of a current position in the stream. The next read operation always starts at that position.

Before starting any input operation, if the character at the input position is a whitespace character, that character is skipped. All leading whitespace characters are skipped. Then the actual read begins.

If the program attempts to read an integer, it grabs the character at the input position, and checks whether it is valid for an integer. If not, the read fails, and the input position does not move. Otherwise, the input operation keeps the character and all subsequent characters that are valid elements of an integer. The input operation interprets the text as an integer and stores the value in the variable. Thus, after reading an integer, you know that the input position points to a character that is *not* a valid integer character.

When reading a string, all the characters are grabbed from the stream until a whitespace character is reached. Thus, the string variable does not contain any whitespace characters. The next read operation will skip over the whitespace, as described earlier.

The input stream ends at the end of the file (if reading from a file), when the user closes the console or terminal, or when the user types a special keystroke sequence to tell the operating system to end the input (such as Control+D on UNIX or Control+Z on DOS or Windows). Once the end of the input stream is reached, all subsequent attempts to read from the stream will fail. This is what caused the loop to end in Exploration 2.

Listing 5-3 shows my version of the name-first program. Naturally, your program will differ in the details, but the basic outline should agree with yours.

**Listing 5-3.** *Getting the User's Name and Age*

```
#include <iostream>
#include <istream>
#include <ostream>
#include <string>

int main()
{
   std::cout << "What is your name? ";
   std::string name;
   std::cin >> name;

   std::cout << "Hello, " << name << ", how old are you? ";
   int age(0);
   std::cin >> age;

   std::cout << "Good-bye, " << name << ". You are " << age << " year";
   if (age != 1)
      std::cout << 's';
   std::cout << " old.\n";
}
```

**Now modify the program to reverse the order of the name and age, and try all the input values again. Explain what you observe.**

_____

_____

_____

When an input operation fails due to malformed input, the stream enters an error state; e.g., the input stream contains the string "Ray" when the program tries to read an integer. All subsequent attempts to read from the stream result in an error being generated without actually trying to read. Even if the stream subsequently tries to read a string, which would otherwise succeed, the error state is sticky, and the string read fails, too.

In other words, when the program cannot read the user's age, it won't be able to read the name, either. That's why the program gets both right or both wrong.

Listing 5-4 shows my version of the age-first program.

**Listing 5-4.** *Getting the User's Age and Then Name*

```
#include <iostream>
#include <istream>
#include <ostream>
#include <string>

int main()
{
   std::cout << "How old are you? ";
```

```
    int age(0);
    std::cin >> age;

    std::cout << "What is your name? ";
    std::string name;
    std::cin >> name;

    std::cout << "Good-bye, " << name << ". You are " << age << " year";
    if (age != 1)
        std::cout << 's';
    std::cout << " old.\n";
}
```

Table 5-2 shows a truncated version of the output (just the name and age) in each situation.

**Table 5-2.** *Interpreting Input the C++ Way*

| Input | Name First | Age First |
|-------|------------|-----------|
| Ray44 | "Ray44", 0 | 0, "" |
| 44Ray | "44Ray", 0 | 44, "Ray" |
| Ray 44 | "Ray", 44 | 0, "" |
| 44 Ray | "44", 0 | 44, "Ray" |
| Ray<br>44 | "Ray", 44 | 0, "" |
| 44<br>Ray | "44", 0 | 44, "Ray" |
| 44#Ray | "44#Ray", 0 | 44, "#Ray" |
| Ray#44 | "Ray#44", 0 | 0, "" |

Handling errors in an input stream requires some more advanced C++, but handling errors in your code is something you can take care of right now. The next Exploration helps you untangle compiler error messages.

■ ■ ■

# Error Messages

**B**y now you've seen plenty of error messages from your C++ compiler. No doubt, some are helpful and others are cryptic—a few are both. This Exploration presents a number of common errors and gives you a chance to see what kinds of messages your compiler issues for these mistakes. The more familiar you are with these messages, the easier it will be for you to interpret them in the future.

Read through Listing 6-1 and keep an eye out for mistakes.

**Listing 6-1.** *Deliberate Errors*

```
 1 #include <iosteam>
 2 #include <istream>
 3 #include <ostream>
 4
 5 int main()
 6 [
 7   std::cout < "This program prints a table of squares.\n";
 8          "Enter the starting value for the table: ";
 9   int start(0);
10   std::cin >> start;
11   std::cout << "Enter the ending value for the table: ";
12   int end(start);
13   std::cin << endl
14   std::cout << "#    #^2\n";
15   int x(start);
16   end = end + 1; // exit loop when x reaches end
17   while (x != end)
18   {
19     std:cout << x << "    " << x*x << "\n";
20     x = x + 1;
21   }
22 }
```

**What errors do you expect the compiler to detect?**

_____

_____

_____

_____

_____

Download the source code and compile Listing 6-1.

**What messages does your compiler actually issue?**

_____

_____

_____

_____

_____

_____

Create three groups: messages that you correctly predicted, messages that you expected but the compiler did not issue, and messages that the compiler issued but you did not expect. **How many messages are in each group?** _____

The program actually contains seven errors, but don't fret if you missed them. Let's take them one at a time.

# Misspelling

Line 1 misspells <iostream> as <iosteam>. Your compiler should give you a simple message, informing you that it could not find <iosteam>. The compiler cannot tell that you meant to type <iostream>, so it cannot give you a suggestion. You need to know the proper spelling of the header name.

At least one compiler gives up completely at this point. If that happens to you, fix this one error then run the compiler again to see some more messages.

If your compiler tries to continue, it does so without the declarations from the misspelled header. In this case, <iostream> declares std::cin and std::cout, so the compiler also issues messages about those names being unknown.

# Bogus Character

The most interesting error is the use of a square bracket character ([) instead of a brace character ({) in line 6. Some compilers may be able to guess what you meant, which can limit the resulting error messages. Others cannot and give a message that may be rather cryptic.

For example, g++ issues many errors, none of which directly points you to the error. Instead, it issues the following messages:

```
list0601.cxx:1:19: error: iosteam: No such file or directory
list0601.cxx:7: error: 'cout' is not a member of 'std'
list0601.cxx:7: error: expected `]' before ';' token
list0601.cxx:8: error: expected unqualified-id before string constant
list0601.cxx:10: error: expected constructor, destructor, or type conversion➡
 before '>>' token
list0601.cxx:11: error: expected constructor, destructor, or type conversion➡
 before '<<' token
list0601.cxx:13: error: expected constructor, destructor, or type conversion➡
 before '<<' token
list0601.cxx:17: error: expected unqualified-id before 'while'
list0601.cxx:22: error: expected declaration before '}' token
```

When you cannot understand the error messages, look at the first message. Search for errors at or near the line number. Ignore the rest of the messages.

On line 7, you may see another error or two. After you fix them, however, a slew of messages still remain. That means you still haven't found the real culprit (which is on line 6).

Once you track down the square bracket and change it to a curly brace, you may get entirely different messages. This is because the substitution of [ for { so sufficiently confuses the compiler that it cannot make any sense of the rest of the program. Correcting that problem straightens out the program for the compiler, but now it may find a whole new set of errors.

# Unknown Operator

The input and output operators (>> and <<) are no different from any other C++ operator, such as addition (+), multiplication (*), or comparison (such as >). Every operator has a limited set of allowed operands. For example, you cannot "add" two I/O streams (e.g., std::cin + std::cout), nor can you use an output operator to "write" a number to a string (e.g., "text" << 3).

On line 7, one error is the use of < instead of <<. The compiler cannot determine that you intended to use <<, and instead issues a message that indicates what is wrong with <. The exact message depends on the compiler, but most likely the message is not something that helps you solve this particular problem. One compiler complains as follows:

```
list0601.cxx: In function 'int main()':
list0601.cxx:7: error: no match for 'operator<' in 'std::cout < "This program➡
 prints a table of squares.\012"'
list0601.cxx:7: note: candidates are: operator<(const char*, const char*) <built-in>
list0601.cxx:7: note:                  operator<(void*, void*) <built-in>
```

This message notifies you that you are using the wrong operator or the wrong operands. You need to determine which one it is.

Once you fix the operator, notice that the compiler does not issue any message for the other mistake, namely, the extraneous semicolon. Strictly speaking, it is not a C++ error. It is a logical error, but the result is a valid C++ program. Some compilers will issue a warning, advising you that line 8 does nothing, which is a hint that you made a mistake. Other compilers will silently accept the program.

The only sure way to detect this kind of mistake is to learn to proofread your code.

# Unknown Name

An easy error for a compiler to detect is when you use a name that the compiler does not recognize at all. In this case, accidentally typing the letter l instead of a semicolon produces the name endl instead of end;. The compiler issues a clear message about this unknown name.

Fix the semicolon, and now the compiler complains about another operator. This time you should be able to zoom in on the problem and notice that the operator is facing the wrong way (<< instead of >>). The compiler may not offer much help, however. One compiler spews out errors of the form:

```
list0601.cxx
list0601.cxx(13) : error C2784: 'std::basic_ostream<char,_Traits> &std::operator➡
<<(std::basic_ostream<char,_Traits> &,unsigned char)' : could not deduce➡
template argument for 'std::basic_ostream<char,_Elem> &' from 'std::istream'
        C:\Program Files\Microsoft Visual C++ Toolkit 2003\include\ostream(887)➡
: see declaration of 'std::operator`<<''
list0601.cxx(13) : error C2784: 'std::basic_ostream<char,_Traits> &std::operator➡
<<(std::basic_ostream<char,_Traits> &,unsigned char)' : could not deduce➡
template argument for 'std::basic_ostream<char,_Elem> &' from 'std::istream'
        C:\Program Files\Microsoft Visual C++ Toolkit 2003\include\ostream(887)➡
: see declaration of 'std::operator`<<''
```

The line number tells you where to look, but it is up to you to find the problem.

# Symbol Errors

But now you run into a strange problem. The compiler complains that it does not know what a name means (cout on line 19), but you know that it does. After all, the rest of the program uses std::cout without any difficulty. What's wrong with line 19 that it causes the compiler to forget?

Small errors can have profound consequences in C++. As it turns out, a single colon means something completely different from a double colon. The compiler sees std:cout as a statement labeled std, followed by the bare name cout. At least the error message points you to the right place. Then it's up to you to notice the missing colon.

# Fun with Errors

After you have fixed all the syntax and semantic errors, compile and run the program to make sure you truly found them all. Then introduce some new errors, just to see what happens. Some suggestions follow:

**Try dropping a semicolon from the end of a statement. What happens?**

_____

_____

**Try dropping a double quote from the start or end of a string. What happens?**

_____

_____

**Try misspelling int as iny. What happens?**

_____

_____

Now I want to you to explore on your own. Introduce one error at a time and see what happens. Try making several errors at once. Sometimes, errors have a way of obscuring each other. Go wild! Have fun! How often does your teacher encourage you to make mistakes?

Now it's time to return to correct C++ code. The next Exploration introduces the for loop.

# EXPLORATION 7

■■■

# For Loops

Explorations 2 and 3 show some simple while loops. This Exploration introduces the while loop's big brother, the for loop.

## Bounded Loops

You've already seen while loops that read from the standard input until no more input is available. That is a classic case of an *unbounded* loop. Unless you know beforehand exactly what the input stream will contain, you cannot define the loop's bounds or limits. Sometimes you know in advance how many times the loop must run; that is, you know the bounds of the loop, making it a *bounded* loop. The for loop is how C++ implements a bounded loop.

Let's start with a simple example. Listing 7-1 shows a program that prints the first ten non-negative integers.

**Listing 7-1.** *Using a* for *Loop to Print Ten Non-Negative Numbers*

```
#include <iostream>
#include <ostream>

int main()
{
  for (int i(0); i != 10; i = i + 1)
    std::cout << i << '\n';
}
```

The for loop crams a lot of information in a small space, so take it one step at a time. Inside the parentheses are three parts of the loop, separated by semicolons. **What do you think these three pieces mean?**

_____

_____

_____

_____

The three parts are: initialization, condition, and postiteration. Take a closer look at each part.

## Initialization

The first part looks similar to a variable definition. It defines an int variable named i, with an initial value of 0. Some C-inspired languages permit only an initialization expression, not a variable definition. In C++, you have a choice: expression or definition. The advantage of defining the loop control variable as part of the initialization is that you cannot accidentally refer to that variable outside the loop. Listing 7-2 demonstrates the advantage of limiting the loop control variable.

**Listing 7-2.** *You Cannot Use the Loop Control Variable Outside the Loop*

```
#include <iostream>
#include <ostream>

int main()
{
  for (int i(0); i != 10; i = i + 1)
    std::cout << i << '\n';
  std::cout << "i=" << i << '\n';        // error: i is undefined outside the loop
}
```

Another consequence of limiting the loop control variable is that you may define and use the same variable name in multiple loops, as shown in Listing 7-3.

**Listing 7-3.** *Using and Reusing a Loop Control Variable Name*

```
#include <iostream>
#include <ostream>

int main()
{
  std::cout << '+';
  for (int i(0); i != 20; i = i + 1)
    std::cout << '-';
  std::cout << "+\n|";
  for (int i(0); i != 3; i = i + 1)
    std::cout << ' ';
  std::cout << "Hello, reader!";
  for (int i(0); i != 3; i = i + 1)
    std::cout << ' ';
  std::cout << "|\n+";
  for (int i(0); i != 20; i = i + 1)
    std::cout << '-';
  std::cout << "+\n";
}
```

**What does Listing 7-3 produce as output?**

_____

_____

_____

If you don't need to perform any initialization, you can leave the initialization part empty.

## Condition

The middle part follows the exact same rules as a `while` loop condition. As you might expect, it controls the loop execution. The loop body executes while the condition is true. If the condition is false, the loop terminates. If the condition is false the first time the loop runs, the loop body never executes.

Sometimes you will see a `for` loop with a missing condition. That means the condition is always true, so the loop runs without stopping. A better way to write a condition that is always true is to be explicit and use `true` as the condition. That way, anyone who needs to read and maintain your code in the future will understand that you deliberately designed the loop to run forever. Think of it as the equivalent of a comment: "This condition deliberately left blank."

## Postiteration

The last part looks like a statement, even though it lacks the trailing semicolon. In fact, it is not a full statement, but only an expression. The expression is evaluated after the loop body (hence the name *post*-iteration) and before the condition is tested again. You can put anything you want here, or leave it blank. Typically, this part of the `for` loop controls the iteration, advancing the loop control variable as needed.

## How a for Loop Works

The flow of control is as follows:

1. The initialization part runs exactly once.

2. The condition is tested. If it is false, the loop terminates and the program continues with the statement that follows the loop body.

3. If the condition is true, the loop body executes.

4. The postiteration part executes.

5. Control jumps to 2.

# Your Turn

Now it's your turn to write a for loop. Listing 7-4 shows a skeleton of a C++ program. **Fill in the missing parts to compute the sum of integers from 10 to 20, inclusive.**

**Listing 7-4.** *Compute Sum of Integers from 10 to 20*

```
#include <iostream>
#include <ostream>

int main()
{
  int sum(0);

  // Fill in the loop here.

  std::cout << "Sum of 10 to 20 = " << sum << '\n';
}
```

Before you test your program, you must first determine how you will know whether the program is correct. In other words, **what is the sum of the integers from 10 to 20, inclusive?**
_____

Okay, now compile and run your program. **What answer does your program produce?**
_____ **Is your program correct?** _____

Compare your program with that shown in Listing 7-5.

**Listing 7-5.** *Compute Sum of Integers from 10 to 20 (Completed)*

```
#include <iostream>
#include <ostream>

int main()
{
  int sum(0);
  for (int i(10); i != 21; i = i + 1)
    sum = sum + i;
  std::cout << "Sum of 10 to 20 = " << sum << '\n';
}
```

A common use of for loops is to format and print tables of information. To accomplish this, you need finer control over output formatting than what you have learned so far. That will be the subject of the next Exploration.

# EXPLORATION 8

■ ■ ■

# Formatted Output

In Exploration 4, you used tab characters to line up output neatly. Tabs are useful, but crude. This Exploration introduces some of the features that C++ offers to format output nicely, such as setting the alignment, padding, and width of output fields.

## The Problem

This Exploration begins a little differently. Instead of reading a program and answering questions about it, you must write your own program to solve a problem. The task is to print a table of squares and cubes (the mathematical variety, not the geometrical shapes) for integers from 1 to 20. The output of the program should look something like the following:

| N | N^2 | N^3 |
|---|-----|-----|
| 1 | 1 | 1 |
| 2 | 4 | 8 |
| 3 | 9 | 27 |
| 4 | 16 | 64 |
| 5 | 25 | 125 |
| 6 | 36 | 216 |
| 7 | 49 | 343 |
| 8 | 64 | 512 |
| 9 | 81 | 729 |
| 10 | 100 | 1000 |
| 11 | 121 | 1331 |
| 12 | 144 | 1728 |
| 13 | 169 | 2197 |
| 14 | 196 | 2744 |
| 15 | 225 | 3375 |
| 16 | 256 | 4096 |
| 17 | 289 | 4913 |
| 18 | 324 | 5832 |
| 19 | 361 | 6859 |
| 20 | 400 | 8000 |

To help you get started, Listing 8-1 gives you a skeleton program. You need only fill in the loop body.

**Listing 8-1.** *Print a Table of Squares and Cubes*

```
#include <iomanip>
#include <iostream>
#include <ostream>

int main()
{
  std::cout << " N    N^2     N^3\n";
  for (int i = 1; i != 21; ++i)
  {
    // fill in the loop body here
  }
}
```

This is a trick problem, so don't worry if you had difficulties. The point of this exercise is to demonstrate how difficult formatted output actually is. If you've learned that much, you successfully completed this exercise, even if you didn't finish the program. Perhaps you tried using tab characters at first, but that aligns the numbers on the left:

| N | N^2 | N^3 |
|---|---|---|
| 1 | 1 | 1 |
| 2 | 4 | 8 |
| 3 | 9 | 27 |
| 4 | 16 | 64 |
| 5 | 25 | 125 |
| 6 | 36 | 216 |
| 7 | 49 | 343 |
| 8 | 64 | 512 |
| 9 | 81 | 729 |
| 10 | 100 | 1000 |

Left-alignment is not the way we usually write numbers. Tradition dictates that numbers should align to the right (or on decimal points, when applicable—more on that in the section, "Alignment," later in this Exploration). Right-aligned numbers are easier to read.

C++ offers some simple but powerful techniques to format output. To format the table of powers, you need to define a field for each column. A field has a width, an alignment, and a pad character. The following sections explain these concepts in depth.

# Field Width

Before exploring how you would specify alignment, first you need to know how to set the width of an output field. I gave you a hint in Listing 8-1. **What is the hint?**

The first line of the program is #include <iomanip>, which you have not seen before. This header declares some useful tools, including std::setw, which sets the minimum width of an output field. For example, to print a number so that it occupies at least three character positions, call std::setw(3). If the number requires more space than that—say the value is 314159—the actual output will take up as much space as needed. In this case, the spacing turned out to be six character positions.

To use setw, call the function as part of an output statement. The statement looks like you are trying to print setw, but in fact, nothing is printed, and all you are doing is manipulating the state of the output stream. That's why setw is called an *I/O manipulator*. The <iomanip> header declares several manipulators, which you will learn about in due course.

Listing 8-2 shows the table of powers program, using setw to set the width of each field in the table.

**Listing 8-2.** *Printing a Table of Powers the Right Way*

```
#include <iomanip>
#include <iostream>
#include <ostream>

int main()
{
  std::cout << " N    N^2     N^3\n";
  for (int i = 1; i != 21; ++i)
    std::cout << std::setw(2) << i
              << std::setw(6) << i*i
              << std::setw(7) << i*i*i
              << '\n';
}
```

The first column of the table requires two positions, to accommodate numbers up to 20. The second column needs some space between columns, and room for numbers up to 400; setw(6) uses three spaces between the N and the N^2 columns, and three character positions for the number. The final column also uses three spaces between columns, and four character positions, to allow numbers up to 8000.

The default field width is zero, which means everything you print takes up the exact amount of space it needs, no more, no less.

After printing one item, the field width automatically resets to zero. For instance, if you wanted to use a uniform column width of six for the entire table, you could not call setw(6) once, and leave it at that. Instead, you must call setw(6) before each output operation:

```
std::cout << std::setw(6) << i
          << std::setw(6) << i*i
          << std::setw(6) << i*i*i
          << '\n';
```

# Padding

By default, values are padded, or filled, with space characters (' '). You can set the fill character to be any that you choose, such as zero ('0') or an asterisk ('*'). Listing 8-3 shows a fanciful use of both fill characters in a program that prints a check.

**Listing 8-3.** *Using Alternative Fill Characters*

```
#include <iomanip>
#include <iostream>
#include <ostream>

int main()
{
  using namespace std;

  int day(14);
  int month(3);
  int year(2006);
  int dollars(42);
  int cents(7);

  // Print date in USA order. Later in the book, you will learn how to
  // handle internationalization.
  cout << "Date: " << setfill('0') << setw(2) << month
                   << '/' << setw(2) << day
                   << '/' << setw(2) << year << '\n';
  cout << "Pay to the order of: CASH\n";
  cout << "The amount of $" << setfill('*') << setw(8) << dollars << '.'
                   << setfill('0') << setw(2) << cents << '\n';
}
```

Notice that unlike setw, setfill is sticky. That is, the output stream remembers the fill character and uses that character for all output fields until you set a different fill character.

# std Prefix

Another new feature in Listing 8-3 is the declaration, using namespace std;. All those std:: prefixes can sometimes make the code hard to read. The important parts of the names become lost in the clutter. By starting your program with using namespace std;, you are instructing the compiler to treat names that it doesn't recognize as though they began with std::.

As the keyword indicates, std is called a *namespace*. Almost every name in the standard library is part of the std namespace. You are not allowed to add anything to the std namespace, nor are any third-party library vendors. Thus, if you see std::, you know that what follows is part of the standard library (so you can look it up in any decent reference). More important, you know that most names you invent in your own program will not conflict with any name in the standard library, and vice versa. Namespaces keep your names separate from the standard library names. Later in the book, you will learn to create your own namespaces, which help organize libraries and manage large applications.

On the other hand, `using namespace std;` is a dangerous declaration, and one I use sparingly. Without the `std::` qualifier before every standard library name, you have opened the door to confusion. Imagine, for example, if your program defines a variable named `cout` or `setw`. The compiler has strict rules for interpreting names and would not be confused at all, but the human reader certainly would be. It is always best to avoid names that collide with those in the standard library, with or without `using namespace std;`.

# Alignment

C++ lets you align output fields to the right or the left. If you want to center a number, you are on your own. To force the alignment to be left or right, use the `left` and `right` manipulators (declared in `<ios>`).

The default alignment is to the right, which might strike you as odd. After all, the first attempt at using tab characters to align the table columns produced left-aligned values. As far as C++ is concerned, however, it knows nothing about your table. Alignment is within a field. The `setw` manipulator specifies the width, and the alignment determines whether the fill characters are added on the right (left-alignment) or on the left (right-alignment). The output stream has no memory of other fields. So, for example, if you want to align a column of numbers on their decimal points, you must do that by hand (or ensure that every value in the column has the same number of digits after the decimal point).

# Exploring Formatting

Now that you know the rudiments of formatting output fields, it is time to explore a little, and help you develop a thorough understanding of how field width, padding, and alignment interact. **Read the program in Listing 8-4 and predict its output.**

**Listing 8-4.** *Exploring Field Width, Padding, and Alignment*

```cpp
#include <iomanip>
#include <ios>
#include <iostream>
#include <ostream>

int main()
{
  using namespace std;
  cout << '|' << setfill('*') << setw(6) <<  1234 << '|' << '\n';
  cout << '|' << left <<        setw(6) <<  1234 << '|' << '\n';
  cout << '|' <<                setw(6) << -1234 << '|' << '\n';
  cout << '|' << right <<       setw(6) << -1234 << '|' << '\n';
}
```

**What do you expect as the output from Listing 8-6?**

_____

_____

_____

_____

**Now write a program that will produce the following output.** Don't cheat and simply print a long string. Instead, print only integers and newlines, throwing in the field width, padding, and alignment manipulators you need to achieve the desired output.

```
000042
420000
42
-42-
```

Lots of different programs can achieve the same goal. My program, shown in Listing 8-5, is only one possibility of many.

**Listing 8-5.** *Program to Produce Formatted Output*

```cpp
#include <iomanip>
#include <ios>
#include <iostream>
#include <ostream>

int main()
{
  using namespace std;

  cout << setfill('0') << setw(6) << 42 << '\n';
  cout << left        << setw(6) << 42 << '\n';
  cout << 42 << '\n';
  cout << setfill('-') << setw(4) << -42 << '\n';
}
```

The manipulators that take arguments, such as setw and setfill are declared in <iomanip>. The manipulators without arguments, such as left and boolalpha, are declared in <ios>. If you can't remember, include both headers. If you include a header that you don't really need, you might see a slightly slower compilation time, but no other ill effects will befall you.

# Alternative Syntax

I like to use manipulators because they are concise, clear, and easy to use. You can also apply functions to the output stream object, using the dot operator (.). For example, to set the fill character, you can call std::cout.fill('*'). The fill function is called a *member function* because it is a member of the output stream's type. You cannot apply it to any other kind of object. Only some types have member functions, and each type defines the member functions that it allows. A large part of any C++ library reference is taken up with the various types and their member functions. (The member functions of an output stream are declared in <ostream> along with the output operators. An input stream's member functions are declared in <istream>.)

When setting sticky properties, such as fill character or alignment, you might prefer using member functions instead of manipulators. You can also use member functions to query the current fill character, alignment and other flags, and field width—something you can't do with manipulators.

The member function syntax uses the stream object, a dot (.), and the function call, e.g., cout.fill('0'). Setting the alignment is a little more complicated. Listing 8-6 shows the same program as Listing 8-5, but uses member functions instead of manipulators.

**Listing 8-6.** *A Copy of Listing 8-5, But Using Member Functions*

```cpp
#include <iostream>
#include <ostream>

int main()
{
  using namespace std;

  cout.fill('0');
  cout.width(6);
  cout << 42 << '\n';
  cout.setf(ios_base::left, ios_base::adjustfield);
  cout.width(6);
  cout << 42 << '\n';
  cout << 42 << '\n';
  cout.fill('-');
  cout.width(4);
  cout << -42 << '\n';
}
```

To query the current fill character, call cout.fill(). That's the same function name you use to set the fill character, but when you call the function with no arguments, it returns the current fill character. Similarly, cout.width() returns the current field width. Obtaining the flags is slightly different. You call setf to set flags, such as the alignment, but you call flags() to return the current flags. The details are not important at this time, but if you're curious, consult any library reference.

# On Your Own

Now it is time for you to write a program from scratch. Feel free to look at other programs to make sure you have all the necessary parts. Write this program to produce a multiplication table for the integers from 1 to 10, inclusive:

```
 *|  1   2   3   4   5   6   7   8   9  10
----+---------------------------------------
 1|  1   2   3   4   5   6   7   8   9  10
 2|  2   4   6   8  10  12  14  16  18  20
 3|  3   6   9  12  15  18  21  24  27  30
 4|  4   8  12  16  20  24  28  32  36  40
 5|  5  10  15  20  25  30  35  40  45  50
 6|  6  12  18  24  30  36  42  48  54  60
 7|  7  14  21  28  35  42  49  56  63  70
 8|  8  16  24  32  40  48  56  64  72  80
 9|  9  18  27  36  45  54  63  72  81  90
10| 10  20  30  40  50  60  70  80  90 100
```

After you finish your program, and have made sure it produces the correct output, compare your program with mine, which is shown in Listing 8-7.

**Listing 8-7.** *Printing a Multiplication Table*

```cpp
#include <iomanip>
#include <iostream>
#include <ostream>

int main()
{
  using namespace std;

  int const low(1);        ///< Minimum value for the table
  int const high(10);      ///< Maximum value for the table
  int const colwidth(4);   ///< Fixed width for all columns

  // All numbers must be right-aligned.
  cout << right;

  // First print the header.
  cout << setw(colwidth) << '*'
       << '|';
  for (int i(low); i <= high; i = i + 1)
    cout << setw(colwidth) << i;
  cout << '\n';

  // Print the table rule by using the fill character.
  cout << setfill('-')
       << setw(colwidth) << ""                      // one column's worth of "-"
       << '+'                                        // the vert. & horz. intersection
       << setw((high-low+1) * colwidth) << ""        // the rest of the line
       << '\n';
```

```
  // Reset the fill character.
  cout << setfill(' ');

  // For each row...
  for (int row(low); row <= high; row = row + 1)
  {
    cout << setw(colwidth) << row << '|';
    // Print all the columns.
    for (int col(low); col <= high; col = col + 1)
      cout << setw(colwidth) << row * col;
    cout << '\n';
  }
}
```

My guess is that you wrote your program a little differently than how I wrote mine, or perhaps you wrote it very differently. That's okay. Most likely, you used a hardcoded string for the table rule (the line that separates the header from the table), or perhaps you used a for loop. I used I/O formatting just to show you what is possible. Printing an empty string with a non-zero field width is a quick and easy way to print a repetition of a single character.

Another new feature I threw in for good luck is the const keyword. Use this keyword in a definition to define the object as a constant instead of a variable. The compiler makes sure you do not accidentally assign anything to the object. As you know, named constants make programs easier to read and understand than littering the source code with numbers.

Loops sure are fun! What data structure do you think of first when you think of loops? I hope you picked arrays because that is the subject of the next Exploration.

# EXPLORATION 9

■■■

# Arrays and Vectors

**N**ow that you understand the basics, it is time to start moving on to more exciting challenges. Let's write a real program, something nontrivial, but still simple enough to master this early in the book. Your job is to write a program that reads integers from the standard input, sorts them into ascending order, and then prints the sorted numbers, one per line.

At this point, the book has not quite covered enough material for you to solve this problem, but it is instructive to think about the problem and the tools you may need to solve it. Your first task in this Exploration is to **write pseudo-code for the program.** Write C++ code where you can, and make up whatever you need to tackle the problem.

# Using Vectors for Arrays

You need an array to store the numbers. Given only that much new information, you can write a program to read, sort, and print numbers, but only by hand-coding the sort code. Those of you who suffered through a college algorithms course may remember how to write a bubble sort or quick sort, but why should you need to muck about with such low-level code? Surely, you say, there's a better way. There is: the C++ standard library has a fast sort function that can sort just about anything. Jump straight into the solution in Listing 9-1.

**Listing 9-1.** *Sorting Integers*

```
 1 #include <algorithm>
 2 #include <iostream>
 3 #include <istream>
 4 #include <ostream>
 5 #include <vector>
 6
 7 int main()
 8 {
 9   std::vector<int> data;      // initialized to be empty
10   int x(0);
11
12   // Read integers one at a time.
13   while (std::cin >> x)
14     // Store each integer in the vector.
15     data.push_back(x);
16
17   // Sort the vector.
18   std::sort(data.begin(), data.end());
19
20   // Print the vector, one number per line.
21   for (std::vector<int>::size_type i(0); i != data.size(); i = i + 1)
22     std::cout << data.at(i) << '\n';
23 }
```

Notice anything unusual about the program? Where is the array? C++ has a type called vector, which is like a resizable array. The next section explains it all to you.

# Vectors

Line 9 defines the variable data, of type std::vector<int>. C++ has several container types; that is, data structures that can contain a bunch of objects. One of those containers is vector, which is the closest type C++ has to a conventional array. All C++ containers require an element type; that is, the type of object that you intend to store in the container. In this case, the element type is int. Specify the element type in angle brackets: <int>. That tells the compiler that you want data to be a vector and that the vector will store integers.

**What's missing from the definition?**

___

The vector has no size. Conventional arrays require a size, but `vector` is resizable at runtime. Thus, `data` is initially empty. Like `std::string`, `vector` is a library type, and it has a well-defined initial value, namely, empty.

You can specify an initial size for the `vector`, if you wish, by providing the size as the initial value of the vector. By default, all elements of the vector are filled with zero, but you can specify a different value as the second argument to the initializer.

```
std::vector<int> full_of_zero(10);    // vector of 10 zeros
std::vector<int> full_of_ten(42, 10); // vector of 42 tens
```

A `vector` can change size at runtime, expanding or contracting to any size you need it to be. You can insert and erase items at any position in the vector, although the performance is best when you only add items to, or erase them from the end. That's how the program stores values in `data`: by calling `push_back`, which adds an element to the end of a `vector` (line 15). The "back" of a vector is the end, with the highest index. The "front" is the beginning, so `back()` returns the last element of the vector, and `front()` returns the first. (Just don't call these functions if the `vector` is empty.) If you want to refer to a specific element, use `at(n)`, where n is a zero-based index, as shown on line 22. The `size()` function (line 21) returns the number of elements in the vector. Therefore, valid indices range from 0 to `size() - 1`.

When you read C++ programs, you will most likely see square brackets (`data[n]`) used to access elements of a vector. The difference between square brackets and the `at` function is that the `at` function provides an additional level of safety. If the index is out of bounds, the program will terminate cleanly. On the other hand, using square brackets with an invalid index will result in undefined behavior: you don't know what will happen. Most dangerous is that your program will not terminate, but will continue to run with the bad data. That's why I recommend using `at` for now.

As you can tell from the `std::` prefix, the `vector` type is part of the standard library and is not built into the compiler. Therefore, you need to `#include <vector>`, as shown on line 5. No surprises there.

All the functions mentioned so far are member functions; that is, you must supply a `vector` object on the left-hand side of the dot operator (`.`), and the function call on the right-hand side. Another kind of function does not use the dot operator and is free from any particular object. In most languages, this is the typical kind of function, but sometimes C++ programmers call them "free" functions, to distinguish them from member functions. Line 18 shows an example of a free function, `std::sort`.

**How would you define a vector of strings?**

___

Substitute `std::string` for `int` to get `std::vector<std::string>`. To define a `vector` of vectors, there is one trick; try changing Listing 9-1 to define a `vector` of `std::vector<int>`. (Ignore the compilation error for line 22: you cannot print an entire vector using an output operator. Instead, heed only the compilation error on line 9.)

**What happens?**

_____

_____

_____

C++ builds multicharacter symbols by grabbing as many characters as it can to form a valid token. Thus, any time it sees two greater-than signs next to each other, it automatically considers them to form a single operator (>>).To define a vector of vectors, you must make sure a space character separates the two closing angle brackets, as shown in the following:

```
std::vector<std::vector<int> >  nested_vector;
```

Don't worry if you can't remember this rule. These early Explorations do not use nested vectors, and by the time you get around to using them, you will be more comfortable with C++ syntax rules.

# Iterators

The `std::sort` function sorts stuff, as you can tell from the name. In some other object-oriented language, you might expect `vector` to have a `sort()` member function. Alternatively, the standard library could have a `sort` function that can sort anything the library can throw at it. The C++ library is different.

The `std::sort` function can sort any sequence of objects that can be compared using the less-than (<) operator: numbers, strings, user-defined types, and more. You specify the sequence to sort by providing the starting position (such as `data.begin()`) and one-past-the-end position (`data.end()`).

These "positions" are called *iterators*. An iterator is an object that can refer to an element of a sequence. The sequence might be elements of a vector, or they could be data in a file or database, or nodes in a tree. The implementation of the sequence is irrelevant, and the `std::sort` function knows nothing about it. Instead, the `sort` function sees only the iterators.

Iterators present a simple interface, even if their implementation is complicated. The * operator returns the value to which the iterator refers (`*iter`), and you can advance an iterator to the next element of the sequence (`++iter`). You can compare two iterators to see if they refer to the same element (`iter1 == iter2`). Iterators come in different flavors, and some flavors let you modify the element or move backward in the sequence.

The notion of "one-past-the-end" is a common idiom in the C++ library and programs. A bounded loop needs a starting and ending position. One way to specify these for a vector is to specify the positions of the first and last elements, but that raises a thorny issue of what to do with an empty vector. Long ago, computer scientists invented the concept of a sentry or guard. Sometimes, the sentry was a real element added after the last element of a container, marking the position one-past-the-last element. In that case, a container with only the sentry element was empty. Iterators work similarly, but instead of using an explicit sentry element in the container, the iterator has a sentry value that denotes the position just past the last true element of the sequence.

Thus, `data.begin()` returns an iterator that refers to the first element of data, and `data.end()` returns an iterator with the special one-past-the-end value, as shown in Figure 9-1.

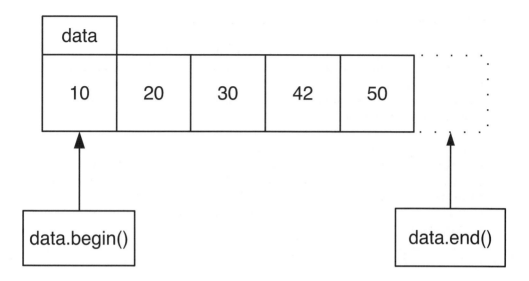

**Figure 9-1.** *Iterators pointing to positions in a vector*

**What is the value of data.begin() if data.size() is zero?**

---

That's right. If the vector is empty, data.begin() returns the same value as data.end(). Because you can compare two iterators, one way to determine if a vector is empty is to test, as demonstrated in the following code:

```
data.begin() == data.end()
```

A better way, however, is to call data.empty(), which returns true if the vector is empty and false if the vector contains at least one element.

Iterators have many uses beyond accessing elements of a vector, and you will see them used often in this book, for input, output, and more.

# Algorithms

The std::sort function is an example of a *generic algorithm*, so named because these functions implement common algorithms and they operate generically. That is, they work for just about anything you can express as a sequence. Most of the standard algorithms are declared in the <algorithm> header, although a few that are numerically oriented are declared in the <numeric> header.

The standard algorithms run the gamut of common programming activities: sorting, searching, copying, comparing, modifying, and more. Searches can be linear or binary. A number of functions, including std::sort, reorder elements within a sequence. No matter what they do, all generic algorithms share some common features.

Almost all the generic algorithms operate on iterators. (The sole exceptions are std::max and std::min, which return the maximum and minimum of two values, respectively.) Earlier, I mentioned that iterators come in different flavors, each flavor having different capabilities.

Although C++ has five flavors in all, you can broadly group them into two categories: read and write.

A read iterator refers to a position in a sequence of values that enables reading from the sequence. The algorithms use read iterators for input, but do not modify the values. Typically, you must specify a range with a pair of read iterators: start and one-past-the-end.

A write iterator refers to a position in a sequence where the algorithm is to write its output. Typically, you specify only the starting position of the output sequence. The algorithm does not and cannot check for overflow, so you must ensure the output sequence has enough room to accommodate everything the algorithm will write.

For example, the std::copy algorithm copies values from an input sequence to an output sequence. The function takes three arguments: two read iterators to specify the input range and one write iterator to specify the start of the output range. You must ensure the output has enough capacity. For example, you might specify the initial size of a vector when you define it, as shown in Listing 9-2.

**Listing 9-2.** *Demonstrating the* std::copy *Function*

```
#include <algorithm>
#include <cassert>
#include <vector>

int main()
{
  std::vector<int> input(3);
  std::vector<int> output(3);
  input.at(0) = 10;
  input.at(1) = 20;
  input.at(2) = 30;
  std::copy(input.begin(), input.end(), output.begin());
  // Now output has a complete copy of input.
  assert(input == output);
}
```

The assert function is a quick way to verify that what you think is true, actually is true. You assert a logical statement, and if you are wrong, the program terminates with a message that identifies the assertion. The assert function is declared in <cassert>; the c means the C++ library inherits this header from the C standard library. Note that assert is one of the rare exceptions to the rule that standard library members begin with std::.

If the program is correct, it runs and exits normally. But if we make a mistake, the assertion triggers and the programs fails with a message.

**Test the program in Listing 9-2.** Just to see what happens when an assertion fails, **comment out the call to std::copy and run it again. Write down the message you get.**

_____

_____

# Member Types

Line 21 of Listing 9-1 looks worse than it is. The definition in the first part of the for loop is particularly scary, even for experienced C++ programmers. In addition to member functions, a C++ class can have member classes. In this case, the parent class, std::vector<int>, has a member type named size_type. Use this type whenever you need to store a size or index for a vector.

The size_type is like an int, but not really. In particular, you cannot assign a negative value to size_type (after all, what kind of vector has a negative size?). Or rather, the language rules let you assign a negative value, but you won't get the result you want or expect. A good compiler warns you that you are making a mistake. Until you learn enough C++ to appreciate the subtleties of size_type, the best strategy is to use size_type only for loop control, for storing the size of a vector, and for storing indices. Don't try to perform arithmetic with size_type values beyond simply incrementing a loop control variable.

Line 21 uses size_type to define the variable i, which is the loop control variable. The loop increments i from 0 up to the vector size, at which point it exits. This is a common idiom for looping through a vector when you need the vector indices. Most programs, in fact, do not need to use the vector indices. I wrote Listing 9-1 that way only to demonstrate the at member function.

A better way to write the program in Listing 9-1 is to use iterators instead of indices and the at() member function. To define an iterator, substitute the member type iterator for size_type in the definition of the loop control variable. Initialize the loop control variable to data.begin(), and end with loop when the iterator equals data.end(). Use the ++ operator to advance the iterator, and * to obtain the vector element to which the iterator refers. Put these pieces together and **rewrite lines 21 and 22 of Listing 9-1 to use iterators.**

_____

_____

Compare your response to Listing 9-3. (For your convenience, I repeat the entire program. That makes it easy for you to compile and test the program.)

**Listing 9-3.** *Sorting Integers, Using Iterators to Print the Results*

```
1 #include <algorithm>
2 #include <iostream>
3 #include <istream>
4 #include <ostream>
5 #include <vector>
6
7 int main()
8 {
9    std::vector<int> data;      // initialized to be empty
10   int x(0);
11
12   // Read integers one at a time.
13   while (std::cin >> x)
14     // Store each integer in the vector.
```

```
15     data.push_back(x);
16
17   // Sort the vector.
18   std::sort(data.begin(), data.end());
19
20   // Print the vector, one number per line.
21   for (std::vector<int>::iterator i(data.begin()); i != data.end(); ++i)
22       std::cout << *i << '\n';
23 }
```

Using iterators instead of indices has many advantages:

- The code works with other kinds of containers (such as linked lists), even if they don't have the at member function.

- The optimizer has more opportunities to produce high-performance code.

- You have fewer chances for mistakes, such as buffer overruns.

- The code is easier to read, especially for experienced C++ programmers.

# Using Iterators and Algorithms

Loops over iterator ranges are so common that many generic algorithms implement the most common actions that you may need to take in a program. With a couple of helpers, you can re-implement the program using only generic algorithms, as shown in Listing 9-4.

**Listing 9-4.** *Sorting Integers by Using Only Generic Algorithms and Iterator Adapters*

```
1 #include <algorithm>
2 #include <iostream>
3 #include <istream>
4 #include <iterator>
5 #include <ostream>
6 #include <vector>
7
8 int main()
9 {
10   std::vector<int> data;
11
12   // Read integers one at a time.
13   std::copy(std::istream_iterator<int>(std::cin),
14            std::istream_iterator<int>(),
15            std::back_inserter(data));
16
17   // Sort the vector.
18   std::sort(data.begin(), data.end());
19
20   // Print the vector, one number per line.
```

```
21   std::copy(data.begin(), data.end(),
22             std::ostream_iterator<int>(std::cout, "\n"));
23 }
```

A std::istream_iterator creates a read iterator that reads from an input stream. Every time you read a value from the iterator, the istream_iterator object uses the >> operator to read a value from the stream. You must supply the type in angle brackets, so that the compiler knows what type of information you want to read from the stream, which you pass as a function argument. With no argument, std::istream_iterator<int>() returns a special one-past-the-end iterator. When the input stream iterator equals this special one-past-the-end iterator, the program has reached the end of the stream, and no more input is available.

The std::back_inserter function takes a vector (or any object that has a push_back function) and wraps it in a write iterator. Any time you assign a value to the iterator, the back insert iterator calls the push_back function to add the value to the object. Using back_inserter, you can guarantee that the program will not overrun the output buffer.

Finally, an ostream_iterator is the counterpart to istream_iterator. It takes an output stream and wraps it in a write iterator. Any value that you assign to the iterator is written to the stream using the << operator. You can pass an optional string argument, and the ostream_iterator writes that string after each value. In this case, the string contains just a newline character, so each number is written on its own line.

All these special iterators are declared in <iterator>. You don't need this header to use an ordinary iterator, such as that returned from a vector's begin() function, but you do need it if you use a special iterator, such as istream_iterator.

Until you are accustomed to using the generic algorithms, iterators, and special iterators, this style of programming can seem unusual. Once you are familiar with these unique C++ library members, you will find such code easier to read and write than more traditional programming styles

It's now time for you to practice using iterators and algorithms.

**Write a program that reads integers from the standard input into a vector. Modify the vector by multiplying each element by 2. Then print the vector, one value per line.**

Test your program using the following input:

68
100
42

**What output do you expect?**

_____

_____

_____

**What output do you actually get?**

_____

_____

_____

Now try running the program with no input at all. **What do you expect?**

_____

**What do you get?**

_____

Listing 9-5 shows one way to write this program using explicit loops. Notice how the *
operator means multiplication when used as a binary (two-operand) operator, and it means
"dereference the iterator" when used as a unary, prefix operator.

**Listing 9-5.** *Doubling Input Values in a Vector*

```
#include <iostream>
#include <istream>
#include <ostream>
#include <vector>

int main()
{
   std::vector<int> data;
   int x(0);

   while (std::cin >> x)
      data.push_back(x);

   for (std::vector<int>::iterator i(data.begin()); i != data.end(); ++i)
      *i = *i * 2;

   for (std::vector<int>::iterator i(data.begin()); i != data.end(); ++i)
      std::cout << *i << '\n';
}
```

Listing 9-6 shows another way, this time using algorithms and iterators for the input and
output loops.

**Listing 9-6.** *Doubling Input Values in a Vector*

```
#include <algorithm>
#include <iostream>
#include <istream>
#include <iterator>
#include <ostream>
#include <vector>

int main()
{
   std::vector<int> data;
```

```
std::copy(std::istream_iterator<int>(std::cin),
          std::istream_iterator<int>(),
          std::back_inserter(data));

for (std::vector<int>::iterator i = data.begin(); i != data.end(); ++i)
   *i = *i * 2;

std::copy(data.begin(), data.end(),
          std::ostream_iterator<int>(std::cout, "\n"));
}
```

The ++ operator is new in this Exploration. The next Exploration takes a closer look at this handy operator.

■■■

# Increment and Decrement

The previous Exploration introduced the increment (++) operator to advance an iterator. This operator works on numeric types, as well. Not surprisingly, it has a decrement counterpart: --. This Exploration takes a closer look at these operators, which appear so often they are part of the language name.

---

**Note** I know that you C, Java, etc., programmers have been waiting for this Exploration ever since I wrote i = i + 1 in Exploration 7. As you saw in the previous Exploration, the ++ operator means more in C++ than what you're used to. That's why I waited until now to introduce it.

---

## Increment

The ++ operator is familiar to C, Java, Perl, and many other programmers. C was the first wide-spread language to introduce this operator to mean "increment" or "add 1." C++ expanded the usage it inherited from C; the standard library uses the ++ operator in several new ways, such as advancing an iterator (as you saw in the previous Exploration).

The increment operator comes in two flavors: prefix and postfix. The best way to understand the difference between these two flavors is with a demonstration, as shown in Listing 10-1.

**Listing 10-1.** *Demonstrating the Difference Between Prefix and Postfix Increment*

```
#include <iostream>
#include <ostream>

int main()
{
  int x = 42;

  std::cout << "x   = " << x   << "\n";
  std::cout << "++x = " << ++x << "\n";
  std::cout << "x   = " << x   << "\n";
```

```
  std::cout << "x++ = " << x++ << "\n";
  std::cout << "x   = " << x   << "\n";
}
```

**Predict the output of the program.**

_____

_____

_____

_____

_____

**What is the actual output?**

_____

_____

_____

_____

_____

**Explain the difference between prefix (++x) and postfix (x++) increment.**

_____

_____

_____

Described briefly, the prefix operator increments the variable first: the value of the expression is the value after incrementing. The postfix operator saves the old value, increments the variable, and uses the old value as the value of the expression.

As a general rule, use prefix instead of postfix unless you need the postfix functionality. Rarely is the difference significant, but the postfix operator must save a copy of the old value, which may impose a small performance cost. If you don't need to use postfix, why pay that price?

# Decrement

The increment operator has a decrement counterpart: --. The decrement operator subtracts one instead of adding one. Decrement also has a prefix and postfix flavor. The prefix operator predecrements, and the postfix operator postdecrements.

You can increment and decrement any variable with a numeric type; however, only some iterators permit decrement.

For example, all write iterators move forward only. You can use the increment operator (prefix or postfix), but not decrement. Test this for yourself. Write a program that uses std::ostream_iterator, and try to use the decrement operator on the iterator. (If you need a hint, look at Listing 9-4. Save the ostream_iterator object in a variable. Then use the decrement operator. It doesn't matter that the program makes no sense; it won't get past the compiler, anyway.)

**What error message do you get?**

_____

_____

Different compilers issue different messages, but the essence of the message should be that the -- operator is not defined. If you need help with the program, see Listing 10-2.

**Listing 10-2.** *Erroneous Program that Applies Decrement to an Output Iterator*

```cpp
#include <iostream>
#include <iterator>
#include <ostream>
#include <vector>

int main()
{
  std::vector<int> data;
  data.push_back(10);
  data.push_back(42);
  std::ostream_iterator<int> out(std::ostream_iterator<int>(std::cout, ""));
  std::copy(data.begin(), data.end(), out);
  --out;
}
```

## INITIALIZING A VECTOR

Listing 10-2 stores numbers in data by defining an empty vector then adding values to it by calling push_back. Many C++ programmers don't like this style, and the next major revision to the C++ language will permit a more graceful initialization method:

```cpp
std::vector<int> data({ 10, 42 });
```

You may be using a compiler that conforms to the new standard. Even if the standard is not yet released, your compiler may implement the new syntax as an extension. Some compiler vendors are experimenting with language features as part of the effort to revise the standard. If you have a new compiler, give the new syntax a whirl, and see how you like it.

This book covers the current standard, so all the examples will work even if your compiler obeys the current language standard, but a little extra credit never hurts, so feel free to explore some of the new language features that I will mention along the way.

A vector's iterators allow increment and decrement. Using increment and decrement operators on iterators, **write a program that reads integers from the standard input into**

**a vector, reverses the order of the vector, and writes the result.** (No fair peeking in a language reference and using the std::reverse algorithm. Use two iterators: one pointing to the start of the vector, and the other pointing to the end. Stop the loop when the iterators meet. Make sure they don't pass each other, and make sure your program does not try to dereference the one-past-the-end iterator.)

Test your program on input with both an even and an odd number of integers. Compare your program with the one in Listing 10-3.

**Listing 10-3.** *Reversing the Input Order*

```
#include <algorithm>
#include <iostream>
#include <istream>
#include <iterator>
#include <ostream>
#include <vector>

int main()
{
  std::vector<int> data;
  int x;
  while (std::cin >> x)
    data.push_back(x);

  for (std::vector<int>::iterator start(data.begin()), end(data.end());
       start != end;
       /*empty*/)
  {
    --end;
    if (start != end)
    {
      int tmp = *start;
      *start = *end;
      *end = tmp;
      ++start;
    }
  }

  std::copy(data.begin(), data.end(), std::ostream_iterator<int>(std::cout, "\n"));
}
```

The start iterator points to the beginning of the data vector, and end initially points to one-past-the-end. If the vector is empty, the for loop terminates without executing the loop body. The loop body decrements end, so it points to an actual element of the vector. If the vector contains an even number of elements, the if condition is true, so *start and *end swap values, and the program advances start one position.

Notice that the program is careful to compare start != end after each increment or decrement operation. If the program had only one comparison, it would be possible for start and end to pass each other. The loop condition would never be true, and the program would exhibit undefined behavior, so the sky would fall, the earth would swallow me, or worse.

Also note how the for loop has an empty postiteration part. The iteration logic appears in different places in the loop body, which is not the preferred way to write a loop, but is necessary in this case.

You can rewrite the loop so the postiteration logic appears only in the loop header. Some programmers argue that distributing the increment and decrement in the loop body makes the loop harder to understand, and in particular, harder to prove the loop terminates correctly. On the other hand, cramming everything in the loop header makes the loop condition especially tricky to understand, as you can see in Listing 10-4.

**Listing 10-4.** *Rewriting the* for *Loop*

```
#include <algorithm>
#include <iostream>
#include <istream>
#include <iterator>
#include <ostream>
#include <vector>

int main()
{
  std::vector<int> data;
  int x;
  while (std::cin >> x)
    data.push_back(x);

  for (std::vector<int>::iterator start(data.begin()), end(data.end());
       start != end and start != --end;
       ++start)
  {
    int tmp = *start;
    *start = *end;
    *end = tmp;
  }

  std::copy(data.begin(), data.end(), std::ostream_iterator<int>(std::cout, "\n"));
}
```

To keep all the logic in the loop header, it was necessary to use a new operator: and. You will learn more about this operator in the next Exploration; meanwhile, just believe that it implements a logical and operation and keep reading.

Most experienced C++ programmers will probably prefer Listing 10-4, whereas most beginners will probably prefer Listing 10-3. Hiding a decrement in the middle of a condition makes the code harder to read and understand. It's too easy to overlook the decrement. As you gain experience with C++, however, you will become more comfortable with increments and decrements, and Listing 10-4 will start to grow on you.

---

**■Note** I prefer Listing 10-3 over Listing 10-4. I really don't like to bury increment and decrement operators in the middle of a complicated condition.

---

So what else would experienced C++ programmers do? Because they have broader knowledge of the C++ standard library, they would make better use of it. In particular, they would use the std::reverse algorithm, which reverses the elements in a range.

```
std::reverse(data.begin(), data.end());
```

Another idea is to use istream_iterator, which you learned about in Exploration 9. This time you will use it a little differently. Instead of using back_inserter and the copy algorithm, Listing 10-5 calls the insert member function, which copies values from any iterator range into the vector. The values are inserted before the position given by the first argument (data.end() in this case).

**Listing 10-5.** *Taking Advantage of the Standard Library*

```
#include <algorithm>
#include <iostream>
#include <istream>
#include <iterator>
#include <ostream>
#include <vector>

int main()
{
  std::vector<int> data;

  // Read integers from the standard input, and append them to the end of data.
  data.insert(data.end(),
            std::istream_iterator<int>(std::cin), std::istream_iterator<int>());

  // Reverse the order of the contents of data.
  std::reverse(data.begin(), data.end());
  // Print data, one number per line.
  std::copy(data.begin(), data.end(), std::ostream_iterator<int>(std::cout, "\n"));
}
```

As you learn more C++, you will find other aspects of this program that lend themselves to improvement. I encourage you to revisit old programs and see how your new techniques can often simplify the programming task. I'll do the same as I revisit examples throughout this book.

Listing 10-4 introduced the and operator. The next Exploration takes a closer look at this operator as well as other logical operators and their use in conditions.

# EXPLORATION 11

███

# Conditions and Logic

**Y**ou first met the bool type in Exploration 2. This type has two possible values: true and false, which are reserved keywords (unlike in C). Although most Explorations have not needed to use the bool type, many have used logical expressions in loop and if-statement conditions. This Exploration examines the many aspects of the bool type and logical operators.

## I/O and bool

C++ I/O streams permit reading and writing bool values. By default, streams treat them as numeric values: true is 1 and false is 0. The manipulator std::boolalpha (declared in <ios>) tells a stream to interpret bool values as words. By default, the words are true and false. (In Exploration 17, you'll discover how to use a language other than English.) You use the std::boolalpha manipulator the same way you do any other manipulator (as you saw in Exploration 8). For an input stream, use an input operator with the manipulator.

**Write a program that demonstrates how C++ formats and prints bool values, numerically and textually.**

Compare your program with Listing 11-1.

**Listing 11-1.** *Printing* bool *Values*

```
#include <ios>
#include <iostream>
#include <ostream>

int main()
{
  std::cout << "true=" << true << '\n';
  std::cout << "false=" << false << '\n';
  std::cout << std::boolalpha;
  std::cout << "true=" << true << '\n';
  std::cout << "false=" << false << '\n';
}
```

**How do you think C++ handles bool values for input?**

_____

**Write a program to test your assumptions. Were you correct? _____ Explain how an input stream handles bool input:**

_____

_____

By default, when an input stream needs to read a bool value, it actually reads an integer, and if the integer's value is 1, the stream interprets that as true. The value 0 is false, and any other value results in an error

With the std::boolalpha manipulator, the input stream requires the exact text true or false. Integers are not allowed, nor are any case differences. The input stream accepts only those exact words.

Use the std::noboolalpha manipulator to revert to the default numeric Boolean values. Thus, you can mix alphabetic and numeric representations of bool in a single stream:

```
bool a(true), b(false);
std::cin >> std::boolalpha >> a >> std::noboolalpha >> b;
std::cout << std::boolalpha << a << ' ' << std::noboolalpha << b;
```

Reading and writing bool values does not actually happen all that often in most programs, but you needed to learn how to write bool values before you can continue this Exploration.

# Boolean Type

C++ automatically converts many different types to bool, so you can use integers, I/O stream objects, and other values whenever you need a bool, such as in a loop or if-statement condition. You can see this for yourself in Listing 11-2.

**Listing 11-2.** _Automatic Type Conversion to_ bool

```
 1 #include <ios>
 2 #include <iostream>
 3 #include <ostream>
 4
 5 int main()
 6 {
 7   bool b;
 8   std::cout << std::boolalpha;
 9   b = false;              std::cout << b << ' ';
10   b = true;               std::cout << b << ' ';
11   b = false;              std::cout << b << ' ';
12   b = true;               std::cout << b << ' ';
13   b = 42;                 std::cout << b << ' ';
14   b = 3.1415926535897;    std::cout << b << ' ';
15   b = 0;                  std::cout << b << ' ';
16   b = -0.0;               std::cout << b << ' ';
```

```
17   b = -1;              std::cout << b << ' ';
18   b = "1";             std::cout << b << ' ';
19   b = "0";             std::cout << b << ' ';
20   b = "false";         std::cout << b << ' ';
21   b = "";              std::cout << b << ' ';
22   b = '0';             std::cout << b << ' ';
23   b = '\0';            std::cout << b << ' ';
24   b = std::cout;       std::cout << b << ' ';
25   b = std::cin;        std::cout << b << ' ';
26   std::cout << '\n';
27 }
```

**Predict the output from Listing 11-2:**

_____

Check your answer. **Were you right?** _____

You may have been fooled by lines 18 through 21. C++ does not interpret the contents of string literals to decide whether to convert the string to true or false. All character strings are true, even empty ones. (The C++ language designers did not do this to be perverse. There's a good reason that strings are true, but you will need to learn quite a bit more C++ in order to understand why.)

On the other hand, character literals are completely different from string literals. The compiler converts the escape character '\0' to false. All other characters are true.

Recall from many previous examples (especially in Exploration 3) that loop conditions often depend on an input operation. If the input succeeds, the loop condition is true. What is actually happening is that C++ knows how to convert a stream object (such as std::cin) to bool. Every I/O stream keeps track of its internal state, and if any operation fails, the stream remembers that fact. When you convert a stream to bool, if the stream is in a failure state, the result is false. Not all complex types can be converted to bool, however.

**What do you expect to happen when you compile and run Listing 11-3?**

_____

**Listing 11-3.** *Converting a* std::string *to* bool

```
#include <iostream>
#include <ostream>
#include <string>

int main()
{
  std::string empty;
  bool b;

  b = empty;
  std::cout << b << '\n';
}
```

The compiler reports an error because it does not know how to convert std::string to bool.

---

**▪Note** If you think the standard library should support such a conversion, consider how you would define the conversion. Would it be like character strings: everything is true? That doesn't seem particularly useful, so you would probably choose to interpret the string. Perhaps "0" and "false" could be false, and everything else would be true. So should "no" be false, also? What about "maybe"? Or "faux"? Or "FALSE"? Such decisions are best left to the application programmer (who can use the c_str() member of std::string if he wants to force the issue), not the language designer.

---

What about std::vector? **Do you think C++ defines a conversion from std::vector to bool?** _____ Write a program to test your hypothesis. **What is your conclusion?**

---

This is another case in which no general solution is feasible. Should an empty vector be false whereas all others are true? Maybe a std::vector<int> that contains only 0 elements should be false. Only the application programmer can make these decisions, so the C++ library designers wisely chose not to make them for you; therefore you cannot convert std::vector to bool. However, there are ways of obtaining the desired result by using member functions.

# Logic Operators

Real-world conditions are often more complicated than merely converting a single value to bool. To accommodate this, C++ offers the usual logical operators: and, or, and not (which are reserved keywords). They have their usual meaning from mathematical logic, namely that and is false unless both operands are true, or is true unless both operands are false, and not inverts the value of its operand.

More important, however, is that the built-in and and or operators do not evaluate their right-hand operand unless they need to. The and operator needs to evaluate its right-hand operand only if the left-hand operand is true. (If the left-hand operand is false, the entire expression is false, and there is no need to evaluate the right-hand operand.) Similarly, the or operator evaluates its right-hand operand only if the left-hand operand is true. Stopping the evaluation early like this is known as *short-circuiting*.

For example, suppose you are writing a simple loop to examine all the elements of a vector to determine whether they are all equal to zero. The loop ends when you reach the end of the vector or when you find an element not equal to zero.

**Write a program that reads numbers into a vector, searches the vector for a non-zero element, and prints a message about whether the vector is all zero.**

You can solve this problem without using a logical operator, but try to use one, just for practice. Take a look at Listing 11-4 to see one way to solve this problem.

**Listing 11-4.** *Using Short-Circuiting to Test for Non-Zero Vector Elements*

```
 1 #include <iostream>
 2 #include <istream>
 3 #include <iterator>
 4 #include <ostream>
 5 #include <vector>
 6
 7 int main()
 8 {
 9   std::vector<int> data;
10   data.insert(data.begin(),
11               std::istream_iterator<int>(std::cin),
12               std::istream_iterator<int>());
13
14   std::vector<int>::iterator iter;
15   for (iter = data.begin(); iter != data.end() and *iter == 0; ++iter)
16     /*empty*/;
17   if (iter == data.end())
18     std::cout << "data contains all zeroes\n";
19   else
20     std::cout << "data does not contain all zeroes\n";
21 }
```

Line 15 is the key. The iterator advances over the vector and tests for zero-valued elements.

**What happens when the iterator reaches the end of the vector?**

_____

_____

The condition iter != data.end() becomes false at the end of the vector. Because of short-circuiting, C++ never evaluates the *iter == 0 part of the expression, which is good.

**Why is this good? What would happen if short-circuiting did not take place?**

_____

_____

Imagine that iter != data.end() is false; in other words the value of iter is data.end(). That means *iter is just like *data.end(), which is bad—really bad. You are not allowed to dereference the one-past-the-end iterator. If you are lucky, it would crash your program. If you are unlucky, your program will continue to run, but with completely unpredictable and erroneous data; and therefore, unpredictable and erroneous results.

Short-circuiting guarantees that C++ will not evaluate *iter when iter equals data.end(), which means iter will always be valid when the program dereferences it, which is good. Some languages (such as Ada) use different operators for short-circuiting and non–short-circuiting operations. C++ does not. The built-in logical operators always perform short-circuiting, so you never accidentally use non–short-circuiting when you intended to use the short-circuiting operator.

# Old-Fashioned Syntax

The logical operators have symbolic versions: && for and, || for or, and ! for not. The keywords are clearer, easier to read, easier to understand, and less error-prone. That's right, less error-prone. You see, && means and, but & is also an operator. Similarly, | is a valid operator. Thus, if you accidentally write & instead of &&, your program will compile and even run. It might seem to run correctly for a while, but it will eventually fail because & and && mean different things. (You'll learn about & and | later in this book.) New C++ programmers aren't the only ones to make this mistake. I've seen highly experienced C++ programmers write & when they mean && or | instead of ||. Avoid this error by using only the keyword logical operators.

I was hesitant about even mentioning the symbolic operators, but I can't ignore them. Most C++ programs use the symbolic operators instead of the keyword equivalents. Most C++ programmers, having grown up with the symbols, prefer to continue to use the symbols over the keywords. This is your chance to become a trend-setter. Eschew the old-fashioned, harder-to-read, harder-to-understand, error-prone symbols, and embrace the keywords.

# Comparison Operators

The built-in comparison operators always yield bool results, regardless of their operands. You have already seen == and != for equality and inequality. You also saw < for less than, and you can guess that > means greater than. Similarly, you probably already know that <= means less-than-or-equal and >= means greater-than-or-equal.

These operators produce the expected results when you use them with numeric operands. You can even use them with vectors of numeric types.

**Write a program that demonstrates how < works with a vector of int.** (If you're having trouble writing the program, take a look at Listing 11-5.) **What are the rules that govern < for a vector?**

_____

_____

_____

_____

C++ compares vectors at the element level. That is, the first elements of two vectors are compared. If one element is smaller than the other, its vector is considered less than the other. If one vector is a prefix of the other (that is, the vectors are identical up to the length of the shorter vector), the shorter vector is less than the longer one.

**Listing 11-5.** _Comparing Vectors_

```
#include <iostream>
#include <ostream>
#include <vector>

int main()
{
    std::vector<int> a, b;
```

```
    a.push_back(10);
    a.push_back(20);
    a.push_back(30);
    b.push_back(10);
    b.push_back(20);
    b.push_back(30);
    if (a != b) std::cout << "wrong: a != b\n";
    if (a < b)  std::cout << "wrong: a < b\n";
    if (a > b)  std::cout << "wrong: a > b\n";
    if (a == b) std::cout << "okay: a == b\n";
    if (a >= b) std::cout << "okay: a >= b\n";
    if (a <= b) std::cout << "okay: a <= b\n";

    a.push_back(40);
    if (a != b) std::cout << "okay: a != b\n";
    if (a < b)  std::cout << "wrong: a < b\n";
    if (a > b)  std::cout << "okay: a > b\n";
    if (a == b) std::cout << "wrong: a == b\n";
    if (a >= b) std::cout << "okay: a >= b\n";
    if (a <= b) std::cout << "wrong: a <= b\n";

    b.push_back(42);
    if (a != b) std::cout << "okay: a != b\n";
    if (a < b)  std::cout << "okay: a < b\n";
    if (a > b)  std::cout << "wrong: a > b\n";
    if (a == b) std::cout << "wrong: a == b\n";
    if (a >= b) std::cout << "wrong: a >= b\n";
    if (a <= b) std::cout << "okay: a <= b\n";
}
```

C++ uses the same rules when comparing `std::string` types, but not when comparing two character string literals.

**Write a program that demonstrates how C++ compares two `std::string` objects by comparing their contents.**

Compare your solution with mine in Listing 11-6.

**Listing 11-6.** *Demonstrating How C++ Compares Strings*

```
#include <iostream>
#include <ostream>
#include <string>

int main()
{
    std::string a("abc"), b("abc");
    if (a != b) std::cout << "wrong: abc != abc\n";
    if (a < b)  std::cout << "wrong: abc < abc\n";
    if (a > b)  std::cout << "wrong: abc > abc\n";
```

```
    if (a == b) std::cout << "okay: abc == abc\n";
    if (a >= b) std::cout << "okay: abc >= abc\n";
    if (a <= b) std::cout << "okay: abc <= abc\n";

    a.push_back('d');
    if (a != b) std::cout << "okay: abcd != abc\n";
    if (a < b)  std::cout << "wrong: abcd < abc\n";
    if (a > b)  std::cout << "okay: abcd > abc\n";
    if (a == b) std::cout << "wrong: abcd == abc\n";
    if (a >= b) std::cout << "okay: abcd >= abc\n";
    if (a <= b) std::cout << "wrong: abcd <= abc\n";

    b.push_back('e');
    if (a != b) std::cout << "okay: abcd != abce\n";
    if (a < b)  std::cout << "okay: abcd < abce\n";
    if (a > b)  std::cout << "wrong: abcd > abce\n";
    if (a == b) std::cout << "wrong: abcd == abce\n";
    if (a >= b) std::cout << "wrong: abcd >= abce\n";
    if (a <= b) std::cout << "okay: abcd <= abce\n";
}
```

Testing how C++ compares quoted strings is more difficult. Instead of using the contents of the string, the compiler uses the location of the strings in memory, which is a detail of the compiler's internal workings and has no bearing on anything practical. Thus, unless you know how the compiler works, you cannot predict how it will compare two quoted strings. In other words, don't do that. Make sure you create std::string objects before you compare strings. It's okay if only one operand is std::string. The other can be a quoted string, and the compiler will automatically create a std::string from the quoted string, as demonstrated in the following example:

```
if ("help" > "hello") std::cout << "Bad. Bad. Bad. Don't do this!\n";
if (std::string("help") > "hello") std::cout << "this works\n";
if ("help" > std::string("hello")) std::cout << "this also works\n";
if (std::string("help") > std::string("hello")) std::cout << "and this works\n";
```

The next Exploration does not relate directly to Boolean logic and conditions. Instead, it shows how to write compound statements, which you need in order to write any kind of useful conditional statement.

# Compound Statements

You have already used compound statements (that is, lists of statements enclosed in curly braces) in many programs. Now it's time to learn some of the special rules and uses for compound statements, which are also known as *blocks*.

## Statements

C++ has some hairy, scary syntax rules. By comparison though, the syntax for statements is downright simplistic. The C++ grammar defines most statements in terms of other statements. For example, the rule for while statements is:

**while (** *condition* **)** *statement*

In this example, bold elements are required, such as the while keyword. *Italic* elements stand for other syntax rules. As you can likely deduce from the example, a while statement can have any statement as the loop body, including another while statement.

The reason most statements appear to end with a semicolon is because the most fundamental statement in C++ is just an expression followed by a semicolon.

*expression* **;**

This kind of statement is called an *expression statement*.

I haven't discussed the precise rules for expressions yet, but they work the way they do in most other languages, with a few differences. Most significant is that assignment is an expression in C++ (as it is in C, Java, C#, etc., but not in Pascal, Basic, Fortran, etc.). Consider the following:

```
while (std::cin >> x)
  sum = sum + x;
```

This example demonstrates a single while statement. Part of the while statement is another statement: in this case, an expression statement. The expression in the expression statement is sum = sum + x. Expressions in expression statements are often assignments or function calls, but the language permits any expression. The following, therefore, is a valid statement:

```
42;
```

**What do you think happens if you use this statement in a program?**

_____

**Try it. What actually happens?**

_____

Modern compilers are usually able to detect statements that serve no useful purpose and eliminate them from the program. Typically, the compiler tells you what it's doing, but you might need to supply an extra option to tell the compiler to be extra picky. For example, try the -Wall option for g++ or /Wall for Microsoft Visual C++. (That's Wall as in all warnings, not the thing holding up your roof.)

The syntax rule for a compound statement is

```
{ statement* }
```

where * means zero-or-more occurrences of the preceding rule (statement). Notice that the closing curly brace has no semicolon.

**How does C++ parse the following?**

```
while (std::cin >> x)
{
    sum = sum + x;
    ++count;
}
```

_____

_____

_____

Once again, you have a while statement, so the loop body must be a single statement. In this example, the loop body is a compound statement. The compound statement consists of two expression statements. Figure 12-1 shows a tree view of the same information.

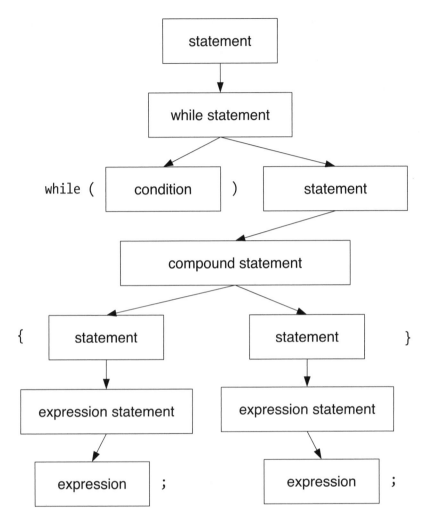

**Figure 12-1.** *Simplified parse tree for C++ statements*

Consider the body of main( ), such as the one in Listing 12-1. What do you see? That's right, it's a compound statement. It's an ordinary block, and it follows the same rules as any other block. In case you were wondering, the body of main( ) must be a compound statement. This is one of the few circumstances in which C++ requires a specific kind of statement, instead of allowing any statement whatsoever.

**Find and fix the errors in Listing 12-1.** Visually locate as many errors as you can by reading the code. When you think you found and fixed them all, try compiling and running the program.

**Listing 12-1.** *Finding Statement Errors*

```
 1 #include <iostream>
 2 #include <ostream>
 3 #include <vector>
 4
 5 int main()
 6 {
 7   std::vector<int> positive_data, negative_data;
 8
 9   for (int x(0); std::cin >> x ;) {
10     if (x < 0);
11     {
12       negative_data.push_back(x)
13     };
14     else
15     {
16       positive_data.push_back(x)
17     }
18   };
19 }
```

Record all the errors in Listing 12-1:

_____

_____

_____

**Did you find them all without the compiler's help?** _____

The errors are:

- Extra semicolon on line 10

- Extra semicolon on line 13

- Missing semicolon from the end of lines 12 and 16

- Extra semicolon on line 18

For extra credit, **which errors are not syntax violations (the compiler will not alert you to them) and do not affect the program's behavior?**

_____

_____

If you answered "the extra semicolon on line 18", give yourself a star. Strictly speaking, the extra semicolon represents an empty, do-nothing statement, called a *null statement.* Such a statement sometimes has a use in a loop, especially a for loop that does all its work in the loop header, leaving nothing for the loop body to do. (See an example in Listing 11-4.)

Thus, the way the compiler interprets line 10 is that the semicolon is the statement body for the if statement. The next statement is a compound statement, which is followed by an else, which has no corresponding if, hence the error. Every else must be a counterpart to an earlier if in the same statement. In other words, every if condition must be followed by exactly one statement then by an optional else keyword and another statement. You cannot use else in any other way.

As written, the if statement on line 10 is followed by three statements: a null statement, a compound statement, and another null statement. The solution is to delete the null statements by deleting the semicolons on lines 10 and 13.

The statements that make up a compound statement can be any statements, including other compound statements. The next section explains why you might want to nest a compound statement within another compound statement.

# Local Definitions and Scope

Compound statements do more than simply group multiple statements into a single statement. You can also group definitions within the block. Any variable that you define in a block is visible only within the confines of the block. The region where you can use a variable is known as the variable's *scope*. A good programming practice is to limit the scope to as small a region as possible. Limiting the scope of a variable serves several purposes:

- *Preventing mistakes*: You can't accidentally use a variable's name outside of its scope.

- *Communicating intent*: Anyone who reads your code can tell how a variable is used. If variables are defined at the broadest scope possible, whoever reads your code must spend more time and effort trying to determine where different variables are used.

- *Reusing names*: How many times can you use the variable i as a loop control variable? You can use and reuse it as often as you like, provided each time you limit the variable's scope to its loop.

Listing 12-2 shows some examples of local definitions. The lines highlighted in bold indicate local definitions.

**Listing 12-2.** *Local Variable Definitions*

```
#include <algorithm>
#include <cassert>
#include <iostream>
#include <iterator>
#include <ostream>
#include <string>
#include <vector>

int main()
{
  std::vector<int> data;
```

```
data.insert(data.begin(), std::istream_iterator<int>(std::cin),
                          std::istream_iterator<int>());

// Silly way to sort a vector. Assume that the initial portion
// of the vector has already been sorted, up to the iterator iter.
// Find where *iter belongs in the already sorted portion of the vector.
// Erase *iter from the vector and re-insert it at its sorted position.
// Use binary search to speed up the search for the proper position.
// Invariant: elements at indices [0, i) are already sorted.
for (std::vector<int>::iterator iter(data.begin()); iter != data.end(); )
{
  // Find where data.at(iter) belongs by calling the standard algorithm
  // lower_bound, which performs a binary search and returns an iterator
  // that points into data at a position where the value should be inserted.
  int value(*iter);
  std::vector<int>::iterator here(std::lower_bound(data.begin(), iter, value));
  iter = data.erase(iter);
  data.insert(here, value);
}

// Debugging code: check that the loop is actually sorted. Do this by comparing
// each element with the preceding element in the vector.
for (std::vector<int>::iterator iter(data.begin()), prev(data.end());
     iter != data.end();
     ++iter)
{
  if (prev != data.end())
    assert(not (*iter < *prev));
  prev = iter;
}

// Print the sorted vector all on one line. Start the line with "{" and
// end it with "}". Separate elements with commas.
// An empty vector prints as "{ }".
std::cout << '{';
std::string separator(" ");
for (std::vector<int>::iterator iter(data.begin()); iter != data.end(); ++iter)
{
  std::cout << separator << *iter;
  separator = ", ";
}
std::cout << " }\n";
}
```

Listing 12-2 has a lot of new functions and features, so let's look at the code one section at a time.

The definition of data is a local definition in a block. True, almost all your definitions have been at this outermost level, but a compound statement is a compound statement, and any definition in a compound statement is a local definition. That begs the question of whether you can define a variable outside of all blocks. The answer is yes, but you rarely want to. C++ permits global variables, but no program in this book has needed to define any yet. I'll cover global variables when the time is right (which would be Exploration 38).

A for loop has its own special scope rules. As you learned in Exploration 7, the initialization part of a for loop can, and often does, define a loop control variable. The scope of that variable is limited to the for loop, as though the for statement was enclosed in an extra set of curly braces.

The value variable is also local to the for loop's body. If you try to use this variable outside of the loop, the compiler issues an error message. In this case, you have no reason to use this variable outside the loop, so define the variable inside the loop.

The lower_bound algorithm performs a binary search that tries to find a value in a range of sorted values. It returns an iterator that points to the first occurrence of the value in the range, or if the value is not found, the position where you can insert the value and keep the range in order. This is exactly what this program needs to sort the data vector.

The erase member function deletes an element from a vector, reducing the vector's size by one. Pass an iterator to erase to designate which element to delete, and save the return value, which is an iterator that refers to the new value at that position in the vector. The insert function inserts a value (the second argument) just before the position designated by an iterator (the first argument).

You can define more than one variable at a time by separating the variables with a comma. Each variable gets its own initializer.

Notice how you can use and reuse the name iter. Each loop has its own distinct variable named iter. Each iter is local to its loop. If you were to write sloppy code and fail to initialize iter, the variable's initial value would be junk. It is not the same variable as the one defined earlier in the program, so its value is not the same as the old value of the old variable.

The separator variable holds a separator string to print between elements when printing the vector. It too is a local variable, but local to the main program's block. However, by defining it just before it is used, you communicate the message that this variable is not needed earlier in main. It helps prevent mistakes that can arise if you reuse a variable from one part of main in another part.

Another way you can help limit the scope of variable such as separator is to define it in a block within a block, as shown in Listing 12-3. (This version of the program replaces the loops with calls to standard algorithms, which is a better way to write C++ programs when you are not trying to make a point.)

**Listing 12-3.** *Local Variable Definitions in a Nested Block*

```
#include <algorithm>
#include <cassert>
#include <iostream>
#include <iterator>
#include <ostream>
#include <string>
#include <vector>

int main()
{
```

```cpp
std::vector<int> data;
data.insert(data.begin(), std::istream_iterator<int>(std::cin),
                          std::istream_iterator<int>());

std::sort(data.begin(), data.end());

{
  // Print the sorted vector all on one line. Start the line with "{" and
  // end it with "}". Separate elements with commas. An empty vector prints
  // as "{ }".
  std::cout << '{';
  std::string separator(" ");
  for (std::vector<int>::iterator iter(data.begin()); iter != data.end(); ++iter)
  {
    std::cout << separator << *iter;
    separator = ", ";
  }
  std::cout << " }\n";
}
// Cannot use separator out here.
}
```

Most C++ programmers nest blocks infrequently. As you learn more C++, you will learn a variety of techniques that improve on nested blocks and keep your main program from looking so cluttered.

# Definitions in for Loop Headers

What if you did not define loop control variables inside the for loop header, but defined them outside the loop, instead? Try it.

**Rewrite Listing 12-2 so you don't define any variables in the for loop headers.**

What do you think? **Does the new code look better or worse than the original?** _____
**Why?**

_____

_____

_____

Personally, I find for loops can become cluttered very easily. Nonetheless, keeping loop control variables local to the loop is critical for clarity and code comprehension. When faced with a large, unknown program, one of the difficulties you face in understanding that program is knowing when and how variables can take on new values. If a variable is local to a loop, you know the variable cannot be modified outside the loop. That is valuable information. If you still need convincing, try reading and understanding Listing 12-4.

**Listing 12-4.** *Mystery Function*

```cpp
#include <algorithm>
#include <cassert>
#include <iostream>
#include <iterator>
#include <ostream>
#include <string>
#include <vector>

int main()
{
  int v;
  std::vector<int> data;
  std::vector<int>::iterator i, p;
  std::string s;

  std::copy(std::istream_iterator<int>(std::cin),
            std::istream_iterator<int>(),
            std::back_inserter(data));
  i = data.begin();

  while (i != data.end())
  {
    v = *i;
    p = std::lower_bound(data.begin(), i, v);
    i = data.erase(i);
    data.insert(p, v);
  }

  s = " ";
  for (p = i, i = data.begin(); i != data.end(); p = i, ++i)
  {
    if (p != data.end())
      assert(not (*i < *p));
  }

  std::cout << '{';
  for (i = data.begin(); i != data.end(); ++i)
  {
    v = *p;
    std::cout << s << v;
    s = ", ";
  }
  std::cout << " }\n";
}
```

Well, that wasn't too hard, was it? After all, you recently finished reading Listing 12-2, so you can see that Listing 12-4 is intended to do the same thing, but is reorganized slightly. The difficulty is in keeping track of the values of p and i, and ensuring that they have the correct value at each step of the program. Try compiling and running the program. **Record your observations:**

_____

_____

_____

**What went wrong?**

_____

_____

_____

I made a mistake and wrote v = *p instead of v = *i. Congratulations if you spotted this error before you ran the program. If the variables had been properly defined local to their respective scopes, this error could never have occurred.

The next Exploration introduces file I/O, so your exercises can read and write files instead of using console I/O. I'm sure your fingers will appreciate it.

■ ■ ■

# Introduction to File I/O

**R**eading from standard input and writing to standard output works fine for many trivial programs, and it is a standard idiom for UNIX and related operating systems. Nonetheless, real programs must be able to open named files for reading, writing, or both. This Exploration introduces the basics of file I/O. Later Explorations will tackle more sophisticated I/O issues.

## Reading Files

The most common file-related task in these early Explorations will involve reading from a file instead of from the standard input stream. One of the greatest benefits of this is it saves a lot of tedious typing. Some IDEs make it difficult to redirect input and output, so it's easier to read from a file and sometimes write to a file. Listing 13-1 shows a rudimentary program that reads integers from a file named *list1301.txt* and writes them, one per line, to the standard output stream. If the program cannot open the file, it prints an error message.

**Listing 13-1.** *Copying Integers from a File to Standard Output*

```
#include <cstdio>
#include <fstream>
#include <iostream>
#include <istream>
#include <ostream>

int main()
{
  std::ifstream in("list1301.txt");
  if (not in)
    std::perror("list1301.txt");
  else
  {
    int x(0);
    while (in >> x)
      std::cout << x << '\n';
    in.close();
  }
}
```

The <fstream> header declares ifstream, which is the type you use to read from a file. To open a file, simply name the file in ifstream's initializer. If the file cannot be opened, the ifstream object is left in an error state; a condition for which you can test using an if statement. When you are done reading from the file, call the close() member function. After closing the stream, you cannot read from it any more.

Once the file is open, read from it the same way you read from std::cin. All the input operators that are declared in <istream> work equally well for an ifstream as they do for std::cin.

The std::perror (declared in <cstdio>) function prints an error message. If the file cannot be opened, the exact reason is saved in a global variable, and perror uses that variable to decide which message to print. It also prints its argument.

**Run the program when you know the input file does not exist. What message does the program display?**

_____

If you can, create the input file then change the protection on the file so you can no longer read it. Run the program.

**What message do you get this time?**

_____

# Writing Files

As you have probably guessed, to write to a file, you define an ofstream object. To open the file, simply name the file in the variable's initializer. If the file does not exist, it will be created. If the file does exist, its old contents are discarded in preparation for writing new contents. If the file cannot be opened, the ofstream object is left in an error state, so remember to test it before you try to use it. Use an ofstream object the same way you use std::cout.

**Modify Listing 13-1 to write the numbers to a named file.** This time, name the input file _list1302.in_ and name the output file _list1302.out_. Compare your solution with mine in Listing 13-2.

**Listing 13-2.** _Copying Integers from a Named File to a Named File_

```
#include <cstdio>
#include <fstream>
#include <istream>
#include <ostream>

int main()
{
  std::ifstream in("list1302.in");
  if (not in)
    std::perror("list1302.in");
  else
  {
```

```
    std::ofstream out("list1302.out");
    if (not out)
      std::perror("list1302.out");
    else
    {
      int x(0);
      while (in >> x)
        out << x << '\n';
      out.close();
      in.close();
    }
  }
}
```

Notice that my program no longer includes <iostream>. Remember that <iostream> declares the names std::cin and std::cout. Listing 13-2 doesn't use these names, therefore it doesn't need the header. It still needs <istream> for the >> operator and <ostream> for the << operator. The ofstream type is declared in <fstream>.

The program opens the input file first. If that succeeds, it opens the output file. If the order were reversed, the program might create the output file then fail to open the input file, and the result would be a wasted, empty file. Always open input files first.

Also notice that the program does not close the input file if it cannot open the output file. Don't worry: it closes the input file just fine. When in is destroyed at the end of main, the file is automatically closed.

I know what you're thinking: "If in is automatically closed, why call close at all? Why not let in close automatically in all cases?" For an input file, that's actually okay. Feel free to delete the in.close(); statement from the program. For an output file, however, doing so is unwise.

Some output errors do not arise until the file is closed, and the operating system flushes all its internal buffers and does all the other clean up it needs to do when closing a file. Thus, an output stream object might not receive an error from the operating system until you call close(). Detecting and handling these errors is an advanced skill. The first step toward developing that skill is to adopt the habit of calling close() explicitly for output files. When it comes time to add the error-checking, you will have a place where you can add it.

Try running the program in Listing 13-2 in various error scenarios. Create the output file, *list1302.out*, and then use the operating system to mark the file as read-only. **What happens?**

---

If you noticed that the program does not check whether the output operations succeed, congratulations for having sharp eyes! C++ offers a few different ways to check for output errors, but they all have drawbacks. The easiest is to test whether the output stream is in an error state. You can check the stream after every output operation, but that approach is cumbersome, and few people write code that way. Another way lets the stream check for an error condition after every operation, and alert your program with an exception. You'll learn about this technique in Exploration 43. A frighteningly common technique is to ignore output errors altogether. As a compromise, I recommend testing for errors after calling close(). Listing 13-3 shows the final version of the program.

**Listing 13-3.** *Copying Integers, with Minimal Error-Checking*

```
#include <cstdio>
#include <fstream>
#include <istream>
#include <ostream>

int main()
{
  std::ifstream in("list1302.in");
  if (not in)
    std::perror("list1302.in");
  else
  {
    std::ofstream out("list1302.out");
    if (not out)
      std::perror("list1302.out");
    else
    {
      int x(0);
      while (in >> x)
        out << x << '\n';
      out.close();
      if (not out)
        std::perror("list1302.out");
    }
  }
}
```

Basic I/O is not difficult, but it can quickly become a morass of gooey, complicated code when you start to throw in sophisticated error-handling, international issues, binary I/O, and so on. Later Explorations will introduce most of these topics, but only when the time is ripe. For now, however, go back to earlier programs and practice modifying them to read and write named files instead of the standard input and output streams. For the sake of brevity (if for no other reason), the examples in the book will continue to use the standard I/O streams. If your IDE interferes with redirecting the standard I/O streams, or if you just prefer named files, you now know how to change the examples to meet your needs.

■■■

# The Map Data Structure

**N**ow that you understand the basics, it's time to move on to more exciting challenges. Let's write a real program—something non-trivial, but still simple enough to master this early in the book. Your task is to write a program that reads words and counts the frequency of each unique word. For the sake of simplicity, a word is a string of non-space characters separated by whitespace. Be aware, however, that by this definition, words end up including punctuation characters, but we'll worry about fixing that problem later.

This is a complicated program, touching on everything you've learned about C++ so far. If you want to exercise your new understanding of file I/O, read from a named file. If you prefer the simplicity, read from the standard input. Before jumping in and trying to write a program, take a moment to think about the problem and the tools you need to solve it. **Write pseudo-code for the program.** Try to write C++ code where you can, and make up whatever else you need to tackle the problem. Keep it simple: and don't dwell on trying to get syntax details correct.

# Using Maps

The title of this Exploration tells you what C++ feature will help provide an easy solution to this problem. What C++ calls a *map*, some languages and libraries call a *dictionary* or *association*. A map is simply a data structure that stores pairs of keys and values, indexed by the key. In other words, it maps a key to a value. Within a map, keys are unique. Thus, the heart of the program is a map that stores strings as keys and number of occurrences as the associated value for each key.

Naturally, your program needs the <map> header. The map datatype is called std::map. To define a map, you need to specify the key and value type within angle brackets (separated by a comma), as shown in the following example:

```
std::map<std::string, int> counts;
```

You can use almost any type as the key and value types, even another map. As with vector, if you do not initialize a map, it starts out empty.

The simplest way to use a map is to look up values using square brackets. For example, counts["the"] returns the value associated with the key "the". If the key is not present in the map, it is added with an initial value of zero. If the value type were std::string, the initial value would be an empty string.

Armed with this knowledge, you can write the first part of the program—collecting the word counts—as shown in Listing 14-1. (Feel free to modify the program to read from a named file, as you learned in Exploration 13.)

**Listing 14-1.** *Counting Occurrences of Unique Words*

```
#include <iostream>
#include <istream>
#include <map>
#include <ostream>
#include <string>

int main()
{
  std::map<std::string, int> counts;
  std::string word;
  while (std::cin >> word)
    ++counts[word];
  // TODO: Print the results.
}
```

In Listing 14-1, the ++ operator increments the count that the program stores in counts. In other words, when counts[word] retrieves the associated value, it does so in a way that lets you modify the value. You can use it as a target for an assignment or apply the increment or decrement operator.

For example, suppose you wanted to reset a count to zero.

```
counts["something"] = 0;
```

That was easy. Now all that's left to do is to print the results. Like vectors, maps also use iterators, but because an iterator refers to a key/value pair, they are a little more complicated to use than a vector's iterators.

# Iterators

The best way to extract information from a map is to use iterators. A map iterator refers to one element of the map: that is, one pair, which consists of a key and its associated value.

The value of a map iterator is a pair object. It has two parts, named first and second. The first part is the key and the second part is the value.

---

**Note**  The two parts of the map iterator's value are not named key and value because the std::pair type is a generic part of the C++ library. The library uses this type in several different places. Thus, the names of the parts of a pair are also generic, and not tied specifically to map.)

---

As you know, the * operator dereferences an iterator, and so returns the pair object. Use a dot (.) operator to access a member of the pair. C++ has one twist, however: the dot operator has higher precedence than *, so the compiler thinks *iter.first means *(iter.first), which doesn't work. Instead, you must write (*iter).first to make sure that the compiler dereferences the iterator before accessing the first member. Some programmers find that a little ugly and hard to read. They prefer the shorthand, iter->first. Both mean the same thing; choose the style that you prefer, and stick with it.

The next question is what to do with each pair. To keep things simple, print the output as the key, followed by a tab character, followed by the count, all on one line. Putting all these pieces together, you end up with the finished program, as presented in Listing 14-2.

**Listing 14-2.** *Printing Word Frequencies*

```cpp
#include <iostream>
#include <istream>
#include <map>
#include <ostream>
#include <string>

int main()
{
  using namespace std;

  map<string, int> counts;
  string word;

  // Read words from the standard input and count the number of times
  // each word occurs.
```

```
  while (cin >> word)
    ++counts[word];

  // For each word/count pair...
  for (map<string,int>::iterator iter(counts.begin()); iter != counts.end(); ++iter)
    // Print the word, tab, the count, newline.
    cout << iter->first << '\t' << iter->second << '\n';
}
```

Recall from Exploration 8 that `using namespace std;` is a shorthand that lets us drop the `std::` prefix from standard library names.

Using the knowledge you gained in Exploration 8, you know how to format the output as two neat columns. All that is required is to find the size of the longest key. In order to right-align the counts, you can try to determine the number of places required by the largest count, or you can simply use a very large number, such as 10.

**Rewrite Listing 14-2 to line up the output neatly, according to the size of the longest key.**

Naturally, you will need to write another loop to visit all the elements of `counts` and test the size of each element. In Exploration 9, you learned that `vector` has a `size()` member function that returns the number of elements in the vector. Would you be surprised to learn that `map` and `string` also have `size()` member functions? The designers of the C++ library did their best to be consistent with names. The `size()` member function returns an integer of type `size_type`.

---

■**Tip**  Remember `size_type` from Exploration 9? If not, go back and refresh your memory; Exploration 9 has some important admonitions about `size_type`.

---

Compare your program with Listing 14-3.

**Listing 14-3.** *Aligning Words and Counts Neatly*

```
#include <iomanip>
#include <ios>
#include <iostream>
#include <istream>
#include <map>
#include <ostream>
#include <string>

int main()
{
  using namespace std;

  map<string, int> counts;
  string word;
```

```
// Read words from the standard input and count the number of times
// each word occurs.
while (cin >> word)
  ++counts[word];

// Determine the longest word.
string::size_type longest(0);
for (map<string,int>::iterator iter(counts.begin()); iter != counts.end(); ++iter)
  if (iter->first.size() > longest)
    longest = iter->first.size();

// For each word/count pair...
const int count_size(10); // Number of places for printing the count
for (map<string,int>::iterator iter(counts.begin()); iter != counts.end(); ++iter)
  // Print the word, count, newline. Keep the columns neatly aligned.
  cout << setw(longest)    << left  << iter->first <<
          setw(count_size) << right << iter->second << '\n';
}
```

If you want some sample input, try the file *explore14.txt*, which you can download from this book's web site. Notice how the word is left-aligned and the count is right-aligned. We expect numbers to be right-aligned, and words are customarily left-aligned (in Western cultures). And remember const from Exploration 8? That simply means count_size is a constant.

# Searching in Maps

A map stores its data in sorted order by key. Searching in a map, therefore, is pretty fast (logarithmic time). Because a map keeps its keys in order, you can use any of the standard binary search algorithms (such as lower_bound, to which you were introduced in Exploration 12), but even better is to use map's member functions. These member functions have the same names as the standard algorithms, but can take advantage of their knowledge of a map's internal structure. The member functions also run in logarithmic time, but with less overhead than the standard algorithms.

For example, suppose you want to know how many times the word "the" appears in an input stream. You can read the input and collect the counts in the usual way then call find("the") to see if "the" is in the map, and if so, get an iterator that points to its key/value pair. If the key is not in the map, find() returns the end() iterator. If the key is present, you can extract the count. You have all the knowledge and skills you need to solve this problem, so go ahead and **write the program to print the number of occurrences of the word "the"**. Once again, you can use *explore14.txt* as sample input. If you don't want to use redirection, modify the program to read from the *explore14.txt* file.

**What count does your program print when you provide this file as the input?** _____
The program presented in Listing 14-4 detects 10 occurrences.

**Listing 14-4.** *Searching for a Word in a Map*

```
#include <iomanip>
#include <iostream>
#include <istream>
#include <map>
#include <ostream>
#include <string>

int main()
{
  using namespace std;

  map<string, int> counts;
  string word;

  // Read words from the standard input and count the number of times
  // each word occurs.
  while (cin >> word)
    ++counts[word];

  map<string,int>::iterator the(counts.find("the"));
  if (the == counts.end())
    cout << "\"the\": not found\n";
  else if (the->second == 1)
    cout << "\"the\": occurs " << the->second << " time\n";
  else
    cout << "\"the\": occurs " << the->second << " times\n";
}
```

I don't know about you, but I find map<string, int>::iterator to be unwieldy. Throw in
the std:: prefixes, and it becomes downright burdensome. Fortunately, C++ (like C) offers
a way out: type synonyms, which just happens to be the subject of the next Exploration.

■ ■ ■

# Type Synonyms

Using types such as `std::vector<std::string>::size_type` or `std::map<std::string,int>::iterator` can be clumsy, prone to typographical errors, and just plain annoying to type and read. Fortunately, C++ lets you define short synonyms for clumsy types. You can also use type synonyms to provide meaningful names for generic types. (The standard library has quite a few synonyms of the latter variety.) These synonyms are often referred to as typedefs because the keyword you use to declare them is `typedef`.

## typedef Declarations

C++ inherits the basic syntax and semantics of `typedef` from C, so you might already be familiar with this keyword. If so, please bear with me while I bring other readers up to speed.

The idea of a `typedef` is to create a synonym, or alias, for another type. There are two compelling reasons for creating type synonyms:

- They create a short synonym for a long type name. For example, you may want to use `count_iter` as a type synonym for `std::map<std::string,int>::iterator`.

- They create a mnemonic synonym. For example, a program might declare `height` as a synonym for `int` to emphasize that variables of type `height` store a height value. This information helps the human reader understand the program.

The basic syntax for a `typedef` declaration is like defining a variable, except you start with the `typedef` keyword, and the name of the type synonym takes the place of the variable name.

```
typedef std::map<std::string,int>::iterator count_iter;
typedef int height;
```

Revisit Listing 14-3 and simplify the program by judicious use of `typedef` declarations. Compare your result with Listing 15-1.

**Listing 15-1.** *Counting Words, with a Clean Program That Uses* `typedef`

```
#include <iomanip>
#include <ios>
#include <iostream>
#include <istream>
#include <map>
```

```
#include <ostream>
#include <string>

int main()
{
  using namespace std;
  typedef map<string, int>    count_map;
  typedef count_map::iterator count_iter;
  typedef string::size_type   str_size;

  count_map counts;
  string word;

  // Read words from the standard input and count the number of times
  // each word occurs.
  while (cin >> word)
    ++counts[word];

  // Determine the longest word.
  str_size longest(0);
  for (count_iter iter(counts.begin()); iter != counts.end(); ++iter)
    if (iter->first.size() > longest)
      longest = iter->first.size();

  // For each word/count pair...
  const int count_size(10); // Number of places for printing the count
  for (count_iter iter(counts.begin()); iter != counts.end(); ++iter)
    // Print the word, count, newline. Keep the columns neatly aligned.
    cout << setw(longest)    << left << iter->first <<
            setw(count_size) << right << iter->second << '\n';
}
```

I like the new version of this program. The for loops are much easier to read when using a typedef name instead of the full iterator type name. You might think str_size is superfluous, but I wanted to demonstrate as many uses of typedef as I could without being ridiculous.

# Common typedefs

The standard library makes heavy use of typedefs, as you have already seen. For example, std::vector<int>::size_type is a typedef for an integer type. You don't know which integer type (C++ has several, which you will learn about in Exploration 23), nor does it matter. All you need to know is that size_type is the type to use if you want to store a vector size or index in a variable.

Most likely, size_type is a typedef for std::size_t, which is itself a typedef. The size_t typedef is a synonym for an integer type that is suitable for representing a size. In particular, C++ has an operator, sizeof, which returns the size in bytes of a type or object. The result of sizeof is an integer of type size_t, however a compiler-writer chooses to implement sizeof and size_t.

---

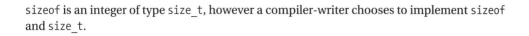

**Note** A "byte" is defined as the size of type char. So, by definition, sizeof(char) == 1. The size of other types depends on the implementation. On most popular desktop workstations, sizeof(int) == 4, but 2 and 8 are also likely candidates.

---

That was short and sweet, wasn't it? Now you can return to the problem of counting words. This program has a number of usability flaws.

**What can you think of to improve the word-counting program?**

At the top of my list are the following two items:

- Ignore punctuation marks
- Ignore case differences

In order to implement these additional features, you need to learn some more C++. For example, the C++ standard library has functions to test whether a character is punctuation, a digit, an uppercase letter, a lowercase letter, and so on. The next Exploration begins by exploring characters more closely.

■■■

# Characters

In Exploration 2, I introduced you to character literals in single quotes, such as '\n' to end a line of output, but I have not yet taken the time to explain these fundamental building blocks. Now is the time to explore characters in greater depth.

## Character Type

The char type represents a single character. Internally, all computers represent characters as integers. The *character set* defines the mapping between characters and numeric values. Common character sets are ISO 8859-1 (also called Latin-1) and ISO 10646 (same as Unicode), but many, many, other character sets are in wide use.

The C++ standard does not mandate any particular character set. The literal '4' represents the digit 4, but the actual value that the computer uses internally is up to the implementation. You should not assume any particular character set. For example, in ISO 8859-1 (Latin-1), '4' has the value 52, but in EBCDIC, it has the value 244.

Similarly, given a numeric value, you cannot assume anything about the character that value represents. If you know a char variable stores the value 169, the character may be 'z' (EBCDIC), '©' (Unicode), or 'Љ' (ISO 8859-5).

C++ does not try to hide the fact that a character is actually a number. You can compare char values with int values, assign a char to an int variable, or do arithmetic with chars. Performing arithmetic is fraught with danger unless you know the actual character set, but C++ guarantees that any character set your compiler and library support represents digit characters with contiguous values, starting at '0'. Thus, for example, the following is true for all C++ implementations:

```
'0' + 7 == '7'
```

Read Listing 16-1. **What does the program do?** (Hint: the get member function reads a single character from the stream. It does not skip over white space or treat any character specially. Extra hint: what happens if you subtract '0' from a character that you know to be a digit?)

_____

_____

_____

_____

**Listing 16-1.** *Working and Playing with Characters*

```
#include <iostream>
#include <istream>
#include <ostream>

int main()
{
  int value(0);
  bool have_value(false);
  char ch(' ');

  while (std::cin.get(ch))
  {
    if (ch >= '0' and ch <= '9')
    {
      value = ch - '0';
      have_value = true;
      while (std::cin.get(ch) and ch >= '0' and ch <= '9')
        value = value * 10 + ch - '0';
    }
    if (ch == '\n')
    {
      if (have_value)
      {
        std::cout << value << '\n';
        have_value = false;
      }
    }
    else if (ch != ' ' and ch != '\t')
    {
      std::cout << '\a';
      while (std::cin.get(ch) and ch != '\n')
        /*empty*/;
    }
  }
}
```

Briefly, this program reads numbers from the standard input and echoes the values to the standard output. If the program reads any invalid characters, it alerts the user (with \a, which I describe later in this Exploration) and ignores the rest of the line of input. Leading and trailing blank and tab characters are allowed. The program prints the saved numeric value only after reaching the end of an input line. This means if a line contains more than one valid number, the program prints only the last value.

The get function takes a character variable as an argument. It reads one character from the input stream then stores the character in that variable. The get function does not skip over white space. When you use get as a loop condition, it returns true if it successfully reads a character, and the program should keep reading. It returns false if no more input is available or some kind of input error occurred.

All the digit characters have contiguous values, so the inner loop tests to determine if a character is a digit character by comparing it to the values for '0' and '9'. If it is a digit, subtracting the value of '0' from it leaves you with an integer in the range 0 to 9.

The final loop reads characters and does nothing with them. The loop terminates when it reads a new line character. In other words, the final loop reads and ignores the rest of the input line.

Programs that need to handle white space on their own (such as Listing 16-1) can use get, or you can tell the input stream not to skip over white space prior to reading a number or anything else. The next section discusses character I/O in more detail.

# Character I/O

You just learned that the get function reads a single character without treating white space specially. You can do the same thing with a normal input operator, but you must use the std::noskipws manipulator. To restore the default behavior, use the std::skipws manipulator (declared in <ios>).

```
// Read two adjacent characters.
char left, right;
std::cin >> left >> std::noskipws >> right >> std::skipws;
```

After turning off the skipws flag, the input stream does not skip over leading white space characters. For instance, if you were to try to read an integer, and the stream is positioned at white space, the read would fail. If you were to try to read a string, the string would be empty, and the stream position would not advance. So you need to carefully consider whether to skip white space. Typically, you would do that only when reading individual characters.

Remember that an input stream uses the >> operator (Exploration 5), even for manipulators. Using >> for manipulators seems to break the mnemonic of transferring data to the right, but it follows the convention of always using >> with an input stream. If you forget, the compiler will remind you.

**Write a program that reads the input stream one character at a time and echoes the input to the standard output stream verbatim.** This is not a demonstration of how to copy streams, but an example of working with characters. Compare your program with Listing 16-2.

**Listing 16-2.** *Echoing Input to Output, One Character at a Time*

```
#include <ios>
#include <iostream>
#include <istream>
#include <ostream>

int main()
{
  std::cin >> std::noskipws;
  char ch;
```

```
    while (std::cin >> ch)
        std::cout << ch;
}
```

You can also use the get member function, in which case you don't need the noskipws manipulator.

Let's try something a little more challenging. Suppose you need to read a series of points. The points are defined by a pair of *x*, *y* coordinates, separated by a comma. White space is allowed before and after each number and around the comma. Read the points into a vector of *x* values and a vector of *y* values. Terminate the input loop if a point does not have a proper comma separator. Print the vector contents, one point per line. I know this is a bit dull, but the point is to experiment with character input. If you prefer, do something special with the data. Compare your result with Listing 16-3.

**Listing 16-3.** *Finding the Points with the Largest* x *and* y *Values*

```cpp
#include <algorithm>
#include <iostream>
#include <istream>
#include <limits>
#include <ostream>
#include <vector>

int main()
{
    typedef std::vector<int>  intvec;
    typedef intvec::iterator  iterator;

    intvec xs, ys;          // store the xs and ys

    { // local block to keep I/O variables local
        int x(0), y(0);         // variables for I/O
        char sep(' ');
        // Loop while the input stream has an integer (x), a character (sep),
        // and another integer (y); then test that the separator is a comma.
        while (std::cin >> x >> sep and sep == ',' and std::cin >> y)
        {
            xs.push_back(x);
            ys.push_back(y);
        }
    }

    for (iterator x(xs.begin()), y(ys.begin()); x != xs.end(); ++x, ++y)
        std::cout << *x << ',' << *y << '\n';
}
```

The while loop is the key. The loop condition reads an integer and a character and tests to determine if the character is a comma before reading a second integer. The loop terminates if the input is invalid or ill-formed or if the loop reaches the end of file. A more sophisticated program would distinguish between these two cases, but that's a side issue for the moment.

## Newlines and Portability

You've probably noticed that Listing 16-3 and every other program I've presented so far, prints '\n' at the end of each line of output. We have done so without considering what this really means. Different environments have different conventions for end-of-line characters. UNIX uses a line feed ('\x0a'); MacOS uses a carriage return ('\x0d'); DOS and Microsoft Windows use a combination of a carriage return followed by a line feed ('\x0d\x0a'); and some operating systems don't use line terminators, but instead have record-oriented files, in which each line is a separate record.

In all these cases, the C++ I/O streams automatically convert a native line ending to a single '\n' character. When you print '\n' to an output stream, the library automatically converts it to a native line ending (or terminates the record).

In other words, you can write programs that use '\n' as a line ending and not concern yourself with native OS conventions. Your source code will be portable to all C++ environments.

## Character Escapes

In addition to '\n', C++ offers several other *escape sequences*, such as '\t' for horizontal tab. Table 16-1 lists all the character escapes. Remember that you can use these escapes in character literals and string literals.

**Table 16-1.** *Character Escape Sequences*

| Escape | Meaning |
|---|---|
| \a | Alert: ring a bell or otherwise signal the user |
| \b | Backspace |
| \f | Formfeed |
| \n | Newline |
| \r | Carriage return |
| \t | Horizontal tab |
| \v | Vertical tab |
| \\ | Literal \ |
| \? | Literal ? |
| \' | Literal ' |
| \" | Literal " |
| \OOO | Octal (base 8) character value |
| \xXX... | Hexadecimal (base 16) character value |

The last two items are the most interesting. An escape sequence of one to three octal digits (0 to 7) specifies the value of the character. Which character the value represents is up to the implementation.

Understanding all the caveats from the first section of this Exploration, there are times when you need to specify an actual character value. The most common is '\0', which is the character with value zero, also called a *null character*, which you may utilize to initialize char variables. It has some other uses as well, especially when interfacing with C functions and the legacy C standard library.

The final escape sequence (\x) lets you specify a character value in hexadecimal. Typically, you would use two hexadecimal digits, because this is all that fits in the typical, 8-bit char. (The purpose of longer \x escapes is for wide characters, the subject of Exploration 52.)

The next section continues the exploration of characters by examining how C++ classifies characters according to letter, digit, punctuation, etc.

■ ■ ■

# Character Categories

**E**xploration 16 introduced and discussed characters. This Exploration continues that discussion with character classification, which as you will see, turns out to be more complicated than you might have expected.

## Character Sets

As you learned in Exploration 16, the numeric value of a character, such as `'A'`, depends on the character set. The compiler must decide which character set to use at compile time and at runtime. This is typically based on preferences that the end user selects in the host operating system.

Character set issues rarely arise for the basic subset of characters—such as letters, digits, and punctuation symbols—that are used to write C++ source code. Although it is conceivable that you could compile a program using ISO 8859-1 and run that program using EBCDIC, you would need to work pretty hard to arrange such a feat. Most likely, you will find yourself using one or more character sets that share some common characteristics. For example, all ISO 8859 character sets use the same numeric values for the letters of the Roman alphabet, digits, and basic punctuation. Even most Asian character sets preserve the values of these basic characters.

Thus, most programmers blithely ignore the character set issue. We use character literals, such as `'%'` and assume the program will function the way we expect it to, on any system, anywhere in the world—and we are usually right. But not always.

Assuming the basic characters are always available in a portable manner, we can modify the word-counting program to treat only letters as characters that make up a word. The program would no longer count `right` and `right?` as two distinct words. The `string` type offers several member functions that can help us: search in strings, extract substrings, and so on.

For example, you can build a string that contains only the letters and any other characters that you want to consider to be part of a word (such as `'-'`). After reading each word from the input stream, make a copy of the word, but keep only the characters that are in the string of acceptable characters. Use the `find` member function to try to find each character; `find` returns the zero-based index of the character if found, or `std::string::npos` if not found.

**Using the `find` function, rewrite Listing 15-1 to clean up the word string prior to inserting it in the map.** Test the program with a variety of input samples. How well does it work? Compare your program with Listing 17-1.

**Listing 17-1.** *Counting Words: Restricting Words to Letters and Letter-like Characters*

```cpp
#include <iomanip>
#include <ios>
#include <iostream>
#include <istream>
#include <map>
#include <ostream>
#include <string>

int main()
{
  using namespace std;
  typedef map<string, int>    count_map;
  typedef count_map::iterator count_iter;
  typedef string::size_type   str_size;

  count_map counts;
  string word;

  // Read words from the standard input and count the number of times
  // each word occurs.
  string okay("ABCDEFGHIJKLMNOPQRSTUVWXYZ"
              "abcdefghijklmnopqrstuvwxyz"
              "0123456789-_");
  while (cin >> word)
  {
    // Make a copy of word, keeping only the characters that appear in okay.
    string copy;
    for (string::iterator w(word.begin()); w != word.end(); ++w)
      if (okay.find(*w) != string::npos)
        copy.push_back(*w);
    // The "word" might be all punctuation, so the copy would be empty.
    // Don't count empty strings.
    if (not copy.empty())
      ++counts[copy];
  }

  // Determine the longest word.
  str_size longest(0);
  for (count_iter iter(counts.begin()); iter != counts.end(); ++iter)
    if (iter->first.size() > longest)
      longest = iter->first.size();

  // For each word/count pair...
  const int count_size(10); // Number of places for printing the count
  for (count_iter iter(counts.begin()); iter != counts.end(); ++iter)
    // Print the word, count, newline. Keep the columns neatly aligned.
```

```
cout << setw(longest)    << left << iter->first <<
      setw(count_size) << right << iter->second << '\n';
}
```

Some of you may have written a program very similar to mine. Others among you—particularly those living outside the United States—may have written a slightly different program. Perhaps you included other characters in your string of acceptable characters.

For example, if you are French and using Microsoft Windows (and the Windows 1252 character set), you may have defined the okay object as follows:

```
string okay("ABCDEFGHIJKLMNOPQRSTUVWXYZÀÁÄÇÈÉÊËÎÏÔÙÛÜŒŸ"
            "abcdefghijklmnopqrstuvwxyzàáäçèéêëîïöùûüœÿ"
            "0123456789-_");
```

But what if you then try to compile and run this program in a different environment, particularly one that uses the ISO 8859-1 character set (popular on UNIX systems)? ISO 8859-1 and Windows 1252 share many character codes, but differ in a few significant ways. In particular, the characters 'Œ', 'œ', and 'Ÿ' are missing from ISO 8859-1. As a result, the program may not compile successfully in an environment that uses ISO 8859-1 for the compile-time character set.

What if you want to share the program with a German user. Surely that user would want to include characters such as 'Ö', 'ö', and 'ß' as letters. What about Greek, Russian, and Japanese users?

We need a better solution. Wouldn't it be nice if C++ provided a simple function that would notify us if a character is a letter, without forcing us to hardcode exactly which characters are letters? Fortunately, it does.

# Character Categories

An easier way to write the program in Listing 17-1 is to call the isalnum function (declared in <locale>). This function indicates whether a character is alphanumeric in the runtime character set. The advantages of using isalnum is that you don't need to enumerate all the possible alphanumeric characters; you don't need to worry about differing character sets; and you don't need to worry about accidentally omitting a character from the approved string.

**Rewrite Listing 17-1 to call isalnum instead of find**. The first argument to isalnum is the character to test, and the second is locale(""). (Don't worry yet about what that means. Have patience: I'll get to that soon.)

Try running the program with a variety of alphabetic input, including accented characters. Compare the results with the results from your original program. The files that accompany this book include some samples that use a variety of character sets. Choose the sample that matches your everyday character set and run the program again, redirecting the input to that file.

If you need help with the program, see my version of the program in Listing 17-2. For the sake of brevity, I eliminated the neat-output part of the code, reverting to simple strings and tabs. Feel free to restore the pretty output, if you desire.

**Listing 17-2.** *Testing a Character by Calling* isalnum

```
#include <iostream>
#include <istream>
#include <locale>
#include <map>
#include <ostream>
#include <string>

int main()
{
  using namespace std;
  typedef map<string, int>    count_map;
  typedef count_map::iterator count_iter;

  count_map counts;
  string word;

  // Read words from the standard input and count the number of times
  // each word occurs.
  while (cin >> word)
  {
    // Make a copy of word, keeping only alphabetic characters.
    string copy;
    for (string::iterator w(word.begin()); w != word.end(); ++w)
      if (isalnum(*w, locale("")))
        copy.push_back(*w);
    // The "word" might be all punctuation, so the copy would be empty.
    // Don't count empty strings.
    if (not copy.empty())
      ++counts[copy];
  }

  // For each word/count pair, print the word & count on one line.
  for (count_iter iter(counts.begin()); iter != counts.end(); ++iter)
    cout << iter->first << '\t' << iter->second << '\n';
}
```

Now let's turn your attention to the locale("") argument. The locale directs isalnum to the character set it should use to test the character. As you saw in Exploration 16, the character set determines the identity of a character, based on its numeric value. A user can change character sets while a program is running, so the program must keep track of the user's actual character set, and not depend on the character set that was active when you compiled the program.

Download the files that accompany this book and find the text files whose names begin with sample. **Find the one that best matches the character set you use every day, and select that file as the redirected input to the program.** Look for the appearance of the special characters in the output.

Change locale("") to locale() in the boldface line of Listing 17-2. Now compile and run the program with the same input. **Do you see a difference?** _____ **If so, what is the difference?**

_____

_____

Without knowing more about your environment, I can't tell you what you should expect. If you are using a Unicode character set, you won't actually see any difference. The program would not treat any of the special characters as letters, even when you can plainly see they are letters. This is due to the way Unicode is implemented, and Exploration 52 will discuss this topic in depth.

Other users will notice that only one or two strings make it to the output. Western Europeans who use ISO 8859-1 may notice that ÁÇÐÈ is considered a word. Greek users of ISO 8859-7 will see ΑΒΓΔΕ as a word.

Power users who know how to change their character sets on the fly can try several different options. You must change the character set that programs use at runtime and the character set that your console uses to display text.

What is most noticeable is that the characters the program considers to be letters vary from one character set to another. But after all, that's the idea of different character sets. The knowledge of which characters are letters in which character sets is embodied in the locale.

# Locales

In C++, a *locale* is a collection of information pertaining to a culture, region, and language. The locale includes information about:

- formatting numbers, currency, dates, and time

- classifying characters (letter, digit, punctuation, etc.)

- converting characters from uppercase to lowercase and *vice versa*

- sorting text (e.g., is 'A' less than, equal to, or greater than 'Å'?)

- message catalogs (for translations of strings that your program uses)

Every C++ program begins with a minimal, standard locale, which is known as the *classic* or "C" locale. The std::locale::classic() function returns the classic locale. The unnamed locale, (std::locale("")), is the user's preferences that C++ obtains from the host operating system. The locale with the empty-string argument is often known as the *native* locale.

The advantage of the classic locale is that its behavior is known and fixed. If your program must read data in a fixed format, you don't want the user's preferences getting in the way. By contrast, the advantage of the native format is that the user chose those preferences for a reason, and wants to see program output follow that format. A user who always specifies a date as day/month/year doesn't want a program printing month/day/year simply because that's the convention in the programmer's home country.

Thus, the classic format is often used for reading and writing data files, and the native format is used to interpret input from the user and to present output directly to the user.

Every I/O stream has its own `locale` object. To affect the stream's `locale`, call its `imbue` function, passing the `locale` object as the sole argument.

---

**Note** You read that correctly: `imbue`, not `setlocale`, or `setloc`—given that the `getloc` function returns a stream's current locale—or anything else that might be easy to remember. On the other hand, `imbue` is such an unusual name for a member function, you may remember it for that reason alone.

---

In other words, when C++ starts up, it initializes each stream with the classic locale as follows:

```
std::cin.imbue(std::locale::classic());
std::cout.imbue(std::locale::classic());
```

Suppose you want to change the output stream to adopt the user's native locale. Do this using the following statement at the start of your program:

```
std::cout.imbue(std::locale(""));
```

For example, suppose you need to write a program that reads a list of numbers from the standard input and computes the sum. The numbers are raw data from a scientific instrument, so they are written as digit strings. Therefore, you should continue to use the classic locale to read the input stream. The output is for the user's benefit, so the output should use the native locale.

**Write the program and try it with very large numbers, so the output will be greater than one thousand. What does the program print as its output?** _____

See Listing 17-3 for my approach to solving this problem.

**Listing 17-3.** *Using the Native Locale for Output*

```
#include <iostream>
#include <istream>
#include <locale>
#include <ostream>

int main()
{
  std::cout.imbue(std::locale(""));
  int sum(0);
  int x;
  while (std::cin >> x)
    sum = sum + x;
  std::cout << "sum = " << sum << '\n';
}
```

When I run the program in Listing 17-3, in my default locale (United States), I get the following result:

sum = 1,234,567

Notice the commas that separate thousands. In some European countries, you might see the following instead:

sum = 1.234.567

You should obtain a result that conforms to native customs, or at least follows the preferences that you set in your host operating system.

When you use the native locale, I recommend defining a variable of type std::locale in which to store it. You can pass this variable to isalnum, imbue, or other functions. By creating this variable and distributing copies of it, your program needs to query the operating system for your preferences only once, not every time you need the locale. Thus, the main loop ends up looking something like Listing 17-4.

**Listing 17-4.** *Creating and Sharing a Single Locale Object*

```cpp
#include <iostream>
#include <istream>
#include <locale>
#include <map>
#include <ostream>
#include <string>

int main()
{
  using namespace std;
  typedef map<string, int>    count_map;
  typedef count_map::iterator count_iter;

  locale native("");          // get the native locale
  cin.imbue(native);          // interpret the input and output according to
  cout.imbue(native);         // the native locale

  count_map counts;
  string word;

  // Read words from the standard input and count the number of times
  // each word occurs.
  while (cin >> word)
  {
    // Make a copy of word, keeping only alphabetic characters.
    string copy;
    for (string::iterator w(word.begin()); w != word.end(); ++w)
      if (isalnum(*w, native))
        copy.push_back(*w);
```

```
  // The "word" might be all punctuation, so the copy would be empty.
  // Don't count empty strings.
  if (not copy.empty())
    ++counts[copy];
}

// For each word/count pair, print the word & count on one line.
for (count_iter iter(counts.begin()); iter != counts.end(); ++iter)
  cout << iter->first << '\t' << iter->second << '\n';
}
```

The next step toward improving the word-counting program is to ignore case differences, so the program does not count the word The as different from the. It turns out this problem is trickier than it first appears, so it deserves an entire Exploration of its own.

■■■

# Case-Folding

Picking up where we left off in Exploration 17, the next step to improving the word-counting program is to update it so it ignores case differences when counting. For example, the program should count The just as it does the. This is a classic problem in computer programming. C++ offers some rudimentary help, but lacks some important fundamental pieces. This Exploration takes a closer look at this deceptively tricky issue.

## Simple Cases

Western European languages have long made use of capital (or majuscule) letters and minuscule letters. The more familiar terms—uppercase and lowercase—arise from the early days of typesetting when the type slugs for majuscule letters were kept in the upper cases of large racks containing all the characters used to make a printing plate. Beneath them were the cases, or boxes, that stored the minuscule letter slugs.

In the <locale> header, C++ declares the isupper and islower functions. They take a character as the first argument and a locale as the second argument. The return value is a bool: true if the character is uppercase (or lowercase, respectively) and false if the character is lowercase (or uppercase) or not a letter.

```
std::isupper('A', std::locale("")) == true
std::islower('A', std::locale("")) == false
std::isupper('Æ', std::locale("")) == true
std::islower('Æ', std::locale("")) == false
std::islower('½', std::locale("")) == false
std::isupper('½', std::locale("")) == false
```

The <locale> header also declares two functions to convert case: toupper converts lowercase to uppercase. If its character argument is not a lowercase letter, toupper returns the character as is. Similarly, tolower converts to lowercase if the character in question is an uppercase letter. Just like the category testing functions, the second argument is a locale object.

Now you can **modify the word-counting program to fold uppercase to lowercase, and count all words in lowercase.** Modify your program from Exploration 17, or start with Listing 17-4. If you have difficulty, take a look at Listing 18-1.

**Listing 18-1.** *Folding Uppercase to Lowercase Prior to Counting Words*

```cpp
#include <iostream>
#include <istream>
#include <locale>
#include <map>
#include <ostream>
#include <string>

int main()
{
  using namespace std;
  typedef map<string, int>    count_map;
  typedef count_map::iterator count_iter;

  locale native("");             // get the native locale
  cin.imbue(native);             // interpret the input and output according to
  cout.imbue(native);            // the native locale

  count_map counts;
  string word;

  // Read words from the standard input and count the number of times
  // each word occurs.
  while (cin >> word)
  {
    // Make a copy of word, keeping only alphabetic characters.
    string copy;
    for (string::iterator w(word.begin()); w != word.end(); ++w)
      if (isalnum(*w, native))
        copy.push_back(tolower(*w, native));
    // The "word" might be all punctuation, so the copy would be empty.
    // Don't count empty strings.
    if (not copy.empty())
      ++counts[copy];
  }

  // For each word/count pair, print the word & count on one line.
  for (count_iter iter(counts.begin()); iter != counts.end(); ++iter)
    cout << iter->first << '\t' << iter->second << '\n';
}
```

That was easy. So what's the problem?

# Harder Cases

Some of you—especially German readers—already know the problem. Several languages have letter combinations that do not map easily between upper and lowercase, or one character maps to two characters. The German eszet, 'ß', is a lowercase letter; when you convert it to uppercase, you get two characters: "SS". Thus, if your input file contains "ESSEN" and "eßen", you want them to map to the same word so they're counted together, but that just isn't feasible with C++. The way the program currently works, it maps "ESSEN" to "essen", which is counted as a different word from "eßen". A naïve solution would be to map "essen" to "eßen", but not all uses of "ss" are equivalent to 'ß'.

Greek readers are familiar with another kind of problem. Greek has two forms of lowercase sigma: use 'ς' at the end of a word and 'σ' elsewhere. Our simple program maps 'Σ' (uppercase sigma) to 'σ', so some words in all uppercase will not convert to a form that matches its lowercase version.

Sometimes, accents are lost during conversion. Mapping 'é' to uppercase usually yields 'É', but may also yield 'E'. Mapping uppercase to lowercase has fewer problems in that 'É' maps to 'é', but what if that 'E' (which maps to 'e'), really means 'É', and you want it to map to 'é'? The program has no way of knowing the writer's intentions, so all it can do is map the letters it receives.

Some character sets are more problematic than others. For example, ISO 8859-1 has a lowercase 'ÿ', but not an uppercase equivalent ('Ÿ'). Windows 1252, on the other hand, extends ISO 8859-1, and one of the new code points is 'Ÿ'.

---

■**Tip** *Code point* is a fancy way of saying "numeric value that represents a character." Although most programmers don't use "code point" in everyday speech, those programmers who work closely with character set issues use it all the time, so you may as well get used to it. Mainstream programmers should become more accustomed to using this phrase.

---

In other words, converting case is impossible to do correctly using only the standard C++ library.

If you know your alphabet is one that C++ handles correctly, then go ahead and use toupper and tolower. For example, if you are writing a command line interpreter, within which you have full control over the commands, and you decide that the user should be able to enter commands in any case, simply make sure the commands map correctly from one case to another. This is easy to do as all character sets can map the 26 letters of the Roman alphabet without any problems.

On the other hand, if your program accepts input from the user and you want to map that input to uppercase or lowercase, you cannot and must not use standard C++. For example, if you are writing a word processor, and you decide you need to implement some case-folding functions, you must write or acquire a non-standard function to implement the case-folding logic correctly. Most likely, you would need a library of character and string functions to implement your word processor; case-folding would simply be one small part of this hypothetical library. (See this book's web site for some links to non-hypothetical libraries that can help you.)

What about our simple program? It isn't always practical to handle the full, complete, correct handling of cases and characters when you just want to count a few words. The case-handling code would dwarf the word-counting code.

In this case (pun intended), you must accept the fact that your program will sometimes produce incorrect results. Our poor little program will never recognize that "ESSEN" and "eßen" are the same word, but in different cases. You can work around some of the multiple mappings (such as with Greek sigma) by mapping to uppercase then to lowercase. On the other hand, this can introduce problems with some accented characters. And I still have not touched upon the issue of whether "naïve" is the same word as "naive". In some locales, the accents are significant, which would cause "naïve" and "naive" to be interpreted as two different words. In other locales, they are the same word and should be counted together.

In some character sets, accented characters can be composed from separate non-accented characters followed by the desired accent. For example, you can write "nai¨ve", which is the same as "naïve".

I hope by now you are completely scared away from manipulating cases and characters. Far too many naïve programmers (again, pun intended) become entangled in this web, or worse, simply write bad code. I was tempted to wait until much later in the book before throwing all this at you, but I know that many readers will want to improve the word-counting program by ignoring case, so I decided to tackle the problem early.

Well, now you know better.

That doesn't mean you can't keep working on the word-counting program. The next Exploration returns to the realm of the realistic and feasible, as I finally show you how to write your own functions.

# EXPLORATION 19

■■■

# Writing Functions

**A**t last, it's time to embark on the journey toward writing your own functions. In this Exploration, you'll begin by improving the word-counting program you've been crafting over the past four Explorations, writing functions to implement separate aspects of the program's functionality.

## Functions

You've been using functions since the very first program you wrote. In fact, you've been writing functions, too. You see, `main()` is a function, and you should view it the same as you would any other function (well sort of, `main()` actually has some key differences from ordinary functions, but they needn't concern you yet).

A function has a return type, a name, and parameters in parentheses. Following that is a compound statement, which is the function body. If the function has no parameters, the parentheses are empty. Each parameter is like a variable declaration: type and name. Parameters are separated by commas, so you cannot declare two parameters after a single type name. Instead you must specify the type explicitly for each parameter.

A function usually has at least one `return` statement, which causes the function to discontinue execution and return control to its caller. A return statement's structure begins with the `return` keyword, followed by an expression, and ending with a semicolon, as demonstrated in the following example:

```
return 42;
```

You can use a `return` statement anywhere you need a statement, and you can use as many `return` statements as you need or want. The only requirement is that every execution path through the function must have a `return` statement. Many compilers will warn you if you forget.

Some languages distinguish between functions, which return a value, and procedures or subroutines, which do not. C++ calls them all functions. If a function has no return value, declare the return type as `void`. Omit the value in the `return` statements in a `void` function.

```
return;
```

You can also omit the `return` statement entirely. In this circumstance, control returns to the caller when execution reaches the end of the function body. Listing 19-1 presents some function examples.

**Listing 19-1.** *Examples of Functions*

```cpp
#include <iostream>
#include <istream>
#include <ostream>
#include <string>

/** Ignore the rest of the input line. */
void ignore_line()
{
  char c;
  while (std::cin.get(c) and c != '\n')
    /*empty*/;
}

/** Prompt the user, then read a number, and ignore the rest of the line.
 * @param prompt the prompt string
 * @return the input number or 0 for end-of-file
 */
int prompted_read(std::string prompt)
{
  std::cout << prompt;
  int x(0);
  std::cin >> x;
  ignore_line();
  return x;
}

/** Print the statistics.
 * @param count the number of values
 * @param sum the sum of the values
 */
void print_result(int count, int sum)
{
  if (count == 0)
  {
    std::cout << "no data\n";
    return;
  }

  std::cout << "\ncount = " << count;
  std::cout << "\nsum   = " << sum;
  std::cout << "\nmean  = " << sum/count << '\n';
}

/** Main program.
 * Read integers from the standard input and print statistics about them.
 */
```

```
int main()
{
  int sum(0);
  int count(0);

  while (std::cin)
  {
    int x(prompted_read("Value: "));
    if (std::cin)
    {
      sum = sum + x;
      ++count;
    }
  }
  print_result(count, sum);
}
```

**What does Listing 19-1 do?**

_____

_____

The ignore_line function reads and discards characters from std::cin until it reaches the end of the line or the end of the file. It takes no arguments and returns no values to the caller.

The prompted_read function prints a prompt to std::cout then reads a number from std::cin. It then discards the rest of the input line. Because x is initialized to 0, if the read fails, the function returns 0. The caller cannot distinguish between a failure and a real 0 in the input stream, so the main() function tests std::cin to know when to terminate the loop. (The value 0 is unimportant; feel free to initialize x to any value.) The sole argument to the function is the prompt string. The return type is int, and the return value is the number read from std::cin.

The print_result function takes two arguments, both of type int. It returns nothing: it simply prints the results. Notice how it returns early if the input contains no data.

Finally, the main() function puts it all together, repeatedly calling prompted_read and accumulating the data. Once the input ends, main() prints the results, which in this example are the sum, count, and average of the integers it read from the standard input.

# Function Call

In a function call, all arguments are evaluated before the function is called. Each argument is copied to the corresponding parameter in the function then the function body begins to run. When the function executes a return statement, the value in the statement is copied back to the caller, which can then use the value in an expression, assign it to a variable, and so on.

In this book, I try to be careful about terminology: *arguments* are the expressions in a function call, and *parameters* are the variables in a function's header. I've also seen the phrase *actual argument* used for arguments and *formal argument* used for parameters. I find these confusing, so I recommend you stick with arguments and parameters.

# Declarations and Definitions

I wrote the functions in bottom-up fashion because C++ needs to know about a function
before it can compile any call to that function. The easiest way to achieve this in a simple
program is to write every function before you call it—that is, write the function earlier in the
source file than the point at which you call the function.

If you prefer, you can code in a top-down manner and write main() first, followed by the
functions it calls. The compiler still needs to know about the functions before you call them,
but you don't need to provide the complete function. Instead, you provide only what the compiler needs: the return type, name, and a comma-separated list of parameters in parentheses.
Listing 19-2 shows this new arrangement of the source code.

**Listing 19-2.** *Separating Function Declarations from Definitions*

```
#include <iostream>
#include <istream>
#include <ostream>
#include <string>

void ignore_line();
int prompted_read(std::string prompt);
void print_result(int count, int sum);

/** Main program.
 * Read integers from the standard input and print statistics about them.
 */
int main()
{
  int sum(0);
  int count(0);

  while (std::cin)
  {
    int x(prompted_read("Value: "));
    if (std::cin)
    {
      sum = sum + x;
      ++count;
    }
  }
  print_result(count, sum);
}

/** Prompt the user, then read a number, and ignore the rest of the line.
 * @param prompt the prompt string
 * @return the input number or -1 for end-of-file
 */
int prompted_read(std::string prompt)
```

```
{
  std::cout << prompt;
  int x(-1);
  std::cin >> x;
  ignore_line();
  return x;
}

/** Ignore the rest of the input line. */
void ignore_line()
{
  char c;
  while (std::cin.get(c) and c != '\n')
    /*empty*/;
}

/** Print the statistics.
 * @param count the number of values
 * @param sum the sum of the values
 */
void print_result(int count, int sum)
{
  if (count == 0)
  {
    std::cout << "no data\n";
    return;
  }

  std::cout << "\ncount = " << count;
  std::cout << "\nsum   = " << sum;
  std::cout << "\nmean  = " << sum/count << '\n';
}
```

Writing the function in its entirety is known as providing a *definition*. Writing the function header by itself—that is, the return type, name, and parameters, followed by a semicolon—is known as a *declaration*. In general, a declaration tells the compiler how to use a name: what part of a program the name is (typedef, variable, function, etc.), the type of the name, and anything else (such as function parameters) that the compiler needs in order to make sure your program uses that name correctly. The definition provides the body or implementation for a name. A function's declaration must match its definition: the return types, name, and the types of the parameters must be the same. However, the parameter names can differ.

A definition is also a declaration because the full definition of an entity also tells C++ how to use that entity.

The distinction between declaration and definition is crucial in C++. So far, our simple programs have not needed to face the difference, but that will soon change. Remember: a declaration describes a name to the compiler, and a definition provides all the details the compiler needs for the entity you are defining.

A variable definition notifies the compiler of the variable's type, name, and possibly its initial value. The definition instructs the compiler to set aside memory for the variable, and if necessary, to generate code to initialize the variable.

In order to use a variable, such as a function parameter, the compiler needs only the name and the type. For a local variable, however, the compiler needs a definition so it knows to set aside memory to store the variable. The definition can also provide the variable's initial value. Even without an explicit initial value, the compiler may generate code to initialize the variable, such as ensuring that a `string` or `vector` is properly initialized as empty.

# Counting Words, Again

Your turn: **rewrite the word-counting program (last seen in Exploration 18), this time making use of functions.** For example, you can restore the pretty-printing utility by encapsulating it in a single function. Here's a hint: you may want to use the `typedef` names in multiple functions. If so, declare them before the first function, following the `#include` directives.

Test the program to ensure that your changes have not altered its behavior.

Compare your program with Listing 19-3.

**Listing 19-3.** *Using Functions to Clarify the Word-Counting Program*

```
#include <iomanip>
#include <ios>
#include <iostream>
#include <istream>
#include <locale>
#include <map>
#include <ostream>
#include <string>

typedef std::map<std::string, int>  count_map;  ///< Map words to counts
typedef count_map::iterator         count_iter; ///< Iterate over a @c count_map
typedef std::string::size_type      str_size;   ///< String size type

/** Initialize the I/O streams by imbuing them with
 * the given locale. Use this function to imbue the streams
 * with the native locale. C++ initially imbues streams with
 * the classic locale.
 * @param locale the native locale
 */
void initialize_streams(std::locale locale)
{
  std::cin.imbue(locale);
  std::cout.imbue(locale);
}

/** Find the longest key in a map.
 * @param map the map to search
```

```
 * @returns the size of the longest key in @p map
 */
str_size get_longest_key(count_map map)
{
  str_size result(0);
  for (count_iter iter(map.begin()); iter != map.end(); ++iter)
    if (iter->first.size() > result)
      result = iter->first.size();
  return result;
}


/** Print the word, count, newline. Keep the columns neatly aligned.
 * Rather than the tedious operation of measuring the magnitude of all
 * the counts and then determining the necessary number of columns, just
 * use a sufficiently large value for the counts column.
 * @param iter an iterator that points to the word/count pair
 * @param longest the size of the longest key; pad all keys to this size
 */
void print_pair(count_iter iter, str_size longest)
{
  const int count_size(10); // Number of places for printing the count
  std::cout << std::setw(longest)    << std::left  << iter->first <<
               std::setw(count_size) << std::right << iter->second << '\n';
}


/** Print the results in neat columns.
 * @param counts the map of all the counts
 */
void print_counts(count_map counts)
{
  str_size longest(get_longest_key(counts));

  // For each word/count pair...
  for (count_iter iter(counts.begin()); iter != counts.end(); ++iter)
    print_pair(iter, longest);
}


/** Sanitize a string by keeping only alphabetic characters.
 * @param str the original string
 * @param loc the locale used to test the characters
 * @return a santized copy of the string
 */
std::string sanitize(std::string str, std::locale loc)
{
  std::string result;
  for (std::string::iterator s(str.begin()); s != str.end(); ++s)
    if (std::isalnum(*s, loc))
```

```
      result.push_back(std::tolower(*s, loc));
  return result;
}


/** Main program to count unique words in the standard input. */
int main()
{
  std::locale native("");              // get the native locale
  initialize_streams(native);

  count_map counts;
  std::string word;

  // Read words from the standard input and count the number of times
  // each word occurs.
  while (std::cin >> word)
  {
    std::string copy(sanitize(word, native));

    // The "word" might be all punctuation, so the copy would be empty.
    // Don't count empty strings.
    if (not copy.empty())
      ++counts[copy];
  }

  print_counts(counts);
}
```

By using functions, you can read, write, and maintain a program in discrete chunks, or modules. Instead of being overwhelmed by one long main(), you can read, understand, and internalize one function at a time, and then move on to the next function. The compiler keeps you honest by ensuring that the function calls match the function declarations, the function definitions and declarations agree, you haven't mistyped a name, and the function return types match the contexts where the functions are called.

# The main() Function

Now that you know more about functions, you can answer the question that you may have already asked yourself: **What is special about the** main() **function?**

_____

_____

One way that main() differs from ordinary functions is immediately obvious. All the main() functions in this book lack a return statement. An ordinary function that returns an int must have at least one return statement, but main() is special. If you don't supply your own return statement, the compiler inserts a return 0; statement at the end of main(). If control reaches the end of the function body, the effect is the same as return 0;, which returns a success status to the operating system. If you want to signal an error to the operating system, you can return a non-zero value from `main()`. How the operating system interprets the value depends on the implementation. The only portable values to return are `0`, `EXIT_SUCCESS`, and `EXIT_FAILURE`. `EXIT_SUCCESS` means the same thing as `0`—namely, success, but its actual value can be different from `0`. The names are declared in `<cstdlib>`.

The next Exploration continues to examine functions by taking a closer look at the arguments in function calls.

# EXPLORATION 20

■ ■ ■

# Function Arguments

This Exploration continues the examination of functions introduced in Exploration 19 by focusing on argument-passing. Take a closer look. Remember that *arguments* are the expressions that you pass to a function in a function call. *Parameters* are the variables that you declare in the function declaration.

## Argument Passing

Read through Listing 20-1 then answer the questions that follow it.

**Listing 20-1.** *Function Arguments and Parameters*

```cpp
#include <algorithm>
#include <iostream>
#include <istream>
#include <iterator>
#include <ostream>
#include <vector>

void modify(int x)
{
  x = 10;
}

int triple(int x)
{
  return 3 * x;
}

void print_vector(std::vector<int> v)
{
  std::cout << "{ ";
  std::copy(v.begin(), v.end(), std::ostream_iterator<int>(std::cout, " "));
  std::cout << "}\n";
}
```

```
void add(std::vector<int> v, int a)
{
  for (std::vector<int>::iterator i(v.begin()); i != v.end(); ++i)
    *i = *i + a;
}

int main()
{
  int a(42);
  modify(a);
  std::cout << "a=" << a << '\n';

  int b(triple(14));
  std::cout << "b=" << b << '\n';

  std::vector<int> data;
  data.push_back(10);
  data.push_back(20);
  data.push_back(30);
  data.push_back(40);

  print_vector(data);
  add(data, 42);
  print_vector(data);
}
```

**Predict what the program will print.**

_____

_____

_____

_____

Now compile and run the program. **What does it actually print?**

_____

_____

_____

_____

**Were you correct?** _____ **Explain why the program behaves as it does.**

_____

_____

When I run the program, I get the following results:

```
a=42
b=42
{ 10 20 30 40 }
{ 10 20 30 40 }
```

Expanding on these results, you may have noticed the modify function does not actually modify the variable a in main( ), and the add function does not modify data.

As you can see, C++ passes arguments *by value*—that is, it copies the argument value to the parameter. The function can do whatever it wants with the parameter, but when the function returns, the parameter goes away, and the caller never sees any changes the function made.

If you want to return a value to the caller, use a return statement, as was done in the triple function.

**Rewrite the add function so it returns the modified vector to the caller.**

_____

_____

_____

_____

_____

_____

_____

_____

Compare your solution with the following code block:

```cpp
std::vector<int> add(std::vector<int> v, int a)
{
  std::vector<int> result;
  for (std::vector<int>::iterator i(v.begin()); i != v.end(); ++i)
    result.push_back(*i + a);
  return result;
}
```

To call the new add, you must assign the function's result to a variable.

```cpp
data = add(data, 42);
```

**What is the problem with this new version of add?**

_____

_____

Consider what would happen when you call add with a very large vector. The function makes an entirely new copy of its argument, consuming twice as much memory as it really ought to.

# Pass-by-Reference

Instead of passing large objects (such as vectors) by value, C++ lets you pass them *by reference*. Add an ampersand (&) after the type name in the function parameter declaration. **Change Listing 20-1 to pass vector parameters by reference.** Also change the modify function, but leave the other int parameters alone. **What do you predict will be the output?**

_____

_____

_____

_____

Now compile and run the program. **What does it actually print?**

_____

_____

_____

_____

**Were you correct?** _____ **Explain why the program behaves as it does.**

_____

_____

Listing 20-2 shows the new version of the program.

**Listing 20-2.** *Pass Parameters by Reference*

```
#include <algorithm>
#include <iostream>
#include <istream>
#include <iterator>
#include <ostream>
#include <vector>

void modify(int& x)
{
  x = 10;
}

int triple(int x)
{
  return 3 * x;
}
```

```
void print_vector(std::vector<int>& v)
{
  std::cout << "{ ";
  std::copy(v.begin(), v.end(), std::ostream_iterator<int>(std::cout, " "));
  std::cout << "}\n";
}

void add(std::vector<int>& v, int a)
{
  for (std::vector<int>::iterator i(v.begin()); i != v.end(); ++i)
    *i = *i + a;
}

int main()
{
  int a(42);
  modify(a);
  std::cout << "a=" << a << '\n';

  int b(triple(14));
  std::cout << "b=" << b << '\n';

  std::vector<int> data;
  data.push_back(10);
  data.push_back(20);
  data.push_back(30);
  data.push_back(40);

  print_vector(data);
  add(data, 42);
  print_vector(data);
}
```

When I run the program, I get the following results:

```
a=10
b=42
{ 10 20 30 40 }
{ 52 62 72 82 }
```

This time the program modified the x parameter in modify and updated the vector's contents in add.

**Change the rest of the parameters to use pass-by-reference. What do you expect to happen?**

_____

_____

Try it. **What actually happens?**

_____

_____

The compiler does not allow you to call `triple(14)` when `triple`'s parameter is a reference. Consider what would happen if `triple` attempted to modify its parameter. You can't assign to a number, only to a variable. In C++ terms, a variable is called an *lvalue*, which in rough translation means it can appear on the left-hand side of an assignment. An integer literal is an example of an *rvalue*, which again, loosely translated, means it can appear only on the right-hand side of an assignment.

When a parameter is a reference, the argument in the function call must be an lvalue. If the parameter is call-by-value, you can pass an rvalue.

**Can you pass an lvalue to a call-by-value parameter?** _____

You've seen many examples that you can pass an lvalue. C++ automatically converts any lvalue to an rvalue when it needs to. **Can you convert an rvalue to an lvalue?**

_____

If you aren't sure, try to think of the problem in more concrete terms: can you convert an integer literal to a variable? That means you cannot convert an rvalue to an lvalue. Except, sometimes you can, as the next section will explain.

# const References

In the new program, the `print_vector` function takes its parameter by reference, but it doesn't modify the parameter. This opens a window for programming errors: you can accidentally write code to modify the vector. To prevent such errors, you can revert to call-by-value, but you would still have a memory problem if the argument is large. Ideally, you would be able to pass an argument by reference, but still prevent the function from modifying its parameter. Well, as it turns out, such a method does exist: remember `const`? C++ lets you declare a function parameter `const`, too:

```
void print_vector(std::vector<int> const& v)
{
  std::cout << "{ ";
  std::copy(v.begin(), v.end(), std::ostream_iterator<int>(std::cout, " "));
  std::cout << "}\n";
}
```

Read the parameter declaration by starting at the parameter name and working your way from right to left: the parameter name is `v`; it is a reference; the reference is to a `const` object; and the object type is `std::vector<int>`. Sometimes, C++ can be hard to read, especially for a newcomer to the language, but with practice, you will soon read such declarations with ease.

## CONST WARS

Many C++ programmers put the const keyword in front of the type, as demonstrated in the following:

```
void print_vector(const std::vector<int>& v)
```

For simple definitions, the const placement is not critical. For example, to define a named constant, you might use

```
const int max_width(80); // maximum line width before wrapping
```

The difference between that and

```
int const max_width(80); // maximum line width before wrapping
```

is small. But with a more complicated declaration, such as the parameter to print_vector, the difference is more significant. I find my technique much easier to read and understand. My rule of thumb is to keep the const keyword as close as possible to whatever it is modifying.

More and more C++ programmers are coming around to adopt the const-near-the-name style instead of const-out-in-front. Again, this is an opportunity for you to be in the vanguard of the most up-to-date C++ programming trends. But you need to get used to reading code with const out in front, because you're going to see a lot of it.

So, v is a reference to a const vector. Because the vector is const, the compiler prevents the print_vector function from modifying it (adding elements, erasing elements, changing elements, and so on). Go ahead and try it. See what happens if you throw in any one of the following lines:

```
data.push_back(10); // add an element
data.pop_back();    // remove the last element
data.front() = 42;  // modify an element
```

The compiler stops you from modifying a const parameter.

Standard practice is to use references to pass any large data structure, such as vector, map, or string. If the function has no intention of making changes, declare the reference as a const. For small objects, such as int, use pass-by-value.

If a parameter is a reference to const, you can pass an rvalue as an argument. This is the exception that lets you convert an rvalue to an lvalue. To see how this works, change triple's parameter to be a reference to const.

```
int triple(int const& x)
```

Convince yourself that you can pass an rvalue (such as 14) to triple. Thus, the more precise rule is that you can convert an rvalue to a const lvalue, but not to a non-const lvalue.

# const_iterator

One additional trick you need to know when using const parameters: if you need an iterator, use const_iterator instead of iterator. An ordinary iterator lets you modify the element by assigning to *iterator. Because the object is const, you cannot modify its elements, so you cannot use an iterator. A const_iterator lets you read values but not modify them; this means you can safely use a const_iterator.

```cpp
void print_vector(std::vector<int> const& v)
{
  std::cout << "{ ";
  std::string separator("");
  for (std::vector<int>::const_iterator i(v.begin()); i != v.end(); ++i)
  {
    std::cout << *i << separator;
    separator = ", ";
  }
  std::cout << "}\n";
}
```

# Output Parameters

You've already seen how to return a value from a function. Sometimes, you want to return a large object, or you need to return multiple values. In that case, you may want to call-by-reference, which is how C++ implements output parameters. For example, you may want to write a function that populates a vector with data read from the standard input, as shown in the following:

```cpp
void read_data(std::vector<int>& data)
{
  std::copy(std::istream_iterator<int>(std::cin),
            std::istream_iterator<int>(),
            std::back_inserter(data));
}
```

Now that you know how to pass strings, vectors, and whatnot to a function, you can begin to make further improvements to the word-counting program, as you will see in the next Exploration.

■ ■ ■

# Using Algorithms

So far, your use of the standard algorithms has been limited to a few calls to copy, the occasional use of sort, and so on. The main limitation has been that many of the more interesting algorithms require you to supply a function. This Exploration takes a look at these more advanced algorithms. In addition, we'll revisit some of the algorithms you already know to show you how they too can be used in a more advanced manner.

## Transforming Data

Several programs that you've read and written have a common theme: copying a sequence of data, such as a vector or string, and applying some kind of transformation to each element (converting to lowercase, doubling the values in an array, and so on). The standard algorithm, transform, is ideal for applying an arbitrarily complex transformation to the elements of a sequence.

For example, recall Listing 9-5, which doubled all the values in an array. Listing 21-1 presents a new way to write this same program, but using transform.

**Listing 21-1.** *Calling* transform *to Apply a Function to Each Element of an Array*

```
#include <algorithm>
#include <iostream>
#include <istream>
#include <iterator>
#include <ostream>
#include <vector>

int times_two(int i)
{
  return i * 2;
}

int main()
{
    std::vector<int> data;
```

```
        std::copy(std::istream_iterator<int>(std::cin),
                  std::istream_iterator<int>(),
                  std::back_inserter(data));

        std::transform(data.begin(), data.end(), data.begin(), times_two);

        std::copy(data.begin(), data.end(),
                  std::ostream_iterator<int>(std::cout, "\n"));
}
```

The transform function takes four arguments: the first two specify the input range (as start and one-past-the-end iterators), the third argument is an output iterator, and the final argument is the name of a function.

Regarding the third argument, as usual, it is your responsibility to ensure the output sequence has enough room to accommodate the transformed data. In this case, the transformed data overwrite the original data, so the start of the output range is the same as the start of the input range. The fourth argument is just the name of a function that you must have declared or defined earlier in the source file. In this example, the function takes one int parameter and returns an int. The general rule for a transform function is that its parameter type must match the input type, which is the type of the element to which the input iterators refer. The return value must match the output type, which is the type to which the result iterator refers. The transform algorithm calls this function once for each element in the input range. It copies to the output range the value returned by the function.

Rewriting the word-counting program is a little harder. Recall from Listing 19-3 that the sanitize function transforms a string by removing non-letters and converting all uppercase letters to lowercase. The purpose of the C++ standard library is not to provide a zillion functions that cover all possible programming scenarios, but rather, to provide the tools you need to build your own functions with which you can solve your problems. Thus, you would search the standard library in vain for a single algorithm that copies, transforms, and filters. Instead, you can combine two standard functions: one that transforms and one that filters.

A further complication, however, is that you know that the filtering and transforming functions will rely on a locale. Solve the problem for now by setting your chosen locale to global. In that way, the functions you write can use the global locale without needing to pass locale objects around. Listing 21-2 demonstrates how to rewrite Listing 18-3 to set the global locale to the native locale, and then to use the global locale in the rest of the program.

**Listing 21-2.** *New* main *Function That Sets the Global Locale*

```
#include <iomanip>
#include <ios>
#include <iostream>
#include <istream>
#include <locale>
#include <map>
#include <ostream>
#include <string>
```

```cpp
typedef std::map<std::string, int>  count_map;  ///< Map words to counts
typedef count_map::iterator          count_iter; ///< Iterate over a @c count_map
typedef std::string::size_type       str_size;   ///< String size type

/** Initialize the I/O streams by imbuing them with
 * the global locale. Use this function to imbue the streams
 * with the native locale. C++ initially imbues streams with
 * the classic locale.
 */
void initialize_streams()
{
  std::cin.imbue(std::locale());
  std::cout.imbue(std::locale());
}

/** Find the longest key in a map.
 * @param map the map to search
 * @returns the size of the longest key in @p map
 */
str_size get_longest_key(count_map map)
{
  str_size result(0);
  for (count_iter iter(map.begin()); iter != map.end(); ++iter)
    if (iter->first.size() > result)
      result = iter->first.size();
  return result;
}

/** Print the word, count, newline. Keep the columns neatly aligned.
 * Rather than the tedious operation of measuring the magnitude of all
 * the counts and then determining the necessary number of columns, just
 * use a sufficiently large value for the counts column.
 * @param iter an iterator that points to the word/count pair
 * @param longest the size of the longest key; pad all keys to this size
 */
void print_pair(count_iter iter, str_size longest)
{
  const int count_size(10); // Number of places for printing the count
  std::cout << std::setw(longest)    << std::left  << iter->first <<
               std::setw(count_size) << std::right << iter->second << '\n';
}

/** Print the results in neat columns.
 * @param counts the map of all the counts
 */
void print_counts(count_map counts)
```

```
{
  str_size longest(get_longest_key(counts));

  // For each word/count pair...
  for (count_iter iter(counts.begin()); iter != counts.end(); ++iter)
    print_pair(iter, longest);
}

/** Sanitize a string by keeping only alphabetic characters.
 * @param str the original string
 * @return a santized copy of the string
 */
std::string sanitize(std::string str)
{
  using namespace std;
  string result;
  for (string::iterator s(str.begin()); s != str.end(); ++s)
    if (isalnum(*s, locale()))
      result.push_back(tolower(*s, locale()));
  return result;
}

/** Main program to count unique words in the standard input. */
int main()
{
  // Set the global locale to the native locale.
  std::locale::global(std::locale(""));
  initialize_streams();

  count_map counts;
  std::string word;

  // Read words from the standard input and count the number of times
  // each word occurs.
  while (std::cin >> word)
  {
    std::string copy(sanitize(word));

    // The "word" might be all punctuation, so the copy would be empty.
    // Don't count empty strings.
    if (not copy.empty())
      ++counts[copy];
  }

  print_counts(counts);
}
```

Now it's time to rewrite the sanitize function to take advantage of algorithms. Use transform to convert characters to lowercase. Use remove_if to get rid of non-alphabetic characters from the string. The remove_if algorithm calls a function for each element of a sequence. If the function returns true, remove_if eliminates that element from the sequence—well, it kind of does.

One curious side effect of how iterators work in C++ is that the remove_if function does not actually erase anything from the sequence. Instead, it rearranges the elements and returns an iterator that points to the position one past the end of the elements to be preserved. You can then call the erase member function to delete the elements that were removed, or you can make sure your function keeps track of the new logical end of the sequence.

Figure 21-1 illustrates how remove_if works with a *before* and *after* view of a string. Notice how the remove_if function does not alter the size of the string, but the characters after the new end are not meaningful. They are junk.

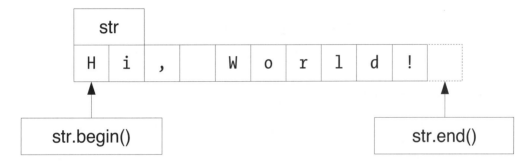

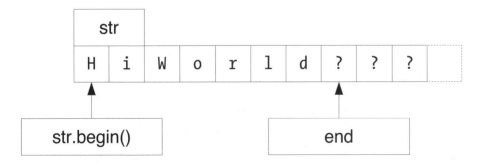

**Figure 21-1.** *Removing elements from a sequence*

Take a look at Listing 21-3 to see how remove_if works in code.

**Listing 21-3.** *Sanitizing a String by Transforming It*

```
/** Test for non-letter.
 * @param ch the character to test
 * @return true if @p ch is not a character that makes up a word
 */
bool non_letter(char ch)
```

```
{
  return not isalnum(ch, std::locale());
}


/** Convert to lowercase.
 * Use a canonical form by converting to uppercase first,
 * and then to lowercase.
 * @param ch the character to test
 * @return the character converted to lowercase
 */
char lowercase(char ch)
{
  return std::tolower(ch, std::locale());
}


/** Sanitize a string by keeping only alphabetic characters.
 * @param str the original string
 * @return a santized copy of the string
 */
std::string sanitize(std::string str)
{
  // Remove all non-letters from the string, and then erase them.
  str.erase(std::remove_if(str.begin(), str.end(), non_letter),
            str.end());

  // Convert the remnants of the string to lowercase.
  std::transform(str.begin(), str.end(), str.begin(), lowercase);

  return str;
}
```

The erase member function takes two iterators as arguments and erases all the elements within that range. The remove_if function returns an iterator that points to one-past-the-end of the new string, which means it also points to the first position of the elements to be erased. Passing str.end() as the end of the range instructs erase to get rid of all the removed elements.

The remove/erase idiom is common in C++, so you should get used to seeing it. The standard library has several remove-like functions, all of which work the same way. It takes a little while to get used to this approach, but once you do, you will find it quite easy to use.

# Predicates

The non_letter function is an example of a *predicate*. A predicate is a function that returns a bool result. These functions have many uses in the standard library.

For example, the sort function sorts values in ascending order. What if you wanted to sort data in descending order? The sort function lets you provide a predicate to compare items. The ordering predicate (call it pred) must meet the following qualifications:

- pred(a, a) must be false (a common error is to implement <= instead of <, which violates this requirement)

- If pred(a, b) is true, and pred(b, c) is true, then pred(a, c) must also be true

- The parameter types must match the element type to be sorted

- The return type must be bool or something that C++ can convert automatically to bool

If you don't provide a predicate, sort uses the < operator as the default.

**Write a predicate to compare two integers for sorting in descending order.**

_____

_____

_____

_____

_____

_____

Write a program to test your function. **Did it work?** _____
Compare your solution with Listing 21-4.

**Listing 21-4.** *Sorting into Descending Order*

```cpp
#include <algorithm>
#include <iostream>
#include <istream>
#include <iterator>
#include <ostream>
#include <vector>

/** Predicate for sorting into descending order. */
int descending(int a, int b)
{
  return a > b;
}

int main()
{
  std::vector<int> data;
  data.insert(data.begin(), std::istream_iterator<int>(std::cin),
                            std::istream_iterator<int>());

  std::sort(data.begin(), data.end(), descending);

  std::copy(data.begin(), data.end(), std::ostream_iterator<int>(std::cout, "\n"));
}
```

The default comparison that sort uses (the < operator) is the standard for comparison throughout the standard library. The standard library uses < as the ordering function for anything and everything that can be ordered. For example, map uses < to compare keys. The lower_bound functions (which you used in Exploration 12) use the < operator to perform a binary search.

The standard library even uses < to compare objects for equality when dealing with ordered values, such as a map or a binary search. (Algorithms and containers that are not inherently ordered use == to determine when two objects are equal.) To test if two items, a and b, are the same, these library functions use a < b and b < a. If both comparisons are false, then a and b must be the same, or in C++ terms, *equivalent*. If you supply a comparison predicate (pred), the library considers a and b to be equivalent if pred(a, b) is false and pred(b, a) is false.

**Modify your descending-sort program (or Listing 21-4) to use == as the comparison operator. What do you expect to happen?**

_____

_____

**Run the new program with a variety of inputs. What actually happens?**

_____

_____

**Were you correct?** _____

The equivalence test is broken because descending(a,a) is true, not false. Because the predicate does not work properly, sort is not guaranteed to work properly, or at all. The results are undefined. Whenever you write a predicate, be sure the comparison is strict (that is, you can write a valid equivalence test) and the transitive property holds (if a < b and b < c, then a < c is also true).

# Other Algorithms

The standard library contains too many useful algorithms to cover in this book, but I'll take a few moments in this section to introduce you to at least some of them. Refer to a comprehensive language reference to learn about the other algorithms.

Let's explore algorithms by looking for palindromes. A palindrome is a word or phrase that reads the same forward and backward, ignoring punctuation, such as:

*Madam, I'm Adam.*

The program reads one line of text at a time by calling the getline function. This function reads from an input stream into a string, stopping when it reads a delimiter character. The default delimiter is '\n', so it reads one line of text. It does not skip over initial or trailing white space.

The first step is to remove non-letter characters, but you already know how to do that.

The next step is to test whether the resulting string is a palindrome. The reverse function transposes the order of elements in a range, such as characters in a string.

The equal function compares two sequences to determine whether they are the same. It takes two iterators for the first range and a starting iterator for the second range. It assumes the two ranges are the same size, and it compares one element at a time and works for any kind of sequence. In this case, the comparison must be case-insensitive, so provide a predicate that converts all text to a canonical case and then compares them.

Go ahead. **Write the program.** A simple web search should deliver up some juicy palindromes with which to test your program. If you don't have access to the web, try the following:

Eve

Deed

Hannah

Leon saw I was Noel

If you need some hints, here are my recommendations:

- Write a function called is_palindrome that takes a string as a parameter and returns a bool.

- This function uses the remove_if function to clean up the string.

- There's no need to erase the removed elements, however. Instead, save the end iterator returned by remove_if and use that instead of str.end().

- Define a new string, rev, which is a copy of the sanitized string. Copy only the desired part of the test string by taking only up to the iterator that was returned from remove_if.

- Next, call reverse.

- Write a predicate, same_char, to compare two characters after converting them both to uppercase and then to lowercase.

- Call the equal function with same_char as its predicate to compare the original string with the reversed copy.

- The main program sets the global locale to the native locale, and imbues the input and output streams with the new global locale.

- The main program calls getline(std::cin, line) until the function returns false (meaning error or end-of-file) then calls is_palindrome for each line.

Listing 21-5 shows my version of the completed program.

**Listing 21-5.** *Testing for Palindromes*

```
#include <algorithm>
#include <iostream>
#include <istream>
#include <iterator>
#include <locale>
#include <ostream>
#include <string>
```

```cpp
/** Test for non-letter.
 * @param ch the character to test
 * @return true if @p ch is not a letter
 */
bool non_letter(char ch)
{
  return not isalpha(ch, std::locale());
}


/** Convert to lowercase.
 * Use a canonical form by converting to uppercase first,
 * and then to lowercase.
 * @param ch the character to test
 * @return the character converted to lowercase
 */
char lowercase(char ch)
{
  return std::tolower(ch, std::locale());
}

/** Compare two characters without regard to case. */
bool same_char(char a, char b)
{
  return lowercase(a) == lowercase(b);
}


/** Determine whether @p str is a palindrome.
 * Only letter characters are tested. Spaces and punctuation don't count.
 * Empty strings are not palindromes because that's just too easy.
 * @param str the string to test
 * @return true if @p str is the same forward and backward
 */
bool is_palindrome(std::string str)
{
  std::string::iterator end(std::remove_if(str.begin(), str.end(), non_letter));
  std::string rev(str.begin(), end);
  std::reverse(rev.begin(), rev.end());
  return not rev.empty() and std::equal(str.begin(), end, rev.begin(), same_char);
}

int main()
{
  std::locale::global(std::locale(""));
  std::cin.imbue(std::locale());
  std::cout.imbue(std::locale());
```

```
  std::string line;
  while (std::getline(std::cin, line))
    if (is_palindrome(line))
      std::cout << line << '\n';
}
```

You may have noticed that some algorithms have more than one form. The sort function, for example, can take two iterators as arguments, or it can take two iterators and a predicate. Using one name for more than one function is called *overloading*. This is the subject of the next Exploration.

■ ■ ■

# Overloading Function Names

In C++, multiple functions can have the same name, provided the functions have a different number of arguments or different argument types. Using the same name for multiple functions is called *overloading* and is common in C++.

## Overloading

All programming languages use overloading at one level or another. For example, most languages use + for integer addition as well as for floating-point addition. Some languages, such as Pascal, use different operators for integer division (div) and floating-point division (/), but others, such as C and Java, uses the same operator (/).

C++ takes overloading one step further, letting you overload your own function names. Judicious use of overloading can greatly reduce complexity in a program and make your programs easier to read and understand.

For example, C++ inherits several functions from the standard C library that compute an absolute value: abs takes an int argument, fabs takes a floating-point argument, and labs takes a long integer argument.

---

**■Note** Don't be concerned that we have not yet covered these other types. All that matters for the purpose of this discussion is that they are distinct from int. The next Exploration will begin to examine them more closely, so please be patient.

---

C++ also has its own complex type for complex numbers, which has its own absolute value function. In C++, however, they all have the same name, abs. Using different names for different types merely clutters the mental landscape and contributes nothing to the clarity of the code.

The sort function, just to name one example, has two overloaded forms.

```
std::sort(start, end);
std::sort(start, end, compare);
```

The first form sorts in ascending order, comparing elements with the < operator, and the second form compares elements by calling compare. Overloading appears in many other places in the standard library. For example, when you create a locale object, you can copy the global locale by passing no arguments

```
std::isalpha('X', std::locale());
```

or create a native locale object by passing an empty string argument

```
std::isalpha('X', std::locale(""));
```

Overloading functions is easy, so why not jump in? **Write a set of functions, all named print.** They all have a void return type and take various parameters:

- One takes an int as a parameter. It prints the parameter to the standard output.

- Another takes two int parameters. It prints the first parameter to the standard output and uses the second parameter as the field width.

- Another takes a vector<int> as the first parameter, followed by three string parameters. Print the first string parameter then each element of the vector (by calling print), with the second string parameter between elements, and the third string parameter after the vector. If the vector is empty, print the first and third string parameters only.

- Another has the same parameters as the vector form, but also takes an int as the field width for each vector element.

**Write a program to print vectors using the print functions.** Compare your functions and program with mine in Listing 22-1.

**Listing 22-1.** *Printing Vectors by Using Overloaded Functions*

```cpp
#include <algorithm>
#include <iostream>
#include <istream>
#include <iterator>
#include <ostream>
#include <string>
#include <vector>

void print(int i)
{
  std::cout << i;
}

void print(int i, int width)
{
  std::cout.width(width);
  std::cout << i;
}
```

```
void print(std::vector<int> const& vec, int width,
std::string const& prefix, std::string const& separator, std::string const& postfix)
{
  bool print_prefix(true);
  for (std::vector<int>::const_iterator v(vec.begin()); v != vec.end(); ++v)
  {
    if (print_prefix)
      std::cout << prefix;
    else
      std::cout << separator;
    print_prefix = false;
    std::cout.width(width);
    std::cout << *v;
  }
  if (print_prefix)
    std::cout << prefix;
  std::cout << postfix;
}

void print(std::vector<int> const& vec,
std::string const& prefix, std::string const& separator, std::string const& postfix)
{
  print(vec, 0, prefix, separator, postfix);
}

int main()
{
  std::vector<int> data;
  data.insert(data.begin(),
              std::istream_iterator<int>(std::cin), std::istream_iterator<int>());

  std::cout << "columnar data:\n";
  print(data, 10, "", "", "\n");
  std::cout << "row data:\n";
  print(data, "{", ", ", "}\n");
}
```

The C++ library often uses overloading. For example, you can change the size of a vector by calling its resize member function. You can pass one or two arguments: the first argument is the new size of the vector. If you pass a second argument, it is a value to use for new elements in case the new size is larger than the old size.

```
data.resize(10);      // if the old size < 10, use default of 0 for new elements
data.resize(20, -42); // if the old size < 20, use -42 for new elements
```

Library-writers often employ overloading, but applications programmers use it less often. **Practice writing libraries by writing the following functions:**

### bool is_alpha(char ch)

Returns true if ch is an alphabetic character in the global locale; if not, returns false.

### bool is_alpha(std::string const& str)

Returns true if str contains only alphabetic characters in the global locale, or false if any character is not alphabetic. Returns true if str is empty.

### char to_lower(char ch)

Returns ch after converting it to lowercase, if possible; otherwise returns ch. Use the global locale.

### std::string to_lower(std::string str)

Returns a copy of str after converting its contents to lowercase, one character at a time. Copies verbatim any character that cannot be converted to lowercase.

### char to_upper(char ch)

Returns ch after converting it to uppercase, if possible; otherwise returns ch. Use the global locale.

### std::string to_upper(std::string str)

Returns a copy of str after converting its contents to uppercase, one character at a time. Copies verbatim any character that cannot be converted to uppercase.

Compare your solution with mine, which is shown in Listing 22-2.

**Listing 22-2.** *Overloading Functions in the Manner of a Library-Writer*

```
#include <algorithm>
#include <iostream>
#include <istream>
#include <locale>
#include <ostream>

bool is_alpha(char ch)
{
  return std::isalpha(ch, std::locale());
}

bool is_alpha(std::string const& str)
{
  for (std::string::const_iterator iter(str.begin()); iter != str.end(); ++iter)
```

```
    if (not is_alpha(*iter))
      return false;
  return true;
}


char to_lower(char ch)
{
  return std::tolower(ch, std::locale());
}


std::string to_lower(std::string str)
{
  for (std::string::iterator iter(str.begin()); iter != str.end(); ++iter)
    *iter = to_lower(*iter);
  return str;
}


char to_upper(char ch)
{
  return std::toupper(ch, std::locale());
}


std::string to_upper(std::string str)
{
  for (std::string::iterator iter(str.begin()); iter != str.end(); ++iter)
    *iter = to_upper(*iter);
  return str;
}


int main()
{
  std::string str;
  while (std::cin >> str)
  {
    if (is_alpha(str))
      std::cout << "alpha\n";
    else
      std::cout << "not alpha\n";
    std::cout << "lower: " << to_lower(str) << "\nupper: " << to_upper(str) << '\n';
  }
}
```

After waxing poetic about the usefulness of standard algorithms, such as transform, I turned around and wrote my own loops. If you tried to use a standard algorithm, I applaud you for your effort and apologize for tricking you.

If you want to pass an overloaded function to a standard algorithm, the compiler needs to be able to tell which overloaded function you really mean. For some rather complicated reasons, the compiler has difficulty understanding situations such as the following:

```
std::string to_lower(std::string str)
{
  std::transform(str.begin(), str.end(), str.begin(), to_lower);
  return str;
}
```

C++ has ways to help the compiler understand what you mean, but it involves some nasty-looking code, and I'd rather you stay away from it for the time being. If you really insist on punishing yourself, look at code that works, but don't try to sprain your brain understanding it.

```
std::string to_lower(std::string str)
{
  std::transform(str.begin(), str.end(), str.begin(),
               static_cast<char (*)(char)>(to_lower));
  return str;
}
```

If you look closely at to_upper and to_lower, you'll notice another technique that's different from other, similar functions. Can you spot it? **If so, what is it?**

_____

_____

The to_lower and to_upper string functions do not take const references, but take plain strings as parameters. This means the argument is passed by value, which in turn means the compiler arranges to copy the string when passing the argument to the function. The function needs the copy, so this technique helps the compiler generate optimal code for copying the argument, and it saves you a step in writing the function. It's a small trick, but a useful one. This technique will be especially useful later in the book—so don't forget it.

The is_alpha string function does not modify its parameter, so it can take a const reference. Remember that when the parameter is const, you must use const_iterator instead of iterator.

A common use of overloading is to overload a function for different types, including different integer types, such as a long integer. The next Exploration takes a look at these other types.

# Big and Little Numbers

**A**nother common use for overloading is to write functions that work with large and small integers just as well as with plain integers. C++ has four different integer types: byte, short, plain, and long. This Exploration takes a look at the details.

## The Long and Short of It

The size of an int is the natural size of an integer on the host platform. For your desktop computer, that probably means 32 bits or 64 bits. Not too long ago, it meant 16 bits or 32 bits. I've also used computers with 36-bit and 60-bit integers. In the realm of desktop computers and workstations, 32-bit and 64-bit processors dominate today's computing landscape, but don't forget specialized devices, such as digital signal processors (DSPs ) and other embedded chips, where 16-bit architectures are still common. The purpose of leaving the standard flexible is to ensure maximum performance for your code. The C++ standard guarantees that an int can represent, at a minimum, any number in the range –32,767 to 32,767, inclusive.

Although your desktop computer most likely uses two's complement representation for integers, C++ does not mandate that format, only that the representation be binary. In other words, you should treat an integer as a number, not a bit pattern. (Wait for Exploration 61 if you need to work at the bit level.)

To discover the number of bits in an integer, use numeric_limits, as you did way back in Listing 2-3. **Try that same program, but substitute int for bool. What do you get for the output?** _____

Most likely, you got 31, although some of you may have seen 15 or 63. The reason for this is digits does not count the sign bit. No matter what representation your computer uses for an integer, one of those bits must indicate whether the number is negative or positive. Thus, for a type that represents a signed quantity, such as int, you must add one to digits, and for a type with no sign, such as bool, use digits without further modification. Fortunately, numeric_limits offers is_signed, which is true for a signed type and false for an unsigned type. **Rewrite Listing 2-3 to use is_signed to determine whether to add one to digits and print the number of bits per int and per bool.**

Check your answers. **Are they correct?** _____ Compare your program with Listing 23-1.

**Listing 23-1.** *Discovering the Number of Bits in an Integer*

```
#include <iostream>
#include <limits>
#include <ostream>

int main()
{
  std::cout << "bits per int = ";
  if (std::numeric_limits<int>::is_signed)
    std::cout << std::numeric_limits<int>::digits + 1 << '\n';
  else
    std::cout << std::numeric_limits<int>::digits << '\n';

  std::cout << "bits per bool = ";
  if (std::numeric_limits<bool>::is_signed)
    std::cout << std::numeric_limits<bool>::digits + 1 << '\n';
  else
    std::cout << std::numeric_limits<bool>::digits << '\n';
}
```

# Long Integers

Sometimes, you need more bits than int can handle. In this case, add long to the definition to get a long integer.

```
long int lots_o_bits(2147483647);
```

You can even drop the int, as shown in the following:

```
long lots_o_bits(2147483647);
```

The standard guarantees that a long int can handle numbers in the range –2,147,483,647 to 2,147,483,647, but C++ does not guarantee that a long int is actually longer than a plain int. On some platforms, int might be 32 bits and long might be 64. When I first used a PC at home, an int was 16 bits and long was 32 bits. But at work, I used systems for which int and long were both 32 bits. I'm writing this book on a machine that uses 32 bits for int and for long.

Use long if you want to store numbers as large as possible, and are willing to pay a small performance penalty (on some systems), or if you need to ensure portability and need to represent numbers outside the range ±32,767 (which is all C++ guarantees for type int).

---

## EXTRA-LONG INTEGERS

The next revision to the C++ standard will sport another type: long long int. This type can handle values in the range –9,223,372,036,854,775,807 to 9,223,372,036,854,775,807. As with plain long, you can drop the int and write the type as merely long long. Many compilers already support this type as an extension to the standard. Write a long long literal with two Ls as a suffix, e.g., 42LL.

# Short Integers

Sometimes, you don't need the full range of an int, and reducing memory consumption is more important. In this case, use a short int, or just short, which has a guaranteed range of at least –32,767 to 32,767, inclusive. As I just mentioned, short may be the same size as int. On the other hand, most modern implementations define short to be smaller than int.

As is done with long, you define a type as short int or short.

```
short int answer(42);
short zero(0);
```

Modify Listing 23-1 to print the number of bits in a **long** and a **short**, too. How many bits are in a **long** on your system? _____ How many in a **short**? _____

When I run the program in Listing 23-2. I get 16 bits in a short, 32 in an int, and 32 in a long. On a friend's 64-bit processor, I get 16 bits in a short, 32 in an int, and 64 in a long.

**Listing 23-2.** *Revealing the Number of Bits in Short and Long Integers*

```cpp
#include <iostream>
#include <limits>
#include <ostream>

int main()
{
  std::cout << "bits per int = ";
  if (std::numeric_limits<int>::is_signed)
    std::cout << std::numeric_limits<int>::digits + 1 << '\n';
  else
    std::cout << std::numeric_limits<int>::digits << '\n';

  std::cout << "bits per bool = ";
  if (std::numeric_limits<bool>::is_signed)
    std::cout << std::numeric_limits<bool>::digits + 1 << '\n';
  else
    std::cout << std::numeric_limits<bool>::digits << '\n';

  std::cout << "bits per short int = ";
  if (std::numeric_limits<short>::is_signed)
    std::cout << std::numeric_limits<short>::digits + 1 << '\n';
  else
    std::cout << std::numeric_limits<short>::digits << '\n';

  std::cout << "bits per long int = ";
  if (std::numeric_limits<long>::is_signed)
    std::cout << std::numeric_limits<long>::digits + 1 << '\n';
  else
    std::cout << std::numeric_limits<long>::digits << '\n';
}
```

# Integer Literals

When you write an integer literal, the type depends on its value. If the value fits in an int, the type is int; otherwise, the type is long. If the value is too big even for a long, the compiler should issue an error message. You can force a literal to have type long by adding l or L (the letter L in lowercase or uppercase) after the digits. (Curiously, C++ has no way for you to type a short literal.) I always use uppercase L because a lowercase l looks too much like the digit 1. The compiler can always tell the difference, but every year it gets a little harder for me to see the difference between 1 and l.

**Devise a way for a program to print int=, followed by the value, for an int literal, and print long=, followed by the value, for a long literal.** (Hint: what was the topic of the previous Exploration?) Write a program to demonstrate your idea and test it with some literals. If you can, run the program on platforms that use different sizes for int and long. Compare your program to that of Listing 23-3.

**Listing 23-3.** *Using Overloading to Distinguish Types of Integer Literals*

```
#include <iostream>
#include <locale>
#include <ostream>

void print(int i)
{
  std::cout << "int=" << i << '\n';
}

void print(long l)
{
  std::cout << "long=" << l << '\n';
}

int main()
{
  std::cout.imbue(std::locale(""));
  print(0);
  print(0L);
  print(32768);
  print(-32768);
  print(2147483647);
  print(-2147483647);
  // The following lines might work on your system.
  // If you are feeling adventuresome, uncomment the next 3 lines:
  // print(2147483648);
  // print(9223372036854775807);
  // print(-9223372036854775807);
}
```

The last three lines work only on 64-bit systems, and result in compiler errors on 32-bit systems. In other words, a program that works perfectly fine on one system may not even compile on another. That's why the C++ standard sets down some guaranteed ranges for each of the integer types. If you stick to the guaranteed ranges, your program will compile and run everywhere; outside the range, you're taking your chances. Library-writers need to be especially careful. You never know when someone working on a small, embedded processor might like your code and want to use it.

# Byte-Sized Integers

The smallest integer type that C++ offers is signed char. The type name looks similar to the character type, char, but the type acts differently. It usually acts like an integer. By definition, the size of signed char is one byte, which is the smallest size that your C++ compiler supports for any type. The guaranteed range of signed char is –127 to 127.

In spite of the name, you should try not to think of signed char as a mutated character type; instead, think of it as a misspelled integer type. Many programs have a typedef similar to this

```
typedef signed char byte;
```

to make it easier for you to think of this type as a byte-sized integer type.

There is no easy way to write a signed char literal. Character literals have type char, not signed char. Besides, some characters may be out of range for signed char.

Although the compiler does its best to help you remember that signed char is not a char, the I/O stream library is less helpful. It tries to treat signed char values as characters. Somehow, you need to inform the stream that you want to print an integer, not a character. You also need a solution to create signed char (and short) literals. Fortunately, the same solution lets you use signed char constants and print signed char numbers: type casting.

# Type Casting

Although you cannot write a short or arbitrary signed char literal directly, you can write a constant expression that has type short or signed char, and can take any suitable value. The trick is to use a plain int and tell the compiler exactly what type you want.

```
static_cast<signed char>(-1)
static_cast<short int>(42)
```

The expression does not have to be a literal, as demonstrated in the following:

```
int x(42);
static_cast<short>(x);
```

The static_cast expression is known as a *type cast*. The operator, static_cast, is a reserved keyword. It converts an expression from one type to another. The "static" in its name means the type is static, or fixed, at compile time.

You can convert any integer type to any other integer type. If the value is out of range for the target type, you get junk as a result—for example, the high-order bits may be discarded.

Thus, you should always be careful when using static_cast. Be absolutely sure that you are not discarding important information.

If you cast a number to bool, the result is false if the number is zero or true if the number is not zero (just like the conversion that takes place when you use an integer as a condition).

**Rewrite Listing 23-3 to overloading print for short and signed char values, too.** Use type casting to force various values to different types and ensure that the results match your expectations. Take a look at Listing 23-5 to see one possible solution.

**Listing 23-4.** *Using Type Casts*

```cpp
#include <iostream>
#include <locale>
#include <ostream>

typedef signed char byte;

void print(byte b)
{
  // The << operator treats signed char as a mutant char, and tries to
  // print a character. In order to print the value as an integer, you
  // must cast it to an integer type.
  std::cout << "byte=" << static_cast<int>(b) << '\n';
}

void print(short s)
{
  std::cout << "short=" << s << '\n';
}

void print(int i)
{
  std::cout << "int=" << i << '\n';
}

void print(long l)
{
  std::cout << "long=" << l << '\n';
}

int main()
{
  std::cout.imbue(std::locale(""));
  print(0);
  print(0L);
  print(static_cast<short>(0));
  print(static_cast<byte>(0));
  print(static_cast<byte>(255));
  print(static_cast<short>(65535));
```

```
    print(32768);
    print(32768L);
    print(-32768);
    print(2147483647);
    print(-2147483647);
    // The following lines might work on your system.
    // If you are feeling adventuresome, uncomment the next 3 lines:
    // print(2147483648);
    // print(9223372036854775807);
    // print(-9223372036854775807);
}
```

When I run Listing 23-4, I get -1 for static_cast<short>(65535) and static_cast<byte> (255). That's because the values are out of range for the target types. The resulting value is mere coincidence. In this case, it is related to the bit patterns that my particular compiler and platform happen to use. Different environments will yield different values.

# Integer Arithmetic

When you use signed char and short values or objects in an expression, the compiler always turns them into type int. It then performs the arithmetic or whatever operation you wanted to do. This is known as type *promotion*. The compiler *promotes* a short to an int. The result of arithmetic operations is also an int.

You can mix int and long in the same expressions. C++ converts the smaller type to match the larger type, and the larger type is the type of the result. This is known as type *conversion*, which is different from type promotion. (The distinction may seem arbitrary or trivial, but it's important. The next section will explain one of the reasons.) Remember: *promote* signed char and short to int; *convert* int to long.

```
long big(2147483640);
short small(7);
std::cout << big + small; // promote small to type int; then convert it to long;
                          // the sum has type long
```

When you compare two integers, the same promotion and conversion happens: the smaller argument is promoted or converted to the size of the larger argument. The result is always bool.

The compiler can convert any numeric value to bool; it considers this a conversion on the same level as any other integer conversion.

# Overload Resolution

The two-step type conversion process may puzzle you. It matters when you have a set of over-loaded functions, and the compiler needs to decide which function to call. The first thing the compiler tries is to find an exact match. If it can't find one, it searches for a match after type promotion. Only if that fails does it search for a match allowing type conversion. Thus, it con-siders a match based only on type promotion to be better than type conversion. Listing 23-5 demonstrates the difference.

**Listing 23-5.** *Overloading Prefers Type Promotion over Type Conversion*

```cpp
#include <iostream>
#include <ostream>

// print is overloaded for signed char, short, int and long
void print(signed char b)
{
  std::cout << "print(signed char = " << static_cast<int>(b) << ")\n";
}

void print(short s)
{
  std::cout << "print(short = " << s << ")\n";
}

void print(int i)
{
  std::cout << "print(int = " << i << ")\n";
}

void print(long l)
{
  std::cout << "print(long = " << l << ")\n";
}

// guess is overloaded for bool, int, and long
void guess(bool b)
{
  std::cout << "guess(bool = " << b << ")\n";
}

void guess(int i)
{
  std::cout << "guess(int = " << i << ")\n";
}

void guess(long l)
{
  std::cout << "guess(long = " << l << ")\n";
}

// error is overloaded for bool and long
void error(bool b)
{
  std::cout << "error(bool = " << b << ")\n";
}
```

```
void error(long l)
{
  std::cout << "error(long = " << l << ")\n";
}

int main()
{
  signed char byte(10);
  short shrt(20);
  int i(30);
  long lng(40);

  print(byte);
  print(shrt);
  print(i);
  print(lng);

  guess(byte);
  guess(shrt);
  guess(i);
  guess(lng);

  error(byte); // expected error
  error(shrt); // expected error
  error(i);    // expected error
  error(lng);
}
```

The first four lines of main call the print function. The compiler always finds an exact match and is happy. The next four lines call guess. When called with signed char and short arguments, the compiler promotes the arguments to int, and finds an exact match with guess(int i).

The last four lines call the aptly-named function, error. The problem is that the compiler promotes signed char and short to int, and then must convert int to either long or bool. It treats all conversions equally, thus it cannot decide which function to call, so it reports an error. Delete the three lines that I marked with "expected error," and the program works just fine, or add an overload for error(int), and everything will work.

The problem of ambiguous overload resolution is a difficult hurdle for new C++ programmers. It's also a difficult hurdle for most experienced C++ programmers. The exact rules for how C++ resolves overloaded names are complicated and subtle. Avoid being clever about overloaded functions, and keep it simple. Most overloading situations are straightforward, but if you find yourself writing an overload for type long, be certain you also have an overload for type int.

Knowing about big integers helps with some programs, but others need to represent even larger numbers. The next Exploration examines how C++ works with floating point values.

# EXPLORATION 24
■■■

# Very Big and Very Little Numbers

**E**ven the longest `long` cannot represent truly large numbers, such as Avogadro's number ($6.02 \times 10^{23}$) or extremely small numbers, such as the mass of an electron ($9.1 \times 10^{-31}$ kg). Scientists and engineers use scientific notation, which consists of a mantissa (such as 6.02 or 9.1) and an exponent (such as 23 or –31), relative to a base (10).

Computers represent very large and very small numbers using a similar representation, known as *floating-point*. I know many of you have been waiting eagerly for this exploration, as you've probably grown tired of using only integers, so let's jump in.

## Floating-Point Numbers

Computers use floating-point numbers for very large and very small values. By sacrificing precision, you can gain a greatly extended range. However, never forget that the range and precision are limited. Floating-point numbers are not the same as mathematical real numbers, although they can often serve as useful approximations of real numbers.

Like its scientific notation counterpart, a floating-point number has a mantissa, also called a *significand*, a sign, and an exponent. The mantissa and exponent use a common *base* or *radix*. Although integers in C++ are always binary in their representation, floating-point numbers can use any base. Binary is a popular base, but some computers use 16 or even 10 as the base. The precise details are, as always, dependent upon the implementation. In other words, each C++ implementation uses its native floating-point format, for maximum performance.

Floating-point values often come in multiple flavors. C++ offers single, double, and extended precision, called `float`, `double`, and `long double`, respectively. The difference is that `float` usually has less precision and a smaller range than `double`, and `double` usually has less precision and smaller range than `long double`. In exchange, `long double` usually requires more memory and computation time than `double`, which usually takes up more memory and computation time than `float`. On the other hand, an implementation is free to use the same representation for all three types.

Use `double` unless there is some reason not to: use `float` when memory is at a premium and you can afford to lose precision, or `long double` when you absolutely need the extra precision or range and can afford to give up memory and performance.

A common binary representation of floating-point numbers is the IEC 60559 standard, which is better known as IEEE 754. Most likely, your desktop system has hardware that implements the IEC 60559 standard. For the sake of convenience, the following discussion describes only IEC 60559, but never forget that C++ permits many floating-point representations. Mainframes and DSPs, for example, often use other representations.

An IEC 60559 `float` occupies 32 bits, of which 23 bits make up the mantissa, 8 bits form the exponent, leaving one bit for the mantissa's sign. The radix is 2, so the range of an IEC 60559 float is roughly $2^{-127}$ to $2^{127}$, or $10^{-38}$ to $10^{38}$. (I lied. Smaller numbers are possible, but the details are not germane to C++. If you are curious, this book's web site has some links, or just look up *denormalization* in your favorite computer science reference.)

The IEC 60559 standard reserves some bit patterns for special values. In particular, if the exponent is all ones, and the mantissa is all zeros, the value is considered "infinity." It's not quite a mathematical infinity, but it does its best to pretend. Adding any finite value to infinity, for example, yields an answer of infinity. Positive infinity is always greater than any finite value, and negative infinity is always smaller than finite values.

If the exponent is all ones and the mantissa is not all zeros, the value is considered as not-a-number, or *NaN*. NaN comes in two varieties: quiet and signaling. Arithmetic with quiet NaN always yields a NaN result. Using a signaling NaN results in a machine interrupt. How that interrupt manifests itself in your program is up to the implementation. In general, you should expect your program to terminate abruptly. Consult your compiler's documentation to learn the details. Certain arithmetic operations that have no meaningful result can also yield NaN, such as adding positive infinity to negative infinity.

Some floating-point representations do not have infinity or NaN, so you cannot write portable code that relies on these special values. Also, the C++ standardization committee neglected to include any functions for testing whether a value is infinity or NaN, so you must use a platform-specific function (or write your own), which is just one more reason not to use the special values in any code that must be portable. (The next major language revision will likely remedy this oversight.)

A `double` is similar in structure to a `float`, except it takes up 64 bits: 52 bits for the mantissa, 11 bits for the exponent, and 1 sign bit. A `double` can also have infinity and NaN values, with the same structural representation (that is, exponent all ones).

A `long double` is even longer than `double`. The IEC 60559 standard permits an extended double-precision format that requires at least 79 bits. Many desktop and workstation systems implement extended-precision, floating-point numbers using 80 bits (63 for the mantissa and 16 for the exponent).

# Floating-Point Literals

Any numeric literal with a decimal point or a decimal exponent represents a floating-point number. The decimal point is always '`.`', regardless of locale. The exponent starts with the letter e or E and can be signed. No spaces are permitted in a numeric literal.

```
3.1415926535897
31415926535897e-13
0.000314159265e4
```

By default, a floating-point literal has type double. To write a float literal, add the letter f or F after the number. For a long double, use the letter l or L.

```
3.141592f
31415926535897E-13l
0.000314159265E+4L
```

As with long int literals, I prefer uppercase L to avoid confusion with the digit 1. Feel free to use f or F, but I recommend you pick one and stick with it.

If a floating-point literal exceeds the range of the type, the compiler will tell you. If you ask for a value at greater precision than the type supports, the compiler will silently give you as much precision as it can. Another possibility is that you request a value that the type cannot represent exactly. In that case, the compiler gives you the next higher or lower value.

For example, your program may have the literal 0.2F, which seems like a perfectly fine real number, but as a binary floating-point value, it has no exact representation. Instead, it is approximately $0.0011001100_2$. The difference between the decimal value and the internal value can give rise to unexpected results, the most common of which is when you expect two numbers to be equal and they are not. **Read Listing 24-1 and predict the outcome.**

**Listing 24-1.** *Floating-Point Numbers Do Not Always Behave as You Expect*

```cpp
#include <cassert>
int main()
{
  float a(0.03f);
  float b(10.0f);
  float c(0.3f);
  assert(a * b == c);
}
```

**What is your prediction?**

_____

**What is the actual outcome?**

_____

**Were you correct?** _____

The problem is that 0.03 and 0.3 do not have exact representations in binary, so if your floating-point format is binary (and most are), the values the computer uses are approximations of the real values. Multiplying 0.03 by 10 gives a result that is very close to 0.3, but the binary representation differs from that obtained by converting 0.3 to binary. (In IEC 60559 single-precision format, 0.03 * 10.0 gives $0.0111001100110011001100100_2$ and 0.3 is $0.0111001100110011001101000_2$. The numbers are very close, but they differ in the 22^nd significant bit.

Some programmers mistakenly believe that floating-point arithmetic is therefore "imprecise." On the contrary, floating-point arithmetic is exact. The problem lies only in the programmer's expectations if you anticipate floating-point arithmetic to follow the rules of real-number arithmetic. If you realize that the compiler converts your decimal literals to other values, and computes with those other values, and if you understand the rules that the processor uses when it performs limited-precision arithmetic with those values, you can know exactly what the results will be. If this level of detail is critical for your application, you need to take the time to perform this level of analysis.

The rest of us, however, can continue to pretend that floating-point numbers and arithmetic are nearly real without worrying overmuch about the differences. Just don't compare floating-point numbers for exact equality. (How to compare numbers for approximate equality is beyond the scope of this book. Visit the web site for links and references.)

# Floating-Point Traits

You can query `numeric_limits` to reveal the size and limits of a floating-point type. You can also determine whether the type allows infinity or NaN. Listing 24-2 shows some code that displays information about a floating-point type.

**Listing 24-2.** *Discovering the Attributes of a Floating-Point Type*

```cpp
#include <ios>
#include <iostream>
#include <limits>
#include <locale>
#include <ostream>

int main()
{
  using namespace std;
  cout.imbue(locale(""));
  cout << boolalpha;
  // Change float to double or long double to learn about those types.
  typedef float T;
  cout << "min=" << numeric_limits<T>::min() << '\n'
       << "max=" << numeric_limits<T>::max() << '\n'
       << "IEC 60559? " << numeric_limits<T>::is_iec559 << '\n'
       << "max exponent=" << numeric_limits<T>::max_exponent << '\n'
       << "min exponent=" << numeric_limits<T>::min_exponent << '\n'
       << "mantissa places=" << numeric_limits<T>::digits << '\n'
       << "radix=" << numeric_limits<T>::radix << '\n'
       << "has infinity? " << numeric_limits<T>::has_infinity << '\n'
       << "has quiet NaN? " << numeric_limits<T>::has_quiet_NaN << '\n'
       << "has signaling NaN? " << numeric_limits<T>::has_signaling_NaN << '\n';

  if (numeric_limits<T>::has_infinity)
  {
    T zero(0.0);
    T one(1.0);
    T inf(numeric_limits<T>::infinity());
```

```
    if (one/zero == inf)
      cout << "1.0/0.0 = infinity\n";
    if (inf + inf == inf)
      cout << "infinity + infinity = infinity\n";
  }
  if (numeric_limits<T>::has_quiet_NaN)
  {
    // There's no guarantee that your environment produces quiet NaNs for
    // these illegal arithmetic operations. It's possible that your compiler's
    // default is to produce signaling NaNs, or to terminate the program
    // in some other way.
    T zero(0.0);
    T inf(numeric_limits<T>::infinity());
    cout << "zero/zero = " << zero/zero << '\n';
    cout << "inf/inf = " << inf/inf << '\n';
  }
}
```

Modify the program so it prints information about **double**. Run it. Modify it again for **long double**, and run it. **Do the results match your expectations?** _____

# Floating-Point I/O

Reading and writing floating-point values depends on the locale. In the classic locale, the input format is the same as for an integer or floating-point literal. In a native locale, you must write the input according to the rules of the locale. In particular, the decimal separator must be that of the locale. Thousands-separators are optional, but if you use them, you must use the locale-specific character and correct placement.

Output is more complicated.

In addition to the field width and fill character, floating-point output also depends on the precision—the number of places after the decimal point—and the format, which can be fixed-point (without an exponent), scientific (with an exponent), or general (use an exponent only when necessary). The default is general. Depending on the locale, the number may include separators for groups of thousands.

In the scientific and fixed formats, the precision is the number of digits after the decimal point. In the general format, it is the maximum number of significant digits. Set the stream's precision with the precision member function or setprecision manipulator. The default precision is six.

```
double const pi = 3.141592653589792;
std::cout.precision(12);
std::cout << pi << '\n';
std::cout << std::setprecision(4) << pi << '\n';
```

In scientific format, the exponent is printed with a lowercase 'e' (or 'E' if you use the uppercase manipulator), followed by the base 10 exponent. The exponent always has a sign (+ or -), and at least two digits, even if the exponent is zero. The mantissa is written with one digit before the decimal point. The precision determines the number of places after the decimal point.

In fixed format, no exponent is printed. The number is printed with as many digits before the decimal point as needed. The precision determines the number of places after the decimal point. The decimal point is always printed.

The default format is the general format, which means printing numbers nicely without sacrificing information. If the exponent is less than or equal to –4, or if it is greater than the precision, the number is printed in scientific format. Otherwise, it is printed without an exponent. However, unlike conventional fixed-point output, trailing zeros are removed after the decimal point. If after removal of the trailing zeros the decimal point becomes the last character, it is also removed.

When necessary, values are rounded off to fit within the allotted precision.

The easiest way to specify a particular output format is with a manipulator: scientific or fixed (declared in <ios>). Like the precision, the format persists in the stream's state until you change it. (Only width resets after an output operation.) Unfortunately, once you set the format, there is no easy way to revert to the default general format. To do that, you must use a member function, and a clumsy one at that, as shown in the following:

```
std::cout << std::scientific << large_number << '\n';
std::cout << std::fixed << small_number << '\n';
std::cout.unsetf(std::ios_base::floatfield);
std::cout << number_in_general_format << '\n';
```

**Complete Table 24-1, showing exactly how each value would be printed in each format, in the classic locale.** I filled in the first row for your convenience.

**Table 24-1.** *Floating-Point Output*

|  | Precision | Scientific | Fixed | General |
|---|---|---|---|---|
| 123456.789 | 6 | 1.234568e5 | 123456.789000 | 123457 |
| 1.23456789 | 4 | _____ | _____ | _____ |
| 123456789 | 2 | _____ | _____ | _____ |
| –1234.5678e9 | 5 | _____ | _____ | _____ |

After you have filled in the table with your predictions, **write a program that will test your predictions** then run it and see how well you did. Compare your program with Listing 24-3.

**Listing 24-3.** *Demonstrating Floating-Point Output*

```
#include <ios>
#include <iostream>
#include <ostream>

/// Print a floating-point number in three different formats.
/// @param precision the precision to use when printing @p value
```

```cpp
/// @param value the floating-point number to print
void print(int precision, float value)
{
  std::cout.precision(precision);
  std::cout << std::scientific << value << '\t'
            << std::fixed      << value << '\t';

  // Set the format to general.
  std::cout.unsetf(std::ios_base::floatfield);
  std::cout << value << '\n';
}

/// Main program.
int main()
{
  print(6, 123456.789f);
  print(4, 1.23456789f);
  print(2, 123456789.f);
  print(5, -1234.5678e9f);
}
```

The precise values can differ from one system to another depending on the floating-point representation. For example, float on most systems cannot support the full precision of nine decimal digits, so you should expect some fuzziness in the least significant digits of the printed result. In other words, unless you want to sit down and do some serious binary computation, you cannot easily predict exactly what the output will be in every case. Table 24-2 shows the output from Listing 24-3, when run on a typical IEC 60559–compliant system.

**Table 24-2.** *Results of Printing Floating-Point Numbers*

| Value | Precision | Scientific | Fixed | General |
|-------|-----------|------------|-------|---------|
| 123456.789 | 6 | 1.234568e+05 | 123456.789062 | 123457 |
| 1.23456789 | 4 | 1.2346e+00 | 1.2346 | 1.235 |
| 123456789 | 2 | 1.23e+08 | 123456792.00 | 1.2e+08 |
| −1234.5678e9 | 5 | −1.23457e+12 | −1234567823360.00000 | −1.2346e+12 |

Some applications never need to use floating-point numbers; others need it a lot. Scientists and engineers, for example, depend on floating-point arithmetic and math functions and must understand the subtleties of working with these numbers. C++ has everything you need for computation-intensive programming. Although the details are beyond the scope of this book, interested readers should consult a reference for the <cmath> header, and the transcendental and other functions that it provides.

The next Exploration takes a side trip to a completely different topic, explaining the strange comments—the extra slashes (///) and stars (/**)—that I've used in so many programs.

■ ■ ■

# Documentation

This exploration is a little different from the others. Instead of covering part of the C++ standard, it examines a third-party tool called Doxygen. Feel free to skip this Exploration, but understand that this is where I explain the strange comments you sometimes see in the code listings.

## Doxygen

Doxygen is a free, open-source tool that reads your source code, looks for comments that follow a certain structure, and extracts information from the comments and from the code to produce documentation. It produces output in a number of formats: HTML, RTF (rich text format), LaTeX, UNIX man pages, and XML.

Java programmers may be familiar with a similar tool called javadoc. The javadoc tool is standard in the Java Software Development Kit, whereas Doxygen has no relationship with the C++ standard or with any C++ vendor. C++ lacks a standard for structured documentation, so you are free to do anything you want. For example, Microsoft defines its own conventions for XML tags in comments, which is fine if you plan to work entirely within the Microsoft .NET environment. For other programmers, I recommend using tools that have more widespread and portable usage. The most popular solution is Doxygen, and I think every C++ programmer should know about it, even if you decide not to use it. That's why I include this Exploration in the book.

## Structured Comments

Doxygen heeds comments that follow a specific format:

- One-line comments start with an extra slash or exclamation mark: /// or //!

- Multi-line comments start with an extra asterisk or exclamation mark: /** or /*!

Also, Doxygen recognizes some widespread comment conventions. For example, it ignores a line of slashes.

/////////////////////////////////////////////////////////////////////////////////

A multi-line comment can begin with a row full of asterisks

```
*****************************************************************************
```

and a line in a multi-line comment can begin with an asterisk

```
/****************************************************************************
 * This is a structured comment for Doxygen.                                *
 ****************************************************************************/
```

Within a structured comment is where you document the various entities in your program: functions, types, variables, and so on.

The convention is that the comment immediately before a declaration or definition applies to the entity being declared or defined. Sometimes, you want to put the comment after the declaration, such as a one-line description of a variable. To do that, use a "less-than" (<) sign at the start of the comment.

```
double const c = 299792458.0;              ///< speed of light in m/sec
```

# Documentation Tags

Doxygen has its own markup language that utilizes *tags*. A tag can start with a backslash character (\return) or an "at-sign" (@return). Some tags take arguments and some don't. The most useful tags are:

### @b word

Mark up *word* in boldface. You can also use HTML markup: *phrase*, which is helpful when *phrase* contains spaces.

### @brief one-sentence-description

Describe an entity briefly. Entities have brief and detailed documentation. Depending on how you configure Doxygen, the brief documentation can be the first sentence of the entity's full documentation, or you can require an explicit @brief tag. In either case, the rest of the comment is the detailed documentation for the entity.

### @c word

Treat *word* as a code fragment and set it in a fixed-pitch typeface. You can also use HTML markup: <tt>*phrase*</tt>, which is helpful when *phrase* contains spaces.

### @em word

Emphasize *word* in italics. You can also use HTML tags: *phrase*, which is helpful when *phrase* contains spaces.

## @file filename

Presents an overview of the source file. The detailed description can describe the purpose of the file, revision history, and other global documentation. The *filename* is optional; without it, Doxygen uses the file's real name. Except for advanced Doxygen uses, this tag is required.

## @link entity text @endlink

Create a hyperlink to the named *entity*, such as a file. I use @link on my @mainpage to create a table of contents to the most important files in the project, or to the sole file.

## @mainpage title

Present an overview of the entire project for the index or cover page. You can put @mainpage in any source file, or even set aside a separate file just for the comment. In small projects, I place @mainpage in the same source file as the main function, but in large projects, I use a separate file.

## @p name

Set *name* in a fixed-pitch typeface to distinguish it as a function parameter.

## @par title

Start a new paragraph. If you supply a one-line *title*, it becomes the paragraph heading. A blank line also separates paragraphs.

## @param name description

Document a function parameter named *name*. If you want to refer to this parameter elsewhere in the function's documentation, use @p *name*.

## @post postcondition

Document a postcondition for a function. A postcondition is a Boolean expression that the function asserts will be true when the function returns (assuming all preconditions were true). C++ lacks any formal mechanism for enforcing postconditions (other than assert), so documenting postconditions is crucial, especially for library writers.

## @pre precondition

Document a precondition for a function. A precondition is a Boolean expression that must be true before the function is called, or else the function is not guaranteed to work properly. C++ lacks any formal mechanism for enforcing preconditions (other than assert), so documenting preconditions is crucial, especially for library writers.

## @return description

Document what a function returns.

## @see xref

Insert a cross-reference to an entity named *xref*. Doxygen looks for references to other documented entities within the structured comment. When it finds one, it inserts a hyperlink (or text cross reference, depending on the output format). Sometimes, however, you need to insert an explicit reference to an entity that is not named in the documentation, so you can use @see.

You can suppress automatic hyperlink creation by prefacing a name with %.

## @&, @@, @\, @%, @<

Escapes a literal character (&, @, \, %, or <), to prevent interpretation by Doxygen or HTML.

Doxygen supports many other tags and HTML markup. If the output format is not HTML, Doxygen converts HTML tags to the desired output format. This book's web site has links to the main Doxygen page where you can find more information about the tool and download the software. Most Linux users already have Doxygen; other users can download Doxygen for their favorite platform.

Listing 25-1 shows a few of the many ways you can use Doxygen.

**Listing 25-1.** *Documenting Your Code with Doxygen*

```
/** @file
 * @brief Test strings to see whether they are palindromes.
 * Read lines from the input, strip non-letters, and check whether
 * the result is a palindrome. Ignore case differences when checking.
 * Echo palindromes to the standard output.
 */


/** @mainpage Palindromes
 * Test input strings to see whether they are palindromes.
 *
 * A palindrome is a string that reads the same forward and backward.
 * To test for palindromes, this program needs to strip punctuation and
 * other non-essential characters from the string, and compare letters without
 * regard to case differences.
 *
 * This program reads lines of text from the standard input and echos
 * to the standard output those lines that are palindromes.
 *
 * Source file: @link palindrome.cpp palindrome.cpp @endlink
 *
 * @date 14-June-2006
 * @author Ray Lischner
 * @version 1.0
 */
#include <algorithm>
#include <iostream>
#include <istream>
```

```
#include <iterator>
#include <locale>
#include <ostream>
#include <string>

/** @brief Test for non-letter.
 * Test the character @p ch in the global locale.
 * @param ch the character to test
 * @return true if @p ch is not a letter
 */
bool non_letter(char ch)
{
  return not isalnum(ch, std::locale());
}


/** @brief Convert to lowercase.
 * Use a canonical form by converting to uppercase first,
 * and then to lowercase. This approach does not solve the eszet
 * problem (German eszet is a lowercase character that converts
 * to two uppercase characters), but it's the best we can do in
 * standard C++.
 *
 * All conversions use the global locale.
 *
 * @param ch the character to test
 * @return the character converted to lowercase
 */
char lowercase(char ch)
{
  return std::tolower(ch, std::locale());
}

/** @brief Compare two characters without regard to case.
 * The comparison is limited by the lowercase() function.
 * @param a one character to compare
 * @param b the other character to compare
 * @return @c true if the characters are the same in lowercase,
 *         @c false if they are different.
 */
bool same_char(char a, char b)
{
  return lowercase(a) == lowercase(b);
}

/** @brief Determine whether @p str is a palindrome.
 * Only letter characters are tested. Spaces and punctuation don't count.
 * Empty strings are not palindromes because that's just too easy.
```

```
 * @param str the string to test
 * @return @c true if @p str is the same forward and backward
 */
bool is_palindrome(std::string str)
{
  std::string::iterator end(std::remove_if(str.begin(), str.end(), non_letter));
  std::string rev(end - str.begin(), ' ');
  std::reverse_copy(str.begin(), end, rev.begin());
  return not rev.empty() and std::equal(str.begin(), end, rev.begin(), same_char);
}


/** @brief Main program.
 * Set the global locale to the user's native locale. Then imbue the I/O streams
 * with the native locale.
 */
int main()
{
  std::locale::global(std::locale(""));
  std::cin.imbue(std::locale());
  std::cout.imbue(std::locale());

  std::string line;
  while (std::getline(std::cin, line))
    if (is_palindrome(line))
      std::cout << line << '\n';
}
```

Figure 25-1 shows the main page as it appears in a web browser.

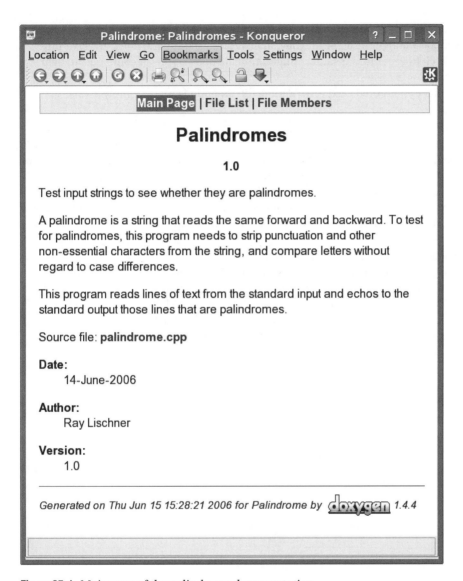

**Figure 25-1.** *Main page of the palindrome documentation*

# Using Doxygen

Instead of taking lots of command-line arguments, Doxygen uses a configuration file, typically named *Doxyfile*, in which you can put all that juicy information. Among the information in the configuration file is the name of the project, which files to examine for comments, which output format or formats to generate, and a variety of options you can use to tweak and adjust the output.

Because of the plethora of options, Doxygen comes with a wizard, *doxywizard*, to help generate a suitable configuration file, or you can just run the command line *doxygen* utility, with the -g switch to generate a default configuration file that has lots of comments to help you understand how to customize it.

Once you have configured Doxygen, running the program is trivial. Simply invoke

```
$ doxygen
```

and away it goes. Doxygen does a reasonable job at parsing C++, which is a complicated and difficult language to parse, but it sometimes gets confused. Pay attention to the error messages to see if it had any difficulties with your source files.

The configuration file dictates the location of the output. Typically, each output format resides in its own subdirectory. For example, the default configuration file stores HTML output in the *html* directory. Open the *html/index.html* file in your favorite browser to check out the results.

**Download and install Doxygen on your system.**

**Add Doxygen comments to one of your programs. Configure and run Doxygen.**

Future programs will continue to use Doxygen comments sporadically, when I think the comments help you understand what the program does. In general, however, I try to avoid them in the book because the text usually explains things well enough, and I don't want to waste any space. The programs that accompany the book, however, have more complete Doxygen comments.

■■■

# Project 1: Body-Mass Index

It's project time! Body-mass index (BMI) is a measurement model health-care professionals use to determine whether a person is overweight, and if so, by how much. To compute BMI, you need a person's weight in kilograms and height in meters. The BMI is simply weight/height$^2$, converted to a unitless value.

Your task is to write a program that reads records, prints the records, and computes some statistics. The program should start by asking for a threshold BMI. Only records with a BMI greater than or equal to the threshold will be printed. Each record needs to consist of a person's name (which may contain spaces), weight in kilograms, height in centimeters (not meters), and the person's sex ('M' or 'F'). Let the user enter the sex in uppercase or lowercase. Ask the user to enter the height in centimeters so you can compute the BMI using integers. You will need to adjust the formula to allow for centimeters instead of meters.

Print each person's BMI immediately after reading their record. After collecting information for everyone, print two tables—one for men, one for women—based on the data. Use an asterisk after the BMI rating to mark records for which the number meets or exceeds the threshold. After each table, print the mean (average) and median BMI. (Median is the value at which half the BMI values are less than the median and half are greater than the median. If the user enters an even number of records, take the mean of the two values in the middle.) Compute individual BMI values as integers. Compute the mean and median BMI values as floating point numbers, and print the mean with one place after the decimal point.

Listing 26-1 shows a sample user session. User input is in **boldface**.

**Listing 26-1.** *Sample User Session with the BMI Program*

```
$ bmi
Enter threshold BMI: 25
Enter name, height (in cm), and weight (in kg) for each person:
Name 1: Ray Lischner
Height (cm): 180
Weight (kg): 90
Sex (m or f): m
BMI = 27
Name 2: A. Nony Mouse
Height (cm): 120
Weight (kg): 42
Sex (m or f): F
```

```
BMI = 29
Name 3: Mick E. Mouse
Height (cm): 30
Weight (kg): 2
Sex (m or f): M
BMI = 22
Name 4: A. Nony Lischner
Height (cm): 150
Weight (kg): 55
Sex (m or f): m
BMI = 24
Name 5: No One
Height (cm): 250
Weight (kg): 130
Sex (m or f): f
BMI = 20
Name 6: ^Z

Male data
Ht(cm) Wt(kg) Sex  BMI  Name
   180     90  M    27* Ray Lischner
    30      2  M    22  Mick E. Mouse
   150     55  M    24  A. Nony Lischner
Mean BMI = 24.3
Median BMI = 24

Female data
Ht(cm) Wt(kg) Sex  BMI  Name
   120     42  F    29* A. Nony Mouse
   250    130  F    20  No One
Mean BMI = 24.5
Median BMI = 24.5
```

# Hints

Here are some hints, in case you need them:

- Keep track of the data in separate vectors, e.g., `heights`, `weights`, `sexes`, `names`, `bmis`.
- Use the native locale for all input and output.
- Divide the program into functions, e.g., `compute_bmi` to compute the BMI from weight and height.

- You can write this program using nothing more than the techniques that we have covered so far, but if you know other techniques, feel free to use them. The next set of Explorations will present language features that will greatly facilitate writing this kind of program.

- The complete source code for my solution is available with the other files that accompany this book, but don't peek until after you have written the program yourself.

# PART 2

# Custom Types

■ ■ ■

# Custom Types

Oне of the key design goals for C++ was that you should be able to custom define brand new types that look and act similar to the built-in types. Do you need tri-state logic? Write your own `tribool` type. Need arbitrary-precision arithmetic? Write your own `bigint` type. This exploration introduces some of the language features that let you define custom types. Subsequent explorations delve deeper into these topics.

## Defining a New Type

Let's consider a scenario in which you want to define a type, `rational`, to represent rational numbers (fractions). A rational number has a numerator and a denominator, both integers. Ideally, you would be able to add, subtract, multiply, and divide rational numbers in the same fashion you can with the built-in numeric types. You should also be able to mix rational numbers and other numeric types in the same expression.

The I/O streams should be able to read and write rational numbers in some reasonable manner. The input operator should accept as valid input anything the output operator produces. The I/O operators should heed the stream's flags and related settings, such as field width and fill character, so you can format neatly aligned columns of rational numbers the same way you did for integers in Exploration 8.

You should be able to assign any numeric value to a `rational` variable, and convert a `rational` value to any built-in numeric type. Naturally, converting a rational number to an integer variable would result in truncation to an integer. One can argue that conversion should be automatic, similar to conversion from floating-point to integer. A counter argument is that automatic conversions that discard information were a mistake in the original C language design, and one not to be duplicated. Instead, conversions that discard information should be made explicit and clear. I prefer the latter approach.

This is a lot to tackle at once, so let's begin slowly.

The first step is to decide how to store a rational number. You need to store a numerator and a denominator, both as integers. What about negative numbers? Choose a convention, such as the numerator gets the sign of the entire value, and the denominator is always positive. Listing 27-1 shows a basic `rational` type definition.

**Listing 27-1.** *Defining a Custom* rational *Type*

```
/// Represent a rational number.
struct rational
{
  int numerator;      ///< numerator gets the sign of the rational value
  int denominator;    ///< denominator is always positive
};
```

The definition starts with the struct keyword. C programmers recognize this as a structure definition—but hang on, there's much more to follow.

The contents of the rational type look like definitions for variables named numerator and denominator, but they work a little differently. Remember that Listing 27-1 shows a type definition. In other words, the compiler remembers that rational names a type, but it does not allocate any memory for an object, for numerator, or for denominator. In C++ parlance, numerator and denominator are called *data members*; some other languages call them instance variables or fields.

Notice the semicolon that follows the closing curly brace. Type definitions are different from compound statements. If you forget the semicolon, the compiler will remind you, sometimes quite rudely, while referring to a line number several lines after the one where the semicolon belongs.

When you define an object with type rational, the object stores the numerator and denominator members. Use the dot (.) operator to access the members, (which you have been doing throughout this book) as shown in Listing 27-2.

**Listing 27-2.** *Using a Class and Its Members*

```
#include <iostream>
#include <ostream>

/// Represent a rational number.
struct rational
{
  int numerator;      ///< numerator gets the sign of the rational value
  int denominator;    ///< denominator is always positive
};

int main()
{
  rational pi;
  pi.numerator = 355;
  pi.denominator = 113;
  std::cout << "pi is about " << pi.numerator << "/" << pi.denominator << '\n';
}
```

That's not terribly exciting, is it? The rational type just sits there, lifeless. You know that many types in the standard library have member functions, such as std::ostream's width member function, which allows you to write std::cout.width(4). The next section shows how to write your own member functions.

# Member Functions

Let's add a member function to rational that reduces the numerator and denominator by their greatest common divisor. Listing 27-3 shows the sample program, with the reduce() member function.

**Listing 27-3.** *Adding the* reduce *Member Function*

```
#include <cassert>
#include <cstdlib>
#include <iostream>
#include <ostream>

/// Compute the greatest common divisor of two integers, using Euclid's algorithm.
int gcd(int n, int m)
{
  n = abs(n);
  while (m != 0) {
    int tmp(n % m);
    n = m;
    m = tmp;
  }
  return n;
}

/// Represent a rational number.
struct rational
{
  /// Reduce the numerator and denominator by their GCD.
  void reduce()
  {
    assert(denominator != 0);
    int div(gcd(numerator, denominator));
    numerator = numerator / div;
    denominator = denominator / div;
  }

  int numerator;      ///< numerator gets the sign of the rational value
  int denominator;    ///< denominator is always positive
};

int main()
{
  rational pi;
  pi.numerator = 1420;
  pi.denominator = 452;
  pi.reduce();
  std::cout << "pi is about " << pi.numerator << "/" << pi.denominator << '\n';
}
```

Notice how the reduce() member function looks just like an ordinary function, except its definition appears within the rational type definition. Also notice how reduce() can refer to the data members of rational. When you call the reduce() member function, you must supply an object as the left-hand operand of the dot (.) operator (such as pi in Listing 27-3). When the reduce() function refers to a data member, the data member is taken from that left-hand operand. Thus, numerator = numerator / div has the effect of pi.numerator = pi.numerator / div.

The gcd function is a free function. You can call it with any two integers, unrelated to rational numbers. I could have also made gcd be a member function, but nothing about the function ties it to rational numbers. It does not access any members of rational. By making it a free function, you can reuse it throughout your program, anywhere you need to compute the greatest common divisor of two integers. If you aren't sure whether a function should be free or a member, err on the side of making it free.

A member function can also call other member functions that are defined in the same type. Try it yourself: **add the assign member function**, which takes a numerator and denominator as two parameters, and assigns them to their respective data members and calls reduce(). This spares the user of rational the additional step (and possible error of neglecting the call to reduce()). Let the return type be void. **Write your member function below:**

_____

_____

_____

_____

_____

_____

Listing 27-4 presents the entire program, with my assign member function in boldface.

**Listing 27-4.** *Adding the* assign *Member Function*

```
#include <cassert>
#include <cstdlib>
#include <iostream>
#include <ostream>

/// Compute the greatest common divisor of two integers, using Euclid's algorithm.
int gcd(int n, int m)
{
  n = abs(n);
  while (m != 0) {
    int tmp(n % m);
    n = m;
    m = tmp;
  }
  return n;
}
```

```
/// Represent a rational number.
struct rational
{
  /// Assign a numerator and a denominator, then reduce to normal form.
  /// @param num numerator
  /// @param den denominator
  /// @pre denominator > 0
  void assign(int num, int den)
  {
    numerator = num;
    denominator = den;
    reduce();
  }

  /// Reduce the numerator and denominator by their GCD.
  void reduce()
  {
    assert(denominator != 0);
    int div(gcd(numerator, denominator));
    numerator = numerator / div;
    denominator = denominator / div;
  }

  int numerator;      ///< numerator gets the sign of the rational value
  int denominator;    ///< denominator is always positive
};

int main()
{
  rational pi;
  pi.assign(1420, 452);
  std::cout << "pi is about " << pi.numerator << "/" << pi.denominator << '\n';
}
```

Notice how simple the main program is now. Hiding details, such as reduce(), helps keep the code clean, readable, and maintainable.

Notice one other subtle detail: the definition of assign() precedes reduce(), even though it calls reduce(). We need one minor adjustment to the rule that the compiler must see at least a declaration of a name before you can use that name; members of a new type can refer to other members, regardless of the order of declaration within the type. In all other situations, you must supply a declaration prior to use.

Being able to assign a numerator and denominator in one step is a fine addition to the rational type, but even more important is being able to initialize a rational object. Recall from Exploration 5 my admonishment to ensure that all objects are properly initialized. The next section demonstrates how to add support for initializers to rational.

# Constructors

Wouldn't it be nice to be able to initialize a rational object with a numerator and denominator, and have them properly reduced automatically? You can do that by writing a special member function that looks and acts a little like assign, except the name is the same as the name of the type (rational), and the function has no return type or return value. Listing 27-5 shows how to write this special member function.

**Listing 27-5.** *Adding the Ability to Initialize a* rational *Object*

```
#include <cassert>
#include <cstdlib>
#include <iostream>
#include <ostream>

/// Compute the greatest common divisor of two integers, using Euclid's algorithm.
int gcd(int n, int m)
{
  n = abs(n);
  while (m != 0) {
    int tmp(n % m);
    n = m;
    m = tmp;
  }
  return n;
}

/// Represent a rational number.
struct rational
{
  /// Construct a rational object, given a numerator and a denominator.
  /// Always reduce to normal form.
  /// @param num numerator
  /// @param den denominator
  /// @pre denominator > 0
  rational(int num, int den)
  : numerator(num), denominator(den)
  {
    reduce();
  }

  /// Assign a numerator and a denominator, then reduce to normal form.
  /// @param num numerator
  /// @param den denominator
  /// @pre denominator > 0
  void assign(int num, int den)
  {
    numerator = num;
```

```
    denominator = den;
    reduce();
  }

  /// Reduce the numerator and denominator by their GCD.
  void reduce()
  {
    assert(denominator != 0);
    int div(gcd(numerator, denominator));
    numerator = numerator / div;
    denominator = denominator / div;
  }

  int numerator;      ///< numerator gets the sign of the rational value
  int denominator;    ///< denominator is always positive
};

int main()
{
  rational pi(1420, 452);
  std::cout << "pi is about " << pi.numerator << "/" << pi.denominator << '\n';
}
```

Notice the definition of the pi object. The variable takes arguments that look just like function arguments, and indeed they work just like function arguments, too. However, instead of calling an ordinary function, the initialization results in a call to the special initialization function of the rational type. This special member function is called a *constructor*.

A constructor looks very much like a normal function, except that it doesn't have a return type. Also, you can't choose a name, but must use the type name. And then there's that extra line that starts with a colon. This extra bit of code initializes the data members in the same manner as initializing a variable. After all the data members are initialized, the body of the constructor runs in the same manner as any member function body.

The initializer list is optional. Without it, data members are left uninitialized—this is a bad thing, so don't do it.

**Modify the rational type so it accepts a negative denominator.** If the denominator is negative, change it to positive, and also change the sign of the numerator. Thus, rational(-710, -226) would have the same value as rational(710, 226).

You can choose to perform the modification in any one of a number of places. Good software design practice dictates that the change should occur in exactly one spot, and all other functions should call that one. Therefore, I suggest modifying reduce(), as shown in Listing 27-6.

**Listing 27-6.** *Modifying the* reduce *Member Function to Accept a Negative Denominator*

```
  /// Reduce the numerator and denominator by their GCD.
  void reduce()
  {
    assert(denominator != 0);
```

```
  if (denominator < 0)
  {
    denominator = -denominator;
    numerator = -numerator;
  }
  int div(gcd(numerator, denominator));
  numerator = numerator / div;
  denominator = denominator / div;
}
```

# Overloading Constructors

You can overload a constructor the same way you overload an ordinary function. All the overloaded constructors have the same name (that is, the name of the type), and they must differ in the number or type of the parameters. For example, you can add a constructor that takes a single integer argument, implicitly using 1 as the denominator. **Add a constructor rational(int num) to the type.** Compare your solution with mine in Listing 27-7.

**Listing 27-7.** *Constructing a Rational Object from an Integer*

```
rational(int num)
: numerator(num), denominator(1)
{}
```

Note that you don't need to call reduce() because you know the value is already in its reduced form, with a denominator of 1.

I'm sure you can see many deficiencies in the current state of the rational type. It has several that you probably missed, too. Hang on, the next exploration starts improving the type. For example, you may want to test your modification by comparing two rational objects to see if they are equal. To do so, however, you need to write a custom == operator, which is the subject of the next Exploration.

■ ■ ■

# Overloading Operators

This Exploration continues the study of writing custom types. An important aspect of making a custom type behave seamlessly with built-in types is ensuring that the custom types support all the expected operators—arithmetic types must support arithmetic operators, readable and writable types must support I/O operators, and so on. Fortunately, C++ lets you overload operators in much the same manner as overloading functions.

## Comparing Rational Numbers

In the previous Exploration, you began to write a `rational` type. After making a modification to it, an important step is testing the modified type, and an important aspect of internal testing is the equality (`==`) operator. C++ lets you define a custom implementation for almost every operator, provided at least one operand has a custom type. In other words, you can't redefine integer division to yield a `rational` result, but you can define division of an integer by a `rational` number, and vice versa.

To implement a custom operator, you need to write a normal function, but for the function name, use the `operator` keyword followed by the operator symbol, as shown in the code excerpt in Listing 28-1.

**Listing 28-1.** *Overloading the Equality Operator*

```
/// Represent a rational number.
struct rational
{
  /// Construct a rational object, given a numerator and a denominator.
  /// Always reduce to normal form.
  /// @param num numerator
  /// @param den denominator
  /// @pre denominator > 0
  rational(int num, int den)
  : numerator(num), denominator(den)
  {
    reduce();
  }
```

```
/// Assign a numerator and a denominator, then reduce to normal form.
/// @param num numerator
/// @param den denominator
/// @pre denominator > 0
void assign(int num, int den)
{
  numerator = num;
  denominator = den;
  reduce();
}

/// Reduce the numerator and denominator by their GCD.
void reduce()
{
  assert(denominator != 0);
  if (denominator < 0)
  {
    denominator = -denominator;
    numerator = -numerator;
  }
  int div(gcd(numerator, denominator));
  numerator = numerator / div;
  denominator = denominator / div;
}

  int numerator;      ///< numerator gets the sign of the rational value
  int denominator;    ///< denominator is always positive
};

/// Compare two rational numbers for equality.
/// @pre @p a and @p b are reduced to normal form
bool operator==(rational const& a, rational const& b)
{
  return a.numerator == b.numerator and a.denominator == b.denominator;
}

/// Compare two rational numbers for inequality.
/// @pre @p a and @p b are reduced to normal form
bool operator!=(rational const& a, rational const& b)
{
  return not (a == b);
}
```

One of the benefits of reducing all rational numbers is that it makes comparison easier. Instead of checking whether 3/3 is the same as 6/6, both numbers are automatically reduced to 1/1, so it is just a matter of comparing the numerators and denominators. Another trick is defining != in terms of ==. There's no point in your making extra work for yourself, so confine the actual logic of comparing rational objects to one function, and call it from another function. If you worry about the performance overhead of calling an extra layer of functions, use the inline keyword, as shown in Listing 28-2.

**Listing 28-2.** *Using inline for Trivial Functions*

```
/// Compare two rational numbers for equality.
/// @pre @p a and @p b are reduced to normal form
bool operator==(rational const& a, rational const& b)
{
  return a.numerator == b.numerator and a.denominator == b.denominator;
}

/// Compare two rational numbers for inequality.
/// @pre @p a and @p b are reduced to normal form
inline bool operator!=(rational const& a, rational const& b)
{
  return not (a == b);
}
```

The inline keyword is a hint to the compiler that you would like the function expanded at the point of call. If the compiler decides to heed your wish, the resulting program will not have any identifiable function named operator!= in it. Instead, every place where you use the != operator with rational objects, the function body is expanded there, resulting in a call to operator==.

To implement the < operator, you need a common denominator. Once you implement operator<, you can implement all other relational operators in terms of <. You can choose any of the relational operators (<, >, <=, >=) as the fundamental operator, and implement the others in terms of the fundamental. The convention is to start with <. Listing 28-3 demonstrates < and <=.

**Listing 28-3.** *Implementing the < Operator for rational*

```
/// Compare two rational numbers for less-than.
bool operator<(rational const& a, rational const& b)
{
  return a.numerator * b.denominator < b.numerator * a.denominator;
}

/// Compare two rational numbers for less-than-or-equal.
inline bool operator<=(rational const& a, rational const& b)
{
  return not (b < a);
}
```

Implement > and >= in terms of <.
Compare your operators with Listing 28-4.

**Listing 28-4.** *Implementing the > and >= Operators in Terms of <*

```
/// Compare two rational numbers for greater-than.
inline bool operator>(rational const& a, rational const& b)
{
  return b < a;
}

/// Compare two rational numbers for greater-than-or-equal.
inline bool operator>=(rational const& a, rational const& b)
{
  return not (b > a);
}
```

**Then write a test program.** To help you write your tests, download the *test.hpp* file and add #include "test.hpp" to your program. Call the test() function as many times as you need, passing a Boolean expression as the sole argument. If the argument is true, the test passed. If the argument is false, the test failed and the test function prints a suitable message. Thus, you may write tests, such as the following:

```
test(rational(2, 2) == rational(5, 5));
test(rational(6,3) > rational(10, 6));
```

How the test function works is beyond the scope of this book, but it's useful to have around; you'll be using it for future test harnesses. Compare your test program with Listing 28-5.

**Listing 28-5.** *Testing the rational Comparison Operators*

```
#include <cassert>
#include <cstdlib>
#include <iostream>
#include <ostream>
#include "test.hpp"

struct rational
{
... omitted for brevity ...
};

int main()
{
  rational a(60, 5);
  rational b(12, 1);
  rational c(-24, -2);
  test(a == b);
  test(a >= b);
  test(a <= b);
  test(b <= a);
```

```
    test(b >= a);
    test(b == c);
    test(b >= c);
    test(b <= c);
    test(a == c);
    test(a >= c);
    test(a <= c);

    rational d(109, 10);
    test(d < a);
    test(d <= a);
    test(d != a);
    test(a > d);
    test(a >= d);
    test(a != d);

    rational e(241, 20);
    test(e > a);
    test(e >= a);
    test(e != a);
    test(a < e);
    test(a <= e);
    test(a != e);
}
```

# Arithmetic Operators

Comparison is fine, but arithmetic operators are much more interesting. You can overload any or all of the arithmetic operators. Binary operators take two parameters, and unary operators take one parameter. You can choose any return type that makes sense. Listing 28-6 shows the binary addition operator and the unary negation operator.

**Listing 28-6.** *Addition Operator for the rational Type*

```
rational operator+(rational const& lhs, rational const& rhs)
{
  return rational(lhs.numerator * rhs.denominator + rhs.numerator * lhs.denominator,
                  lhs.denominator * rhs.denominator);
}

rational operator-(rational const& r)
{
  return rational(-r.numerator, r.denominator);
}
```

**Write the other arithmetic operators: -, \*, and /.** Ignore for the moment the issue of division by zero. Compare your functions with mine, which are presented in Listing 28-7.

**Listing 28-7.** *Arithmetic Operators for the rational Type*

```
rational operator-(rational const& lhs, rational const& rhs)
{
  return rational(lhs.numerator * rhs.denominator - rhs.numerator * lhs.denominator,
                  lhs.denominator * rhs.denominator);
}

rational operator*(rational const& lhs, rational const& rhs)
{
  return rational(lhs.numerator * rhs.numerator, lhs.denominator * rhs.denominator);
}

rational operator/(rational const& lhs, rational const& rhs)
{
  return rational(lhs.numerator * rhs.denominator, lhs.denominator * rhs.numerator);
}
```

Adding, subtracting, etc., with rational numbers is fine, but more interesting is the issue of mixing types. For example, what is the value of 3 * rational(1, 3)? **Try it.** Collect the definition of the rational type with all the operators, and write a main() function that computes that expression and stores it somewhere. Choose a type for the result variable that makes sense to you then determine how best to print that value to std::cout.

**Do you expect the expression to compile without errors?** _____

**What is the result type of the expression?** _____

**What value do you expect as the result?** _____

**Explain your observations.**

_____

_____

_____

_____

It turns out that rational's one-argument constructor tells the compiler it can construct a rational from an int any time it needs to do so. It does so automatically, so the compiler sees the integer 3, and a multiplication of an int and a rational object. It knows about operator* between two rationals, and it knows it cannot use the built-in * operator with a rational operand. Thus, the compiler decides its best response is to convert the int to a rational (by invoking rational(3)), and then it can apply the custom operator* that multiplies two rational objects, yielding a rational result, namely, rational(1, 1). It does all this automatically on your behalf. Listing 28-8 illustrates one way to write the test program.

**Listing 28-8.** *Test Program for Multiplying an Integer and a Rational Number*

```
#include <cassert>
#include <cstdlib>
#include <iostream>
#include <ostream>

struct rational
{
... omitted for brevity ...
};

int main()
{
  rational result(3 * rational(1, 3));
  std::cout << result.numerator << '/' << result.denominator << '\n';
}
```

Being able to construct a rational object automatically from an int is a great convenience. You can easily write code that performs operations on integers and rational numbers without concerning yourself with type conversions all the time. You'll find this same convenience when mixing integers and floating-point numbers. For example, you can write 1+2.0 without needing to perform a type cast: static_cast<double>(1)+2.0.

On the other hand, all this convenience can be too convenient. The compiler happily converts floating point numbers to integers, so it accepts rational(3.14159) by converting the floating point argument to an int then calling rational's constructor. The solution is to provide constructors for floating-point arguments. Ideally, rational(3.14159) would be equal to rational(314159, 100000), but getting the details right is quite tricky. Because this is a book on C++, not numerical analysis, I provide only one simple implementation in Listing 28-9. A better solution uses numeric_limits to determine the number of decimal digits of precision double can support, and try to preserve as much precision as possible. An even better solution uses the radix of the floating-point implementation, instead of working in base 10.

**Listing 28-9.** *Constructing a Rational Number from a Floating-Point Argument*

```
struct rational
{
  rational(double r)
  : numerator(static_cast<int>(r * 10000)), denominator(10000)
  {
    reduce();
  }

... omitted for brevity ...

};
```

If you want to optimize a particular function for a particular argument type, you can do that, too, by taking advantage of ordinary function overloading. You'd better make sure it's worth the extra work, however. Remember that the int operand can be the right-hand or left-hand operand, so you will need to overload both forms of the function, as shown in Listing 28-10.

**Listing 28-10.** *Optimizing Operators for a Specific Operand Type*

```
rational operator*(rational const& rat, int mult)
{
  return rational(rat.numerator * mult, rat.denominator);
}

inline rational operator*(int mult, rational const& rat)
{
  return rat * mult;
}
```

In such a simple case, it's not worth the added trouble to avoid a little extra arithmetic However, in more complicated situations, you may need to write such code.

# Math Functions

The C++ standard library offers a number of mathematical functions, such as abs, which computes absolute values. The C++ standard prohibits you from overloading these standard functions to operate on custom types, but you can still write functions that perform similar operations. In Exploration 50, you'll learn about namespaces, which will enable you to use the real function name. Whenever you write a custom numeric type, you should consider which math functions you should provide. In this case, absolute value makes perfect sense. **Write an absolute value function that works with rational numbers. Call it absval.**

Your absval function should take a rational parameter by value and return a rational result. As with the arithmetic operators I wrote, you may opt to use call-by-reference for the parameter; if so, make sure you declare the reference to be const. Listing 28-11 shows my implementation of absval.

**Listing 28-11.** *Computing the Absolute Value of a Rational Number*

```
rational absval(rational const& r)
{
  return rational(abs(r.numerator), r.denominator);
}
```

That was easy. What about the other math functions, such as sqrt, for computing square roots? Most of the other functions are overloaded for floating-point arguments. If the compiler knew how to convert a rational number to a floating-point number automatically, you could simply pass a rational argument to any of the existing floating-point functions with no further work. **So which floating-point type should you use?** _____

This question has no easy answer. A reasonable first choice might be double, which is the "default" floating-point type (e.g., floating-point literals have type double). On the other hand, what if someone really wants the extra precision long double offers? Or what if that person doesn't need much precision and prefers to use float?

The solution is to abandon the possibility of automatic conversion to a floating-point type, and instead offer three functions that explicitly compute the floating-point value of the rational number. **Write as_float, as_double, and as_long_double.** Each of these member functions computes and returns the floating-point approximation for the rational number. The function name identifies the return type. You will need to cast the numerator and denominator to the desired floating-point type using static_cast, as you learned in Exploration 23. Listing 28-12 shows how I wrote these functions, with a sample program that demonstrates their use.

**Listing 28-12.** *Converting to Floating-Point Types*

```
struct rational
{
  float as_float()
  {
    return static_cast<float>(numerator) / denominator;
  }

  double as_double()
  {
    return numerator / static_cast<double>(denominator);
  }

  long double as_long_double()
  {
    return static_cast<long double>(numerator) /
           static_cast<long double>(denominator);
  }

... omitted for brevity ...

};

int main()
{
  rational pi(355, 113);
  rational bmi(90*100*100, 180*180); // Body-mass index of 90 kg, 180 cm
  double circumference(0), radius(10);

  circumference = 2 * pi.as_double() * radius;
  std::cout << "circumference of circle with radius " << radius << " is about "
            << circumference << '\n';
  std::cout << "bmi = " << bmi.as_float() << '\n';
}
```

As you can see, if either argument to / (or any other arithmetic or comparison operator) is floating point, the other operand is converted to match. You can cast both operands or just one or the other. Pick the style that suits you best, and stick with it.

One more task would make it easier to write test programs: overloading the I/O operators. That is the topic for the next Exploration.

# Custom I/O Operators

Wouldn't it be nice to be able to read and write rational numbers directly, for example, std::cout << rational(355, 113)? In fact, C++ has everything you need, although the job is a little trickier than perhaps it should be. This Exploration introduces some of the pieces you need to accomplish this.

## Input Operator

The I/O operators are just like any other operators in C++, and you can overload them the way you overload any other operator. The input operator, also known as an *extractor* (because it extracts data from a stream), takes std::istream& as its first parameter. It must be a non-const reference because the function will modify the stream object. The second parameter must also be a non-const reference because you will store the input value there. By convention, the return type is std::istream&, and the return value is the first parameter. That lets you combine multiple input operations in a single expression. (Go back to Listing 16-3 for an example.)

The body of the function must do the work of reading the input stream, parsing the input, and deciding how to interpret that input. Proper error handling is difficult, but the basics are easy. Every stream has a state mask that keeps track of errors. Table 29-1 lists the available state flags (declared in <ios>).

If the input is not valid, the input function sets failbit in the stream's error state. When the caller tests whether the stream is okay, it tests the error state; if failbit is set, the check fails. (The test also fails if an unrecoverable error occurs, such as a hardware malfunction, but that's not pertinent to the current topic.)

**Table 29-1.** *I/O State Flags*

| Flag | Description |
| --- | --- |
| badbit | Unrecoverable error |
| eofbit | End of file |
| failbit | Invalid input or output |
| goodbit | No errors |

Now you need to decide on a format for rational numbers. The format should be one that is flexible enough for a human to read and write easily, but simple enough for a function to read and parse quickly. The input format must be able to read the output format, and might be able to read other formats, too.

Let's define the format as an integer, a slash (/), and another integer. White space can appear before or after any of these elements unless the white space flag is disabled in the input stream. If the input contains an integer that is not followed by a slash, the integer becomes the resulting value (that is, the implicit denominator is one). The input operator needs to "unread" the character, which may be important to the rest of the program. The unget() member function does exactly that. The input operator for integers does the same thing: read as many characters as possible until reading a character that is not part of the integer, then unget that last character.

Putting all these pieces together requires a little care, but is not all that difficult. Listing 29-1 presents the input operator.

**Listing 29-1.** *Input Operator*

```
#include <ios>      // declares failbit, etc.
#include <istream>  // declares std::istream and the necessary >> operators

std::istream& operator>>(std::istream& in, rational& rat)
{
  int n(0), d(0);
  char sep('\0');
  if (not (in >> n >> sep))
    // Error reading the numerator or the separator character.
    in.setstate(std::cin.failbit);
  else if (sep != '/')
  {
    // Read numerator successfully, but it is not followed by /.
    // Push sep back into the input stream, so the next input operation
    // will read it.
    in.unget();
    rat.assign(n, 1);
  }
  else if (in >> d)
    // Successfully read numerator, separator, and denominator.
    rat.assign(n, d);
  else
    // Error reading denominator.
    in.setstate(std::cin.failbit);

  return in;
}
```

Notice how rat is not modified until the function has successfully read both the numerator and the denominator from the stream. The goal is to ensure that if the stream enters an error state, the function does not alter rat.

The input stream automatically handles white space. By default, the input stream skips leading white space in each input operation, which means the rational input operator skips white space before the numerator, the slash separator, and the denominator. If the program turns off the ws flag, the input stream does not skip white space, and all three parts must be contiguous.

# Output Operator

Writing the output operator, or *inserter* (so named because it inserts text into the output stream), has a number of hurdles due to the plethora of formatting flags. You want to heed the desired field width and alignment, and you need to insert fill characters as needed. Like any other output operator, you want to reset the field width, but not change any other format settings.

The key to writing a complicated output operator is to use a temporary output stream that stores its text in a string. The std::ostringstream type is declared in the <sstream> header. Use ostringstream the way you would use any other output stream, such as cout. When you are done, the str() member function returns the finished string.

To write the output operator for a rational number, create an ostringstream, and then write the numerator, separator, and denominator. Next, write the resulting string to the actual output stream. Let the stream itself handle the width, alignment, and fill issues when it writes the string. If you had written the numerator, slash, and denominator directly to the output stream, the width would apply only to the numerator, and the alignment would be wrong. Similar to an input operator, the first parameter has type std::ostream&, which is also the return type. The return value is the first parameter. The second parameter can use call-by-value or you can pass a reference to const, as you can see in Listing 29-2.

**Listing 29-2.** *Output Operator*

```
#include <ostream>  // declares the necessary << operators
#include <sstream>  // declares the std::ostringstream type

std::ostream& operator<<(std::ostream& out, rational const& rat)
{
  std::ostringstream tmp;
  tmp << rat.numerator;
  if (rat.denominator != 1)
    tmp << '/' << rat.denominator;
  out << tmp.str();

  return out;
}
```

# Error State

The next step is to write a test program. Ideally, the test program should be able to continue when it encounters an invalid-input error. So now is a good time to take a closer look at how an I/O stream keeps track of errors.

As you learned earlier in this Exploration, every stream has a mask of error flags (see Table 29-1). You can test these flags, set them, or clear them. Testing the flags is a little unusual, however, so pay attention.

The way most programs in this book test for error conditions on a stream is to use the stream itself or an input operation as a condition. As you learned, an input operator function returns the stream, so these two approaches are equivalent. A stream converts to a bool result by returning the inverse of its fail() function, which returns true if failbit or badbit are set.

In the normal course of an input loop, the program progresses until the input stream is exhausted. The stream sets eofbit when it reaches the end of the input stream. The stream's state is still good in that fail() returns false, so the loop continues. However, the next time you try to read from the stream, it sees that no more input is available, sets failbit, and returns an error condition. The loop condition is false, and the loop exits.

The loop might also exit if the stream contains invalid input, such as non-numeric characters for integer input, or the loop can exit if there is a hardware error on the input stream (such as a disk failure). Until now, the programs in this book didn't bother to test why the loop exited. To write a good test program, however, you need to know the cause.

First, you can test for a hardware or similar error by calling the bad() member function, which returns true if badbit is set. That means something terrible happened to the file, and the program can't do anything to fix the problem.

Next, test for normal end-of-file by calling the eof() member function, which is true only when eofbit is set. If bad() and eof() are both false and fail() is true, this means the stream contains invalid input. How your program should handle an input failure depends on your particular circumstances. Some programs must exit immediately; others may try to continue. For example, your test program can reset the error state by calling the clear() member function then continue running. After an input failure, you may not know the stream's position, so you don't know what the stream is prepared to read next. This simple test program skips to the next line.

Listing 29-3 demonstrates a test program that loops until end-of-file or an unrecoverable error occurs. If the problem is merely invalid input, the error state is cleared, and the loop continues.

**Listing 29-3.** *Testing the I/O Operators*

```
... omitted for brevity ...

/// Tests for failbit only
bool iofailure(std::istream& in)
{
  return in.fail() and not in.bad();
}

int main()
{
  rational r(0);

  while (std::cin)
  {
    if (std::cin >> r)
      // Read succeeded, so no error state is set in the stream.
      std::cout << r << '\n';
    else if (iofailure(std::cin))
```

```
    {
      // Only failbit is set, meaning invalid input. Clear the error state,
      // and then skip the rest of the input line.
      std::cin.clear();
      std::cin.ignore(std::numeric_limits<int>::max(), '\n');
    }
  }

  if (std::cin.bad())
    std::cerr << "Unrecoverable input error\n";
}
```

The rational type is nearly finished. The next Exploration tackles assignment operators, and seeks to improve the constructors.

■■■

# Assignment and Initialization

The final step needed to complete this stage of the rational type is to write assignment operators and to improve the constructors. It turns out C++ does some work for you, but you often want to fine tune that work. Let's find out how.

## Assignment Operator

Until now, all the rational operators have been free functions. The assignment operator is different. The C++ standard requires that it be a member function. One way to write this function is shown in Listing 30-1.

**Listing 30-1.** *First Version of the Assignment Operator*

```
struct rational
{
... omitted for brevity ...
  rational& operator=(rational const& rhs)
  {
    numerator = rhs.numerator;
    denominator = rhs.denominator;
    return *this;
  }
};
```

Several points need further explanation. When you implement an operator as a free function, you need one parameter per operand. Thus, binary operators require a two-parameter function, and unary operators require a one-parameter function. Member functions are different because the object itself is an operand (always the left-hand operand), and the object is implicitly available to all member functions, therefore you need one fewer parameter. Binary operators require a single parameter (as you can see in Listing 30-1), and unary operators require no parameters (examples to follow).

The convention for assignment operators is to return a reference to the enclosing type; the value to return is the object itself. You can obtain the object with the expression *this (this is a reserved keyword).

Because *this is the object itself, another way to refer to members is to use the dot operator (e.g., (*this).numerator) instead of the basic numerator. Recall from Exploration 14 that another way to write (*this).numerator is this->numerator. The meaning is the same; the alternative syntax is mostly a convenience. Writing this-> is not necessary for these simple functions, but it's often a good idea. When you read a member function, and you have trouble discerning the members from the non-members, that's a signal that you need to help the reader by using this-> before all the member names. Listing 30-2 shows the assignment operator with explicit use of this->.

**Listing 30-2.** *Assignment Operator with Explicit Use of* this->

```
struct rational
{
... omitted for brevity ...
  rational& operator=(rational const& that)
  {
    this->numerator = that.numerator;
    this->denominator = that.denominator;
    return *this;
  }
};
```

The right-hand operand can be anything you want it to be. For example, you may want to optimize assignment of an integer to a rational object. The way the assignment operator works with the compiler's rules for automatic conversion, the compiler treats such an assignment (e.g., r = 3) as an implicit construction of a temporary rational object, followed by an assignment of one rational object to another.

**Write an assignment operator that takes an int parameter.** Compare your solution with mine, which is shown in Listing 30-3.

**Listing 30-3.** *Assignment of an Integer to a Rational*

```
struct rational
{
... omitted for brevity ...
  rational& operator=(int num)
  {
    this->numerator = num;
    this->denominator = 1;
    return *this;
  }
};
```

If you do not write an assignment operator, the compiler writes one for you. In the case of the simple rational type, it turns out that the compiler writes one that works exactly like the one in Listing 30-2, so there was actually no need to write it yourself (except for instructional purposes).

# Constructors

The compiler also writes a constructor automatically, specifically one that constructs a rational object by copying all the data members from another rational object. This is called a *copy constructor*. Any time you pass a rational argument by value to a function, the compiler uses the copy constructor to copy the argument value to the parameter. Any time you define a rational variable and initialize it with the value of another rational value, the compiler constructs the variable by calling the copy constructor.

As with the assignment operator, the compiler's default implementation is exactly what we would write ourselves, so there is no need to write the copy constructor.

If you don't write any constructors for a type, the compiler also creates a constructor that takes no arguments, called a *default constructor*. The compiler uses the default constructor when you define a variable and do not provide an initializer for it. The compiler's implementation of the default constructor merely calls the default constructor for each data member. If a data member has a built-in type, the member is left uninitialized. In other words, if we did not write any constructors for rational, any rational variable would be uninitialized, so its numerator and denominator would contain garbage values. That's bad—very bad. All the operators assume the rational object has been reduced to normal form. They would fail if you passed an uninitialized rational object to them. The solution is simple: don't let the compiler write its default constructor. Instead, you write one.

All you need to do is write any constructor at all. This will prevent the compiler from writing its own default constructor. (It will still write its own copy constructor. The only way to prevent that is to write your own copy constructor.)

Early on, we wrote a constructor for the rational type, but it was not a default constructor. As a result, you could not define a rational variable and leave it uninitialized. (You may have run into that issue when writing your own test program.) Uninitialized data is a bad idea, but having default constructors is a good idea. So write a default constructor to make sure a rational variable that has no initializer has a well-defined value nonetheless. What value should you use? I recommend zero, which is in keeping with the spirit of the default constructors for types such as string and vector. **Write a default constructor for rational to initialize the value to zero.**

Compare your solution with mine, which is presented in Listing 30-4.

**Listing 30-4.** *Overloaded Constructors for rational*

```
struct rational
{
  rational()
  : numerator(0), denominator(1)
  {/*empty*/}

  rational(int num)
  : numerator(num), denominator(1)
  {/*empty*/}

  rational(int num, int den)
  : numerator(num), denominator(den)
  {
```

```
    reduce();
  }
... omitted for brevity ...
};
```

# Putting It All Together

Before we take leave of the `rational` type (only temporarily, we will return), let's put all the pieces together so you can see what you've accomplished over the past four Explorations. Listing 30-5 shows the complete definition of `rational` and the related operators.

**Listing 30-5.** *Complete Definition of rational and Its Operators*

```
#include <cassert>
#include <cstdlib>
#include <istream>
#include <ostream>
#include <sstream>

/// Compute the greatest common divisor of two integers, using Euclid's algorithm.
int gcd(int n, int m)
{
  n = std::abs(n);
  while (m != 0) {
    int tmp(n % m);
    n = m;
    m = tmp;
  }
  return n;
}

/// Represent a rational number (fraction) as a numerator and denominator.
struct rational
{
  rational()
  : numerator(0), denominator(1)
  {/*empty*/}

  rational(int num)
  : numerator(num), denominator(1)
  {/*empty*/}

  rational(int num, int den)
  : numerator(num), denominator(den)
  {
    reduce();
  }
```

```cpp
rational(double r)
: numerator(static_cast<int>(r * 10000)), denominator(10000)
{
  reduce();
}

rational& operator=(rational const& that)
{
  this->numerator = that.numerator;
  this->denominator = that.denominator;
  return *this;
}

float as_float()
{
  return static_cast<float>(numerator) / denominator;
}

double as_double()
{
  return static_cast<double>(numerator) / denominator;
}

long double as_long_double()
{
  return static_cast<long double>(numerator) /
         denominator;
}

/// Assign a numerator and a denominator, then reduce to normal form.
void assign(int num, int den)
{
  numerator = num;
  denominator = den;
  reduce();
}

/// Reduce the numerator and denominator by their GCD.
void reduce()
{
  assert(denominator != 0);
  if (denominator < 0)
  {
    denominator = -denominator;
    numerator = -numerator;
  }
  int div(gcd(numerator, denominator));
```

```
    numerator = numerator / div;
    denominator = denominator / div;
  }

  int numerator;
  int denominator;
};

/// Absolute value of a rational number.
rational abs(rational const& r)
{
  return rational(std::abs(r.numerator), r.denominator);
}

/// Unary negation of a rational number.
rational operator-(rational const& r)
{
  return rational(-r.numerator, r.denominator);
}

/// Add rational numbers.
rational operator+(rational const& lhs, rational const& rhs)
{
  return rational(lhs.numerator * rhs.denominator + rhs.numerator * lhs.denominator,
              lhs.denominator * rhs.denominator);
}

/// Subtraction of rational numbers.
rational operator-(rational const& lhs, rational const& rhs)
{
  return rational(lhs.numerator * rhs.denominator - rhs.numerator * lhs.denominator,
              lhs.denominator * rhs.denominator);
}

/// Multiplication of rational numbers.
rational operator*(rational const& lhs, rational const& rhs)
{
  return rational(lhs.numerator * rhs.numerator, lhs.denominator * rhs.denominator);
}

/// Division of rational numbers.
/// TODO: check for division-by-zero
rational operator/(rational const& lhs, rational const& rhs)
{
  return rational(lhs.numerator * rhs.denominator, lhs.denominator * rhs.numerator);
}
```

```
/// Compare two rational numbers for equality.
bool operator==(rational const& a, rational const& b)
{
  return a.numerator == b.numerator and a.denominator == b.denominator;
}

/// Compare two rational numbers for inequality.
inline bool operator!=(rational const& a, rational const& b)
{
  return not (a == b);
}
/// Compare two rational numbers for less-than.
bool operator<(rational const& a, rational const& b)
{
  return a.numerator * b.denominator < b.numerator * a.denominator;
}

/// Compare two rational numbers for less-than-or-equal.
inline bool operator<=(rational const& a, rational const& b)
{
  return not (b < a);
}
/// Compare two rational numbers for greater-than.
inline bool operator>(rational const& a, rational const& b)
{
  return b < a;
}

/// Compare two rational numbers for greater-than-or-equal.
inline bool operator>=(rational const& a, rational const& b)
{
  return not (b > a);
}

/// Read a rational number.
/// Format is @em integer @c / @em integer.
std::istream& operator>>(std::istream& in, rational& rat)
{
  int n(0), d(0);
  char sep('\0');
  if (not (in >> n >> sep))
    // Error reading the numerator or the separator character.
    in.setstate(in.failbit);
  else if (sep != '/')
  {
    // Push sep back into the input stream, so the next input operation
    // will read it.
```

```
    in.unget();
    rat.assign(n, 1);
  }
  else if (in >> d)
    // Successfully read numerator, separator, and denominator.
    rat.assign(n, d);
  else
    // Error reading denominator.
    in.setstate(in.failbit);

  return in;
}

/// Write a rational numbers.
/// Format is @em numerator @c / @em denominator.
std::ostream& operator<<(std::ostream& out, rational const& rat)
{
  std::ostringstream tmp;
  tmp << rat.numerator << '/' << rat.denominator;
  out << tmp.str();

  return out;
}
```

I encourage you to add tests to the program in Listing 28-5 to exercise all the latest features of the rational class. Make sure everything works the way you expect it. Then put aside rational for the next Exploration, which takes a closer look at the foundations of writing custom types.

■ ■ ■

# Writing Classes

The `rational` type is an example of a *class*. Now that you've seen a concrete example of writing your own class, it's time to understand the general rules that govern all classes. This Exploration and the next four lay the foundation for this important aspect of C++ programming.

## Anatomy of a Class

A class has a name and *members*—data members, member functions, and even member typedefs and nested classes. You start a class definition with the `struct` keyword. (You might wonder why you would not start a class definition with the `class` keyword. Please be patient; all will become clear in Exploration 33.) Use curly braces to surround the body of the class definition, and the definition ends with a semicolon. Within the curly braces, you list all the members. Declare data members in a manner similar to a local variable definition, with no initializer. You write member functions in the same manner as you would a free function. Listing 31-1 shows a simple class definition that contains only data members.

**Listing 31-1.** *Class Definition for a Cartesian Point*

```
struct point
{
  double x;
  double y;
};
```

Listing 31-2 demonstrates how C++ lets you list multiple data members in a single declaration. Except for trivial classes, this style is uncommon. I prefer to list each member separately so I can include a comment explaining the member, what it's used for, what constraints apply to it, and so on. Even without the comment, a little extra clarity goes a long way.

**Listing 31-2.** *Multiple Data Members in One Declaration*

```
struct point
{
  double x, y;
};
```

As with any other name in a C++ source file, before you can use a class name, the compiler must see its declaration or definition. You can use the name of a class within its own definition.

Use the class name as a type name to define local variables, function parameters, function return types, and even other data members. The compiler knows about the class name from the very start of the class definition, so you can use its name as a type name inside the class definition.

When you define a variable using a class type, the compiler sets aside enough memory so the variable can store its own copy of every data member of the class. For example, define an object with type point, and the object contains the x and y members. Define another object of type point, and that object contains its own, separate x and y members.

Use the dot (.) operator to access the members, as you have been doing throughout this book. The object is the left-hand operand and the member name is the right-hand operand, as shown in Listing 31-3.

**Listing 31-3.** *Using a Class and Its Members*

```
#include <iostream>
#include <ostream>

struct point
{
  double x;
  double y;
};

int main()
{
  point origin, unity;
  origin.x = 0;
  origin.y = 0;
  unity.x = 1;
  unity.y = 1;
  std::cout << "origin = (" << origin.x << ", " << origin.y << ")\n";
  std::cout << "unity  = (" << unity.x  << ", " << unity.y  << ")\n";
}
```

# Member Functions

In addition to data members, you can have member functions. Member function definitions look very similar to ordinary function definitions, except you define them as part of a class definition. Also, a member function can call other member functions of the same class and can access data members of the same class. Listing 31-4 shows some member functions added to class point.

**Listing 31-4.** *Member Functions for Class point*

```
#include <cmath> // for sqrt and atan
struct point
{
  /// Distance to the origin.
  double distance()
  {
    return std::sqrt(x*x + y*y);
  }
  /// Angle relative to x-axis.
  double angle()
  {
    return std::atan2(y, x);
  }

  /// Add an offset to x and y.
  void offset(double off)
  {
    offset(off, off);
  }
  /// Add an offset to x and an offset to y
  void offset(double  xoff, double yoff)
  {
    x = x + xoff;
    y = y + yoff;
  }

  /// Scale x and y.
  void scale(double mult)
  {
    this->scale(mult, mult);
  }
  /// Scale x and y.
  void scale(double xmult, double ymult)
  {
    this->x = this->x * xmult;
    this->y = this->y * ymult;
  }
  double x;
  double y;
};
```

For each member function, the compiler generates a hidden parameter named this. When you call a member function, the compiler passes the object as the hidden argument. In a member function, you can access the object with the expression *this. The C++ syntax rules specify that the member operator (.) has higher precedence than the * operator, so you need parentheses around *this (e.g., (*this).x). As a syntactic convenience, another way to write the same expression is this->x, several examples of which you can see in Listing 31-4.

The compiler is smart enough to know when you use a member name, so the use of this-> is optional. If a name has no local definition, and it is the name of a member, the compiler assumes you want to use the member. Some programmers prefer to always include this-> for the sake of clarity—in a large program, you can easily lose track of which names are member names. Other programmers find the extra this-> to be clutter and use it only when necessary. My recommendation is the latter. You need to learn to read C++ classes, and one of the necessary skills is to be able to read a class definition, find the member names, and keep track of those names while you read the class definition.

A number of programmers employ a more subtle technique, which involves using a special prefix or suffix to denote data member names. For example, a common technique is to use the prefix m_ for all data members ("m" is short for member). Another common technique is a little less intrusive: using a plain underscore (_) suffix. I prefer a suffix to a prefix because suffixes interfere less than prefixes, so they don't obscure the important part of a name. From now on, I will adopt the practice of appending an underscore to every data member name.

---

### NO LEADING UNDERSCORE

If you want to use an underscore to denote members, use it as a suffix, not a prefix. The C++ standard sets aside certain names and prohibits you from using them. The actual rules are somewhat lengthy because C++ inherits a number of restrictions from the C standard library. For example, you should not use any name that begins with E and is followed by a digit or an uppercase letter. (That rule seems arcane, but the C standard library defines several error code names, such as ERANGE, for a range error in a math function. This rule lets the library add new names in the future, and lets those who implement libraries add vendor-specific names.)

I like simplicity, so I follow three basic rules. These rules are slightly more restrictive than the official C++ rules, but not in any burdensome way:

- Do not use any name that contains two consecutive underscores (like__this).
- Do not use any name that starts with an underscore (_like_this).
- Do not use any name that is all uppercase (LIKE_THIS).

Using a reserved name results in undefined behavior. The compiler may not complain, but the results are unpredictable. Typically, a standard library implementation must invent many additional names for its internal use. By defining certain names that the application programmer cannot use, C++ ensures the library-writer can use these names within the library. If you accidentally use a name that conflicts with an internal library name, the results could be chaos or merely a subtle shift in a function's implementation.

---

# Constructor

As I mentioned earlier, data member declarations do not take initializers. The way to initialize a data member is in a *constructor*, which you learned about in Exploration 30. Recall that a constructor is a special member function. You cannot call a constructor directly; instead, when you define a variable of class type, the compiler automatically generates code to call the appropriate constructor. Which constructor it calls depends on the arguments you supply to the variable's initializer (if any), according to the usual rules for overloading functions.

Write a constructor almost the same way you would an ordinary member function, but with a few differences:

- Omit the return type.

- Use plain `return`; (return statements that do not return values).

- Use the class name as the function name.

- Add an initializer list after a colon to initialize the data members.

Listing 31-5 shows several examples of constructors added to class `point`.

**Listing 31-5.** *Constructors for Class point*

```
struct point
{
  point()
  : x_(0.0), y_(0.0)
  {}
  point(double x, double y)
  : x_(x), y_(y)
  {}
  point(point const& pt)
  : x_(pt.x_), y_(pt.y_)
  {}
  double x_;
  double y_;
};
```

Constructors take arguments the same way ordinary functions do. When you define an object of class type, you pass arguments to initialize the object. The compiler passes the arguments to the constructor, just as though you were calling the constructor as a function. If you omit the constructor argument list, you must also omit the parentheses; the compiler calls the no-argument constructor (called the *default* constructor), as shown in the following:

```
point origin;          // invokes point()
point unit(1.0, 1.0);  // invokes point(double x, double y)
point copy(origin);    // invokes point(point const& pt)
```

Initialization is one of the key differences between class types and built-in types. If you define an object of built-in type without an initializer, you get a garbage value, but objects of class type are always initialized by calling a constructor. You always get a chance to initialize the object's data members. The difference between built-in types and class types are also evident in the rules C++ uses to initialize data members in a constructor.

A constructor's initializer list is optional, but I recommend you always provide it. It appears after a colon, which follows the closing parenthesis of the constructor's parameter list. The initializer list initializes each data member in the same order in which you declare them in the class definition, ignoring the order in the initializer list. I further recommend that to avoid confusion, you always write the initializer list in the same order as the data members. Member initializers are separated by commas and can spill onto as many lines as you need. Each member initializer provides the initial value of a single data member. List the member name, followed by the initial value in parentheses.

The compiler treats class-type data members differently from data members with built-in type. Each member initializer can have one of three kinds of values:

- The member is missing: you omitted the member from the initializer list, or you left out the entire initializer list. Members of built-in type are left uninitialized; members of class type are initialized by calling their default constructors, as demonstrated in the following:

```
struct demo
{
  demo() {}  // invoke point() to initialize pt_, but u_ is uninitialized
  point pt_;
  int u_;
};
```

- The initializer is missing: the member is in the initializer list, but the parentheses are empty. (You must always include the parentheses after the member name.) Members are *value-initialized*: A member of built-in type is value-initialized by initializing it to zero, cast to the appropriate type (0, 0.0, false). A member of class type—when the class has at least one explicit constructor—is value-initialized by calling its default constructor. If the class has at least one constructor, but no default constructor, the compiler issues an error message. A member of class type with no explicit constructor is value-initialized by value-initializing its members individually. (I don't like the name value-initialize, but that's what the standard calls it, and that's what C++ experts call it, so you may as well get used to it.)

```
struct demo
{
  demo() : pt_(), z_() {}    // zero-initialize z_; zero-initialize pt_ if
                             // point has no constructors; otherwise invoke
                             // point's default constructor
  point pt_;
  int z_;
};
```

- The initializer has a list of one or more arguments, separated by commas (as in a function call): members of built-in type must have only one argument, and that argument is the initial value. Members of class type are initialized by passing the arguments to a suitable constructor. The compiler chooses a constructor based on the number and type of the arguments, using the normal rules for resolving overloaded functions, as shown in the following:

```
struct demo {
  demo(int x, int y) : pt_(x, y), x_(42) {}
  point pt_;
```

```
    int x_;
  };
```

If you don't write any constructors for your class, the compiler writes its own default constructor. The compiler's default constructor is just like a constructor that omits an initializer list.

```
struct point {
  point() {} // x_ and y_ are uninitialized
  double x_;
  double y_;
};
```

When the compiler writes a constructor for you, the constructor is *implicit*. When you write your own constructor, it is explicit. The distinction matters when value-initializing an object, as I explained earlier.

In some applications, you may want to avoid the overhead of initializing the data members of point because your application will immediately assign a new value to the point object. Most of the time, however, caution is best. For that reason, I wrote the default constructor for point to initialize the data members to 0.0.

A *copy* constructor is one that takes a single argument of the same type as the class, passed by reference. The compiler automatically generates calls to the copy constructor when you pass objects by value to functions, or when functions return objects. You can also initialize a point object with the value of another point object, and the compiler generates code to invoke the copy constructor.

```
point pt1;        // default constructor
point p2(pt1);    // copy constructor
```

If you don't write your own copy constructor, the compiler writes one for you. The automatic copy constructor calls the copy constructor for every data member, just like the one in Listing 31-5. Because I wrote one that is exactly like the one the compiler writes implicitly, there is no reason to write it explicitly. Let the compiler do its job.

To help you visualize how the compiler calls constructors, read Listing 31-6. Notice how it prints a message for each constructor use.

**Listing 31-6.** *Visual Constructors*

```
#include <iostream>
#include <ostream>

struct demo
{
  demo()      : x_(0) { std::cout << "default constructor\n"; }
  demo(int x) : x_(x) { std::cout << "constructor(" << x << ")\n"; }
  demo(demo const& that)
  : x_(that.x_)
  {
    std::cout << "copy constructor(" << x_ << ")\n";
  }
```

```
   int x_;
};

demo addone(demo d)
{
  ++d.x_;
  return d;
}

int main()
{
  demo d1;
  demo d2(d1);
  demo d3(42);
  demo d4(addone(d3));
}
```

**Predict the output from running the program in Listing 31-6.**

_____

_____

_____

_____

_____

_____

_____

Check your prediction. **Were you correct?** _____

The compiler is allowed to perform some minor optimizations when passing arguments to functions and accepting return values. For example, instead of copying a demo object to the addone return value, and then copying the return value to initialize d4, the C++ standard permits compilers to remove unnecessary calls to the copy constructor. Not all compilers perform this optimization, and not all do so in the same manner. Most compilers require a command line switch or project option to be set before it optimizes. Thus, the exact number of calls to the copy constructor can vary slightly from one compiler or platform to another, or from one set of command line switches to another. When I run the program, I get the following:

```
default constructor
copy constructor(0)
constructor(42)
copy constructor(42)
copy constructor(43)
```

That was easy. The next Exploration starts with a real challenge.

■ ■ ■

# More About Member Functions

Member functions and constructors are even more fun than what you've learned so far. This Exploration continues to uncover their mysteries.

## Invoking the Default Constructor

Let's begin with a challenge. Read the program in Listing 32-1.

**Listing 32-1.** *Mystery Program*

```
#include <iostream>
#include <ostream>

struct point
{
  point()
  : x_(0.0), y_(0.0)
  {
    std::cout << "default constructor\n";
  }
  point(double x, double y)
  : x_(x), y_(y)
  {
    std::cout << "constructor(" << x << ", " << y << ")\n";
  }

  double x_;
  double y_;
};

int main()
{
  point pt();
}
```

**Predict the output from the program in Listing 32-1.**

_____

_____

_____

Okay, I confess. I played a trick on you. You probably expected to see the message

```
default constructor
```

but you didn't, did you? So, what happened? To better understand, **try adding a line to print the value of pt.x_.**

```
int main()
{
  point pt();
  std::cout << pt.x_ << '\n';
}
```

Now what happens?

_____

_____

More tricks, I'm afraid. The problem is that the program does not actually define a variable named pt, constructed with the default constructor. Instead, you have inadvertently declared a function named pt, which takes no arguments and returns a point value.

The C++ language is complicated, and the grammar in particular has a number of subtle complexities. In this case, the grammar is ambiguous and permits two different interpretations of the declaration of pt. The semantic rules resolve the syntactic ambiguity, but not in the way you probably predicted. Imagine for a moment that you change the type from point to int, and the name from pt to size.

```
int size();
```

Now it looks like a function declaration, doesn't it? And that's exactly how the compiler sees it: a declaration (not a definition) of a function named size that takes no arguments and returns type int. Listing 32-1 contains a declaration of a function named pt that takes no arguments and returns type point.

The proper way to define an object named pt that invokes the default constructor is to omit the parentheses, as shown in the following:

```
point pt;
```

This issue often trips up new C++ programmers. Fortunately, the compiler detects the mistake and issues an error message. Unfortunately, the message is often cryptic because the compiler's interpretation of what you wrote is so very different from your intention, and the message typically arises where you use pt, not where you declare it. Fortunately, with a little experience, you will quickly learn to recognize this coding pattern.

Subtle semantic problems arise in other ways. The most notable trap arises when you try to construct objects, such as vectors, only the compiler doesn't see it that way at all. Types such as vector have a plethora of constructors. One constructor takes two read iterators and initializes the vector by copying all the elements from the iterator range. Listing 32-2 shows a simple program that reads integers from the standard input, then finds the first instance of zero in the data, and constructs a new vector, starting at the zero and extending to the end of the original vector. The only point of this program is to demonstrate vector's two-iterator constructor.

**Listing 32-2.** *Constructing a vector from Two Read Iterators*

```
#include <algorithm>
#include <iostream>
#include <istream>
#include <iterator>
#include <ostream>
#include <vector>

int main()
{
  using namespace std;
  vector<int> orig;
  orig.insert(orig.begin(), istream_iterator<int>(cin), istream_iterator<int>());
  vector<int>::iterator zero(find(orig.begin(), orig.end(), 0));
  vector<int> from_zero(zero, orig.end());
  copy(from_zero.begin(), from_zero.end(), ostream_iterator<int>(cout, "\n"));
}
```

You can use the same constructor to construct the orig object, too. Instead of using the default constructor and a separate call to the insert member function, you can directly construct orig with the values that istream_iterator reads from cin. Consider the program in Listing 32-3.

**Listing 32-3.** *Problem with* istream *Iterators*

```
#include <algorithm>
#include <iostream>
#include <istream>
#include <iterator>
#include <ostream>
#include <vector>

int main()
{
  using namespace std;
  vector<int> orig(istream_iterator<int>(cin), istream_iterator<int>());
  vector<int>::iterator zero(find(orig.begin(), orig.end(), 0));
  vector<int> from_zero(zero, orig.end());
  copy(from_zero.begin(), from_zero.end(), ostream_iterator<int>(cout, "\n"));
}
```

The constructor for orig looks just like the constructor for from_zero, except that the two read iterators are istream_iterator objects. At least that's what the program looks like at first. **What does the program actually do?**

_____

_____

_____

Instead of defining a variable named orig that is initialized by calling a two-argument constructor with two istream_iterator<int> objects as arguments, the program actually declares a function named orig that takes two parameters of type istream_iterator<int>. The first parameter is named cin, and the second has no name. The parentheses around the parameter name (or lack of name) are redundant, so the compiler ignores them.

Once again, the compiler sees a function declaration instead of a variable definition. The grammar is again ambiguous, and the language rules opt in favor of the function declaration.

In past Explorations, I've avoided this particular problem by defining an empty vector, and then copying the data into the vector by calling the insert member function or the copy algorithm. Another way to get around the compiler's interpretation of the declaration is to surround each argument in its entirety in parentheses, as demonstrated in the following:

```
vector<int> data((istream_iterator<int>(cin)), (istream_iterator<int>()));
```

These extra parentheses force the compiler to see the declaration as a variable definition, not a function declaration. You may find this style a little hard to read, but once you get used to it, you can easily see this idiom and how it works.

# Revisiting Project 1

What did you find most frustrating about Project 1 (Exploration 26)? If you are anything like me (although I hope you're not, for your own sake), you may have been disappointed that you had to define several separate vectors to store one set of records. However, without knowing about classes, that was the only feasible approach. Now that you've been introduced to classes, you can fix the program. **Write a class definition to store one record.** Refer back to Exploration 26 for details. To summarize, each record keeps track of an integer height in centimeters, an integer weight in kilograms, the calculated BMI (which you can round off to an integer), the person's sex (letter 'M' or 'F'), and the person's name (a string).

Next, **write a read member function that reads a single record from an istream**. It takes two arguments: an istream and an integer. Prompt the user for each piece of information by writing to std::cout. The integer argument is the record number, which you can use in the prompts. **Write a print member function that prints one record**; it takes an ostream and an integer threshold as arguments.

**Finally, modify the program to take advantage of the new class you wrote.** Compare your solution to that of mine, shown in Listing 32-4.

**Listing 32-4.** *New BMI Program*

```cpp
#include <algorithm>
#include <cstdlib>
#include <iomanip>
#include <ios>
#include <iostream>
#include <istream>
#include <limits>
#include <locale>
#include <ostream>
#include <string>
#include <vector>

/// Compute body-mass index from height in centimeters and weight in kilograms.
int compute_bmi(int height, int weight)
{
    return static_cast<int>(weight * 10000 / (height * height) + 0.5);
}

/// Skip the rest of the input line.
void skip_line(std::istream& in)
{
  in.ignore(std::numeric_limits<int>::max(), '\n');
}

/// Represent one person's record, storing the person's name, height, weight,
/// sex, and body-mass index (BMI), which is computed from the height and weight.
struct record
{
  record() : height_(0), weight_(0), bmi_(0), sex_('?'), name_()
  {}

  /// Get this record, overwriting the data members.
  /// Error-checking omitted for brevity.
  /// @return true for success or false for eof or input failure
  bool read(std::istream& in, int num)
  {
    std::cout << "Name " << num << ": ";
    std::string name;
    if (not std::getline(in, name))
      return false;

    std::cout << "Height (cm): ";
    int height;
    if (not (in >> height))
      return false;
    skip_line(in);
```

```
      std::cout << "Weight (kg): ";
      int weight;
      if (not (in >> weight))
        return false;
      skip_line(in);

      std::cout << "Sex (M or F): ";
      char sex;
      if (not (in >> sex))
        return false;
      skip_line(in);
      sex = std::toupper(sex, std::locale());

      // Store information into data members only after reading
      // everything successfully.
      name_ = name;
      height_ = height;
      weight_ = weight;
      sex_ = sex;
      bmi_ = compute_bmi(height_, weight_);
      return true;
    }

    /// Print this record to @p out.
    void print(std::ostream& out, int threshold)
    {
      out << std::setw(6) << height_
          << std::setw(7) << weight_
          << std::setw(3) << sex_
          << std::setw(6) << bmi_;
      if (bmi_ >= threshold)
        out << '*';
      else
        out << ' ';
      out << ' ' << name_ << '\n';
    }

    int height_;       ///< height in centimeters
    int weight_;       ///< weight in kilograms
    int bmi_;          ///< Body-mass index
    char sex_;         ///< 'M' for male or 'F' for female
    std::string name_; ///< Person's name
};


/** Print a table.
 * Print a table of height, weight, sex, BMI, and name.
```

```
 * Print only records for which sex matches @p sex.
 * At the end of each table, print the mean and median BMI.
 */
void print_table(char sex, std::vector<record>& records, int threshold)
{
  std::cout << "Ht(cm) Wt(kg) Sex  BMI  Name\n";

  float bmi_sum(0);
  long int bmi_count(0);
  std::vector<int> tmpbmis; // store only the BMIs that are printed
                            // in order to compute the median
  for (std::vector<record>::iterator iter(records.begin());
       iter != records.end();
       ++iter)
  {
    if (iter->sex_ == sex)
    {
      bmi_sum = bmi_sum + iter->bmi_;
      ++bmi_count;
      tmpbmis.push_back(iter->bmi_);
      iter->print(std::cout, threshold);
    }
  }

  // If the vectors are not empty, print basic statistics.
  if (bmi_count != 0)
  {
    std::cout << "Mean BMI = "
              << std::setprecision(1) << std::fixed << bmi_sum / bmi_count
              << '\n';

    // Median BMI is trickier. The easy way is to sort the
    // vector and pick out the middle item or items.
    std::sort(tmpbmis.begin(), tmpbmis.end());
    std::cout << "Median BMI = ";
    // Index of median item.
    int i(tmpbmis.size() / 2);
    if (tmpbmis.size() % 2 == 0)
      std::cout << (tmpbmis.at(i) + tmpbmis.at(i-1)) / 2.0 << '\n';
    else
      std::cout << tmpbmis.at(i) << '\n';
  }
}

/** Main program to compute BMI. */
int main()
{
```

```
std::locale::global(std::locale(""));
std::cout.imbue(std::locale());
std::cin.imbue(std::locale());

std::vector<record> records;
int threshold;

std::cout << "Enter threshold BMI: ";
if (not (std::cin >> threshold))
  return EXIT_FAILURE;
skip_line(std::cin);

std::cout << "Enter name, height (in cm),"
             " and weight (in kg) for each person:\n";
record rec;
while (rec.read(std::cin, records.size()+1))
{
  records.push_back(rec);
  std::cout << "BMI = " << rec.bmi_ << '\n';
}

// Print the data.
std::cout << "\n\nMale data\n";
print_table('M', records, threshold);
std::cout << "\nFemale data\n";
print_table('F', records, threshold);
}
```

That's a lot to swallow, so take your time. I'll wait here until you're done. When faced with a new class that you need to read and understand, start by reading the comments (if any). One approach is to first skim lightly over the class to identify the members (function and data) then re-read the class to understand the member functions in depth. Tackle one member function at a time.

You may be asking yourself why I didn't overload the >> and << operators to read and write record objects. The requirements of the program are a little more complicated than what these operators offer. For example, reading a record also involves printing prompts, and each prompt includes an ordinal so the user knows which record to type. Some records are printed differently than others, depending on the threshold. The >> operator has no convenient way to specify the threshold. Overloading I/O operators is great for simple types, but usually is not appropriate for more complicated situations.

# const Member Functions

Take a closer look at the print_table function. Notice anything unusual or suspicious about its parameters? The records argument is passed by reference, but the function never modifies it, so you really should pass it as a reference to const. Go ahead and make that change. **What happens?**

_____

_____

You should see an error from the compiler. I often make this particular mistake in my code, so I'm glad it's easy to fix. You are not allowed to use a plain `iterator` with a `const` container. You must use `const_iterator` instead. (See Exploration 20.) Change the `for` loop to use a `const_iterator`. **Now what happens?**

_____

_____

Hmmm, still no go. Remember that every member function has a hidden parameter, `this`, that refers to the object. In this case, `print_table` calls the `print` member function, but after the change, `this` refers to a `const` object. _You_ know that the `print` function does not modify any data members, but the compiler doesn't. You need to instruct the compiler that it can call `print()` with a `const` object, and you do so by adding a `const` modifier between the function header and the function body. Listing 32-5 shows the new definition of the `print` member function.

**Listing 32-5.** _Adding the const Modifier to print_

```
/// Print this record to @p out.
void print(std::ostream& out, int threshold)
const
{
  out << std::setw(6) << height_
      << std::setw(7) << weight_
      << std::setw(3) << sex_
      << std::setw(6) << bmi_;
  if (bmi_ >= threshold)
    out << '*';
  else
    out << ' ';
  out << ' ' << name_ << '\n';
}
```

As a general rule, use the `const` modifier for any member function that does not change any data members. This ensures that you can call the member function when you have a `const` object. **Copy the code from Listing 30-4 and modify it to add const modifiers where appropriate.** Compare your result with mine in Listing 32-6.

**Listing 32-6.** _const Member Functions for Class point_

```
#include <cmath> // for sqrt and atan
struct point
{
  /// Distance to the origin.
  double distance()
  const
```

```
  {
    return std::sqrt(x*x + y*y);
  }
  /// Angle relative to x-axis.
  double angle()
  const
  {
    return std::atan2(y, x);
  }


  /// Add an offset to x and y.
  void offset(double off)
  {
    offset(off, off);
  }
  /// Add an offset to x and an offset to y
  void offset(double  xoff, double yoff)
  {
    x = x + xoff;
    y = y + yoff;
  }


  /// Scale x and y.
  void scale(double mult)
  {
    this->scale(mult, mult);
  }
  /// Scale x and y.
  void scale(double xmult, double ymult)
  {
    this->x = this->x * xmult;
    this->y = this->y * ymult;
  }
  double x;
  double y;
};
```

The scale and offset functions modify data members, so they cannot be const. The angle and distance member functions don't modify any members, so they are const.

Given a point variable, you can call any member function. If the object is const, however, you can call only const member functions. The most common situation is when you find your-self with a const object within another function, and the object was passed by reference to const, as illustrated in Listing 32-7.

**Listing 32-7.** *Calling const and Non-const Member Functions*

```
#include <cmath>
#include <iostream>
#include <ostream>

// Use the same point definition as Listing 32-6
... omitted for brevity ...

void print_polar(point const& pt)
{
  std::cout << "{ r=" << pt.distance() << ", angle=" << pt.angle() << " }\n";
}

void print_cartesian(point const& pt)
{
  std::cout << "{ x=" << pt.x << ", y=" << pt.y << " }\n";
}

int main()
{
  point p1, p2;
  double const pi = 3.141592653589792;
  p1.x = std::cos(pi / 3);
  p1.y = std::sin(pi / 3);
  print_polar(p1);
  print_cartesian(p1);
  p2 = p1;
  p2.scale(4.0);
  print_polar(p2);
  print_cartesian(p2);
  p2.offset(0.0, -2.0);
  print_polar(p2);
  print_cartesian(p2);
}
```

Another common use for member functions is to restrict access to data members. Imagine what would happen if a program that used the BMI record type accidentally modified the bmi_ member. A better design would let you call a bmi() function to obtain the BMI, but hide the bmi_ data member to prevent accidental modification. You can prevent such accidents, and the next Exploration shows you how.

# EXPLORATION 33

■■■

# Access Levels

**E**veryone has secrets, some of us more than others. Classes have secrets, too. For example: throughout this book you have used the std::string class without having any notion of what goes on inside the class. The implementation details are secrets—not closely guarded secrets, but secrets nonetheless. You cannot directly examine or modify any of string's data members. Instead, it presents quite a few member functions that make up its public interface. You are free to use any of the publicly available member functions, but only the publicly available member functions. This Exploration explains how you can do the same with your classes.

## Public vs. Private

The author of a class determines which members are secrets (for use only by the class's own member functions), and which members are freely available for use by any other bit of code in the program. Secret members are called *private*, and the members that anyone can use are *public*. The privacy setting is called the *access level*.

To specify an access level, use the private keyword or the public keyword, followed by a colon. All subsequent members in the class definition have that accessibility level until you change it with a new access level keyword. Listing 33-1 shows the point class with access level specifiers.

**Listing 33-1.** *The point Class with Access Level Specifiers*

```
struct point
{
public:
  point() : x_(0.0), y_(0.0) {}
  point(double x, double y) : x_(x), y_(y) {}

  double x() const { return x_; }
  double y() const { return y_; }

  double angle()    const { return std::atan2(y(), x()); }
  double distance() const { return std::sqrt(x()*x() + y()*y()); }

  void move_cartesian(double x, double y)
  {
```

```
    x_ = x;
    y_ = y;
  }
  void move_polar(double r, double angle)
  {
    move_cartesian(r * std::cos(angle), r * std::sin(angle));
  }

  void scale_cartesian(double s)        { scale_cartesian(s, s); }
  void scale_cartesian(double xs, double ys)
  {
    move_cartesian(x() * xs, y() * ys);
  }
  void scale_polar(double r)            { move_polar(distance() * r, angle()); }
  void rotate(double a)                 { move_polar(distance(), angle() + a); }
  void offset(double o)                 { offset(o, o); }
  void offset(double xo, double yo)     { move_cartesian(x() + xo, y() + yo); }

private:
  double x_;
  double y_;
};
```

The data members are private, so the only functions that can modify them are point's own member functions. Public member functions provide access to the position with the public x() and y() member functions.

---

▓**Tip** Always keep data members private, and provide access only through member functions.

---

To modify a position, notice that point does not let the user arbitrarily assign a new *x* or *y* value. Instead, it offers several public member functions to move the point to an absolute position, or relative to the current position.

The public member functions let you work in Cartesian coordinates—that is, the familiar *x* and *y* positions, or in polar coordinates, specifying a position as an angle (relative to the x-axis) and a distance from the origin. Both representations for a point have their uses, and both can uniquely specify any position in two-dimensional space. Some users prefer polar notation while others prefer Cartesian. Neither user has direct access to the data members, so it doesn't matter how the point class actually stores the coordinates. In fact, you can change the implementation of point to store the distance and angle as data members by changing only a few member functions. **Which member functions would you need to change?**

---

---

Changing the data members from x_ and y_ to r_ and angle_ necessitate a change to the x, y, angle, and distance member functions just for access to the data members. You also need to change the two move functions: move_polar and move_cartesian. Finally, you need to modify the constructors. No other changes are necessary. Because the scale and offset functions do not access data members directly, but instead call other member functions, they are insulated from changes to the class implementation. **Rewrite the point class to store polar coordinates in its data members.** Compare your class with mine, which is shown in Listing 33-2.

**Listing 33-2.** *The point Class Changed to Store Polar Coordinates*

```
struct point
{
public:
  point() : r_(0.0), angle_(0.0) {}
  point(double x, double y) : r_(0.0), angle_(0.0) { move_cartesian(x, y); }

  double x() const { return distance() * std::cos(angle()); }
  double y() const { return distance() * std::sin(angle()); }

  double angle()    const { return angle_; }
  double distance() const { return r_; }

  void move_cartesian(double x, double y)
  {
    move_polar(std::sqrt(x*x + y*y), std::atan2(y, x));
  }
  void move_polar(double r, double angle)
  {
    r_ = r;
    angle_ = angle;
  }

  void scale_cartesian(double s)         { scale_cartesian(s, s); }
  void scale_cartesian(double xs, double ys)
  {
    move_cartesian(x() * xs, y() * ys);
  }
  void scale_polar(double r)              { move_polar(distance() * r, angle()); }
  void rotate(double a)                   { move_polar(distance(), angle() + a); }
  void offset(double o)                   { offset(o, o); }
  void offset(double xo, double yo)       { move_cartesian(x() + xo, y() + yo); }

private:
  double r_;
  double angle_;
};
```

One small difficulty is the constructor. Ideally, point should have two constructors, one taking polar coordinates and the other taking Cartesian coordinates. The problem is that both coordinates are pairs of numbers, and overloading cannot distinguish between the arguments. This means you can't use normal overloading for these constructors. Instead, you can add a third parameter: a flag that indicates whether to interpret the first two parameters as polar coordinates or Cartesian coordinates.

```
class polar
{
public:
  polar(double a, double b, bool is_polar)
  {
    if (is_polar)
      move_polar(a, b);
    else
      move_cartesian(a, b);
  }
... omitted for brevity ...
};
```

It's something of a hack, but it will have to do for now. Later in the book, you will learn cleaner techniques to accomplish this task.

# class vs. struct

Exploration 32 hinted that the class keyword was somehow involved in class definitions, even though every example in this book so far uses the struct keyword. Now is the time to learn the truth.

The truth is quite simple. The struct and class keywords both start class definitions. The only difference is the default access level: private for class and public for struct. That's all.

By convention, programmers tend to use class for class definitions. Also by convention, class definitions begin with the public interface, tucking away the private members at the bottom of the class definition. Listing 33-3 shows the latest incarnation of the point class, this time defined using the class keyword.

**Listing 33-3.** *The point Class Defined with the class Keyword*

```
class point
{
public:
  point() : r_(0.0), angle_(0.0) {}

  double x() const { return distance() * std::cos(angle()); }
  double y() const { return distance() * std::sin(angle()); }

  double angle()    const { return angle_; }
  double distance() const { return r_; }
```

```
// ... other member functions omitted for brevity ...

private:
  double r_;
  double angle_;
};
```

# Plain Old Data

So what good is the struct keyword? Authors of introductory books like it because we can gradually introduce concepts such as classes without miring the reader in too many details, such as access levels, all at once. But what about real-world programs?

The struct keyword plays a crucial role in C-compatibility. C++ is a distinct language from C, but many programs must interface with the C world. C++ has a couple of key features to interface with C; one of those features is POD. That's right, POD, short for Plain Old Data.

A POD type is one that stores data but doesn't really do much else with it. For example, the built-in types are POD types. They don't have member functions. An int just sits there and exists as an int with all the behavior of an int. It's up to your code to do something interesting with it. An int is plain, old data.

A class that has only public POD types as data members, with no constructors, and no overloaded assignment operator, is a POD type. A class with a private member, a member with reference or other non-POD type, a constructor, or an assignment operator is not POD.

The importance of POD types is that legacy C functions in the C++ library, in third-party libraries, or operating system interfaces, require POD types. This book won't go into the details of any of these functions, but if you find yourself needing to call memcpy, fwrite, ReadFileEx, or any one of the myriad related functions, you will need to make sure you are using POD classes.

By defining POD classes with struct, you achieve two goals: data members are public by default so you don't need any access level specifiers, and it's a hint to the human reader that the class is not a normal class. Not everyone uses struct to mean POD, but it's a convention I use in my own code. I use class for all other cases to remind the human reader that the class can take advantage of C++ features and is not required to maintain compatibility with C.

# Public or Private?

Usually, you can easily determine which members should be public and which should be private. Sometimes, however, you need to stop and ponder. Consider the rational class (last seen in Exploration 31). **Rewrite the rational class to take advantage of access levels.**

Did you decide to make reduce() public or private? I chose private because there is no need for any outside caller to call reduce(). Instead, the only member functions to call reduce() are the ones that change the data members themselves. Thus, reduce() is hidden from outside view and serves as an implementation detail. The more details you hide, the better because it makes your class easier to use.

When you added access functions, did you let the caller change the numerator only? Did you write a function to change the denominator only? Or did you ask that the user assign both at the same time? The user of a rational object should treat it as a single entity, a number. You can't assign only a new exponent to a floating-point number, and you shouldn't be able to assign only a new numerator to a rational number. On the other hand, I see no reason not to let the caller examine just the numerator or just the denominator. For example, you may want to write your own output formatting function, which requires knowing the numerator and denominator separately.

A good sign that you have made the right choices is that you can rewrite all the operator functions easily. These functions should not need to access the data members of `rational`, but use only the public functions. If you tried to access any private members, you learned pretty quickly that the compiler wouldn't let you. That's what privacy is all about.

Compare your solution with my solution, presented in Listing 33-4.

**Listing 33-4.** *The Latest Rewrite of the rational Class*

```
#include <cassert>
#include <cstdlib>
#include <istream>
#include <ostream>
#include <sstream>

/// Compute the greatest common divisor of two integers, using Euclid's algorithm.
int gcd(int n, int m)
{
  n = std::abs(n);
  while (m != 0) {
    int tmp(n % m);
    n = m;
    m = tmp;
  }
  return n;
}

/// Represent a rational number (fraction) as a numerator and denominator.
class rational
{
public:
  rational(): numerator_(0), denominator_(1)  {}
  rational(int num): numerator_(num), denominator_(1) {}

  rational(int num, int den)
  : numerator_(num), denominator_(den)
  {
    reduce();
  }

  rational(double r)
  : numerator_(static_cast<int>(r * 10000)), denominator_(10000)
  {
    reduce();
  }
```

```cpp
  int numerator()    const { return numerator_; }
  int denominator() const { return denominator_; }
  float as_float()
  const
  {
    return static_cast<float>(numerator()) / denominator();
  }

  double as_double()
  const
  {
    return static_cast<double>(numerator()) / denominator();
  }

  long double as_long_double()
  const
  {
    return static_cast<long double>(numerator()) /
           denominator();
  }

  /// Assign a numerator and a denominator, then reduce to normal form.
  void assign(int num, int den)
  {
    numerator_ = num;
    denominator_ = den;
    reduce();
  }
private:
  /// Reduce the numerator and denominator by their GCD.
  void reduce()
  {
    assert(denominator() != 0);
    if (denominator() < 0)
    {
      denominator_ = -denominator();
      numerator_ = -numerator();
    }
    int div(gcd(numerator(), denominator()));
    numerator_ = numerator() / div;
    denominator_ = denominator() / div;
  }

  int numerator_;
  int denominator_;
};
```

```
/// Absolute value of a rational number.
rational abs(rational const& r)
{
  return rational(abs(r.numerator()), r.denominator());
}

/// Unary negation of a rational number.
rational operator-(rational const& r)
{
  return rational(-r.numerator(), r.denominator());
}

/// Add rational numbers.
rational operator+(rational const& lhs, rational const& rhs)
{
  return rational(
         lhs.numerator() * rhs.denominator() + rhs.numerator() * lhs.denominator(),
         lhs.denominator() * rhs.denominator());
}

/// Subtraction of rational numbers.
rational operator-(rational const& lhs, rational const& rhs)
{
  return rational(
         lhs.numerator() * rhs.denominator() - rhs.numerator() * lhs.denominator(),
         lhs.denominator() * rhs.denominator());
}

/// Multiplication of rational numbers.
rational operator*(rational const& lhs, rational const& rhs)
{
  return rational(lhs.numerator() * rhs.numerator(),
               lhs.denominator() * rhs.denominator());
}

/// Division of rational numbers.
/// TODO: check for division-by-zero
rational operator/(rational const& lhs, rational const& rhs)
{
  return rational(lhs.numerator() * rhs.denominator(),
               lhs.denominator() * rhs.numerator());
}

/// Compare two rational numbers for equality.
bool operator==(rational const& a, rational const& b)
{
```

```
  return a.numerator() == b.numerator() and a.denominator() == b.denominator();
}


/// Compare two rational numbers for inequality.
inline bool operator!=(rational const& a, rational const& b)
{
  return not (a == b);
}
/// Compare two rational numbers for less-than.
bool operator<(rational const& a, rational const& b)
{
  return a.numerator() * b.denominator() < b.numerator() * a.denominator();
}


/// Compare two rational numbers for less-than-or-equal.
inline bool operator<=(rational const& a, rational const& b)
{
  return not (b < a);
}
/// Compare two rational numbers for greater-than.
inline bool operator>(rational const& a, rational const& b)
{
  return b < a;
}


/// Compare two rational numbers for greater-than-or-equal.
inline bool operator>=(rational const& a, rational const& b)
{
  return not (b > a);
}


/// Read a rational number.
/// Format is @em integer @c / @em integer.
std::istream& operator>>(std::istream& in, rational& rat)
{
  int n(0), d(0);
  char sep('\0');
  if (not (in >> n >> sep))
    // Error reading the numerator or the separator character.
    in.setstate(in.failbit);
  else if (sep != '/')
  {
    // Push sep back into the input stream, so the next input operation
    // will read it.
    in.unget();
    rat.assign(n, 1);
  }
```

```
  else if (in >> d)
    // Successfully read numerator, separator, and denominator.
    rat.assign(n, d);
  else
    // Error reading denominator.
    in.setstate(in.failbit);

  return in;
}

/// Write a rational numbers.
/// Format is @em numerator @c / @em denominator.
std::ostream& operator<<(std::ostream& out, rational const& rat)
{
  std::ostringstream tmp;
  tmp << rat.numerator() << '/' << rat.denominator();
  out << tmp.str();

  return out;
}
```

Classes are one of the fundamental building blocks of object-oriented programming. Now that you know how classes work, you can see how they apply to this style of programming, which is the subject of the next Exploration.

■ ■ ■

# Introduction to Object-Oriented Programming

This Exploration takes a break from C++ programming to turn to the topic of object-oriented programming (OOP). You may already be familiar with this topic, but I urge you to continue reading. You may learn something new. To everyone else, this Exploration introduces some of the foundations of OOP in general terms. Later Explorations will show how C++ implements OOP principles.

## Books and Magazines

**What is the difference between a book and a magazine?** Yes, I really want you to write down your answer. Write down as many differences as you can think of:

_____

_____

_____

**What are the similarities between books and magazines?** Write down as many similarities as you can think of:

_____

_____

_____

If you can, compare your lists with the lists that other people write. They don't need to be programmers; everyone knows what books and magazine are. Ask your friends and neighbors, stop strangers at the bus stop and ask them. Try to find a core set of commonalities and differences.

Many items on the lists will be qualified. For instance, "most books have at least one author," "many magazines are published monthly," and so on. That's fine. When solving real problems, we often map "maybe" and "sometimes" into "never" or "always," according to the specific needs of the problem at hand. Just remember that this is an OOP exercise, not a bookstore or library exercise.

Now categorize the commonalities and the differences. I'm not telling you how to categorize them. Just try to find a small set of categories that covers the diverse items on your lists. Some less useful categorizations are: group by number of words, group by last letter. **Try to find useful categories. Write them down.**

_____

_____

_____

_____

I came up with two broad categories: attributes and actions. *Attributes* describe the physical characteristics of books and magazines:

- Books and magazines have size (number of pages) and cost.

- Most books have an ISBN (international standard book number).

- Most magazines have an ISSN (international standard serial number).

- Magazines have a volume number and issue number.

Books and magazines have a title and publisher. Books have authors. Magazines typically don't. (Magazine articles have authors, but the magazine as a whole rarely lists an author.) *Actions* describe how a book or magazine acts or how you interact with them:

- You can read a book or magazine. A book or magazine can be open or closed.

- You can purchase a book or magazine.

- You can subscribe to a magazine.

The key distinction between attributes and actions is that attributes are specific to a single object. Actions are shared by all objects of a common class. Sometimes, actions are called *behaviors*. All dogs exhibit the behavior called panting; they all pant in pretty much the same manner and for the same reasons. All dogs have the attribute color, but one dog is golden, another dog is black, and the dog over there next to the tree, is white with black spots.

In programming terms, a *class* describes the behaviors or actions and the types of attributes for all the objects of that class. Each *object* has its own values for the attributes that the class enumerates. In C++ terms, member functions implement actions and provide access to attributes, and data members store attributes.

# Classification

Books and magazines don't do much on their own. Instead, their "actions" depend on how we interact with them. A bookstore interacts with books and magazines by selling, stocking, and advertising them. A library's actions include lending and returning. Other kinds of objects have actions they initiate on their own. For example, **what are some of the behaviors of a dog?**

_____
_____
_____
_____
_____

**What are the attributes of a dog?**

_____
_____
_____
_____
_____

What about a cat? **Do cats and dogs have significantly different behaviors? _____
Attributes? _____ Summarize the differences:**

_____
_____

I don't own dogs or cats, so my observations are limited. From where I sit, dogs and cats have many similar attributes and behaviors. I expect that many readers are much more astute observers than I, and can enumerate quite a few differences between the two.

Nonetheless, I maintain that once you consider the differences closely, you will see that many of them are not attributes or behaviors unique to one type of animal or the other, but are merely different values of a single attribute or different details of a single behavior. Cats may be more fastidious, but dogs and cats both exhibit grooming behavior. Dogs and cats come in different colors, but they both have colored furs (with rare exceptions).

In other words, when trying to enumerate the attributes and behaviors of various objects, your job can be made simpler by classifying similar objects together. For critters, biologists have already done the hard work for us, and they have devised a rich and detailed taxonomy of animals. Thus, a species (*catus* or *familiaris*) belongs to a genus (*Felis* or *Canis*), which is part of a family (Felidae or Canidae). These are grouped yet further into an order (Carnivora), a class (Mammalia), and so on, up to the animal (Metazoa) kingdom. (Taxonomists: please forgive my oversimplification.)

So what happens to attributes and behaviors as you ascend the taxonomy tree? **Which attributes and behaviors are the same as for the general class of mammals?**

_____
_____
_____

**All animals?**

_____

_____

_____

_____

As the classification became broader, the attributes and behavior also became more general. Among the attributes of dogs and cats are color of fur, length of tail, weight, and much more. Not all mammals have fur or tails, so you need broader attributes for the entire class. Weight still works, but instead of overall length, you may want to use length or height. Instead of color of fur, you need only generic coloring. For all animals, the attributes are quite broad: size, weight, single-cell vs. multi-cell, etc.

Behaviors are similar. You may list that cats purr, dogs pant, both animals can walk and run, and so on. All mammals eat and drink. Female mammals nurse their young. For all animals, you are left with a short, general list: eat and reproduce. It's hard to be more specific than that when you are trying to list the behaviors common to all animals, from amoebae to zebras.

A classification tree helps biologists understand the natural world. Class trees (or _class hierarchies_, as they are often called because big words make us feel important) help programmers model the natural world in software (or model the unnatural world, as so often happens in many of our projects). Instead of trying to name each level of the tree, programmers prefer a local, recursive view of any class hierarchy. Going up the tree, toward the root, each class has a _base_ class, also called a superclass or parent class. Thus _animal_ is a base class of _mammal_, which is a base class of _dog_. Going toward the leaves of the tree are _derived_ classes, also called subclasses or child classes. _Dog_ is a derived class of _mammal_. Figure 34-1 illustrates a class hierarchy. Arrows point from derived class to base class.

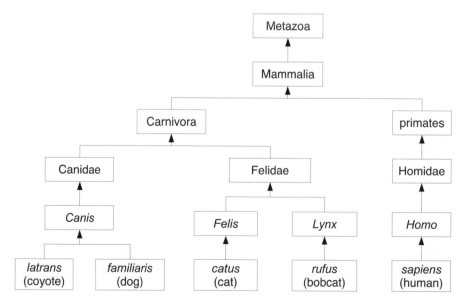

**Figure 34-1.** _A class diagram_

An *immediate* base class is one with no intervening base classes. For example, the immediate base class of *catus* is *Felis*, which has an immediate base class of Felidae, which has an immediate base class of Carnivora. Metazoa, Mammalia, Carnivora, Felidae, and *Felis* are all base classes of *catus*, but only *Felis* is its immediate base class.

# Inheritance

Just as a mammal has all the attributes and behaviors of an animal, and a dog has the attributes and behaviors of all mammals, in an OOP language, a derived class has all the behaviors and attributes of all of its base classes. The term most often used is *inheritance*: the derived class *inherits* the behaviors and attributes of its base class. This term is somewhat unfortunate because OOP inheritance is nothing like real-world inheritance. When a derived class inherits behaviors, the base class retains its behaviors. In the real world, classes don't inherit anything; objects do. In the real world, a person object inherits the value of certain attributes (cash, stock, real estate, etc.) from a deceased ancestor object. In the OOP world, a person class inherits behaviors from a base class by sharing the single copy of those behavior functions that are defined in the base class. A person class inherits the attributes of a base class, so objects of the derived class contain values for all the attributes defined in its class and in all of its base classes. In time, the inheritance terminology will become natural to you.

Because inheritance creates a tree structure, tree terminology also pervades discussion of inheritance. As is so common in programming, tree diagrams are drawn upside down, with the root at the top, and leaves at the bottom (as you saw in Figure 34-1). Some OOP languages (Java, Smalltalk, Delphi) have a single root, which is the ultimate base class for all classes. Others, such as C++, do not. Any class can be the root of its own inheritance tree.

So far, the main examples for inheritance involved some form of specialization. *Cat* is more specialized than *mammal*, which is more specialized than *animal*. The same is true in computer programming. For example, class frameworks for graphical user interfaces (GUIs) often use a hierarchy of specialized classes. Figure 34-2 shows a selection of some of the more important classes that make up wxWidgets, which is an open-source C++ framework that supports many platforms.

Even though C++ does not require a single root class, some frameworks do; wxWidgets is one that does require a single root class. Most wxWidgets classes derive from wxObject. Some objects are straightforward, such as wxPen and wxBrush. Interactive objects derive from wxEvtHandler (short for "event handler"). Thus, each step in the class tree introduces another degree of specialization.

Later in the book, you will see other uses for inheritance, but the most common and most important use is to create specialized derived classes from more general base classes.

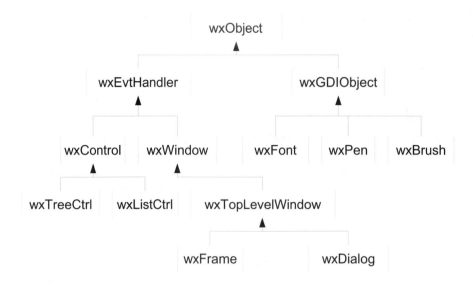

**Figure 34-2.** *Excerpt from the wxWidgets class hierarchy*

# Liskov's Substitution Principle

When a derived class specializes the behavior and attributes of a base class (which is the common case), any code that you write involving the base class should work equally well with an object of the derived class. In other words, the act of feeding a mammal is, in broad principles, the same regardless of the specific kind of animal.

Barbara Liskov and Jeannette Wing formalized this fundamental principle of object-oriented programming, which is often known today as the Substitution Principle or Liskov's Substitution Principle. Briefly, the Substitution Principle states that if you have base class *B* and derived class *D*, in any situation that calls for an object of type *B*, you can substitute an object of type *D* with no ill effects. In other words, if you need a mammal, any mammal, and someone hands you a dog, you should be able to use that dog. If someone hands you a cat, a horse, or a cow, you can use that animal. If someone hands you a fish, however, you are allowed to reject the fish in any manner that you deem suitable.

The Substitution Principle helps you write programs, but it also imposes a burden. It helps because it frees you to write code that depends on base class behavior without concerning yourself about any derived classes. For example, in a GUI framework, the base wxEvtHandler class might be able to recognize a mouse click and dispatch it to an event-handler. The click handler does not know or care whether the control is actually a wxListCtrl control, a wxTreeCtrl control, or a wxButton. All that matters is that wxEvtHandler accepts a click event, acquires the position, determines which mouse button was clicked, and so on, and then dispatches this event to the event handler.

The burden is on the authors of the wxButton, wxListCtrl, and wxTreeCtrl classes to ensure that their click behavior meets the requirements of the Substitution Principle. The easiest way to meet the requirements is to let the derived class inherit the behavior of the base class. Sometimes, however, the derived class has additional work to do. Instead of inheriting, it provides new behavior. In that case, the programmer must ensure that the behavior is a valid substitution for the base class behavior. The next few Explorations will show concrete examples of this abstract principle.

# Type Polymorphism

Before returning to C++-land, I want to present one more general principle. Suppose I hand you a box labeled "Mammal." Inside the box can be any mammal: a dog, a cat, a person, etc. You know the box cannot contain a bird, a fish, a rock, or a tree. It must contain a mammal. Programmers call the box *polymorphic*, from the Greek meaning many forms. The box can hold any one of many forms, that is, any one mammal, regardless of which form of mammal it is.

Although many programmers use the general term polymorphism, this specific kind of polymorphism is *type polymorphism*, also called *subtyping polymorphism*. That is, the type of a variable (or a box) determines which kinds of objects it can contain. A polymorphic variable (or box) can contain one of a number of different types of objects.

In particular, a variable with a base class type can refer to an object of the base class type or to an object of any type that is derived from that base class. According to the substitution principle, you can write code to use the base-class variable, calling any of the member functions of the base class, and that code will work regardless of the object's true, derived type.

Now that you have a fundamental understanding of the principles of OOP, it is time to see how these principles play out in C++.

■ ■ ■

# Inheritance

The previous Exploration introduced general OOP principles. Now it's time to see how to apply those principles to C++.

## Deriving a Class

Defining a derived class is just like defining any other class, except that you include a base class access level and name after a colon. See Listing 35-1 for an example of some simple classes to support a library. Every item in the library is a work of some kind: a book, a magazine, a movie, and so on. To keep things simple, the class work has only two derived classes, book and periodical.

**Listing 35-1.** *Defining a Derived Class*

```
class work
{
public:
  work() : id_(), title_() {}
  work(std::string const& id, std::string const& title) : id_(id), title_(title) {}
  std::string const& id()    const { return id_; }
  std::string const& title() const { return title_; }
private:
  std::string id_;
  std::string title_;
};

class book : public work
{
public:
  book() : author_(), pubyear_(0) {}
  book(std::string const& id, std::string const& title, std::string const& author,
      int pubyear)
  : work(id, title), author_(author), pubyear_(pubyear)
  {}
  std::string const& author() const { return author_; }
  int pubyear()              const { return pubyear_; }
```

```
private:
  std::string author_;
  int pubyear_; ///< year of publication
};

class periodical : public work
{
public:
  periodical() : volume_(0), number_(0), date_() {}
  periodical(std::string const& id, std::string const& title, int volume,
              int number,
  std::string const& date)
    : work(id, title), volume_(volume), number_(number), date_(date)
  {}
  int volume()              const { return volume_; }
  int number()              const { return number_; }
  std::string const& date() const { return date_; }
private:
  int volume_;      ///< volume number
  int number_;      ///< issue number
  std::string date_; ///< publication date
};
```

When you define a class using the struct keyword, the default access level is public; for the class keyword, the default is private. These keywords also affect derived classes. Except in rare circumstances, public is the right choice here, which is how I wrote the classes in Listing 35-1.

Also in Listing 35-1, notice there is something new about the initializer lists. A derived class can (and should) initialize its base class by listing the base class name and any arguments you want to pass to the base class's constructor. You can call any constructor by passing the right arguments. If you omit the base class from the initializer list, the compiler uses the base class's default constructor.

**What do you think happens if the base class does not have a default constructor?**

_____

Try it. Comment out work's default constructor and try to compile the code for Listing 35-1. (Add a trivial main() to ensure that you write a complete program, and be certain to #include all necessary headers.) **What happens?**

_____

That's right; the compiler complains. The exact error message or messages you receive vary from compiler to compiler. I get something like the following:

```
$ g++ -ansi -pedantic list3501err.cpp
list3501err.cpp: In constructor 'book::book()':
list3501err.cpp:22: error: no matching function for call to 'work::work()'
```

```
list3501err.cpp:11: note: candidates are: work::work(const std::string&,➥
   const std::string&)
list3501err.cpp:8: note:                    work::work(const work&)
list3501err.cpp: In constructor 'periodical::periodical()':
list3501err.cpp:36: error: no matching function for call to 'work::work()'
list3501err.cpp:11: note: candidates are: work::work(const std::string&,➥
   const std::string&)
list3501err.cpp:8: note:                    work::work(const work&)
```

Base classes are always initialized before members, starting with the root of the class tree. You can see this for yourself by writing classes that print messages from their constructors, as demonstrated in Listing 35-2.

**Listing 35-2.** *Printing Messages from Constructors to Illustrate Order of Construction*

```cpp
#include <iostream>
#include <ostream>

class base
{
public:
  base() { std::cout << "base::base()\n"; }
};

class middle : public base
{
public:
  middle() { std::cout << "middle::middle()\n"; }
};

class derived : public middle
{
public:
  derived() { std::cout << "derived::derived()\n"; }
};

int main()
{
  derived d;
}
```

**What output do you expect from the program in Listing 35-2?**

_____

_____

_____

Try it. **What output did you actually get?**

_____

_____

_____

**Were you correct?** _____ In the interest of being thorough, I receive the following:

```
base::base()
middle::middle()
derived::derived()
```

Remember that if you omit the base class from the initializers, or you omit the initializer list entirely, the base class's default constructor is called. Listing 35-2 contains only default constructors, so what happens is the constructor for derived first invokes the default constructor for middle. The constructor for middle invokes the default constructor for base first, and the constructor for base has nothing to do except execute its function body. Then it returns, and the constructor body for middle executes and returns, finally letting derived run its function body.

# Destructors

When an object is destroyed—perhaps because the function in which it is defined ends and returns—sometimes you need to do some cleanup. A class has another special member function that performs cleanup when an object is destroyed. This special member function is called a *destructor*.

Like constructors, destructors do not have return values. A destructor name is the class name preceded by a tilde (~). Listing 35-3 adds destructors to the example classes from Listing 35-2.

**Listing 35-3.** *Order of Calling Destructors*

```cpp
#include <iostream>
#include <ostream>

class base
{
public:
  base()  { std::cout << "base::base()\n"; }
  ~base() { std::cout << "base::~base()\n"; }
};

class middle : public base
{
public:
  middle()  { std::cout << "middle::middle()\n"; }
```

```
  ~middle() { std::cout << "middle::~middle()\n"; }
};

class derived : public middle
{
public:
  derived()  { std::cout << "derived::derived()\n"; }
  ~derived() { std::cout << "derived::~derived()\n"; }
};

int main()
{
  derived d;
}
```

**What output do you expect from the program in Listing 35-3?**

_____

_____

_____

_____

_____

_____

Try it. **What do you actually get?**

_____

_____

_____

_____

_____

**Were you correct?** _____ When a function returns, it destroys all local objects in the reverse order of construction. When a destructor runs, it destroys the most-derived class first by running the destructor's function body. It then invokes the immediate base class destructor. Hence, the destructors run in opposite order of construction in this example:

```
base::base()
middle::middle()
derived::derived()
derived::~derived()
middle::~middle()
base::~base()
```

If you don't write a destructor, the compiler writes a trivial one for you. After every destructor body finishes, the compiler arranges to call the destructor for every data member then execute the destructor for the base classes, starting with the most-derived. For simple classes in these examples, the compiler's destructors work just fine. Later, you will find more interesting uses for destructors. For now, the main purpose is just to visualize the life cycle of an object.

Read Listing 35-4 carefully.

**Listing 35-4.** *Constructors and Destructors*

```cpp
#include <iostream>
#include <ostream>
#include <vector>

class base
{
public:
  base(int value) : value_(value) { std::cout << "base(" << value << ")\n"; }
  base() : value_(0) { std::cout << "base()\n"; }
  base(base const& copy)
   : value_(copy.value_)
   { std::cout << "copy base(" << value_ << ")\n"; }

  ~base() { std::cout << "~base(" << value_ << ")\n"; }
  int value() const { return value_; }
  base& operator++()
  {
    ++value_;
    return *this;
  }
private:
  int value_;
};

class derived : public base
{
public:
  derived(int value): base(value) { std::cout << "derived(" << value << ")\n"; }
  derived() : base() { std::cout << "derived()\n"; }
  derived(derived const& copy)
   : base(copy)
   { std::cout << "copy derived(" << value() << "\n"; }
  ~derived() { std::cout << "~derived(" << value() << ")\n"; }
};

derived make_derived()
{
  return derived(42);
}
```

```
base increment(base b)
{
  ++b;
  return b;
}

void increment_reference(base& b)
{
  ++b;
}

int main()
{
  derived d(make_derived());
  base b(increment(d));
  increment_reference(d);
  increment_reference(b);
  derived a(d.value() + b.value());
}
```

**Fill in the left-hand column of Table 35-1 with the output you expect from the program.**

**Table 35-1.** *Expected and Actual Results of Running the Program in Listing 35-4*

| Expected Output | Actual Output |
| --- | --- |
|  |  |
|  |  |
|  |  |
|  |  |
|  |  |
|  |  |
|  |  |
|  |  |
|  |  |
|  |  |
|  |  |
|  |  |
|  |  |

Try it. Fill in the right-hand column of Table 35-1 with the actual output and compare the two columns. **Did you get everything correct?** _____

Below is the output generated on my system, along with some commentary. Remember that compilers have some leeway in optimizing away extra calls to the copy constructor. You may get one or two extra copy calls in the mix.

```
base(42)              // inside make_derived()
derived(42)           // finish constructing in make_derived()
copy base(42)         // copy to b in call to increment()
copy base(43)         // copy return value from increment to b in main
~base(43)             // destroy temporary return value
base(87)              // construct a in main
derived(87)           // construct a in main
~derived(87)          // end of main: destroy a
~base(87)             // destroy a
~base(44)             // destroy b
~derived(43)          // destroy d
~base(43)             // finish destroying d
```

Note how pass-by-reference (`increment_reference`) does not invoke any constructors because no objects are being constructed. Instead, references are passed to the function, and the referenced object is incremented.

By the way, I have not yet shown you how to overload the increment operator, but you probably guessed that's how it works (in class `base`). Decrement is similar.

# Access Level

At the start of this Exploration, I told you to use `public` before the base class name, but never explained why. Now is the time to fill you in on the details.

Access levels affect inheritance the same way they affect members. *Public inheritance* occurs when you use the `struct` keyword to define a class or the `public` keyword before the base class name. Public inheritance means the derived class inherits every member of the base class at the same access level that the members have in the base class. Except in rare circumstances, this is exactly what you want. Remember that the convention is that `struct` is reserved for C compatibility and other POD data types. Inheritance is not POD. Thus, you tend to see `class` definitions with explicit public inheritance. It seems more verbose than using `struct` with `private` access specifiers where necessary, but the `struct`/`class` distinction between POD and non-POD serves a useful purpose, even if the compiler doesn't care.

*Private inheritance* occurs when you use the `private` keyword, and is the default when you define a class using the `class` keyword. Private inheritance keeps every member of the base class private and inaccessible to users of the derived class. The compiler still calls the base class constructor and destructor when necessary, and the derived class still inherits all the members of the base class. The derived class can call any of the base class's public member functions, but no one else can call them through the derived class. It's as though the derived class redeclares all inherited members as `private`. I recommend that you not use private inheritance. If the compiler complains about inaccessible members, most likely you forgot to include a `public` keyword in the class definition. Try compiling Listing 35-5 to see what I mean.

**Listing 35-5.** *Accidentally Inheriting Privately*

```
class base
{
public:
  base(int v) : value_(v) {}
  int value() const { return value_; }
private:
  int value_;
};

class derived : base
{
public:
  derived() : base(42) {}
};

int main()
{
  base b(42);
  int x(b.value());
  derived d;
  int y(d.value());
}
```

When you read C++ code, you may see another access level, `protected`. I'll cover that one later. Two access levels are more than enough to begin with.

# Programming Style

When in doubt, make data members and member functions private unless and until you know you need to make a member public. Once a member is part of the public interface, anyone using your class is free to use that member, and you have one more code dependency. Changing a public member means finding and fixing all those dependencies. Keep the public interface as small as possible. If you need to add members later, you can, but it's much harder to remove a member, or change it from public to private. Anytime you need to add members to support the public interface, make the supporting functions and data members private.

Use public inheritance, not private inheritance. Remember that inherited members also becomes part of the derived class's public interface. If you change which class is the base class, you may need to write additional members in the derived class, to make up for members that were in the original base class but are missing from the new base class. The next Exploration continues the discussion of how derived classes work with base classes to provide important functionality.

# Virtual Functions

**D**eriving classes is fun, but there's not a lot you can do with them—at least, not yet. The next step is to see how C++ implements type polymorphism, and this Exploration starts you on that journey.

## Type Polymorphism

Recall from Exploration 34 that type polymorphism is the ability for a variable of type B to take the "form" of any class derived from B. The obvious question is: "How?" The key in C++ is to declare a function in a base class with a magic keyword, and also implement the function in a derived class. The magic keyword tells the compiler that you want to invoke type polymorphism. The compiler implements the polymorphism magic. Simply initialize a variable of type reference-to-base class with an object of derived-class type. When you call the polymorphic function for the object, the compiled code checks the object's true type, and calls the derived-class implementation of the function. The magic word to turn a function into a polymorphic function is `virtual`.

For example, suppose you want to be able to print any kind of work in the library (see Listing 35-1) using standard (more or less) bibliographical format. For books, I use the format:

*author, title, year.*

For periodicals, I use:

*title, volume(number), date.*

Add a `print` member function to each class to print this information. Because this function has different behavior in each derived class, the function is polymorphic, so use the `virtual` keyword before each declaration of `print`, as shown in Listing 36-1.

**Listing 36-1.** *Adding a Polymorphic print Function to Every Class Derived from work*

```
class work
{
public:
  work() : id_(), title_() {}
  work(std::string const& id, std::string const& title) : id_(id), title_(title) {}
  virtual ~work() {}
  std::string const& id()    const { return id_; }
```

```cpp
  std::string const& title() const { return title_; }
  virtual void print(std::ostream& out) const {}
private:
  std::string id_;
  std::string title_;
};

class book : public work
{
public:
  book() : author_(), pubyear_(0) {}
  book(std::string const& id, std::string const& title, std::string const& author,
       int pubyear)
  : work(id, title), author_(author), pubyear_(pubyear)
  {}
  std::string const& author() const { return author_; }
  int pubyear()               const { return pubyear_; }
  virtual void print(std::ostream& out) const
  {
    out << author() << ", " << title() << ", " << pubyear() << ".";
  }
private:
  std::string author_;
  int pubyear_; ///< year of publication
};

class periodical : public work
{
public:
  periodical() : volume_(0), number_(0), date_() {}
  periodical(std::string const& id, std::string const& title, int volume,
             int number,
  std::string const& date)
  : work(id, title), volume_(volume), number_(number), date_(date)
  {}
  int volume()               const { return volume_; }
  int number()               const { return number_; }
  std::string const& date() const { return date_; }
  virtual void print(std::ostream& out) const
  {
    out << title() << ", " << volume() << '(' << number() << "), " <<
           date() << ".";
  }
private:
  int volume_;        ///< volume number
  int number_;        ///< issue number
  std::string date_; ///< publication date
};
```

A program that has a reference to a work can call the print member function to print that work, and because print is polymorphic, or virtual, the C++ environment performs its magic to ensure that the correct print is called, depending on whether the work object is actually a book or a periodical. To see this demonstrated, read the program in Listing 36-2.

**Listing 36-2.** *Calling the print Function*

```cpp
#include <iostream>
#include <ostream>
#include <string>

// All of Listing 36-1 belongs here
... omitted for brevity ...

void showoff(work const& w)
{
  w.print(std::cout);
  std::cout << '\n';
}

int main()
{
  book sc("1", "The Sun Also Crashes", "Ernest Lemmingway", 2000);
  book ecpp("2", "Exploring C++", "Ray Lischner", 2008);
  periodical pop("3", "Popular C++", 13, 42, "January 1, 2000");
  periodical today("4", "C++ Today", 1, 1, "January 13, 1984");

  showoff(sc);
  showoff(ecpp);
  showoff(pop);
  showoff(today);
}
```

**What output do you expect?**

_____

_____

_____

_____

Try it. **What output do you actually get?**

_____

_____

_____

_____

The showoff function does not need to know about the book or periodical classes. As far as it is concerned, w is a reference to a work object. The only member functions you can call are those declared in the work class. Nonetheless, when showoff calls print, it will invoke book's print or periodical's print if the object's true type is book or periodical.

**Write an output operator (operator<<) that prints a work object by calling its print member function.** Compare your solution with my solution, as shown in Listing 36-3.

**Listing 36-3.** *Output Operator for Class work*

```
std::ostream& operator<<(std::ostream& out, work const& w)
{
  w.print(out);
  return out;
}
```

Writing the output operator is perfectly normal. Just be certain you declare w as a reference. Polymorphic magic does not occur with ordinary objects, only references. With this operator, you can write any work-derived object to an output stream, and it will print using its print function.

# Virtual Functions

A polymorphic function is called a *virtual function* in C++ due to the virtual keyword. Once a function is defined as virtual, it remains so in every derived class. You don't need the virtual keyword in the derived classes, but I like to include it as an aid and reminder to the human reader trying to distinguish virtual functions. In every derived class, the virtual function must have the same name, the same return type, and the same number and type of parameters (but the parameters can have different names).

A derived class is not required to implement a virtual function. If it doesn't, it inherits the base class function the same way it does for a non-virtual function. When a derived class implements a virtual function, it is said to *override* the function because the derived class's behavior overrides the behavior that would have been inherited from the base class.

**Add a class, movie, to the library classes.** The movie class represents a movie or film recording on tape or disc. Like book and periodical, the movie class derives from work. For the sake of simplicity, define a movie as having an integer running time (in minutes) in addition to the members it inherits from work. Do not override print yet. Compare your class to Listing 36-4.

**Listing 36-4.** *Adding a Class movie*

```
class movie : public work
{
public:
  movie() : runtime_(0) {}
  movie(std::string const& id, std::string const& title, int runtime)
  : work(id, title), runtime_(runtime)
  {}
  int runtime() const { return runtime_; }
```

```
private:
  int runtime_; ///< running length in minutes
};
```

**Now modify the test program from Listing 36-2 to create and print a movie object.** If you want, you can take advantage of the new output operator instead of calling showoff. Compare your program with Listing 36-5.

**Listing 36-5.** *Using the New movie Class*

```
#include <iostream>
#include <ostream>
#include <string>

// All of Listing 36-1 belongs here
// All of Listing 36-3 belongs here
// All of Listing 36-4 belongs here
... omitted for brevity ...

int main()
{
  book sc("1", "The Sun Also Crashes", "Ernest Lemmingway", 2000);
  book ecpp("2", "Exploring C++", "Ray Lischner", 2006);
  periodical pop("3", "Popular C++", 13, 42, "January 1, 2000");
  periodical today("4", "C++ Today", 1, 1, "January 13, 1984");
  movie tr("5", "Lord of the Token Ring", 314);

  std::cout << sc << '\n';
  std::cout << ecpp << '\n';
  std::cout << pop << '\n';
  std::cout << today << '\n';
  std::cout << tr << '\n';
}
```

**What do you expect as the last line of output?**

Try it. **What do you get?**

Because movie does not override print, it inherits the implementation from the base class, work. The definition of print in the work class does nothing, so printing the tr object prints nothing.

**Fix the problem by adding print to the movie class.** Now your movie class should look something like Listing 36-6.

**Listing 36-6.** *Adding a print Member Function to the movie Class*

```
class movie : public work
{
public:
  movie() : runtime_(0) {}
  movie(std::string const& id, std::string const& title, int runtime)
  : work(id, title), runtime_(runtime)
  {}
  int runtime() const { return runtime_; }
  virtual void print(std::ostream& out) const
  {
    out << title() << " (" << runtime() << " min)";
  }
private:
  int runtime_; ///< running length in minutes
};
```

Convince yourself that the virtual keyword is optional in the derived class. Modify the movie class to remove the virtual keyword from the print function. **Does the program still work the way you expect it to?** _____ The key is that the base class must declare the function and must use the virtual keyword. The compiler ensures that all calls to a virtual function via a reference are polymorphic calls. However, if you call the function from an ordinary object, not from a reference, the call is not polymorphic, and the compiler ignores the virtual keyword, as you will see in the next section.

# References and Slices

The showoff function in Listing 36-2 and the output operator in Listing 36-3 declare their parameter as a reference to const work. **What do you expect to happen if you were to change them to pass-by-value?**

_____

_____

_____

Try it. Delete the ampersand in the declaration of the output operator, as shown in the following:

```
std::ostream& operator<<(std::ostream& out, work w)
{
  w.print(out);
  return out;
}
```

Run the test program from Listing 36-5. What is the actual output?

_____

_____

_____

_____

_____

**Explain what happened.**

_____

_____

_____

When you pass an argument by value, or assign a derived-class object to a base-class variable, you lose polymorphism. For instance, instead of a movie, the result is an honest-to-goodness, genuine, no-artificial-ingredients, work—with no memory of movie-ness whatsoever. Thus, the output operator ends up calling work's version of print every time the output operator calls it. That's why the program's output is a bunch of empty lines. When you pass a book object to the output operator, not only do you lose polymorphism, but you also lose all sense of book-ness. In particular, you lose the author_ and pubyear_ data members. The data members that a derived class adds are *sliced* away when the object is copied to a base class variable. Another way to look at it is this: because the derived-class members are sliced away, what is left is only a work object, so you cannot have polymorphism. The same thing happens with assignment.

```
work w;
book nuts("7", "C++ in a Nutshell", "Ray Lischner", 2003);
w = nuts; // slices away the author_ and pubyear_; copies only id_ and title_
```

Slicing is easy to avoid when writing functions (pass all arguments by reference), but harder to cope with for assignment. The techniques you need to manage assignment come much later in this book; for now, I will focus on writing polymorphic functions.

# Pure Virtual Functions

The class work defines the print function, but the function doesn't do anything useful. In order to be useful, every derived class must override print. The author of a base class, such as work, can ensure that every derived class properly overrides a virtual function by omitting the body of the function and substituting the tokens, = 0, instead. These tokens mark the function as a *pure virtual function*, which means the function has no implementation to inherit, and derived classes must override the function.

**Modify the work class to make print a pure virtual function. Then delete the book class's print function, just to see what happens. What does happen?**

_____

_____

The compiler enforces the rules for pure virtual functions. A class that has at least one pure virtual function is said to be *abstract*. You cannot define an object of abstract type. **Fix the program.** The new work class should look something like Listing 36-7.

**Listing 36-7.** *Defining work As an Abstract Class*

```
class work
{
public:
  work() : id_(), title_() {}
  work(std::string const& id, std::string const& title) : id_(id), title_(title) {}
  virtual ~work() {}
  std::string const& id()    const { return id_; }
  std::string const& title() const { return title_; }
  virtual void print(std::ostream& out) const = 0;
private:
  std::string id_;
  std::string title_;
};
```

# Virtual Destructors

Although most classes you are writing at this time do not need destructors, I want to mention an important implementation rule. Any class that has virtual functions must declare its destructor to be virtual, too. This rule is a programming guideline, not a semantic requirement, so the compiler will not help you by issuing a message when you break it (although some compilers may issue a warning). Instead, you need to enforce this rule yourself through discipline.

I will repeat the rule when you begin to write classes that require destructors. If you try any experiments on your own, please be mindful of this rule, or else your programs could be subject to subtle problems—or not-so-subtle crashes.

The next Exploration continues the discussion of classes and their relationship in the C++ type system.

■■■

# Classes and Types

**O**ne of the main design goals for C++ was to give the programmer the ability to define custom types that look and act nearly identically to the built-in types. The combination of classes and overloaded operators gives you that power. This Exploration takes a closer look at the type system and how your classes can best fit into the C++ world.

## Classes vs. typedefs

Suppose you are writing a function to compute body-mass index (BMI) from an integer height in centimeters and an integer weight in kilograms. You have no difficulty writing such a function (which you can copy from your work in Explorations 26 and 32). For added clarity, you decide to add typedefs for height and weight, which allows the programmer to define variables for storing and manipulating these values with extra clarity to the human reader. Listing 37-1 shows a simple use of the compute_bmi() function and the associated typedefs.

**Listing 37-1.** *Computing BMI*

```
#include <iostream>
#include <ostream>

typedef int height;
typedef int weight;
typedef int bmi;

bmi compute_bmi(height h, weight w)
{
  return w * 10000 / (h * h);
}

int main()
{
  std::cout << "Height in centimeters: ";
  height h;
  std::cin >> h;

  std::cout << "Weight in kilograms: ";
```

```
    weight w;
    std::cin >> w;

    std::cout << "Body-mass index = " << compute_bmi(w, h) << '\n';
}
```

Test the program. **What's wrong?**

_____

_____

   If you haven't spotted it yet, take a closer look at the call to `compute_bmi`, on the last line of code in `main()`. Compare the arguments with the parameters in the function definition. Now do you see the problem?

   In spite of the extra clarity that the `height` and `weight` typedefs offer, I still made a fundamental mistake and reversed the order of the arguments. In this case, the error is easy to spot because the program is small. Also, the program's output is so obviously wrong that testing quickly reveals the problem. Don't relax too much, though; not all mistakes are so obvious.

   The problem here is that a `typedef` does not define a new type, but instead creates an alias for an existing type. The original type and its `typedef` alias are completely interchangeable. Thus, a `height` is the same as an `int`, is the same as a `weight`. Because the programmer is able to mix up `height` and `weight`, the typedefs don't actually help much.

   More useful would be to create distinct types called `height` and `weight`. As distinct types, you would not be able to mix them up, and you would have full control over the operations that you allow. For example, dividing two `weight`s should yield a plain, unit-less `int`. Adding a `height` to a `weight` should result in an error message from the compiler. Listing 37-2 shows simple `height` and `weight` classes that impose these restrictions.

**Listing 37-2.** *Defining Classes for height and weight*

```
#include <iostream>
#include <ostream>

/// Height in centimeters
class height
{
public:
  height(int h) : value_(h) {}
  int value() const { return value_; }
private:
  int value_;
};

/// Weight in kilograms
class weight
{
public:
  weight(int w) : value_(w) {}
```

```
  int value() const { return value_; }
private:
  int value_;
};

/// Body-mass index
class bmi
{
public:
  bmi() : value_(0) {}
  bmi(height h, weight w) : value_(w.value() * 10000 / (h.value()*h.value())) {}
  int value() const { return value_; }
private:
  int value_;
};
height operator+(height a, height b)
{
  return height(a.value() + b.value());
}
int operator/(height a, height b)
{
  return a.value() / b.value();
}
std::istream& operator>>(std::istream& in, height& h)
{
  int tmp;
  if (in >> tmp)
    h = tmp;
  return in;
}
std::ostream& operator<<(std::ostream& out, bmi i)
{
  out << i.value();
  return out;
}
// Implement other operators similarly, but implement only
// the ones that make sense.
weight operator-(weight a, weight b)
{
  return weight(a.value() - b.value());
}
... omitted for brevity ...

int main()
{
  std::cout << "Height in centimeters: ";
  height h(0);
  std::cin >> h;
```

```
    std::cout << "Weight in kilograms: ";
    weight w(0);
    std::cin >> w;

    std::cout << "Body-mass index = " << bmi(h, w) << '\n';
}
```

The new classes prevent mistakes such as that in Listing 37-1, but at the expense of more code. For instance, you need to write suitable I/O operators. You also need to decide which arithmetic operators to implement. And don't forget the comparison operators. Most of these functions are trivial to write, but you can't neglect them. In many applications, however, the work will pay off many times over by removing potential sources of error.

I'm not suggesting that you do away with unadorned integers and other built-in types, and replace them with clumsy wrapper classes. In fact, I agree with you (don't ask how I know what you're thinking) that the BMI example is rather artificial. If I were writing a real, honest-to-goodness program for computing and managing BMIs, I would use plain int variables, and rely on careful coding and proofreading to prevent and detect errors. I use wrapper classes, such as height and weight, when they add some primary value. For example, I might use them if I were to add some error checking to them, impose constraints on the domain of values they can represent, or otherwise help me do my job as a programmer. Nonetheless, it's best to start simple, and add complexity slowly and carefully. The next section explains in greater detail what behavior you must implement to make a useful and meaningful custom class.

# Value Types

The height and weight types are examples of *value types*—that is, types that behave as ordinary values. Contrast them with the I/O stream types, which behave very differently. For instance, you cannot copy or assign streams; you must pass them by reference to functions. Nor can you compare streams, or perform arithmetic on them. Value types, by design, behave similarly to the built-in types, such as int and float. One of the important characteristics of value types is that you can store them in containers, such as vector and map. This section explains the general requirements for value types.

The basic guideline is to make sure your type behaves "like an int." When it comes to copying, comparing, and performing arithmetic, avoid surprises by making your custom type look, act, and work as much like the built-in types as possible.

## Copying

Copying an int yields a new int that is indistinguishable from the original. Your custom type should behave the same way.

Consider the example of string. Many implementations of string are possible. Some of these use copy-on-write to optimize frequent copying and assignment. In a copy-on-write implementation, the actual string contents are kept separately from the string object; copies of the string object do not copy the contents until and unless a copy is needed, which happens when the string contents must be modified. Many uses of strings are read-only, so copy-on-write avoids unnecessary copies of the contents, even when the string objects themselves are copied frequently.

Other implementations optimize for small strings by using the string object to store their contents, but storing large strings separately. Copying small strings is fast, but copying large strings is slower. Most programs use only small strings. In spite of these differences in implementation, when you copy a string (such as passing a string by value to a function), the copy and the original are indistinguishable: just like an int.

Usually, the automatic copy constructor does what you want, and you don't need to write any code. Nonetheless, you need to think about copying, and assure yourself that the compiler's automatic (also called *implicit*) copy constructor does exactly what you want.

## Assigning

Assigning objects is similar to copying them. After an assignment, the target and source must contain identical values. The key difference between assignment and copying is that copying starts with a blank slate: a newly constructed object. Assignment begins with an existing object, and you may need to clean up the old value before you can assign the new value. Simple types such as height have nothing to clean up, but later in this book, you will learn how to implement more complicated types, such as string, which require careful cleanup.

Most simple types work just fine with the compiler's implicit assignment operator, and you don't need to write your own. Nonetheless, you need to consider the possibility, and make sure the implicit assignment operator is exactly what you want.

## Comparing

I defined copying and assignment in a way that requires meaningful comparison. If you can't determine whether two objects are equal, you can't verify whether you copied or assigned them correctly. C++ has several different ways to check whether two objects are the same.

- The first and most obvious way is to compare objects with the == operator. Value types should overload this operator. Make sure the operator is transitive—that is, if a == b and b == c, then a == c. Make sure the operator is commutative, that is, if a == b, then b == a. Finally, the operator should be reflexive: a == a.

- Standard algorithms such as find compare items by one of two methods: with operator== or with a caller-supplied predicate. Sometimes, you may want to compare objects with a custom predicate, for example, a person class might have operator== that compares every data member (name, address, etc.), but you want to search a container of person objects by checking only last names, which you do by writing your own comparison function. The custom predicate must obey the same transitive and commutative restrictions as the == operator. If you are using the predicate with a specific algorithm, that algorithm calls the predicate in a particular way, so you know the order of the arguments. You don't need to make your predicate reflexive, and in some cases, you wouldn't want to.

- Containers such as map store their elements in sorted order. Some standard algorithms, such as binary_search, require their input range to be in sorted order. The ordered containers and algorithms use the same conventions. By default, they use the < operator, but you can also supply your own comparison predicate. These containers and algorithms never use the == operator to determine whether two objects are the same. Instead, they check for equivalence—that is, a is equivalent to b if a < b is false and b < a is false.

  If your value type can be ordered, you should overload the < operator. Ensure that the operator is transitive (if a < b and b < c, then a < c). Also, the ordering must be strict: a < a is always false.

- Containers and algorithms that check for equivalence also take a custom predicate instead of the < operator. The custom predicate must obey the same transitive and strictness restrictions as the < operator.

Not all types are comparable with a less-than relationship. If your type cannot be ordered, do not implement the < operator, but you must also understand that you will not be able to store objects of that type in a map, or use any of the binary search algorithms. Sometimes, you may want to impose an artificial order, just to permit these uses. For example, a color type may represent colors such as red, green, or yellow. Although nothing about red or green inherently defines one as being "less than" another, you may want to define an arbitrary order just so you can use these values as keys in a map. One immediate suggestion is to write a comparison function that compares colors as integers, using the < operator.

On the other hand, if you have a value that should be compared (such as rational), you should implement operator== and operator<. You can then implement all other comparison operators in terms of these two. (See Exploration 30 for an example of how the rational class does this.)

**Implement a color class that describes a color as three components**: red, green, and blue, which are integers in the range 0 to 255. Define comparison functions, order_color, to permit storing colors as map keys. **For extra credit, devise a suitable I/O format and overload the I/O operators, too.** Don't worry about error-handling yet—for instance, what if the user tries to set red to 1000, blue to 2000, and green to 3000. You'll get to that soon enough.

Compare your solution with mine, which is presented in Listing 37-3.

**Listing 37-3.** *The* color *Class*

```
class color
{
public:
  color() : red_(0), green_(0), blue_(0) {}
  color(int r, int g, int b) : red_(r), green_(g), blue_(b) {}
  int red() const { return red_; }
  int green() const { return green_; }
  int blue() const { return blue_; }
  /// Because red(), green(), and blue() are supposed to be in the range [0,255],
  /// it should be possible to add them together in a single long integer.
  /// TODO: handle errors if any color component is out of range
  long int combined() const { return ((red() * 256L + green()) * 256) + blue(); }
```

```
private:
  int red_, green_, blue_;
};

inline bool operator==(color const& a, color const& b)
{
  return a.combined() == b.combined();
}

inline bool operator!=(color const& a, color const& b)
{
  return not (a == b);
}

inline bool order_color(color const& a, color const& b)
{
  return a.combined() < b.combined();
}

/// Write a color in HTML format: #RRGGBB.
std::ostream& operator<<(std::ostream& out, color const& c)
{
  std::ostringstream tmp;
  // The hex manipulator tells a stream to write or read in hexadecimal (base 16).
  tmp << '#' << std::hex << std::setw(6) << std::setfill('0') << c.combined();
  out << tmp.str();
  return out;
}

class ioflags
{
public:
  /// Save the formatting flags from @p stream.
  ioflags(std::basic_ios<char>& stream) : stream_(stream), flags_(stream.flags()) {}
  /// Restore the formatting flags.
  ~ioflags() { stream_.flags(flags_); }
private:
  std::basic_ios<char>& stream_;
  std::ios_base::fmtflags flags_;
};

std::istream& operator>>(std::istream& in, color& c)
{
  ioflags flags(in);

  char hash;
  if (not (in >> hash))
```

```
    return in;
  if (hash != '#')
  {
    // malformed color: no leading # character
    in.unget();                    // return the character to the input stream
    in.setstate(in.failbit);    // set the failure state
    return in;
  }
  // Read the color number, which is hexadecimal: RRGGBB.
  int combined;
  in >> std::hex >> std::noskipws;
  if (not (in >> combined))
    return in;
  // Extract the R, G, and B bytes.
  int red, green, blue;
  blue = combined % 256;
  combined = combined / 256;
  green = combined % 256;
  combined = combined / 256;
  red = combined % 256;

  // Assign to c only after successfully reading all the color components.
  c = color(red, green, blue);

  return in;
}
```

Listing 37-3 introduced a new trick with the ioflags class. The next section explains all.

# Resource Acquisition Is Initialization

A programming idiom that goes by the unwieldy name of Resource Acquisition Is Initialization (RAII) takes advantage of constructors, destructors, and automatic destruction of objects when a function returns. Briefly, the RAII idiom means a constructor acquires a resource: it opens a file, connects to a network, or even just copies some flags from an I/O stream. The acquisition is part of the object's initialization. The destructor releases the resource: closes the file, disconnects from the network, or restores any modified flags in the I/O stream.

To use an RAII class, all you need to do is define an object of that type. That's all. The compiler takes care of the rest. The RAII class's constructor takes whatever arguments it needs to acquire its resources. When the surrounding function returns, the RAII object is automatically destroyed, thereby releasing the resources. It's that simple.

You don't even need to wait until the function returns. Define an RAII object in a compound statement, and the object is destroyed when the statement finishes and control leaves the compound statement.

The ioflags class in Listing 37-3 is an example of using RAII. It throws some new items at you; let's take them one at a time:

- The `std::basic_ios<char>` class is the base class for all I/O stream classes, such as `istream` and `ostream`. Thus, `ioflags` works the same with input and output streams.

- The `std::ios_base::fmtflags` type is the type for all the formatting flags.

- The `flags()` member function with no arguments returns all the current formatting flags.

- The `flags()` member function with one argument sets all the flags to its argument.

The way to use `ioflags` is simply to define a variable of type `ioflags` in a function or compound statement, passing a stream object as the sole argument to the constructor. The function can change any of the stream's flags. In this case, the input operator sets the input radix (or base) to hexadecimal with the `std::hex` manipulator. The input radix is stored with the formatting flags. The operator also turns off the `skipws` flag. By default, this flag is enabled, which instructs the standard input operators to skip initial white space. By turning this flag off, the input operator does not permit any white space between the pound sign (#) and the color value.

When the input function returns, the `ioflags` object is destroyed, and its destructor restores the original formatting flags. Without the magic of RAII, the `operator>>` function would need to restore the flags manually at all four return points, which is burdensome and prone to error.

RAII is a common programming idiom in C++. The more you learn about C++, the more you will come to appreciate its beauty and simplicity.

As you can see, our examples are becoming more complicated, and it's becoming harder and harder for me to fit entire examples in a single code listing. Your next task is to understand how to separate your code into multiple files, which makes my job and yours much easier. The first step for this new task is to take a closer look at declarations, definitions, and the distinctions between them.

■ ■ ■

# Declarations and Definitions

**E**xploration 19 introduced the distinction between declarations and definitions; this is a good time to remind you of the difference and to explore declarations and definitions of classes and their members.

## Declaration vs. Definition

Recall that a *declaration* furnishes the compiler with the basic information it needs so you can use a name in a program. In particular, a function declaration tells the compiler about the function's name, return type, and parameter types.

A *definition* is a particular kind of declaration that also provides the full implementation details for an entity. For example, a function definition includes all the information of a function declaration, plus the function body. Classes, however, add another layer of complexity because you can declare or define the class's members independently of the class definition itself. A class definition must declare all of its members. Sometimes, you can also define a member function as part of a class definition (which is the style I've been using until now), but most programmers prefer to declare member functions inside the class, and define the member functions separately, outside of the class definition.

As with any function declaration, a member function declaration includes the return type (possibly with a `virtual` specifier), the function name, the function parameters, and an optional `const` modifier. If the function is a pure virtual function, you must include the `= 0` token marks as part of the function declaration, and you don't define the function.

The function definition is like any other function definition, with a few exceptions. The definition must follow the declaration—that is, the member function definition must come later in the source file than the class definition that declares the member function. In the definition, omit the `virtual` specifier. The function name must start with the class name, followed by the scope operator (`::`) and the function name so the compiler knows which member function you are defining. Write the function body the same way you would write it if you provided the function definition inside the class definition. Listing 38-1 shows some examples.

**Listing 38-1.** *Declarations and Definitions of Member Functions*

```
class rational
{
public:
  rational();
```

```
  rational(int num);
  rational(int num, int den);
  void assign(int num, int den);
  int numerator() const;
  int denominator() const;
  rational& operator=(int num);
private:
  void reduce();
  int numerator_;
  int denominator_;
};

rational::rational()
: numerator_(0), denominator_(1)
{}

rational::rational(int num)
: numerator_(num), denominator_(1)
{}

rational::rational(int num, int den)
: numerator_(num), denominator_(den)
{
  reduce();
}

void rational::assign(int num, int den)
{
  numerator_ = num;
  denominator_ = den;
  reduce();
}

void rational::reduce()
{
  assert(denominator_ != 0);
  if (denominator_ < 0)
  {
    denominator_ = -denominator_;
    numerator_ = -numerator_;
  }
  int div(gcd(numerator_, denominator_));
  numerator_ = numerator_ / div;
  denominator_ = denominator_ / div;
}
```

```
int rational::numerator()
const
{
  return numerator_;
}

int rational::denominator()
const
{
  return denominator_;
}

rational& rational::operator=(int num)
{
  numerator_ = num;
  denominator_ = 1;
  return *this;
}
```

Because each function name begins with the class name, the full constructor name is rational::rational, and member function names have the form rational::numerator, rational::operator=, etc. The C++ term for the complete name is *qualified name*.

Programmers have many reasons to define member functions outside the class. The next section presents one way that functions differ depending on where they are defined, and the next Exploration will focus on this thread in detail.

# Inline Functions

In Exploration 28, I introduced the inline keyword, which is a hint to the compiler that it should optimize speed over size by trying to expand a function at its point of call. You can use inline with member functions, too. Indeed, for trivial functions, such as those that return a data member and do nothing else, making the function inline can improve speed and program size.

When you define a function inside the class definition, the compiler automatically adds the inline keyword. If you separate the definition from the declaration, you can still make the function inline by adding the inline keyword to the function declaration or definition. Common practice is to place the inline keyword only on the definition, but I recommend putting the keyword in both places to help the human reader.

Remember that inline is just a hint. The compiler does not have to heed the hint. Modern compilers are becoming better and better at making these decisions for themselves.

My personal guideline is to define one-line functions in the class definition. Longer functions or functions that are complicated to read belong outside the class definition. Some functions are too long to fit in the class definition, but are short and simple enough that they should be inline. Organizational coding styles usually include guidelines for inline functions. For example, directives for large projects may eschew inline functions because they increase compilation time. Thus inline may be allowed only on a function-by-function basis, when performance measurements demonstrate their need.

**Rewrite the rational class from Listing 38-1 to use inline functions judiciously.** Compare your solution with that of mine, shown in Listing 38-2.

**Listing 38-2.** *The rational Class with inline Member Functions*

```
class rational
{
public:
  rational(int num) : numerator_(num), denominator_(1) {}
  inline rational(int num, int den);
  void assign(int num, int den);
  int numerator() const                    { return numerator_; }
  int denominator() const                  { return denominator_; }
  rational& operator=(int num);
private:
  void reduce();
  int numerator_;
  int denominator_;
};

inline rational::rational(int num, int den)
: numerator_(num), denominator_(den)
{
  reduce();
}

void rational::assign(int num, int den)
{
  numerator_ = num;
  denominator_ = den;
  reduce();
}

void rational::reduce()
{
  assert(denominator_ != 0);
  if (denominator_ < 0)
  {
    denominator_ = -denominator_;
    numerator_ = -numerator_;
  }
  int div(gcd(numerator_, denominator_));
  numerator_ = numerator_ / div;
  denominator_ = denominator_ / div;
}

rational& rational::operator=(int num)
{
```

```
  numerator_ = num;
  denominator_ = 1;
  return *this;
}
```

Don't agonize over deciding which functions should be inline. When in doubt, don't bother. Make functions inline only if performance measures show that the function is called often, and the function-call overhead is significant. In all other aspects, I regard the matter as one of aesthetics and clarity: I find one-line functions are easier to read when they are inside the class definition.

# Variable Declarations and Definitions

Ordinary data members have declarations, not definitions. Local variables in functions and blocks have definitions, but not separate declarations. This can be a little confusing, but don't be concerned, I'll unravel it and make it clear.

A definition of a named object instructs the compiler to set aside memory for storing the object's value and to generate the necessary code to initialize the object. Some objects are actually subobjects—not entire objects on their own (entire objects are called *complete* objects in C++ parlance). A subobject doesn't get its own definition; instead, its memory and lifetime are dictated by the complete object that contains it. That's why a data member doesn't get a definition of its own. Instead, the definition of an object with class type causes memory to be set aside for all of the object's data members. Thus, a class definition contains declarations of data members, but not definitions.

You define a variable that is local to a block. The definition specifies the object's type, name, whether it is const, and the initial value (if any). You can't declare a local variable without defining it, but there are other kinds of declarations.

You can declare a local reference as a synonym for a local variable. Declare the new name as a reference in the same manner as a reference parameter, but initialize it with an existing object. If the reference is const, you can use any expression (of a suitable type) as the initializer. For a non-const reference, you must use an lvalue (remember those from Exploration 20?), such as another variable. Listing 38-3 illustrates these principles.

**Listing 38-3.** *Declaring and Using References*

```
#include <iostream>
#include <ostream>

int main()
{
  int answer(42);     // definition of a named object, also an lvalue
  int& ref(answer);   // declaration of a reference named ref
  ref = 10;           // changes the value of answer
  std::cout << answer << '\n';
  int const& cent(ref * 10); // declaration; must be const to initialize with expr
  std::cout << cent << '\n';
}
```

A local reference is not a definition because no memory is allocated, and no initializers are run. Instead, the reference declaration creates a new name for an old object. One common use for a local reference is to create a short name for an object that is obtained from a longer expression, and another is to save a const reference to an expression so you can use the result multiple times. Listing 38-4 shows a silly program that reads a series of integers into a vector, sorts the data, and searches for all the elements that equal a magic value. It does this by calling the equal_range algorithm, which returns a pair (first described in Exploration 14) of iterators that delimit a range of equal values.

**Listing 38-4.** *Finding the Mode of a Data Set*

```
#include <algorithm>
#include <iostream>
#include <istream>
#include <iterator>
#include <ostream>
#include <utility>
#include <vector>

int main()
{
  using namespace std;
  typedef vector<int>::iterator vec_iterator;

  vector<int> data((istream_iterator<int>(cin)), istream_iterator<int>());
  sort(data.begin(), data.end());
  // Find all values equal to 42
  pair<vec_iterator, vec_iterator> const& range(
    equal_range(data.begin(), data.end(), 42)
  );
  if (range.first != range.second)
  {
    // Print the range indices only if at least one value is found.
    cout << "index of start of range: " << range.first  - data.begin() << '\n';
    cout << "index of end of range:   " << range.second - data.begin() << '\n';
  }
  cout << "size of range:           " << range.second - range.first << '\n';
}
```

If you define range as a local variable instead of declaring it as a reference, the program would work just fine, but it would also make an unneeded copy of the result that equal_range returns. In this program, the extra copy is irrelevant and unnoticeable, but in other programs, the cost savings can add up.

**What happens if you delete the const from the declaration of range?**

_____

_____

The result that `equal_range` returns is an rvalue, not an lvalue, so you must use `const` when initializing a reference to that result. Because you are free to modify an object via a non-`const` reference, only lvalue objects are allowed. Usually, the values returned from functions are rvalues, not lvalues, so references must be `const`.

# Static Variables

Local variables are *automatic*. This means when the function begins or a local block (compound statement) is entered, memory is allocated and the object is constructed. When the function returns or when control exits the block, the object is destroyed and memory is reclaimed. All automatic variables are allocated on the program stack, so memory allocation and release is trivial and typically handled by the host platform's normal function call instructions.

Remember that `main()` is like a function and follows many of the same rules as other functions. Thus, variables that you define in `main()` seem to last for the entire lifetime of the program, but they are automatic variables, allocated on the stack, and the compiler treats them the same as it treats any other automatic variables.

The behavior of automatic variables permits idioms such as RAII (see Exploration 37) and greatly simplifies typical programming tasks. Nonetheless, it is not suited for every programming task. Sometimes you need a variable's lifetime to persist across function calls. For example, suppose you need a function that generates unique identification numbers for a variety of objects. It starts a serial counter at 1 and increments the counter each time it issues an ID. Somehow, the function needs to keep track of the counter value, even after it returns. Listing 38-5 demonstrates one way to do it.

**Listing 38-5.** *Generating Unique Identification Numbers*

```
int generate_id()
{
  static int counter(0);
  ++counter;
  return counter;
}
```

The `static` keyword informs the compiler that the variable is not automatic but *static*. The first time the program calls `generate_id()`, the variable `counter` is initialized. The memory is not automatic and is not allocated on the program stack. Instead, all static variables are kept off to the side somewhere so they never go away. When `generate_id()` returns, `counter` is not destroyed and therefore retains its value.

**Write a program to call `generate_id()` multiple times to see that it works and generates new values each time you call it.** Compare your program with mine, which is shown in Listing 38-6.

**Listing 38-6.** *Calling* generate_id *to Demonstrate Static Variables*

```
#include <iostream>
#include <ostream>

int generate_id()
{
  static int counter(0);
  ++counter;
  return counter;
}

int main()
{
  for (int i = 0; i != 10; ++i)
    std::cout << generate_id() << '\n';
}
```

You can also declare a variable outside of any function. Because it is outside of all functions, it is not inside any block, thus it cannot be automatic, and so its memory must be static. You don't need to use the static keyword for such a variable. **Rewrite Listing 38-6 to declare counter outside of the generate_id function.** Do not use the static keyword. Assure yourself that the program still works correctly. Listing 38-7 shows my solution.

**Listing 38-7.** *Declaring* counter *Outside of the* generate_id *Function*

```
#include <iostream>
#include <ostream>

int counter;

int generate_id()
{
  ++counter;
  return counter;
}

int main()
{
  for (int i = 0; i != 10; ++i)
    std::cout << generate_id() << '\n';
}
```

Unlike automatic variables, all static variables without initializers start out filled with zero, even if the variable has a built-in type. If the class has a custom constructor, the default constructor is then called to initialize static variables of class type. Thus, you don't need to specify an initializer for counter, but you can if you want to.

One of the difficulties in working with static variables in C++ is that you have little control over *when* static variables are initialized. The standard offers two basic guarantees:

- Static objects are initialized in the same order as their order of appearance in the file.

- Static objects are initialized before their first use in main(), or any function called from main().

Prior to the start of main(), however, you have no guarantee that a static object will be initialized when you expect it to be. In practical terms, this means a constructor for a static object should not refer to other static objects because those other objects may not be initialized yet. All names in C++ are lexically scoped; a name is visible only within its scope. The scope for a name declared within a function is the block that contains the declaration (including the statement header of for, if, and while statements). The scope for a name declared outside of any function is a little trickier. The name of a variable or function is global and can be used only for that single entity throughout the program. On the other hand, you can use it only in the source file where it is declared, from the point of declaration to the end of the file. (The next Exploration will go into more detail about working with multiple source files.)

The common term for variables that you declare outside of all functions is *global variables*. That's not the standard C++ terminology, but it will do for now.

If you declare counter globally, you can refer to it and modify it anywhere else in the program, which may not be what you want. It's always best to limit the scope of every name as narrowly as possible. By declaring counter inside generate_id, you guarantee that no other part of the program can accidentally change its value. In other words, if only one function needs to access a static variable, keep the variable's definition local to the function. If multiple functions must share the variable, define the variable globally.

# Static Data Members

The static keyword has many uses. You can use it before a member declaration in a class to declare a *static data member*. A static data member is one that is not part of all objects of the class, but instead, is separate from all objects. All objects of that class type (and derived types) share a sole instance of the data member. A common use for static data members is to define useful constants. For example, the std::string class has a static data member, npos, which roughly means "no position." Member functions return npos when they cannot return a meaningful position, such as find when it cannot find the string for which it was looking. You can also use static data members to store shared data the same way a globally static variable can be shared. By making the shared variable a data member, however, you can restrict access to the data member using the normal class access levels.

Define a static data member the way you would any other global variable, but qualify the member name with the class name. Use the static keyword only in the data member's declaration, not in its definition. Because static data members are not part of objects, do not list them in a constructor's initializer list. Instead, initialize static data members the way you would an ordinary global variable, but remember to qualify the member name with the class name. Qualify the name when you use a static data member, too. Listing 38-8 shows some simple uses of static data members.

**Listing 38-8.** *Declaring and Defining Static Data Members*

```cpp
#include <iostream>
#include <ostream>

class rational {
public:
  rational();
  rational(int num);
  rational(int num, int den);
  int numerator() const { return numerator_; }
  int denominator() const { return denominator_; }
  // Some useful constants
  static const rational zero;
  static const rational one;
  static const rational pi;
private:
  void reduce();
  int numerator_;
  int denominator_;
};

rational::rational() : numerator_(0), denominator_(1) {}
rational::rational(int num) : numerator_(num), denominator_(1) {}
rational::rational(int num, int den)
: numerator_(num), denominator_(den)
{
  reduce();
}

std::ostream& operator<<(std::ostream& out, rational const& r);

const rational rational::zero;
const rational rational::one(1);
const rational rational::pi(355, 113);

int main()
{
  std::cout << "pi = " << rational::pi << '\n';
}
```

A static const data member with an integral type is a little odd, however. Only these data members can have an initial value specified inside the class definition, as part of the data member's declaration. The value does not change the declaration into a definition, and you still need a definition of the data member, outside the class definition. However, by providing a value in the declaration, you can use the static const data member as a constant value elsewhere in the program, anywhere a constant integer is needed.

To specify the value of an integral static const data member, follow the member name with an equal sign (=) and a constant expression. For example, the declaration for std::string::npos is as follows:

```
class string {
...
   static size_type const npos = -1;
...
```

Like other collection types, string declares size_type as a suitable integer type for representing sizes and indices. The implementation of the string class needs to define this data member, but without an initial value.

```
string::size_type const string::npos;
```

Listing 38-9 shows some examples of static data members in a more sophisticated id-generator. This one uses a prefix as part of the IDs it produces and then uses a serial counter for the remaining portion of each ID. You can initialize the prefix to a random number to generate IDs that are unique even across multiple runs of the same program. (The code is not meant to show off a high-quality ID generator, just static data members.) Using a different prefix for every run is fine for production software, but greatly complicates testing. Therefore, this version of the program uses the fixed quantity 1. A comment shows the intended code.

**Listing 38-9.** *Using Static Data Members for an ID Generator*

```
#include <iostream>
#include <ostream>

class generate_id
{
public:
  generate_id() : counter_(0) {}
  long next();
private:
  short counter_;
  static short prefix_;
  // The counter rolls over at a fairly low value (32,767), to ensure the code
  // is completely portable to all systems. Real code can use a higher value
  // before rolling over, but that involves C++ features that the book has not
  // yet covered.
  static long int const max_counter_ = 32767;
};

// Switch to random-number as the initial prefix for production code.
// short generate_id::prefix_(static_cast<short>(std::rand()));
short generate_id::prefix_(1);
long const generate_id::max_counter_;
```

```
long generate_id::next()
{
  if (counter_ == max_counter_)
    counter_ = 0;
  else
    ++counter_;
  return prefix_ * (max_counter_ + 1) + counter_;
}

int main()
{
  generate_id gen;            // Create an ID generator
  for (int i = 0; i != 10; ++i)
    std::cout << gen.next() << '\n';
}
```

# Declarators

As you've already seen, you can define multiple variables in a single declaration, as demonstrated in the following:

```
int x(42), y(0), z(x+y);
```

The entire declaration contains three *declarators*. Each declarator declares a single name, whether that name is for a variable, function, or type. Most C++ programmers don't use this term in everyday conversation, but C++ experts often do. You need to know official C++ terminology so if you need to ask for help from the experts, you can understand them.

The most important reason to know about separating declarations from definitions is so you can put a definition in one source file and a declaration in another. The next Exploration shows how to work with multiple source files.

■■■

# Using Multiple Source Files

**R**eal programs rarely fit into a single source file, and I know you've been champing at the bit, eager to explore how C++ works with multiple source files that make up a single program. This Exploration shows you the basics. Advanced techniques, such as shared libraries (DLLs, shared objects, etc.) are beyond the scope of this book and sometimes involve compiler-specific features that extend the language beyond the standard. You need to consult your compiler documentation for details.

## Multiple Source Files

The basic principle is that you can put any function or global object in any source file. The compiler does not care which file contains what. As long as it has a declaration for every name it needs, it can compile a source file to an object file. (In this unfortunate case of convergent terminology, *object* files are unrelated to *objects* in a C++ program.) To create the final program, you need to link all the object files together. The linker doesn't care which file contains which definition; it simply needs to find a definition for every name reference that the compiler generates.

The previous Exploration presented a simple program in Listing 38-6, which generated unique ID numbers. Let's rewrite the program to put the generate_id class in one file called *generate_id.cpp*, and main in another file called *main.cpp*. Listing 39-1 shows the *generate_id.cpp* file.

**Listing 39-1.** *The Definition of generate_id's Members in generate_id.cpp*

```
class generate_id
{
public:
  generate_id() : counter_(0) {}
  long next();
private:
  short counter_;
  static short prefix_;
  static long int const max_counter_ = 32767;
};
```

```
// Switch to random-number as the initial prefix for production code.
// short generate_id::prefix_(static_cast<short>(std::rand()));
short generate_id::prefix_(1);
long const generate_id::max_counter_;

long generate_id::next()
{
  if (counter_ == max_counter_)
    counter_ = 0;
  else
    ++counter_;
  return prefix_ * (max_counter_ + 1) + counter_;
}
```

You can compile the *generate_id.cpp* file, but not link it. To create a valid C++ program, you must have a main function, which is presented in Listing 39-2. Because main makes use of the generate_id class, it needs the class definition, but not the definitions of the class's members.

**Listing 39-2.** *The main Function for the ID-generating Program in the main.cpp File*

```
#include <iostream>
#include <ostream>

class generate_id
{
public:
  generate_id() : counter_(0) {}
  long next();
private:
  short counter_;
  static short prefix_;
  static long int const max_counter_ = 32767;
};

int main()
{
  generate_id gen;          // Create an ID generator
  for (int i = 0; i != 10; ++i)
    std::cout << gen.next() << '\n';
}
```

Now compile the two source files and link them together to produce a working C++ program. An IDE takes care of the details for you, provided both source files are part of the same project. If you are using command-line tools, typically, you can invoke the same compiler, but instead of listing source file names on the command line, list only the object file names. Alternatively, you can compile and link at the same time, by listing all the source file names in one compilation. Verify that the program's behavior is identical to that from Listing 38-6.

That's the basic idea, But the details, of course, are a little trickier. For the remainder of this Exploration, we'll take a closer look at those details.

# Declarations and Definitions

At first glance, you will notice that both source files contain an identical definition of the generate_id class. That immediately raises the question: "What happens if the definition changes in one file but not in the other?" Let's find out. Rename the next() function to next_id(), as shown in Listing 39-3.

**Listing 39-3.** *Renaming a Member Function Only in main.cpp*

```cpp
#include <iostream>
#include <ostream>

class generate_id
{
public:
  generate_id() : counter_(0) {}
  long next_id();
private:
  short counter_;
  static short prefix_;
  static long int const max_counter_ = 32767;
};

int main()
{
  generate_id gen;            // Create an ID generator
  for (int i = 0; i != 10; ++i)
    std::cout << gen.next_id() << '\n';
}
```

Leave the other source file alone. **What do you expect to happen?**

_____

_____

Compile and link the program. **What actually happens?**

_____

_____

When compiling *main.cpp*, the compiler sees the declaration of next_id and the call to next_id. As far as it can tell, everything is just fine. The linker, however, sees a call to next_id in the *main* object file, but no definition of next_id in the *generate_id* object file. Thus, the linker issues an error message and refuses to create the executable program file.

A more subtle change is to add a new data member before counter, as shown in Listing 39-4.

**Listing 39-4.** *Adding a New Data Member Only in main.cpp*

```cpp
#include <iostream>
#include <ostream>

class generate_id
{
public:
  generate_id() : counter_(0) {}
  long next();
private:
  int unused_;
  short counter_;
  static short prefix_;
  static long int const max_counter_ = 32767;
};

int main()
{
  generate_id gen;            // Create an ID generator
  for (int i = 0; i != 10; ++i)
    std::cout << gen.next() << '\n';
}
```

Leaving the other source file untouched, **what do you expect to happen?**

_____

_____

Compile, link, and run the program. **What actually happens?**

_____

_____

Remember that the program should produce identical results. The exact numeric sequence should be the same between this program and earlier incarnations. The problem is that you have stumbled once again into undefined behavior.

Even though the main function thinks the unused_ data member is indeed unused, the next() function's idea of the counter_ data member happens to be at the same address as the unused_ data member. This is bad—really bad. But if you weren't watching closely, you might have missed it. Although anything is possible, most likely the program generated a sequence of unique IDs, and if you hadn't looked at the actual values, but simply used the generate_id class in a program, you might never have noticed. At least, not until you ported the program to a different environment. A different compiler or linker may be able to detect this error.

A different operating system may cause the program to crash. Once you enter the realm of undefined behavior, anything goes.

A class or function definition must be identical in all files, or else the results are undefined. The compiler and linker are not required to detect this kind of error.

You have been warned.

To avoid these kinds of problems, you need to host the definition of the generate_id class in a single file, and somehow use that file in every source file that makes use of the class. This way, you can assure yourself that every source file is using the same definition of generate_id.

You need to write your own #include file.

# #include Files

Remember that the compiler needs only a function's declaration, not its definition in order to call the function. If you put the declaration in its own file then #include that file in every source file that calls the function, you ensure that the compiler sees the same declaration every time, allowing it to generate the correct code for calling the function. The same is true for a class. Put only the class definition in its own file, and then #include the file in every source file that needs it. Listing 39-5 shows you the #include file that contains the generate_id class. Common conventions for #include files are to use extensions such as *.h* or *.hpp* (for header, or C++ header), or sometimes *.hh* or *.hxx*. Some files need to preserve compatibility with C, and these typically use *.h* as the extension. For all other files, I prefer *.hpp* because it is a nice parallel to the extension *.cpp* I use for C++ source files. Thus, name this file *generate_id.hpp*. If you use *.cc* for source files, you may like *.hh* for header files; ditto for *.cxx* and *.hxx*.

**Listing 39-5.** *The #include File for the generate_id Class*

```
/// Class for generating a unique ID number.
class generate_id
{
public:
  generate_id() : counter_(0) {}
  long next();
private:
  short counter_;
  static short prefix_;
  static long int const max_counter_ = 32767;
};
```

To use the *generate_id.hpp* file, you need to #include it in the source files, but use double quotes instead of angle brackets. Listing 39-6 displays the new version of *generate_id.cpp*.

**Listing 39-6.** *Rewrite of generate_id.cpp to #include the generate_id.hpp File*

```
#include "generate_id.hpp"

// Switch to random-number as the initial prefix for production code.
// short generate_id::prefix_(static_cast<short>(std::rand()));
```

```
short generate_id::prefix_(1);
long const generate_id::max_counter_;

long generate_id::next()
{
  if (counter_ == max_counter_)
    counter_ = 0;
  else
    ++counter_;
  return prefix_ * (max_counter_ + 1) + counter_;
}
```

**Rewrite *main.cpp* similarly.** Compile both source files and link the resulting object files to create your program (or let the IDE do it for you). Make sure the program behaves the same as it did originally. Compare your rewrite of *main.cpp* with mine, which is presented in Listing 39-7.

**Listing 39-7.** *Rewriting main.cpp to #include the generate_id.hpp File*

```
#include <iostream>
#include <ostream>

#include "generate_id.hpp"

int main()
{
  generate_id gen;            // Create an ID generator
  for (int i = 0; i != 10; ++i)
    std::cout << gen.next() << '\n';
}
```

## Quotes and Brackets

Now you're wondering why I told you to use quotes instead of angle brackets for the #include directives. The difference is that you should use angle brackets only for the standard library headers, although some third-party libraries recommend the use of angle brackets, too. Use double quotes for everything else. The C++ standard is vague about this distinction to give compiler vendors maximum flexibility. As a result, vendors of add-on libraries have all taken different approaches concerning naming their library files and whether they require angle brackets or double quotes.

For your own files, the important aspect is that the compiler must be able to find all your #include files. The easiest way to do that is to keep them in the same directory or folder as your source files. As your projects become larger and more complex, you probably will want to move all the #include files to a separate area. In this case, you need to consult your compiler documentation to learn how to inform the compiler about that separate area. Users of *g++* and other UNIX and UNIX-like command-line tools typically use the -I option. Microsoft's command-line compiler uses /I. IDEs have a project option with which you can add a directory or folder to the list of places to search for #include files.

For many compilers, the only difference between angle brackets and quotes is where it looks for the file. A few compilers have additional differences that are specific to that compiler.

In a source file, I like to list all the standard headers together, in alphabetical order, and list them first, followed by the #include files that are specific to the program (also in alphabetical order). This organization makes it easy for me to determine whether a source file #includes a particular header and helps me add or remove #include directives as needed.

## Nested #include Directives

One #include file can #include another. For example, consider the vital_stats class (similar to the record class in Listing 31-3, for recording a person's vital statistics, including body-mass index) in Listing 39-8.

**Listing 39-8.** *The* vital_stats *Class to Record a Person's Vital Statistics*

```
#include <istream>
#include <ostream>
#include <string>

class vital_stats
{
public:
  vital_stats() : height_(0), weight_(0), bmi_(0), sex_('?'), name_()
  {}

  bool read(std::istream& in, int num);
  void print(std::ostream& out, int threshold) const;

private:
  int compute_bmi() const; ///< Return BMI, based on height_ and weight_
  int height_;             ///< height in centimeters
  int weight_;             ///< weight in kilograms
  int bmi_;                ///< Body-mass index
  char sex_;               ///< 'M' for male or 'F' for female
  std::string name_;       ///< Person's name
};
```

Because the vital_stats class uses std::string, the *vital_stats.hpp* file should #include <string>. Similarly, std::istream is defined in <istream> and std::ostream in <ostream>. By adding all the necessary #include directives to the *vital_stats.hpp* file, you remove one burden from the programmer who makes use of *vital_stats.hpp*.

The standard library headers work the same way. Any particular header may #include other headers. An implementation of the standard library is free to #include any, all, or none of the other standard headers. Thus, suppose you #include <string> and forget the I/O stream headers. With one compiler and library, your project may compile and run successfully because that particular implementation of <string> happens to #include <istream> and <ostream>. You never notice your mistake until you move the source code to a different platform. This other implementation may work differently. Suddenly and unexpectedly, your compiler issues a slew of error messages for source code that worked perfectly on the first plat-form. The mistake is easy to fix and also easy to avoid by checking all your files to be sure each file #includes all the headers it needs.

One consequence of headers including other headers is that any single header can be included many times in a single source file. For example, suppose your source file includes <string>, but so does *generate_id.hpp*. This means your source file includes the same header, <string>, more than once. In the case of the standard library headers, including the same header more than once is harmless. What about your files? **What would happen if *generate_id.cpp* were to #include "generate_id.hpp" more than once?**

_____

_____

**Try it. What happens?**

_____

_____

C++ does not allow you to define a class, function, or object more than once in the same source file, and *generate_id.hpp* contains a class definition. Thus, if you #include that file more than once, the compiler issues an error message. The next section explains how to prevent this problem.

## Include Guards

You cannot define the same class, function, or object more than once in a source file. On the other hand, you cannot prevent anyone from including your header more than once. Some-how, you need to ensure that the compiler sees the definitions only once, even if a source file includes your header more than once. Fortunately, C++ offers additional # directives to help you.

The most widely-used idiom is to pick a name to uniquely identify your header, such as VITAL_STATS_HPP_ or GENERATE_ID_HPP_, and then use that name to control the compilation of your header. Use the following two lines as the first two lines of the header file:

```
#ifndef GENERATE_ID_HPP_
#define GENERATE_ID_HPP_
```

Next, use the following as the last line of the header file:

```
#endif
```

Convention is to use all capital letters because no other names in your program should be made up of all capital letters. I use the file name, but change dot (.), and other characters that aren't allowed in C++ identifiers, into underscores (_). I use a trailing underscore to further ensure that I avoid collisions with other names.

The #ifndef directive means "if not defined." The directive controls whether the compiler compiles the source code normally or skips the entire section of the file. If the name is not defined, compilation proceeds normally. If it is defined, the compiler skips rapidly over the file until it finds #endif, thereby ignoring the definitions that you want to protect.

The #define directive defines a name. Thus, the first time the compiler processes this header, the name is not defined, the #ifndef condition is true, and the compiler processes the definitions normally. Among the code it processes normally is the #define. If the file is included more than once, the second and subsequent times the name is defined, the #ifndef directive is false, so the compiler skips the bulk of the file, and does not try to compile the definitions more than once.

## BAD ADVICE

Some books and programmers recommend putting the conditional directives in the file that does the #include-ing. For example, they maintain that main.cpp should begin like this:

```
#ifndef GENERATE_ID_HPP_
#include "generate_id.hpp"
#endif
```

They are wrong. The name GENERATE_ID_HPP_ is an internal, private detail of the included file. You should never use it outside of that file, and no one else should ever use that name. The purported reason to export the guard name and use it outside of the file is to improve compilation speed by eliminating the compiler's need to open and process the file that would otherwise be included. With modern compilers, the improvement is negligible. A better solution is for you to use precompiled headers.

With large, complicated programs, much of the compiler's time and effort is spent compiling included files. In other words, the compiler spends a lot of its time recompiling the same definitions over and over again. The idea of using precompiled headers is that the compiler saves some information about the definitions it sees in an included file. When you include the same file in other source files, the compiler fetches its precompiled data, and saves time by avoiding a recompilation of the same definitions. This compiler hack is completely unrelated to the C++ language, and is purely an artifact of the compiler program. Check your compiler's documentation to learn how to set up and use precompiled headers.

## Documentation

Recall the doxygen tool from Exploration 25. With headers, you now face the problem that you have two places to document certain entities: the declaration in the header file, and the definition in the source file. One option is to put the documentation in the header file. The documentation is usually aimed at the user of the entity, and the header is the proper place to document the interface.

Another option is to document the public interface in the header file and the private implementation details in the source file. The doxygen tool cannot merge documentation from two sources for a single entity. Instead, you should take advantage of its conditional processing features to compile a set of interface documentation and a separate set of implementation documentation. Listing 39-9 shows the final version of the *vital_stats.hpp* header file.

**Listing 39-9.** *The vital_stats.hpp Header File*

```
#ifndef VITAL_STATS_HPP_
#define VITAL_STATS_HPP_

#include <istream>
#include <ostream>
#include <string>

class vital_stats
{
public:
  /// Constructor. Initialize everything to zero or other "empty" value.
  vital_stats() : height_(0), weight_(0), bmi_(0), sex_('?'), name_()
  {}

  /// Get this record, overwriting the data members.
  /// Error-checking omitted for brevity.
  /// @param in the input stream
  /// @param num a serial number, for use when prompting the user
  /// @return true for success or false for eof or input failure
  bool read(std::istream& in, int num);
  /// Print this record to @p out.
  /// @param out the output stream
  /// @param threshold mark records that have a BMI >= this threshold
  void print(std::ostream& out, int threshold) const;

  /// Return the BMI.
  int bmi() const { return bmi_; }
  /// Return the height in centimeters.
  int height() const { return height_; }
  /// Return the weight in kilograms.
  int weight() const { return weight_; }
  /// Return the sex: 'M' for male or 'F' for female
  char sex() const { return sex_; }
  /// Return the person's name.
  std::string const& name() const { return name_; }

private:
  /// Return BMI, based on height_ and weight_
  /// This is called only from read().
  int compute_bmi() const;
  int height_;          ///< height in centimeters
  int weight_;          ///< weight in kilograms
  int bmi_;             ///< Body-mass index
  char sex_;            ///< 'M' for male or 'F' for female
```

```
    std::string name_;          ///< Person's name
};

#endif
```

Listing 39-10 presents the implementation in *vital_stats.cpp*.

**Listing 39-10.** *The vital_stats.cpp Source File*

```
#include <iomanip>
#include <istream>
#include <limits>
#include <locale>
#include <ostream>
#include <string>

#include "vital_stats.hpp"

/// Skip the rest of the input line.
/// @param in the input stream
void skip_line(std::istream& in)
{
  in.ignore(std::numeric_limits<int>::max(), '\n');
}

int vital_stats::compute_bmi()
const
{
   return static_cast<int>(weight_ * 10000 / (height_ * height_) + 0.5);
}

bool vital_stats::read(std::istream& in, int num)
{
  std::cout << "Name " << num << ": ";
  if (not std::getline(in, name_))
    return false;

  std::cout << "Height (cm): ";
  if (not (in >> height_))
    return false;
  skip_line(in);

  std::cout << "Weight (kg): ";
  if (not (in >> weight_))
    return false;
  skip_line(in);
```

```
  std::cout << "Sex (M or F): ";
  if (not (in >> sex_))
    return false;
  skip_line(in);
  sex_ = std::toupper(sex_, std::locale());

  bmi_ = compute_bmi();
  return true;
}

void vital_stats::print(std::ostream& out, int threshold)
const
{
  out << std::setw(6) << height_
      << std::setw(7) << weight_
      << std::setw(3) << sex_
      << std::setw(6) << bmi_;
  if (bmi_ >= threshold)
    out << '*';
  else
    out << ' ';
  out << ' ' << name_ << '\n';
}
```

# extern Variables

If you define a global variable, and you want to use it in multiple files, you need a declaration in every file that uses the variable. The most common use for global objects is for useful constants. For example, one of the omissions many scientific programmers notice when they first begin to use C++ is that the standard math header, <cmath>, lacks a definition for $\pi$. Suppose you decide to remedy this oversight by creating your own header file, *math.hpp*. This header file contains the declarations for pi and other useful constants. Declare a global variable by using the extern keyword, followed by the variable's type and name.

   **Write *math.hpp*, with proper #include guards and a declaration for a double constant named pi.** Compare your file with Listing 39-11.

**Listing 39-11.** *Simple Header for Math Constants*

```
#ifndef MATH_HPP_
#define MATH_HPP_

extern double const pi;

#endif
```

   One source file in the project must define pi. Call the file *math.cpp*. **Write *math.cpp*.** Compare your file with Listing 39-12.

**Listing 39-12.** *Definitions of Math Constants*

```
#include "math.hpp"

// More digits that typical implementations of double support.
double const pi(3.14159265358979323846264338327);
```

# Inline Functions

Typically, you declare functions in a header file and define them in a separate source file, which you then link with your program. This is true for free functions and for member functions. Thus, most member functions are defined separately from the class.

Inline functions follow different rules than ordinary functions. Any source file that calls an inline function needs the function's definition. Each source file that uses an inline function must have no more than one definition of that inline function, and every definition in the program must be the same. Thus, the rule for functions in header files is slightly more complicated: the header file contains declarations for non-inline functions and definitions for inline functions. The separate source file defines only the non-inline functions.

Inline functions have their uses, but they also have some significant drawbacks:

- Increased compilation time. With inline functions, the header file is larger, and the compiler does more work for every compilation in the project. The problem grows as the number of source files grows.

- Increased recompilation. If you modify a function body, only that body really needs to be recompiled. However, if the function body is in a header file, you end up recompiling every source file that includes that header. By putting function bodies in a separate source file, only that file needs to be recompiled, and you can save time. In large projects, the amount of time you save can be enormous.

Separating function declarations and definitions makes sense in real programs, but it complicates this book. Instead of a single code listing, sometimes I will need multiple code listings. Nonetheless, I'll do my best to demonstrate good programming practices in the judicious use of inline functions and the separation of declarations and definitions.

# One-Definition Rule

The compiler enforces the rule that permits one definition of a class, function, or object per source file. Another rule is that you can have only one definition of a function or global object in the entire program. You can define a class in multiple source files, provided the definition is the same in all source files.

As mentioned in the previous section, inline functions follow different rules than ordinary functions. You can define an inline function in multiple source files. Each source file must have no more than one definition of the inline function, and every definition in the program must be the same.

These rules are collectively known as the One-Definition Rule (ODR).

The compiler enforces the ODR within a single source file. However, the standard does not require a compiler or linker to detect any ODR violations that span multiple source files. If you make such a mistake, the problem is all yours to find and fix.

Imagine that you are maintaining a program, and part of the program is the header file shown in Listing 39-13.

**Listing 39-13.** *The Original point.hpp File*

```
#ifndef POINT_HPP_
#define POINT_HPP_
class point
{
public:
  point() : x_(0), y_(0) {}
  point(int x, int y) : x_(x), y_(y) {}
  int x() const { return x_; }
  int y() const { return y_; }
private:
  int y_, x_;
};
#endif // POINT_HPP_
```

The program works just fine. One day, however, you upgrade compiler versions and when recompiling the program, the new compiler issues a warning, such as the following, that you've never seen before:

```
point.hpp: In constructor 'point::point()':
point.hpp:13: warning: 'point::x_' will be initialized after
point.hpp:13: warning:    'int point::y_'
point.hpp:8: warning:    when initialized here
```

The problem is that the order of the data member declarations is different from the order of the data members in the constructors' initializer lists. It's a minor error, but one that can lead to confusion or worse in more complicated classes. It's a good idea to ensure the orders are the same. You decide to fix the problem by reordering the data members.

Then you recompile the program, but the program fails in mysterious ways. Some of your regression tests pass and some fail, including trivial tests that have never failed in the past.

**What went wrong?**

_____

_____

_____

With such limited information, you can't determine for certain what went wrong, but the most likely candidate is that the recompilation failed to capture all the source files. Some part of the program (not necessarily the part that is failing) is still using the old definition of the point class, and other parts of the program use the new definition. The program fails to adhere to the ODR, resulting in undefined behavior. Specifically, when the program passes a point object from one part of the program to another, one part of the program stores a value in x_, and another part reads the same data member as y_.

This is only one small example of how ODR violations can be both subtle and terrible at the same time. By ensuring that all class definitions are in their respective header files, and that any time you modify a header file you recompile all dependent source files, you can avoid most accidental ODR violations.

Now that you have the tools needed to start writing some serious programs, it's time to embark on some more advanced techniques. The next Exploration introduces function objects—a powerful technique for using the standard algorithms.

■ ■ ■

# Function Objects

**C**lasses have many, many uses in C++ programs. This Exploration introduces one powerful use of classes to replace functions. This style of programming is especially useful with the standard algorithms.

## The Function Call Operator

The first step is to take a look at an unusual "operator," the function call operator, which lets an object behave as a function. Overload this operator the same way you would any other. Its name is operator(). It takes any number of parameters, and can have any return type. Listing 40-1 shows another iteration of the generate_id class (last seen in Listing 39-5), this time replacing the next() member function with the function call operator. In this case, the function has no parameters, so the first set of empty parentheses is the operator name and the second set is the empty parameter list.

**Listing 40-1.** *Rewriting generate_id to Use the Function Call Operator*

```
#ifndef GENERATE_ID_HPP_
#define GENERATE_ID_HPP_

/// Class for generating a unique ID number.
class generate_id
{
public:
  generate_id() : counter_(0) {}
  long operator()();
private:
  short counter_;
  static short prefix_;
  static long int const max_counter_ = 32767;
};

#endif
```

Listing 40-2 displays the implementation of the function call operator (and `prefix_`, which also needs a definition).

**Listing 40-2.** *Implementation of the* generate_id *Function Call Operator*

```
#include "generate_id.hpp"

short generate_id::prefix_(1);

long generate_id::operator()()
{
  if (counter_ == max_counter_)
    counter_ = 0;
  else
    ++counter_;
  return prefix_ * (max_counter_ + 1) + counter_;
}
```

In order to use the function call operator, you must first declare an object of the class type then use the object name as though it were a function name. Pass arguments to this object the way you would to an ordinary function. The compiler sees the use of the object name as a function and invokes the function call operator. Listing 40-3 shows a sample program that uses a generate_id function call operator to generate id codes for new library works (remember the work class from Exploration 36?). Assume that int_to_id converts an integer identification into the string format that work requires, and that accession adds a work-derived object to the library's database.

**Listing 40-3.** *Using a generate_id Object's Function Call Operator*

```
#include <iostream>
#include <ostream>

#include "generate_id.hpp"
#include "library.hpp"

bool get_movie(std::string& title, int& runtime)
{
  std::cout << "Movie title: ";
  if (not std::getline(std::cin, title))
    return false;
  std::cout << "Runtime (minutes): ";
  if (not (std::cin >> runtime))
    return false;
  return true;
}

int main()
{
```

```
generate_id gen;            // Create an ID generator
std::string title;
int runtime;
while (get_movie(title, runtime))
{
  movie m(int_to_id(gen()), title, runtime);
  accession(m);
}
```

# Function Objects

A *function object* or *functor* is an object of class type for a class that overloads the function call operator. Informally, programmers sometimes also speak of the class as a "function object," with the understanding that the actual function objects are the variables defined with that class type.

The power of a function object is that the object can maintain state information, as you saw with *generate_id*. Stateful objects are much more powerful and flexible than plain, ordinary functions.

Recall the std::transform algorithm from Exploration 21. The goal was to transform a string by converting the case of each character in the string. The problem was that transform did not make it easy to call the standard toupper or tolower function. Using a function object, however, the task becomes simpler. Refer back to Listing 21-3, and **rewrite the sanitize function so it makes use of non_letter and lowercase function objects instead of functions.**

Need a hint? The constructors take a locale object as an argument.

Compare your solution with that of mine in Listing 40-4.

**Listing 40-4.** *Rewriting the sanitize Function to Make Use of Function Objects*

```
/** Test for non-letter. */
class non_letter
{
public:
  non_letter(std::locale loc) : locale_(loc) {}
  bool operator()(char ch)
  const
  {
    return not isalnum(ch, locale_);
  }
private:
  std::locale locale_;
};

/** Convert to lowercase.
 * Use a canonical form by converting to uppercase first,
 * and then to lowercase.
 */
class lowercase
```

```
{
public:
  lowercase(std::locale loc) : locale_(loc) {}
  char operator()(char ch)
  const
  {
    return std::tolower(ch, locale_);
  }
private:
  std::locale locale_;
};


/** Sanitize a string by keeping only alphabetic characters.
 * @param str the original string
 * @return a santized copy of the string
 */
std::string sanitize(std::string str)
{
  // Remove all non-letters from the string, and then erase them.
  str.erase(std::remove_if(str.begin(), str.end(), non_letter(std::locale())),
            str.end());

  // Convert the remnants of the string to lowercase.
  std::transform(str.begin(), str.end(), str.begin(), lowercase(std::locale()));

  return str;
}
```

At first glance, you don't seem to have gained much by using function objects instead of functions (the code is actually longer). If you aren't used to seeing function objects, the code seems more complicated. On the other hand, the program is not fetching the global locale three times for every single character. Instead, the program fetches the global locale twice for an entire word. By creating the function objects in main() and passing them as arguments to sanitize, the program could fetch the desired locale once for the entire program.

**Implement this suggested optimization.**

Listing 40-5 shows my solution. I wrote a new function object, sanitizer, which has a constructor that takes a locale as an argument. The sanitizer in turn creates two function objects, non_letter and lowercase, and uses them as before.

**Listing 40-5.** *Rewriting the sanitize Function As a Function Object*

```
// Copy the initial portion of Listing 21-2 here, including print_counts,
// but stopping just before sanitize.
... omitted for brevity ...


/** Base class to hold a locale object. */
class function
{
```

```
public:
  function(std::locale loc) : locale_(loc) {}
  bool isalnum(char ch) const { return std::isalnum(ch, locale()); }
  char tolower(char ch) const { return std::tolower(ch, locale()); }
private:
  std::locale const& locale() const { return locale_; }
  std::locale locale_;
};
/** Test for non-letter. */
class non_letter : public function
{
public:
  non_letter(std::locale loc) : function(loc) {}
  bool operator()(char ch)
  const
  {
    return not isalnum(ch);
  }
};


/** Convert to lowercase.
 * Use a canonical form by converting to uppercase first,
 * and then to lowercase.
 */
class lowercase : public function
{
public:
  lowercase(std::locale loc) : function(loc) {}
  char operator()(char ch)
  const
  {
    return tolower(ch);
  }
};

/** Sanitize a string by keeping only alphabetic characters. */
class sanitizer : public function
{
public:
  sanitizer(std::locale loc) : function(loc), non_letter_(loc), lowercase_(loc) {}
  std::string operator()(std::string str)
  {
    // Remove all non-letters from the string, and then erase them.
    str.erase(std::remove_if(str.begin(), str.end(), non_letter_), str.end());

    // Convert the remnants of the string to lowercase.
    std::transform(str.begin(), str.end(), str.begin(), lowercase_);
```

```
      return str;
   }
private:
  non_letter non_letter_;
  lowercase lowercase_;
};


/** Main program to count unique words in the standard input. */
int main()
{
  // Fetch the native locale only once.
  std::locale native(std::locale(""));
  // Use the native locale as the global locale.
  std::locale::global(native);
  initialize_streams();

  count_map counts;
  std::string word;
  sanitizer sanitize(native);

  // Read words from the standard input and count the number of times
  // each word occurs.
  while (std::cin >> word)
  {
    std::string copy(sanitize(word));

    // The "word" might be all punctuation, so the copy would be empty.
    // Don't count empty strings.
    if (not copy.empty())
      ++counts[copy];
  }

  print_counts(counts);
}
```

Notice how the main program requires very few changes.

I also factored out a common base class, function, for all the function objects. The base class manages the locale object and hides it from the derived classes by presenting its own tolower and isalnum functions. Thus, if you later find a way to further improve the performance of these functions, you can hide the details in the base class.

Another advantage to using function objects is that function call operators can be expanded inline. For a small function that a program calls often, the savings can be considerable. Using a sample file that contains about 12 MB of text, Listing 21-3 ran in 6.2 seconds and Listing 40-5 ran in 4.8 seconds on the same platform.

# Recycling Member Functions

You don't always need to write brand new classes for your function objects. Sometimes, you can recycle existing member functions. The standard library has a function, mem_fun_ref (in the <functional> header), which wraps a member function in a special functor, enabling you to use that member function easily with standard algorithms or anywhere else you need a function object.

Suppose you have a vector of vital_stats objects (see Listing 39-8), and you want to copy only the bmi() values to another vector so you can perform some statistical analysis on the BMI data. Listing 40-6 shows how to use mem_fun_ref with the bmi member function.

**Listing 40-6.** *Extracting BMI Values*

```cpp
#include <algorithm>
#include <iostream>
#include <istream>
#include <locale>
#include <ostream>
#include <string>
#include <vector>

#include "vital_stats.hpp"

int main()
{
  std::cout.imbue(std::locale(""));
  std::cin.imbue(std::locale(""));

  std::vector<vital_stats> data;

  std::cout << "Enter name, height (in cm),"
              " and weight (in kg) for each person:\n";
  vital_stats stats;
  while (stats.read(std::cin, data.size()+1))
    data.push_back(stats);

  // Copy only the BMI values to bmi_data.
  std::vector<int> bmi_data(data.size());
  std::transform(data.begin(), data.end(), bmi_data.begin(),
                 std::mem_fun_ref(&vital_stats::bmi));

  // Do stuff with bmi_data.
... omitted for brevity ...
}
```

The key is the call to mem_fun_ref. The sole argument is the address of a member function—in this case the bmi member function of the vital_stats class—written with the qualified class name, vital_stats::bmi. The & operand informs the compiler that you are not calling the member function, but need its location in memory. The `mem_fun_ref` function takes the member function address and creates a functor with one parameter, with type `vital_stats`. The functor's function call operator calls the `bmi()` member function. The exact implementation of `mem_fun_ref` is a detail best left to the library author, but the resulting functor class looks something like the class presented in Listing 40-7.

**Listing 40-7.** *The Functor Class Created by* `mem_fun_ref`

```
class mem_fun_ref_class
{
public:
  int operator()(vital_stats const& obj)
  const
  {
    return obj.bmi();
  }
};
```

The actual class name is an implementation detail; it will not collide with any name that you use in your code. You supply the parameter type (`vital_stats`) and the member function name (`bmi`) in the argument to `mem_fun_ref`. The compiler determines everything else; such as the return type (`int`) and that the function can be `const`. If the `bmi` member function were not `const`, the functor class would not have a `const` function call operator and `obj` parameter.

The `<functional>` header provides several other standard functors and wrappers of various shapes and sizes. They can be complicated to use correctly, but if you're curious, any complete language reference will spell out all the details for you. In this book, I'll stick with `mem_fun_ref`.

# Generator Functor

Suppose you need a vector that contains integers of increasing value. For example, a vector of size 10 would contain the values 1, 2, 3, ..., 8, 9, 10. The `generate` algorithm takes an iterator range and calls a function or functor for each element of the range, assigning the result of the functor to successive elements. **Write a functor class to generate successive integers so the functor can be used with the `generate` algorithm.** Name the class `sequence`. The constructor takes two arguments: the first specifies the initial value of the sequence and the second is the increment. Each time you call the function call operator, it returns the generator value then increments that value, which will be the value returned on the next invocation of the function call operator. Listing 40-8 shows the main program. Write your solution in a separate file, *sequence.hpp*, using only inline functions (so you don't need to compile a separate *sequence.cpp* source file).

**Listing 40-8.** *The Main Program for Generating Successive Integers*

```
#include <algorithm>
#include <iostream>
#include <istream>
#include <iterator>
```

```
#include <ostream>
#include <vector>

#include "sequence.hpp"

int main()
{
  int size;
  std::cout << "How many integers do you want? ";
  std::cin >> size;
  int first;
  std::cout << "What is the first integer? ";
  std::cin >> first;
  int step;
  std::cout << "What is the interval between successive integers? ";
  std::cin >> step;

  std::vector<int> data(size);
  // Generate the integers to fill the vector.
  std::generate(data.begin(), data.end(), sequence(first, step));

  // Print the resulting integers, one per line.
  std::copy(data.begin(), data.end(),
          std::ostream_iterator<int>(std::cout, "\n"));
}
```

Compare your solution with mine, shown in Listing 40-9.

**Listing 40-9.** *The sequence.hpp File*

```
#ifndef SEQUENCE_HPP_
#define SEQUENCE_HPP_

/// Generate a sequence of integers.
class sequence
{
public:
  /// Construct the functor.
  /// @param start the first value the generator returns
  /// @param step increment the value by this much for each call
  sequence(int start, int step ) : value_(start), step_(step) {}
  sequence(int start) : value_(start), step_(1) {}
  sequence() : value_(0), step_(1) {}
  /// Return the current value in the sequence, and increment the value.
  int operator()()
  {
    int result(value_);
    value_ = value_ + step_;
```

```
    return result;
  }
private:
  int value_;
  int const step_;
};
```

```
#endif
```

The generate algorithm has a partner, generate_n, which specifies an input range with an iterator for the start of the range and an integer for the size of the range. The next Exploration examines this and several other useful algorithms.

# EXPLORATION 41

■ ■ ■

# Useful Algorithms

The standard library includes a suite of functions, which the library calls *algorithms*, to simplify many programming tasks that involve repeated application of operations over sequential data. The data can be a container of objects, a portion of a container, values read from an input stream, or any other sequence of objects that you can express with iterators. I've been introducing various algorithms when appropriate; this Exploration takes a closer look at a number of the most useful algorithms.

## Searching

The standard algorithms include many flavors of searching, divided into two broad categories: linear and binary. The linear searches examine every element in a range, starting from the first, and proceeding to subsequent elements until reaching the end (or the search ends because it is successful). The binary searches require the elements be sorted in ascending order using the < operator, or according to a custom predicate, that is, a function or a function object that returns a Boolean result.

### Linear Search Algorithms

The most basic linear search is the find function. It searches a range of read iterators for a value. It returns an iterator that refers to the first matching element in the range. If find cannot find a match, it returns a copy of the end iterator. Listing 41-1 shows an example of its use. The program reads integers into a vector, searches for the value 42, and if found, changes that element to 0.

**Listing 41-1.** *Searching for an Integer*

```
#include <algorithm>
#include <iostream>
#include <ostream>

#include "data.hpp"

int main()
{
  intvector data;
```

331

```
  read_data(data);
  write_data(data);
  intvector::iterator iter(std::find(data.begin(), data.end(), 42));
  if (iter == data.end())
    std::cout << "Value 42 not found\n";
  else
  {
    *iter = 0;
    std::cout << "Value 42 changed to 0:\n";
    write_data(data);
  }
}
```

Listing 41-2 shows the *data.hpp* file, which provides a few utilities for working with vectors of integers. Most of the examples in this Exploration will #include this file.

**Listing 41-2.** *The data.hpp File to Support Integer Data*

```
#ifndef DATA_HPP_
#define DATA_HPP_

#include <algorithm>
#include <iostream>
#include <iterator>
#include <ostream>
#include <vector>

/// Convenient shorthand for a vector of integers.
typedef std::vector<int> intvector;

/// Convenient shorthand for an intvector's iterator.
typedef intvector::iterator intvec_iterator;

/// Read a series of integers from the standard input into @p data,
/// overwriting @p data in the process.
/// @param[in,out] data a vector of integers
void read_data(intvector& data)
{
  data.clear();
  data.insert(data.begin(), std::istream_iterator<int>(std::cin),
                            std::istream_iterator<int>());
}

/// Write a vector of integers to the standard output. Write all values on one
/// line, separated by single space characters, and surrounded by curly braces,
/// e.g., { 1 2 3 }.
/// @param data a vector of integers
void write_data(intvector const& data)
```

```
{
  std::cout << "{ ";
  std::copy(data.begin(), data.end(),
            std::ostream_iterator<int>(std::cout, " "));
  std::cout << "}\n";
}
```

```
#endif
```

A companion to the find algorithm is find_if. Instead of searching for a matching value, find_if takes a predicate function or function object (from now on, I will write *functor* to mean a free function or a function object). It calls the functor for every element in the range until the functor returns true (or any value that can be converted automatically to true, such as a nonzero numeric value). If the functor never returns true, find_if returns the end iterator.

Every search algorithm comes in two forms. The first compares items using an operator (== for linear searches and < for binary searches). The second form uses a caller-supplied functor instead of the operator. For most algorithms, the functor is an additional argument to the algorithm, so overloading distinguishes the two forms. In a few cases, both forms take the same number of arguments, and the library uses distinct names because overloading cannot distinguish between the two forms. In these cases, the functor form has _if added to the name, such as find and find_if.

Suppose you want to search a vector of integers, not for a single value, but for any value that falls within a certain range. You can write a custom predicate to test a hard-coded range, but a more useful solution is to write a general-purpose functor that compares an integer against any range. You use this functor by supplying the range limits as argument to the constructor. **Write the intrange functor.** The constructor takes two int arguments. The function call operator takes a single int argument; it returns true if the argument falls within the inclusive range specified in the constructor, or false if the argument lies outside the range.

Listing 41-3 shows my implementation of intrange. As an added bonus, I decided to allow the caller to specify the range limits in either order. That way I neatly avoid the issue of error checking and error handling if the caller tries to use a meaningless range, such as [10, 0].

**Listing 41-3.** *Functor intrange to Test Whether an Integer Lies Within a Certain Range*

```
#ifndef INTRANGE_HPP_
#define INTRANGE_HPP_

#include <algorithm>

/// Check whether an integer lies within an inclusive range.
class intrange
{
public:
  inline intrange(int low, int high);
  inline bool operator()(int test) const;
private:
  int const low_;
```

```
  int const high_;
};

/// Construct an integer range.
/// If the parameters are in the wrong order,
/// swap them to the right order.
/// @param low the lower bound of the inclusive range
/// @param high the upper bound of the inclusive range
inline intrange::intrange(int low, int high)
: low_(std::min(low, high)), high_(std::max(low, high))
{}

/// Check whether a value lies within the inclusive range.
/// @param test the value to test
inline bool intrange::operator()(int test)
const
{
  return (test >= low_ and test <= high_);
}

#endif
```

The < operator form of the std::min function takes two arguments and returns the
smaller. The std::max function also takes two arguments and returns the larger. Both functions compare their arguments with the < operator; like other algorithms, you can call a
functor form of both functions, passing a comparison functor to use instead of the < operator.
The types of the first two arguments must be the same, and the return type matches that of the
arguments.

**Write a test program** that reads integers from the standard input and then uses find_if
and intrange to find the first value that lies within the range [10, 20]. Compare your solution
with mine in Listing 41-4.

**Listing 41-4.** *Using find_if and intrange to Find an Integer That Lies Within a Range*

```
#include <algorithm>
#include <iostream>
#include <ostream>

#include "data.hpp"
#include "intrange.hpp"

int main()
{
  intvector data;
  read_data(data);
  write_data(data);
  intvec_iterator iter(std::find_if(data.begin(), data.end(), intrange(10, 20)));
  if (iter == data.end())
```

```
      std::cout << "No values in [10,20] found\n";
   else
      std::cout << "Value " << *iter << " in range [10,20].\n";
}
```

The search function is similar to find, except it searches for a matching subrange. That is, you supply an iterator range to search and an iterator range to match. The search algorithm looks for the first occurrence of a sequence of elements that equals the entire match range. Listing 41-5 shows a silly program that generates a large vector of random integers in the range 0 to 9, and then searches for a subrange that matches the first four digits of π.

**Listing 41-5.** *Finding a Subrange that Matches the First Four Digits of* π

```
#include <algorithm>
#include <cstdlib>
#include <iostream>
#include <iterator>
#include <ostream>
#include <vector>

#include "data.hpp"
#include "randomint.hpp"

int main()
{
  intvector pi(4);
  pi.at(0) = 3;
  pi.at(1) = 1;
  pi.at(2) = 4;
  pi.at(3) = 1;

  intvector data(10000);
  // The randomint functor generates random numbers in the range [0, 9].
  // The details are not germane to this exploration, but feel free to
  // consult the code in randomint.hpp on the book's web site.
  std::generate(data.begin(), data.end(), randomint(0, 9));

  intvec_iterator iter(std::search(data.begin(), data.end(), pi.begin(), pi.end()));
  if (iter == data.end())
    std::cout << "The integer range does not contain the digits of pi.\n";
  else
  {
    std::cout << "Easy as pi: ";
    std::copy(iter, iter+pi.size(), std::ostream_iterator<int>(std::cout, " "));
    std::cout << '\n';
  }
}
```

# Binary Search Algorithms

The map container stores its elements in sorted order, so you can use any of the binary search algorithms, but map also has member functions that can take advantage of access to the internal structure of a map, and so offer improved performance. Thus, the binary search algorithms are typically used on sequential containers, such as vector, when you know that they contain sorted data. If the input range is not properly sorted, the results are undefined: you might get the wrong answer, the program might crash, or something even worse might happen.

The binary_search function simply tests whether a sorted range contains a particular value. By default, values are compared using only the < operator. Another form of binary_search takes a comparison functor as an additional argument to perform the comparison.

## WHAT'S IN A NAME?

The find function performs a linear search for a single item. The search function performs a linear search for a matching series of items. So why isn't binary_search called binary_find? On the other hand, find_end searches for the rightmost match of a range of values, so why isn't it called search_end? The equal function is completely different from equal_range, in spite of the similarity in their names.

In spite of efforts by the C++ committee to apply uniform rules for algorithm names, such as appending _if to functions that take a functor argument but cannot be overloaded, they goofed with a number of names. What this means for you is that you need to keep a reference close at hand. Don't judge a function by its name, but read the description of what the function does and how it does it before you decide whether it's the right function to use.

The lower_bound function is similar to binary_search, except it returns an iterator. The iterator points to the first occurrence of the value or it points to a position where the value belongs if you want to insert the value into the vector and keep the vector in sorted order. The upper_bound function is similar to lower_bound except it returns an iterator that points to the last position where you can insert the value and keep it in sorted order; if the value is found, that means upper_bound points to one position past the last occurrence of the value in the vector. To put it another way, the range [lower_bound, upper_bound) is the subrange of every occurrence of the value in the sorted range. As with any range, if lower_bound == upper_bound, the result range is empty, which means the value is not in the search range.

Listing 41-6 shows a variation on Listing 41-1, sorting the integer vector and searching for a value using lower_bound to perform a binary search.

**Listing 41-6.** *Searching for an Integer Using Binary Search*

```
#include <algorithm>
#include <iostream>
#include <ostream>
```

```
#include "data.hpp"

int main()
{
  intvector data;
  read_data(data);
  std::sort(data.begin(), data.end());
  write_data(data);
  intvec_iterator iter(std::lower_bound(data.begin(), data.end(), 42));
  if (iter == data.end())
    std::cout << "Value 42 not found\n";
  else
  {
    *iter = 0;
    std::cout << "Value 42 changed to 0:\n";
    write_data(data);
  }
}
```

Only two lines changed: one insertion to sort the vector, and changing find to lower_
bound. To better understand how lower_bound and upper_bound really work, it helps to write a
test program. The program reads some integers from the user into a vector, sorts the vector,
and clears the I/O state bits on the standard input (std::cin.clear()) so you can enter some
test values. The program then repeatedly ask for integers from the user, and searches for each
value using lower_bound and upper_bound. To help you understand exactly what these functions return, call the distance function to determine an iterator's position in a vector:

```
intvec_iterator iter(std::lower_bound(data.begin(), data.end(), 42));
std::cout << "Index of 42 is " << std::distance(data.begin(), iter) << '\n';
```

The distance function (declared in <iterator>) takes an iterator range and returns the
number of elements in the range. The return type is the iterator's difference_type, which is
just an integer type, although the exact type (e.g., int or long int) depends on the implementation.

**Write the test program.** Then run the program with the following sample input:

9 4 2 1 5 4 3 6 2 7 4

**What should the program print as the sorted vector?**

_____

Fill in Table 41-1 with the expected values for the lower and upper bounds of each value.
Then run the program to check your answers.

**Table 41-1.** *Results of Testing Binary Search Functions*

| Value | Expected Lower Bound | Expected Upper Bound | Actual Lower Bound | Actual Upper Bound |
|---|---|---|---|---|
| 3 | | | | |
| 4 | | | | |
| 8 | | | | |
| 0 | | | | |
| 10 | | | | |

Compare your test program with mine in Listing 41-7.

**Listing 41-7.** *Exploring the* lower_bound *and* upper_bound *Functions*

```
#include <algorithm>
#include <iostream>
#include <istream>
#include <vector>

#include "data.hpp"

int main()
{
  intvector data;
  read_data(data);
  std::sort(data.begin(), data.end());
  write_data(data);

  std::cin.clear();
  int test;
  while (std::cin >> test)
  {
    intvec_iterator lb(std::lower_bound(data.begin(), data.end(), test));
    intvec_iterator ub(std::upper_bound(data.begin(), data.end(), test));
    std::cout << "lower bound = " << std::distance(data.begin(), lb) << '\n' <<
                 "upper bound = " << std::distance(data.begin(), ub) << '\n';
  }
}
```

Other useful linear functions include count, which takes an iterator range and value and returns the number of occurrences of the value in the range. Its counterpart count_if takes a predicate instead of a value and returns the number of times the predicate returns true.

The min_element function takes a range and returns an iterator that refers to the smallest element in the range. It has a counterpart, max_element, which returns an iterator that refers to the largest element in the range. Both come in the usual overloaded forms: one uses the < operator and the other takes an additional argument for a comparison predicate.

# Comparing

To check whether two ranges are equal, that is, that they contain the same values, call the
equal algorithm. This algorithm takes a start and one-past-the-end iterator for one range and
the start of the second range, assuming the two ranges have the same size. It returns true if
every element of the two ranges are equal or false if any element doesn't match. The function
has two forms: pass only the iterators to equal, and it compares elements with the == operator;
pass a comparison functor as the last argument, and equal compares elements by calling the
functor. The first argument to the functor is the element from the first range and the second
argument is the element from the second range.

The mismatch function is the opposite. It compares two ranges and returns a std::pair
(introduced in Exploration 14) of iterators that refer to the first elements that do not match.
The first iterator in the pair refers to an element in the first range and the second iterator refers
to the second range. If the two ranges are equal, the return value is a pair of end iterators.

The lexicographical_compare algorithm sets the record for the longest algorithm name.
It compares two ranges and determines whether the first range is "less than" the second. It
does this by comparing the ranges one element at a time. If the ranges are equal, the function
returns false. If the ranges are equal up to the end of one range, and the other range is longer,
the shorter range is less than the longer range. If an element mismatch is found, whichever
range contains the smaller element is the smaller range. All elements are compared using the
< operator (or a caller-supplied predicate) and checked for equivalence, not equality. Recall
that elements a and b are equivalent if the following is true:

```
not (a < b) and not (b < a)
```

If you apply lexicographical_compare to two strings, you get the expected less-than relationship, which explains the name. In other words, if you call this algorithm with the strings
"hello" and "help", it returns true; if you call it with "help" and "hello", it returns false; and if
you call it with "hel" and "hello", it returns true.

**Write a test program** that reads two sequences of integers into separate vectors. (Remember to clear the state after reading the first vector's data.) Then test the equal, mismatch, and
lexicographical_compare functions on the two ranges. Remember that equal and mismatch
require their input ranges to have the same size. You can ensure that you compare only the
number of elements in the shorter vector by computing the end iterator instead of calling the
end() member function:

```
std::equal(data1.begin(),
           data1.begin() + std::min(data1.size(), data2.size()),
           data2.begin())
```

Not all iterators allow addition, but a vector's iterators do allow it. Adding an integer n
to begin() offsets the iterator as though you had advanced it n times with the ++ operator.
(Discover more about iterators in the next Exploration.)

Table 41-2 lists some suggested input data sets.

**Table 41-2.** *Suggested Data Sets for Testing Comparison Algorithms*

| Data Set 1 | Data Set 2 |
|---|---|
| 1 2 3 4 5 | 1 2 3 |
| 1 2 3 | 1 2 3 4 5 |
| 1 2 3 4 5 | 1 2 4 5 |
| 1 2 3 | 1 2 3 |

Compare your test program with mine in Listing 41-8.

**Listing 41-8.** *Testing Various Comparison Algorithms*

```
#include <algorithm>
#include <iostream>
#include <ostream>
#include <vector>

#include "data.hpp"

int main()
{
  intvector data1;
  intvector data2;

  read_data(data1);
  std::cin.clear();
  read_data(data2);

  std::cout << "data1: ";
  write_data(data1);
  std::cout << "data2: ";
  write_data(data2);

  intvec_iterator data1_end(data1.begin() + std::min(data1.size(), data2.size()));

  std::cout << std::boolalpha;
  std::cout << "equal(data1, data2) = " <<
    equal(data1.begin(), data1_end, data2.begin()) << '\n';

  std::pair<intvec_iterator, intvec_iterator>
    result(mismatch(data1.begin(), data1_end, data2.begin()));

  std::cout << "mismatch(data1, data2) = index " <<
   std::distance(data1.begin(), result.first) << '\n';
```

```
    std::cout << "lex_comp(data1, data2) = " <<
        std::lexicographical_compare(data1.begin(), data1.end(),
                                     data2.begin(), data2.end()) << '\n';
}
```

# Rearranging Data

You've already seen the sort algorithm many times. Other algorithms are also adept at rearranging values in a range. The merge algorithm merges two sorted input ranges into a single output range. As always, you must ensure the output range has enough room to accept the entire merged result from both input ranges. The two input ranges can be different sizes, so merge takes five or six arguments: two for the first input range, two for the second input range, one for the start of the output range, and an optional argument for a functor to use instead of the < operator.

The replace algorithm scans an input range and replaces every occurrence of an old value with a new value. The replacement occurs in place, so you specify the range with the usual pair of iterators, but no write iterator. The replace_if function is similar, but takes a predicate instead of an old value. **Write a program that reads a vector of integers, and replaces all occurrences of values in the range [10, 20] with 0.** Be sure to reuse the intrange functor class. Compare your program with mine in Listing 41-9.

**Listing 41-9.** *Using replace_if and intrange to Replace All Integers in [10, 20] with 0*

```
#include <algorithm>

#include "data.hpp"
#include "intrange.hpp"

int main()
{
  intvector data;
  read_data(data);
  write_data(data);
  std::replace_if(data.begin(), data.end(), intrange(10, 20), 0);
  write_data(data);
}
```

A fun algorithm is random_shuffle, which shuffles elements in place into random order. This function takes two arguments, specifying the range to shuffle. Another form of the function takes three arguments. The final argument is a functor that returns a random number in the range [0, n), where n is the size of the input range.

**Use the *sequence.hpp* file (from Listing 40-9) and generate a vector of 100 sequential integers. Then shuffle it into random order and print it.** Compare your solution with mine in Listing 41-10.

**Listing 41-10.** *Shuffling Integers into Random Order*

```
#include <algorithm>

#include "data.hpp"
#include "sequence.hpp"

int main()
{
  intvector data(100);
  std::generate(data.begin(), data.end(), sequence(1, 1));
  write_data(data);
  std::random_shuffle(data.begin(), data.end());
  write_data(data);
}
```

Unless you peeked ahead or used a library reference, your solution probably uses a loop to call the sequence function call operator 100 times. That's a fine solution, and is such a common idiom the standard library has an algorithm to do it for you. The generate algorithm repeatedly calls a functor with no arguments and copies the return value into an output range. It calls the functor once per element in the range, overwriting every element. The generate_n function takes an iterator for the start of a range and an integer for the size of the range. It then calls a functor (the third argument) once for each element of the range, copying the return value into the range. It is your responsibility to ensure the range actually has that many elements in it. To use generate_n instead of generate in Listing 41-10, you could write

```
std::generate_n(data.begin(), data.size(), sequence(1, 1));
```

If you don't need to call a functor for every item of a range, but instead want to fill a range with copies of the same value, call fill, passing a pair of iterators that specify a range, and a value. The value is copied into every element in the range. The fill_n function takes a starting iterator and an integer size to specify the target range.

The only other algorithm that has a counted form is search_n, which is the counted counterpart of search.

The transform algorithm modifies items by calling a functor for each item in an input range. It writes the results to an output range, which can be the same as the input range, resulting in modifying the range in place. You've seen this algorithm at work already, so I won't add much to what you already know. The function has two forms: unary and binary. The unary form takes one input range, the start of an output range, and a functor. It calls the functor for each element of the input range, copying the result to the output range. The output range can be the same as the input range, or it can be a separate range. As with all algorithms, you need to ensure that the output range is large enough to store the results.

The binary form takes an input range, the start of a second input range (it assumes the size is the same as the size of the first input range), the start of an output range, and a binary functor. The functor is called for each element in the input ranges; the first argument comes from the first input range, and the second argument comes from the second input range. As with the unary form, the function copies the result to the output range, which can be the same as either input range. Note that the types of the two input ranges do not have to be the same.

# Copying Data

Some algorithms operate in place, and others copy their results to an output range. For example, `reverse` reverses items in place, and `reverse_copy` leaves the input range intact and copies the reversed items to an output range. If a copying form of an algorithm exists, its name has `_copy` appended. (Unless it is also a predicate form of a function, in which case it has `_if` appended after `_copy`, as in `replace_copy_if`.)

In addition to just plain `copy`, which you've seen many times already, the standard library offers `copy_backward` which makes a copy, but starts at the end and works toward the beginning, preserving the original order. Distinguish `copy_backward` from `reverse_copy`. The latter starts at the beginning and works toward the end of the input range, but copies the values into reverse order.

As with all algorithms that write output, it is your responsibility to ensure the output range is large enough to handle everything you write to it. Some implementations of the standard library offer debugging modes to help detect violations of this rule. If your library offers such a feature, by all means, take full advantage of it.

# Deleting Elements

The trickiest algorithms to use are those that "remove" elements. As you learned in Exploration 21, algorithms such as `remove` don't actually delete anything. Instead, they rearrange the elements in the range so that all the elements slated for removal are packed at the end of the range. You can then decide to use the subrange of elements you want to keep, or erase the "removed" elements by calling the `erase` member function.

The `remove` function takes an iterator range and a value, and it removes all elements equal to that value. You can also use a predicate with `remove_if`, to remove all elements for which a predicate returns true. These two functions have copying counterparts, which don't rearrange anything, but merely copy the elements that are not being removed: `remove_copy` copies all the elements that are not equal to a certain value, and `remove_copy_if` copies all elements for which a predicate returns false.

I often find situations in which I want to copy elements that meet some condition. Ideally, I would write a predicate for the condition and call the `copy_if` algorithm. The only problem is that `copy_if` is not in the standard library. Instead, you can reverse the logic of your predicate and call `remove_copy_if`. (The `copy_if` function is one of several new algorithms slated to appear in the next revision of the C++ standard.)

Another algorithm that removes elements is `unique` (and `unique_copy`). It takes an input range and removes all adjacent duplicates, thereby ensuring that every item in the range is unique. (If the range is sorted, then all duplicates are adjacent.) Both functions can take a comparison functor instead of using the default `==` operator.

**Write a program that reads integers into a vector, erases all elements equal to zero, copies only those elements that lie in the range [24, 42] to another vector, sorts the other vector, and removes duplicates. Print the resulting vector.** My solution is in Listing 41-11.

**Listing 41-11.** *Erasing Elements from a Vector*

```cpp
#include <algorithm>
#include "data.hpp"
#include "intrange.hpp"

class outofrange
{
public:
  outofrange(int low, int high) : range_(low, high) {}
  bool operator()(int test) const { return not range_(test); }
private:
  intrange range_;
};

int main()
{
  intvector data;
  read_data(data);
  data.erase(std::remove(data.begin(), data.end(), 0), data.end());
  intvector copy;
  std::remove_copy_if(data.begin(), data.end(), std::back_inserter(copy),
                      outofrange(24, 42));
  std::sort(copy.begin(), copy.end());
  copy.erase(std::unique(copy.begin(), copy.end()), copy.end());
  write_data(copy);
}
```

# Iterators

Algorithms and iterators are closely related. All the algorithms (except min and max) take two or more iterators as arguments. To use algorithms effectively, you must understand iterators. Therefore, the next Exploration will help you master iterators, all five flavors. That's right. Iterators come in five different varieties. Keep reading to learn more.

■■■

# Iterators

Iterators provide element-by-element access to a sequence of things. The things can be numbers, characters, or objects of almost any type. The standard containers, such as `vector`, provide iterator access to the container contents, and other standard iterators let you access input streams and output streams, for example. The standard algorithms use iterators exclusively for operating on sequences of things.

Until now, your view and use of iterators has been somewhat limited. Sure, you've used them, but do you really understand them? This Exploration helps you understand what's really going on with iterators.

## Kinds of Iterators

So far, you have seen that iterators come in multiple varieties, in particular, read and write. The `copy` function, for example, takes two read iterators to specify an input range and one write iterator to specify the start of an output range. As always, specify the input range as a pair of read iterators: one that refers to the first element of the range and one that refers to one-past-the-end element of the input range. The `copy` function returns a write iterator: the value of the result iterator after the copy is complete.

```
WriteIterator copy(ReadIterator start, ReadIterator end, WriteIterator result);
```

All this time, however, I've oversimplified the situation by referring to "read" and "write" iterators. In fact, C++ has five different categories of iterators: input, output, forward, bidirectional, and random access. Input and output iterators have the least functionality, and random access has the most. You can substitute an iterator with more functionality anywhere that calls for an iterator with less. Figure 42-1 illustrates the substitutability of iterators. Don't be misled by the figure, however. It does not show class inheritance. What makes an iterator an iterator is its behavior. If it fulfills all the requirements of an input iterator, for example, it is an input iterator, regardless of its type.

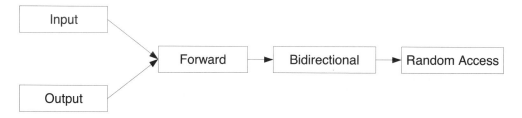

**Figure 42-1.** *Substitution tree for iterators*

All iterators can be copied and assigned freely. The result of a copy or an assignment is a new iterator that refers to the same item as the original iterator. The other characteristics depend on the iterator category, as described in the following sections.

## Input Iterators

An input iterator, unsurprisingly, supports only input. You can read from the iterator (using the unary * operator) only once per iteration. You cannot modify the item that the itera-tor refers to. The ++ operator advances to the next input item. You can compare iterators for equality and inequality, but the only meaningful comparison is to compare an iterator with an end iterator. You cannot, in general, compare two input iterators to see if they refer to the same item.

That's about it. Input iterators are quite limited, but they are also extremely useful. Almost every standard algorithm expresses an input range in terms of two input iterators: the start of the input range and one-past-the-end of the input range.

The istream_iterator type is an example of an input iterator. You can also treat any con-tainer's iterator as an input iterator; e.g., the iterator that a vector's begin() member function returns.

## Output Iterators

An output iterator supports only output. You can assign to an iterator item (by applying the * operator to the iterator on the left-hand side of an assignment), but you cannot read from the iterator. You can modify the iterator value only once per iteration. The ++ operator advances to the next output item.

You *cannot* compare output iterators for equality or inequality.

In spite of the limitations on output iterators, they, too, are widely used by the standard algorithms. Every algorithm that copies data to an output range takes an output iterator to specify the start of the range.

One caution when dealing with output iterators is that you must ensure that wherever the iterator is actually writing has enough room to store the entire output. Any mistakes result in undefined behavior. Some implementations offer debugging iterators that can check for this kind of mistake, and you should certainly take advantage of such tools when they are avail-able. Don't rely solely on debugging libraries, however. Careful code design, careful code implementation, and careful code review are absolutely necessary to ensure safety when using output (and other) iterators.

The `ostream_iterator` type is an example of an output iterator. You can also treat many container's iterators as output iterators; e.g., the iterator that a vector's `begin()` member function returns.

## Forward Iterators

A forward iterator has all the functionality of an input iterator and an output iterator, and then some. You can freely read from and write to an iterator item (still using the unary * operator), and you can do so as often as you wish. The ++ operator advances to the next item, and the == and != operators can compare iterators to see if they refer to the same item or to the end position.

Some algorithms require forward iterators instead of input iterators. I glossed over that detail in the previous Explorations because it rarely affects you. For example, the binary search algorithms require forward iterators to specify the input range because they might need to refer to a particular item more than once. That means you cannot directly use an `istream_iterator` as an argument to, say, `lower_bound`, but then, you aren't likely to try that in a real program. All the containers' iterators meet the requirements of forward iterators, so in practical terms, this restriction has little impact.

## Bidirectional Iterators

A bidirectional iterator has all the functionality of a forward iterator, but it also supports the -- operator, which moves the iterator backward one position to the previous item. As with any iterator, you are responsible for ensuring that you never advance the iterator past the end of the range or before the beginning.

The `reverse` and `reverse_copy` algorithms (and a few others) require bidirectional iterators. All the containers' iterators meet at least the requirements of bidirectional iterators, so you rarely have to worry about this restriction.

## Random Access Iterators

A random access iterator is the most powerful iterator. It has all the functionality of all other iterators, plus you can move the iterator an arbitrary amount by adding or subtracting an integer.

You can subtract two iterators (provided they refer to the same sequence of objects) to obtain the distance between them. Recall from Exploration 41 that the `distance` function returns the distance between two iterators. If you pass forward or bidirectional iterators to the function, it advances the starting iterator one step at a time until it reaches the end iterator. Only then will it know the distance. If you pass random access iterators, it merely subtracts the two iterators and immediately returns the distance between them.

You can compare random access iterators for equality or inequality. If the two iterators refer to the same sequence of objects, you can also use any of the relational operators. For random access iterators, a < b means a refers to an item earlier in the sequence than b.

Algorithms such as `sort` require random access iterators. The `vector` type provides random access iterators, but not all containers do. The `list` container, for example, implements a doubly-linked list. It has only bidirectional iterators. Because you can't use the `sort` algorithm, the list container has its own `sort` member function. Learn more about `list` in Exploration 51.

Now that you know vectors supply random access iterators, and you can compare random access iterators using relational operators, revisit Listing 10-4. Can you think of an easier way to write that program? (Hint: consider a loop condition of start < end.) See my rewrite in Listing 42-1.

**Listing 42-1.** *Comparing Iterators by Using the < Operator*

```cpp
#include <algorithm>
#include <iostream>
#include <istream>
#include <iterator>
#include <ostream>
#include <vector>

int main()
{
  std::vector<int> data;
  int x;
  while (std::cin >> x)
    data.push_back(x);

  for (std::vector<int>::iterator start(data.begin()), end(data.end());
       start < end;
       ++start)
  {
    --end; // now end points to a real position, possibly start
    int tmp = *start;
    *start = *end;
    *end = tmp;
  }

  std::copy(data.begin(), data.end(), std::ostream_iterator<int>(std::cout, "\n"));
}
```

So input, forward, bidirectional, and random access iterators all qualify as "read" iterators, and output, forward, bidirectional, and random access iterators all qualify as "write" iterators. An algorithm, such as copy, might require only input and output iterators. That is, the input range requires two input iterators; you can use any iterator that meets the requirements of an input iterator: input, forward, bidirectional, or random access. For the start of the output range, use any iterator that meets the requirements of an output iterator: output, forward, bidirectional, or random access.

# Working with Iterators

The most common sources for iterators are the begin() and end() member functions that all containers (such as map and vector) provide. The begin() member function returns an iterator that refers to the first element of the container, and end() returns an iterator that refers to the position one-past-the-end element of the container.

### What does begin() return for an empty container?

---

If the container is empty, begin() returns the same value as end(), that is, a special value that represents "past the end" and cannot be dereferenced. One way to test whether a container is empty is to test whether begin() == end(). (Even better, especially when you are writing a real program and not trying to illustrate the nature of iterators, is to call the empty() member function, which every container provides.)

The type of a container's iterator is always named iterator. The name is a nested member, so you refer to the iterator name by prefixing it with the container type.

```
std::map<std::string, int>::iterator map_iter;
std::vector<int>::iterator vector_iter;
```

Each container implements its iterator differently. All that matters to you is that the iterator fulfills the requirements of one of the standard categories.

The exact category of iterator depends on the container. A vector returns random access iterators. A map returns bidirectional iterators. Any library reference will tell you exactly what category of iterator each container supports.

A number of algorithms and container member functions also return iterators. For example, almost every function that performs a search returns an iterator that refers to the desired item. If the function cannot find the item, it returns the end iterator. The type of the return value is usually the same as the type of the iterators in the input range. Algorithms that copy elements to an output range return the result iterator.

Once you have an iterator, you can dereference it with * to obtain the value that it refers to (except for an output iterator, which you dereference only to assign a new value; and except for the end iterators, which you can never dereference). If the iterator refers to an object, and you want to access a member of the object, you can use the shorthand -> notation.

```
std::vector<std::string> lines(2, "hello");
std::string first(*lines.begin());   // dereference the first item
int size(lines.begin()->size());     // dereference and call a member function
```

You can advance an iterator to a new position by calling the advance function (declared in <iterator>). The first argument is the iterator you want to advance, and the second is the number of positions. If the iterator is bidirectional or random access, the second argument can be negative to go backward. You can advance an input iterator but not an output iterator. Reusing the sequence functor from Exploration 40, read the program in Listing 42-2.

**Listing 42-2.** *Advancing an Iterator*

```
#include <algorithm>
#include <iostream>
#include <iterator>
#include <ostream>
#include <vector>

#include "data.hpp"
#include "sequence.hpp"
```

```
int main()
{
  intvector data(10);
  std::generate(data.begin(), data.end(), sequence(0, 2)); // fill with even numbers
  intvec_iterator iter(data.begin());
  std::advance(iter, 4);
  std::cout << *iter << ", ";
  std::advance(iter, -2);
  std::cout << *iter << '\n';
}
```

**What does the program print?**

_____

The data vector is filled with even numbers, starting at 0. The iterator, iter, initially refers to the first element of the vector, namely, 0. The iterator advances four positions, to value 8, and then back two positions to 4. So the output is

8, 4

Declaring variables to store iterators is clumsy. The type names are long and cumbersome. A good idea, therefore, is to use typedef declarations to create shorter aliases for the long, clumsy type names:

```
typedef std::vector<std::string>::iterator strvec_iterator;

std::vector<std::string> lines(2, "hello");
strvec_iterator iter(lines.begin());
std::string first(*iter);    // dereference the first item
int size(iter->size());      // dereference and call a member function
```

## SIMPLER, SHORTER DECLARATIONS

The next revision to the C++ standard will make it easier to declare iterators. The auto keyword will deduce the type of an object automatically. Thus, a definition of the form

```
auto iter(lines.begin());
```

directs the compiler to use the return type of lines.begin() as the type of iter. Typedefs are still useful in many cases, but this new use of the auto keyword will reduce the size of many a for loop. Look for this feature soon in a compiler near you.

# const_iterator vs. const iterator

A frequent source of confusion is the difference between a `const_iterator` and `const iterator`. An output iterator (and any iterator that also meets the requirements of an output iterator, namely, forward, bidirectional, and random access) lets you modify the item it references. For some forward iterators (and bidirectional and random access), you want to treat the data in the range as read only. Even though the iterator itself meets the requirements of a forward iterator, your immediate need might be only for an input iterator.

You might think that declaring the iterator `const` would help. After all, that's how you ask the compiler to help you by preventing accidental modification of a variable: declare the variable with the `const` specifier. What do you think? **Will it work?** _____

If you aren't sure, try a test. Read Listing 42-3 and **predict its output**.

**Listing 42-3.** *Printing the Middle Item of a Series of Integers*

```
#include <iostream>
#include <ostream>

#include "data.hpp"

int main()
{
  intvector data;
  read_data(data);
  const intvec_iterator iter(data.begin());
  std::advance(iter, data.size() / 2); // move to middle of vector
  if (not data.empty())
    std::cout << "middle item = " << *iter << '\n';
}
```

Can you see why the compiler refuses to compile the program? Maybe you can't see the precise reason, buried in the compiler's error output. (The next section will discuss this problem at greater length.) The error is that the variable `iter` is `const`. You cannot modify the iterator, so you cannot advance it to the middle of the vector.

Instead of declaring the iterator itself as `const`, you need to tell the compiler that you want the iterator to refer to `const` data. If the vector itself were `const`, the `begin()` function would return exactly such an iterator. You could freely modify the iterator's position, but you could not modify the value that the iterator references. The name of the iterator that this function returns is `const_iterator` (with underscore).

In other words, every container actually has two different `begin()` functions. One is a `const` member function and returns `const_iterator`. The other is not a `const` member function; it returns a plain `iterator`. As with any `const` or non-const member function, the compiler chooses one or the other depending on whether the container itself is `const`. If the container is not `const`, you get the non-`const` version of `begin()`, which returns a plain `iterator`, and you can modify the container contents through the iterator. If the container is `const`, you get the `const` version of `begin()`, which returns a `const_iterator`, which prevents you from modifying the container's contents.

Rewrite Listing 42-3 to use a const_iterator. Your program should look something like Listing 42-4.

**Listing 42-4.** *Really Printing the Middle Item of a Series of Integers*

```
#include <iostream>
#include <ostream>

#include "data.hpp"

int main()
{
  intvector data;
  read_data(data);
  intvector::const_iterator iter(data.begin());
  std::advance(iter, data.size() / 2); // move to middle of vector
  if (not data.empty())
    std::cout << "middle item = " << *iter << '\n';
}
```

Prove to yourself that you cannot modify the data when you have a const_iterator. **Make a further modification to your program to negate the middle value.** Now your program should look like Listing 42-5.

**Listing 42-5.** *Negating the Middle Value in a Series of Integers*

```
#include <iostream>
#include <ostream>

#include "data.hpp"

int main()
{
  intvector data;
  read_data(data);
  intvector::const_iterator iter(data.begin());
  std::advance(iter, data.size() / 2); // move to middle of vector
  if (not data.empty())
    *iter = - *iter;
  write_data(data);
}
```

If you change const_iterator to iterator, the program works. **Do it.**

# Error Messages

When you compiled Listing 42-3, the compiler issued an error message, or *diagnostic* as the C++ standard writers call it. For example, the compiler that I use every day, g++, prints the following:

```
/usr/include/c++/4.0.2/bits/stl_iterator_base_funcs.h: In function void➥
std::__advance(_RandomAccessIterator&, _Distance,➥
std::random_access_iterator_tag) [with _RandomAccessIterator = const➥
__gnu_cxx::__normal_iterator<int*, std::vector<int, std::allocator<int> > >,➥
_Distance = unsigned int]:
/usr/include/c++/4.0.2/bits/stl_iterator_base_funcs.h:175:   instantiated from➥
void std::advance(_InputIterator&, _Distance) [with _InputIterator = const➥
__gnu_cxx::__normal_iterator<int*, std::vector<int, std::allocator<int> > >,➥
_Distance = unsigned int]
list4102.cxx:13:   instantiated from here
/usr/include/c++/4.0.2/bits/stl_iterator_base_funcs.h:155: error: no match for➥
operator+= in __i += __n
/usr/include/c++/4.0.2/bits/stl_iterator.h:649: note: candidates are:➥
__gnu_cxx::__normal_iterator<_Iterator, _Container>&➥
__gnu_cxx::__normal_iterator<_Iterator, _Container>::operator+=(const typename➥
std::iterator_traits<_Iterator>::difference_type&) [with _Iterator = int*,➥
_Container = std::vector<int, std::allocator<int> >] <near match>
```

So what does all that gobbledygook mean? Although a C++ expert can figure it out, it may not be much help to you. Buried in the middle is the line number and source file that identify the source of the error. That's where you need to start looking. The compiler didn't detect the error until it started working through various #include files. These file names depend on the implementation of the standard library, so you can't always tell from those file names what is the actual error.

In this case, the error arises from within the std::advance function. That's when the compiler detects that it has a const iterator, but it does not have any functions that work with a const iterator. Instead of complaining about the const-ness, however, all it manages to do is to complain that it lacks a "match" for the function it seeks. That means it is looking for argument types that match the parameter types to resolve an overloaded operator. Because a const argument cannot match a non-const parameter, the compiler failed to find an overload that matches the arguments.

Don't give up hope for ever understanding C++ compiler error messages. By the end of the book, you will have gained quite a bit more knowledge that will help you understand how the compiler and library really work, and that understanding will help you make sense of these error messages.

My advice for dealing with the deluge of confusing error messages is to start by finding the first mention of your source file. That should tell you the line number that gives rise to the problem. Check the source file. You might see an obvious mistake. If not, check the error message text. Ignore the "instantiated from here" and similar messages. Try to find the real error message.

# Specialized Iterators

The <iterator> header defines a number of useful, specialized iterators, such as back_
inserter, which you've seen several times already. Strictly speaking, back_inserter is
a function that returns an iterator, but you rarely need to know the exact iterator type.

In addition to back_inserter, you can also use front_inserter, which also takes a container as an argument and returns an output iterator. Every time you assign a value to the
dereferenced iterator, it calls the container's push_front member function to insert the value
at the start of the container.

The inserter function takes a container and an iterator as arguments. It returns an output
iterator that calls the container's insert function. The insert member function requires an
iterator argument, specifying the position at which to insert the value. The inserter iterator
initially passes its second argument as the insertion position. After each insertion, it updates
its internal iterator, so subsequent insertions go into subsequent positions. In other words,
inserter just does the right thing.

Other specialized iterators include istream_iterator and ostream_iterator, which you've
also seen. An istream_iterator is an input iterator that extracts values from a stream when
you dereference the iterator. With no arguments, the istream_iterator constructor creates an
end-of-stream iterator. An iterator is equal to the end-of-stream iterator when an input operation fails.

An ostream_iterator is an output iterator. The constructor takes an output stream and an
optional string as arguments. Assigning to the dereferenced iterator writes a value to the output stream, optionally followed by the string (from the constructor).

Another specialized iterator is reverse_iterator. It adapts an existing iterator (called the
*base* iterator), which must be bidirectional (or random access). When the reverse iterator goes
forward (++), the base iterator goes backward (--). Containers that support bidirectional iterators have rbegin() and rend() member functions, which return reverse iterators. The rbegin()
function returns a reverse iterator that points to the last element of the container, and rend()
returns a special reverse iterator value that represents one position before the beginning of the
container. Thus, you treat the range [rbegin(), rend()) as a normal iterator range, expressing
the values of the container in reverse order.

C++ doesn't permit an iterator to point to "one-before-the-beginning," so reverse iterators
have a somewhat funky implementation. Ordinarily, implementation details don't matter, but
reverse_iterator exposes this particular detail in its base() member function, which returns
the base iterator.

I could tell you what the base iterator actually is, but that would take the fun away from
you. **Write a program to reveal the nature of the reverse_iterator's base iterator.** (Hint: fill
a vector with a sequence of integers. Use a reverse iterator to get to the middle value. Compare
with the value of the iterator's base() iterator.)

**If a reverse_iterator points to position $x$ of a container, what does its base() iterator
point to?**

_____

If you did not answer $x + 1$, try running the program in Listing 42-6.

**Listing 42-6.** *Revealing the Implementation of* reverse_iterator

```
#include <algorithm>
#include <cassert>
#include <iostream>
#include <ostream>

#include "data.hpp"
#include "sequence.hpp"

int main()
{
  intvector data(10);
  std::generate(data.begin(), data.end(), sequence(1));
  write_data(data);                          // prints { 1 2 3 4 5 6 7 8 9 10 }
  intvector::iterator iter(data.begin());
  iter = iter + 5;                           // iter is random access
  std::cout << *iter << '\n';                // prints 5

  intvector::reverse_iterator rev(data.rbegin());
  std::cout << *rev << '\n';                 // prints 10
  rev = rev + 4;                             // rev is also random access
  std::cout << *rev << '\n';                 // prints 6
  std::cout << *rev.base() << '\n';          // prints 7
  std::cout << *data.rend().base() << '\n';  // prints 0
  assert(data.rbegin().base() == data.end());
  assert(data.rend().base()   == data.begin());
}
```

Now do you see? The base iterator always points to one position *after* the reverse itera-tor's position. That's the trick that allows rend() to point to a position "before the beginning," even though that's not allowed. Under the hood, the rend() iterator actually has a base iterator that points at the first item in the container, and the reverse_iterator's implementation of the * operator performs the magic of taking the base iterator, retreating one position, and then dereferencing the base iterator.

# The Importance of Being Iterator

At this point, you might be a little bewildered and wondering why I'm bothering to reveal this magician's secrets. The problem is that a number of important member functions, such as insert and erase, require an iterator as an argument—not const_iterator and not reverse_iterator, but just plain iterator.

Fully understanding the point requires more C++ than you've learned so far. If you still feel iffy about your C++ skills, you can skip this section. It provides a little bit of explanation about problems that can crop up when using iterators, and eventually, you will need to under-stand this material. If you stick with the way I use iterators in this book, you won't run into any problems. I raise these issues in case you venture off and start using iterators in new and different ways, which I encourage you to do. This section is just an introduction to the problems. If you want to know more, I recommend Scott Meyers' book, *Effective STL* (Addison-Wesley, 2001).

Consider the program in Listing 42-7.

**Listing 42-7.** *You Can't erase with a const_iterator*

```
#include <algorithm>
#include "data.hpp"

// Find the answer in data.
intvector::const_iterator find_answer(intvector const& data)
{
  return std::find(data.begin(), data.end(), 42);
}

int main()
{
  intvector data;
  read_data(data);
  // find the answer, and erase all elements from that point onward
  data.erase(find_answer(data), data.end());
}
```

Can you see what's wrong with this simple program? Don't be discouraged if you can't. The problem is subtle.

The erase member function takes an iterator for its arguments, but find_answer returns a const_iterator. The standard lets you convert an iterator to a const_iterator, but not vice versa. Thus, the compiler complains because one of the arguments to erase is const_iterator, which is not allowed.

The solution, in this case, is to remove the const specifier in find_answer and change const_iterator to iterator. Although I recommend using const because it promotes safe programming, when dealing with iterators, you should use a plain iterator whenever possible, and use const_iterator only when you absolutely have to.

Similarly, you can't use a reverse_iterator or a const_reverse_iterator (which is just like a normal reverse_iterator, except you cannot modify the data) when a plain iterator is called for. Unlike const_iterator, you can convert a reverse_iterator into an iterator with the base() member function. As you saw, however, the position is off by one, so be careful if you want to use the base iterator in a call to erase.

As you can see, iterators are a little more complicated than they initially seem to be. Once you understand how they work, however, you will see that they are actually quite simple, powerful, and easy to use. But first, it's time to pick up a few more important C++ programming techniques. The next Exploration introduces exceptions and exception-handling, necessary topics for properly handling programmer and user errors.

# Exceptions

**Y**ou may have been dismayed by the lack of error checking and error handling in the Explorations so far. That's about to change. C++, like most modern programming languages, supports exceptions as a way to jump out of the normal flow of control in response to an error or other exceptional condition. This Exploration introduces exceptions: how to throw them, how to catch them, when the language and library use them, and when and how you should use them.

## Introducing Exceptions

Exploration 9 introduced vector's at member function, which retrieves a vector element at a particular index. At the time, I wrote that most programs you read would use square brackets instead. Now is a good time to take a close look at the difference between square brackets and the at function. First, take a look at two programs. Listing 43-1 shows a simple program that uses a vector.

**Listing 43-1.** *Accessing an Element of a Vector*

```
#include <vector>

int main()
{
  std::vector<int> data;
  data.push_back(10);
  data.push_back(20);
  data.at(5) = 0;
}
```

**What do you expect to happen when you run this program?**

_____

Try it. **What actually happens?**

_____

The vector index, 5, is out of bounds. The only valid indices for data are 0 and 1, so it's no wonder that the program terminates with a nastygram. Now consider the program in Listing 43-2.

**Listing 43-2.** *A Bad Way to Access an Element of a Vector*

```
#include <vector>

int main()
{
  std::vector<int> data;
  data.push_back(10);
  data.push_back(20);
  data[5] = 0;
}
```

**What do you expect to happen when you run this program?**

_____

Try it. **What actually happens?**

_____

The vector index, 5, is still out of bounds. If you still get a nastygram, you get a different one than before. On the other hand, the program might run to completion without indicating any error. You might find that disturbing, but such is the case of undefined behavior. Anything can happen.

That, in a nutshell, is the difference between using subscripts ([ ]) and the at member function. If the index is invalid, the at member function causes the program to terminate in a predictable, controlled fashion. You can write additional code and avoid termination, take appropriate actions to clean up prior to termination, or let the program end.

The subscript operator, on the other hand, results in undefined behavior if the index is invalid. Anything can happen, so you have no control—none whatsoever. If the software is controlling, say, an airplane, then "anything" involves many options that are too unpleasant to imagine. On a typical desktop workstation, a more likely scenario is that the program crashes, which is a good thing because it tells you that something went wrong. The worst possible consequence is that nothing obvious happens, and the program silently uses a garbage value and keeps running.

The at member function, and many other functions, can *throw exceptions* to signal an error. When a program throws an exception, the normal, statement-by-statement progression of the program is interrupted. Instead, a special exception-handling system takes control of the program. The standard gives some leeway in how this system actually works, but you can imagine that it forces functions to end and destroys local objects and parameters, although the functions do not return a value to the caller. Instead, functions are forcefully ended, one at a time, and a special code block *catches* the exception. Use the try-catch statement to set up these special code blocks in a program. A catch block is also called an *exception handler*. Normal code execution resumes after the handler finishes its work.

When a program throws an exception (with the throw keyword), it throws a value, called an exception object, which can be an object of nearly any type. By convention, exceptions inherit from the std::exception class or one of several subclasses that the standard library provides. Third-party class libraries sometimes introduce their own exception base class.

An exception handler also has an object declaration, which has a type, and the handler accepts only exception objects of the same type or of a derived type. If no exception handler has a matching type, or if you don't write any handler at all, the program terminates as happens with Listing 43-1. The remainder of this Exploration examines each aspect of exception handling in detail.

# Catching Exceptions

An exception handler is said to *catch* an exception. Write an exception handler at the end of a try: the try keyword is followed by a compound statement (it must be compound), followed by a series of *handlers*. Each handler starts with a catch keyword, followed by parentheses that enclose the declaration of an exception-handler object. After the parentheses is a compound statement that is the body of the exception handler.

When the type of the exception object matches the type of the exception-handler object, the handler is deemed a match, and the exception object is copied to the handler object, or the handler declaration can be a reference, which sometimes saves you one extra copy of the exception object. Most handlers don't need to modify the exception object, so the handler declaration is typically a reference to const. A "match" is when the exception object's type is the same as the handler's declared type or a class derived from the handler's declared type, ignoring whether the handler is const or a reference.

The exception-handling system destroys all objects that it constructed in the try part of the statement prior to throwing the exception, then it transfers control to the handler, so the handler's body runs normally, and control resumes with the statement after the end of the entire try-catch statement; that is, after the statement's last catch handler. The handler types are tried in order, and the first match wins. Thus, you should always list the most specific types first, and base class types later.

A base class exception handler type matches any exception object of a derived type. To handle all exceptions that the standard library might throw, write the handler to catch std::exception (declared in <exception>), which is the base class for all standard exceptions. Listing 43-3 demonstrates some of the exceptions that the std::string class can throw. Try out the program by typing strings of varying length.

**Listing 43-3.** *Forcing a string to Throw Exceptions*

```cpp
#include <exception>
#include <iostream>
#include <istream>
#include <ostream>
#include <stdexcept>
#include <string>

int main()
{
  std::string line;
  while (std::getline(std::cin, line))
```

```
{
  try
  {
    line.at(10) = ' ';                         // can throw out_of_range
    for (std::string::size_type size(line.size());
         size < line.max_size();
         size = size * 2)
    {
      line.resize(size);                       // can throw bad_alloc
    }
    line.resize(line.max_size());              // can throw bad_alloc
    line.push_back('x');                       // throws length_error
    std::cout << "okay\n";
  }
  catch (std::out_of_range const& ex)
  {
    std::cout << ex.what() << '\n';
    std::cout << "string index (10) out of range.\n";
  }
  catch (std::length_error const& ex)
  {
    std::cout << ex.what() << '\n';
    std::cout << "maximum string length (" << line.max_size() << ") exceeded.\n";
  }
  catch (std::exception const& ex)
  {
    std::cout << "other exception: " << ex.what() << '\n';
  }
  catch (...)
  {
    std::cout << "Unknown exception type. Program terminating.\n";
    std::terminate();
  }
}
}
```

If you type a line that contains ten or fewer characters, the line.at(10) expression throws a std::out_of_range exception. If the string has more than ten characters, the program tries to increase the string size, using ever-growing sizes. Most likely, the size will eventually exceed available memory, in which case the resize() function will throw std::bad_alloc. If you have lots and lots of memory, the next error situation is forcing the string size to the limit that string supports, and then trying to add another character to the string, which causes the push_back function to throw std::length_error. (The max_size member function returns the maximum number of elements that a container, such as std::string, can contain.)

The base class handler catches any exceptions that the first two handlers miss; in particular, it catches std::bad_alloc. The what() member function returns a string that describes the exception. The exact contents of the string vary by implementation. As a general rule, I do not recommend showing the what() string to users. Instead, use the type of the exception object to format a suitable error message, and use the what() string merely to add additional information, such as a file name. Unfortunately, C++ lacks a universal convention for exception messages, and different libraries use what() strings differently. A better solution would be to write an explicit handler to catch bad_alloc, but I want to demonstrate a handler for a base class.

The final catch handler uses an ellipsis (. . .) instead of a declaration. This is a catch-all handler that matches any exception. If you use it, it must be last because it matches every exception object, of any type. Because the handler doesn't know the type of the exception, it has no way to access the exception object. This catch-all handler prints a message and then calls std::terminate() (declared in <exception>), which terminates the program by calling std::abort(). Because the std::exception catches all standard library exceptions, the final catch-all handler is not really needed, but I wanted to show you how it works.

# Throwing Exceptions

A *throw expression* throws an exception. The expression consists of the throw keyword followed by an expression, namely, the exception object. The standard exceptions all take a string argument, which becomes the value returned from the what() member function.

```
throw std::out_of_range("index out of range");
```

The messages that the standard library uses for its own exceptions are implementation-defined, so you cannot rely on them to provide any useful information.

You can throw an exception anywhere an expression can be used, sort of. The type of a throw expression is void, which means it has no type. Type void is not allowed as an operand for any arithmetic, comparison, etc., operator. Thus, realistically, a throw expression is typically used in an expression statement, all by itself.

You can throw an exception inside a catch handler, which low-level code and libraries often do. You can throw the same exception object or a brand new exception. To rethrow the same object, use the throw keyword without any expression.

```
catch (std::out_of_range const& ex)
{
  std::cout << "index out of range\n";
  throw;
}
```

A common case for rethrowing an exception is inside a catch-all handler. The catch-all handler performs some important clean-up work, and then propagates the exception so the program can handle it

If you throw a new exception, the exception-handling system takes over normally. Control leaves the try-catch block immediately, so the same handler cannot catch the new exception.

# Program Stack

To understand what happens when a program throws an exception, you must first understand the nature of the *program stack*, sometimes called the *execution stack*. Procedural and similar languages use a stack at runtime to keep track of function calls, function arguments, and local variables. The C++ stack also helps keep track of exception handlers.

When a program calls a function, the program pushes a *frame* onto the stack. The frame has information such as the instruction pointer and other registers, arguments to the function, and possibly some memory for the function's return value. When a function starts, it might set aside some memory on the stack for local variables. Each local scope pushes a new frame onto the stack. (The compiler might be able to optimize away a physical frame for some local scopes, or even an entire function. Conceptually, however, the following applies.)

While a function executes, it typically constructs a variety of objects: function arguments, local variables, temporary objects, and so on. The compiler keeps track of all the objects the function must create, so it can properly destroy them when the function returns. Local objects are destroyed in the opposite order of their creation.

Frames are dynamic, that is, they represent function calls and the flow of control in a program, not the static representation of source code. Thus, a function can call itself, and each call results in a new frame on the stack, and each frame has its own copy of all the function arguments and local variables.

When a program throws an exception, the normal flow of control stops, and the C++ exception-handling mechanism takes over. The exception object is copied to a safe place, off the execution stack. The exception-handling code looks through the stack for a try statement. When it finds a try statement, it checks the types for each handler in turn, looking for a match. If it doesn't find a match, it looks for the next try statement, farther back in the stack. It keeps looking until it finds a matching handler or it runs out of frames to search.

When it finds a match, it pops frames off the execution stack, calling destructors for all local objects in each popped frame, and continues to pop frames until it reaches the handler. Popping frames from the stack is also called *unwinding* the stack.

After unwinding the stack, the exception object initializes the handler's exception object, and then the catch body is executed. After the catch body exits normally, the exception object is freed, and execution continues with the statement that follows the end of the last sibling catch block.

If the handler throws an exception, the search for a matching handler starts anew. A handler cannot handle an exception that it throws, nor can any of its sibling handlers in the same try statement.

If no handler matches the exception object's type, the std::terminate function is called, which aborts the program. Some implementations will pop the stack and free local objects prior to calling terminate, but others won't.

Listing 43-4 can help you visualize what is going on inside a program when it throws and catches an exception.

**Listing 43-4.** *Visualizing an Exception*

```
1 #include <exception>
2 #include <iostream>
3 #include <istream>
4 #include <ostream>
```

```
5 #include <string>
6
7 /// Make visual the construction and destruction of objects.
8 class visual
9 {
10 public:
11    visual(std::string const& what)
12    : id_(serial_), what_(what)
13    {
14      ++serial_;
15      print("");
16    }
17    visual(visual const& ex)
18    : id_(ex.id_), what_(ex.what_)
19    {
20      print("copy ");
21    }
22    ~visual()
23    {
24      print("~");
25    }
26    void print(std::string const& label)
27    const
28    {
29      std::cout << label << "visual(" << what_ << ": " << id_ << ")\n";
30    }
31 private:
32    static int serial_;
33    int const id_;
34    std::string const what_;
35 };
36
37 int visual::serial_(0);
38
39 void count_down(int n)
40 {
41    std::cout << "start count_down(" << n << ")\n";
42    visual v("count_down local");
43    try
44    {
45      if (n == 3)
46        throw visual("exception");
47      else if (n > 0)
48        count_down(n - 1);
49    }
50    catch (visual ex)
51    {
```

```
52      ex.print("catch ");
53      throw;
54    }
55    std::cout << "end count_down(" << n << ")\n";
56 }
57
58 int main()
59 {
60   try
61   {
62     count_down(2);
63     count_down(4);
64   }
65   catch (visual const ex)
66   {
67     ex.print("catch ");
68   }
69   std::cout << "All done!\n";
70 }
```

The visual class helps show when and how objects are constructed, copied, and destroyed. The count_down function throws an exception when its argument equals 3, and it calls itself when its argument is positive. The recursion stops for non-positive arguments. To help you see function calls, it prints the argument upon entry to and exit from the function.

The first call to count_down does not trigger the exception, so you should see normal creation and destruction of the local visual object. **Write exactly what the program should print as a result of line 62 (count_down(2)):**

_____

_____

_____

_____

_____

_____

_____

_____

_____

_____

_____

The next call to count_down from main (line 63) allows count_down to recurse once before throwing an exception. So count_down(4) calls count_down(3). The local object, v, is constructed inside count_down(4), and a new instance of v is constructed inside count_down(3). Then the exception object is created and thrown. (See Figure 43-1.)

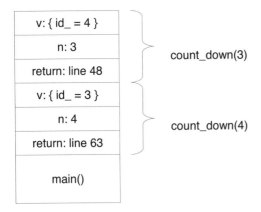

**Figure 43-1.** *Program stack when the exception is thrown*

The exception is caught inside count_down, so its frame is not popped. The exception object is then copied to ex (line 50), and the exception handler begins. It prints a message and then rethrows the original exception object (line 53). The exception-handling mechanism treats this exception the same way it treats any other: the try statement's frame is popped, and then the count_down function's frame is popped. Local objects are destroyed (including ex and v). The final statement in count_down does not execute.

The stack is unwound, and the try statement inside the call to count_down(4) is found, and once again, the exception object is copied to a new instance of ex. (See Figure 43-2.) The exception handler prints a message, and rethrows the original exception. The count_down(4) frame is popped, returning control to the try statement in main. Again, the final statement in count_down does not execute.

```
ex: visual { id_= 5 }


        main()
```

**Figure 43-2.** *Program stack after rethrowing exception*

The exception handler in main gets its turn, and this handler prints the exception object one last time (line 65). After the handler prints a message, and the catch body reaches its end, the local exception object and the original exception object are destroyed. Execution then continues normally on line 69. The final output is:

```
start count_down(2)
visual(count_down local: 0)
start count_down(1)
visual(count_down local: 1)
```

```
start count_down(0)
visual(count_down local: 2)
end count_down(0)
~visual(count_down local: 2)
end count_down(1)
~visual(count_down local: 1)
end count_down(2)
~visual(count_down local: 0)
start count_down(4)
visual(count_down local: 3)
start count_down(3)
visual(count_down local: 4)
visual(exception: 5)
copy visual(exception: 5)
catch visual(exception: 5)
~visual(exception: 5)
~visual(count_down local: 4)
copy visual(exception: 5)
catch visual(exception: 5)
~visual(exception: 5)
~visual(count_down local: 3)
copy visual(exception: 5)
catch visual(exception: 5)
~visual(exception: 5)
~visual(exception: 5)
```

# Standard Exceptions

The standard library defines several standard exception types. The base class, exception, is declared in the <exception> header. Most of the other exception classes are defined in the <stdexcept> header. If you want to define your own exception class, I recommend deriving it from one of the standard exceptions in <stdexcept>.

The standard exceptions are divided into two categories (with two base classes that derive directly from exception):

- Runtime errors (std::runtime_error) are exceptions that you cannot detect or prevent merely by examining the source code. They arise from conditions that you can antici-pate, but not prevent.

- Logical errors (std::logic_error) are the result of programmer error. They represent violations of preconditions, invalid function arguments, and other errors that the pro-grammer should prevent in code.

The other standard exception classes in <stdexcept> derive from these two. Most standard library exceptions are logic errors. For example, out_of_range inherits from logic_error. The at member function (and others) throws out_of_range when the index is out of range. After all, you should check indices and sizes to be sure your vector and string usage are correct, and not

rely on exceptions. The exceptions are there to provide clean, orderly shutdown of your program when you do make a mistake (and we all make mistakes).

Any decent library reference tells you which functions throw which exceptions, such as
at can throw out_of_range. Any function might throw other, undocumented exceptions, too,
depending on the library's and compiler's implementation. In general, however, the standard
library uses few exceptions. Instead, most of the library yields undefined behavior when you
provide bad input. The I/O streams do not ordinarily throw any exceptions, but you arrange
for them to throw exceptions when bad errors happen, as I explain in the next section.

# I/O Exceptions

You learned about I/O stream state bits in Exploration 29. State bits are important, but checking them repeatedly is cumbersome. In particular, many programs fail to check the state bits
of output streams, especially when writing to the standard output. That's just plain, old-fashioned laziness. Fortunately, C++ offers an avenue for programmers to gain I/O safety without
much extra work: the stream can throw an exception when I/O fails.

In addition to state bits, each stream also has an *exception mask*. The exception mask
tells the stream to throw an exception if a corresponding state bit changes value. For example,
you could set badbit in the exception mask, and never write an explicit check for this unlikely
occurrence. If a serious I/O error were to occur, causing badbit to become set, the stream
would throw an exception. You can write a handler at a high level to catch the exception and
terminate the program cleanly, as shown in Listing 43-5.

**Listing 43-5.** *Using an I/O Stream Exception Mask*

```
#include <ios>
#include <iostream>
#include <istream>
#include <ostream>

int main()
{
  std::cin.exceptions(std::ios_base::badbit);
  std::cout.exceptions(std::ios_base::badbit);

  int x(0);
  try
  {
    while (std::cin >> x)
      std::cout << x << '\n';
    if (not std::cin.eof()) // failure without eof means invalid input
      std::cerr << "Invalid integer input. Program terminated.\n";
  }
  catch(std::ios_base::failure const& ex)
  {
    std::cerr << "Major I/O failure! Program terminated.\n";
```

```
      std::terminate();
   }
}
```

As you can see, the exception class is named `std::ios_base::failure`. Also note a new output stream: `std::cerr`. The `<iostream>` header actually declares several standard I/O streams. So far, I've used only `cin` and `cout` because that's all we've needed. The `cerr` stream is an output stream dedicated to error output. In this case, separating normal output (to `cout`) from error output (to `cerr`) is important because `cout` might have a fatal error (say, a disk is full), so any attempt to write an error message to `cout` would be futile. Instead, the program writes the message to `cerr`. There's no guarantee that writing to `cerr` would work, but at least there's a chance, for example, the user might redirect the standard output to a file (and thereby encounter a disk full error), while allowing the error output to appear on a console.

Recall that when an input stream reaches the end of the input, it sets `eofbit` in its state mask. Although you can also set this bit in the exceptions mask, I can't see any reason why you would want to. If an input operation does not read anything useful from the stream, the stream sets `failbit`. The most common reasons that the stream might not read anything is end of file (`eofbit` is set) or an input formatting error (e.g., text in the input stream when the program tries to read a number). Again, it's possible to set `failbit` in the exception mask, but most programs rely on ordinary program logic to test the state of an input stream. Exceptions are for exceptional conditions, and end-of-file is a normal occurrence when reading from a stream.

The loop ends when `failbit` is set, but you need to test further to discover whether `failbit` is set because of a normal end-of-file condition or because of malformed input. If `eofbit` is also set, you know the stream is at its end. Otherwise, `failbit` must be due to malformed input.

As you can see, exceptions are not the solution for every error situation. Thus, `badbit` is the only bit in the exception mask that makes sense for most programs, especially for input streams. An output stream sets `failbit` if it cannot write the entire value to the stream. Usually, such a failure occurs because of an I/O error that sets `badbit`, but it's at least theoretically possible for output failure to set `failbit` without also setting `badbit`. In most situations, any output failure is cause for alarm, so you might want to throw an exception for `failbit` with output streams and `badbit` with input streams:

```
std::cin.exceptions(std::ios_base::badbit);
std::cout.exceptions(std::ios_base::failbit);
```

# Custom Exceptions

Exceptions simplify coding by removing exceptional conditions from the main flow of control. You can and should use exceptions for many different error situations. For example, the rational class (most recently appearing in Exploration 38) has, so far, completely avoided the issue of division by zero. A better solution than invoking undefined behavior (which is what happens when you divide by zero) is to throw an exception anytime the denominator is zero. Define your own exception class by deriving from one of the standard exception base classes, as shown in Listing 43-6. By defining your own exception class, any user of rational can easily distinguish its exceptions from other exceptions.

**Listing 43-6.** *Throwing an Exception for a Zero Denominator*

```
#ifndef RATIONAL_HPP_
#define RATIONAL_HPP_

#include <stdexcept>
#include <string>

class rational
{
public:
  class zero_denominator : public std::logic_error
  {
  public:
    zero_denominator(std::string const& what_arg) : logic_error(what_arg) {}
  };

  rational() : numerator_(0), denominator_(1) {}
  rational(int num) : numerator_(num), denominator_(1) {}
  rational(int num, int den) : numerator_(num), denominator_(den)
  {
    if (denominator_ == 0)
      throw zero_denominator("zero denominator");
    reduce();
  }
... omitted for brevity ...
};
#endif
```

Notice how the zero_denominator class nests within the rational class. The nested class is a perfectly ordinary class. It has no connection with the outer class (as with a Java inner class), except the name. The nested class gets no special access to private members in the outer class, nor does the outer class get special access to the nested class name. The usual rules for access levels determine the accessibility of the nested class. Some nested classes are private helper classes, so you would declare them in a private section of the outer class definition. In this case, zero_denominator must be public so callers can use the class in exception handlers.

To use a nested class name outside the outer class, you must use the outer class and the nested class names, separated by a scope operator (::). The nested class name has no significance outside of the outer class's scope. Thus, nested classes help avoid name collisions. They also provide clear documentation for the human reader who sees the type in an exception handler:

```
catch (rational::zero_denominator const& ex) {
  std::cerr << "zero denominator in rational number\n";
}
```

**Find all other places in the rational class that need to check for a zero denominator, and add appropriate error-checking code to throw zero_denominator.**

All roads lead to reduce(), so one approach is to replace the assertion with a check for a zero denominator, and throw the exception there. You don't need to modify any other functions, and even the extra check in the constructor (illustrated in Listing 43-6) is unnecessary. Listing 43-7 shows the latest implementation of reduce().

**Listing 43-7.** *Checking for a Zero Denominator in reduce()*

```
void rational::reduce()
{
  if (denominator_ == 0)
    throw zero_denominator("denominator is zero");
  if (denominator_ < 0)
  {
    denominator_ = -denominator_;
    numerator_ = -numerator_;
  }
  int div(gcd(numerator_, denominator_));
  numerator_ = numerator_ / div;
  denominator_ = denominator_ / div;
}
```

# Exceptional Advice

The basic mechanics of exceptions are easy to grasp, but their proper use is more difficult. The applications programmer has three distinct tasks: catching exceptions, throwing exceptions, and avoiding exceptions.

You should write your programs to catch all exceptions, even the unexpected ones. One approach is for your main program to have a master try statement around the entire program body. Within the program, you might use targeted try statements to catch specific exceptions. The closer you are to the source of the exception, the more contextual information you have, and the better you can ameliorate the problem, or at least present the user with more useful messages.

This outermost try statement catches any exceptions that other statements miss. It is a last-ditch attempt to present a coherent and helpful error message before the program terminates abruptly. At a minimum, tell the user that the program is terminating because of an unexpected exception.

In an event-driven program, such as a GUI application, exceptions are more problematic. The outermost try statement shuts down the program, closing all windows. Most event handlers should have their own try statement to handle exceptions for that particular menu pick, keystroke event, and so on.

Within the body of your program, better than catching exceptions is avoiding them. Use the at member function to access elements of a vector, but you should write the code so you are confident that the index is always valid. Index and length exceptions are signs of programmer error.

When writing low-level code, throw exceptions for most error situations that should not happen or that otherwise reflect programmer error. Some error conditions are especially dangerous. For example, in the rational class, a denominator should never be zero or negative after reduce() returns. If a condition arises when the denominator is indeed zero or negative, the internal state of the program is corrupt. If the program were to attempt a graceful shutdown, saving all files, etc., it might end up writing bad data to the files. Better to terminate immediately, and rely on the most recent backup copy, which your program made while its state was still known to be good. Use assertions, not exceptions, for such emergencies.

Ideally, your code should validate user input, check vector indices, and make sure all arguments to all functions are valid before calling the functions. If anything is invalid, your program can tell the user with a clear, direct message, and avoid exceptions entirely. Exceptions are a safety net when your checks fail or you forget to check for certain conditions.

As a general rule, libraries should throw exceptions, not catch them. Applications tend to catch exceptions more than throw them. As programs grow more complex, I will highlight situations that call for exceptions, throwing or catching.

Now that you know how to write classes, overload operators, and handle errors, you need only learn about some additional operators before you can start implementing fully functional classes of your own. The next Exploration revisits some familiar operators and introduces a few new ones.

# EXPLORATION 44

■ ■ ■

# More Operators

**C**++ has lots of operators. Lots and lots. So far, I've introduced the basic operators that you need for most programs: arithmetic, comparison, assignment, subscript, and function call. Now it's time to introduce some more: additional assignment operators, the conditional operator (which is like having an if statement in the middle of an expression), and the comma operator (most often used in for loops).

## Conditional Operator

The conditional operator is a unique entry in the C++ operator bestiary, being a ternary operator, that is, an operator that takes three operands.

```
condition ? true-part : false-part
```

The *condition* is a Boolean expression. If it evaluates to true, the result of the entire expression is the *true-part*. If the condition is false, the result is the *false-part*. As with an if statement, only one part is evaluated; the branch not taken is skipped. For example, the following statement is perfectly safe:

```
std::cout << (x == 0 ? 0 : y / x);
```

If x is zero, the y / x expression is not evaluated, and division by zero never occurs. The conditional operator has very low precedence, so you often see it written inside parentheses. Assignment has lower precedence, so you can safely use conditional operators as the source of an assignment statement.

```
x = test ? 42 : 24;
```

The *true-part* and *false-part* are expressions that have the same or compatible types, that is, the compiler can automatically convert one type to the other, ensuring that the entire conditional expression has a well-defined type. For example, you can mix an integer and a floating-point number; the expression result is a floating-point number. The following statement prints 10.000000 if x is positive:

```
std::cout << std::fixed << (x > 0 ? 10 : 42.24) << '\n';
```

Do not use the conditional operator as a replacement for if statements. If you have a choice, use an if statement because a statement is almost always easier to read and understand than a conditional expression. Use conditional expressions in situations when if statements are infeasible. Initializing a data member in a constructor, for example, does not permit the use of an `if` statement. Although you can use a member function for complicated conditions, you can also use a conditional expression for simple conditions.

The `rational` class (last seen in Exploration 43) for example, takes a numerator and a denominator as constructor arguments. The class ensures that its denominator is always positive; if the denominator is negative, it negates the numerator and denominator. In past Explorations, I loaded the `reduce()` member function with additional responsibilities, such as checking for a zero denominator and checking for a negative denominator to reverse the signs of the numerator and denominator. This design has the advantage of centralizing all code needed to convert a rational number to canonical form. An alternate design is to separate the responsibility, and let the constructor check the denominator prior to calling `reduce()`. If the denominator is zero, the constructor throws an exception; if the denominator is negative, the constructor negates the numerator and the denominator. This alternative design makes `reduce()` simpler, and simple functions are less error prone than complicated functions. Listing 44-1 shows how you can do this using conditional operators.

**Listing 44-1.** *Using Conditional Expressions in a Constructor's Initializer*

```
/// Construct a rational object from a numerator and a denominator.
/// If the denominator is zero, throw zero_denominator. If the denominator
/// is negative, normalize the value by negating the numerator and denominator.
/// @post denominator_ > 0
/// @throws zero_denominator
rational::rational(int num, int den)
: numerator_(den < 0 ? -num : num),
  denominator_(den == 0 ? throw zero_denominator("0 denominator") :
                      (den < 0 ? -den : den))
{
  reduce();
}
```

A `throw` expression has type `void`, but the compiler knows it doesn't return, so you can use it as one (or both) of the parts of a conditional expression. The type of the overall expression is that of the nonthrowing part (or `void` if both parts throw an exception).

In other words, if `den` is zero, the *true-part* of the expression throws an exception. If the condition is false, the *false-part* executes, which is another conditional expression that evaluates the absolute value of `den`. The initializer for the numerator also tests `den`, and if negative, it negates the numerator, too.

Like me, you might find the use of conditional expressions makes the code harder to read. The conditional operator is widely used in C++ programs, so you must get used to reading it. If you decide that the conditional expressions are just too complicated, write a separate, private member function to do the work, and initialize the member by calling the function, as shown in Listing 44-2.

**Listing 44-2.** *Using a Function and Conditional Statements Instead of Conditional Expressions*

```
/// Construct a rational object from a numerator and a denominator.
/// If the denominator is zero, throw zero_denominator. If the denominator
/// is negative, normalize the value by negating the numerator and denominator.
/// @post denominator_ > 0
/// @throws zero_denominator
rational::rational(int num, int den)
: numerator_(den < 0 ? -num : num), denominator_(init_denominator(den))
{
  reduce();
}

/// Return an initial value for the denominator_ member. This function is used
/// only in a constructor's initializer list.
int rational::init_denominator(int den)
{
  if (den == 0)
    throw zero_denominator("0 denominator");
  else if (den < 0)
    return -den;
  else
    return den;
}
```

When writing new code, use the technique that you like best, but get used to reading both programming styles.

# Short-Circuit Operators

C++ lets you overload the and and or operators, but you must resist the temptation. By over-loading these operators, you defeat one of their key benefits: short-circuiting.

Recall from Exploration 11 that the and and or operators do not evaluate their right-hand operands if they don't need to. That's true of the built-in operators, but not if you overload them. When you overload the Boolean operators, they become normal functions, and C++ always evaluates function arguments before calling a function. Therefore, overloaded and and or operators behave differently from the built-in operators, and this difference makes them significantly less useful.

**Tip** Do not overload the and and or operators.

# Comma Operator

The comma (,) serves many roles: it separates arguments in a function call, parameters in a function declaration, declarators in a declaration, and initializers in a constructor's initializer list. In all these cases, the comma is a punctuator, that is, a symbol that is part of the syntax that serves only to show where one thing (argument, declarator, etc.) ends and another thing begins. It is also an operator in its own right (briefly introduced in Exploration 12), which is a completely different use for the same symbol. The comma as operator separates two expressions; it causes the left-hand operand to be evaluated, then the result is discarded, and then the right-hand operand is evaluated, which becomes the result of the entire expression.

At first, this operator seems a little pointless. After all, what's the purpose of writing, say,

```
x = 1 + 2, y = x + 3, z = y + 4
```

instead of

```
x = 1 + 2;
y = x + 3;
z = y + 4;
```

The comma operator is not meant to be a substitute for writing separate statements. There is one situation, however, when multiple statements are not possible, but multiple expressions need to be evaluated. I speak of none other than the `for` loop.

Suppose you want to implement the `search` algorithm. Implementing a fully generic algorithm requires techniques that you haven't learned yet, but you can write this function so that it works with the iterators of a `vector<int>`. The basic idea is simple, `search` looks through a search range, trying to find a sequence of elements that equal elements in a match range. It steps through the search range one element at a time, testing whether a match starts at that element. If so, it returns an iterator that refers to the start of the match. If no match is found, `search` returns the end iterator. To check for a match, use a nested loop to compare successive elements in the two ranges. Listing 44-3 shows one way to implement this function.

**Listing 44-3.** *Searching for a Matching Subrange in a Vector of Integers*

```
#include <vector>

typedef std::vector<int>::iterator viterator;
typedef std::vector<int>::difference_type vdifference;

viterator search(viterator first1,viterator last1,viterator first2,viterator last2)
{
   // s1 is the size of the untested portion of the first range
   // s2 is the size of the second range
   // End the search when s2 > s1 because a match is impossible if the remaining
   // portion of the search range is smaller than the test range. Each iteration
   // of the outer loop shrinks the search range by one, and advances the first1
   // iterator. The inner loop searches for a match starting at first1.
   for (vdifference s1(last1-first1), s2(last2-first2); s2 <= s1; --s1, ++first1)
   {
```

```
    // Is there a match starting at first1?
    viterator f2(first2);
    for (viterator f1(first1);
         f1 != last1 and f2 != last2 and *f1 == *f2;
         ++f1, ++f2)
    {
        // The subsequence matches so far, so keep checking.
        // All the work is done in the loop header, so the body is empty.
    }
    if (f2 == last2)
      return first1;        // match starts at first1
  }
  // no match
  return last1;
}
```

The boldface lines demonstrate the comma operator. The initialization portion of the first for loop does not invoke the comma operator. The comma in the declaration is just a separator between declarators. The comma operator appears in the post-iteration part of the loops. Because the post-iteration part of a for loop is an expression, you cannot use multiple statements to increment multiple objects. Instead, you need to do it in a single expression. Hence, the need for the comma operator.

On the other hand, some programmers prefer to avoid the comma operator because the resulting code can be hard to read. **Rewrite Listing 44-3 so that it does not use the comma operator. Which version of the function do you prefer?** _____ Listing 44-4 shows my version of search without the comma operator.

**Listing 44-4.** *The search Function Without Using the Comma Operator*

```
#include <vector>

typedef std::vector<int>::iterator viterator;
typedef std::vector<int>::difference_type vdifference;

viterator search(viterator first1,viterator last1,viterator first2,viterator last2)
{
  // s1 is the size of the untested portion of the first range
  // s2 is the size of the second range
  // End the search when s2 > s1 because a match is impossible if the remaining
  // portion of the search range is smaller than the test range. Each iteration
  // of the outer loop shrinks the search range by one, and advances the first1
  // iterator. The inner loop searches for a match starting at first1.
  for (vdifference s1(last1-first1), s2(last2-first2); s2 <= s1; --s1)
  {
    // Is there a match starting at first1?
    viterator f2(first2);
    for (viterator f1(first1); f1 != last1 and f2 != last2 and *f1 == *f2; )
    {
```

```
      ++f1;
      ++f2;
    }
    if (f2 == last2)
      return first1;      // match starts at first1
    ++first1;
  }
  // no match
  return last1;
}
```

The comma operator has very low precedence, even lower than assignment. If a loop needs to advance objects by steps of 2, for example, you can use assignment expressions with the comma operator.

```
for (int i(0), j(size-1); i < j; i += 2, j -= 2) do_something(i, j);
```

By the way, C++ lets you overload the comma operator, but you shouldn't take advantage of this feature. The comma is so basic, C++ programmers quickly grasp its standard use. If the comma does not have its usual meaning, readers of your code will be confused, bewildered, and stymied when they try to understand it.

# Arithmetic Assignment Operators

In addition to the usual arithmetic operators, C++ has assignment operators that combine arithmetic with assignment: +=, -=, *=, /=, and %=. The assignment operator x += y is shorthand for x = x + y, and the same applies to the other special assignment operators. Thus, the following three expressions are all equivalent:

```
x = x + 1
x += 1
++x
```

The advantage of the special assignment operator is that x is evaluated only once, which can be a boon if x is a complicated expression. If data has type std::vector<int>, which of the two equivalent expressions do you find easier to read and understand:

```
data.at(data.size() / 2) = data.at(data.size() / 2) + 10;
data.at(data.size() / 2) += 10;
```

Listing 44-5 shows a sample implementation of *= for the rational class.

**Listing 44-5.** *Implementing the Multiplication Operator*

```
rational& rational::operator*=(rational const& rhs)
{
  numerator_ *= rhs.numerator();
  denominator_ *= rhs.denominator();
  reduce();
  return *this;
}
```

The return type of operator*= is a reference, rational&. The return value is *this. Although the compiler lets you use any return type and value, the convention is for assignment operators to return a reference to the object, that is, an lvalue. Even if your code never uses the return value, many programmers use the result of an assignment, so don't use void as a return type:

```
rational r;
while ((r += rational(1,10)) != 2) do_something(r);
```

Often, implementing an arithmetic operator, such as +, is easiest to do by implementing the corresponding assignment operator first. Then implement the free operator in terms of the assignment operator, as shown in Listing 44-6 for the rational class.

**Listing 44-6.** *Reimplementing Multiplication in Terms of an Assignment Operator*

```
rational operator*(rational const& lhs, rational const& rhs)
{
  rational result(lhs);
  result *= rhs;
  return result;
}
```

**Implement the /=, +=, and -= operators for class rational.** You can implement these operators in many different ways. I recommend putting the arithmetic logic in the assignment operators and reimplementing the /, +, and - operators to use the assignment operators, as I did with the multiplication operators. My solution appears in Listing 44-7.

**Listing 44-7.** *Other Arithmetic Assignment Operators*

```
rational& rational::operator+=(rational const& rhs)
{
  numerator_ = numerator() * rhs.denominator() + rhs.numerator() * denominator();
  denominator_ *= rhs.denominator();
  reduce();
  return *this;
}

rational& rational::operator-=(rational const& rhs)
{
  numerator_ = numerator() * rhs.denominator() - rhs.numerator() * denominator();
  denominator_ *= rhs.denominator();
  reduce();
  return *this;
}

rational& rational::operator/=(rational const& rhs)
{
  if (rhs.numerator() == 0)
    throw zero_denominator("divide by zero");
```

```
numerator_ *= rhs.denominator();
denominator_ *= rhs.numerator();
if (denominator_ < 0)
{
  denominator_ = -denominator_;
  numerator_ = -numerator_;
}
reduce();
return *this;
}
```

Because reduce() no longer checks for a negative denominator, any function that might change the denominator to negative must check. Because the denominator is always positive, you know that operator+= and operator-= cannot cause the denominator to become negative. Only operator/= introduces that possibility, so only that function needs to check.

# Increment and Decrement

Let's add increment (++) and decrement (--) operators to the rational class. Because these operators modify the object, I suggest implementing them as member functions, although C++ lets you use free functions, too. **Implement the prefix increment operator for class rational.** Compare your function with mine in Listing 44-8.

**Listing 44-8.** *The Prefix Increment Operator for rational*

```
rational& rational::operator++()
{
  numerator_ += denominator_;
  return *this;
}
```

I am confident that you can implement the decrement operator with no additional help. Like the arithmetic assignment operators, the prefix operator++ returns the object as a reference. Thus, you can use the ++ operator on the left-hand side of an assignment statement.

That leaves the postfix operators. Implementing the body of the operator is easy, and requires only one additional line of code. However, you need to take care with the return type. The postfix operators cannot simply return *this because they return the original value of the object, not its new value. Thus, these operators cannot return a reference. Instead, they must return a plain rational rvalue.

But how do you declare the function? A class can't have two separate functions with the same name (operator++) and arguments. Somehow, you need a way to tell the compiler that one implementation of operator++ is prefix and another is postfix.

The solution is that when the compiler calls a custom postfix increment or decrement operator, it passes the integer 0 as an extra argument. The postfix operators don't need the value of this extra parameter; it's just a placeholder to distinguish prefix from postfix.

Thus, when you declare operator++ with an extra parameter of type int, you are declaring the postfix operator. When you declare the operator, omit the name for the extra parameter. That tells the compiler that the function doesn't use the parameter, so the compiler won't bother you with messages about unused function parameters. **Implement the postfix increment and decrement operators for rational.** Listing 44-9 shows my solution.

**Listing 44-9.** *Postfix Increment and Decrement Operators*

```
rational rational::operator++(int)
{
  rational result(*this);
  numerator_ += denominator_;
  return result;
}

rational rational::operator--(int)
{
  rational result(*this);
  numerator_ -= denominator_;
  return result;
}
```

Once all the dust settles from our rehabilitation project, behold the new, improved rational class definition in Listing 44-10.

**Listing 44-10.** *The rational Class Definition*

```
#ifndef RATIONAL_HPP_
#define RATIONAL_HPP_

#include <istream>
#include <ostream>
#include <stdexcept>
#include <string>

/// Represent a rational number (fraction) as a numerator and denominator.
class rational
{
public:
  class zero_denominator : public std::logic_error
  {
  public:
    zero_denominator(std::string const& what) : logic_error(what) {}
  };
  rational(): numerator_(0), denominator_(1) {}
  rational(int num): numerator_(num), denominator_(1) {}
  rational(int num, int den);
  rational(double r);

  int numerator()             const { return numerator_; }
  int denominator()           const { return denominator_; }
```

```
  float as_float()           const;
  double as_double()         const;
  long double as_long_double() const;

  rational& operator=(int); // optimization to avoid an unneeded call to reduce()
  rational& operator+=(rational const& rhs);
  rational& operator-=(rational const& rhs);
  rational& operator*=(rational const& rhs);
  rational& operator/=(rational const& rhs);
  rational& operator++();
  rational& operator--();
  rational operator++(int);
  rational operator--(int);

private:
  /// Reduce the numerator and denominator by their GCD.
  void reduce();
  /// Reduce the numerator and denominator, and normalize the signs of both,
  /// that is, ensure denominator is not negative.
  void normalize();
  /// Return an initial value for denominator_. Throw a zero_denominator
  /// exception if @p den is zero. Always return a positive number.
  int init_denominator(int den);
  int numerator_;
  int denominator_;
};

/// Compute the greatest common divisor of two integers, using Euclid's algorithm.
int gcd(int n, int m);

rational abs(rational const& r);
rational operator-(rational const& r);
rational operator+(rational const& lhs, rational const& rhs);
rational operator-(rational const& lhs, rational const& rhs);
rational operator*(rational const& lhs, rational const& rhs);
rational operator/(rational const& lhs, rational const& rhs);

bool operator==(rational const& a, rational const& b);
bool operator<(rational const& a, rational const& b);

inline bool operator!=(rational const& a, rational const& b)
{
  return not (a == b);
}

inline bool operator<=(rational const& a, rational const& b)
{
```

```
  return not (b < a);
}

inline bool operator>(rational const& a, rational const& b)
{
  return b < a;
}

inline bool operator>=(rational const& a, rational const& b)
{
  return not (b > a);
}

std::istream& operator>>(std::istream& in, rational& rat);
std::ostream& operator<<(std::ostream& out, rational const& rat);

#endif
```

The next Exploration is your second project. Now that you know about classes, inheritance, operator overloading, and exceptions, you are ready to tackle some serious C++ coding.

# Project 2: Fixed-Point Numbers

**Y**our task for Project 2 is to implement a simple fixed-point number class. The class represents fixed-point numbers using an integer type. The number of places after the decimal point is a fixed constant, four. For example, represent the number 3.1415 as the integer 31415 and 3.14 as 31400. You must overload the arithmetic, comparison, and I/O operators to maintain the fixed-point fiction.

Name the class `fixed`. It should have the following members:

## value_type

A typedef for the underlying integer type, such as `int` or `long`. By using the `value_type` typedef throughout the `fixed` class, you can easily switch between `int` and `long` by changing only the declaration of `value_type`.

## places

A `static const int` equal to 4, or the number of places after the decimal point. By using a named constant instead of hard coding the value 4, you can easily change the value to 2 or something else in the future. Using a named constant instead of a member function that returns 4 gives the compiler more flexibility for optimization because it knows the value at compile time. If the value were returned from a member function, the compiler would not know the value at compile time.

## places10

A `static const int` equal to $10^{places}$, or the scale factor for the fixed point values. Divide the internal integer by `places10` to obtain the true value. Multiply a number by `places10` to scale it to an integer that the `fixed` object stores internally.

## fixed()

Default constructor.

## fixed(value_type integer, value_type fraction)

A constructor to make a fixed-point value from an integer part and a fractional part. For example, to construct the fixed-point value 10.0020, use `fixed(10, 20)`.

Throw std::invalid_argument if fraction < 0. If fraction >= places10, discard digits to the right, rounding off the result, so fixed(3, 14159) == fixed(3, 1416) and fixed(31, 415926) == fixed(31, 4159).

## fixed(double val)

A constructor to make a fixed-point value from a floating-point number. Round-off the fraction and discard excess digits. Thus, fixed(12.3456789) == fixed(12, 3456789) == fixed(12, 3457).

Implement the arithmetic operators, arithmetic assignment operators, comparison operators, and I/O operators. Don't concern yourself with overflow. Do your best to check for errors when reading fixed-point numbers. Be sure to handle integers without decimal points (42) and values with too many decimal points (3.14159).

Implement a member function to convert the fixed-point value to std::string.

## as_string()

Convert the value to a string representation; e.g., 3.1416 becomes "3.1416" and –21 becomes "-21.0000".

To convert to an integer means discarding information. To make it abundantly clear to the user, call the function round(), to emphasize that the fixed-point value must be rounded off to become an integer.

## round()

Round off to the nearest integer. If the fractional part is exactly 5000, round to the nearest even integer (banker's rounding). Be sure to handle negative and positive numbers.

Other useful member functions give you access to the raw value (good for debugging, implementing additional operations, etc.), or the parts of the fixed-point value: the integer part and the fractional part.

## integer()

Return just the integer part, without the fractional part.

## fraction()

Return just the fraction part, without the integer part. The fraction part is always in the range [0, places10).

Be sure to write a header file (*fixed.hpp*) with #include guards. Write a separate implementation file (*fixed.cpp*). Decide which member functions should be inline (if any), and be sure to define all inline functions in *fixed.hpp*, not *fixed.cpp*. After you finish, review your solution carefully and run some tests, comparing your results to mine, which you can download from the book's web site.

If you need help testing your code, try linking your *fixed.cpp* file with the test program in Listing 45-1. The test program makes use of the test function, declared in *test.hpp*. The details are beyond the scope of this book. Just call test with a Boolean argument. If the argument is true, the test passed. Otherwise, the test failed, and test prints a message. Thus, if the program produces no output, all tests passed.

**Listing 45-1.** *Testing the fixed Class*

```
#include <iostream>
#include <istream>
#include <ostream>
#include <sstream>
#include <stdexcept>

#include "test.hpp"
#include "fixed.hpp"

int main()
{
  fixed f1;
  test(f1.value() == 0);
  fixed f2(1);
  test(f2.value() == 10000);
  fixed f3(3, 14162);
  test(f3.value() == 31416);
  fixed f4(2, 14159265);
  test(f4.value() == 21416);
  test(f2 + f4 == f1 + f3);
  test(f2 + f4 <= f1 + f3);
  test(f2 + f4 >= f1 + f3);
  test(f1 < f2);
  test(f1 <= f2);
  test(f1 != f2);
  test(f2 > f1);
  test(f2 >= f1);
  test(f2 != f1);

  test(f2 + f4 == f3 - f1);
  test(f2 * f3 == f3);
  test(f3 / f2 == f3);
  f4 += f2;
  test(f3 == f4);
  f4 -= f1;
  test(f3 == f4);
  f4 *= f2;
  test(f3 == f4);
  f4 /= f2;
  test(f3 == f4);

  test(-f4 == f1 - f4);
  test(-(-f4) == f4);
  --f4;
  test(f4 + 1 == f3);
  f4--;
```

```
test(f4 + 2 == f3);
++f4;
test(f4 + 1 == f3);
f4++;
test(f4 == f3);
++f3;
test(++f4 == f3);
test(f4-- == f3);
test(f4++ == --f3);
test(--f4 == f3);

test(f4 / f3 == f2);
test(f4 - f3 == f1);

test(f4.as_string() == "3.1416");
test(f4.integer() == 3);
f4 += fixed(0,4584);
test(f4 == 3.6);
test(f4.integer() == 3);
test(f4.round() == 4);

test(f3.integer() == 3);
test((-f3).integer() == -3);
test(f3.fraction() == 1416);
test((-f3).fraction() == 1416);

test(fixed(7,4999).round() == 7);
test(fixed(7,5000).round() == 8);
test(fixed(7,5001).round() == 8);
test(fixed(7,4999).round() == 7);
test(fixed(8,5000).round() == 8);
test(fixed(8,5001).round() == 9);

test(fixed(123,2345500) == fixed(123,2346));
test(fixed(123,2345501) == fixed(123,2346));
test(fixed(123,2345499) == fixed(123,2345));
test(fixed(123,2346500) == fixed(123,2346));
test(fixed(123,2346501) == fixed(123,2347));
test(fixed(123,2346499) == fixed(123,2346));
test(fixed(123,2346400) == fixed(123,2346));
test(fixed(123,2346600) == fixed(123,2347));

test(fixed(-7,4999).round() == -7);
test(fixed(-7,5000).round() == -8);
test(fixed(-7,5001).round() == -8);
test(fixed(-7,4999).round() == -7);
test(fixed(-8,5000).round() == -8);
test(fixed(-8,5001).round() == -9);
```

```
test(fixed(-3.14159265).value() == -31416);
test(fixed(123,456789).value() == 1234568);
test(fixed(123,4).value() == 1230004);
test(fixed(-10,1111).value() == -101111);

std::ostringstream out;
out << f3 << " 3.14159265 " << fixed(-10,12) << " 3 421.4 end";
fixed f5;
std::istringstream in(out.str());
test(in >> f5);
test(f5 == f3);
test(in >> f5);
test(f5 == f3);
test(in >> f5);
test(f5.value() == -100012);
test(in >> f5);
test(f5.value() == 30000);
test(in >> f5);
test(f5.value() == 4214000);
test(not (in >> f5));

test(fixed(31.4159265) == fixed(31, 4159));
test(fixed(31.41595) == fixed(31, 4160));

bool okay(false);
try {
  fixed f6(1, -1);
} catch (std::invalid_argument const& ex) {
  okay = true;
} catch (...) {
}
test(okay);
}
```

If you need a hint, I implemented `fixed` so it stores a single integer, with an implicit decimal place `places`10 positions from the right. Thus, I store the value 1 as 10000. Addition and subtraction are easy. When multiplying or dividing, you need to scale the result. (Even better is to scale the operands prior to multiplication, which avoids some overflow situations, but you need to be careful about not losing precision.)

# PART 3

# Generic Programming

# Function Templates

**Y**ou saw in Exploration 22 that the magic of overloading lets C++ implement an improved interface to the absolute value function. Instead, of three different names (abs, labs, and fabs), C++ has a single name for all three functions. Overloading helps the programmer who needs to call the abs function, but it doesn't help the implementor much, who still has to write three separate functions that all look and act the same. Wouldn't it be nice if the library author could write the abs function once instead of three times? After all, the three implementations are identical, differing only in the return type and parameter type. This Exploration introduces this style of programming, called generic programming.

## Generic Functions

Sometimes, you want to provide overloaded functions for integer and floating-point types, but the implementation is essentially the same. Absolute value is the obvious example; for any type T, the function looks the same (I'm using the name absval to avoid any confusion or conflict with the standard library's abs), as shown in Listing 46-1.

**Listing 46-1.** *Writing an Absolute Value Function*

```
T absval(T x)
{
  if (x < 0)
    return -x;
  else
    return x;
}
```

Substitute int for T, double for T, or use any other numeric type. You can even substitute rational for T, and the absval function still works the way you expect it to. So why waste your precious time writing, rewriting, and re-rewriting the same function? With a simple addition to the function definition, you can turn the function into a generic function, that is, a function that work with any suitable type T, which you can see in Listing 46-2.

**Listing 46-2.** *Writing a Function Template*

```
template<class T>
T absval(T x)
{
  if (x < 0)
    return -x;
  else
    return x;
}
```

The first line is the key. The `template` keyword means that what follows is a template, in this case, a *function template* definition. The angle brackets delimit a comma-separated list of template parameters. A function template is a pattern for creating functions, according to the parameter type, T. Within the function template definition, T represents a type, potentially any type. The caller of the `absval` function determines the template argument that will substitute for T.

When you define a function template, the compiler remembers the template, but does not generate any code. The compiler waits until you use the function template, and then it generates a real function. You can imagine the compiler taking the source text of the template, substituting the template argument, such as `int`, for the template parameter, T, and then compiling the resulting text. The next section tells you more about how to use a function template.

# Using Function Templates

Using a function template is easy, at least in most situations. Just call the `absval` function, and the compiler will automatically determine the template arguments based on the function argument type. It might take you a little while to get comfortable with the notion of template parameters and template arguments, which are quite different from function parameters and function arguments.

In the case of `absval`, the template parameter is T, and the template argument must be a type. You can't pass a type as a function argument, but templates are different. You aren't really "passing" anything in the program. Template magic occurs at compile time. The compiler sees the template definition of `absval`, and later it sees an invocation of the `absval` function template. The compiler examines the type of the function argument, and from the function argument's type, determines the template argument. The compiler substitutes that template argument for T, and generates a new instance of the `absval` function, customized for the template argument type. Thus, if you write

```
int x(-42);
int y(absval(x));
```

the compiler sees that x has type `int`, so it substitutes `int` for T. The compiler generates a function just as though the library implementor has written

```
int absval(int x)
{
  if (x < 0)
    return -x;
```

```
    else
        return x;
}
```

Later, in the same program, perhaps you call absval on a rational object.

```
rational r(-420, 10);
rational s(absval(r));
```

The compiler generates a new instance of absval.

```
rational absval(rational x)
{
    if (x < 0)
        return -x;
    else
        return x;
}
```

In this new instance of absval, the < operator is the overloaded operator that takes rational arguments. The negation operator is also a custom operator that takes a rational argument. In other words, when the compiler generates an instance of absval, it does so by compiling the source code pretty much just as the template author wrote it.

Write a sample program that contains the **absval** function template definition and some test code to call **absval** with a variety of argument types. Convince yourself that function templates actually work. Compare your test program with mine in Listing 46-3.

**Listing 46-3.** *Testing the absval Function Template*

```
#include <iostream>
#include <ostream>

#include "rational.hpp"

template<class T>
T absval(T x)
{
    if (x < 0)
        return -x;
    else
        return x;
}

int main()
{
    std::cout << absval(-42) << '\n';
    std::cout << absval(-4.2) << '\n';
    std::cout << absval(42) << '\n';
    std::cout << absval(4.2) << '\n';
    std::cout << absval(-42L) << '\n';
```

```
  std::cout << absval(rational(42, 5)) << '\n';
  std::cout << absval(rational(-42, 5)) << '\n';
  std::cout << absval(rational(42, -5)) << '\n';
}
```

# Writing Function Templates

Writing function templates is harder than writing ordinary functions. When you write a template such as absval, the problem is that you don't know what type or types T will actually be. So the function must be generic. C++ has no simple way for you to impose any overt restrictions on T, such as requiring that it be a built-in type or a numeric type. Instead, the restrictions are implicit by the way the template body uses T.

**C++ REVISION WILL HELP TEMPLATE AUTHORS**

The next major revision of the C++ language will let you write explicit restrictions, such as requiring that T have a copy constructor or that the < operator be usable with values of type T. The compiler will be able to issue clear, direct, and helpful error messages. The new feature is called a *concept*. The standard library will include a set of standard concepts, such as Copyable and LessThanComparable, and you will be able to define your own. A template author will use those concepts in a template parameter declaration to constrain the set of template arguments that you can use to instantiate the template. The standard library will use concepts for all the standard containers and algorithms. Look for concepts soon in a compiler near you!

In particular, absval imposes the following restrictions on T:

- T must be copyable. That means you must be able to copy an object of type T, so arguments can be passed to the function and a result can be returned. If T is a class type, the class must have an accessible copy constructor, that is, the copy constructor must not be private.

- T must be comparable with 0 using the < operator. You might overload the < operator, or the compiler can convert 0 to T, or T to an int.

- Unary operator - must be defined for an operand of type T. The result type must be T or something the compiler can convert automatically to T.

The built-in numeric types all meet these requirements. The rational type also meets these requirements because of the custom operators it supports. The string type, just to name one example, does not because it lacks a comparison operator when the right-hand operand is an integer, and it lacks a unary negation (-) operator. Suppose you tried to call absval on a string.

```
std::string test("-42");
std::cout << absval(test) << '\n';
```

**What do you think would happen?**

_____

_____

**Try it. What really happens?**

_____

_____

The compiler complains about the lack of the comparison and negation operators for `std::string`. One difficulty in delivering helpful error messages when working with templates is whether to give you the line number where the template is used or the line number in the template definition. Sometimes, you will get both. Sometimes, the compiler cannot report an error in the template definition unless you try to use the template. Other errors it can report immediately. **Read Listing 46-4 carefully.**

**Listing 46-4.** *Mystery Function Template*

```
template<class T>
T add(T lhs, T rhs)
{
  return lhs + rhs
}

int main()
{
}
```

**What is the error?**

_____

**Does your compiler report it?**

_____

Some compilers report the missing semicolon and some do not. You might have a program that is working just fine, and one day, you add a line of code, and the compiler reports an error. You check that line of code over and over again, but you don't see the problem. The real problem lies somewhere else entirely, in a template definition. The compiler probably gives you the right file and line number in a different error message, so you can find the true error.

**How can you force your compiler to report the error?**

_____

Add a line of code to use the template. For example, add the following to `main`:

```
return add(0, 0);
```

Every compiler will now report the missing semicolon in the template definition.

# Template Parameters

Whenever you see T in a C++ program, most likely, you are looking at a template. Look backward in the source file until you find the template header, that is, the part of the declaration that starts with the template keyword. That's where you should find the template parameters. The use of T as a template parameter name is merely a convention, but its use is nearly universal. The use of class to declare T may seem a little strange, especially because you've seen several examples when the template argument is not, in fact, a class.

Instead of class to declare a template parameter type, some programmers use an alternate keyword, typename, which means the same thing in this one context. The advantage of typename over class is that it avoids any confusion over nonclass types. The disadvantage is that typename has more than one use in a template context, which can confuse human readers in more complicated template definitions. Learn to read both styles, and pick the one you like best.

Sometimes, you will see parameter names that are more specific than T. If the template has more than one parameter, every parameter must have a unique name, so you will definitely see names other than T. For example, the copy algorithm is a function template with two parameters: the input iterator type and the output iterator type. The definition of copy, therefore, might look something like Listing 46-5.

**Listing 46-5.** *One Way to Implement the copy Algorithm*

```
template<class InputIterator, class OutputIterator>
OutputIterator copy(InputIterator start, InputIterator end, OutputIterator result)
{
  for ( ; start != end; ++start, ++result)
    *result = *start;
  return result;
}
```

Pretty simple, isn't it? (The real copy function is probably more complicated, with optimizations for certain types. Somewhere in the optimized implementation, however, is probably a function that looks just like Listing 46-5, albeit with different parameter names.)

When you use the copy algorithm, the compiler determines the value of InputIterator and OutputIterator according to the function argument types. As you saw with absval, the function's requirements on the template arguments are all implicit: InputIterator must allow the following operators: !=, prefix ++, and unary *. OutputIterator must allow prefix ++ and unary * operators. Now, perhaps, you can start to see why the requirements on iterators (Exploration 42) are written the way they are. Instead of mandating, say, that all iterators must derive from some base iterator class, the requirements are defined solely in terms of allowed operators.

**Write a simple implementation of the find algorithm.** This algorithm takes three arguments: the first two are input iterators that specify a range to search. The third argument is a value. Successive items in the range are compared with the value (using ==), and when an item matches, the function returns an iterator that refers to the matching position. If the item is not found, the end iterator is returned. Compare your solution with Listing 46-6.

**Listing 46-6.** *Implementing the find Algorithm*

```
template<class InputIterator, class T>
InputIterator find(InputIterator start, InputIterator end, T value)
{
  for ( ; start != end; ++start)
    if (*start == value)
      return start;
  return end;
}
```

Many of the standard algorithms are quite simple at their heart. Modern implementations are heavily optimized, and as is the nature of hand-optimized code, the results often bear little resemblance to the original code, and the optimized code can be much harder to read. Nonetheless, the simplicity remains in the architecture of the standard library, which relies extensively on templates.

# Template Arguments

Templates are easiest to use when the compiler automatically deduces the template arguments from the function arguments. It can't always do so, however, so you might need to tell the compiler explicitly what you want. The simple form of the min and max standard algorithms, for example, take a single template parameter. Listing 46-7 shows the min function, for reference.

**Listing 46-7.** *The std::min Algorithm*

```
template<class T>
T min(T a, T b)
{
  if (a < b)
    return a;
  else
    return b;
}
```

If both argument types are the same, the compiler can deduce the desired type, and everything just works.

```
int x(10), y(20), z(std::min(x, y));
```

On the other hand, if the function argument types are different, the compiler can't tell which type to use for the template argument.

```
int x(10);
long y(20);
std::cout << std::min(x, y); // error
```

Why is that? Suppose you wrote your own function as a nontemplate.

```
long my_min(long a, long b)
{
  if (a < b)
    return a;
  else
    return b;
}
```

The compiler could handle my_min(x, y) by converting x from an int to a long. As a template, however, the compiler does not perform any automatic type conversion. The compiler cannot read your mind and know that you want the template parameter to have the type of the first function argument or the second, or sometimes the first and sometimes the second. Instead, the compiler requires you to write exactly what you mean. In this case, you can tell the compiler what type to use for the template parameter by enclosing the desired type in angle brackets.

```
int x(10);
long y(20);
std::cout << std::min<long>(x, y); // okay: compiler converts x to type long
```

If a template takes multiple arguments, separate the arguments with a comma. For example, Listing 46-8 shows the input_sum function, which reads items from the standard input, and accumulates them by means of the += operator. The accumulator can have a different type than the item type. Because the item and accumulator types are not used in the function arguments, the compiler cannot deduce the parameter arguments, so you must supply them explicitly.

**Listing 46-8.** *Multiple Template Arguments*

```
#include <iostream>
#include <istream>
#include <ostream>

template<class T, class U>
U input_sum(std::istream& in)
{
  T x;
  U sum(0);
  while (in >> x)
    sum += x;
  return sum;
}

int main()
{
  long sum(input_sum<int, long>(std::cin));
  std::cout << sum << '\n';
}
```

**Rewrite the gcd function (from Listing 33-4) to be a function template**, so you can use the same function template for int, short, or long arguments. Compare your solution with mine in Listing 46-9. Remember to use the template parameter to declare the temporary variable.

**Listing 46-9.** *The gcd Function Template*

```
#ifndef GCD_HPP_
#define GCD_HPP_

#include <cstdlib> // for std::abs

template<class T>
/// Compute the greatest common divisor of two integers, using Euclid's algorithm.
T gcd(T n, T m)
{
  n = std::abs(n);
  while (m != 0) {
    T tmp(n % m);
    n = m;
    m = tmp;
  }
  return n;
}
#endif
```

# Declarations and Definitions

I can't seem to stop talking about declarations and definitions. Templates introduce yet another twist to this plot. When you work with templates, the rules change. The compiler needs to see more than just a declaration before you can use a function template. The compiler usually needs the full function template definition. In other words, if you define a template in a header file, that header file must include the body of that function template. Suppose you want to share the gcd function among many projects. Ordinarily, you would put the function declaration in a header file, say, *gcd.hpp*, and put the full definition in a separate source file, say, *gcd.cpp*.

When you convert gcd to a function template, however, you usually put the definition in the header file, as you saw in Listing 46-9. In order for the compiler to create concrete functions from the template, say, for gcd<int> or gcd<long>, it needs the body of the function template. A few compilers let you keep the template definitions in a separate file, using the export keyword. Most compilers do not support export, however, so I don't cover it in this book. There are also techniques that let you set up template instances in separate files, but they are tricky to get right, so I don't cover these techniques, either. For the purposes of this book, be sure your header files contain the bodies of all function templates.

# Member Function Templates

The rational class has three nearly identical functions: as_long_double, as_double, and as_float. They all do the same thing: divide the numerator by the denominator after converting to the destination type. Whenever you have multiple functions doing the same thing, in the same way, using the same code, you have a candidate for a template.

```
template<class T, class R>
T convert(R const& r)
{
   return static_cast<T>(r.numerator()) / r.denominator();
}
```

As with any function template, the only requirement on R is that objects of type R have member functions named numerator() and denominator(), and that these functions have return types suitable for use with operator/ (which could be overloaded). To use the convert function, you must supply the target type, T, as an explicit template argument, but you can let the compiler deduce R from the function argument:

```
rational r(42, 10);
double x( convert<double>(r) );
```

You can omit template arguments that the compiler can deduce, starting from the rightmost argument. As you saw earlier in this chapter, if the compiler can deduce all the arguments, you can leave out the angle brackets entirely.

A function template can be a member function, too. Instead of passing the rational object as an argument, you might prefer to use a member function template.

```
rational r(42, 10);
double x( r.convert<double>() );
```

A member function template avoids collisions with other free functions that might be named convert. For normal (nontemplate) functions, ordinary overloading rules often help to keep collisions to a minimum. It is unlikely that another function named convert would take a rational object as an argument. But templates are more problematic. Nothing about the template restricts the argument to rational, so the template convert collides with every other function named convert that takes one argument, even if that argument has nothing to do with rational. (Concepts, to be introduced in the new C++ revision, will let you restrict a function template's arguments to the rational template, neatly solving this problem. The standardization committee is still polishing the details as I write this book, but the standard may be complete when you read it.)

The details are more complicated than I've described, but the short version will do for now as a justification for writing a member function template instead of a free function template. Listing 46-10 shows how you might write the convert member function template.

**Listing 46-10.** *Implementing a Member Function Template*

```
class rational
{
public:
  rational() : numerator_(0), denominator_(1) {}
  rational(int num) : numerator_(num), denominator_(1) {}
  rational(int num, int den);
  rational(double r);

  template<class T>
  T convert()
  const
  {
    return static_cast<T>(numerator()) / static_cast<T>(denominator());
  }

... omitted for brevity ...
};
```

Generic programming is a powerful technique, and as you learn more about it in the next several Explorations, you will see how expressive and useful this programming paradigm is.

■ ■ ■

# Class Templates

**A** class can be a template, which makes all of its members templates. Every program in this book has used class templates because much of the standard library relies on templates: the standard I/O streams, strings, vectors, and maps are all class templates. This Exploration takes a look at simple class templates.

## Parameterizing a Type

Consider a simple point class, which stores an x and y coordinate. A graphics device driver might use int for the member types.

```
class point {
public:
   point(int x, int y) : x_(x), y_(y) {}
   int x() const { return x_; }
   int y() const { return y_; }
private:
   int x_, y_;
};
```

On the other hand, a calculus tool probably prefers to use double.

```
class point {
public:
   point(double x, double y) : x_(x), y_(y) {}
   double x() const { return x_; }
   double y() const { return y_; }
private:
   double x_, y_;
};
```

Imagine adding much more functionality to the point classes: computing distances between two point objects, rotating one point around another by some angle, etc. The more functionality you dream up, the more you must duplicate in both classes.

Wouldn't your job be simpler if you could write the point class once, and use that single definition for both situations and other not-yet-dreamed-of templates to the rescue. Listing 47-1 shows the point class template.

**Listing 47-1.** *The point Class Template*

```
template<class T>
class point {
public:
    point(T x, T y) : x_(x), y_(y) {}
    T x() const { return x_; }
    T y() const { return y_; }
    void move_to(T x, T y);        ///< Move to absolute coordinates (x, y)
    void move_by(T x, T y);        ///< Add (x, y) to current position
private:
    T x_, y_;
};

template<class T>
void point<T>::move_to(T x, T y)
{
    x_ = x;
    y_ = y;
}
```

Just as with function templates, the template keyword introduces a class template. The class template is a pattern for making classes, which you do by supplying template arguments; e.g., point<int>.

The member functions of a class template are themselves function templates, using the same template parameters, except that you supply the template arguments to the class, not the function, as you can see in the point<T>::move_to function. **Write the move_by member function.** Compare your solution with Listing 47-2.

**Listing 47-2.** *The move_by Member Function*

```
template<class T>
void point<T>::move_by(T x, T y)
{
    x_ += x;
    y_ += y;
}
```

Every time you use a different template argument, the compiler generates a new class instance, with new member functions. That is, point<int>::move_by is one function and point<double>::move_by is another, which is exactly what would happen if you had written the functions by hand. If two different source files both use point<int>, the compiler and linker ensure that they share the same template instance. Different tools have different ways of sharing the template instances; however, the details are beyond the scope of this book.

# Parameterizing the rational Class

A simple point class is easy. What about something more complicated, such as the rational class? Suppose someone likes your rational class, but wants more precision. You decide to change the type of the numerator and denominator from int to long. Someone else then complains that rational takes up too much memory, and asks for a version that uses short as the base type. You could make three copies of the source code, one each for types short, int, and long. Or you could define a class template, as illustrated by the simplified rational class template in Listing 47-3.

**Listing 47-3.** *The rational Class Template*

```
1 #ifndef RATIONAL_HPP_
2 #define RATIONAL_HPP_
3 template<class T>
4 class rational
5 {
6 public:
7   typedef T value_type;
8   rational() : numerator_(0), denominator_(1) {}
9   rational(T num) : numerator_(num), denominator_(1) {}
10   rational(T num, T den);
11
13   void assign(T num, T den);
13
14   template<class U>
15   U convert()
16   const
17   {
18     return static_cast<U>(numerator()) / static_cast<U>(denominator());
19   }
20
21   T numerator() const { return numerator_; }
22   T denominator() const { return denominator_; }
23 private:
24   void reduce();
25   T numerator_;
26   T denominator_;
27 };
28
29 template<class T>
30 rational<T>::rational(T num, T den)
31 : numerator_(num), denominator_(den)
32 {
33   reduce();
34 }
35
36 template<class T>
```

```
37 void rational<T>::assign(T num, T den)
38 {
39   numerator_ = num;
40   denominator_ = den;
41   reduce();
42 }
43
44 template<class T>
45 bool operator==(rational<T> const& a, rational<T> const& b)
46 {
47   return a.numerator()   == b.numerator() and
48          a.denominator() == b.denominator();
49 }
50
51 template<class T>
52 inline bool operator!=(rational<T> const& a, rational<T> const& b)
53 {
54   return not (a == b);
55 }
56
57 #endif
```

The typedef of value_type (line 7) is a useful convention. Many class templates that use a template parameter as some kind of subordinate type expose the parameter under a well-defined name. For example, vector<char>::value_type is a typedef for its template parameter, namely, char.

Look at the definition of the constructor on line 29. When you define a member outside of its class template, you need to repeat the template header. The full name of the type includes the template parameter, rational<T> in this case. Inside the class scope, use just the class name, without the template parameter. Also, once the compiler sees the fully qualified class name, it knows it is inside the class scope, and you can also use the template parameter by itself, which you can see in the parameter declarations

Because the name T is already in use, the convert member function (line 14) needs a new name for its template parameter. U is a common convention, provided you don't take it too far. More than two or three single-letter parameters, and you start to need more meaningful names, just to help keep straight which parameter goes with which template.

In addition to the class template itself, you need to convert all the free functions that support the rational type to be function templates. Listing 47-3 keeps things simple by showing only operator== and operator!=. Other operators work similarly.

# Using Class Templates

Unlike function templates, the compiler cannot deduce the template argument of a class template. That means you must supply the argument explicitly, inside angle brackets.

```
rational<short> zero;
rational<int> pi1(355, 113);
rational<long> pi2(80143857L, 25510582L);
```

Notice anything familiar? Does `rational<int>` look like `vector<int>`? All the collection types, such as `vector` and `map`, are class templates. The standard library makes heavy use of templates throughout, and you will discover other templates when the time is right.

If a class template takes multiple arguments, separate the arguments with a comma, as in `map<long, int>`. A template argument can even be another template. For example, suppose you want to store vectors in a vector, as shown in Listing 47-4.

**Listing 47-4.** *Trying to Use a Vector of Vectors*

```
#include <vector>

int main()
{
  std::vector<std::vector<int>> matrix;
}
```

**What happens when you try to compile Listing 47-4?**

_____

_____

**Most of you will get an error message. Can you explain this message?**

_____

If you need a hint, go back to Exploration 9, where I first explained it.

The root problem is that the C++ compiler always builds the longest possible token it can from adjacent characters. Only after it has tokenized the input does it try to make sense of that input. In this case, the compiler sees `>>` as the input operator, not as two separate closing angle brackets. The solution is to leave a space between the angle brackets, to ensure the compiler sees two separate tokens.

```
std::vector<std::vector<int> > matrix;
```

## MINOR TWEAK TO THE LANGUAGE

The next revision to the C++ language changes the interpretation of `>>` in a template argument list. The compiler sees `>>` as two separate `>` symbols. It's a minor change, but one that many C++ programmers welcome.

Some compilers offer this capability now as an extension to the standard. I recommend sticking to the standard. It is always correct to keep the space, regardless of which version of the compiler you are using. If you are using the new revision, and have no need for compatibility with the first revision, go ahead and elide the space. Everyone else should keep it.

Starting with *rational.hpp* from Listing 47-3, **add the I/O operators**. Write a simple test program that reads rational objects and echoes the values, one per line, to the standard output. Try changing the template argument to different types (short, int, long). Your test program might look something like Listing 47-5.

**Listing 47-5.** *Simple I/O Test of the rational Class Template*

```
#include <iostream>
#include <istream>
#include <ostream>

#include "rational.hpp"

int main()
{
  rational<int> r;
  while (std::cin >> r)
    std::cout << r << '\n';
}
```

Now modify the test program to print only nonzero values. The program should look something like Listing 47-6.

**Listing 47-6.** *Testing rational Comparison Operator*

```
#include <iostream>
#include <istream>
#include <ostream>

#include "rational.hpp"

int main()
{
  rational<int> r;
  while (std::cin >> r)
    if (r != 0)
      std::cout << r << '\n';
}
```

The program should work, right? Remember that with the old rational class, the compiler knew how to construct a rational object from an integer. Thus, it could convert the 0 to rational(0) and then call the overloaded == operator to compare two rational objects.

# Overloaded Operators

Remember from the previous Exploration that the compiler does not perform automatic type conversion for a function template. To solve this problem, you need to add some additional comparison operators:

```
template<class T> bool operator==(rational<T> const& lhs, T rhs);
template<class T> bool operator==(T lhs, rational<T> const& rhs);
template<class T> bool operator!=(rational<T> const&  lhs, T rhs);
template<class T> bool operator!=(T lhs, rational<T> const& rhs);
```

and so on, for all of the comparison and arithmetic operators. On the other hand, you need to consider whether that's what you really want. To better understand the limitations of this approach, go ahead and try it. You don't need all the comparison operators yet, just operator!=, so you can compile the test program. **Compile the test program with a template parameter of long. What happens?**

---

---

Once again, the compiler complains that it can't find any suitable function for the != operator. The problem is that an overloaded != operator exists for the template parameter, namely, type long, but the type of the literal 0 is int, not long. You can try to solve this problem by defining operators for all the built-in types, but that quickly gets out of hand. So your choices are

- define only operators that take two rational arguments. Force the caller to convert arguments to the desired rational type.

- define operators in triples: one that takes two rational arguments, and two others that mix one rational and one base type (T).

- define operators to cover all the bases. For the built-in types (signed char, char, short, int, long, plus some types that I haven't covered yet). Thus, each operator needs 11 functions.

You might be interested in knowing how the C++ standard library addresses this issue. Among the types in the standard library is a class template, complex, which represents a complex number. The standardization committee opted for the second choice, that is, three overloaded function templates.

```
template<class T> bool operator==(complex<T> const& a, complex<T> const& b);
template<class T> bool operator==(complex<T> const& a, T const& b);
template<class T> bool operator==(T const& a, complex<T> const& b);
```

This solution works well enough, and later in the book, you'll learn techniques to reduce the amount of work involved in defining all these functions.

Another dimension to this problem is the literal 0. Using a literal of type int is fine when you know the base type of rational is also int. How do you express a generic zero for use in a template? The same issue arises when testing for a zero denominator. That was easy when you knew that the type of the denominator was int. When working with templates, you don't know the type. Recall from Listing 44-6 that the division assignment operator checked for a zero divisor and threw an exception in that case. If you don't know the type T, how do you know how to express the value zero? You can try using the literal 0 and hope that T has a suitable constructor (single argument of type int). A better solution is to invoke the default constructor for type T, as shown in Listing 47-7.

**Listing 47-7.** *Invoking a Default Constructor of a Template Parameter*

```
template<class T>
rational<T>& rational<T>::operator/=(rational const& rhs)
{
  if (rhs.numerator() == T())
    throw zero_denominator("divide by zero");
  numerator_ *= rhs.denominator();
  denominator_ *= rhs.numerator();
  if (denominator_ < T())
  {
    denominator_ = -denominator_;
    numerator_ = -numerator_;
  }
  reduce();
  return *this;
}
```

If the type T is a class type, T() yields an object that is initialized using T's default constructor. If T is a built-in type, the value of T() is zero (i.e., 0, 0.0, or false). Initializing the local variables in the input operator is a little trickier.

Most likely, when you converted the old rational code to the new template code, you didn't change the way the local variables were initialized. In my version, I initialized the local numerator and denominator to zero as follows:

```
T n(0), d(0);
```

Recall from Exploration 32 that simply changing the definition to use empty parentheses doesn't work.

```
T n(), d(); // does not invoke default constructors
```

Instead of invoking default T constructors, you are declaring two functions, named n and d, which take no arguments and return type T. Another approach might be to change the 0 to T(), which worked in Listing 47-7.

```
T n(T()), d(T());
```

Too bad that still doesn't work. What you've declared are two functions again, this time taking a single argument of type T.

One solution is to wrap the argument in parentheses.

```
T n((T())), d((T()));
```

But I find that difficult to read. You can clean it up a little with some extra spaces, and debates have run hot about exactly where and when to insert extra spaces. My preferred solution is to use an alternative syntax for initializing objects in a definition.

```
T n = T(), d = T();
```

If you have a single initializer value, instead of enclosing the value in parentheses, you can use an equal sign followed by the initial value. You saw a similar syntax with static const data members.

The equal sign in the definition is not an assignment operator. It is merely another syntax for initializing an object. In addition to the syntactic difference between the equal sign and parentheses, there is a subtle semantic difference. Using the equal sign, the compiler might invoke two constructors to initialize each value: first, it calls T(), then it can call a copy constructor to construct n from the temporary value T(). Most compilers eliminate the copy constructor as an optimization, but the standard grants some flexibility to the compilers. Using parentheses initializes the object directly and does not need an extra call to the copy constructor. Thus, initializing with the equal sign is called *copy initialization*, and using parentheses is called *direct initialization*. My recommendation is to use direct initialization as much as possible, but don't hesitate to use copy initialization when it enhances readability.

# Mixing Types

As you know, you can assign an int value to a long object or *vice versa*. It seems reasonable, therefore, that you should be able to assign a rational<int> value to a rational<long> object. Try it. **Write a simple program to perform an assignment that mixes base types.** Your program might look a little bit like Listing 47-8, but many other programs are equally reasonable.

**Listing 47-8.** *Trying to Mix* rational *Base Types*

```
#include "rational.hpp"

int main()
{
  rational<int> little;
  rational<long> big;
  big = little;
}
```

**What happens when you compile your program?**

_____

_____

The only assignment operator for the new rational class template is the compiler's implicit operator. Its parameter type is rational<T> const, so the base type of the source expression must be the same as the base type of the assignment target. You can fix this easily with a member function template. Add the following declaration to the class template:

```
template<class U>
rational& operator=(rational<U> const& rhs);
```

Inside the rational class template, the unadorned name, rational, means the same thing as rational<T>. The complete name of the class includes the template argument, so the proper name of the constructor is rational<T>. Because rational means the same as rational<T>, I was able to shorten the constructor name, and many other uses of the type name throughout the class template definition. But the assignment operator's parameter is `rational<U>`. It uses a completely different template argument. Using this assignment operator, you can freely mix different `rational` types in an assignment statement.

**Write the definition of the assignment operator.** Don't worry about overflow that might result from assigning large values to small. It's a difficult problem, and distracts from the main task at hand, which is practicing writing class templates and function templates. Compare your solution with Listing 47-9.

**Listing 47-9.** *Defining the Assignment Operator Function Template*

```
template<class T>
template<class U>
rational<T>& rational<T>::operator=(rational<U> const& rhs)
{
  assign(rhs.numerator(), rhs.denominator());
  return *this;
}
```

The first template header tells the compiler about the `rational` class template. The next template header tells the compiler about the assignment operator function template. Note that the compiler will be able to deduce the template argument for U from the type of the assignment source (rhs). After adding this operator to the `rational` class template, you should now be able to make your test program work.

**Add a member template constructor that works similarly to the assignment operator.** In other words, add to `rational` a constructor that looks like a copy constructor, but isn't really. A copy constructor copies only objects of the same type, or `rational<T>`. This new constructor copies rational objects with a different base type, `rational<U>`. Compare your solution with Listing 47-10.

**Listing 47-10.** *Defining a Member Constructor Template*

```
template<class T>
template<class U>
rational<T>::rational(rational<U> const& copy)
: numerator_(copy.numerator()), denominator_(copy.denominator())
{}
```

**Finish the *rational.hpp* header by completing all the operators.** The new file is too big to include here, but as always, you can download the completed file from the book's web site.

Programming with templates and type parameters opens a new world of programming power and flexibility. A template lets you write a function or class once, and lets the compiler generate actual functions and classes for different template arguments. Sometimes, however, one size does not fit all, and you need to grant exceptions to the rule. The next Exploration takes a look at how you do that by writing template specializations.

# EXPLORATION 48

■ ■ ■

# Template Specialization

The ability to write a template and then use that template multiple times, with different template arguments each time, is one of the great features of C++. Even better is the ability to carve out exceptions to the rule. That is, you can tell the compiler to use a template for most template arguments, except that for certain argument types, it should use a different template definition. This Exploration introduces this feature.

## Instantiation and Specialization

Template terminology is tricky. When you use a template, it is known as *instantiating* the template. A *template instance* is a concrete function or class that the compiler creates by applying the template arguments to the template definition. Another name for a template instance is a *specialization*. Thus, rational<int> is a specialization of the template rational<>.

Therefore, specialization is the realization of a template for a specific set of template arguments. C++ lets you define a custom specialization for one particular set of template arguments; that is, you can create an exception to the rule set down by the template. When you define the specialization instead of letting the compiler instantiate the template for you, it is known as *explicit specialization*. Thus, a specialization that the compiler creates automatically would be an *implicit specialization*. (Explicit specialization is also called *full specialization*, for reasons that will become clear in the next Exploration.) For example, suppose you define a simple class template, point, to represent an (*x, y*) coordinate and made it into a template to accept any numeric type as the type for *x* and *y*. Because some types are large, you decide to pass values by const reference whenever possible, as shown in Listing 48-1.

**Listing 48-1.** *The point Class Template*

```
template<class T>
class point
{
public:
  typedef T value_type;
  point(T const& x, T const& y) : x_(x), y_(y) {}
  point() : x_(), y_() {}
  T const& x() const { return x_; }
  T const& y() const { return y_; }
  void move_absolute(T const& x, T const& y) {
```

**415**

```
    x_ = x;
    y_ = y;
  }
  void move_relative(T const& dx, T const& dy) {
    x_ += dx;
    y_ += dy;
  }
private:
  T x_;
  T y_;
};
```

The point template works with int, double, rational, and any type that behaves the same way as the built-in numeric types. If you had, say, an arbitrary-precision numeric type, you could use that, too, and because such objects are potentially very large, passing by reference is a good choice for default behavior.

On the other hand, point<int> is a fairly common usage, especially in graphical user interfaces. In a mathematical context, point<double> might be more common. In either case, you might decide that passing values by reference is actually wasteful. You can define an explicit specialization for point<int> to pass arguments by value, as shown in Listing 48-2.

**Listing 48-2.** *The point<int> Specialization*

```
template<>
class point<int>
{
public:
  typedef int value_type;
  point(int x, int y) : x_(x), y_(y) {}
  point() : x_(), y_() {}
  int x() const { return x_; }
  int y() const { return y_; }
  void move_absolute(int x, int y) {
    x_ = x;
    y_ = y;
  }
  void move_relative(int dx, int dy) {
    x_ += dx;
    y_ += dy;
  }
private:
  int x_;
  int y_;
};
```

Start an explicit specialization with template<> (notice the empty angle brackets), which tells the compiler that you are writing an explicit specialization. Next is the definition. Notice how the class name is the specialized template name: point<int>. That's how the compiler knows what you are specializing. Before you can specialize a template, you must tell the compiler about the class template with a declaration of the class template name or a full definition of the class template. Typically, you would put the class template declaration followed by its specializations in a single header, in the right order.

Your explicit specialization completely replaces the template declaration for that template argument (or arguments: if the template takes multiple arguments, you must supply a specific value for each one). Although convention dictates that point<int> should define all the same members as the primary template, point<>, the compiler imposes no such limitation.

**Write an explicit specialization for point<double>.** Add a debugging statement to the primary template and to the specialization so you can prove to yourself that the compiler really does choose the specialization. Write a main program to use point<double> and point<short>, and check that the correct debugging statements execute. Listing 48-3 shows how the program looks when I write it.

**Listing 48-3.** *Specializing point<double> and Testing the Code*

```cpp
#include <iostream>
#include <ostream>

template<class T>
class point
{
public:
  typedef T value_type;
  point(T const& x, T const& y) : x_(x), y_(y) {}
  point() : x_(), y_() { std::cout << "point<>()\n"; }
  T const& x() const { return x_; }
  T const& y() const { return y_; }
  void move_absolute(T const& x, T const& y) {
    x_ = x;
    y_ = y;
  }
  void move_relative(T const& dx, T const& dy) {
    x_ += dx;
    y_ += dy;
  }
private:
  T x_;
  T y_;
};

template<>
class point<double>
{
public:
  typedef double value_type;
  point(double  x, double y) : x_(x), y_(y) {}
  point() : x_(), y_() { std::cout << "point<double> specialization\n"; }
  double x() const { return x_; }
```

```
  double y() const { return y_; }
  void move_absolute(double x, double y) {
    x_ = x;
    y_ = y;
  }
  void move_relative(double dx, double dy) {
    x_ += dx;
    y_ += dy;
  }
private:
  double x_;
  double y_;
};

int main()
{
  point<short> s;
  point<double> d;
  s.move_absolute(10, 20);
  d.move_absolute(1.23, 4.56);
}
```

If you really want to get fancy, include the <typeinfo> header, and, in the primary template, call typeid(T).name() to obtain a string that describes the type T. The exact contents of the string depend on the implementation. The typeid keyword returns a typeinfo object (defined in <typeinfo>) that describes a type, or you can apply the keyword to an expression to obtain information on the expression's type. You can't do much with a typeinfo object. It's not a reflection mechanism, but you can call the name() member function to get a name. This is a handy debugging technique when you have a complicated template situation, and you aren't quite sure what the compiler thinks the template argument is. Thus, write the constructor as follows:

```
point() : x_(), y_() { std::cout << "point<" << typeid(T).name() << ">()\n"; }
```

One compiler I have prints

```
point<short>()
point<double> specialization
```

Another prints

```
point<s>()
point<double> specialization
```

# Custom Comparators

The map container lets you provide a custom comparator. The default behavior is for map to use a template class, std::less<>, which is a functor that uses the < operator to compare keys. If you want to store a type that cannot be compared with <, you can specialize std::less for your type. For example, suppose you have a person class, which stores a person's name, address, and telephone number. You want to store a person in a map, ordered by name. All you need to do is write a template specialization, std::less<person>, as shown in Listing 48-4.

**Listing 48-4.** *Specializing* std::less *to Compare person Objects by Name*

```cpp
#include <functional>
#include <iostream>
#include <map>
#include <ostream>
#include <string>

class person {
public:
   person() : name_(), address_(), phone_() {}
   person(std::string const& name,
          std::string const& address,
          std::string const& phone)
   : name_(name), address_(address), phone_(phone)
   {}
   std::string const& name()    const { return name_; }
   std::string const& address() const { return address_; }
   std::string const& phone()   const { return phone_; }
private:
   std::string name_, address_, phone_;
};

namespace std {
   template<>
   struct less<person> {
      bool operator()(person const& a, person const& b) const {
         return a.name() < b.name();
      }
   };
}

int main()
{
   std::map<person, int> people;
   people[person("Ray", "123 Erewhon", "555-5555")] = 42;
   people[person("Arthur", "456 Utopia", "123-4567")] = 10;
   std::cout << people.begin()->first.name() << '\n';
}
```

You are allowed to specialize templates that are defined in the `std` namespace, but you cannot add new declarations to `std`. The `std::less` template is declared in the `<functional>` header. This header defines comparator templates for all the relational and equality operators, and some more besides. Consult a language reference for details. What matters right now is what the `std::less` primary template looks like, that is, the main template that C++ uses when it cannot find an explicit specialization (such as `std::less<person>`). **Write the definition of a class template, `less`, that would serve as a primary template to compare any comparable objects with the `<` operator.** Compare your solution with Listing 48-5.

**Listing 48-5.** *The Primary* `std::less` *Class Template*

```
template<class T>
struct less {
    bool operator()(T const& a, T const& b) const { return a < b; }
};
```

Take a peek into your standard library's `<functional>` header. It might be in another file that `<functional>` includes, and it might be more complicated than Listing 48-5, but you should be able to find something you can recognize and understand.

# Specializing Function Templates

You can specialize a function template, but you should prefer overloading to templates. For example, let's keep working with the template form of `absval` (Exploration 46). Suppose you have an arbitrary-precision integer class, `integer`, and it has an efficient absolute value function (that is, it simply clears the sign bit, so there's no need to compare the value with zero). Instead of the template form of `absval`, you want to use the efficient method for taking the absolute value of `integer`. Although C++ permits you to specialize the `absval<>` function template, a better solution is to override the `absval` function (not template).

```
integer absval(integer i)
{
    i.clear_sign_bit();
    return i;
}
```

When the compiler sees a call to `absval`, it examines the type of the argument. If the type matches the parameter type used in a nontemplate function, the compiler arranges to call that function. If it can't match the argument type with the parameter type, it checks template functions. The precise rules are complicated, and I will discuss them later in the book. For now, just remember that the compiler prefers nontemplate functions to template functions, but it will use a template function instead of a nontemplate function if it can't find a good match between the argument types and the parameter types of the nontemplate function.

Sometimes, however, you need to write a template function, even if you just want to overload the `absval` function. For example, suppose you want to improve the absolute value function for the `rational<T>` class template. There is no need to compare the entire value with zero; just compare the numerator, and avoid unnecessary multiplications.

```
template<class T>
rational<T> absval(rational<T> const& r)
{
  if (r.numerator() < 0) // to avoid unnecessary multiplications in operator<
    return -r;
  else
    return r;
}
```

When you call absval, pass it an argument in the usual way. If you pass an int, double, or other built-in numeric type, the compiler instantiates the original function template. If you pass an integer object, the compiler calls the overloaded nontemplate function, and if you pass a rational object, the compiler instantiates the overloaded function template.

# Traits

Another use of specialization is to define a template that captures the characteristics, or *traits*, of a type. You've already seen one example of a traits template: std::numeric_limits. The <limits> header defines a class template named std::numeric_limits. The primary template is rather dull, saying that the type has zero digits of precision, a radix of zero, and so on. The only way this template makes any sense is to specialize it. Thus, the <limits> header also defines explicit specializations of the template for all the built-in types. Thus, you can discover the smallest int by calling std::numeric_limits<int>::min() or determine the floating-point radix with std::numeric_limits<double>::radix, and so on. Every specialization declares the same members, but with values that are particular to the specialization.

You can define your own specialization when you create a numeric type, such as rational. Defining a template of a template involves some difficulties that I will cover in the next Exploration, so for now, go back to Listing 44-9 and the old-fashioned nontemplate rational class, which hardcoded int as the base type. Listing 48-6 shows how to specialize numeric_limits for this rational class.

**Listing 48-6.** *Specializing numeric_limits for the rational Class*

```
namespace std {
template<>
class numeric_limits<rational>
{
public:
  static bool const is_specialized = true;
  static rational min() throw() { return rational(numeric_limits<int>::min()); }
  static rational max() throw() { return rational(numeric_limits<int>::max()); }
  static int const digits = 2 * numeric_limits<int>::digits;
  static int const digits10 = numeric_limits<int>::digits10;
  static bool const is_signed = true;
  static bool const is_integer = false;
  static bool const is_exact = true;
  static int const radix = 2;
  static bool const is_bounded = true;
```

```
    static bool const is_modulo = false;
    static bool const traps = std::numeric_limits<int>::traps;

    static rational epsilon() throw()
    { return rational(1, numeric_limits<int>::max()-1); }
    static rational round_error() throw()
    { return rational(1, numeric_limits<int>::max()); }
    static float_round_style const round_style = round_to_nearest;

    // The following are meaningful only for floating-point types.
    static int const min_exponent = 0;
    static int const min_exponent10 = 0;
    static int const max_exponent = 0;
    static int const max_exponent10 = 0;
    static bool const has_infinity = false;
    static bool const has_quiet_NaN = false;
    static bool const has_signaling_NaN = false;
    static float_denorm_style const has_denorm = denorm_absent;
    static bool const has_denorm_loss = false;
    // The following are meant only for floating-point types, but you have
    // to define them, anyway, even for nonfloating-point types. The values
    // they return do not have to be meaningful.
    static rational infinity() throw() { return rational(); }
    static rational quiet_NaN() throw() { return rational(); }
    static rational signaling_NaN() throw() { return rational(); }
    static rational denorm_min() throw() { return rational(); }
    static bool const is_iec559 = false;
    static bool const tinyness_before = false;
};

}
```

This example has a few new things. They aren't important right now, but in C++, you have to get all the tiny details right or the compiler voices its stern disapproval. The first line, which starts namespace std is how you put names in the standard library. You are not allowed to add new names to the standard library (although the standard does not require a compiler to issue an error message if you break this rule), but you are allowed to specialize templates that the standard library has already defined. Notice the opening curly brace, which has a corresponding closing curly brace on the last line of the listing. The member functions all have throw() between their names and bodies. This tells the compiler that the function must not throw an exception. If the function does actually throw an exception at runtime, the program terminates by calling the unexpected() function, which in turns calls abort(), which aborts your program unceremoniously, without calling any destructors.

Template specialization has many other uses, but before we get carried away, the next Exploration takes a look at a particular kind of specialization, where your specialization still requires template parameters, called partial specialization.

# Partial Specialization

Explicit specialization requires you to specify a template argument for every template parameter, leaving no template parameters in the template header. Sometimes, however, you want to specify only some of the template arguments, leaving one or more template parameters in the header. C++ lets you do just that and more, but only for class templates, as this Exploration describes.

## Degenerate Pairs

The standard library defines the `std::pair<T, U>` class template in the `<utility>` header. This class template is a trivial holder of a pair of objects. The template arguments specify the types of these two objects. Listing 49-1 depicts the definition of this simple template.

**Listing 49-1.** *The* `std::pair` *Class Template*

```
template<class T, class U>
struct pair {
    typedef T first_type;
    typedef U second_type;
    T first;
    U second;
    pair();
    pair(T const& first, U const& second);
    template<class T2, class U2>
    pair(pair<T2, pair U2> const& other);
};
```

As you can tell, the `pair` class template doesn't do much. The `std::map` class template can use `std::pair` to store keys and values. A few functions return a `pair` in order to return two pieces of information. In other words, `pair` is a useful, if dull, part of the standard library.

**What happens if T or U is void?**

_____

Although `void` has popped up here and there, usually as a function's return type, I haven't discussed it much. The `void` type means "no type." That's useful for returning from a function, but you cannot declare an object with void type, nor does the compiler permit you to use void for a data member. Thus, pair<int, void> results in an error.

As you start to use templates more and more, you will find yourself in unpredictable situations. A template contains a template, which contains another template, and suddenly you find a template, such as pair, being instantiated with template arguments that you never imagined before. So let's add specializations for pair that permit one or two void template arguments, just for the sake of completeness. (The standard permits specializations of library templates only if a template argument is a user-defined type. Therefore, specializing pair for the void type results in undefined behavior. If your compiler is picky, you can copy the definition of pair out of the <utility> header and into your own file, using a different namespace. Then proceed with the experiment. Most readers will be able to work in the std namespace without incurring the wrath of the compiler.)

**Write an explicit specialization for pair<void, void>.** It cannot store anything, but you can declare objects of type pair<void, void>. Compare your solution with Listing 49-2.

**Listing 49-2.** *Specializing pair<> for Two void Arguments*

```
template<>
struct pair<void, void> {
   typedef void first_type;
   typedef void second_type;
   // The implicity default and copy constructors work for this specialization.
};
```

More difficult is the case of one void argument. You still need a template parameter for the other part of the pair. That calls for *partial specialization*.

# Partial Specialization

When you write a template specialization that involves some, but not all, of the template arguments, it is called *partial specialization*. Some programmers call explicit specialization *full specialization* to help distinguish it from partial specialization. Partial specialization is explicit, so the phrase full specialization is more descriptive, and I will use it for the rest of this book.

Begin a partial specialization with a template header that lists the template parameters you are not specializing. Then define the specialization. Notice how you name the class that you are specializing by listing all the template arguments. Some of the template arguments depend on the specialization's parameters, and some are fixed with specific values. That's what makes this specialization partial.

As with full specialization, the definition of the specialization completely replaces the primary template for a particular set of template arguments. By convention, you keep the same interface, but the actual implementation is up to you.

Listing 49-3 shows a partial specialization of pair if the first template argument is void.

**Listing 49-3.** *Specializing pair for One void Argument*

```
template<class U>
struct pair<void, U> {
   typedef void first_type;
```

```
    typedef U second_type;
    U second;
    pair();
    pair(U second);
    template<class U2>
    pair(pair<void, U2> const& other);
};
```

Based on Listing 49-3, **write a partial specialization of pair with a void second argument**. Compare your solution with Listing 49-4.

**Listing 49-4.** *Specializing pair for the Other void Argument*

```
template<class T>
struct pair<T, void> {
    typedef T first_type;
    typedef void second_type;
    T first;
    pair();
    pair(T first);
    template<class T2>
    pair(pair<T2, void> const& other);
};
```

Regardless of the presence or absence of any partial or full specializations, you still use the pair template the same way: always with two type arguments. The compiler examines those template arguments and determines which specialization to use.

# Partially Specializing Function Templates

You cannot partially specialize a function template. Full specialization is allowed, as described in the previous Exploration, but partial specialization is not. Sorry. Use overloading instead, which is usually better than template specialization, anyway.

# Value Template Parameters

Before I present the next example of partial specialization, I want to introduce a new template feature. Templates typically use types as parameters, but they can also use values. Declare a value template parameter with a type and optional name, much the same way that you would declare a function parameter. Value template parameters are limited to types for which you can specify a compile-time constant: bool, char, int, etc. Floating-point types and classes are not allowed.

For example, suppose you want to modify the fixed class that you wrote for Exploration 45 so the developer can specify the number of digits after the decimal place. While you're at it, you can also use a template parameter to specify the underlying type, as shown in Listing 49-5.

**Listing 49-5.** *Changing fixed from a Class to a Class Template*

```
template<class T, int N>
class fixed
{
public:
    typedef T value_type;
    static const T places = N;
    static const T places10;
    fixed();
    fixed(T const& integer, T const& fraction);
    fixed& operator=(fixed const& rhs);
    fixed& operator+=(fixed const& rhs);
    fixed& operator*=(fixed const& rhs);
    // and so on...
private:
    T value_; // scaled to N decimal places
};

template<class T, int N>
bool operator==(fixed<T,N> const& a, fixed<T,N> const& b);
template<class T, int N>
fixed<T,N> operator+(fixed<T,N> const& a, fixed<T,N> const& b);
template<class T, int N>
fixed<T,N> operator*(fixed<T,N> const& a, fixed<T,N> const& b);
// and so on...
```

The key challenge in converting the fixed class to a class template is defining places10. Defining places10 as a compile-time constant requires template trickery that is beyond what I've covered so far. (I will cover advanced template trickery, but not until Exploration 67.) A simpler approach is to initialize places10 in *fixed.cpp*.

```
template<class T, int N>
T fixed<T, N>::places10 = static_cast<T>(std::pow(10.0, N));
```

Otherwise, the conversion is mostly mechanical: adding template headers and changing the name fixed to fixed<T, N>.

Suppose you have an application that instantiates fixed<long, 0>. This degenerate case is no different from a plain long, but with overhead for managing places10, even though the value of places10 is 1. Suppose further that performance measurements of your application reveal that this overhead has a measurable impact on the overall performance of the application. Therefore, you decide to use partial specialization for the case of fixed<T, 0>. Use a partial specialization so the template still takes a template argument for the underlying type.

You might wonder why the application programmer doesn't simply replace fixed<long, 0> with plain long. In some cases, that is the correct solution. Other times, however, the use of fixed<long, 0> might be buried inside another template. The issue becomes, therefore, one of which template to specialize. For the sake of this Exploration, we are specializing fixed.

Remember that any specialization must provide a full implementation. You don't need to specialize the free functions, too. By specializing the fixed class template, we get the performance boost we need. Listing 49-6 shows the partial specialization of fixed.

**Listing 49-6.** *Specializing fixed for N == 0*

```
template<class T>
class fixed<T, 0>
{
public:
    typedef T value_type;
    static const T places = 0;
    static const T places10 = 1;
    fixed() : value_() {}
    fixed(T const& integer, T const&) : value_(integer) {}
    fixed& operator=(fixed const& rhs) { value_ = rhs; }
    fixed& operator+=(fixed const& rhs) { value_ += rhs; }
    fixed& operator*=(fixed const& rhs) { value_ *= rhs; }
    // and so on...
private:
    T value_; // no need for scaling
};
```

The next Exploration introduces a language feature that helps you manage your custom types: namespaces.

■■■

# Names and Namespaces

**N**early every name in the standard library begins with std::, and only names in the standard library are permitted to start with std::. For your own names, you can define other prefixes, which is a good idea and an excellent way to avoid name collisions. Libraries and large programs in particular benefit from proper partitioning and naming. However, templates and names have some complications, and this Exploration helps clarify the issues.

## Namespaces

The name std is an example of a *namespace*, which is a C++ term for a named scope. A namespace is a way to keep names organized. When you see a name that begins with std::, you know it's in the standard library. Good third-party libraries use namespaces. The open-source Boost project (http://www.boost.org/), for example, uses the boost namespace, to ensure names, such as boost::mem_fun_ref, do not interfere with similar names in the standard library, such as std::mem_fun_ref. Applications can take advantage of namespaces, too. For example, different project teams can place their own names in different namespaces, so members of one team are free to name functions and classes without the need to check with other teams. For example, the GUI team might use the namespace gui and define a gui::tree class, which manages a tree widget in a user interface. The database team might use the db namespace. Thus, db::tree might represent a tree data structure that is used to store database indexes on disk. A database debugging tool can use both tree classes because there is no clash between db::tree and gui::tree. The namespaces keep the names separate.

To create a namespace and declare names within it, you must define the namespace. A namespace definition begins with the namespace keyword followed by an optional identifier that names the namespace. This in turn is followed by declarations within curly braces. Unlike a class definition, a namespace definition does not end with a semicolon after the closing curly brace. All the declarations within the curly braces are in the scope of the namespace. You must define a namespace outside of any function. Listing 50-1 defines the namespace numeric and within it, the rational class template.

**Listing 50-1.** *Defining the* rational *Class Template in the* numeric *Namespace*

```
#ifndef RATIONAL_HPP_
#define RATIONAL_HPP_

namespace numeric
{
  template<class T>
  class rational
  {
    // you know what goes here...
  };
  template<class T>
  bool operator==(rational<T> const& a, rational<T> const& b);
  template<class T>
  rational<T> operator+(rational<T> const& a, rational<T> const& b);
  // and so on...
}

#endif
```

Namespace definitions can be discontiguous. This means you can have many separate namespace blocks that all contribute to the same namespace. Therefore, multiple header files can each define the same namespace, and every definition adds names to the same, common namespace. Listing 50-2 illustrates how to define the fixed class template within the same numeric namespace, even in a different header (say, *fixed.hpp*).

**Listing 50-2.** *Defining the* fixed *Class Template in the* numeric *Namespace*

```
#ifndef FIXED_HPP_
#define FIXED_HPP_

namespace numeric
{
  template<class T, int N>
  class fixed
  {
    // copied from Exploration 49...
  };
  template<class T, int N>
  bool operator==(fixed<T,N> const& a, fixed<T,N> const& b);
  template<class T, int N>
  fixed<T,N> operator+(fixed<T,N> const& a, fixed<T,N> const& b);
  // and so on...
}

#endif
```

Note how the free functions and operators that are associated with the class templates are defined in the same namespace. I'll explain exactly why later in the Exploration, but I wanted to point it out now because it's very important.

When you declare but don't define an entity (such as a function) in a namespace, you have a choice for how to define that entity, as described in the following:

- Use the same or another namespace definition, and define the entity within the namespace definition.

- Define the entity outside of the namespace, and prefix the entity name with the namespace name and the scope operator (`::`).

Listing 50-3 illustrates both styles of definition. (The declarations are in Listings 50-1 and 50-2.)

**Listing 50-3.** *Defining Entities in a Namespace*

```
namespace numeric
{
  template<class T>
  rational<T> operator+(rational<T> const& a, rational<T> const& b)
  {
    rational<T> result(a);
    a += b;
    return a;
  }
}

template<class T>
numeric::rational<T> numeric::operator*(rational<T> const& a, rational<T> const& b)
{
  rational<T> result(a);
  a *= b;
  return a;
}
```

The first form is straightforward. As always, the definition must follow the declaration. In a header file, you might define an inline function or function template using this syntax.

In the second form, the compiler sees the namespace name (`numeric`) followed by the scope operator and knows to look up the subsequent name (`operator*`) in that namespace. The compiler considers the rest of the function to be in the namespace scope, so you don't need to specify the namespace name in the remainder of the declaration (that is, the function parameters and the function body). The function's return type comes before the function name, which places it outside the namespace scope, so you still need to use the namespace name. To avoid ambiguity, you are not allowed to have a namespace and a class with the same name in a single namespace.

Traditionally, when you define a namespace in a header, the header contains a single namespace definition, which contains all the necessary declarations and definitions. When you implement functions and other entities in a separate source file, I find it most convenient to write an explicit namespace and define the functions inside the namespace, but some programmers prefer to omit the namespace definition. Instead, they use the namespace name and scope operator when defining the entities. An entity name that begins with the namespace name and scope operator is an example of a *qualified* name—that is, a name that explicitly tells the compiler where to look to find the name's declaration.

The name `rational<int>::value_type` is qualified because the compiler knows to look up `value_type` in the class template `rational`, specialized for `int`. Inside a member function, `this->value_` is qualified because it instructs the compiler to look up `value_` as a member of the class or one of its base classes. The name `std::vector` is a qualified name because the compiler looks up `vector` in the namespace `std`. On the other hand, where does the compiler look up the name `std`? Before I can answer that question, I need to delve into the general subject of nested namespaces.

# Nested Namespaces

Namespaces can nest, that is, you can define a namespace inside another namespace, as demonstrated in the following:

```
namespace exploring_cpp
{
  namespace numeric {
    template<class T> class rational
    {
      // and so on ...
    };
  }
}
```

To use a nested namespace, the qualifier lists all the namespaces in order, starting from the outermost namespace. Separate each namespace with the scope operator (`::`).

```
exploring_cpp::numeric::rational<int> half(1, 2);
```

A top-level namespace, such as `std` or `exploring_cpp`, is actually a nested namespace. Its outer namespace is called the *global namespace*. All entities that you declare outside of any function are in a namespace—in an explicit namespace or in the global namespace. Thus, names outside of functions are said to be at *namespace scope*. The phrase *global scope* refers to names that are declared in the implicit global namespace, which means outside of any explicit namespace. Qualify global names by prefixing the name with a scope operator.

```
::exploring_cpp::numeric::rational<int> half(1, 2);
```

Most programs you read will not use an explicit global scope operator. Instead, programmers tend to rely on the normal C++ rules for looking up names, letting the compiler find global names on its own. So far, every function you've written has been global; every call to these functions has been unqualified; the compiler has never had a problem with the unqualified names. If you have a situation in which a local name hides a global name, you can refer to the global name explicitly. Listing 50-4 demonstrates the kind of trouble you can wreak through poor choice of names, and how to use qualified names to extricate yourself.

**Listing 50-4.** *Coping with Conflicting Names*

```
1 #include <cmath>
2 #include <numeric>
3 #include <vector>
4
5 namespace stats {
6   // Really bad name for a functor to compute sum of squares,
7   // for use in determining standard deviation.
8   class std
9   {
10  public:
11    std(double mean) : mean_(mean) {}
12    double operator()(double acc, double x)
13    const
14    {
15      return acc + square(x - mean_);
16    }
17    double square(double x) const { return x * x; }
18  private:
19    double mean_;
20  };
21
22  // Really bad name for a function in the stats namespace.
23  // It computes standard deviation.
24  double stats(::std::vector<double> const& data)
25  {
26    double std(0.0); // Really, really bad name for a local variable
27    if (not data.empty())
28    {
29      double sum(::std::accumulate(data.begin(), data.end(), 0.0));
30      double mean(sum / data.size());
31      double sumsq(::std::accumulate(data.begin(), data.end(), 0.0,
32                    stats::std(mean)));
33      double variance(sumsq / data.size() - mean * mean);
34      std = ::std::sqrt(variance);
35    }
36    return std;
37  }
38 }
```

The local variable `std` does not conflict with the namespace of the same name because the compiler knows that only class and namespace names can appear on the left-hand side of a scope operator. On the other hand, the class `std` does conflict, so the use of a bare `std::` qualifier is ambiguous. You must use `::std` (for the standard library namespace) or `stats::std` (for the class). References to the local variable must use a plain `std`.

The name `stats` on line 24 refers to a function, so it does not conflict with the namespace `stats`. Therefore, the use of `stats::std` on line 32 is not ambiguous.

The `accumulate` algorithm in Listing 50-4 does exactly what its name suggests. It adds all the elements in a range to a starting value either by invoking the + operator or by calling a binary functor that takes the sum and a value from the range as arguments.

**Remove the global scope operators from `::std::accumulate` (lines 29 and 31) to give `std::accumulate`. Recompile the program. What messages does your compiler give you?**

_____

_____

_____

Restore the file to its original form. **Remove the first `::` qualifier from `::std::vector` (line 24). What message does the compiler give you?**

_____

_____

_____

Restore the file to its original form. **Remove the `stats::` qualifier from `stats::std` (line 32). What message does the compiler give you?**

_____

_____

_____

Sane and rational people do not deliberately name a class `std` in a C++ program, but we all make mistakes. (Maybe you have a class that represents a building element in an architectural CAD system, and you accidentally omitted the letter `u` from `stud`.) By seeing the kinds of messages that the compiler issues when it runs into name conflicts, you can better recognize these errors when you accidentally create a name that conflicts with a name invented by a third-party library or another team working on your project.

Most application programmers don't need to use the global scope prefix because you can be careful about choosing names that don't conflict. Library authors, on the other hand, never know where their code will be used, or what names that code will use. Therefore, cautious library authors always use the global scope prefix.

# Global Namespace

Names that you declare outside of all namespaces are _global_. In the past, I used global to mean outside of any function, but that was before you knew about namespaces. C++ programmers refer to names declared at _namespace scope_, which is our way of saying, "outside of any function." Such a name can be declared in a namespace or outside of any explicit namespace.

A program's `main` function must be global. If you define another function named `main` in a namespace, it does not interfere with the global `main`, but it will confuse anyone who reads your program.

# The std Namespace

As you know, the standard library uses the std namespace. You are not allowed to define any names in the std namespace, but you can specialize templates that are defined in std, provided at least one template argument is a user-defined type.

The C++ standard library inherits some functions, types, and objects from the C standard library. You can recognize the C-derived headers because their names begin with an extra letter c; e.g., <cmath> is the C++ equivalent of the C header <math.h>. Some C names, such as EOF, do not follow namespace rules. These names are usually written in all capital letters to warn you that they are special. You don't need to concern yourself with the details; just be aware that you cannot use the scope operator with these names, and the names are always global. When you look up a name in a language reference, these special names are called *macros*. (You've already seen one example: assert, declared in the <cassert> header.)

The C++ standard grants some flexibility in how a library implementation inherits the C standard library. In particular, all C names in the std namespace are also reserved in the global namespace. For example, std::size_t is a typedef for an integral type that is suitable for representing a size or index. (The choice of integer type depends on the implementation and need not concern us here.) Because size_t comes from the C standard library, the name ::size_t is also reserved. Not all implementations will define ::size_t, but if a library does, the definition must be identical to std::size_t.

C function names are reserved, so functions such as abs are also reserved in the global namespace. For example, the C header <cstdlib> declares std::abs, which means the standard library also reserves ::abs. Thus, you are not allowed to define your own function ::abs, but you can define abs in an explicit namespace. The standard does not guarantee that ::abs and std::abs are the same function in the same way it does for types. Instead, it reserves the global names and prohibits you from using them.

My recommendation is not to get caught up in which names originate in the C standard library and which are unique to C++. Instead, consider any name in the standard library off-limits. The only exception is when you want to use the same name for the same purpose, but in your own namespace. For example, you may want to overload the abs function to work with rational or fixed objects. Do so in their respective namespaces, alongside all the overloaded operators and other free functions.

---

■**Caution** Many C++ references omit the C portions of the standard library. As you can see, however, the C portions are most problematic when it comes to name clashes. Thus, make sure your C++ reference is complete or supplement your incomplete C++ reference with a complete C library reference.

---

# Using Namespaces

In order to use any name, the C++ compiler must be able to find it, which means identifying the scope where it is declared. The most direct way to use a name from a namespace, such as rational or fixed, is to use a qualified name—that is, the namespace name as a prefix; e.g., numeric, followed by the scope operator(::).

```
numeric::rational<long> pi_r(80143857L, 25510582L);
numeric::fixed<long, 6> pi_f(3, 141593);
```

When the compiler sees the namespace name and the double colons (::), it knows to look up the subsequent name in that namespace. There is no chance of a collision with the same entity name in a different namespace.

Sometimes, however, you end up using the namespace a lot, and brevity becomes a virtue. The next two sections describe a couple of options.

## The *using* Directive

You've seen a *using* directive before, but in case you need a refresher, take a look at the following:

```
using namespace std;
```

The syntax is as follows: the using keyword, the namespace keyword, and a namespace name. A *using* directive instructs the compiler to treat all the names in the namespace as though they were global. (The precise rule is slightly more complicated. However, unless you have a nested hierarchy of namespaces, the simplification is accurate.) You can list multiple *using* directives, but you run the risk of introducing name collisions among the namespaces. A *using* directive affects only the scope in which you place it. Because it can have a big impact on name lookup, restrict *using* directives to the narrowest scope you can; typically this would be an inner block.

Although a *using* directive has its advantages—and I use them in this book—you must be careful. They hinder the key advantage of namespaces: avoidance of name collisions. Names in different namespaces don't ordinarily collide, but if you try to mix namespaces that declare a common name, the compiler will complain.

If you are careless with *using* directives, you can accidentally use a name from the wrong namespace. If you're lucky, the compiler will tell you about your mistake because your code uses the wrong name in a way that violates language rules. If you aren't lucky, the wrong name will coincidentally have the same syntax, and you won't notice your mistake until much, much later.

Never place a *using* directive in a header. That ruins namespaces for everyone who includes your header. Keep *using* directives as local as possible, in the smallest scope possible.

In general, I try to avoid *using* directives. You should get used to reading fully qualified names. On the other hand, sometimes, long names interfere with easy comprehension of complicated code. Rarely do I use more than one *using* directive in the same scope. So far, the only times I've ever done so is when all the namespaces are defined by the same library, so I know they work together, and I won't run into naming problems. Listing 50-5 illustrates how *using* directives work.

**Listing 50-5.** *Examples of* using *Directives*

```
1 #include <iostream>
2 #include <ostream>
3
4 void print(int i)
5 {
```

```cpp
 6    std::cout << "int: " << i << '\n';
 7  }
 8
 9  namespace labeled
10  {
11    void print(double d)
12    {
13      std::cout << "double: " << d << '\n';
14    }
15  }
16
17  namespace simple
18  {
19    void print(int i)
20    {
21      std::cout << i << '\n';
22    }
23    void print(double d)
24    {
25      std::cout << d << '\n';
26    }
27  }
28
29  void test_simple()
30  {
31    using namespace simple;
32    print(42);                // ???
33    print(3.14159);           // finds simple::print(double)
34  }
35
36  void test_labeled()
37  {
38    using namespace labeled;
39    print(42);                // find ::print(int)
40    print(3.14159);           // finds labeled::print(double)
41  }
42
43  int main()
44  {
45    test_simple();
46    test_labeled();
47  }
```

**What will happen if you try to compile Listing 50-5?**

_____

_____

_____

The error is on line 32. The *using* directive effectively merges the simple namespace with the global namespace. Thus, you now have two functions named print that take a single int argument, and the compiler doesn't know which one you want. Fix the problem by qualifying the call to print(42) (on line 32) so it calls the function in the simple namespace. **What do you expect as the program output?**

_____

_____

_____

_____

Try it. Make sure you get what you expect. Line 32 should now look like the following:

```
simple::print(42);
```

# The *using* Declaration

More specific, and therefore less dangerous, than a *using* directive is a *using* declaration. A *using* declaration imports a single name from another namespace into a local scope, as demonstrated in the following:

```
using numeric::rational;
```

A *using* declaration adds the name to the local scope as though you had declared it explicitly. Thus, within the scope where you place the *using* declaration, you can use the declared name without qualification (e.g., rational). Listing 50-6 shows how *using* declarations help avoid the problems you encountered with *using* directives in Listing 50-5.

**Listing 50-6.** *Examples of* using *Declarations with Namespaces*

```
 1 #include <iostream>
 2 #include <ostream>
 3
 4 void print(int i)
 5 {
 6   std::cout << "int: " << i << '\n';
 7 }
 8
 9 namespace labeled
10 {
11   void print(double d)
12   {
```

```
13      std::cout << "double: " << d << '\n';
14    }
15 }
16
17 namespace simple
18 {
19    void print(int i)
20    {
21      std::cout << i << '\n';
22    }
23    void print(double d)
24    {
25      std::cout << d << '\n';
26    }
27 }
28
29 void test_simple()
30 {
31    using simple::print;
32    print(42);
33    print(3.14159);
34 }
35
36 void test_labeled()
37 {
38    using labeled::print;
39    print(42);
40    print(3.14159);
41 }
42
43 int main()
44 {
45    test_simple();
46    test_labeled();
47 }
```

**Predict the program's output.**

_____

_____

_____

_____

This time, the compiler can find `simple::print(int)` because the *using* declaration injects names into the local scope. Thus, the local names do not conflict with the global `print(int)` function. On the other hand, the compiler does not call `::print(int)` for line 39. Instead, it calls `labeled::print(double)`, converting 42 to 42.0.

Are you puzzled by the compiler's behavior? Let me explain. When the compiler tries to resolve an overloaded function or operator name, it looks for the first scope that declares a matching name. It then collects all overloaded names from that scope, and only from that scope. Finally, it resolves the name by choosing the best match (or reporting an error if it cannot find exactly one good match). Once the compiler finds a match, it stops looking in other scopes or outer namespaces.

In this case, the compiler sees the call to `print(42)` and looks first in the local scope, where it finds a function named `print`, which was imported from the `labeled` namespace. So it stops looking for namespaces and tries to resolve the name `print`. It finds one function, which takes a `double` argument. The compiler knows how to convert an `int` to a `double`, so it deems this function a match and calls it. The compiler never even looks at the global namespace.

**How would you instruct the compiler to also consider the global `print` function?**

---

Add a *using* declaration for the global `print` function. Between lines 38 and 39, insert the following:

```
using ::print;
```

When the compiler tries to resolve `print(int)`, it finds `labeled::print(double)` and `::print(int)`, both imported into the local scope. It then resolves the overload by considering both functions. The `print(int)` function is the best match for an `int` argument.

Now add `using simple::print;` at the same location. **What do you expect to happen when you compile this example now?**

---

Now the compiler has too many choices—and they conflict. A *using* directive doesn't cause this kind of conflict because it simply changes the namespaces where the compiler looks for a name. A *using* declaration, however, adds a declaration to the local scope. If you add too many declarations, those declarations can conflict, and the compiler would complain.

When a *using* declaration names a template, the template name is brought into the local scope. The compiler keeps track of full and partial specializations of a template. The *using* declaration affects only whether the compiler finds the template at all. Once it finds the template and decides to instantiate it, the compiler will find the proper specialization. That's why you can specialize a template that is defined in the standard library—that is, in the `std` namespace.

A key difference between a *using* directive and a *using* declaration is that a *using* directive does not affect the local scope. A *using* declaration, however, introduces the unqualified name into the local scope. This means you cannot declare your own name in the same scope. Listing 50-7 illustrates the difference.

**Listing 50-7.** *Comparing a* using *Directive with a* using *Declaration*

```
#include <iostream>
#include <ostream>

void demonstrate_using_directive()
{
    using namespace std;
```

```
    typedef int ostream;
    ostream x(0);
    std::cout << x << '\n';
}

void demonstrate_using_declaration()
{
    using std::ostream;
    typedef int ostream;
    ostream x(0);
    std::cout << x << '\n';
}
```

The local declaration of ostream interferes with the *using* declaration, but not the *using* directive. A local scope can have only one object or type with a particular name, and a *using* declaration adds the name to the local scope, whereas a *using* directive does not.

## The *using* Declaration in a Class

A *using* declaration can also import a member of a class. This is different from a namespace *using* declaration because you can't just import any old member into any old class, but you can import a name from a base class into a derived class. There are several reasons why you may want to do this. Two immediate reasons are:

- The base class declares a function, and the derived class declares a function with the same name, and you want overloading to find both functions. The compiler looks for overloads only in a single class scope. With a *using* declaration to import the base class function into the derived class scope, overloading can find both functions in the derived class scope and so choose the best match.

- When inheriting privately, you can selectively expose members by placing a *using* declaration in a public section of the derived class.

Listing 50-8 illustrates *using* declarations. You will learn more advantages of *using* declarations as you learn more advanced C++ techniques.

**Listing 50-8.** *Examples of* using *Declarations with Classes*

```
#include <iostream>
#include <ostream>

class base
{
public:
  void print(int i) { std::cout << "base: " << i << '\n'; }
};

class derived1 : public base
{
public:
```

```
  void print(double d) { std::cout << "derived: " << d << '\n'; }
};

class derived2 : public base
{
public:
  using base::print;
  void print(double d) { std::cout << "derived: " << d << '\n'; }
};

int main()
{
  derived1 d1;
  derived2 d2;

  d1.print(42);
  d2.print(42);
}
```

**Predict the output from the program.**

_____

_____

The class derived1 has a single member function named print. Calling d1.print(42) converts 42 to 42.0 and calls that function. Class derived2 imports print from the base class. Thus, overloading determines the best match for d2.print(42) and calls print in the base class. The output appears as follows:

```
derived: 42
base: 42
```

# Unnamed Namespaces

A name is optional in a namespace definition. The names in an ordinary, named namespace are shared among all files that make up a program, but names in an unnamed namespace are private to the source file that contains the namespace definition.

```
namespace {
  // Version control ID string is different in every file.
  const std::string id("$Id$");
}
```

If a header file contains an unnamed namespace, every source file that includes the header is furnished with its own private copy of everything defined in that namespace. When you want to keep various helper functions and other implementation details private, define them in an unnamed namespace (sometimes called an *anonymous* namespace). This ensures that their names will not collide with the same names in any other source files. (Note to C programmers: use anonymous namespaces instead of global `static` functions and objects.)

The only tricky aspect of the unnamed namespace is that you cannot qualify names to refer to names that you defined in the anonymous namespace. You must rely on ordinary name lookup for unqualified names. The next section discusses name lookup issues in greater depth.

# Name Lookup

In the absence of namespaces, looking up a function or operator name is simple. The compiler looks first in the local block then in outer blocks, until finally, the compiler searches global declarations. It stops searching in the first block that contains a matching declaration. If the compiler is looking for a function or operator, the name may be overloaded, so the compiler considers all the matching names that are declared in the same scope.

Looking up a member function is slightly different. When the compiler looks up an unqualified name in a class context, it starts by searching in the local block and enclosing blocks, as described earlier. The search continues by considering members of the class, then its base class, and so on for all ancestor classes. Again, when looking up an overloaded name, the compiler considers all the matching names that it finds in the same scope—that is, the same class or block.

Namespaces complicate the name lookup rules. Suppose you want to use the `rational` type, which is defined in the `exploring_cpp::numeric` namespace. You know how to use a qualified name for the type, but what about, for instance, addition or the I/O operators, such as those in the following:

```
exploring_cpp::numeric::rational<int> r;
std::cout << r + 1 << '\n';
```

The full name of the addition operator is `exploring_cpp::numeric::operator+`. But normally, you use the addition operator without specifying the namespace. Therefore, the compiler needs some help to determine which namespace contains the operator declaration. The trick is that the compiler checks the types of the operands and looks for the overloaded operator in the namespaces that contain those types. This is known as argument-dependent lookup (ADL). It is also called Koenig Lookup, after Andrew Koenig, who first described ADL.

The compiler creates several sets of scopes to search. It first determines which scopes to search using the ordinary lookup rules, described at the beginning of this section. For each function argument or operator operand, the compiler also collects a set of namespaces based on the argument types. If a type is a class type, the compiler selects the namespace that contains the class declaration and the namespaces that contain all of its ancestor classes. If the type is a specialization of a class template, the compiler selects the namespace that contains the primary template and the namespaces of all the template arguments. The compiler forms the union of all these scopes, and then searches them for the function or operator. As you can see, the goal of ADL is to be inclusive. The compiler tries hard to discover which scope declares the operator or function name.

To better understand the importance of ADL, take a look at Listing 50-9.

**Listing 50-9.** *Reading and Writing Tokens*

```cpp
#include <algorithm>
#include <iostream>
#include <istream>
#include <iterator>
#include <ostream>
#include <string>
#include <vector>

namespace parser
{
  class token
  {
  public:
    token() : text_() {}
    token(std::string& s) : text_(s) {}
    token& operator=(std::string const& s) { text_ = s; return *this; }
    std::string text() const { return text_; }
  private:
    std::string text_;
  };
}

std::istream& operator>>(std::istream& in, parser::token& tok)
{
  std::string str;
  if (in >> str)
    tok = str;
  return in;
}

std::ostream& operator<<(std::ostream& out, parser::token const& tok)
{
  out << tok.text();
  return out;
}

int main()
{
  using namespace parser;
  using namespace std;

  vector<token> tokens;
  copy(istream_iterator<token>(std::cin), istream_iterator<token>(),
       back_inserter(tokens));
  copy(tokens.begin(), tokens.end(), ostream_iterator<token>(cout, "\n"));
}
```

**What will happen when you compile the program?**

_____

_____

Some compilers, trying to be helpful, fill your console with messages. The core of the problem is that `istream_iterator` and `ostream_iterator` invoke the standard input (`>>`) and output (`<<`) operators. In the case of Listing 50-9, the compiler locates the operators through ordinary lookup as member functions of the `istream` and `ostream` classes. The standard library declares these member function operators for the built-in types, so the compiler cannot find a match for an argument of type `parser::token`. Because the compiler finds a match in a class scope, it never gets around to searching the global scope, so it never finds the custom I/O operators.

The compiler applies ADL and searches the `parser` namespace because the second operand to `<<` and `>>` has type `parser::token`. It searches the `std` namespace because the first operand has type `std::istream` or `std::ostream`. It cannot find a match for the I/O operators in these namespaces because the operators are in the global scope.

Now you see why it's vital that you declare all associated operators in the same namespace as the main type. If you don't, the compiler cannot find them. **Move the I/O operators into the parser namespace and see that the program now works.** Compare your program with Listing 50-10.

**Listing 50-10.** _Move the I/O Operators into the_ parser _Namespace_

```
#include <algorithm>
#include <iostream>
#include <istream>
#include <iterator>
#include <ostream>
#include <string>
#include <vector>

namespace parser
{
  class token
  {
  public:
    token() : text_() {}
    token(std::string& s) : text_(s) {}
    token& operator=(std::string const& s) { text_ = s; return *this; }
    std::string text() const { return text_; }
  private:
    std::string text_;
  };

  std::istream& operator>>(std::istream& in, parser::token& tok)
  {
    std::string str;
```

```
      if (in >> str)
        tok = str;
      return in;
    }

    std::ostream& operator<<(std::ostream& out, parser::token const& tok)
    {
      out << tok.text();
      return out;
    }
  }

int main()
{
  using namespace parser;
  using namespace std;

  vector<token> tokens;
  copy(istream_iterator<token>(std::cin), istream_iterator<token>(),
       back_inserter(tokens));
  copy(tokens.begin(), tokens.end(), ostream_iterator<token>(cout, "\n"));
}
```

To see how the compiler extends its ADL search, **modify the program to change the container from a vector to a map, and count the number of occurrences of each token** (remember from Exploration 21?). Because a map stores pair objects, write an output operator that prints pairs of tokens and counts. This means ostream_iterator calls the << operator with two arguments from namespace std. Nonetheless, the compiler finds your operator (in the parser namespace) because the template argument to std::pair is in parser. Your program may end up looking something like Listing 50-11.

**Listing 50-11.** *Counting Occurrences of Tokens*

```
#include <algorithm>
#include <iostream>
#include <istream>
#include <iterator>
#include <map>
#include <ostream>
#include <string>

namespace parser
{
  class token
  {
  public:
    token() : text_() {}
    token(std::string& s) : text_(s) {}
```

```
    token& operator=(std::string const& s) { text_ = s; return *this; }
    std::string text() const { return text_; }
  private:
    std::string text_;
  };

  // To store tokens in a map.
  bool operator<(token const& a, token const& b)
  {
    return a.text() < b.text();
  }

  std::istream& operator>>(std::istream& in, parser::token& tok)
  {
    std::string str;
    if (in >> str)
      tok = str;
    return in;
  }

  std::ostream& operator<<(std::ostream& out, parser::token const& tok)
  {
    out << tok.text();
    return out;
  }

  std::ostream& operator<<(std::ostream& out,
                           std::pair<const token, long> const& count)
  {
    out << count.first.text() << '\t' << count.second << '\n';
    return out;
  }
}

int main()
{
  using namespace parser;
  using namespace std;

  map<token, long> tokens;
  token tok;
  while (std::cin >> tok)
    ++tokens[tok];
  copy(tokens.begin(), tokens.end(),
       ostream_iterator<pair<const token, long> >(cout));
}
```

Now that you know about templates and namespaces, it's time to look at some of their practical uses. The next several Explorations take a closer look at parts of the standard library, beginning with the standard containers.

■■■

# Containers

So far, the only standard containers you've used have been vector and map. I mentioned list briefly in Exploration 42, but never went into depth. This Exploration introduces the remaining containers and discusses the general nature of containers. When third-party libraries implement additional containers, they usually follow the pattern set by the standard library, and make their containers follow the same requirements.

## Properties of Containers

The container types implement common data structures, such as trees, lists, arrays, and so on. They all serve the common purpose of storing a collection of similar objects in a single container object. You can treat the container as a single entity: compare it, copy it, assign it, and so on. You can also access the individual items in the container. What distinguishes one container type from another is how the container stores the items within it, which in turn affects the speed of accessing and modifying items in the container.

All containers fall into two broad categories: sequence and associative. The difference is that you can control the order of items in a sequence container, but not in an associative container. As a result, associative containers offer improved performance for accessing and modifying their contents. The standard sequence containers are array* (fixed-size), deque (double-ended queue), list (doubly-linked list), and vector (variable-length array).

The associative containers have two subcategories: ordered and unordered*. Ordered containers store keys in a data-dependent order, which is given by the < operator or a caller-supplied functor. Although the standard does not specify any particular implementation, the complexity requirements pretty much dictate that ordered associative containers are implemented as balanced binary trees. Unordered containers store keys in a hash table, so the order is unimportant to your code and is subject to change as you add items to the container.

Another way to divide the associative containers is into sets and maps. Sets are like mathematical sets: they have members and can test for membership. Maps are like sets that store key/value pairs. Sets and maps can require unique keys or permit duplicate keys. The set types are set (unique key, ordered), multiset (duplicate key, ordered), unordered_set*, and unordered_multiset*. The map types are map, multimap, unordered_map*, and unordered_multimap*.

---

\* These types are not yet part of the Standard, but are defined by an addition to the Standard, called Technical Report 1 (TR1), and they will be included in the next revision to the C++ language. See the "Technical Report 1" section later in this chapter for details.

Different containers have different characteristics. For example, vector permits rapid access to any item, but insertion in the middle is slow. A list, on the other hand, offers rapid insertion and erasure of any item, but provides only bidirectional iterators, not random access. The unordered containers do not permit comparing entire containers.

The C++ standard defines container characteristics in terms of *complexity*, which is written in big-O notation. Remember from your introductory algorithms course that $O(1)$ is constant complexity, but without any indication of what the constant might be. $O(n)$ is linear complexity: if the container has $n$ items, performing an $O(n)$ operation takes time proportional to $n$. Operations on sorted data are often logarithmic: $O(\log n)$.

Table 51-1 summarizes all the containers and their characteristics. The Insert, Erase, and Lookup columns show the average-case complexity for these operations, where $N$ is the number of elements in the container. Lookup for a sequence container means looking for an item at a particular index; for an associative container, it means looking for a specific item by value. "No" means the container does not support that operation at all.

**Table 51-1.** *Summary of Containers and Their Characteristics*

| Type | Header | Insert | Erase | Lookup | Iterator |
|---|---|---|---|---|---|
| array | <array> | No | No | $O(1)$ | Random Access |
| deque | <deque> | $O(N)^*$ | $O(N)^*$ | $O(1)$ | Random Access |
| list | <list> | $O(1)$ | $O(1)$ | $O(N)$ | Bidirectional |
| map | <map> | $O(\log N)$ | $O(\log N)$ | $O(\log N)$ | Bidirectional |
| multimap | <map> | $O(\log N)$ | $O(\log N)$ | $O(\log N)$ | Bidirectional |
| multiset | <set> | $O(\log N)$ | $O(\log N)$ | $O(\log N)$ | Bidirectional |
| set | <set> | $O(\log N)$ | $O(\log N)$ | $O(\log N)$ | Bidirectional |
| unordered_map | <unordered_map> | $O(1)$ | $O(1)$ | $O(1)$ | Forward |
| unordered_multimap | <unordered_map> | $O(1)$ | $O(1)$ | $O(1)$ | Forward |
| unordered_multiset | <unordered_set> | $O(1)$ | $O(1)$ | $O(1)$ | Forward |
| unordered_set | <unordered_set> | $O(1)$ | $O(1)$ | $O(1)$ | Forward |
| vector | <vector> | $O(N)^*$ | $O(N)^*$ | $O(1)$ | Random Access |

*\* Complexity is $O(N)$ for insertion and erasure in the middle of the container, but is $O(1)$ at the end of the container, when amortized over many operations. A deque also allows amortized $O(1)$ insertion and erasure at the beginning of the container.*

# Technical Report 1

The array and unordered types are not actually part of the standard library. Instead, they are part of a library extension called Technical Report 1 (TR1). TR1 is the work of the C++ standardization committee, and it has gone through an ISO approval process. In ISO-parlance, TR1 is non-normative, which means support is not mandatory. It is recommended, but not required.

TR1 was approved in 2005, yet as I write this, only one vendor offers a complete implementation of TR1. This is not surprising as TR1 is large and includes many specialized mathematical functions, which are tricky to get right. Don't be surprised if some vendors never get around to supporting the entirety of TR1. However, I do expect that most vendors will offer partial TR1 support, especially for the new containers and some other parts of TR1 that are easy to implement. Even if your particular library does not include any TR1 extensions, you can easily find other implementations of array and the unordered containers. This book's web site has some helpful links.

Names in TR1 are in the std::tr1 namespace. Each vendor is free to organize TR1 headers in a way that best suits their interests, so writing portable code to use TR1 is problematic. If you cannot compile the listings, and you know you have TR1 installed, try inserting tr1/ before the file name—that is, where I have written

```
#include <array>
```

you may need to change it to:

```
#include <tr1/array>
```

As I write this, the C++ committee is nearing completion on the next major revision to the C++ standard. Much of TR1 has become part of the revised standard. Some parts are undergoing improvement based on practical experience with TR1, but I expect the new containers to come through pretty much unscathed. Therefore, anything you learn now about the TR1 containers will apply to the standard containers when the new revision is finally approved and products become widespread. That's why it's a good idea to start learning about TR1 now.

If you are using the next revision to the standard, all the new container types are in the std namespace, e.g., std::array.

Enough about the future. This book is about today's standard, and the emphasis is on the official standard. So I made sure the TR1 sections are all optional. You can skip them if you wish or need to, and still make full use of the rest of the book. On the other hand, TR1 is available today (at least in part), and I highly recommend that you avail yourself of its features. I will mention other useful TR1 extensions when the occasion arises. However, if you cannot obtain TR1 for your compiler and library (or your organization's standards prevent you), you can still get by just fine with the current standard, and feel free to skip over the TR1 sections.

# Member Types

Every container provides a number of useful types and typedefs as members of the container. This section makes frequent use of several of them:

## value_type

This is a synonym for the type that the container stores. For example, value_type for vector<double> is double and std::list<char>::value_type is char. Using a standard typedef makes it easier to write and read container code. The rest of this Exploration uses value_type extensively.

The mapped containers store key/value pairs, so value_type for map<Key, T> (and multimap, unordered_map, and unordered_multimap) is std::pair<const Key, T>.

### key_type

The associative containers declare key_type as a typedef for the template parameter—for instance, map<int, double>::key_type is int. For the set types, key_type and value_type are the same.

### reference

This is a synonym for a reference to value_type. Except in very rare cases, reference is identical to value_type&.

### const_reference

const_reference is a synonym for a reference to const value_type. Except in very rare cases, const_reference is identical to value_type const&.

### iterator

This is the iterator type. It might be a typedef, but more likely, it is a class, the definition of which is implementation-dependent. All that matters is that this type meets the requirements of an iterator. Each container type specifies the iterator category that it implements.

### const_iterator

const_iterator is the iterator type for const items. It might be a typedef, but more likely, it is a class, the definition of which is implementation-dependent. All that matters is that this type meets the requirements of an iterator of const items. Each container type specifies the iterator category that it implements.

### size_type

size_type is a typedef for one of the built-in integer types (which one depends on the implementation). It represents an index for a sequence container, or a container size.

# What Can Go Into a Container

In order to store an item in a container, the item's type must meet some basic requirements. You must be able to copy and assign the item. For the built-in types, this is automatic. For a class type, you usually have that capability. The compiler even writes the copy constructor and assignment operator for you. It's possible, however, for you to write them yourself in the private part of a class. In this case, the constructor or assignment operator is *inaccessible*, so the container cannot copy or assign items, and you can't store that type of item in a container.

The copy constructor and assignment operators must make accurate copies. This means that the newly constructed object or the target of the assignment must be the same as the original, at least as far as the container is concerned. The compiler's implicitly defined constructor and assignment operator usually manage to make good copies, but some specialized classes may violate this requirement, and so prevent you from storing such objects in a container.

Sequence containers themselves do not need to compare items for equality; they just assume that copies are identical to the original and freely make copies and assign items whenever they need to.

Ordered associative containers require an ordering functor. By default, they use a standard functor called std::less<T> (where T is the same base type as that used by the container), which in turn uses the < operator. You can supply a custom functor, provided it implements *strict weak ordering*, which is defined by the following requirements:

- If $a < b$ and $b < c$, then $a < c$
- $a < a$ is always false
- The order does not change after an item is stored in a container

A common error among new C++ programmers is to violate rule 2, typically by implementing <= instead of <. Violations of the strict weak ordering rule result in undefined behavior. Some libraries have a debugging mode that checks your functor to ensure that it is valid. If your library has such a mode, use it.

Unordered associative containers need a hash functor and an equality functor. The default hash functor is std::tr1::hash<T> (declared in <functional>). TR1 provides specializations for the built-in types and string. If you store a custom class in an unordered container, you need to provide your own hash functor. The simplest way to do that is to specialize hash. Listing 51-1 shows how to specialize hash for the rational type. You need to provide only the function call operator, which must return type std::size_t (an implementation-defined integer type).

**Listing 51-1.** *Specializing the hash Template for the rational Type*

```
#include <array>
#include "rational.hpp"
namespace std {
namespace tr1 {

template<class T>
class hash<rational<T> >
{
public:
  std::size_t operator()(rational<T> const& r)
  const
  {
    return hasher_(r.numerator()) + hasher_(r.denominator());
  }
private:
  std::tr1::hash<T> hasher_;
};
} // end of tr1
} // end of std
```

The default equality functor is std::equal_to<T> (declared in <functional>), which uses the == operator. If two items are equal, their hash values must also be equal (but the reverse is not necessarily true).

When you insert an item in a container, the container keeps a copy of the item. When you erase an item, the container destroys the item. When you destroy a container, it destroys all of its elements. The next section discusses insertion and erasure at greater length.

# Inserting and Erasing

I've presented a number of examples of inserting and erasing elements in vectors and maps. This section explores this topic in greater depth. Note that the array type has a fixed size, so it provides none of the insertion or erasure functions. All the other containers follow the specification described in this section.

## Inserting in a Sequence Container

You have a choice of several different member functions with which to insert an item into a sequence container. The most fundamental function is insert, which has three overloaded forms:

    iterator insert(iterator here, value_type const& item)

Inserts item in the collection immediately before the position to which here refers, and returns an iterator that refers to the newly added item. If here is end(), item is appended to the end of the container.

    void insert(iterator here, size_type n, value_type const& item)

Inserts n copies of item immediately before the position to which here refers. If here is end(), the items are appended to the end of the container.

    template<class InputIterator>
    void insert(iterator here, InputIterator first, InputIterator last)

Copies the values from the range [first, last) into the container, starting at the position immediately before here.

Two additional functions add items to the start (push_front) or end (push_back) of a container. The container type provides only the functions that it can implement with constant complexity. Thus, vector provides push_back but not push_front. Both list and deque provide push_back and push_front.

## Erasing From a Sequence Container

The erase function erases, or deletes, items from a container. Sequence containers implement two forms of erase:

    iterator erase(iterator pos)

Erases the item to which pos refers and returns an iterator that refers to the subsequent item. Returns end() if the last item is erased. The behavior is undefined if you try to erase end() or if pos is an iterator for a different container object.

`iterator erase(iterator first, iterator last)`

Erases all the items in the range [first, last) and returns an iterator that refers to the item that immediately followed the last item erased. Returns end() if the last item in the container is erased. The behavior is undefined if the iterators are in the wrong order or refer to a different container object.

The clear() function erases all elements from the container. In addition to the basic erasure functions, sequence containers also provide pop_front to erase the first element and pop_back to erase the last element of a collection. A container implements these two functions only if it can do so with constant complexity. **Which sequence containers implement pop_back?**

**Which sequence containers implement pop_front?**

As with the push functions, vector provides pop_back, and list and deque provide both pop_back and pop_front.

## Inserting in an Associative Container

The insert function has several forms for inserting into an associative container. One key difference from the sequence containers is that you don't need to provide a position (one form does let you provide a position as a hint). The behavior of insert depends on whether the container allows duplicate items. The set, map, unordered_set, and unordered_map types require unique keys; multiset, multimap, unordered_multiset, and unordered_multimap permit duplicate keys.

`iterator insert(value_type const& item)`
`std::pair<iterator, bool> insert(value_type const& item)`

Tries to insert item in the container. If the container permits duplicate keys, insert always succeeds and returns an iterator that refers to the newly inserted item. If the container requires unique keys, insert inserts the item only if it is not already in the container. It returns a pair of an iterator and a bool: the iterator refers to the item in the container (whether pre-existing or newly added), and the bool is true if the item was added or false if the item was already in the container.

`iterator insert(iterator hint, value_type const& item)`

Tries to insert item in the container. If the container permits duplicate keys, insert always succeeds. Otherwise, insert adds item only if it is not already in the container. In all cases, insert returns an iterator that refers to the newly added item or an existing equivalent item.

For an ordered container, if the item's position is immediately after `hint`, the item is added with constant complexity. Otherwise, the complexity is logarithmic. For an unordered container, usage of `hint` is implementation-defined, and complexity is always constant (average-case). In other words, if you need to store many items in an ordered container, and the items are already in order, you can save some time by using the position of the most recently inserted item as the hint.

```
template<class InputIterator>
void insert(InputIterator first, InputIterator last)
```

Copies the values from the range [`first`, `last`) into the container. For the ordered containers, you get optimal performance if the range [`first`, `last`) is already sorted.

**Write a program that reads a list of strings from the standard input into a set of strings.** Use the hinted form of `insert`. Save the return value from `insert` to pass as the hint when inserting the next item. Find a large list of strings to use as input. Make two copies of the list, one in sorted order and one in random order. (See this book's web site if you need help locating or preparing the input files.) **Compare the performance of your program reading the two input files.**

**Write another version of the same program, this time using the simple, one-argument form of `insert`.** Again, run the program with both input files. Compare the performance of all four variations: hinted and unhinted insert, sorted and unsorted input.

Listing 51-2 shows a simple form of the program that uses the hinted form of `insert`.

**Listing 51-2.** *Using a Hint Position When Inserting into a Set*

```
#include <iostream>
#include <istream>
#include <set>
#include <string>

int main()
{
  std::string word;
  std::set<std::string> words;

  std::set<std::string>::iterator hint(words.begin());
  while(std::cin >> word)
    hint = words.insert(hint, word);
}
```

When I run the program with a file of over 200,000 words, the hinted program with sorted input executes in about 1.6 seconds. The unhinted form takes 2.2 seconds. With randomly ordered inputs, both programs run in about 2.3 seconds. As you can see, the hint can make a difference when the input is already sorted. The details depend on the library implementation; your mileage may vary.

## Erasing From an Associative Container

The `erase` function erases, or deletes, items from a container. Associative containers implement two forms of `erase`:

```
void erase(iterator pos)
iterator erase(iterator pos)
```

Erases the item to which `pos` refers; complexity is constant, possibly amortized over many calls. The ordered containers do not return a value; unordered containers return an iterator that refers to the successive value (or `end()`). The behavior is undefined if you try to erase `end()` or if `pos` is an iterator for a different container object.

```
void erase(iterator first, iterator last)
iterator erase(iterator first, iterator last)
```

Erases all the items in the range [`first`, `last`). Ordered containers do not return a value; unordered containers return an iterator that refers to the item that follows the last item erased. Returns `end()` if the last item in the container is erased. The behavior is undefined if the iterators are in the wrong order or refer to a different container object.

As with sequence containers, `clear()` erases all elements of the container.

## Exceptions

The containers do their best to keep order if an exception is thrown. Exceptions have two potential sources: the container itself and the items in the containers. Most member functions do not throw exceptions for invalid arguments, so the most common source of exceptions from the container itself is `std::bad_alloc` if the container runs out of memory and cannot insert a new item. In this case, the insertion fails, and the container is unchanged.

If you try to insert a single item into a container, and the operation fails (perhaps because the item's copy constructor throws an exception, or the container ran out of memory), the container is unchanged.

If you try to insert multiple items, and one of those items throws an exception while it is being inserted into a container (e.g., the item's copy constructor throws an exception), most containers do not roll back the change. Only the `list` type rolls back to its original state. The other containers leave the container in a valid state, and the items that have been inserted successfully remain in the container.

When erasing one or many items, the containers do not throw exceptions themselves, but they may need to copy (or in the case of ordered containers, compare) items; if an item's copy constructor throws an exception, the erasure may be incomplete. No matter what, however, the container remains in a valid state.

In order for these guarantees to remain valid, destructors must not throw exceptions.

---

**Tip** Never throw an exception from a destructor.

---

# Iterators and References

When using containers, one important point that I have not yet covered is the validity of iterators and references. The issue is that when you insert or erase items in a container, some or all iterators for that container can become invalid, and references to items in the container can become invalid. The details of which iterators and references become invalid and under what circumstances depend on the container.

Iterators and references becoming invalid reflect the internal structure of the container. For example, `vector` stores its elements in a single, contiguous chunk of memory. Therefore, inserting or erasing any elements shifts all the elements at higher indices, which invalidates all iterators and references to those elements at higher indices. As a `vector` grows, it may need to allocate a new internal array, which invalidates all extant iterators and references for that `vector`. You never know when that can occur, so it is safest never to hold onto a `vector`'s iterators or references while adding items to the `vector`. (But look up the `reserve` member function in a library reference if you must keep those iterators and references lying around.)

A `list`, on the other hand, implements a doubly linked list. Inserting or erasing an element is simply a matter of inserting or deleting a node, which has no effect on iterators and references to other nodes. For all containers, if you erase a node that an iterator refers to, that iterator necessarily becomes invalid, just as a reference to the erased element must become invalid.

In practical terms, you must take care when inserting and erasing elements. These functions often return iterators that you can use to help maintain your program's logic. Listing 51-3 shows a function template, `erase_less`, which marches through a container and calls `erase` for any element that is less than the value that precedes it. It is a function template, and it works with any class that meets the requirements of a sequence container.

**Listing 51-3.** *Erasing Elements from a Sequence Container*

```
template<class Container>
void erase_less(Container& cont)
{
  typename Container::iterator prev(cont.end());
  typename Container::iterator iter(cont.begin());
  while (iter != cont.end())
  {
    if (prev != cont.end() and not (*prev < *iter))
      iter = cont.erase(iter);
    else
    {
      prev = iter;
      ++iter;
    }
  }
}
```

Notice how `erase_less` moves the iterator, `iter`, through the container. The `prev` iterator refers to the previous item (or `container.end()` when the loop first begins and there is no previous item). As long as `*prev` is less than `*iter`, the loop advances by setting `prev` to `iter` and incrementing iter. If the container is in ascending order, nothing happens to it. If an item is out of place, however, *prev < *iter is false, and the item at position iter is erased. The value that erase returns is an iterator that refers to the item that follows iter prior to its erasure. That's exactly where we want iter to point, so we just set iter to the return value, and let the loop continue.

**Write a test program to see that erase_less works with a list and with a vector. Make sure it works with ascending data, descending data, and mixed data.** Listing 51-4 shows my simple test program.

**Listing 51-4.** *Testing the erase_less Function Template*

```cpp
#include <algorithm>
#include <cassert>
#include <iostream>
#include <istream>
#include <iterator>
#include <list>
#include <ostream>
#include <sstream>
#include <vector>

#include "erase_less.hpp"

/// Extract items from a string and store them in a container.
template<class Container>
void read(std::string const& str, Container& cont)
{
  std::istringstream in(str);
  cont.insert(cont.begin(),
              std::istream_iterator<typename Container::value_type>(in),
              std::istream_iterator<typename Container::value_type>());
}

/// Print items from a container to the standard output.
template<class Container>
void print(std::string const& label, Container const& cont)
{
  std::cout << label;
  std::copy(cont.begin(), cont.end(),
            std::ostream_iterator<typename Container::value_type>(std::cout, " "));
  std::cout << '\n';
}

/// Test erase_less by extracting integers from a string into a container
/// and calling erase_less. Print the container before and after.
/// Double-check that the same results obtain with a list and a vector.
void test(std::string const& str)
{
```

```
  std::list<int> list;
  read(str, list);
  print("before: ", list);
  erase_less(list);
  print("after:  ", list);

  std::vector<int> vector;
  read(str, vector);
  erase_less(vector);

  assert(list.size() == vector.size());
  assert(std::equal(list.begin(), list.end(), vector.begin()));
}

int main()
{
  test("2 3 7 11 13 17 23 29 31 37");
  test("37 31 29 23 17 13 11 7 3 2");
  test("");
  test("42");
  test("10 30 20 40 0 50");
}
```

The typename keyword informs the compiler that what follows is the name of a type. The compiler needs the hint when it compiles a template because it cannot know what Container might actually be at instantiation time, so it cannot know what Container::value_type might be. It might be a type, an object, or a function. If you know the name is a type, you need to notify the compiler by inserting the typename keyword before the name. Use typename only in a template and only for names that the compiler cannot determine on its own, such as members of a template parameter or members of a template that uses a template parameter as an argument.

# Sequence Containers

In this book, the most common use of a container has been to add items to the end of a vector. A program might then use standard algorithms to change the order, such as sorting into ascending order, shuffling into random order, etc. In addition to vector, the other sequence containers are array, deque, and list.

The primary distinguishing feature of the sequence containers is their complexity characteristics. If you often need to insert and erase from the middle of the sequence, you probably want a list. If you need to insert and erase only off one end, use a vector. If the container's size is a fixed, compile-time constant, use an array. (But vector works just as well if you don't have array.) If the elements of the sequence must be stored contiguously (in a single block of memory), use array or vector.

The following sections include some more details about each container type. Each section presents the same program for comparison. The program constructs a deck of playing cards then randomly selects a card for itself and a card for you. The card with the highest value wins. The program plays ten times then exits. The program plays without replacement—that is, it does not return used cards to the deck after each game. Listing 51-5 shows the card class, which the sample programs use.

**Listing 51-5.** *The Card Class, to Represent a Playing Card*

```cpp
#ifndef CARD_HPP_
#define CARD_HPP_

#include <istream>
#include <ostream>

/// Represent a standard western playing card.
class card
{
public:
  typedef char suit;
  static suit const spades   = 4;
  static suit const hearts   = 3;
  static suit const clubs    = 2;
  static suit const diamonds = 1;

  typedef char rank;
  static rank const ace   = 14;
  static rank const king  = 13;
  static rank const queen = 12;
  static rank const jack  = 11;

  card() : rank_(0), suit_(0) {}
  card(rank r, suit s) : rank_(r), suit_(s) {}

  void assign(rank r, suit s);
  suit get_suit() const { return suit_; }
  rank get_rank() const { return rank_; }
private:
  rank rank_;
  suit suit_;
};

bool operator==(card a, card b);
bool operator!=(card a, card b);
std::ostream& operator<<(std::ostream& out, card c);
std::istream& operator>>(std::istream& in, card& c);

/// In some games, Aces are high. In other Aces are low. Use different
/// comparison functors depending on the game.
bool acehigh_compare(card a, card b);
bool acelow_compare(card a, card b);
```

```
/// Generate successive playing cards, in a well-defined order,
/// namely, 2-10, J, Q, K, A. Diamonds first, then Clubs, Hearts, and Spades.
/// Roll-over and start at the beginning again after generating 52 cards.
class card_generator
{
public:
  card_generator();
  card operator()();
private:
  card card_;
};

#endif
```

## The array Class Template

The array type is a fixed-size container, so you cannot call insert or erase. To use array, specify a base type and a size as a compile-time constant expression, as shown in the following:

```
std::tr1::array<double, 5> five_elements;
```

What makes array most unusual is that it is a POD type (Exploration 33). Recall that one of the requirements for a POD class is that it has no custom constructors. Thus, array lacks the constructors that are common to other sequence containers. In exchange, you gain the ability to directly initialize the elements of an array by listing the elements inside curly braces.

```
std::tr1::array<int, 10> digits = { 0, 1, 2, 3, 4, 5, 6, 7, 8, 9 };
```

If you are fortunate enough to have a compiler that implements the new revision to C++, you can use a similar technique to initialize other containers. See Exploration 10 for an introduction to this feature.

If you list fewer values than the array size, remaining values are initialized to zero. If you omit the initializer altogether, the compiler calls the default initializer if the base type is a class type; otherwise it leaves the array elements uninitialized. Because an array cannot change size, you can't simply erase the cards after playing. In order to keep the code simple the program returns cards to the deck after each game. Listing 51-6 shows the high-card program with replacement.

**Listing 51-6.** *Playing High-Card with an array*

```
#include <array>
#include <iostream>
#include <ostream>

#include "card.hpp"
#include "randomint.hpp"

int main()
{
```

```
std::tr1::array<card, 52> deck;
std::generate(deck.begin(), deck.end(), card_generator());

randomint picker(0, deck.size() - 1);

for (int i(0); i != 10; ++i)
{
  card const& computer_card(deck.at(picker()));
  std::cout << "I picked " << computer_card << '\n';

  card const& user_card(deck.at(picker()));
  std::cout << "You picked " << user_card << '\n';

  if (acehigh_compare(computer_card, user_card))
    std::cout << "You win.\n";
  else
    std::cout << "I win.\n";
}
}
```

## The deque Class Template

A deque (pronounced "deck") represents a double-ended queue. Insertion and erasure from the beginning or the end is fast, but the complexity is linear if you need to insert or erase anywhere else. Most of the time, you can use a deque the same way you would use a vector, so **apply your experience with vector to write the high-card program.** Play without replacement: after each game, discard the two cards by erasing them from the container. Listing 51-7 shows how I wrote the high-card program using a deque.

**Listing 51-7.** *Playing High-Card with a deque*

```
#include <deque>
#include <iostream>
#include <ostream>

#include "card.hpp"
#include "randomint.hpp"

int main()
{
  std::deque<card> deck(52);
  std::generate(deck.begin(), deck.end(), card_generator());

  for (int i(0); i != 10; ++i)
  {
    randomint picker(0, deck.size() - 1);
```

```
    card computer_card(deck.at(picker()));
    std::cout << "I picked " << computer_card << '\n';

    card user_card(deck.at(picker()));
    std::cout << "You picked " << user_card << '\n';

    if (acehigh_compare(computer_card, user_card))
      std::cout << "You win.\n";
    else
      std::cout << "I win.\n";

    // Remove the cards, then erase them.
    std::deque<card>::iterator
      end(std::remove(deck.begin(), deck.end(), computer_card));
    end = std::remove(deck.begin(), end, user_card);
    deck.erase(end, deck.end());
  }
}
```

Recall from Exploration 21 that the remove function reorders a container without erasing anything. It returns an iterator that you can treat as the new end of the container. You can then erase from that iterator to the container's end(). In this case, the program saves the return value and passes it as the end-of-range to a second call to remove(). Then the program erases both cards at the same time.

## The list Class Template

A list represents a doubly linked list. Insertion and erasure is fast at any point in the list, but random access is not supported. Thus, the high-card program uses iterators instead of direct access to an element, by means of the advance function (Exploration 42). **Write the high-card program to use list.** Compare your solution with that of mine in Listing 51-8.

**Listing 51-8.** *Playing High-Card with a list*

```
#include <iostream>
#include <list>
#include <ostream>

#include "card.hpp"
#include "randomint.hpp"

int main()
{
  std::list<card> deck(52);
  std::generate(deck.begin(), deck.end(), card_generator());
```

```
  for (int i(0); i != 10; ++i)
  {
    randomint picker(0, deck.size() - 1);

    std::list<card>::iterator computer_pick(deck.begin());
    std::advance(computer_pick, picker());
    std::cout << "I picked " << *computer_pick << '\n';

    std::list<card>::iterator user_pick(deck.begin());
    std::advance(user_pick, picker());
    std::cout << "You picked " << *user_pick << '\n';

    if (acehigh_compare(*computer_pick, *user_pick))
      std::cout << "You win.\n";
    else
      std::cout << "I win.\n";

    // Discard the two cards.
    deck.erase(computer_pick);
    deck.erase(user_pick);
  }
}
```

Because this version of the program keeps track of the actual iterator, not just a copy of the card, it can erase the cards directly, without calling remove.

## The vector Class Template

A vector is an array that can change size at runtime. Appending to the end or erasing from the end is fast, but complexity is linear when inserting or erasing anywhere else in the vector. **Compare the deque and list versions of the high-card program. Pick the one you prefer and modify it to work with vector.** My version of the program is displayed in Listing 51-9.

**Listing 51-9.** *Playing High-Card with a vector*

```
#include <iostream>
#include <ostream>
#include <vector>

#include "card.hpp"
#include "randomint.hpp"

int main()
{
  std::vector<card> deck(52);
  std::generate(deck.begin(), deck.end(), card_generator());
```

```
for (int i(0); i != 10; ++i)
{
  randomint picker(0, deck.size() - 1);

  card computer_card(deck.at(picker()));
  std::cout << "I picked " << computer_card << '\n';

  card user_card(deck.at(picker()));
  std::cout << "You picked " << user_card << '\n';

  if (acehigh_compare(computer_card, user_card))
    std::cout << "You win.\n";
  else
    std::cout << "I win.\n";

  // Remove the cards, then erase them.
  std::vector<card>::iterator
    end(std::remove(deck.begin(), deck.end(), computer_card));
  end = std::remove(deck.begin(), end, user_card);
  deck.erase(end, deck.end());
}
}
```

Notice how you can change the program to use vector instead of a deque just by changing the type names. Their usage is quite similar. One key difference is that deque offers fast (constant complexity) insertion at the beginning of the container; something that vector lacks. The other key difference is that vector stores all of its elements in a single chunk of memory, which can be important when interfacing with external libraries. Neither of these factors matters here.

# Associative Containers

The associative containers offer rapid insertion, deletion, and lookup by controlling the order of elements in the container. The ordered associative containers store elements in a tree, ordered by a comparison functor (default is std::less, which uses <), so insertion, erasure, and lookup occur with logarithmic complexity. The unordered containers use hash tables (according to a caller-supplied hash functor and equality functor) for access with constant complexity in the average case, but with a linear worst-case complexity. Consult any textbook on data structures and algorithms for more information regarding trees and hash tables.

Sets store keys, and maps store key/value pairs. Multisets and multimaps allow duplicate keys. All equivalent keys are stored at adjacent locations in the container. Plain sets and maps require unique keys. If you try to insert a key that is already in the container, the new key is not inserted. Remember that equivalence in an ordered container is determined solely by calling the comparison functor: compare(a, b) is false and compare(b, a) is false means a and b are equivalent. Unordered containers call their equality functor to determine whether a key is a duplicate. The default is std::equal_to (declared in <functional>), which uses the == operator.

Because associative arrays store keys in an order that depends on the keys' contents, you cannot modify the contents of a key that is stored in an associative container. This means you cannot use an associative container's iterators as output iterators. Thus, if you want to implement the high-card program using an associative container, you cannot call generate to fill the deck of cards. Instead, use the inserter function to create an output iterator that fills the container. Listing 51-10 shows how to use set to implement the high-card program.

**Listing 51-10.** *Playing High-Card with a set*

```cpp
#include <iostream>
#include <iterator>
#include <ostream>
#include <set>

#include "card.hpp"
#include "randomint.hpp"

int main()
{
  typedef std::set<card, bool(*)(card, card)> cardset;
  cardset deck(acehigh_compare);
  std::generate_n(std::inserter(deck, deck.begin()), 52, card_generator());

  for (int i(0); i != 10; ++i)
  {
    randomint picker(0, deck.size() - 1);

    cardset::iterator computer_pick(deck.begin());
    std::advance(computer_pick, picker());
    std::cout << "I picked " << *computer_pick << '\n';

    cardset::iterator user_pick(deck.begin());
    std::advance(user_pick, picker());
    std::cout << "You picked " << *user_pick << '\n';

    if (acehigh_compare(*computer_pick, *user_pick))
      std::cout << "You win.\n";
    else
      std::cout << "I win.\n";

    // Discard the two cards.
    deck.erase(computer_pick);
    deck.erase(user_pick);
  }
}
```

When using associative containers, you may experience some difficulty when you use a custom compare functor (for ordered containers) or custom equality and hash functors (for unordered containers). You must specify the functor type as a template argument. When you construct a container object, pass a functor as an argument to the constructor. The functor must be an instance of the type that you specified in the template specialization.

For example, Listing 51-10 uses the acehigh_compare function, which it passes to the constructor for deck. Because acehigh_compare is a function, you must specify a function type as the template argument. The syntax is a little odd: it looks like a function signature, but with (*) instead of a function name. In other words, start with the return type bool, then use (*) as the function name, and then give the function parameter types in parentheses, as shown in the following:

```
bool (*)(card a, card b)
```

Another approach is to specialize the std::less class template for type card. The explicit specialization would implement the function call operator to call acehigh_compare. Taking advantage of the specialization, you could use the default template argument and constructor arguments. The specialization should inherit from std::binary_function (declared in <functional>), which is a class template of three arguments. The first two arguments are the operand types and the third argument is the result type. The functor should provide a function call operator that uses those three types and implements the strict weak ordering function for your container. Listing 51-11 demonstrates yet another version of the high-card program, this time using a specialization of less.

**Listing 51-11.** *Playing High-Card Using an Explicit Specialization of* std::less

```
#include <functional>
#include <iostream>
#include <iterator>
#include <ostream>
#include <set>

#include "card.hpp"
#include "randomint.hpp"

namespace std
{
  template<>
  class less<card> : std::binary_function<card, card, bool>
  {
  public:
    bool operator()(card a, card b) const { return acehigh_compare(a, b); }
  };
}

int main()
{
  typedef std::set<card> cardset;
  cardset deck;
  std::generate_n(std::inserter(deck, deck.begin()), 52, card_generator());
```

```
  for (int i(0); i != 10; ++i)
  {
    randomint picker(0, deck.size() - 1);

    cardset::iterator computer_pick(deck.begin());
    std::advance(computer_pick, picker());
    std::cout << "I picked " << *computer_pick << '\n';

    cardset::iterator user_pick(deck.begin());
    std::advance(user_pick, picker());
    std::cout << "You picked " << *user_pick << '\n';

    if (acehigh_compare(*computer_pick, *user_pick))
      std::cout << "You win.\n";
    else
      std::cout << "I win.\n";

    // Discard the two cards.
    deck.erase(computer_pick);
    deck.erase(user_pick);
  }
}
```

If you have TR1, write an explicit specialization of std::hash<card>. Listing 51-1 should be able to help. The *card.hpp* header already declares operator== for card, so you should be ready to **rewrite the high-card program one last time, this time for unordered_set.** Compare your solution with Listing 51-12.

**Listing 51-12.** *Playing High-Card with an unordered_set*

```
#include <functional>
#include <iostream>
#include <iterator>
#include <ostream>
#include <unordered_set>

#include "card.hpp"
#include "randomint.hpp"

namespace std { namespace tr1
{
  template<>
  class hash<card>
  {
  public:
    std::size_t operator()(card a)
    const
    {
```

```
          return hash<card::suit>()(a.get_suit()) + hash<card::rank>()(a.get_rank());
      }
  };
} }

int main()
{
  typedef std::tr1::unordered_set<card> cardset;
  cardset deck;
  std::generate_n(std::inserter(deck, deck.begin()), 52, card_generator());

  for (int i(0); i != 10; ++i)
  {
    randomint picker(0, deck.size() - 1);

    cardset::iterator computer_pick(deck.begin());
    std::advance(computer_pick, picker());
    std::cout << "I picked " << *computer_pick << '\n';

    cardset::iterator user_pick(deck.begin());
    std::advance(user_pick, picker());
    std::cout << "You picked " << *user_pick << '\n';

    if (acehigh_compare(*computer_pick, *user_pick))
      std::cout << "You win.\n";
    else
      std::cout << "I win.\n";

    // Discard the two cards.
    deck.erase(computer_pick);
    deck.erase(user_pick);
  }
}
```

In the next Exploration, you will embark on a completely different journey, one involving world travels to exotic locations, where natives speak exotic languages and use exotic character sets. The journey also touches on new and interesting uses for templates.

# EXPLORATION 52

▪▪▪

# International Characters

Explorations 16–18 discussed characters, but only hinted at bigger things to come. This Exploration tackles the bigger issues, and what issue could be bigger than the world, its inhabitants, and their languages? (Astronomers need not reply.)

This Exploration introduces wide characters, which are like ordinary (or *narrow*) characters, except that they usually occupy more memory. This means the wide character type can potentially represent many more characters than plain char. During your exploration of wide characters, you will also get to know more about Unicode.

## Why Wide?

As you saw in Exploration 17, the meaning of a particular character value depends on the locale and character set. For instance, in one locale, you can support Greek characters, while in another locale, Cyrillic, depending on the character set. Your program needs to know the locale and the character set in order to determine which characters are letters, which are punctuation, which are uppercase or lowercase, and how to convert uppercase to lowercase and *vice versa*.

What if your program needs to handle Cyrillic and Greek? What if this program needs to handle them both at the same time? And what about Asian languages? Chinese does not use a western-style alphabet, but instead uses thousands of distinct ideographs. Several Asian languages have adopted some Chinese ideographs for their own use. The typical implementation of the char type reaches its limit at only 256 distinct characters, which is woefully inadequate for international demands.

In other words, you can't use plain char and string types if you want to support the majority of the world's population and their languages. C++ solves this problem with *wide characters*, which it represents using the wchar_t type. (Unlike in C, wchar_t is a reserved keyword and is a built-in type, not a typedef.) The intent is that wchar_t can represent characters that don't fit into a char; with larger characters, a program can support Asian character sets.

## Using Wide Characters

In true C++ fashion, the size and other characteristics of wchar_t are left to the implementation. The only guarantees are that wchar_t is at least as big as char, and that wchar_t is the same size as one of the built-in integer types. The <cwchar> header declares a typedef, std::wint_t, for that built-in type. In some implementations, wchar_t may be identical to char, but most desktop and workstation environments use 16 or 32 bits for wchar_t.

Dig up Listing 23-2 and modify it to reveal the size of wchar_t and wint_t in your C++ environment. **How many bits are in wchar_t?** _____ **How many are in wint_t?** _____ They should be the same number. **How many bits are in char?** _____

Wide string objects use the std::wstring type (declared in <string>). A wide string is a string composed of wide characters. In all other ways, wide strings and narrow strings behave similarly; they have the same member functions, and you use them the same way. For example, the size() member function returns the number of characters in the string, regardless of the size of each character.

Wide character and string literals look like their narrow equivalents except that they start with a capital L and they contain wide characters. The best way to express a wide character in a character or string literal is to specify the character's hexadecimal value with the \x escape (introduced in Exploration 16). Thus, you need to know the wide character set that your C++ environment uses, and you need to know the numeric value of the desired character in that character set. If your editor and compiler permit it, you may be able to write wide characters directly in a wide character literal, but your source code will not be portable to other environments. You can also write a narrow character in a wide character or string literal, and the compiler automatically converts the narrow characters to wide ones, as shown in the following:

```
wchar_t capital_a('A');        // the compiler automatically widens narrow characters
std::wstring ray(L"Ray");
wchar_t pi(L'π');              // if your text editor lets you type π as a character
wchar_t pi_unicode(L'\x03c0'); // if wchar_t uses a Unicode encoding, such as UTF-32
std::wstring price(L"\x20ac" L"12345");     // Unicode Euro symbol: €12345
```

Notice how in the last line of the example I divided the string into two parts. Recall from Exploration 16 that the \x escape starts an escape sequence that specifies a character by its value in hexadecimal (base 16). The compiler collects as many characters as it can that form a valid hexadecimal number—that is, digits and the letters A through F (in uppercase or lowercase). It then uses that numeric value as the representation of a single character. If the last line were left as one string, the compiler would try to interpret the entire string as the \x escape. This means the compiler would think the character value is the hexadecimal value, $20AC12345_{16}$. By separating the strings, the compiler knows when the \x escape ends, and compiles the character value $20AC_{16}$, followed by the characters 1, 2, 3, 4, and 5. Just like narrow strings, the compiler assembles adjacent wide strings into a single, wide string. (You are not allowed to place narrow and wide strings next to each other, however. Use all wide strings or all narrow strings, not a mixture of the two.)

# Wide Strings

Everything you know about string also applies to wstring. They are just instances of a common template, basic_string. The <string> header declares string to be a typedef for basic_string<char> and wstring as a typedef for basic_string<wchar_t>. The magic of templates takes care of the details.

Because the underlying implementation of string and wstring is actually a template, any time you write some utility code to work with strings, you should consider making that code a template, too. For example, suppose you want to rewrite the is_palindrome function (from Listing 21-5) so it operates with wide characters. Instead of replacing char with wchar_t, let's turn it into a function template. Begin by rewriting the supporting functions to be function templates, taking a character type as a template argument. **Rewrite the supporting functions for is_palindrome so they function with narrow and wide strings and characters.** My solution is presented in Listing 52-1.

**Listing 52-1.** *Supporting Cast for the is_palindrome Function Template*

```
#include <algorithm>
#include <iostream>
#include <istream>
#include <iterator>
#include <locale>
#include <ostream>
#include <string>

/** Test for non-letter.
 * @param ch the character to test
 * @return true if @p ch is not a letter
 */
template<class Char>
bool non_letter(Char ch)
{
  return not std::isalpha(ch, std::locale());
}

/** Convert to lowercase.
 * Use a canonical form by converting to uppercase first,
 * and then to lowercase.
 * @param ch the character to test
 * @return the character converted to lowercase
 */
template<class Char>
Char lowercase(Char ch)
{
  return std::tolower(ch, std::locale());
}

/** Compare two characters without regard to case. */
template<class Char>
bool same_char(Char a, Char b)
{
  return lowercase(a) == lowercase(b);
}
```

The next task is to rewrite is_palindrome itself. The basic_string template actually takes three template arguments. The first is the character type, and the next two are details that needn't concern us at this time. All that matters is that if you want to templatize your own function that deals with strings, you need to handle all three of the template parameters.

Before starting, however, you need to be aware of a minor hurdle when dealing with functions as arguments to standard algorithms: the argument must be a real function, not the name of a function template. In other words, if you need to work with function templates, such as lowercase and non_letter, you must instantiate the template and pass the template instance. When you pass non_letter and same_char to the remove_if and equal algorithms, be sure to pass the correct template argument, too. If Char is the template parameter for the character type, use non_letter<Char> as the functor argument to remove_if.

**Rewrite the is_palindrome function as a function template with three template parameters.** The first template parameter is the character type: call it Char. Call the second template parameter Traits and the third Allocator. You will need to use all three as arguments to the std::basic_string template. Listing 52-2 shows my version of the is_palindrome function, converted to a template so it can handle narrow and wide strings.

**Listing 52-2.** *Changing* is_palindrome *to a Function Template*

```
/** Determine whether @p str is a palindrome.
 * Only letter characters are tested. Spaces and punctuation don't count.
 * Empty strings are not palindromes because that's just too easy.
 * @param str the string to test
 * @return true if @p str is the same forward and backward
 */
template<class Char, class Traits, class Allocator>
bool is_palindrome(std::basic_string<Char, Traits, Allocator> str)
{
  typedef typename std::basic_string<Char, Traits, Allocator> string;
  typename string::iterator end(
      std::remove_if(str.begin(), str.end(), non_letter<Char>));
  string rev(str.begin(), end);
  std::reverse(rev.begin(), rev.end());
  return not rev.empty() and
          std::equal(str.begin(), end, rev.begin(), same_char<Char>);
}
```

The is_palindrome function never uses the Traits and Allocator template parameters, except to pass them along to basic_string. If you're curious about those parameters, consult a language reference, but be warned that they're a bit advanced.

Calling is_palindrome is easy because the compiler uses automatic type deduction to determine whether you are using narrow or wide strings, and instantiates the templates accordingly. Thus, the caller doesn't need to bother with templates at all.

Without further ado, the non_letter and lowercase functions work with wide character arguments. That's because locales are templates, parameterized on the character type, just like the string and I/O class templates.

However, in order to use wide characters you do need to perform I/O with wide characters, which is the subject of the next section.

# Wide Character I/O

You read wide characters from the standard input by reading from `std::wcin`. Write wide characters by writing to `std::wcout` or `std::wcerr`. Once you read or write anything to or from a stream, the character width of the corresponding narrow and wide streams is fixed and you cannot change it— you must decide whether to use narrow or wide characters, and stay with that choice for the lifetime of the stream. So a program must use `cin` or `wcin`, but not both. Ditto for the output streams. The `<iostream>` header declares the names of all the standard streams, narrow and wide. The `<istream>` header defines all the input stream classes and operators; `<ostream>` defines the output classes and operators. More precisely, `<istream>` and `<ostream>` define templates, and the character type is the first template parameter.

The `<istream>` header defines the `std::basic_istream` class template, parameterized on the character type. The same header declares two typedefs.

```
typedef basic_istream<char>    istream;
typedef basic_istream<wchar_t> wistream;
```

As you can guess, the `<ostream>` header is similar, defining the `basic_ostream` class template and the `ostream` and `wostream` typedefs.

The `<fstream>` header follows the same pattern—`basic_ifstream` and `basic_ofstream` are class templates, with typedefs, as in the following:

```
typedef basic_ifstream<char>    ifstream;
typedef basic_ifstream<wchar_t> wifstream;
typedef basic_ofstream<char>    ofstream;
typedef basic_ofstream<wchar_t> wofstream;
```

**Rewrite the main program from Listing 21-5 to test the `is_palindrome` function template with wide character I/O.** Modern desktop environments should be able to support wide characters, but you may need to learn some new features to figure out how to get your text editor to save a file with wide characters. You may also need to load some additional fonts. Most likely, you can supply an ordinary, narrow-text file as input, and the program will work just fine. If you're having difficulty finding a suitable input file, try the palindrome files that you can download with the other examples in this book. The file names indicate the character set. For example, *palindrome-utf8.txt* contains UTF-8 input. You need to determine what format your C++ environment expects when reading a wide stream and pick the correct file. My solution is shown in Listing 52-3.

**Listing 52-3.** *The main Program for Testing `is_palindrome`*

```
int main()
{
  std::locale::global(std::locale(""));
  std::wcin.imbue(std::locale());
  std::wcout.imbue(std::locale());

  std::wstring line;
  while (std::getline(std::wcin, line))
```

```
      if (is_palindrome(line))
        std::wcout << line << L'\n';
}
```

Reading wide characters from a file or writing wide characters to a file is different from reading or writing narrow characters. All file I/O passes through an additional step of character conversion. C++ always interprets a file as a series of bytes. When reading or writing narrow characters, the conversion of a byte to a narrow character is a no-op, but when reading or writing wide characters, the C++ library needs to interpret the bytes to form wide characters. It does so by accumulating one or more adjacent bytes to form each wide character. The rules for deciding which bytes are elements of a wide character and how to combine the characters are specified by the encoding rules for a *multi-byte character set*.

# Multi-Byte Character Sets

Multi-byte character sets originated in Asia, where demand for characters exceeded the few character slots available in a single-byte character set, such as ASCII. European nations managed to fit their alphabets into 8-bit character sets, but languages such as Chinese, Japanese, Korean, and Vietnamese require far more bits to represent thousands of ideographs, syllables and native characters.

The requirements of Asian languages spurred the development of character sets that used two bytes to encode a character—hence the common term, *double-byte character set* (DBCS), with the generalization to multi-byte character sets (MBCS). Many DBCSes were invented, and sometimes a single character had multiple encodings. For example, in Chinese Big 5, the ideograph, 丁, has the double-byte value, `"\xA4\x42"`. In the EUC-KR character set (which is popular in Korea), the same glyph has a different encoding: `"\xEF\xCB"`.

The typical DBCS uses characters with the most significant bit set (in an 8-bit byte) to represent double characters. Characters with the most significant bit clear would be taken from a single-byte character set (SBCS). Some DBCSes mandate a particular SBCS; others leave it open, so you get different conventions for different combinations of DBCS and SBCS. Mixing single- and double-byte characters in a single character stream is necessary to represent the common use of character streams that mix Asian and Western text. Working with multi-byte characters is more difficult than working with single-byte characters. A string's `size()` function, for example, doesn't tell you how many characters are in a string. You must examine every byte of the string to learn the number of characters. Indexing into a string is more difficult because you must take care not to index into the middle of a double-byte character.

Sometimes a single character stream needs more flexibility than simply switching between one particular SBCS and one particular DBCS. Sometimes, the stream needs to mix multiple double-byte character sets. The ISO 2022 standard is an example of a character set that allows shifting between other, subsidiary character sets. *Shift sequences* (also called *escape sequences*, not to be confused with C++ backslash escape sequences) dictate which character set to use. For example, ISO 2022-JP is widely used in Japan and allows switching between ASCII, JIS X 0201 (a SBCS), and JIS X 0208 (a DBCS). Each line of text begins in ASCII, and a shift sequence changes character sets mid-string. For example, the shift sequence `"\x1B$B"` switches to JIS X 0208-1983.

Seeking to an arbitrary position in a file or text stream that contains shift sequences is clearly problematic. A program that needs to seek in a multi-byte text stream must keep track of shift sequences in addition to stream positions. Without knowing the most recent shift sequence in the stream, a program has no way of knowing which character set to use to interpret the subsequent characters.

A number of variations on ISO 2022-JP permit additional character sets. The point here is not to offer a tutorial on Asian character sets, but to impress on you the complexities of writing a truly open, general, and flexible mechanism that can support the world's rich diversity in character sets and locales. These and similar problems gave rise to the Unicode project.

# Unicode

Unicode is an attempt to get out of the whole character set mess by unifying all major variations into one, big, happy character set. To a large degree, the Unicode Consortium has succeeded. The Unicode character set has been adopted as an international standard as ISO 10646. However, the Unicode project includes more than just the character set; it also specifies rules for case folding, character collation, and more.

Unicode provides over one million possible character values (called *code points*). So far, the Unicode Consortium has assigned about 100,000 code points to characters, so there's plenty of room for expansion. The simplest way to represent a million code points is to use a 32-bit integer, and indeed, this is a common encoding for Unicode. It is not the only encoding, however. The Unicode standard also defines encodings that let you represent a code point using one or two 16-bit integers and one to four 8-bit integers.

The standard way to write a Unicode code point is U+ followed by the code point as a hexadecimal number of at least four places. Thus, '\x41' is the C++ encoding of U+0041 (Latin capital A), and Greek π has code point U+03C0, and ♪ has code point U+266A or U+1D160. The former code point is one of a group of miscellaneous symbols, which happen to include an eighth note. The latter code point is part of a group of musical symbols, which you will need for any significant work with music-related characters.

UTF-32 is the name of the encoding that stores a code point as a 32-bit integer. This format is ideally suited for the wchar_t type, and several C++ environments, such as GNU g++, can utilize UTF-32 for wchar_t. This encoding is the simplest to use because one storage unit represents one character. On the other hand, it takes up the most memory of all Unicode encodings. UTF-32 is best suited for in-memory representation of Unicode text.

If you are using UTF-32, you can encode many familiar characters normally and other characters using their hexadecimal code points and \x escapes. For example, to represent the letter A, use L'A'; for a lowercase Greek π, use L'\x03c0'; and for a musical eighth note ( ♪ ), use L'\x266a' or L'\x1d160'.

Some older environments use UTF-16, which represents a code point using one or two 16-bit integers. In some ways, UTF-16 is the worst of both worlds. You still have the same problem as multi-byte characters, namely, that one storage unit does not necessarily represent a single code point, so UTF-16 is less than ideal as an in-memory representation. In addition, you have the problem that the two bytes of a UTF-16 code point can appear with the most-significant byte first or last. Some hardware platforms prefer one order or the other, but a program must be able to read and work with either order.

---

■**Note** The position of the most-significant byte is called "endianness." A "big-endian" platform is one with the most-significant byte first. A "little-endian" platform puts the least-significant byte first. The popular Intel x86 platform is little-endian.

---

So UTF-16 is not ideal as a file encoding, either. Nonetheless, some major C++ tools and libraries, not to mention a popular operating system, have adopted UTF-16— you might be stuck with it. Again, you need a good library to work with code points instead of storage units.

The majority of common characters fit into a single 16-bit unit, so UTF-16 often requires less memory than UTF-32. For example, π fits into 16 bits, so you can still use L'\x03c0', but 𝄞 requires two 16-bit storage units (called a *surrogate pair*): L"\xD834\xDD1E".

Many programmers cope with the difficulty of working with UTF-16 by ignoring surrogate pairs completely. They assume that size() does indeed return the number of code points in the string. This strategy works for many situations because Unicode's designers kept the most common code points in the lower 16-bit region (called the *Basic Multilingual Plane* or BMP). Without surrogate pairs, you cannot represent any characters with code points greater than U+FFFF. This means you lose access to ancient scripts, specialized alphabets and symbols, and infrequently used ideographs.

Another common encoding for Unicode uses one to four 8-bit units to make up a single code point. Common characters in Western European languages can usually be represented in a single byte, and many other characters take only two bytes. Less common characters require three or four. The result is an encoding that supports the full range of Unicode code points, consumes less memory than UTF-16 for the vast majority of strings, and never needs more space than UTF-32, with a cost of increased complexity in processing. This character set is called UTF-8. Representing a Greek letter π requires only two bytes, as in UTF-16, but with a different encoding: L"\xcf\x80". An eighth note (♪) requires three or four bytes, again with a different encoding than that used in UTF-32: L"\xe2\x99\xaa" or L"\xf0\x9d\x85\xa0".

UTF-8 is a common encoding for files and network transmissions. It has an advantage over UTF-32 and UTF-16 for external representations because you don't need to deal with endianness. The Unicode standard defines a mechanism for encoding and revealing the endianness of a stream of UTF-16 or UTF-32 text, but that just makes extra work for you. Thus, the simplest way to work when you need to use international characters is to use UTF-8 externally and UTF-32 internally. To conserve memory, use UTF-8 exclusively, and use a library for working with UTF-8 in memory.

In C++ terms, a char is a suitable unit for UTF-8, but the string type has no support for multiple units making up a single code point. The wchar_t type may be suitable for UTF-16 or UTF-32, depending on the implementation. The wstring type has no support for multiple units, so it cannot support surrogate pairs directly.

Unicode's popularity continues to increase, but not all C++ environments support Unicode, and wchar_t might use a different character set, such as Chinese Big 5. The only way to guarantee support for Unicode is to use a third-party library. See this book's web pages for some links. Most GUI frameworks provide their own character type, such as Qt's QChar and Microsoft's TCHAR, both of which are 16-bits and implement UTF-16.

Muddying the waters further is the fact that even if your C++ environment has full support for Unicode and you can write programs that use UTF-32, you have no guarantee that the host operating system can support Unicode. In particular, the fonts you have on your system probably don't contain all 100,000 glyphs that make up the Unicode character set. Thus, a program may write `L'\x1d160'` to the standard output, but you probably won't see ♪.

# Universal Character Names

Unicode makes one official appearance in the C++ standard. You can specify a character using its Unicode code point. The compiler maps the code point into a suitable character in the native character set. Use \uXXXX or \UXXXXXXXX, replacing XXXX or XXXXXXXX with the hexadecimal code point. Unlike the \x escape, you must use exactly four hexadecimal digits with \u or eight with \U. These character constructs are called *universal character names*.

Thus, a better way to encode international characters in a string is to use a universal character name. This helps insulate you against vagaries in the native character set. On the other hand, you have no control over the compiler's actions if it cannot map a Unicode code point to a native character. Therefore, if your native character set is ISO 8859-7 (Greek), the following code should initialize the variable pi with the value `'\xf0'`, but if your native character set is ISO 8859-1 (Latin-1), the compiler cannot map it and so might give you a space, a question mark, or something else:

```
char pi('\u03c0');
```

Also note that \u and \U are not escape sequences (unlike \x). You can use them anywhere in a program, not just in a character or string literal.

Most likely, you'll rarely, if ever, find a need to write universal character names. Instead, you will probably seek out tools that let you edit Unicode characters directly. Instead of dealing with Unicode encoding issues, the editor simply reads and writes universal character names. Thus, the programmer edits WYSIWYG international text, and the source code retains maximum portability. Because universal character names are allowed anywhere, you can use international text in comments, too. If you really want to have fun, try using international letters in identifier names. Not all compilers support this feature, although the standard requires it. Thus, you would write a declaration

```
double π(3.14159265358979);
```

and your smart editor would store the following in the source file

```
double \u03c0(3.14159265358979);
```

and your standard-compliant compiler would accept it and let you use π as an identifier. I don't recommend using extended characters in identifiers unless you know that everyone reading your code is using tools that are aware of universal character names. Otherwise, they make the code much harder to read, understand, and maintain.

**Does your compiler support universal character names in strings?** _____
**Does your compiler support universal character names in identifiers?** _____

The character set is only one aspect of an international locale. The next Exploration takes a closer look at locales and how to use them.

# EXPLORATION 53

■■■

# Locales and Facets

**W**ide characters are merely one aspect of working with international locales. As you saw in Exploration 17, C++ offers a complicated system to support internationalization and localization of your code. Even if you don't intend to ship translations of your program in a multitude of languages, you must understand the locale mechanism that C++ uses. Indeed, you have been using it all along because C++ always sends formatted I/O through the locale system. This Exploration will help you understand locales better and make more effective use of them in your programs.

## The Problem

The story of the Tower of Babel is appealing to programmers. Imagine a world that speaks a single language and uses a single alphabet. How much simpler programming would be if we didn't need to deal with character set issues, language rules, or locales.

Alas, the real world has many languages, numerous alphabets and syllabaries, and multitudinous character sets. Somehow, we programmers must cope. It isn't easy, and this Exploration cannot give you all the answers, but it's a start.

Different cultures, languages, and character sets give rise to different methods to present and interpret information, different interpretations of character codes (as you learned in Exploration 16), and different ways of organizing (especially sorting) information. Even with numeric data, you find you need to write the same number in several different ways, depending on the local environment, culture, and language. Table 53-1 presents just a few examples of the ways to write a number according to various cultures, conventions, and locales.

**Table 53-1.** *Various Ways to Write a Number*

| Number | Culture |
|---|---|
| 123456.7890 | Default C++ |
| 123,456.7890 | United States |
| 123 456.7890 | International scientific |
| Rs. 1,23,456.7890 | Indian currency* |
| 123.456,7890 | Germany |

*\* Yes, the commas are correct.*

Other cultural differences can include:

- 12-hour *vs.* 24-hour clock

- How accented characters are sorted relative to non-accented characters (does 'a' come before or after 'á'?)

- Date formats: month/day/year, day/month/year, or year-month-day

- Formatting of currency (¥123,456 or 99¢)

Somehow, the poor application programmer must figure out exactly what is culturally-dependent, collect the information for all the possible cultures where the application might run, and use that information appropriately in the application. Fortunately, the hard work has already been done for you and is part of the C++ standard library.

# Locales to the Rescue

C++ uses a system called *locales* to manage this disparity of styles. Exploration 17 introduced locales as a means to organize character sets and their properties. Locales also organize formatting of numbers, currency, dates, and times (plus some more stuff that I won't get into).

C++ defines a basic locale, known as the *classic* locale, which provides minimal formatting. Each C++ implementation is then free to provide additional locales. Each locale typically has a name, but the C++ standard does not mandate any particular naming convention, which makes it difficult to write portable code. You can rely on only two standard names:

- The *classic* locale is named "C". The classic locale specifies the same basic formatting information for all implementations. When a program starts, the classic locale is the initial locale.

- An empty string ("") means the *default*, or native locale. The default locale obtains formatting and other information from the host operating system in a manner that depends on what the OS can offer. With traditional desktop operating systems, you can assume that the default locale specifies the user's preferred formatting rules and character set information. With other environments, such as embedded systems, the default locale may be identical to the classic locale.

A number of C++ implementations use ISO and POSIX standards for naming locales: an ISO 639 code for the language (e.g., fr for French, en for English, ko for Korean), optionally followed by an underscore and an ISO 3166 code for the region (e.g., CH for Switzerland, GB for Great Britain, HK for Hong Kong). The name is optionally followed by a dot and the name of the character set (e.g., utf8 for Unicode UTF-8, Big5 for Chinese Big 5 encoding). Thus, I use en_US.utf8 for my default locale. A native of Taiwan might use zh_TW.Big5; in French-speaking Switzerland, developers there might use fr_CH.latin1. Read your library documentation to learn how it specifies locale names. **What is your default locale? _____ What are its main characteristics?**

_____

_____

_____

Every C++ application has a global `locale` object. Unless you explicitly change a stream's locale, it starts off with the global locale. (If you later change the global locale, that does not affect streams that already exist, such as the standard I/O streams.) Initially, the global locale is the classic locale. The classic locale is the same everywhere (except for the parts that depend on the character set), so a program has maximum portability with the classic locale. On the other hand, it has minimum local flavor. The next section explores how you can change a stream's locale.

# Locales and I/O

Recall from Exploration 17 that you *imbue* a stream with a locale in order to format I/O according to the locale's rules. Thus, to ensure that you read input in the classic locale, and that you print results in the user's native locale, you need the following:

```
std::cin.imbue(std::locale::classic()); // standard input uses the classic locale
std::cout.imbue(std::locale(""));        // imbue with the user's default locale
```

The standard I/O streams initially use the classic locale. You can imbue a stream with a new locale at any time, but it makes the most sense to do so before performing any I/O.

Typically, you would use the classic locale when reading from, or writing to, files. You usually want the contents of files to be portable and not dependent on a user's OS preferences. For ephemeral output to a console or GUI window, you may want to use the default locale, so the user can be most comfortable reading and understanding it. On the other hand, if there is any chance that another program might try to read your program's output (as happens with UNIX pipes and filters), you should stick with the classic locale in order to ensure portability and a common format. If you are preparing output to be displayed in a GUI, by all means, use the default locale.

# Facets

The way a stream interprets numeric input and formats numeric output is by making requests of the imbued locale. A `locale` object is a collection of pieces, each of which manages a small aspect of internationalization. For example, one piece, called `numpunct`, provides the punctuation symbols for numeric formatting, such as the decimal point character (which is ' . ' in the United States, but ' , ' in France). Another piece, `num_get`, reads from a stream and parses the text to form a number, using information it obtains from `numpunct`. The pieces such as `num_get` and `numpunct` are called *facets*.

For ordinary numeric I/O, you never need to deal with facets. The I/O streams automatically manage these details for you; the `operator<<` function uses the `num_put` facet to format numbers for output, and `operator>>` uses `num_get` to interpret text as numeric input. However, if you want to format currency, dates, or times, you need to use the facets yourself. The `isalpha`, `toupper`, and other character-related functions about which you learned in Exploration 17 also use facets. Any program that needs to do a lot of character testing and converting can benefit by managing its facets directly.

Like strings and I/O streams, facets are class templates, parameterized on the character type. Thus, if your program needs to parse currency for input, it may use `money_get<char>` for narrow characters or `money_get<wchar_t>` for wide characters.

To obtain a facet from a locale, call the use_facet function template. The template argument is the facet you seek, and the function argument is the locale object. The returned facet is const, so the best way to use the result is to initialize a const reference, as demonstrated in the following:

```
std::money_get<char> const&
    mgetter( std::use_facet<std::money_get<char> >(std::locale("")) );
```

Reading from the inside outward, the use_facet function is requesting a reference to the money_get<char> facet. The default locale is passed as the sole argument to the use_facet function. The result returned by use_facet is used to initialize the reference called mgetter. The type of mgetter is a reference to a const money_get<char> facet. It's a little daunting to read at first, but you'll get used to it—eventually.

Once you have a facet, call its member functions to use it. This section introduces the currency facets as an example. A complete library reference tells you about all the facets and their member functions.

The money_get facet has two overloaded functions named get. The get function reads a currency value from an iterator range. It checks the currency symbol, thousands separator, thousands grouping, and decimal point. It extracts the numeric value and stores the value in a double (overloaded form 1) or as a string of digit characters (overloaded form 2). If you choose to use double, take care that you do not run into rounding errors. The get function assumes that the input originates in an input stream, and you must pass a stream object as one of its arguments. It checks the stream's flags to see whether a currency symbol is required (showbase flag is set). And finally, it sets error flags as needed: failbit for input formatting errors and eofbit for end of file.

Similarly, the money_put facet provides the overloaded put function, which formats a double or digit string according to the locale's currency formatting rules and writes the formatted value to an output iterator. If the stream's showbase flag is set, money_put prints the currency symbol. The locale's rules specify the position and formatting of the symbol (in the moneypunct facet). The money facets can use local currency rules or international standards. A bool argument to the get and put functions specifies the choice: true for international and false for local.

Listing 53-1 shows a simple program that imbues the standard I/O streams with the default locale then reads and writes currency values. It hides the complexity of using facets inside classes, which helps keep the main program easy to read. Notice how the reader and writer classes cache the facet so their objects can use the locale repeatedly without the need to fetch it each time. The C++ library offers a means of receiving notification whenever the imbued locale changes. This enables you to reload the facet, but the techniques are beyond the scope of this book. Consult a comprehensive C++ reference for details.

**Listing 53-1.** *Reading and Writing Currency Using the Money Facets*

```
#include <ios>
#include <iostream>
#include <istream>
#include <iterator>
#include <locale>
#include <ostream>
#include <string>
```

```
/// Read monetary values from an input stream.
/// Construct a reader, passing an input stream to its constructor. Call the
/// function call operator every time you want to read a value.
class money_reader
{
public:
  money_reader(std::istream& in);
  bool operator()(std::string& digits);
private:
  std::istream& in_;
  std::money_get<char> const& get_;
};

/// Write monetary values to an output stream.
/// Construct a writer, passing an output stream to its constructor. Call the
/// function call operator every time you want to write a value.
class money_writer
{
public:
  money_writer(std::ostream& out);
  bool operator()(std::string const& digits);
private:
  std::ostream& out_;
  std::money_put<char> const& put_;
};

money_reader::money_reader(std::istream& in)
: in_(in), get_(std::use_facet<std::money_get<char> >(in.getloc()))
{}

bool money_reader::operator()(std::string& digits)
{
  // The sentry flushes prompts prior to reading, and skips leading white space.
  std::istream::sentry sentry(in_);
  if (not in_)
    return in_;

  std::ios_base::iostate error(in_.rdstate());
  get_.get(std::istreambuf_iterator<char>(in_), std::istreambuf_iterator<char>(),
           false, in_, error, digits);
  in_.setstate(error);
  return in_;
}

money_writer::money_writer(std::ostream& out)
: out_(out), put_(std::use_facet<std::money_put<char> >(out.getloc()))
{}
```

```cpp
bool money_writer::operator()(std::string const& digits)
{
  // The sentry flushes prompts prior to writing, and flushes the buffer
  // if the user has set buffering to unit buffering.
  std::ostream::sentry sentry(out_);
  if (not out_)
    return out_;

  std::ios_base::iostate error(out_.rdstate());
  put_.put(std::ostreambuf_iterator<char>(out_), false, out_, error, digits);
  out_.setstate(error);
  return out_;
}

int main()
{
  std::locale native("");
  std::cin.imbue(native);
  std::cout.imbue(native);

  std::cin >> std::noshowbase;  // currency symbol is optional for input
  std::cout << std::showbase;    // always write the currency symbol for output

  money_reader read(std::cin);
  money_writer write(std::cout);
  std::string digits;
  while (read(digits))
  {
    write(digits);
    std::cout << '\n';
  }
  if (not std::cin.eof())
    std::cout << "Invalid input.\n";
}
```

Notice that the reader makes use of istreambuf_iterator, not istream_iterator. The former works at a lower level than the latter. An istreambuf_iterator reads raw characters from a stream without interpreting those characters. Similarly, the writer uses ostreambuf_iterator to write individual characters to the stream.

The sentry objects reflect how the standard I/O streams work. An input sentry skips leading white space if the skipws flag is set (which is the default). An output sentry flushes the output buffer after each write if the unitbuf flag is set.

# Character Categories

This section continues the examination of character sets and locales that you began in Exploration 17. In addition to testing for alphanumeric characters, or lowercase characters, you can test for several different categories. Table 53-2 lists all the classification functions and their behavior in the classic locale. They all take a character (char or wchar_t) as the first argument and a locale as the second; they all return a bool result.

**Table 53-2.** *Character Classification Functions*

| Function | Description | Classic Locale |
|---|---|---|
| isalnum | Alphanumeric | 'a'–'z', 'A'–'Z', '0'–'9' |
| isalpha | Alphabetic | 'a'–'z', 'A'–'Z' |
| iscntrl | Control | Any non-printable character* |
| isdigit | Digit | '0'–'9' (in all locales) |
| isgraph | Graphical | Printable character other than ' '* |
| islower | Lowercase | 'a'–'z' |
| isprint | Printable | Any printable character in the character set* |
| ispunct | Punctuation | Printable character other than alphanumeric or white space* |
| isspace | White space | ' ', '\f', '\n', '\r', '\t', '\v' |
| isupper | Uppercase | 'A'–'Z' |
| isxdigit | Hexadecimal digit | 'a'–'f', 'A'–'F', '0'–'9' (in all locales) |

*\* Behavior depends on the character set, even in the classic locale*

The classic locale has fixed definitions for some categories (such as isupper). Other locales, however, can expand these definitions to include other characters, which may (and probably will) depend on the character set, too. Only isdigit and isxdigit have fixed definitions for all locales and all character sets.

However, even in the classic locale, the precise implementation of some functions, such as isprint, depend on the character set. For example, in the popular ISO 8859-1 (Latin-1) character set '\x80' is a control character, but in the equally popular Windows-1252 character set, it is printable. In UTF-8, '\x80' is invalid, so all the categorization functions would return false.

The interaction between the locale and the character set is one of the areas where C++ underperforms. The locale can change at any time, which potentially sets a new character set, which in turn can give new meaning to certain character values. But, the compiler's view of the runtime character set is fixed. For instance, the compiler treats 'A' as the uppercase Roman letter A, and compiles the numeric code according to its idea of the runtime character set. That numeric value is then fixed forever. If the characterization functions use the same character set, everything is fine. The isalpha and isupper functions return true, isdigit returns false, and all is right with the world. If the user changes the locale and by so doing, changes the character set, those functions may not work with that character variable any more.

488 EXPLORATION 53 ■ LOCALES AND FACETS

Let's consider a concrete example as shown in Listing 53-2. This program encodes locale names, which may not work for your environment. Read the comments and see if your environment can support the same kind of locales, albeit with different names. After reading Listing 53-2, **what do you expect as the result?**

_____

_____

**Listing 53-2.** *Exploring Character Sets and Locales*

```cpp
#include <iomanip>
#include <iostream>
#include <locale>
#include <ostream>

#include "ioflags.hpp"

/// Print a character's categorization in a locale.
void print(int c, std::string const& name, std::locale loc)
{
  // Don't concern yourself with the & operator. I'll cover that later
  // in the book, in Exploration 61. Its purpose is just to ensure
  // the character's escape code is printed correctly.
  std::cout << "\\x" << std::setw(2) << (c & 0xff) <<
               " is " << name << " in " << loc.name() << '\n';
}

/// Test a character's categorization in the locale, @p loc.
void test(char c, std::locale loc)
{
  ioflags save(std::cout);
  std::cout << std::hex << std::setfill('0');
  if (std::isalnum(c, loc))
    print(c, "alphanumeric", loc);
  else if (std::iscntrl(c, loc))
    print(c, "control", loc);
  else if (std::ispunct(c, loc))
    print(c, "punctuation", loc);
  else
    print(c, "none of the above", loc);
}

int main()
{
  // Test the same code point in different locales and character sets.
  char c('\xd7');
```

```
// ISO 8859-1 is also called Latin-1 and is widely used in Western Europe
// and the Americas. It is often the default character set in these regions.
// The country and language are unimportant for this test.
// Choose any that support the ISO 8859-1 character set.
test(c, std::locale("en_US.iso88591"));

// ISO 8859-5 is Cyrillic. It is often the default character set in Russia
// and some Eastern European countries. Choose any language and region that
// support the ISO 8859-5 character set.
test(c, std::locale("ru_RU.iso88595"));

// ISO 8859-7 is Greek. Choose any language and region that
// support the ISO 8859-7 character set.
test(c, std::locale("el_GR.iso88597"));

// ISO 8859-8 contains some Hebrew. It is no longer widely used.
// Choose any language and region that support the ISO 8859-8 character set.
test(c, std::locale("he_IL.iso88598"));
}
```

**What do you get as the actual response?**

_____

_____

_____

_____

In case you had trouble identifying locale names or other problems running the program, Listing 53-3 shows the result when I run it on my system.

**Listing 53-3.** *Result of Running the Program in Listing 53-2*

```
\xd7 is punctuation in en_US.iso88591
\xd7 is alphanumeric in ru_RU.iso88595
\xd7 is alphanumeric in el_GR.iso88597
\xd7 is none of the above in he_IL.iso88598
```

As you can see, the same character has different categories, depending on the locale's character set. Now imagine that the user has entered a string, and your program has stored the string. If your program changes the global locale or the locale used to process that string, you may end up misinterpreting the string.

Listing 53-1 cached its facets. In Listing 53-2, the categorization functions reload their facets every time they are called, but you can rewrite the program so it loads its facet only once. The character type facet is called ctype. It has a function named is that takes a category mask and a character as arguments, and returns a bool: true if the character has a type in the mask. The mask values are specified in std::ctype_base.

> **Note** Notice the convention that the Standard library uses throughout. When a class template needs helper types and constants, they are declared in a non-template base class. The class template derives from the base class, and so gains easy access to the types and constants. Callers gain access to the types and constants by qualifying with the base class name. By avoiding the template in the base class, the Standard library avoids unnecessary instantiations just to use a type or constant that is unrelated to the template argument.

The mask names are the same as the categorization functions, but without the leading is. Listing 53-4 shows how to rewrite the simple character set demonstration to use a single cached ctype facet.

**Listing 53-4.** *Caching the ctype Facet*

```cpp
#include <iomanip>
#include <iostream>
#include <locale>
#include <ostream>

#include "ioflags.hpp"

void print(int c, std::string const& name, std::locale loc)
{
  // Don't concern yourself with the & operator. I'll cover that later
  // in the book. Its purpose is just to ensure the character's escape
  // code is printed correctly.
  std::cout << "\\x" << std::setw(2) << (c & 0xff) <<
              " is " << name << " in " << loc.name() << '\n';
}

/// Test a character's categorization in the locale, @p loc.
void test(char c, std::locale loc)
{
  ioflags save(std::cout);

  std::ctype<char> const& ctype(std::use_facet<std::ctype<char> >(loc));

  std::cout << std::hex << std::setfill('0');
  if (ctype.is(std::ctype_base::alnum, c))
    print(c, "alphanumeric", loc);
  else if (ctype.is(std::ctype_base::cntrl, c))
    print(c, "control", loc);
  else if (ctype.is(std::ctype_base::punct, c))
    print(c, "punctuation", loc);
  else
```

```
    print(c, "none of the above", loc);
}

int main()
{
  // Test the same code point in different locales and character sets.
  char c('\xd7');

  // ISO 8859-1 is also called Latin-1 and is widely used in Western Europe
  // and the Americas. It is often the default character set in these regions.
  // The country and language are unimportant for this test.
  // Choose any that support the ISO 8859-1 character set.
  test(c, std::locale("en_US.iso88591"));

  // ISO 8859-5 is Cyrillic. It is often the default character set in Russia
  // and some Eastern European countries. Choose any language and region that
  // support the ISO 8859-5 character set.
  test(c, std::locale("ru_RU.iso88595"));

  // ISO 8859-7 is Greek. Choose any language and region that
  // support the ISO 8859-7 character set.
  test(c, std::locale("el_GR.iso88597"));

  // ISO 8859-8 contains some Hebrew. It is no longer widely used.
  // Choose any language and region that support the ISO 8859-8 character set.
  test(c, std::locale("he_IL.iso88598"));
}
```

The ctype facet also performs case conversions with the toupper and tolower member functions, which take a single character argument and return a character result. **Copy the program from Listing 40-5, and change the functor classes to use cached facets.** Compare your program with Listing 53-5.

**Listing 53-5.** *Counting Words Again, This Time with Cached Facets*

```
// Copy the initial portion of Listing 21-2 here, including print_counts,
// but stopping just before sanitize.

/** Base class to hold a ctype facet. */
class function
{
public:
  function(std::locale loc) : ctype_(std::use_facet<std::ctype<char> >(loc)) {}
  bool isalnum(char ch) const { return ctype_.is(std::ctype_base::alnum, ch); }
  char tolower(char ch) const { return ctype_.tolower(ch); }
private:
  std::ctype<char> const& ctype_;
```

```
};
// Copy the rest of Listing 40-5 here, starting with the non_letter class,
// and continuing to the end of the listing.
```

Notice how most of the program is unchanged. The simple act of caching the ctype facet reduces this program's runtime by about 15 percent on my system.

# Collation Order

You can use the relational operators (such as <) with characters and strings, but they don't actually compare characters; they compare code points. Most users don't care whether a list of names is sorted in ascending numerical order by code point. They want a list of names sorted in ascending alphabetical order, according to their native collation rules.

For example, which comes first: ångstrom or angle? The answer depends on where you live and what language you speak. In Scandinavia, angle comes first, and ångstrom follows zebra. The collate facet compares strings according to the locale's rules. Its compare function is somewhat clumsy to use, so the locale class template provides a simple interface for determining whether one string is less than another in a locale: use the locale's function call operator. In other words, you can use a locale object itself as the comparison functor for standard algorithms, such as sort. Listing 53-6 shows a program that demonstrates how collation order depends on locale. In order to get the program to run in your environment, you may need to change the locale names.

**Listing 53-6.** *Demonstrating How Collation Order Depends on Locale*

```cpp
#include <algorithm>
#include <iostream>
#include <iterator>
#include <locale>
#include <ostream>
#include <string>
#include <vector>

void sort_words(std::vector<std::string> words, std::locale loc)
{
  std::sort(words.begin(), words.end(), loc);
  std::cout << loc.name() << ":\n";
  std::copy(words.begin(), words.end(),
          std::ostream_iterator<std::string>(std::cout, "\n"));
}

int main()
{
  using namespace std;
  vector<string> words;
  words.push_back("circus");
  words.push_back("\u00e5ngstrom");        // ångstrom
  words.push_back("\u00e7irc\u00ea");      // çircê
```

```
words.push_back("angle");
words.push_back("essen");
words.push_back("ether");
words.push_back("\u00e6ther");          // æther
words.push_back("aether");
words.push_back("e\u00dfen");           // eßen

sort_words(words, locale::classic());
sort_words(words, locale("en_GB.utf8")); // Great Britain
sort_words(words, locale("no_NO.utf8")); // Norway
}
```

The boldface line shows how the locale object is used as a comparison functor to sort the words. Table 53-3 lists the results I get for each locale. Depending on your native character set, you may get different results.

**Table 53-3.** *Collation Order for Each Locale*

| Classic | Great Britain | Norway |
|---------|---------------|--------|
| aether | aether | aether |
| angle | æther | angle |
| circus | angle | çircê |
| essen | ångstrom | circus |
| ether | çircê | essen |
| eßen | circus | eßen |
| ångstrom | essen | ether |
| æther | eßen | æther |
| çircê | ether | ångstrom |

Facets are parameterized on character type, so you can use them with wide characters, too. In fact, if you had trouble running the program in Listing 53-6, or you saw different results, using wide characters may solve your problems. **Rewrite Listing 53-6 to use wstring instead of string, to use wide string literals, and to write results to wcout.** The ostream_iterator class template takes multiple template arguments. As you know, the first is the type of item to write to the output stream. The second is the stream's character type. Because the default type for the second argument is char, we've never needed to specify it before, but now we do. Compare your program with Listing 53-7.

**Listing 53-7.** *Testing Collation Order of Wide Strings*

```
#include <algorithm>
#include <iostream>
#include <iterator>
#include <locale>
#include <ostream>
#include <string>
#include <vector>
```

```
std::wstring widen(std::string const& narrow)
{
  return std::wstring(narrow.begin(), narrow.end());
}

void sort_words(std::vector<std::wstring> words, std::locale loc)
{
  std::sort(words.begin(), words.end(), loc);
  std::wcout << widen(loc.name()) << L":\n";
  std::copy(words.begin(), words.end(),
            std::ostream_iterator<std::wstring, wchar_t>(std::wcout, L"\n"));
}

int main()
{
  using namespace std;
  vector<wstring> words;
  words.push_back(L"circus");
  words.push_back(L"\u00e5ngstrom");        // ångstrom
  words.push_back(L"\u00e7irc\u00ea");      // çircê
  words.push_back(L"angle");
  words.push_back(L"essen");
  words.push_back(L"ether");
  words.push_back(L"\u00e6ther");           // æther
  words.push_back(L"aether");
  words.push_back(L"e\u00dfen");            // eßen

  sort_words(words, locale::classic());
  sort_words(words, locale("en_GB.utf8"));  // Great Britain
  sort_words(words, locale("no_NO.utf8"));  // Norway
}
```

On the other hand, some environments have poor support for wide characters, and the results may be worse than earlier. You need to get to know your compiler, library, and operating system in order to know what works best for you.

The next and final topic in Part 3 is to further your understanding of text I/O.

■ ■ ■

# Text I/O

Input and output have two basic flavors: text and binary. Binary I/O introduces subtleties that are beyond the scope of this book; so all discussion of I/O herein is text-oriented. This Exploration presents a variety of topics related to textual I/O. You've already seen how the input and output operators work with the built-in types as well as with the standard library types, when it makes sense. You've also seen how you can write your own I/O operators for custom types. This Exploration shows some additional details about file modes, reading and writing strings, and converting values to and from strings.

## File Modes

When you open a file stream, you can specify file modes as a second argument, after the file name. The default mode for an ifstream is std::ios_base::in, which opens the file for input. The default mode for ofstream is std::ios_base::out | std::ios_base::trunc. (The | operator combines certain values, such as modes. Exploration 61 will cover this in depth.) The out mode opens the file for output. If the file doesn't exist, it is created. The trunc mode means to truncate the file so you always start with an empty file. If you explicitly specify the mode and omit trunc, the old contents (if any) remain. Therefore, by default, writing to the output stream overwrites the old contents. If you want to position the stream at the end of the old contents, use the ate mode (short for at-end), which sets the stream's initial position to the end of the existing file contents. The default is to position the stream at the start of the file.

Another useful mode for output is app (short for append), which causes every write to append to the file. That is, app affects every write, whereas ate affects only the starting position. The app mode is useful when writing to a log file.

**Write a debug() function that takes a single string as an argument and writes that string to a file named "debug.txt".** Listing 54-1 shows the header that declares the function.

**Listing 54-1.** *Header That Declares a Trivial Debugging Function*

```
#ifndef DEBUG_HPP_
#define DEBUG_HPP_

#include <string>

void debug(std::string const&);

#endif
```

**495**

Append every log message to the file, terminating each message with a newline. To ensure that the debugging information is properly recorded, even if the program crashes, open the file anew every time the debug() function is called. Listing 54-2 shows my solution.

**Listing 54-2.** *Implementing the Debug Function*

```
#include <fstream>
#include <ostream>
#include <string>
#include "debug.hpp"

void debug(std::string const& str)
{
   std::ofstream stream("debug.txt", std::ios_base::out | std::ios_base::app);
   if (not stream)
      throw std::runtime_error("cannot open debug.txt");
   stream.exceptions(std::ios_base::failbit);
   stream << str << '\n';
   stream.close();
}
```

# String Streams

In addition to file streams, C++ offers string streams. The <sstream> header defines istringstream and ostringstream. As you may have guessed, these names are typedefs for template specializations: basic_istringstream<char> and basic_ostringstream<char>. Naturally, wchar_t specializations are also in <sstream>.

A string stream reads from and writes to a std::basic_string object. For input, supply the string as an argument to the istringstream constructor. For output, you can supply a string object, but the more common usage is to let the stream create and manage the string for you. The stream appends to the string, allowing the string to grow as needed. After you are finished writing to the stream, call the str() member function to retrieve the final string.

Suppose you need to read pairs of numbers from a file, representing a car's odometer reading and the amount of fuel needed to fill the tank. The program computes the miles-per-gallon (or liters-per-kilometer if you prefer) at each fill-up, and overall. The file format is simple: each line has the odometer reading followed by the fuel amount on one line, separated by white space.

**Write the program.** Listing 54-3 demonstrates the miles-per-gallon approach.

**Listing 54-3.** *Computing Miles-Per-Gallon*

```
#include <iostream>
#include <istream>
#include <ostream>
```

```
int main()
{
   double fuel, odometer;
   double prev_odometer(0.0);
   double total_fuel(0.0);
   while (std::cin >> odometer >> fuel)
   {
      if (fuel != 0)
      {
         double distance(odometer - prev_odometer);
         std::cout << distance / fuel << '\n';
         total_fuel += fuel;
         prev_odometer = odometer;
      }
   }
   if (total_fuel != 0)
      std::cout << "Net MPG=" << odometer / total_fuel << '\n';
}
```

Listing 54-4 shows the equivalent program, but instead computing liters-per-kilometer. For the remainder of this Exploration, I will use miles-per-gallon; Readers who don't use this method can consult the files that accompany the book for liters-per-kilometer.

**Listing 54-4.** *Computing Liters-Per-Kilometer*

```
#include <iostream>
#include <istream>
#include <ostream>

int main()
{
   double fuel, odometer;
   double prev_odometer(0.0);
   double total_fuel(0.0);
   while (std::cin >> odometer >> fuel)
   {
      double distance(odometer - prev_odometer);
      if (distance != 0)
      {
         std::cout << fuel / distance << '\n';
         total_fuel += fuel;
         prev_odometer = odometer;
      }
   }
   if (odometer != 0)
      std::cout << "Net LPK=" << total_fuel / odometer << '\n';
}
```

**What happens if the user accidentally forgets to record the fuel on one line of the file?**

_____

The input loop doesn't know or care about lines. It resolutely skips over white space in its quest to fulfill each input request. Thus, it reads the subsequent line's odometer reading as a fuel amount. Naturally, the results will be incorrect.

A better solution would be to read each line as a string and extract two numbers from the string. If the string is not formatted correctly, issue an error message and ignore that line. You read a line of text into a std::string by calling the std::getline function (declared in <string>). This function takes an input stream as the first argument and a string object as the second argument. It returns the stream, which means it returns a true value if the read succeeds or false if the read fails, so you can use the call to getline as a loop condition.

Once you have the string, open an istringstream to read from the string. Using the string stream the same way you would use any other input stream. Read two numbers from the string stream; if the string stream does not contain any numbers, ignore that line. If it contains only one number, issue a suitable error message. Listing 54-5 presents the new program.

**Listing 54-5.** _Rewriting the Miles-Per-Gallon Program to Parse a String Stream_

```cpp
#include <iostream>
#include <istream>
#include <ostream>
#include <sstream>
#include <string>

int main()
{
    double prev_odometer(0.0), odometer(0.0);
    double total_fuel(0.0);
    std::string line;
    int linenum(0);
    bool error(false);
    while (std::getline(std::cin, line))
    {
        std::istringstream input(line);
        ++linenum;
        double fuel;
        if (input >> odometer)
        {
            if (not (input >> fuel))
            {
                std::cerr << "Missing fuel consumption on line " << linenum << '\n';
                error = true;
            }
            else if (fuel != 0)
            {
                double distance(odometer - prev_odometer);
                std::cout << distance / fuel << '\n';
```

```
            total_fuel += fuel;
            prev_odometer = odometer;
        }
      }
    }
    if (total_fuel != 0)
    {
        std::cout << "Net MPG=" << odometer / total_fuel;
        if (error)
            std::cout << " (estimated, due to input error)";
        std::cout << '\n';
    }
}
```

Most text file formats allow some form of annotation or commentary. The file format already allows one form of commentary, as a side effect of the program's implementation. **How can you add comments to the input file?**

---

After the program reads the fuel amount from the line, it ignores the rest of the string. You can add comments to any line that contains the proper odometer and fuel data. But that's a sloppy side effect. A better design requires the user to insert an explicit comment marker. Otherwise, the program might misinterpret erroneous input as a valid input followed by a comment, such as accidentally inserting an extra space, as illustrated in the following:

```
12321 10. 23
```

Let's modify the file format. Any line that begins with a pound sign (#) is a comment. Upon reading a comment character, the program skips the entire line. **Add this feature to the program.** A useful function is an input stream's unget() function. After reading a character from the stream, unget() returns that character to the stream, causing the subsequent read operation to read that character again. In other words, after reading a line, read a character from the line, and if it is '#', skip the line. Otherwise, call unget() and continue as before. Compare your result with mine, as shown in Listing 54-6.

**Listing 54-6.** *Parsing Comments in the Miles-Per-Gallon Data File*

```cpp
#include <iostream>
#include <istream>
#include <ostream>
#include <sstream>
#include <string>

int main()
{
    double prev_odometer(0.0), odometer(0.0);
    double total_fuel(0.0);
    std::string line;
    int linenum(0);
    bool error(false);
```

```
   while (std::getline(std::cin, line))
   {
      std::istringstream input(line);
      ++linenum;
      char comment;
      if (input >> comment and comment != '#')
      {
         input.unget();
         double fuel;
         if (input >> odometer)
         {
            if (not (input >> fuel))
            {
               std::cerr << "Missing fuel consumption on line " << linenum << '\n';
               error = true;
            }
            else if (fuel != 0)
            {
               double distance(odometer - prev_odometer);
               std::cout << distance / fuel << '\n';
               total_fuel += fuel;
               prev_odometer = odometer;
            }
         }
      }
   }
   if (total_fuel != 0)
   {
      std::cout << "Net MPG=" << odometer / total_fuel;
      if (error)
         std::cout << " (estimated, due to input error)";
      std::cout << '\n';
   }
}
```

More complicated still is allowing the comment marker to appear anywhere on a line. A comment extends from the # character to the end of the line. The comment marker can appear anywhere on a line, but if the line contains any data, it must contain two valid numbers prior to the comment marker. **Enhance the program to allow comment markers anywhere.** Consider using the find() member function of std::string. It has many forms, one of which takes a character as an argument and returns the zero-based index of the first occurrence of that character in the string. The return type is std::string::size_type. If the character is not in the string, find() returns the magic constant std::string::npos.

Once you find the comment marker, you can delete the comment by calling erase() or copy the non-comment portion of the string by calling substr(). String member functions work with zero-based indices. Substrings are expressed as a starting position and a count of the number of characters affected. Usually, the count can be omitted to mean the rest of the string. Compare your solution with mine, presented in Listing 54-7.

**Listing 54-7.** *Allowing Comments Anywhere in the Miles-Per-Gallon Data File*

```cpp
#include <iostream>
#include <istream>
#include <ostream>
#include <sstream>
#include <string>

int main()
{
   double prev_odometer(0.0), odometer(0.0);
   double total_fuel(0.0);
   std::string line;
   int linenum(0);
   bool error(false);
   while (std::getline(std::cin, line))
   {
      ++linenum;
      std::string::size_type comment(line.find('#'));
      if (comment != std::string::npos)
         line.erase(comment);
      std::istringstream input(line);
      double fuel;
      if (input >> odometer)
      {
         if (not (input >> fuel))
         {
            std::cerr << "Missing fuel consumption on line " << linenum << '\n';
            error = true;
         }
         else if (fuel != 0)
         {
            double distance(odometer - prev_odometer);
            std::cout << distance / fuel << '\n';
            total_fuel += fuel;
            prev_odometer = odometer;
         }
      }
   }
   if (total_fuel != 0)
   {
      std::cout << "Net MPG=" << odometer / total_fuel;
      if (error)
         std::cout << " (estimated, due to input error)";
      std::cout << '\n';
   }
}
```

Now that the file format allows explicit comments on each line, you should add some more error-checking to make sure that each line contains only two numbers, and nothing more (after removing comments). One way to check is to read a single character after reading the two numbers. If the read succeeds, the line contains erroneous text. **Add error-checking to detect lines with extra text.** Compare your solution with my solution, shown in Listing 54-8.

**Listing 54-8.** *Adding Error-Checking for Each Line of Input*

```cpp
#include <iostream>
#include <istream>
#include <ostream>
#include <sstream>
#include <string>

int main()
{
    double prev_odometer(0.0), odometer(0.0);
    double total_fuel(0.0);
    std::string line;
    int linenum(0);
    bool error(false);
    while (std::getline(std::cin, line))
    {
        ++linenum;
        std::string::size_type comment(line.find('#'));
        if (comment != std::string::npos)
            line.erase(comment);
        std::istringstream input(line);
        double fuel;
        if (input >> odometer)
        {
            char check;
            if (not (input >> fuel))
            {
                std::cerr << "Missing fuel consumption on line " << linenum << '\n';
                error = true;
            }
            else if (input >> check)
            {
                std::cerr << "Extra text on line " << linenum << '\n';
                error = true;
            }
            else if (fuel != 0)
            {
                double distance(odometer - prev_odometer);
                std::cout << distance / fuel << '\n';
                total_fuel += fuel;
                prev_odometer = odometer;
```

```
         }
      }
   }
   if (total_fuel != 0)
   {
      std::cout << "Net MPG=" << odometer / total_fuel;
      if (error)
         std::cout << " (estimated, due to input error)";
      std::cout << '\n';
   }
}
```

# Text Conversion

Let me put on my clairvoyance cap for a moment . . . I can see that you have many unanswered questions about C++; and one of those questions is, "How can I convert a number to a string easily, and vice versa?"

Now that you know how to use string streams, you can see one possible solution: use an istringstream to read a number from a string, or use an ostringstream to write a number to a string. The only task is to wrap up the functionality in an appropriate function. Even better is to use a template. After all, reading or writing an int is essentially the same as reading or writing a long, etc.

Listing 54-9 shows the from_string function template, which has a single template parameter, T—the type of object to convert. The function returns type T and takes a single function argument: a string to convert.

**Listing 54-9.** *The from_string Function Extracts a Value from a String*

```cpp
#include <istream> // for the >> operator
#include <sstream> // for ostringstream
#include <string>  // for string
#include "conversion_error.hpp"

template<class T>
T from_string(std::string const& str)
{
  std::istringstream in(str);
  T result;
  if (in >> result)
    return result;
  else
    throw conversion_error(str);
}
```

The conversion_error class is a custom exception class. The details are not relevant to this discussion, but inquisitive readers can satisfy their curiosity with the files that accompany this book. T can be any type that permits reading from an input stream with the >> operator, including any custom operators and types that you write.

Your turn: write the to_string function template, which takes a single template argument and declares the to_string function to take a single function argument of that type. The function converts its argument to a string by writing it to a string stream and returns the resulting string. Compare your solution with mine, presented in Listing 54-10.

**Listing 54-10.** *The to_string Function Converts a Value to a String*

```
#include <ostream> // for the << operator
#include <sstream> // for ostringstream
#include <string>  // for string

template<class T>
std::string to_string(T const& obj)
{
  std::ostringstream out;
  out << obj;
  return out.str();
}
```

**Can you see any particular drawback to these functions? _____ If so, what?**

_____

No doubt, you can see many problems, but in particular, the one I want to point out is that they don't work with wide characters. It would be a shame to waste all that effort you spent in understanding wide characters, so let's add another template parameter for the character type. In fact, the std::string class template has three template parameters: the character type, something called the character traits, and an allocator object to manage any heap memory that the string might use. You don't need to know any of the details of these three types; you need only pass them to the basic_string class template. The basic_ostringstream class template takes the first two template arguments.

Your first attempt at implementing to_string may look a little bit like Listing 54-11.

**Listing 54-11.** *Rewriting to_string As a Template Function*

```
#include <ostream> // for the << operator
#include <sstream> // for ostringstream
#include <string>  // for basic_string

template<class T, class Char, class Traits, class Allocator>
std::basic_string<Char, Traits, Allocator> to_string(T const& obj)
{
  std::basic_ostringstream<Char, Traits> out;
  out << obj;
  return out.str();
}
```

This implementation works. It's correct, but it's clumsy. Try it. **Try to write a simple test program that converts an integer to a narrow string and the same integer to a wide string.** Don't be discouraged if you can't do it. This exercise is a demonstration of how templates in the standard library can lead you astray if you aren't careful. Take a look at my solution in Listing 54-12.

**Listing 54-12.** *Demonstrating the Use of* to_string

```
#include <iostream>
#include <ostream>
#include "to_string.hpp"
#include "from_string.hpp"

int main()
{
    std::string str(
       to_string<int, char, std::char_traits<char>, std::allocator<char> >(42)
    );
    int value(from_string<int>(str));
}
```

Do you see what I mean? How are you supposed to know what to provide as the third and fourth template arguments? Don't worry, we can find a better solution.

One alternative approach is not to return the string, but to take it as an output function argument. The compiler could then use argument-type deduction, and you wouldn't need to specify all those template arguments. **Write a version of to_string that takes the same template parameters** but takes two function arguments: the value to convert and the destination string. **Write a demonstration program** to show how much simpler this function is to use. Listing 54-13 shows my solution.

**Listing 54-13.** *Passing the Destination String As an Argument to* to_string

```
#include <ostream> // for the << operator
#include <sstream> // for ostringstream
#include <string>  // for string
#include "from_string.hpp"

template<class T, class Char, class Traits, class Allocator>
void to_string(T const& obj, std::basic_string<Char, Traits, Allocator>& result)
{
  std::basic_ostringstream<Char, Traits> out;
  out << obj;
  result = out.str();
}

int main()
{
    std::string str;
```

```
        to_string(42, str);
        int value(from_string<int>(str));
}
```

On the other hand, if you want to use the string in an expression, you still need to declare a temporary variable just to hold the string.

Another way to approach this problem is to specify `std::string` or `std::wstring` as the sole template argument. The compiler can deduce the type of the object you want to convert. The `to_string` function returns the string type and takes an argument of the object type. Both types need to be template parameters. **Which parameter should be first?** Listing 54-14 shows the latest incarnation of `to_string`, which now takes two template parameters: the string type, and the object type.

**Listing 54-14.** *Improving the Calling Interface of to_string*

```
#include <ostream> // for the << operator
#include <sstream> // for ostringstream

template<class String, class T>
String to_string(T const& obj)
{
  std::basic_ostringstream<typename String::value_type,
                           typename String::traits_type> out;
  out << obj;
  return out.str();
}
```

(Remember `typename` from Exploration 51?) The `from_string` function does little error checking. For example, it will happily convert "1+2=3" into the integer 1 or "1.2.3.4.5" into the floating-point value 1.2. You can add some error checking by making sure that only white space follows the object after reading it from the string stream. Use the same trick you used in Listing 54-8: try to read a single character. If the read succeeds, you know that additional text remains in the stream. If the read fails, only white space remains. Make this change to `from_string`. Compare your solution with Listing 54-15.

**Listing 54-15.** *Improving from_string by Adding Some Error-Checking*

```
#include <istream> // for the >> operator
#include <sstream> // for ostringstream
#include <string>  // for basic_string
#include "conversion_error.hpp"

template<class T, class Char, class Traits, class Alloc>
T from_string(std::basic_string<Char, Traits, Alloc> const& str)
{
  std::basic_istringstream<Char, Traits> in(str);
  T result;
  Char extra;
  if (in >> result and not (in >> extra))
```

```
      return result;
  else
      throw conversion_error(str);
}
```

# Boost Lexical Cast

The to_string and from_string function templates work, but I don't use them in my own programs. Instead, I use a template from an open-source C++ suite of libraries called Boost (http://www.boost.org/). In particular, I use boost::lexical_cast<>, which replaces both function templates.

I briefly mentioned the Boost project in Exploration 50, but it deserves a more complete explanation. Boost is the most important third-party C++ library extant. Among the many libraries it contains are some that are destined to be incorporated into future revisions of the C++ standard. I also mentioned TR1 in Exploration 51; many of the libraries in TR1 originated in Boost. Boost provides a means of field-testing libraries and gaining practical experience with them prior to standardizing. In this way, the standardization committee has greater confidence that the standard is practical and helpful.

Every library in Boost has been peer reviewed to ensure widespread support. Libraries are documented, although some have better documentation than others. Boost's open-source license further ensures that the libraries can enjoy wide use in open-source and closed-source projects. Boost's authors took great pains to achieve a high degree of portability, even to some fairly broken compilers that fail to implement large swaths of the C++ standard, or implement it incorrectly.

Perhaps most important is that much of Boost was written by C++ experts, including members of the C++ standardization committee. The result is that the interface to the Boost libraries often represents the best that C++ has to offer. The lexical_cast<> template is an example.

The name parallels the name of cast expressions that are built into the C++ language, such as static_cast<> (Exploration 23). For instance, to convert a string to an int, use lexical_cast<int>("42"). To convert an int to a string, use lexical_cast<std::string>(42). It's that simple.

The implementation is not so simple, however. That's why I started with to_string and from_string. The implementation of lexical_cast, like most Boost elements, contains a large amount of code to ensure portability. In a typical Boost header, the portability hacks take up more lines than the real code.

Also, Boost often takes full advantage of templates. You need to be an advanced programmer to make sense of many Boost libraries, but anyone can use Boost without understanding the implementation. (Just as you were able to use std::cin long before you learned about the std::basic_istream template.)

If you don't have Boost available, don't fret. This book does not require it. On the other hand, if you have Boost, I highly recommend that you look into using it.

# EXPLORATION 55

■■■

# Project 3: Currency Type

It's time for another project. You're going to continue building on the fixed type from Project 2, and incorporate what you've learned about locales and I/O. Your task this time is to write a currency type. The value is stored as a fixed-point value. I/O is formatted according to the money_get and money_put facets. You may need a library reference to help you.

Make sure you can add two currency amounts to get a currency value, subtract two currency amounts to get currency, multiply and divide currency by an integer or rational value to get a currency result, and divide two currency values to get a rational result.

As with any project, start small and add functionality as you go. For example, start with the basic data representation then add I/O operators. Add arithmetic operators one at a time. Write each test function before you implement the feature.

# PART 4

■■■

# Real Programming

# EXPLORATION 56

▄▄▄

# Pointers

**F**ew topics cause more confusion, especially for programmers new to C++, than pointers. Necessary, powerful, and versatile, pointers can also be dangerous and the underlying cause of so many bugs, that they are both bane and blessing. Pointers are hard at work behind many of the standard library's features, and any serious application or library inevitably uses pointers in some fashion. When used with care and caution, pointers will become an indispensable tool in your C++ programmer's toolkit.

## The Problem

Before diving into syntax and semantics, consider the following problem. Real-life C++ projects typically contain multiple source files, and each source file includes multiple headers. While you are working, you will compile and recompile the project many times. Each time, it's preferable to recompile only those files that have changed, or that include a header file that has changed. Different development environments have different tools to decide which files to recompile. An IDE typically makes these decisions itself; in other environments, a separate tool, such as *make*, *jam*, or *scons*, examines the files in your project and decides which ones to recompile.

The problem to tackle in this and following Explorations is to write a simple tool that decides which files to compile and pretends to compile them. (Actually invoking an external program is beyond the scope of this book, so you won't learn how to write an entire build tool.)

The essential idea is simple: to make an executable program, you must compile source files into object files and link the object files together to form the program. The executable program is said to *depend on* the object files, which in turn, depend on the source files. Other terminology has the program as the *target* with the object files as its *dependencies*. An object file, in turn, can be a target, with a source file and the header files that it includes as dependencies.

As you know, to compile a single source file into a single object file, the compiler may need to read many additional header files. Each of these header files is a dependency of the object file. Thus, one header file can be a dependency of many object files. In more technical terms, targets and dependencies form a directed acyclic graph (DAG), which I will call the *dependency graph*.

---

**Note**  A cyclic graph, such that A depends on B, and B depends on A, is a really bad idea in the real world. For the sake of simplicity, I will ignore this error condition in this and subsequent Explorations.

---

Anyone who's been around large projects knows that dependency graphs can become extremely complex. Some header files may be generated by other programs, so the header files are targets with the generating programs as dependencies, and the generating programs are targets with their own dependencies.

IDEs and programs, such as *make*, analyze the dependency graph and determine which targets must be built first to ensure every target's dependencies are fulfilled. Thus, if A depends on B, and B depends on C, *make* must build C first (if it is a target), then B, and finally A. The key algorithm that *make* employs to find the correct order in which to build targets is a *topological sort*.

Topological sorts are not included in the typical algorithms coursework of many computer science majors. Nor does the algorithm appear in many textbooks. However, any comprehensive algorithms book includes topological sort.

---

**Note**  A good text on topological sort is *Introduction to Algorithms*, by T. H. Cormen, C. E. Leiserson, and R. L. Rivest, 1990 MIT Press. My solution implements exercise 23.4-5.

---

The C++ standard library does not include a topological sort algorithm because it is not a sequential algorithm. It operates on a graph, and the C++ library has no standard graph classes. (Boost has a graph library that includes topological sort, but to ensure everyone can use this Exploration, we will write our own topological sort function.)

We'll begin this Exploration by writing a pseudo-*make* program—that is, a program that reads a *makefile*: a file that describes a set of targets and their dependencies, performs a topological sort to find the order for building targets, and prints the targets in proper build order. In order to simplify the program somewhat, restrict the input to a text file that declares dependencies as pairs of strings, one pair on a line of text. The first string is the name of a target and the second string is the name of a dependency. If a target has multiple dependencies, the input file must list the target on multiple lines, one per dependency. A target can be a dependency of another target. The order of lines within the input file is not important. The goal is to write a program that will print the targets in order so that a *make*-like program can build the first target first, and proceed in order, such that all targets are built before they are needed as dependencies.

To help clarify terminology, I use the term *artifact* for a string that can be a target, a dependency, or both. If you already know an algorithm for topological sort, go ahead and implement the program now. Otherwise, assume the existence of a function, *topological_ sort*, which performs a topological sort of a DAG. To represent the dependency graph, use a map of sets. The map key is a dependency, and the value is the set of targets that list the key as a dependency. This seems inside out from the way you may usually think about organizing targets and dependencies, but as you can see in Listing 56-1, it makes the topological sort quite easy to implement. Because the *topological_sort()* function is reusable, it is a template function and works with "nodes" instead of artifacts, targets, and dependencies.

**Listing 56-1.** *Topological Sort of a Directed Acyclic Graph*

```
#ifndef TOPOLOGICAL_SORT_HPP_
#define TOPOLOGICAL_SORT_HPP_

#include <queue>
#include <stdexcept>

/// Helper function for topological_sort().
/// Finds all the nodes in the graph with no incoming edges,
/// that is, with empty values. Removes each one from the graph
/// and adds it to the set @p nodes.
/// @param[in,out] graph A map of node/set pairs
/// @param[in,out] nodes A queue of nodes with no incoming edges
template<class Graph, class Nodes>
void topsort_clean_graph(Graph& graph, Nodes& nodes)
{
  for (typename Graph::iterator iter(graph.begin()); iter != graph.end();)
  {
    if (iter->second.empty())
    {
      nodes.push(iter->first);
      graph.erase(iter++);   // advance iterator before erase invalidates it
    }
    else
      ++iter;
  }
}

/// Topological sort of a directed acyclic graph.
/// A graph is a map keyed by nodes, with sets of nodes as values.
/// Edges run from values to keys. The sorted list of nodes
/// is copied to an output iterator in reverse order.
/// @param graph The graph
/// @param sorted The output iterator
/// @throws std::runtime_error if the graph contains a cycle
/// @pre Graph::key_type == Graph::mapped_type::key_type
template<class Graph, class OutIterator>
void topological_sort(Graph graph, OutIterator sorted)
{
  std::queue<typename Graph::key_type> nodes;
  // Start with the set of nodes with no incoming edges.
  topsort_clean_graph(graph, nodes);
```

```
  while (not nodes.empty())
  {
    // Grab the first node to process, output it to sorted,
    // and remove it from the graph.
    typename Graph::key_type n(nodes.front());
    nodes.pop();
    *sorted = n;
    ++sorted;

    // Erase n from the graph
    for (typename Graph::iterator iter(graph.begin()); iter != graph.end(); ++iter)
    {
      iter->second.erase(n);
    }
    // After removing n, find any nodes that no longer
    // have any incoming edges.
    topsort_clean_graph(graph, nodes);
  }
  if (not graph.empty())
    throw std::invalid_argument("Dependency graph contains cycles");
}

#endif // TOPOLOGICAL_SORT_HPP_
```

Now that you have the *topological_sort* function, **implement the pseudo-make program** to read and parse the input, build the dependency graph, call *topological_sort*, and print the sorted result. Keep things simple and treat artifacts (targets and dependencies) as strings. Thus, the dependency graph is a map with std::string as the key type and std::set<std::string> as the value type. Compare your solution with Listing 56-2.

**Listing 56-2.** *First Draft of the Pseudo-Make Program*

```
#include <algorithm>
#include <cstdlib>
#include <iostream>
#include <istream>
#include <iterator>
#include <map>
#include <ostream>
#include <set>
#include <sstream>
#include <stdexcept>
#include <string>
#include <vector>

#include "topological_sort.hpp"
```

```cpp
typedef std::string artifact; ///< A target, dependency, or both

class dependency_graph
{
public:
  typedef std::map<artifact, std::set<artifact> > graph_type;

  void store_dependency(artifact target, artifact dependency)
  {
    graph_[dependency].insert(target);
  }

  graph_type const& graph() const { return graph_; }

  template<class OutIter>
  void sort(OutIter sorted)
  const
  {
    topological_sort(graph_, sorted);
  }

private:
  graph_type graph_;
};

int main()
{
  dependency_graph graph;

  std::string line;
  while (std::getline(std::cin, line))
  {
    std::string target, dependency;
    std::istringstream stream(line);
    if (stream >> target >> dependency)
      graph.store_dependency(target, dependency);
    else if (not target.empty())
      // Input line has a target with no dependency,
      // so report an error.
      std::cerr << "malformed input: target, " << target <<
                   ", must be followed by a dependency name\n";
    // else ignore blank lines
  }

  try {
    // Get the artifacts in reverse order.
    std::vector<artifact> sorted;
```

```
      graph.sort(std::back_inserter(sorted));
      // Then print them in the correct order.
      std::copy(sorted.rbegin(), sorted.rend(),
               std::ostream_iterator<artifact>(std::cout, "\n"));
   } catch (std::runtime_error const& ex) {
      std::cerr << ex.what() << '\n';
      return EXIT_FAILURE;
   }
}
```

So what do DAGs and topological sorts have to do with the topic of this Exploration? I thought you'd never ask. Let's construct a slightly more complicated problem by making it a little more realistic.

A real *make* program needs to keep track of more information about an artifact, especially the time when it was last modified. A target also has a list of actions to perform if any dependency is newer than the target. Thus, a class makes more sense than a string for representing an artifact. You can add to the class whatever functionality you need for your *make* program.

Standard C++ does not have any functions for querying a file's modification time. For now, we'll just sidestep the issue and make up a time for every artifact. The important task at hand is to associate additional information with an artifact. The <ctime> header declares the std::time_t type, which represents a time in an implementation-defined format. Ignoring actions, you might define the artifact type as shown in Listing 56-3.

**Listing 56-3.** *New Definition of an Artifact*

```
#ifndef ARTIFACT_HPP_
#define ARTIFACT_HPP_

#include <ctime>
#include <string>

class artifact
{
public:
   artifact() : name_(), mod_time_(static_cast<time_t>(-1)) {}
   artifact(std::string const& name)
   : name_(name), mod_time_(get_mod_time())
   {}

   std::string const& name()      const { return name_; }
   std::time_t        mod_time() const { return mod_time_; }

   /// Build a target.
   /// After completing the actions (not yet implemented),
   /// update the modification time.
   void build();
```

```
/// Look up the modification time of the artifact.
/// Return static_cast<time_t>(-1) if the artifact does not
/// exist (and therefore must be built) or if the time cannot
/// be obtained for any other reason.
/// Also see boost::file_system::last_write_time.
std::time_t get_mod_time()
{
  // Real programs should get this information from the
  // operating system. This program returns the current time.
  return std::time(0);
}
private:
  std::string name_;
  std::time_t mod_time_;
};
```

```
#endif // ARTIFACT_HPP_
```

Now we run into a problem. In the first draft of this program, what made two strings refer to the same artifact is that the strings had the same content. The target named "program" is the same artifact as the dependency named "program" because they are spelled the same. That scheme falls down now that an artifact is more than just a string. When you build a target and update its modification time, you want all uses of that artifact to be updated. Somehow, every use of an artifact name must be associated with a single artifact object for that name.

Got any ideas? It can be done with your current understanding of C++, but you may need to stop and think about it.

Need a hint? How about storing all artifacts in one big vector? Then make a dependency graph that contains indices into the vector instead of artifact names. **Try it.** Rewrite the program in Listing 56-2 to use the new artifact.hpp header from Listing 56-3. When an artifact name is read from the input file, look up that name in a vector of all artifacts. If the artifact is new, add it to the end. Store vector indices in the dependency graph. Print the final list by looking up the numbers in the vector. Compare your solution with Listing 56-4.

---

■**Note** If the performance of linear look-ups concerns you, congratulations for sharp thinking. Not to worry, however, because the program will continue to grow and evolve throughout this Exploration, and we will eliminate the performance issue before we finish.

---

**Listing 56-4.** *Second Draft, Adding Modification Times to Artifacts*

```
#include <algorithm>
#include <cstdlib>
#include <iostream>
#include <istream>
#include <iterator>
#include <map>
```

```cpp
#include <ostream>
#include <set>
#include <sstream>
#include <stdexcept>
#include <string>
#include <vector>

#include "artifact.hpp"
#include "topological_sort.hpp"

typedef std::size_t artifact_index;

class dependency_graph
{
public:
  typedef std::map<artifact_index, std::set<artifact_index> > graph_type;

  void store_dependency(artifact_index target, artifact_index dependency)
  {
    graph_[dependency].insert(target);
  }

  graph_type const& graph() const { return graph_; }

  template<class OutIter>
  void sort(OutIter sorted)
  const
  {
    topological_sort(graph_, sorted);
  }

private:
  graph_type graph_;
};

std::vector<artifact> artifacts;
artifact_index lookup_artifact(std::string const& name)
{
  for (artifact_index i(0); i != artifacts.size(); ++i)
    if (artifacts[i].name() == name)
      return i;
  // Artifact not found, so add it to the end.
  artifacts.push_back(artifact(name));
  return artifacts.size() - 1;
}
```

```
int main()
{
  dependency_graph graph;

  std::string line;
  while (std::getline(std::cin, line))
  {
    std::string target_name, dependency_name;
    std::istringstream stream(line);
    if (stream >> target_name >> dependency_name)
    {
      artifact_index target(lookup_artifact(target_name));
      artifact_index dependency(lookup_artifact(dependency_name));
      graph.store_dependency(target, dependency);
    }
    else if (not target_name.empty())
      // Input line has a target with no dependency,
      // so report an error.
      std::cerr << "malformed input: target, " << target_name <<
                   ", must be followed by a dependency name\n";
    // else ignore blank lines
  }

  try {
    // Get the sorted artifact indices in reverse order.
    std::vector<artifact_index> sorted;
    graph.sort(std::back_inserter(sorted));
    // Then print the artifacts in the correct order.
    for (std::vector<artifact_index>::reverse_iterator it(sorted.rbegin());
         it != sorted.rend();
         ++it)
    {
      std::cout << artifacts.at(*it).name() << '\n';
    }
  } catch (std::runtime_error const& ex) {
    std::cerr << ex.what() << '\n';
    return EXIT_FAILURE;
  }
}
```

Well, that works, but it's ugly. Looking up indices is sloppy programming. Much better would be to store references to the artifact objects directly in the graph. Ah, there's the rub. You can't store a reference in a standard container. Containers are for storing objects—real objects. The container needs to be able to copy and assign the elements in the container, but it can't do that with references. Copying a reference actually copies the object to which it refers. A reference is not a first-class entity that a program can manipulate.

Wouldn't it be nice if C++ had a language feature that acted like a reference, but let you copy and assign the reference itself (not the referred-to object)? Let's pretend we are inventing the C++ language and we need to add this language feature.

# The Solution

Let's devise a new language feature to solve this programming problem. This new feature is similar to references, but permits use with standard containers. Let's call this feature a *flex-ref*, short for flexible reference.

If a and b are both flex-refs that refer to type int, the statement

```
a = b
```

means the value of a is changed so that a now refers to the same int object to which b refers. Passing a as an argument to a function passes the value of a, so if the function assigns a new value to a, that change is local to the function (just as with any other function argument). Using a suitable operator, however, the function can obtain the int object to which a refers, and read or modify that int.

You need a way to obtain the referred-to value, so we need to invent a new operator. Look at iterators for inspiration: given an iterator, the unary * operator returns the item to which the iterator refers. Let's use the same operator for flex-refs. Thus, the following prints the int value to which a refers:

```
std::cout << *a;
```

In the spirit of the * operator, declare a flex-ref by using * in the same manner that you use & for references.

```
int *a, *b;
```

Use the same syntax when declaring a container. For example, declare a vector of flex-refs that refer to type int.

```
std::vector<int*> vec;
vec.push_back(a);
b = vec.front();
```

All that's left is to provide a way to make a flex-ref refer to an object. For that, let's turn to ordinary references for inspiration and use the & operator. Suppose that c is of type int, the following makes a refer to c:

```
a = &c;
```

As you've guessed by now, flex-refs are pointers. The variables a and b are called "pointers to int." A pointer is an honest-to-goodness lvalue. It occupies memory. The values that are stored in that memory are addresses of other lvalues. You can freely change the value stored in that memory, which has the effect of making the pointer refer to a different object.

A pointer can point to a const object, or it can be a const pointer, or both. The following shows pointer to const int:

```
int const* p;
p = &c;
```

Define a const pointer—that is, a pointer that is itself const and therefore cannot be the target of an assignment, but the dereferenced object can be the target.

```
int * const q(&c);
*q = 42;
```

Like any const object, you must supply an initializer and you cannot modify the pointer. However, you can modify the object to which the pointer points.

You can define a reference to a pointer, just as you can define a reference to anything (except another reference).

```
int const*&r(p);
```

Read this declaration the way you would read any other declaration: start by finding the declarator, r. Then read the declaration from the inside working your way outward. To the left, see &, telling you that r is a reference. To the right is the initializer, (p); r is a reference to p (r is another name for the object p). Continuing to the left, you see *, so r is a reference to a pointer. Finally, int tells you that r is a reference to a pointer to int. Thus, the initializer is valid because its type is pointer to int.

What about the other way around? Can you define a pointer to a reference? The short answer is that you can't. A pointer to a reference makes as little sense as a reference to a reference. References and pointers must refer or point to a real object.

You can define a pointer to a pointer. Or a pointer to a pointer to a pointer to a pointer... Just keep track of the exact type of your pointer. The compiler ensures that you assign only expressions of the correct type, as shown in the following:

```
int x;
int *y;
int **z;
y = &x;
z = &y;
```

**Try z = &x and y = z. What happens?**

_____

Because x has type int, &x has type int*; y has type int*, too, so you can assign &x to y, but not to z, which has type int**. The types must match, so you can't assign z to y, either.

It took me long enough to get to the point (and no, that pun is not my proudest moment), but now you can see how pointers help solve the problem of writing the dependency graph. Before we dive into the code, however, let's take a moment to clarify some terminology.

# Addresses vs. Pointers

Programmers are sticklers for details. The compilers and other tools we use daily force us to be. So let's be absolutely clear about addresses and pointers.

An *address* is a memory location. In C++ parlance, it is an rvalue, so you cannot modify or assign to an address. When a program takes the address of an object (with the & operator), the result is a constant for the lifetime of that object. Like every other rvalue, an address in C++ has a type, which must be a pointer type.

A *pointer type* is more properly called an *address type* because the range of values represented by the type are addresses. Nonetheless, the term pointer type is more common because a pointer object has a pointer type.

A pointer type can denote multiple levels of indirection—it can denote a pointer to a pointer, or a pointer to a pointer to a pointer, etc. You must declare each level of pointer indirection with an asterisk. In other words, int* is the type "pointer to int" and int** is "pointer to pointer to int."

A *pointer* is an lvalue that has a pointer type. A pointer object, like any object, has a location in memory in which the program can store a value. The value must have a type that is compatible with the pointer's type; the value must be an address of the correct type.

# Dependency Graphs

Now let's get back to the dependency graph. The graph can store pointers to artifacts. Each external file corresponds to a single artifact object in the program. That artifact can have many nodes in the graph pointing to it. If you update that artifact, all nodes that point to the artifact see the update. Thus, when a build rule updates an artifact, the file modification time may change. All nodes for that artifact in the graph immediately see the new time because they all point to a single object.

All that's left to figure out is where these artifacts reside. For the sake of simplicity, I recommend a map, keyed by artifact name. The mapped values are artifact objects (not pointers). Take the address of an artifact in the map to obtain pointers to store in the graph. **Go ahead; don't wait for me.** Using the *topological_sort.hpp* and *artifact.hpp* headers, **rewrite 56-4** to store artifact objects in a map, and artifact pointers in the graph. Compare your solution with Listing 56-5.

**Listing 56-5.** *Storing Pointers in the Dependency Graph*

```
#include <algorithm>
#include <cstdlib>
#include <iostream>
#include <istream>
#include <iterator>
#include <map>
#include <ostream>
#include <set>
#include <sstream>
#include <stdexcept>
#include <string>
#include <vector>

#include "artifact.hpp"
#include "topological_sort.hpp"
```

```cpp
class dependency_graph
{
public:
  typedef std::map<artifact*, std::set<artifact*> > graph_type;

  void store_dependency(artifact* target, artifact* dependency)
  {
    graph_[dependency].insert(target);
  }

  graph_type const& graph() const { return graph_; }

  template<class OutIter>
  void sort(OutIter sorted)
  const
  {
    topological_sort(graph_, sorted);
  }

private:
  graph_type graph_;
};

std::map<std::string, artifact> artifacts;

artifact* lookup_artifact(std::string const& name)
{
  return &artifacts[name];
}

int main()
{
  dependency_graph graph;

  std::string line;
  while (std::getline(std::cin, line))
  {
    std::string target_name, dependency_name;
    std::istringstream stream(line);
    if (stream >> target_name >> dependency_name)
    {
      artifact* target(lookup_artifact(target_name));
      artifact* dependency(lookup_artifact(dependency_name));
      graph.store_dependency(target, dependency);
    }
```

```
    else if (not target_name.empty())
      // Input line has a target with no dependency, so report an error.
      std::cerr << "malformed input: target, " << target_name <<
                   ", must be followed by a dependency name\n";
    // else ignore blank lines
  }

  try {
    // Get the sorted artifacts in reverse order.
    std::vector<artifact*> sorted;
    graph.sort(std::back_inserter(sorted));
    // Then print the artifacts in the correct order.
    for (std::vector<artifact*>::reverse_iterator it(sorted.rbegin());
         it != sorted.rend();
         ++it)
    {
      std::cout << (*it)->name() << '\n';
    }
  } catch (std::runtime_error const& ex) {
    std::cerr << ex.what() << '\n';
    return EXIT_FAILURE;
  }
}
```

As you can see, the program requires minimal changes, and the changes are all simplifications. As the program grows more complicated (as real programs inevitably do), the simplicity and elegance of pointers become more and more evident.

Standard containers are extremely helpful, but sometimes a program needs greater control over its objects. It must create and destroy objects on its own schedule, not when functions start and end or when control enters or leaves a block. The next Exploration tackles this problem by introducing dynamic memory.

# EXPLORATION 57

■ ■ ■

# Dynamic Memory

**D**eclaring pointers is all well and good, but real programs need to do more. The next step is to learn how to create new objects on the fly, at runtime. Your program takes full control over the lifetime of these objects, destroying the objects only when the program is done using them. This Exploration details how to allocate and free memory dynamically. It also continues to develop the artifact and related classes from Exploration 56.

I want to warn you however, not to run off immediately and start using dynamic memory in your programs. We still have several more Explorations to go, each one building upon its predecessors. You need the full picture, which will include safer ways to manage pointers and dynamic memory.

## Allocating Memory

A new expression allocates memory for a new object, calls a constructor to initialize that object, and returns the address of the newly allocated and constructed object. The syntax is the new keyword followed by the base type, followed by an optional initializer in parentheses.

```
int *pointer(new int(42));
std::cout << *pointer << '\n'; // prints 42
*pointer = 10;                 // changes the int to 10
```

The new expression returns the address of an lvalue. The type of the lvalue is the type you provide after the new keyword. If the initializer is a set of empty parentheses, the newly allocated object is zero-initialized (see Exploration 31), meaning all members are initialized to known, zero values. If you omit the parentheses entirely, the new object is default-initialized, which means objects of built-in type are left uninitialized. This is usually a bad thing, so I recommend providing an initializer with all new expressions, such as shown in the following:

```
int *good(new int()); // *good == 0
int *bad(new int);    // undefined behavior if you read *bad
```

As with any other initializer, if you are initializing a class-type object, and the constructor takes multiple arguments, separate the arguments with commas.

```
rational* piptr(new rational(355, 113));
```

If the C++ environment runs out of memory and cannot fulfill a new request, it throws the std::bad_alloc exception (declared in <new>).

Once allocated and initialized, a dynamically allocated object lives until you get rid of it with a delete expression (as covered in the next section).

# Freeing Memory

When your program no longer needs an object that it had allocated with a new expression, it must free that object with a delete expression. The syntax is the delete keyword followed by a pointer to the object you want to delete.

```
int *tmp(new int(42));
// use *tmp
delete tmp;
```

After you delete an object, all pointers to it become invalid. It is your responsibility to ensure that you never dereference, copy, or otherwise use these pointers. The only thing you can do with a pointer variable after you delete its object is to assign a new value to the variable.

Dynamic objects are more difficult to work with than other objects because they impose a greater burden on you, the programmer, to manage their lifetimes. Almost any mistake results in undefined behavior. A few of the most common mistakes are:

- Using a pointer after a delete

- Invoking delete more than once on the same object

- Failing to delete an object before the program terminates

Most programmers are familiar with segmentation faults, access violations, and the like. These are the most benign of the actual behavior you might encounter if you fail to follow these rules.

It sure would be nice to be able to test whether a pointer is valid before dereferencing it. Too bad you can't. The only way to ensure that your program never dereferences an invalid pointer or tries to otherwise misuse a pointer is to be very, very careful when you write programs that use pointers and dynamic memory. That's why I waited until late in the book to introduce these topics.

Fortunately, C++ offers one tool to help you: a special pointer value that you can assign to any pointer variable to represent a "pointer to nothing." You cannot dereference a pointer to nothing, but you can copy and assign these pointers, and most important, compare a pointer variable with the "pointer to nothing" value. In other words, when your program deletes an object, it should assign a "pointer to nothing" value to the pointer variable. By ensuring that every pointer variable stores a valid pointer or a "pointer to nothing," you *can* safely test whether a pointer is valid before dereferencing it.

# Pointer to Nothing

A "pointer to nothing" is called a *null pointer* and you write a null pointer as 0. Use a null pointer constant to initialize a pointer variable, as the source of an assignment, or as a function argument, as shown in the following:

```
int* ptr(0);
ptr = 0;
```

Note that the compiler treats the integer expression 0 specially. You cannot assign an arbitrary int-type expression to a pointer. Only an integer constant is permitted, and only the value of zero is permitted. Don't be fooled by the zero value, however; the language representation of a null pointer *constant* has nothing to do with the actual bits stored in a null pointer *value*. In some implementations, a null pointer value may have all zero bits; in another implementation, it may have all one bits. Zero-initializing a pointer stores a null pointer value; default-initializing leaves a pointer with a garbage value.

## A KEYWORD FOR NULL POINTERS

The next revision to the C++ language standard adds a keyword to represent null pointers: nullptr. If you are using a compiler that supports nullptr, you should prefer nullptr to 0.

```
int* ptr(nullptr);
ptr = nullptr;
```

The use of 0 for null pointers has caused much confusion among C++ programmers, and I look forward to the day when throughout the world they toss aside their confusing 0's and embrace the glorious future of nullptr clarity.

You have one guarantee with null pointers: whatever value the C++ environment uses for them, no real object will ever have that value as its address. Thus, you can assign a null pointer to a variable after you delete it as a way to mark the pointer object as no longer pointing to anything.

```
int* ptr(new int(42));
delete ptr;
ptr = 0;
```

A good programming practice is to ensure that no pointer variable ever retains an invalid value. Assigning a null pointer to a pointer variable is one way to accomplish this.

A common idiom is to take advantage of short-circuiting (Exploration 11) to test for a null pointer, and if the pointer is not null, use it:

```
if (ptr != 0 and ptr->needs_work())
    do_work(ptr);
```

A frequent question among newcomers to C++ is why the compiler does not generate code that automatically assigns a null pointer as part of the actions of the delete expression. There are two key reasons:

- The delete expression takes an rvalue as an argument, not necessarily a modifiable pointer. Thus, it may not have anything to modify.

- A program may have multiple pointers that all store the same address. Deleting the object invalidates all of these pointers. The delete expression cannot modify all of these pointers because it doesn't know about them. It knows only about the one address that is the argument to the delete expression. Thus, modifying the argument to delete does not solve this problem. You can minimize the extent of this problem by not copying pointers.

C++ has some of its own uses for null pointers. You can supply a null pointer value to the delete expression, and it safely ignores the delete request. If you wish, you can ask that the new expression return a null pointer instead of throwing an exception when it cannot allocate enough memory for the new object. Just add (std::nothrow) after the new keyword and be sure to check the pointer that new returns. The parentheses are required, and std::nothrow is declared in <new>.

```
int *pointer(new (std::nothrow) int(42));
if (pointer != 0)
  // do something with pointer...
```

Most programs don't need to #include <new>. You need that header only if you use std::nothrow or catch std::bad_alloc.

The <cstdlib> and <cstdio> headers declare the name NULL, which some programmers use as a null pointer constant. C programmers are accustomed to using NULL because it is the easiest way to write a C null pointer constant. In C++, however, the rules are different and 0 is the easiest, clearest, best way to write a null pointer constant (unless you are using the new language revision, in which case, nullptr is the best way). I recommend you avoid using NULL in your C++ programs.

If you define a pointer variable without initializing it, the variable's initial value is garbage. This is bad, and you are courting disaster—don't do it. If you don't have a valid address to use as the pointer's initial value, use a null pointer.

# Implementing Standard Containers

Have you ever wondered how the standard containers actually work? If, for instance, I were to ask you to implement std::map or std::set, could you do it? A full, high-quality implementation of any standard container is surprisingly difficult, but it isn't hard to grasp the basic principles.

The standard mandates logarithmic complexity for the associative containers. That is, lookups and insertion must have logarithmic performance, which pretty much forces a tree implementation. Most standard C++ libraries use red-black trees. A quick trip to the Internet will provide the algorithms—even working code—to implement red-black trees. The details of balancing the trees obscure the interesting use of pointers, so let's pick a simpler container: list.

The list class template implements a common doubly linked list. Start with the definition of the list class template itself, as shown in Listing 57-1.

**Listing 57-1.** *Defining the list Class Template*

```
template<class T>
class list
{
public:
  list()
  : head_(0), tail_(0), size_(0)
  {}
  ~list() { clear(); }

  void clear();              ///< Erase all nodes in the list. Reset size to 0.
  void push_back(T const& x); ///< Add to tail.
  void pop_back();           ///< Erase from tail.
  // Other useful functions omitted for brevity...
private:
  class node
  {
  public:
    node(T const& key)
    : next_(0), prev_(0), value_(key)
    {}
    node* next_;
    node* prev_;
    T     value_;
  };

  node* head_;        ///< Start of the list
  node* tail_;        ///< End of the list
  std::size_t size_;  ///< Number of nodes in the list
};
```

A list has a number of insert and erase functions. For the sake of simplicity, this example implements only push_back and pop_back in Listing 57-2.

**Listing 57-2.** *Implementing list::push_back and list::pop_back*

```
template<class T>
void list<T>::push_back(T const& x)
{
    node* n(new node(x));
    if (tail_ == 0)
        head_ = tail_ = n;
    else
    {
        n->prev_ = tail_;
        tail_->next = n;
```

```
    }
    ++size_;
}

template<class T>
void list<T>::pop_back()
{
    node* n(tail_);
    if (head_ == tail_)
        head_ = tail_ = 0;
    else
    {
        tail_ = tail_->prev_;
        tail_->next_ = 0;
    }
    --size_;
    delete n;
}
```

Notice how pop_back removes the node from the list, ensures that the list is in a valid state, and then deletes the memory. Also notice how pop_back does not need to set n to a null pointer. Instead, the function simply returns; it has no opportunity to refer to the address of the deleted memory. These two techniques are ways that help ensure that your program handles dynamic memory correctly.

# Adding Variables

Now return to the dependencies example that you started in Exploration 56. Let's add a new feature: variables. If an input line contains only one string, and the string contains an equal sign, it is a variable assignment. The variable name is to the left of the equal sign; the value is to the right. In this over-simplified example, no spaces are allowed around the equal sign or in the variable's value.

An artifact can contain a variable reference, which is a dollar sign, followed by the variable name in parentheses. The variable's value replaces the reference in its containing string. If a variable is not defined, automatically define it as an empty string.

```
NUM=1
target$(NUM) source$(NUM)
NUM=2
target$(NUM) source$(NUM)
source1 hdrX
source2 hdrY
all target1
all target2
```

The target all depends on target1 and target2. In turn, target1 depends on source1 and target2 depends on source2. Finally, source1 depends on hdrX and source2 depends on hdrY.

**Add an expand function that takes a string, expands variables, and returns the result.**
What if the expansion of a variable contains further variable references? I suggest expanding all variables and re-expanding the string until no more variables remain to be expanded. The std::string class has a number of helpful member functions: the find() function searches for the first occurrence of a substring or a character and returns the index of the substring or the constant std::string::npos to mean "not found." The index type is std::string::size_type. Pass an optional second argument to specify the position at which the search should begin.

```
string::size_type pos(str.find('$', 4)); // start searching at index 4
```

The substr() member function takes two arguments, a starting position and a length, and returns a substring. The second argument is optional; omit it to mean "the rest of the string." The replace() function has several forms. It replaces a substring with a new string. Pass the starting index and length of the substring to replace, followed by the replacement string.

```
str.replace(start, length, replacement);
```

For now, use a global map to store variables. Call it variables. Listing 57-3 presents my implementation of the expand function.

**Listing 57-3.** *Expanding Variables*

```cpp
std::map<std::string, std::string> variables;

std::string expand(std::string str)
{
   std::string::size_type start(0); // start searching here
   while (true)
   {
      // Find a dollar sign.
      std::string::size_type pos(str.find('$', start));
      if (pos == std::string::npos)
         // No more dollar signs.
         return str;
      if (pos == str.size() - 1 or str[pos + 1] != '(')
         // Not a variable reference. Skip the dollar sign,
         // and keep searching.
         start = pos + 1;
      else
      {
         std::string::size_type end(str.find(')', pos));
         if (end == std::string::npos)
            // No closing parenthesis.
            return str;

         // Get the variable name.
         std::string varname(str.substr(pos + 2, end - pos - 2));
         // Replace the entire variable reference.
         str.replace(pos, end - pos + 1, variables[varname]);
```

```
            // Scan the replacement text for more variables.
            start = pos;
        }
    }
}
```

**Now modify the input function** to recognize a variable definition, parse the definition to extract the variable name and value, and store the variable and its value in the `variables` map. Listing 57-4 illustrates how I rewrote the `main` function to parse variable definitions.

**Listing 57-4.** *Parsing Variable Definitions*

```
void parse_graph(std::istream& in, dependency_graph& graph)
{
  std::string line;
  while (std::getline(in, line))
  {
    std::string target_name, dependency_name;
    std::istringstream stream(line);
    if (stream >> target_name >> dependency_name)
    {
      artifact* target(lookup_artifact(expand(target_name)));
      artifact* dependency(lookup_artifact(expand(dependency_name)));
      graph.store_dependency(target, dependency);
    }
    else if (not target_name.empty())
    {
      std::string::size_type equal(target_name.find('='));
      if (equal == std::string::npos)
        // Input line has a target with no dependency,
        // so report an error.
        std::cerr << "malformed input: target, " << target_name <<
                     ", must be followed by a dependency name\n";
      else
        variables[target_name.substr(0, equal)] = target_name.substr(equal+1);
    }
    // else ignore blank lines
  }
}

int main()
{
  dependency_graph graph;

  parse_graph(std::cin, graph);
```

```
try {
  // Get the sorted artifacts in reverse order.
  std::vector<artifact*> sorted;
  graph.sort(std::back_inserter(sorted));

  // Then print the artifacts in the correct order.
  for (std::vector<artifact*>::reverse_iterator it(sorted.rbegin());
       it != sorted.rend();
       ++it)
  {
    std::cout << (*it)->name() << '\n';
  }
} catch (std::runtime_error const& ex) {
  std::cerr << ex.what() << '\n';
  return EXIT_FAILURE;
}
}
```

This seemed like a good time to factor the input to its own function, **parse_graph**. So far, the modifications have not used dynamic memory, at least not explicitly. (Do you think the std::string class uses dynamic memory in its implementation?) The next step is to permit per-target variables. That is, if the input starts with a target name, and instead of a dependency name, the second string is a variable definition, that definition applies only to that target.

```
NUM=1
target$(NUM)  SRC=1
target$(NUM)  source$(SRC)
target2       source$(NUM)
target2       source$(SRC)
```

The NUM variable is global, so target2 depends on source1. The SRC variable applies only to target1, so target1 depends on source1. On the other hand, target2 depends on source, not source2 because target2 does not have a SRC variable, and unknown variables expand to an empty string.

One implementation is to add a map object to every artifact. Most artifacts do not have variables, however, so that can become wasteful. An alternative implementation uses dynamic memory and allocates a map only if a target has at least one variable. To look up a variable for a target, look only in the global map. To look up a variable for a dependency, first check the target's map then check the global map.

As the program evolves, the difference between a target and a dependency grows. This is to be expected because in real life, they are quite different. Targets get actions, for example, so you can build them. You may well argue that now is a good time for refactoring, to create two derived classes: target and dependency. Only the target class could have a map for variables. I grant you extra credit if you decide to undertake this refactoring now. To keep the solution simple, however, I will make the fewest modifications possible as we go along.

**Start with the new artifact class.** In addition to the new map, add an expand member function, which hides the details of the two-level lookup. Compare your solution with mine, which is shown in Listing 57-5.

**Listing 57-5.** *Adding Variable Storage and Lookup to the artifact Class*

```
#ifndef ARTIFACT_HPP_
#define ARTIFACT_HPP_

#include <ctime>
#include <string>

#include "variables.hpp"

class artifact
{
public:
  artifact()
  : name_(), mod_time_(static_cast<time_t>(-1)), variables_(0)
  {}
  artifact(std::string const& name)
  : name_(name), mod_time_(get_mod_time()), variables_(0)
  {}
  ~artifact()
  {
    delete variables_;
  }

  std::string const& name()     const { return name_; }
  std::time_t        mod_time() const { return mod_time_; }
  std::string        expand(std::string str) const
  {
    return ::expand(str, variables_);
  }

  /// Build a target.
  /// After completing the actions (not yet implemented),
  /// update the modification time.
  void build();

  /// Look up the modification time of the artifact.
  /// Return static_cast<time_t>(-1) if the artifact does not
  /// exist (and therefore must be built) or if the time cannot
  /// be obtained for any other reason.
  std::time_t get_mod_time()
  {
    // Real programs should get this information from the
    // operating system. This program returns the current time.
    return std::time(0);
  }
```

```
  /// Store a per-target variable.
  void store_variable(std::string const& name, std::string const& value)
  {
    if (variables_ == 0)
      variables_ = new variable_map;
    (*variables_)[name] = value;
  }
private:
  std::string name_;
  std::time_t mod_time_;
  variable_map* variables_;
};
```

```
#endif // ARTIFACT_HPP_
```

Note that the new destructor does not need to test whether the variables_ variable is set to anything. The value will be either a null pointer or the address of a map. The delete expression handles both and does the right thing: nothing for a null pointer or deletes the memory for an address. Thus, the destructor is easy to write and understand.

I hid a number of details in the new header, *variables.hpp*, which I present in Listing 57-6.

**Listing 57-6.** *The* variables.hpp *File*

```
#ifndef VARIABLES_HPP_
#define VARIABLES_HPP_

#include <map>
#include <string>

typedef std::map<std::string, std::string> variable_map;
extern variable_map global_variables;

/// Expand variables in a string using a local map
/// and the global map.
/// @param str The string to expand
/// @param local_variables The optional, local map; can be null
/// @return The expanded string
std::string expand(std::string str, variable_map const* local_variables);

#endif // VARIABLES_HPP_
```

The implementation of the new expand function is in *variables.cpp*, shown in Listing 57-7.

**Listing 57-7.** *The* variables.cpp *File Implements the expand Function*

```cpp
#include "variables.hpp"

variable_map global_variables;

// Get a variable's value. Try the local variables first; if not found
// try the global variables. If still not found, define the name with
// an empty string and return an empty string. Subsequent lookups of
// the same name will find the empty string. Exercise for reader:
// print a message the first time the undefined variable's name
// is used.
std::string get_value(std::string const& name, variable_map const* local_variables)
{
   if (local_variables != 0)
   {
      variable_map::const_iterator iter(local_variables->find(name));
      if (iter != local_variables->end())
         return iter->second;
   }
   return global_variables[name];
}

std::string expand(std::string str, variable_map const* local_variables)
{
   std::string::size_type start(0); // start searching here
   while (true)
   {
      // Find a dollar sign.
      std::string::size_type pos(str.find('$', start));
      if (pos == std::string::npos)
         // No more dollar signs.
         return str;
      if (pos == str.size() - 1 or str[pos + 1] != '(')
         // Not a variable reference.
         // Skip the dollar sign, and keep searching.
         start = pos + 1;
      else
      {
         std::string::size_type end(str.find(')', pos));
         if (end == std::string::npos)
            // No closing parenthesis.
            return str;
```

```
      // Get the variable name.
      std::string varname(str.substr(pos + 2, end - pos - 2));
      // Replace the entire variable reference.
      std::string value(get_value(varname, local_variables));
      str.replace(pos, end - pos + 1, value);
      // Scan the replacement text for more variables.
      start = pos;
    }
  }
}
```

The only task that remains is to update the parser. **Modify the parse_graph function to parse target-specific variables.** Compare your solution with that of mine in Listing 57-8.

**Listing 57-8.** *Adding Per-Target Variables to parse_graph*

```
void parse_graph(std::istream& in, dependency_graph& graph)
{
  std::string line;
  while (std::getline(std::cin, line))
  {
    std::string target_name, dependency_name;
    std::istringstream stream(line);
    if (stream >> target_name >> dependency_name)
    {
      artifact* target(lookup_artifact(expand(target_name, 0)));
      std::string::size_type equal(dependency_name.find('='));
      if (equal == std::string::npos)
      {
        // It's a dependency specification
        artifact* dependency(lookup_artifact(target->expand(dependency_name)));
        graph.store_dependency(target, dependency);
      }
      else
        // It's a target-specific variable
        target->store_variable(dependency_name.substr(0, equal-1),
                               dependency_name.substr(equal+1));
    }
    else if (not target_name.empty())
    {
      std::string::size_type equal(target_name.find('='));
      if (equal == std::string::npos)
        // Input line has a target with no dependency,
        // so report an error.
        std::cerr << "malformed input: target, " << target_name <<
                     ", must be followed by a dependency name\n";
      else
```

```
            global_variables[target_name.substr(0, equal)] =
                                     target_name.substr(equal+1);
      }
      // else ignore blank lines
   }
}
```

# Special Member Functions

The program seems to function, but it still needs work. As written, it triggers undefined behavior in the artifact class. To understand what's going on, consider the program in Listing 57-9.

**Listing 57-9.** *Simple Wrapper for Dynamic Memory*

```cpp
#include <iostream>
#include <ostream>

class wrapper
{
public:
   wrapper(int x) : p_(new int(x)) {}
   ~wrapper()                   { delete p_; }
   int value() const            { return *p_; }
private:
   int* p_;
};

void print(wrapper w)
{
   std::cout << w.value() << '\n';
}

wrapper increment(wrapper w)
{
   return wrapper(w.value() + 1);
}

int main()
{
  wrapper w(42);
  print(increment(w));
}
```

**Predict the output from this program.**

The behavior is undefined, so I cannot predict exactly how it will work on your system. Most likely, the program will fail with some kind of memory violation. It is possible that the program will run without any observable sign of failure. It's also possible that it will print a seemingly random value instead of 43.

So what's going on?

The constructor allocates an int; the destructor deletes an int; it all seems correct.

The problem is the copy constructor.

"What copy constructor?" you ask.

"The copy constructor that the compiler creates for you," I answer.

"Oh, that copy constructor," you reply comprehendingly.

The compiler implicitly writes a copy constructor, assignment operator, and destructor for you, performing member-wise copying, assignment, and destruction. In this case, the copy constructor dutifully copies the p_ data member. Thus, the original and the copy both contain identical pointers. The first one to be destroyed deletes the memory, leaving the other with a dangling pointer—an invalid pointer. When that other object is destroyed, it tries to delete p_ again, but it had already been deleted. Deleting the same address more than once is undefined behavior (unless a new expression has subsequently returned that same address).

One solution to this kind of problem is to disallow copying. You can easily do this by declaring an explicit copy constructor and assignment operator as private members. Declare the functions, but don't define them. Because the members are private, no user of the class can copy or assign instances of the class. Because the members are not defined, even if you inadvertently copy or assign instances of the class, the linker will report the missing function definitions, as demonstrated in the following:

```
class nocopy {
public:
    nocopy(int x) : p_(new int(x)) {}
    ~nocopy()                       { delete p_; }
private:
    nocopy(nocopy const&);          // do not implement
    void operator=(nocopy const&);  // do not implement
    int* p_;
};
```

On the other hand, this means you can't copy or assign the objects, which is kind of limiting. Another solution is to make a *deep copy*—that is allocate and copy the dynamic memory. Listing 57-10 shows this solution applied to Listing 57-9.

**Listing 57-10.** *Making a Deep Copy*

```
#include <iostream>
#include <ostream>

class wrapper
{
public:
    wrapper(int x)            : p_(new int(x))          {}
    wrapper(wrapper const& w) : p_(new int(w.value()))) {}
    ~wrapper()                                          { delete p_; }
```

```
    wrapper& operator=(wrapper w)
    {
        swap(w);
        return *this;
    }
    void swap(wrapper& w)
    {
        int* tmp(w.p_);
        w.p_ = p_;
        p_ = tmp;
    }
    int value() const                                  { return *p_; }
private:
    int* p_;
};

void print(wrapper w)
{
    std::cout << w.value() << '\n';
}

wrapper increment(wrapper w)
{
    return wrapper(w.value() + 1);
}

int main()
{
  wrapper w(42);
  print(increment(w));
}
```

The implementation of the assignment operator is interesting, isn't it? You have a choice of many ways to implement this operator. The swap idiom has the advantage of simplicity. The standard library defines swap functions for the standard containers, and any decent library implements swap as a lightweight, fast function (if the container permits it). Typically, these swap functions work similar to wrapper::swap: they copy a few pointers. The trick of the assignment operator is that it takes its argument by value, not by reference. The compiler uses the copy constructor to make a copy of the source of the assignment; the swap function then swaps the current p_ value with the copy. The copy will be freed after the assignment operator returns, thereby cleaning up the original pointer, leaving the object with a deep copy of the assignment source, which is exactly what you want to have happen.

Whenever a class allocates dynamic memory, you need to consider all the special member functions: copy constructor, assignment operator, and destructor. If you find yourself implementing one of them (in this case, the destructor), most likely you need to implement all three, or at least deal with all three.

**Note** If you write any one of the three special member functions—copy constructor, copy assignment operator, or destructor—you must take a look at the others, and most likely implement them, too.

As you can see, dynamic memory involves a number of complications. The next Exploration takes a look at more complications—namely, exceptions. Exceptions can greatly complicate proper handling of dynamic memory, so pay close attention.

# EXPLORATION 58

■■■

# Exception-Safety

$E$xploration 43 introduced exceptions, which you have used in a number of programs since then. Dynamic memory presents a new wrinkle regarding exceptions, and you need to be that much more careful when handling them in order to do so safely and properly in the face of dynamic memory management. In particular, you need to watch for memory leaks and similar problems.

## Memory Leaks

Careless use of dynamic memory and exceptions can result in memory leaks—that is, memory that a program allocates but fails to free. In modern desktop operating systems, when an application terminates, the operating system reclaims all memory that the application used, so it is easy to become complacent about memory leaks. After all, no leak outlives the program invocation. But then your pesky users surprise you and leave your word processor (or whatever) running for days on end. They don't notice the memory leaking until suddenly they can no longer edit documents, and the automatic backup utility cannot allocate enough memory to save the user's work before the program terminates abruptly.

Maybe that's an extreme example, but leaking memory is a symptom of mismanaging memory. If you mismanage memory in one part of the program, you probably mismanage memory in other parts, too. Those other parts may be less benign than a mere memory leak.

Consider the silly program in Listing 58-1.

**Listing 58-1.** *Silly Program to Demonstrate Memory Leaks*

```
#include <iostream>
#include <istream>
#include <ostream>
#include <sstream>
#include <string>

int* read(std::istream& in)
{
  int value;
  if (in >> value)
    return new int(value);
  else
```

```
      return 0;
}

int divide(int x, int y)
{
  return x / y;
}

int main()
{
  std::cout << "Enter pairs of numbers, and I will divide them.\n";
  std::string line;
  while(std::getline(std::cin, line))
  {
    std::istringstream input(line);
    if (int* x = read(input))
      if (int* y = read(input))
        std::cout << divide(*x, *y) << '\n';
  }
}
```

This program introduces a new C++ feature. The if statements in main() define variables inside their conditionals. The rules for this feature are restrictive, so it is not used often. You can define only one declarator. You must use an equal sign to specify an initializer. The value is then implicitly converted to bool, which in this case means comparing to a null pointer. In other words, this conditional is true if the pointer is not null. The scope of the variable is limited to the body of the conditional (including the else portion of an if statement).

Now that you can understand it, **what's wrong with this program?**

_____

_____

_____

The program leaks memory. It leaks memory if a line of text contains only one number. It also leaks memory if a line of text contains two numbers. In short, the program leaks like a termite's rowboat. Adding delete expressions should fix things, right? **Do it.** Your program should now look like Listing 58-2.

**Listing 58-2.** _Adding Delete Expressions to the Silly Program_

```
#include <iostream>
#include <istream>
#include <ostream>
#include <sstream>
#include <string>
```

```
int* read(std::istream& in)
{
  int value;
  if (in >> value)
    return new int(value);
  else
    return 0;
}

int divide(int x, int y)
{
  return x / y;
}

int main()
{
  std::cout << "Enter pairs of numbers, and I will divide them.\n";
  std::string line;
  while(std::getline(std::cin, line))
  {
    std::istringstream input(line);
    if (int* x = read(input))
    {
      if (int* y = read(input))
      {
        std::cout << divide(*x, *y) << '\n';
        delete y;
      }
      delete x;
    }
  }
}
```

Well, that's a little better, but only a little. Let's make the problem more interesting by adding some exceptions.

# Exceptions and Dynamic Memory

Exceptions can be a significant factor for memory errors. You may write a function that carefully matches every new with a corresponding delete, but an exception thrown in the middle of the function will cause that oh-so-carefully-written function to fail, and the program forgets all about that dynamically allocated memory.

Any time you use a new expression, you must be aware of places in your program that may throw an exception. You must have a plan for how to manage the exception to ensure that you don't lose track of the dynamically allocated memory and that the pointer always holds a valid address. Many places can throw exceptions, including new expressions, any I/O statement (if the appropriate exception mask bit is set, as explained in Exploration 43), and a number of other library calls.

To see an example of how exceptions can cause problems, read the program in Listing 58-3.

**Listing 58-3.** *Demonstrating Issues with Exceptions and Dynamic Memory*

```cpp
#include <iostream>
#include <istream>
#include <ostream>
#include <sstream>
#include <stdexcept>
#include <string>

int* read(std::istream& in)
{
  int value;
  if (in >> value)
    return new int(value);
  else
    return 0;
}

int divide(int x, int y)
{
  if (y == 0)
    throw std::runtime_error("integer divide by zero");
  else if (x < y)
    throw std::underflow_error("result is less than 1");
  else
    return x / y;
}

int main()
{
  std::cout << "Enter pairs of numbers, and I will divide them.\n";
  std::string line;
  while(std::getline(std::cin, line))
    try
    {
      std::istringstream input(line);
      if (int* x = read(input))
      {
        if (int* y = read(input))
        {
          std::cout << divide(*x, *y) << '\n';
          delete y;
        }
        delete x;
```

```
    }
  } catch (std::exception const& ex) {
    std::cout << ex.what() << '\n';
  }
}
```

**Now what's wrong with this program?**

_____

_____

_____

The program leaks memory when the divide function throws an exception. In this case, the problem is easy to see, but in a more complicated program, it can be harder to identify. Looking at the input loop, it seems that every allocation is properly paired with a delete expression. But in a more complicated program, the source of exceptions and the try-catch statement may be far apart and unrelated to the input loop.

Ideally, you should be able to manage memory without knowing about exceptions. Fortunately, you can—at least to a certain degree.

# Automatically Deleting Pointers

Keeping track of allocated memory can be tricky, so you should accept any help that C++ can offer. One class template that can help a lot is std::auto_ptr<> (defined in the <memory> header). This template wraps a pointer so that when the auto_ptr object goes out of scope, it automatically deletes the pointer it wraps. The template also guarantees that exactly one auto_ptr object owns a particular pointer. Thus, when you assign one auto_ptr to another, you know exactly which auto_ptr (the target of the assignment) owns the pointer and has responsibility for freeing it. You can assign auto_ptr objects, pass them to functions, and return them from functions; in all cases, ownership passes from one auto_ptr object to another. Like children playing the game of Hot Potato, whoever is left holding the pointer or potato in the end is the loser and must delete the pointer.

The auto_ptr template is particularly helpful when a program throws an exception. When C++ handles the exception, it unwinds the stack and destroys local variables along the way. This means it will destroy local auto_ptr objects in those unwound stack frames, which will delete their pointers. Without auto_ptr, you may get a memory leak.

Thus, a common idiom is to use auto_ptr<> for local variables of pointer type, as well as for data members of pointer type. Equally viable, but less common, is for function parameters and return types to be auto_ptr, as illustrated in Listing 58-4.

**Listing 58-4.** _Using the auto_ptr Class Template_

```
#include <iostream>
#include <memory>
#include <ostream>
```

```
class see_me
{
public:
  see_me(int x) : x_(x) { std::cout <<  "see_me(" << x_ << ")\n"; }
  ~see_me()              { std::cout << "~see_me(" << x_ << ")\n"; }
  int value() const     { return x_; }
private:
  int x_;
};

std::auto_ptr<see_me> nothing(std::auto_ptr<see_me> arg)
{
  return arg;
}

template<class T>
std::auto_ptr<T> make(int x)
{
  return std::auto_ptr<T>(new T(x));
}

int main()
{
  std::cout << "program begin...\n";
  std::auto_ptr<see_me> sm(make<see_me>(42));
  std::auto_ptr<see_me> other;
  other = nothing(sm);
  if (sm.get() == 0)
    std::cout << "sm is null, having lost ownership of its pointer\n";
  if (other.get() != 0)
    std::cout << "other now has ownership of the int, " <<
                 other->value() << '\n';
  std::cout << "program ends...\n";
}
```

As you can see, the get() member function returns the raw pointer value, which you can use to test the pointer or pass to functions that do not expect to gain ownership of the pointer. You can assign a new auto_ptr value, which causes the target of the assignment to delete its old value and take ownership of the new pointer. Dereference the auto_ptr pointer with *, or use -> to access members, the same way you would with an ordinary pointer.

**Use std::auto_ptr to fix the program in Listing 58-3.** Compare your repairs with mine, which are presented in Listing 58-5.

**Listing 58-5.** *Fixing Memory Leaks*

```
#include <iostream>
#include <istream>
#include <memory>
```

```
#include <ostream>
#include <sstream>
#include <stdexcept>
#include <string>

std::auto_ptr<int> read(std::istream& in)
{
  int value;
  if (in >> value)
    return std::auto_ptr<int>(new int(value));
  else
    return std::auto_ptr<int>();
}

int divide(int x, int y)
{
  if (y == 0)
    throw std::runtime_error("integer divide by zero");
  else if (x < y)
    throw std::underflow_error("result is less than 1");
  else
    return x / y;
}

int main()
{
  std::cout << "Enter pairs of numbers, and I will divide them.\n";
  std::string line;
  while(std::getline(std::cin, line))
    try
    {
      std::istringstream input(line);
      std::auto_ptr<int> x(read(input));
      if (x.get() != 0)
      {
        std::auto_ptr<int> y(read(input));
        if (y.get() != 0)
          std::cout << divide(*x, *y) << '\n';
      }
    } catch (std::exception const& ex) {
      std::cout << ex.what() << '\n';
    }
}
```

The restrictions of a conditional declaration prevent its use with auto_ptr because the auto_ptr object has no implicit conversion to bool. Instead, you must explicitly call the get() member function to check whether it is null. Other than that, the changes are minimal, but they vastly increase the safety of this program. No matter what happens in the divide function or elsewhere, this program does not leak any memory.

# What You Can't Do with auto_ptr

The auto_ptr template solves some problems, but it's no panacea. The most glaring restriction in its use is that you cannot store an auto_ptr in a standard container. The standard containers require their contents be assignable and copyable. After the assignment or copy, the source and the target must be identical. That isn't true for auto_ptr because the original gives up the pointer to the target of the assignment or copy.

Because of this key limitation, many C++ programmers avoid auto_ptr. Nonetheless, it has its uses, and if your organization eschews third-party libraries, auto_ptr may be all you have. But the standardization committee feels your pain, and the next revision to the language will deprecate auto_ptr in favor of newer, brighter, shinier class templates. Exploration 60 takes a look at them and similar class templates. But for now, auto_ptr is all we have in the standard, so it behooves us to understand the tools we have, and how best to use them.

# Exceptions and Constructors

Even without auto_ptr, C++ guarantees one level of exception-safety when constructing an object: if a constructor throws an exception, the compiler automatically cleans up base-class portions of the incompletely constructed object. The new expression never completes, so it never returns a pointer to an incomplete object. On the other hand, if the constructor man-aged to initialize some data members but not all, the pointer-type data members will be stranded. Listing 58-6 demonstrates how constructors and exceptions interact.

**Listing 58-6.** *Demonstrating Constructors That Throw Exceptions*

```
#include <iostream>
#include <ostream>

class see_me
{
public:
  see_me(int x) : x_(x) { std::cout <<  "see_me(" << x_ << ")\n"; }
  ~see_me()             { std::cout << "~see_me(" << x_ << ")\n"; }
private:
  int x_;
};

class bomb : public see_me
{
public:
  bomb() : see_me(1), a_(new see_me(2)) { throw 0; }
  ~bomb() {
    delete a_;
  }
```

```
private:
  see_me *a_;
};

int main()
{
  bomb *b(0);
  try {
    b = new bomb;
  } catch(int) {
    if (b == 0)
      std::cout << "b is null\n";
  }
}
```

**Predict the output from this program:**

_____

_____

_____

_____

_____

**Run the program. What is the actual output?**

_____

_____

_____

_____

_____

**Explain your observations.**

_____

_____

_____

_____

_____

The bomb class throws an exception in its constructor. It derives from see_me and has an additional member of type pointer to see_me. The see_me class lets you see the constructors and destructors, so you can see that the data member, see_me(2), is constructed, but never destroyed, which indicates a memory leak. The bomb destructor never runs because the bomb constructor never finishes. Therefore, a_ is never cleaned up. On the other hand, see_me(1) is cleaned up because the base class is automatically cleaned up if a derived-class constructor throws an exception.

The main() function catches the exception and recognizes that the b variable was never assigned. Thus, there's nothing for the main() function to clean up.

What happens if you were to use auto_ptr in the bomb class? **Try and see. What happens?**

_____

_____

_____

Listing 58-7 shows the new program.

**Listing 58-7.** *Using auto_ptr in bomb*

```cpp
#include <iostream>
#include <memory>
#include <ostream>

class see_me
{
public:
  see_me(int x) : x_(x) { std::cout <<  "see_me(" << x_ << ")\n"; }
  ~see_me()              { std::cout << "~see_me(" << x_ << ")\n"; }
private:
  int x_;
};

class bomb : public see_me
{
public:
  bomb() : see_me(1), a_(new see_me(2)) { throw 0; }
  ~bomb() {}
private:
  std::auto_ptr<see_me> a_;
};

int main()
{
  bomb *b(0);
  try {
    b = new bomb;
  } catch(int) {
    if (b == 0)
      std::cout << "b is null\n";
  }
}
```

Notice that all the see_me objects are now properly destroyed. Even though the constructor does not finish before throwing an exception, any data members that have been constructed will be destroyed. Thus, auto_ptr objects are cleaned up. Ta da! Mission accomplished!

Or is it? Even with auto_ptr, you must still be cautious. Consider the program in Listing 58-8.

**Listing 58-8.** *Mystery Program That Uses auto_ptr*

```
#include <iostream>
#include <memory>
#include <ostream>

class mystery
{
public:
  mystery() {}
  mystery(mystery const&) { throw "oops"; }
};

class demo
{
public:
  demo(int* x, mystery m, int* y) : x_(x), m_(m), y_(y) {}
  int x() const { return *x_; }
  int y() const { return *y_; }
private:
  demo(demo const&);              // do not implement
  void operator=(demo const&);    // do not implement
  std::auto_ptr<int> x_;
  mystery            m_;
  std::auto_ptr<int> y_;
};

int main()
{
  demo d(new int(42), mystery(), new int(24));
  std::cout << d.x() << d.y() << '\n';
}
```

**What's wrong with this program?**

_____

_____

_____

To help you understand what the program does, use a see_me object instead of int. Does that help you understand?

The demo class uses auto_ptr to ensure proper lifetime management of its pointers. It properly keeps the copy constructor and assignment operator private and unimplemented, to avoid any problems they may cause.

The problem is the basic design of the demo constructor. By taking two pointer arguments, it opens the possibility of losing track of these pointers before it can safely tuck them away in their auto_ptr wrappers. The mystery class forces an exception, but in a real program, unexpected exceptions can arise from a variety of less explicit sources.

The simplest solution is to force the caller to use auto_ptr by changing the demo constructor, as demonstrated in the following:

```
demo(std::auto_ptr<int> x, mystery m, std::auto_ptr<int> y)
: x_(x), m_(m), y_(y)
{}
```

Exploration 60 will take a closer look at auto_ptr and some of its friends. But first, let's take a side trip and discover the close connection between old-fashioned, C-style arrays and pointers.

# Old-Fashioned Arrays

Throughout this book, I've used std::vector for arrays. As you discovered in Exploration 51, TR1 extends the standard library with std::tr1::array, and the next revision of the language standard will include std::array. Hidden in the implementation of these types is an old-fashioned, crude, and unsafe style of arrays. This Exploration takes a look at this relic from C, not because I want you to ever use it, but because you may need to read code that uses this language construct, and it will help you to understand how the standard library can implement vector, array, and similar types. You may be surprised to learn that C-style arrays have much in common with pointers.

## C-Style Arrays

C++ inherits from C a primitive form of array. Although an application should never need to use C-style arrays, library authors sometimes need to use them. For example, a typical implementation of std::vector makes use of C-style arrays.

The following shows how you define a C-style array object by specifying the array size in square brackets after the declarator name:

```
int data[10];
```

The array size must be a compile-time constant integer expression. The size must be strictly positive; zero-length arrays are not allowed. The compiler sets aside a single chunk of memory that is large enough to store the entire array. After the array definition, your code can use the array name as an address, not as a pointer. The elements of the array are lvalues, so for instance, you can assign to data[0], but not to data itself.

Use square brackets to refer to elements of the array. The array index must be an integer. If the index is out of bounds, the results are undefined. Now you can see why std::vector implements the square bracket operator the way it does—namely, in imitation of C style arrays.

```
int data[10];
std::vector<int> safer_data(10);
data[0] = 42;            // okay
safer_data[0] = 42;      // okay: just like a C-style array
safer_data.at(0) = 42;   // okay: safer way to access vector elements
data[10] = -1;           // error: undefined behavior
safer_data[10] = -1;     // error: also undefined behavior
safer_data.at(10) = -1;  // okay: throws an exception
```

For the moment, C-style arrays offer one key advantage over vectors: you can initialize a C-style array, even letting the compiler count the number of elements in the array. To initialize an array, use an equal sign, followed by a curly brace-delimited list of array elements, separated by commas.

```
int data[10] = { 1, 2, 3, 4, 5, 6, 7, 8, 9, 10 };
point corners[2] = { point(0, 1), point(10, 20) };
```

When you provide initial values, you can omit the array size; the compiler uses the number of initializers as the array size.

```
int data[] = { 1, 2, 3, 4, 5 }; // just like data[5]
```

If you provide an array size, you can omit trailing elements, in which case the compiler zero-initializes the remaining elements.

```
int values[5] = { 3, 2, 1 }; // like { 3, 2, 1, 0, 0 }
int data[10] = { }; // initialize entire array to zero
```

The next revision to the C++ standard, however, will permit the initialization of the standard containers in a similar fashion. (See the sidebar in Exploration 10.)

# Array Limitations

One of the key limitations to a C-style array is that the array doesn't know its own size. The compiler knows the size when it compiles the array definition, but the size is not stored with the array itself, so most uses of the array are not aware of the array size.

If you declare an array type as a function parameter, something strange happens: the compiler ignores the size and treats the array type as a pointer type. In other words, when used as a function parameter, int x[10] means exactly the same thing as int x[1], int x[100000000], and int* x. In practical terms, this means the function has no idea what the array size is. The function sees only a pointer to the start of the array. Thus, functions that take a C-style array as an argument typically have an additional argument to pass the array size, as shown in Listing 59-1.

**Listing 59-1.** *Array Type in Function Parameters*

```
#include <iostream>
#include <ostream>

int sum(int* array, int size);

int main()
{
  int data[5] = { 1, 2, 3, 4, 5 };
  std::cout << sum(data, 5) << '\n';
}
```

```
int sum(int array[], int size)
{
  int result(0);
  while (size-- != 0)
    result += array[size];
  return result;
}
```

Because an array does not store its size, an extern declaration (Exploration 39) of an array doesn't keep track of the array size. Thus, the definition of the array specifies the size, but extern declarations can omit the size. Although you may read code that omits the size, I recommend specifying the size in the extern declaration (which must match the size in the definition), as follows:

```
extern int data[42];
```

However, unlike function arguments and parameters, no conversions take place with extern objects. Arrays are arrays and pointers are pointers. If the extern declaration does not match the object's definition, the results are undefined. The best way to avoid problems is to make the extern declaration match the definition as closely as possible. Be sure to #include the header file that contains the extern declarations in the source file that contains the definitions. In this manner, the compiler checks that the declarations and definitions match.

Another limitation of arrays is that a function cannot return an array. If you need to return a sequence of objects, store them in a container object. Even better is to pass a container by reference, and let the function fill in the values. This way you avoid making extra copies of the container.

```
void get_a_whole_bunch_of_things(std::vector<thing>& fill_me_in);
```

# Dynamically Allocating an Array

A new expression can allocate an array, or more precisely, it allocates one or more contiguous values, invokes the default constructor for each element, and returns the address of the first one. (Remember that default-initializing a built-in type, such as int, leaves the value uninitialized.) Like passing an array to a function, all you get from new is a pointer. It is up to you to keep track of the size. Pass the size in square brackets after the type.

```
int* ptr(new int[10]);
ptr[0] = 9;
ptr[9] = 0;
```

To free the memory, use the delete[] operator. The square brackets are required. Do not pass the size.

```
delete[] ptr;
```

If you allocate a scalar value with new (no square brackets), you must delete the memory with plain delete (no square brackets). If you allocate an array (even if the size is one), delete the memory with delete[]. You cannot mix the array-style new with a non-array delete or vice versa. Because the delete operator and delete[] operator both take a plain pointer as an operand, the compiler cannot, in general, detect errors. A good library can detect errors and report them at runtime, but the standard provides no guarantee.

The auto_ptr type uses plain delete, so you cannot use it to manage dynamically allocated arrays. (But the next Exploration has a few hints if you need to manage one.)

The best way to avoid mismatches between new, new[], delete, and delete[] is to avoid the array forms entirely. Use plain new and delete for single items, and use a vector if you need an array. The advantage of using vector instead of new[] and delete[] is that the vector automatically frees all of its memory when it is destroyed.

**Why should you use std::vector instead of C-style arrays?**

_____

_____

_____

_____

I can think of many reasons. You can pass a vector to a function, return a vector from a function, and use the vector's many member functions for greater functionality and safety. For example, use the at() member function instead of square brackets for safe indexing. Use the size() member function to learn how many elements are in the vector.

**In what way are C-style arrays superior to std::vector?**

_____

_____

_____

_____

When performance is at a premium, std::vector has greater overhead than a C-style array. Sometimes you don't need the array to grow at runtime, and you don't want to pay the performance penalty for that flexibility. Another advantage of a C-style array is that you can directly initialize its elements when you define the array object.

---

**■Note**  The next revision to the standard will let you directly initialize the contents of a vector the way you can initialize a C-style array. For more information on this, go back and read the sidebar in Exploration 10.

---

The C++ standardization committee introduced the array class template in TR1 (see Exploration 51 for more information about Technical Report 1) and plan to include std::array in the next revision of the standard to address these shortcomings. The std::tr1::array or std::arrray class template has the advanced features of std::vector with the performance advantages of a C-style array. If you ever find yourself wishing for a C-style array, you should use tr1::array or std::array instead (whichever one is most readily available to you).

# Multi-Dimensional Arrays

One situation in which you might need to use C-style arrays is when you must work in multiple dimensions. In C++, as in C, a multi-dimensional array is an array of arrays. Thus, define a variable as a 3 × 4 matrix as follows:

```
double matrix[3][4];
```

Read this declaration the way you would any other. Start with the name and work your way from inside to outside: matrix is an array with 3 elements. Each element is an array of 4 elements of type double. Thus, C++ arrays are column-major—that is, the column (right-most) index varies fastest. So another way to define matrix is as follows:

```
typedef double row[4];
row matrix[3];
```

When you pass a matrix to a function, only the leftmost array is converted to a pointer. Thus, if you were to pass matrix to a function, you must declare the function parameter as a pointer to an array of 4 doubles.

```
double sum(double arg[][4]);
```

or

```
double sum(double *arg[4]);
```

or

```
double sum(row* arg);
```

To refer to elements of the matrix, use a separate subscript operator for each index, as follows:

```
void initialize(double matrix[][4], int num_rows)
{
   for (int i = 0; i != num_rows; ++i)
      for (int j = 0; j != 4; ++j)
         matrix[i][j] = 1.0;
}
```

You can also refer to an entire row: matrix[2] returns the address of the last row of the matrix, which has type double[4], which means it is the address of the first element of a 4-element array of double.

# C-Style Strings

Another legacy type that C++ inherits from C is the C-style string, which is little more than a C-style array of char. (A wide C-style string is a C-style array of wchar_t. Everything in this chapter applies equally to wide strings and wchar_t, but mentions only char for the sake of simplicity.) A string literal in C++ is a const array of char. The size of the array is the number of characters in the literal, plus one. The compiler automatically appends the character with value zero ('\0') to the end of the array, as a marker for the end of the string. (Remember that the array does not store the size, so the trailing zero-valued character is the only way to identify the end of the string, and therefore, the length of the string.) The zero-value character is also called a *null character*. In spite of the unfortunate collision of terminology, null characters have nothing to do with null pointers (Exploration 57).

The std::string class has a constructor to construct a C++ string from a C character pointer. Often, the compiler is able to call this constructor automatically, so you can usually use a string literal anywhere that calls for std::string.

Should you ever need to work with C-style strings directly, remember that a string literal contains const elements. A frequent mistake is to treat a string literal as an array of char, not an array of const char. Although you generally cannot know the amount of memory that a character array occupies, you can discover the number of characters by calling the std::strlen function (declared in <cstring>, along with several other functions that are useful for working with C-style strings), passing the start of the character array as an argument.

# Command-Line Arguments

The one and only time you should use a C-style array is to access command-line arguments that the host environment passes to a program when the main() function begins. For historic reasons, the command-line arguments are passed as a C-style array of pointers to C-style character strings. Thus, you can choose to write the main() function as a function of no arguments or a function of two arguments: an int for the number of command-line arguments and a pointer to the first element of an array of pointers to the individual command line arguments, each as an array of char. Listing 59-2 shows an example of *echo*, which echoes command-line arguments to the standard output. Note that the first command-line argument is the program name or path to the program's executable file (the details are defined by the implementation). Note also that std::ostream knows how to print a C-style character pointer.

**Listing 59-2.** *Echoing Command-Line Arguments*

```cpp
#include <iostream>
#include <ostream>

int main(int argc, char* argv[])
{
  char const* separator("");
  while (--argc != 0)
  {
    std::cout << separator << *++argv;
    separator = " ";
  }
}
```

The names argc and argv are conventional, not required. As with any other function parameters, you are free to pick any names you want. The second argument is of type pointer-to-pointer-to-char, and is often written as char* argv[] to emphasize the point that it is an array of char* values; although some programmers also use char** argv, which means the same thing.

The size of the argv array is argc + 1 because its last element is a null pointer, after all the command-line arguments. Thus, some programs loop through command line arguments by counting and comparing with argc, and others loop through argv, until reaching a null pointer.

**Write a program that takes two command-line arguments: an input file and an output file. The program copies the contents of the input file to the output file.** Compare your solution with mine, shown in Listing 59-3.

**Listing 59-3.** *Copying a File Named on the Command Line*

```cpp
#include <cstdio>
#include <cstdlib>
#include <fstream>
#include <iostream>
#include <istream>
#include <ostream>

int main(int argc, char* argv[])
{
  if (argc != 3)
  {
    std::cerr << "usage: " << argv[0] << " INPUT OUTPUT\n";
    return EXIT_FAILURE;
  }
  std::ifstream input(argv[1]);
  if (not input)
  {
    std::perror(argv[1]);
    return EXIT_FAILURE;
  }
  std::ofstream output(argv[2]);
  if (not output)
  {
    std::perror(argv[2]);
    return EXIT_FAILURE;
  }

  input.exceptions(input.badbit);    // throw for serious errors
  output.exceptions(output.failbit); // throw for any error

  try
  {
    // Lots of ways to copy: use std::copy, use a loop to read & write
    // The following is a little-known technique that is probably fastest.
    output << input.rdbuf();
    output.close();
    input.close();
  }
```

```
    catch (std::ios_base::failure const& ex)
    {
      std::cerr << "Can't copy " << argv[1] << " to " << argv[2] << ": " <<
                   ex.what() << '\n';
      return EXIT_FAILURE;
    }
}
```

# Pointer Arithmetic

An unusual feature of C++ pointers (inherited from C) is that you can perform addition and subtraction on pointers. In ordinary usage, these operations work only on pointers that point into arrays. Specifically, you can add or subtract integers and pointers, and you can subtract two pointers to get an integer. You can also compare two pointers using relational operators (less than, greater than, etc.). This section explores what these operations mean.

Briefly, a pointer can point to any object in an array. Add an integer to a pointer to obtain the address of an element of the array. For example, array + 2 points to the third element of the array: the element at index 2. You are allowed to form a pointer to any position in the array, including the position one-past-the-end. Given a pointer into the array, subtract an integer to obtain the address of an element earlier in the array. You are not allowed to form an address that precedes the first element of the array.

Subtract two pointers to obtain the number of array elements that separate them. They must be pointers that point into the same array. When you compare two pointers using relational operators, a pointer a is "less than" a pointer b if a and b both point to the same array and a comes earlier in the array than b.

Ordinarily, you have no reason to use the relational operators on pointers that are not in the same array. But you can use pointers as keys in sets and maps, and these types need to compare pointers to put the keys in order. The std::set and std::map templates use std::less to compare keys (Exploration 48), and std::less uses the < operator. The details are specific to the implementation, but the standard requires std::less to work with all pointers, thereby ensuring that sets and maps work properly when you use pointers as keys.

The compiler and library are not required to enforce the rule that pointers must point to the same array or stay confined to legal indices. Some compilers might try to give you a few warnings, but in general, the compiler cannot tell whether your program follows all the rules. If your program does not follow the rules, it enters the twilight zone of undefined behavior. That's what makes pointers so dangerous: it's easy to fall into undefined behavior territory.

The most common use for pointer arithmetic is to advance through the elements of an array by marching a pointer from the beginning of the array to the end, instead of using an array index. Listing 59-4 illustrates this idiom as well as pointer subtraction by showing one possible implementation of the standard std::strlen function, which returns the length of a C-style string.

**Listing 59-4.** *Using Pointer Arithmetic to Determine the Length of a C String*

```
#include <cstring>

std::size_t my_std_strlen(char const* str)
{
   char const* start(str);      // remember the start of the string
   while (*str != 0)            // while not at the end of the string
      ++str;                    // advance to the next character
   return str - start;          // compute string length by subtracting pointers
}
```

Pointer arithmetic is error-prone, dangerous, and I recommend avoiding it. Instead of C strings, for example, use `std::string`. Instead of C-style arrays, use `std::vector`, `std::tr1::array`, or `std::array`.

However, pointer arithmetic is a common idiom in C++ programs, and therefore unavoidable. Pointer arithmetic is especially prevalent in library implementations. For example, I can almost guarantee that it is used in your library's implementation of the `string`, `vector`, and `array` class templates. Thus, library authors need to be especially vigilant against errors that are difficult or impossible for the compiler to detect, but that effort pays off by making a safer interface available to all other developers.

In the interest of making pointers safer, C++ lets you define a class that looks, acts, and smells like a pointer type, but with bonus features, such as additional checks and safety. These so-called smart pointers are the subjects of the next Exploration.

# EXPLORATION 60

■■■

# Smart Pointers

The std::auto_ptr class template is an example of a so-called *smart pointer*. A smart pointer behaves much like any other pointer, but with extra features and functionality. This Exploration takes a closer look at auto_ptr and other smart pointers.

## Revisiting auto_ptr

Exploration 58 introduced auto_ptr as a way to manage dynamically allocated objects. The auto_ptr class template overloads the dereference (*) and member access (->) operators, which lets you use an auto_ptr object the same way you would use a pointer. At the same time, it extends the behavior of an ordinary pointer such that when the auto_ptr object is destroyed, it automatically deletes the pointer it holds. That's why auto_ptr is called a *smart pointer*—it's just like an ordinary pointer, only smarter. Using auto_ptr helps ensure that memory is properly managed, even in the face of unexpected exceptions.

### C++ REPLACEMENT FOR auto_ptr

The next major revision to the C++ standard deprecates auto_ptr. Instead of auto_ptr, you will have a choice of several smart pointers that serve a variety of purposes. If you are using a compiler and library that implement the new standard, please skip this section, and continue with Copyable Smart Pointers. That section describes shared_ptr, which is one of the smart pointers in the new standard and is much more useful than auto_ptr. See an updated language reference to learn about the other smart pointers.

When used properly, the key feature of auto_ptr is that exactly one auto_ptr object owns a particular pointer. You can copy and assign auto_ptr objects; each time you do, the target of the copy or assignment becomes the new owner of the pointer.

You can also force an auto_ptr to give up ownership of its pointer by calling the release() member function. The release() function returns the raw pointer, as displayed in the following:

```
std::auto_ptr<int> ap(new int(42));
int* ip(ap.release());
delete ip;
```

Call the `reset` member function to tell an `auto_ptr` to take over a different pointer. The `auto_ptr` object deletes its old pointer and takes control of the new pointer (assuming the two pointer values are different). With no argument, `reset()` sets the `auto_ptr` to a null pointer.

```
std::auto_ptr<int> ap(new int(42));
ap.reset(new int(10)); // deletes the pointer to 42
ap.reset();            // deletes the pointer to 10
```

The `get()` member function retrieves the raw pointer without affecting the `auto_ptr`'s ownership. The `auto_ptr` template also overloads the dereference (\*) and member (->) operators so they work the way they do with ordinary pointers. These functions do not affect ownership of the pointer.

```
std::auto_ptr<rational> rp(new rational(420, 10));
int n(rp->numerator());
rational r(*rp);
rational *raw_ptr(rp.get());
```

Because copying an `auto_ptr` transfers ownership, the copy constructor must be able to modify its argument, the source of the copy. This is unconventional and an important point to remember. Usually, a copy constructor declares its parameter as a reference to `const`, but `auto_ptr` requires a non-const reference. This has a number of ramifications that you may find surprising. Consider, for example, Listing 60-1.

**Listing 60-1.** *Copying an auto_ptr Object (Or Not)*

```
#include <memory>

std::auto_ptr<int> does_this_work(std::auto_ptr<int> const& x)
{
  std::auto_ptr<int> y(x);
  return y;
}

int main()
{
  std::auto_ptr<int> a, b;
  a.reset(new int(42));
  b = does_this_work(a);
}
```

Before you run this program, **predict whether you think it will compile and run successfully:** _____. **Try it.** The does_this_work function never assigns to x or otherwise appears to modify it. At first glance, declaring x as a reference to `const` is perfectly normal and acceptable, but the compiler complains anyway.

Remember that copying an `auto_ptr` object transfers ownership of the pointer, so it must modify the source of the copy to tell it to release its pointer. Thus, copying x to y fails because x is const. The proper way to use `auto_ptr` is to pass it by value. Ironically, passing it by value causes the argument to be modified. Ordinarily, passing an object by value prevents the argument from being modified, but `auto_ptr` is special because of its unusual copy constructor.

The implementation is beyond the scope of this book, but you can use it without knowing all the details of its implementation. Take a look at Listing 60-2.

**Listing 60-2.** *The Correct Way to Copy* auto_ptr *Objects*

```
#include <memory>

std::auto_ptr<int> does_this_work(std::auto_ptr<int> x)
{
  std::auto_ptr<int> y(x);
  return y;
}

int main()
{
  std::auto_ptr<int> a, b;
  a.reset(new int(42));
  b = does_this_work(a);
}
```

The new program transfers ownership from a in main to x in does_this_work, then to y, and then to b. When b is destroyed at the end of main, the pointer is deleted.

If you use auto_ptr for data members in a class, you must remember that the compiler imposes the same restrictions on your class. The compiler generates a copy constructor, but because auto_ptr's own copy constructor cannot copy a const source, neither can your class's copy constructor.

Thus, using auto_ptr may free you from thinking about your class's destructor, but you are not excused from thinking about the copy constructor and assignment operators. This is a minor tweak to the guideline that if you need to deal with one, you must deal with all three. The same solutions are available, such as implementing a deep copy, or declaring the special member functions private and not implementing them at all.

One last restriction as a consequence of auto_ptr's semantics is that you cannot store auto_ptr objects in a standard container. The standard containers have few restrictions on the types of objects you can store, but one restriction is absolute: the container must be free to make copies and assign objects such that the source and target of a copy or assignment are equal. That isn't true for auto_ptr, so you can't store auto_ptr objects in a container.

With all these restrictions, it's a wonder that auto_ptr has any utility at all. Indeed, some C++ programmers never use auto_ptr. Instead, they use other smart pointers that have fewer restrictions, such as the std::tr1::shared_ptr class template, which is the subject of the next section.

# Copyable Smart Pointers

A common need is to store pointers in a container, but instead of storing raw pointers, you often want to store smart pointers. In particular, when you erase a pointer from the container, it would be nice to delete the object, too. Calling clear() on the container to erase its entire contents should delete every pointer that it stores. One way to do this is to write template specializations for all the standard containers so that when the element type is a pointer, the container takes ownership of the pointers stored in the container. That's a lot of work, however. You would need to rewrite all the containers in their entirety.

A better solution is to write a smart pointer class that can be stored in a container. The Boost project includes several different smart pointers. This section discusses one of those types, shared_ptr, which the C++ committee accepted into TR1 and the next revision of the C++ standard.

The boost::shared_ptr, std::tr1::shared_ptr, or std::shared_ptr class template is similar in spirit to auto_ptr. Once you deliver a pointer to a shared_ptr, the shared_ptr object owns that pointer. When the shared_ptr object is destroyed, it will delete the pointer. The difference between shared_ptr and auto_ptr is that you can freely copy and assign shared_ptr objects with normal semantics. In other words, after an assignment, the source and target shared_ptrs point to the same object. The shared_ptr object keeps a reference count, so assignment merely increments the reference count without needing to transfer ownership. When a shared_ptr object is destroyed, it decrements the reference count; when the count reaches zero, the pointer is deleted. Thus, you can make as many copies as you like, store shared_ptr objects in a container, pass them to functions, return them from functions, copy them, assign them, and carry on to your heart's content. Each copy increments the reference count; when a copy is destroyed, the reference count decrements. When the count becomes zero, that means no more shared_ptr objects refer to the pointer, so the pointer is deleted. It's that simple. Listing 60-3 shows that copying shared_ptr works in ways that don't work with auto_ptr.

**Listing 60-3.** *Working with shared_ptr*

```
#include <iostream>
#include <memory>
#include <ostream>
#include <vector>

class see_me
{
public:
  see_me(int x) : x_(x) { std::cout <<  "see_me(" << x_ << ")\n"; }
  ~see_me()             { std::cout << "~see_me(" << x_ << ")\n"; }
  int value() const     { return x_; }
private:
  int x_;
};

std::tr1::shared_ptr<see_me> does_this_work(std::tr1::shared_ptr<see_me> x)
{
  std::tr1::shared_ptr<see_me> y(x);
  return y;
}

int main()
{
  std::tr1::shared_ptr<see_me> a, b;
  a.reset(new see_me(42));
```

```
  b = does_this_work(a);
  std::vector<std::tr1::shared_ptr<see_me> > v;
  v.push_back(a);
  v.push_back(b);
}
```

Using shared_ptr, you can reimplement the program from Listing 56-5. The old program used the artifact map to manage the lifetime of all artifacts. Although convenient, there is no reason to tie artifacts to this map because the map is used only for parsing. In a real program, most of its work lies in the actual building of targets, not parsing the input. All the parsing objects should be freed and long gone by the time the program is building targets.

**Rewrite the artifact-lookup portion of Listing 56-5 to allocate artifact objects dynamically, using shared_ptr throughout to refer to artifact pointers.** See Listing 60-4 for my solution.

**Listing 60-4.** *Using Smart Pointers to Manage Artifacts*

```
std::map<std::string, std::tr1::shared_ptr<artifact> > artifacts;

std::tr1::shared_ptr<artifact>
lookup_artifact(std::string const& name)
{
  std::tr1::shared_ptr<artifact> a(artifacts[name]);
  if (a.get() == 0)
  {
    a.reset(new artifact(name));
    artifacts[name] = a;
  }
  return a;
}
```

Once you have shared_ptr, you have no reason to use auto_ptr. However, if your work environment does not permit third-party libraries, or you have other reasons you cannot use Boost or TR1, auto_ptr is better than nothing.

# Smart Arrays

Recall from Exploration 59 that allocating a single object is completely different from allocating an array of objects. Thus, smart pointers must also distinguish between a smart pointer to a single object and a smart pointer to an array of objects. In the C++ standard, the distinction is well defined: auto_ptr and shared_ptr work only with single objects, not arrays. The C++ standard, including TR1, has no smart array pointers.

---

■**Caution**  Do not use the address of an array when constructing an auto_ptr or a shared_ptr.

---

So what if you need to manage an array of objects? Put on your thinking cap. You want automatic management of the lifetime of an array of objects. You may not know the number of objects until runtime. When the container object is destroyed, you want it to destroy all the objects it contains. Ring any bells? Sound familiar? **Which type satisfies these requirements?** _____ How about `std::vector`? If you don't want to incur the overhead of vector—perhaps because your array has a known, fixed size—you can use `shared_ptr` with `std::tr1::array` (see Exploration 51 for a refresher).

That's why the standard library does not have `auto_array` or `shared_array` or anything like that. If you really want to use `shared_array`, the Boost project provides `shared_array` as a companion to `shared_ptr`, but you don't need it, and I suggest you not bother with it.

# Pimpls

No, that's not a spelling error. Although programmers have spoken for years about pimples and warts in their programs, often referring to unsightly but unavoidable bits of code, Herb Sutter combined the name "pointer-to-implementation" with these pimples to come up with the pimpl idiom.

In short, a pimpl is a class that hides implementation details in an implementation class, and the public interface object holds only a pointer to that implementation object. Instead of forcing the user of your class to allocate and deallocate objects, manage pointers, and keep track of object lifetimes, you can expose a class that is easier to use. Specifically, the user can treat instances of the class as values, in the manner of `int` and other built-in types.

The pimpl wrapper manages the lifetime of the pimpl object. It typically implements the big three member functions: copy constructor, assignment operator, and destructor. It delegates most of its other member functions to the pimpl object. The user of the wrapper never needs to be concerned with any of this.

Thus, we will rewrite the `artifact` class so it wraps a pimpl—that is, a pointer to an `artifact_impl` class. The `artifact_impl` class will do the real work, and artifact will merely forward all functions through its pimpl. The language feature that makes pimpls possible is declaring a class name without providing a definition of the class, as illustrated by the following:

```
class artifact_impl;
```

This class declaration, often called a *forward declaration*, informs the compiler that `artifact_impl` is the name of a class. The declaration doesn't provide the compiler with anything more about the class, so the class type is *incomplete*. You face a number of restrictions in what you can do with an incomplete type. In particular, you cannot define any objects or data members of that type, nor can you use an incomplete class as a function parameter or return type. You cannot refer to any members of an incomplete class. But you can define objects, data members, function parameters, and return types that are pointers or references to the type. In particular, you can use a pointer to `artifact_impl` in the `artifact` class.

A normal class definition is a *complete* type definition. You can mix forward declarations with class definitions of the same class name. A common pattern is for a header, such as *artifact.hpp*, to declare a forward declaration; a source file then fills in the complete class definition.

The definition of the `artifact` class, therefore, can have a data member that is a pointer to the `artifact_impl` class, even though the compiler knows only that `artifact_impl` is a class, but doesn't know any details about it. This means the *artifact.hpp* header file is independent of the implementation of artifact_impl. The implementation details are tucked away in a separate file, and the rest of your program can make use of the artifact class completely insulated from artifact_impl. In large projects, this kind of barrier is tremendously important.

Writing the *artifact.hpp* header is not difficult. Start with a forward declaration of artifact_impl. In the artifact class, the declarations of the member functions are the same as in the original class. Change the data members to a single pointer to artifact_impl. Finally, overload operator< for two artifact objects. Implement the comparison by comparing names. Read Listing 60-5 to see one possible implementation of this class.

**Listing 60-5.** *Defining an artifact Pimpl Wrapper Class*

```
#ifndef ARTIFACT_HPP_
#define ARTIFACT_HPP_

#include <ctime>
#include <string>

class artifact_impl;

class artifact
{
public:
  artifact();
  artifact(std::string const& name);
  artifact(artifact const& a);
  ~artifact();

  artifact& operator=(artifact const& a);

  std::string const& name()      const;
  std::time_t        mod_time() const;
  std::string        expand(std::string str) const;

  void build();
  std::time_t get_mod_time();

  void store_variable(std::string const& name, std::string const& value);

private:
  artifact_impl* pimpl_;
};

bool operator<(artifact const& a, artifact const& b)
{
  return a.name() < b.name();
}

#endif // ARTIFACT_HPP_
```

The header defines the artifact class without any mention of artifact_impl, except for the pimpl_ data member.

The next step is to write the source file, *artifact.cpp*. This is where the compiler needs the full definition of the artifact_impl class, thus making artifact_impl a *complete class*, so include the *artifact_impl.hpp* header. The artifact class doesn't do much on its own. Instead, it just delegates every action to the artifact_impl class. The only interesting code is in the constructor, destructor, and assignment operator. They need to manage the pimpl_ pointer, which they do by manipulating a reference count.

If you have TR1, Boost, or the new C++ revision, you can use std::tr1::shared_ptr, boost::shared_ptr, or std::shared_ptr to define the pimpl_ member, as illustrated in the following:

```
shared_ptr<artifact_impl> pimpl_;
```

In this case, you don't need to manipulate the reference count because shared_ptr does that for you. This example sticks with the current standard and nothing but the standard, so artifact_impl manages its own reference count. We'll save the details until it's time to write artifact_impl. Right now, you need to know only that the copy constructor increments the reference count, and the destructor decrements it. The assignment operator increments the count of the source and decrements the count of the assignment target. Be sure to get the order correct: increment the source reference count first. You'll understand why this is important later in this section when we write *artifact_impl.cpp*. See the details in Listing 60-6.

**Listing 60-6.** *Implementing the artifact Class*

```
#include "artifact.hpp"
#include "artifact_impl.hpp"

artifact::artifact() : pimpl_(new artifact_impl()) {}

artifact::artifact(std::string const& name)
: pimpl_(new artifact_impl(name))
{}

artifact::artifact(artifact const& a)
: pimpl_(a.pimpl_)
{
   pimpl_->add_ref();
}

artifact::~artifact()
{
   pimpl_->delete_ref();
}

artifact& artifact::operator=(artifact const& a)
{
   a.pimpl_->add_ref();
   pimpl_->delete_ref();
```

```
    pimpl_ = a.pimpl_;
    return *this;
}

std::string const& artifact::name()
const
{
    return pimpl_->name();
}

std::time_t artifact::mod_time()
const
{
    return pimpl_->mod_time();
}

std::string artifact::expand(std::string str)
const
{
    return pimpl_->expand(str);
}

void artifact::build()
{
    pimpl_->build();
}

std::time_t artifact::get_mod_time()
{
    return pimpl_->get_mod_time();
}

void artifact::store_variable(std::string const& name, std::string const& value)
{
    pimpl_->store_variable(name, value);
}
```

You define the artifact_impl class in the *artifact_impl.hpp* header. This class looks similar to the original artifact class, but with the addition of a reference count and member functions to manage the count. Listing 60-7 shows the artifact_impl class definition.

**Listing 60-7.** *Defining the Artifact Implementation Class*

```
#ifndef ARTIFACT_IMPL_HPP_
#define ARTIFACT_IMPL_HPP_

#include <cstdlib>
#include <ctime>
#include <string>
#include "variables.hpp"

class artifact_impl
{
public:
  artifact_impl();
  artifact_impl(std::string const& name);  ~artifact_impl();

  void add_ref();
  void delete_ref();

  std::string const& name()      const { return name_; }
  std::time_t        mod_time() const { return mod_time_; }

  std::string        expand(std::string str) const;
  void               build();
  std::time_t        get_mod_time();
  void store_variable(std::string const& name, std::string const& value);
private:
  std::size_t ref_count_;
  std::string name_;
  std::time_t mod_time_;
  variable_map* variables_;
};

#endif // ARTIFACT_IMPL_HPP_
```

The artifact_impl class is unsurprising. You already know you need add_ref() and delete_ref(). The reference count is just an integer. I use std::size_t because that's a convenient typedef that the C++ standard defines primarily for sizes, but also for counts, such as reference counts. The fun stuff lies in the implementation, as presented in Listing 60-8.

**Listing 60-8.** *The artifact_impl.cpp Source File*

```
artifact_impl::artifact_impl()
: ref_count_(1), name_(), mod_time_(static_cast<time_t>(-1)), variables_(0)
{}

artifact_impl::artifact_impl(std::string const& name)
: ref_count_(1), name_(name), mod_time_(get_mod_time()), variables_(0)
{}
```

```
artifact_impl::~artifact_impl()
{
    delete variables_;
}

void artifact_impl::add_ref()
{
    ++ref_count_;
}

void artifact_impl::delete_ref()
{
    --ref_count_;
    if (ref_count_ == 0)
      delete this;
}

std::string const& artifact_impl::name()
const
{
    return name_;
}

std::time_t artifact_impl::mod_time()
const
{
    return mod_time_;
}

std::string artifact_impl::expand(std::string str)
const
{
    return ::expand(str, variables_);
}

void artifact_impl::build()
{}

std::time_t artifact_impl::get_mod_time()
{
    // Real programs should get this information from the
    // operating system. This program returns the current time.
    return std::time(0);
}

void artifact_impl::store_variable(std::string const& name,
                                   std::string const& value)
```

```
{
   if (variables_ == 0)
      variables_ = new variable_map;
   (*variables_)[name] = value;
}
```

You can copy the implementation of the original artifact class to artifact_impl then add the reference counting functions.

The add_ref() function is simple: it increments the reference count. The artifact class calls this function when a new artifact class points to a single artifact_impl object.

The delete_ref() member function decrements the reference count. When the count reaches zero, it is a signal that means no artifact objects refer to this artifact_impl any more. The delete_ref function, therefore, deletes the artifact_impl object with delete this. It may seem strange for an object to delete itself, but this is perfectly safe, provided the function does not refer to any data member after deleting this.

Now it's time to rewrite the lookup_artifact function yet again. **Rewrite Listings 57-4, 57-8, and 60-4 to use the new artifact class.** This time, the artifacts map stores artifact objects directly. See Listing 60-9 for one way to rewrite the program.

**Listing 60-9.** *Rewriting the Program to Use the New artifact Value Class*

```
#include <ctime>
#include <iostream>
#include <istream>
#include <ostream>
#include <sstream>
#include <string>

#include "artifact.hpp"
#include "depgraph.hpp"
#include "variables.hpp"

void parse_graph(std::istream& in, dependency_graph& graph)
{
  std::map<std::string, artifact> artifacts;
  std::string line;
  while (std::getline(std::cin, line))
  {
    std::string target_name, dependency_name;
    std::istringstream stream(line);
    if (stream >> target_name >> dependency_name)
    {
      artifact target(artifacts[expand(target_name, 0)]);
      std::string::size_type equal(dependency_name.find('='));
      if (equal == std::string::npos)
      {
        // It's a dependency specification
        artifact dependency(artifacts[target.expand(dependency_name)]);
```

```
          graph.store_dependency(target, dependency);
        }
        else
          // It's a target-specific variable
          target.store_variable(dependency_name.substr(0, equal-1),
                                dependency_name.substr(equal+1));
      }
      else if (not target_name.empty())
      {
        std::string::size_type equal(target_name.find('='));
        if (equal == std::string::npos)
          // Input line has a target with no dependency,
          // so report an error.
          std::cerr << "malformed input: target, " << target_name <<
                       ", must be followed by a dependency name\n";
        else
          global_variables[target_name.substr(0, equal)] =
                                        target_name.substr(equal+1);
      }
      // else ignore blank lines
    }
}

int main()
{
  dependency_graph graph;

  parse_graph(std::cin, graph);

  try {
    // Get the sorted artifacts in reverse order.
    std::vector<artifact> sorted;
    graph.sort(std::back_inserter(sorted));

    // Then print the artifacts in the correct order.
    for (std::vector<artifact>::reverse_iterator it(sorted.rbegin());
         it != sorted.rend();
         ++it)
    {
      std::cout << it->name() << '\n';
    }
  } catch (std::runtime_error const& ex) {
    std::cerr << ex.what() << '\n';
    return EXIT_FAILURE;
  }
}
```

As you can see, the code that uses `artifact` objects is simpler and easier to read. The complexity of managing pointers and lifetimes is pushed down into the `artifact` and `artifact_impl` classes. In this manner, the complexity is kept contained in one place and not spread throughout the application. Because the code that uses `artifact` is now simpler, it is less likely to contain errors. Because the complexity is localized, it is easier to review and test thoroughly. The cost is a little more development time to write two classes instead of one, and a little more maintenance effort because any time a new function is needed in the `artifact` public interface, that function must also be added to `artifact_impl`. In many, many situations, the benefits far outweigh the costs, which is why this idiom is so popular.

# Iterators

Perhaps you've noticed the similarity between iterator syntax and pointer syntax. The C++ committee deliberately designed iterators to mimic pointers. Indeed a pointer meets all the requirements of a random-access iterator, so you can use all the standard algorithms with a C-style array:

```
int data[4];
std::fill(data, data + 4, 42);
```

Thus, iterators are a form of smart pointer. Iterators are especially smart because they come in five distinct flavors (see Exploration 42 for a reminder). Random access iterators are just like pointers; other kinds of iterators have less functionality, so they are smart by being dumb.

Iterators can be just as dangerous as pointers. In their pure form, iterators are nearly as unchecked, wild, and raw as pointers. After all, iterators do not prevent you from advancing too far, from dereferencing an uninitialized iterator, from comparing iterators that point to different containers, etc. The list of unsafe practices with iterators is quite extensive.

Because these errors result in undefined behavior, a library implementor is free to choose any result for each kind of error. In the interest of performance, most libraries do not implement additional safety checks, and push that back on the programmer who can decide on his or her preference for a safety/performance trade-off.

If the programmer prefers safety to performance, some library implementations offer a debugging version that implements a number of safety checks. The debugging version of the standard library can check that iterators do refer to the same container when comparing the iterators, and throw an exception if they do not. An iterator is allowed to check that it is valid before honoring the dereference (*) operator. An iterator can ensure that it does not advance past the end of a container.

Thus, iterators are smart pointers because they can be really, really smart. I highly recommend that you take full advantage of all safety features that your standard library offers. Remove checks one by one only after you have measured the performance of your program and found that one particular check degrades performance significantly, and you have the reviews and tests in place to give you confidence in the less safe code.

This completes your tour of pointers and memory. The next topic gets down into the bits of bytes of C++.

■ ■ ■

# Working with Bits

This Exploration begins a series of Explorations that cover more advanced topics in the C++ type system. The series kicks off with an examination of how to work with individual bits. This Exploration begins with operators that manipulate integers at the bit level then introduces bitfields—a completely different way of working with bits. The final topic is the bitset class template, which lets you work with bitsets of any size.

## Integer As a Set of Bits

A common idiom in computer programming is to treat an integer as a bitmask. The bits can represent a set of small integers, such that a value $n$ is a member of the set if the bit at position $n$ is one; $n$ is not in the set if the corresponding bit is zero. An empty set has the numeric value zero because all bits are zero. To better understand how this works, consider the I/O stream formatting flags (introduced in Exploration 37).

Typically, you use manipulators to set and clear flags. For example, Exploration 16 introduced the skipws and noskipws manipulators. These manipulators set and clear the std::ios_base::skipws flag by calling the setf and unsetf member functions. In other words, the following statement

```
std::cin >> std::noskipws >> read >> std::skipws;
```

is exactly equivalent to

```
std::cin.unsetf(std::ios_base::skipws);
std::cin >> read;
std::cin.setf(std::ios_base::skipws);
```

Other formatting flags include boolalpha (introduced in Exploration 11), showbase (Exploration 54), showpoint (display a decimal point even when it would otherwise be suppressed), and showpos (show a plus sign for positive numbers). Consult a C++ reference to learn about the remaining formatting flags.

A simple implementation of the formatting flags is to store the flags in an int, and assign a specific bit position to each flag. A common way to write flags that you define in this manner is to use hexadecimal notation, as shown in Listing 61-1. Write a hexadecimal integer literal with 0x or 0X, followed by the base 16 value. Letters A through F in upper- or lowercase represent 10 through 15. (The C++ standard does not mandate any particular implementation of the formatting flags. Your library probably implements the formatting flags differently.)

**Listing 61-1.** *An Initial Definition of Formatting Flags*

```
typedef int fmtflags;
fmtflags const showbase  = 0x01;
fmtflags const boolalpha = 0x02;
fmtflags const skipws    = 0x04;
fmtflags const showpoint = 0x08;
fmtflags const showpos   = 0x10;
// etc. for other flags...
```

The next step is to write the setf and unsetf functions. The former function sets specific bits in a flags_ data member (of the std::ios_base class), and the latter clears bits. To set and clear bits, C++ provides some operators that manipulate individual bits in an integer. Collectively, they are called the *bitwise* operators.

The bitwise operators perform the usual arithmetic promotions and conversions (Exploration 23). The operators then perform their operation on successive bits in their arguments. The & operator implements bitwise *and*, the | operator implements bitwise, inclusive *or*; and the ~ operator is a unary operator to perform bitwise complement. Figure 61-1 illustrates the bitwise nature of these operators (using & as an example).

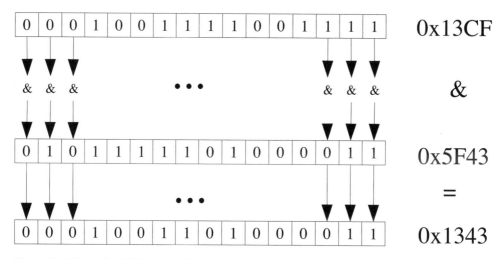

**Figure 61-1.** *How the & (bitwise and) operator works*

**Implement the setf function.** This function takes a single fmtflags argument and sets the specified flags in the flags_ data member. Listing 61-2 shows a simple solution.

**Listing 61-2.** *A Simple Implementation of the setf Member Function*

```
void setf(fmtflags f)
{
    flags_ = flags_ | f;
}
```

The unsetf function is slightly more complicated. It must clear flags, which means setting the corresponding bits to zero. In other words, the argument specifies a bitmask in which each 1 bit means to clear (set to 0) the bit in flags_. **Write the unsetf function.** Compare your solution with Listing 61-3.

**Listing 61-3.** *A Simple Implementation of the unsetf Member Function*

```
void unsetf(fmtflags f)
{
   flags_ = flags_ & ~f;
}
```

Recall from Exploration 44 that various assignment operators combine an arithmetic operator with assignment. Assignment operators also exist for the bitwise functions, so you can write these functions even more succinctly, as shown in Listing 61-4.

**Listing 61-4.** *Using Assignment Operators in the Flags Functions*

```
void setf(fmtflags f)
{
   flags_ |= f;
}

void unsetf(fmtflags f)
{
   flags_ &= ~f;
}
```

Recall from Exploration 54 that the | operator combines I/O mode flags. Now you know that the flags are bits, and the I/O mode is a bitmask. Should the need arise, you can use any of the bitwise operators on I/O modes.

# Bit Masks

Not all the flags are individual bits. The alignment flags, for example, can be left, right, or internal. The floating-point style can be fixed, scientific, or general. To represent three or four values, you need two bits. For these situations, C++ has a two-argument form of the setf function. (Exploration 8). The second argument specifies a mask of which bits to affect; the first argument specifies a mask of bits to set within the field.

Using the same bitwise operators, you can define adjustfield as a two-bit wide bitmask, for instance, 0x300. If both bits are clear, that could mean left-adjustment; one bit set means right-adjustment; the other bit could mean "internal" alignment (align after a sign or 0x in a hexadecimal value). That leaves one more possible value (both bits set), but the standard library defines only three different alignment values.

Listing 61-5 shows one possible implementation of the adjustfield and floatfield masks and their associated values.

**Listing 61-5.** *Declarations for Formatting Fields*

```
fmtflags const adjustfield = 0x300;
fmtflags const left       = 0x000;
fmtflags const right      = 0x100;
fmtflags const internal   = 0x200;
fmtflags const floatfield = 0xC00;
fmtflags const scientific = 0x400;
fmtflags const fixed      = 0x800;
// general does not have a name; its value is zero
```

Thus, to set the alignment to right, one calls setf(right, adjustfield). **Write the two-argument form of the setf function.** Compare your solution with Listing 61-6.

**Listing 61-6.** *Two-Argument Form of the setf Function*

```
void setf(fmtflags flags_to_set, fmtflags field)
{
   flags_ &= ~field;
   flags_ |= flags_to_set;
}
```

One difficulty with defining bitfields in this fashion is that the numeric values can be hard to read unless you've spent a lot of time working with hexadecimal values. Another solution is to use more familiar integers for all flags and fields, and let the computer do the hard work by shifting those values into the correct positions.

# Shifting Bits

Listing 61-7 shows another way to define the formatting fields. They represent the exact same values as shown in Listing 61-1, but they are a little easier to proofread.

**Listing 61-7.** *Using Shift Operators to Define the Formatting Fields*

```
int boolalpha_pos = 0;
int showbase_pos  = 1;
int showpoint_pos = 2;
int showpos_pos   = 3;
int skipws_pos    = 4;
int adjust_pos    = 5;
int adjust_size   = 2;
int float_pos     = 7;
int float_size    = 2;

fmtflags boolalpha  = 1 << boolalpha_pos;
fmtflags showbase   = 1 << showbase_pos;
fmtflags showpos    = 1 << showpos_pos;
fmtflags showpoint  = 1 << showpoint_pos;
fmtflags skipws     = 1 << showpoint_pos;
```

```
fmtflags adjustfield = 3 << adjust_pos;
fmtflags floatfield  = 3 << float_pos;

fmtflags left     = 0 << adjust_pos;
fmtflags right    = 1 << adjust_pos;
fmtflags internal = 2 << adjust_pos;

fmtflags fixed      = 1 << float_pos;
fmtflags scientific = 2 << float_pos;
```

The << operator (which looks just like the output operator) is the left-shift operator. It shifts its left-hand operator (which must be an integer) by the number of bit positions specified by the right-hand operator (also an integer). Vacated bits are filled with zero.

```
1 << 2 == 4
10 << 3 == 80
```

Although this style is more verbose, you can clearly see that the bits are defined with adjacent values. You can also easily see the size of multi-bit masks. If you need to add a new flag, you can do so without the need to recompute any other fields or flags.

**What is the C++ right-shift operator?** _____ That's right: >>, which is also the input operator.

If the right-hand operand is negative, that reverses the direction of the shift. That is, a left shift by a negative amount is the same as right-shifting by a positive amount, and vice versa. You can use the shift operators on integers, but not on floating-point numbers. The right-hand operand cannot be greater than the number of bits in the left-hand operand. (Use the numeric_ limits class template, introduced in Exploration 23, to determine the number of bits in a type, such as int.)

The C++ standard library overloads the shift operators for the I/O stream classes to implement the I/O operators. Thus, the >> and << operators were designed for shifting bits in an integer, and were later usurped for I/O. As a result, the operator precedence is not quite right for I/O. In particular, the shift operators have a higher precedence than the bitwise operators because that makes the most sense for manipulating bits. As a consequence, if for instance you want to print the result of a bitwise operation, you must enclose the expression in parentheses.

```
std::cout << "5 & 3 = " << (5 & 3) << '\n';
```

One caution when using the right-shift operator: the value of the bits that are filled in is implementation-defined. This can be particularly problematic with negative numbers. The value -1 >> 1 may be positive on some implementations and negative on others. Fortunately, C++ has a way to avoid this uncertainty, as the next section explains.

# Safe Shifting with Unsigned Types

Every primitive integer type has a corresponding type that you declare with the unsigned keyword. These types are known—not surprisingly—as *unsigned* types. One key difference between ordinary (or signed) integer types and their unsigned equivalents is that unsigned types always shift in a zero when right-shifting. For this reason, unsigned types are preferable to signed types for implementing bit fields.

```
typedef unsigned int fmtflags;
```

**Write a program to determine how your C++ environment right-shifts negative values. Compare this with shifting unsigned values.** Your program will certainly look different from mine, which is shown in Listing 61-8, but you should be able to recognize the key similarities.

**Listing 61-8.** *Exploring How Negative and Unsigned Values Are Shifted*

```cpp
#include <iostream>
#include <ostream>
#include <string>

template<class T>
void print(std::string const& label, T value)
{
   std::cout << label << " = ";
   std::cout << std::dec << value << " = ";
   std::cout.width(8);
   std::cout.fill('0');
   std::cout << std::hex << std::internal << std::showbase << value << '\n';
}

int main()
{
   int i(~0); // all bits set to 1; on most systems, ~0 == -1
   unsigned int u(~0); // all bits set to 1
   print("int >> 15", i >> 15);
   print("unsigned >> 15", u >> 15);
}
```

On my Linux x86 system, I see the following output:

```
int >> 15 = -1 = 0xffffffff
unsigned >> 15 = 131071 = 0x01ffff
```

which means right-shifting a signed value fills in the vacated bits with copies of the sign bit (a process known as *sign extension*), and that right-shifting an unsigned value works correctly by shifting in zero bits.

## Signed and Unsigned Types

The plain int type is shorthand for signed int. That is, the int type has two sign flavors: signed int and unsigned int, the default being signed int. Similarly, short int is the same as signed short int and long int is the same as signed long int. Thus, you have no reason to use the signed keyword with the integer types.

Like too many rules, however, this one has an exception: signed char. The char type comes in three flavors, not two: char, signed char, and unsigned char. All three types occupy the same amount of space (one byte). The plain char type has the same representation as either signed char or unsigned char, but it remains a distinct type. The choice is left to the compiler; consult your compiler's documentation to learn the equivalent char type for your implementation. Thus, the signed keyword has a use for the signed char type; the most common use for signed char is to represent a tiny, signed integer when conserving memory is important. Use plain char for text, signed char for tiny integers, and unsigned char for tiny bitmasks.

Unfortunately, the I/O stream classes treat signed char and unsigned char as text, not tiny integers or bitmasks. Thus, reading and writing tiny integers is harder than it should be, as demonstrated in the following:

```
signed char real_value(42);
std::cout << static_cast<unsigned>(real_value) << '\n';

int tmp;
std::cin >> tmp;
if (tmp >= std::numeric_limits<signed char>::min() and
    tmp <= std::numeric_limits<signed char>::max())
{
  real_value = static_cast<signed char>(tmp);
  // do something with real_value
}
else // handle the error
```

## Unsigned Literals

If an integer literal does not fit in a signed int, the compiler tries to make it fit into an unsigned int. If that works, the literal's type is unsigned int. If the value is too big for unsigned int, the compiler tries long, and then unsigned long before giving up and issuing an error message. (The next version of the C++ standard will try the long long and unsigned long long types before issuing an error message.)

You can force an integer to be unsigned with the u or U suffix. The U and L suffixes can appear in any order for an unsigned long literal.

```
1234u
4321UL
0xFFFFlu
```

One consequence of this flexibility is that you can't always know the type of an integer literal. For instance, the type of 0xFFFFFFFF might be int on a 64-bit system. On some 32-bit systems, the type might be unsigned int and on others, it might be unsigned long. The moral is to make sure you write code that works correctly regardless of the precise type of an integer literal, which isn't difficult. For example, all the programs and fragments in this book work on any C++ compiler, regardless of the size of an int.

## Type Conversions

A signed type and its unsigned counterpart always occupy the same amount of space. You can use static_cast (Exploration 23) to convert one to the other, or you can let the compiler implicitly perform the conversion, which can result in surprises if you aren't careful. Consider the following example:

```
int i(-1);
unsigned u(i);
std::cout << i << '\n' << u << '\n';
```

This results in the following output on my system:

```
-1
4294967295
```

If you mix signed and unsigned values in an expression (usually a bad idea), the compiler converts the signed value to unsigned, which often results in more surprises. This kind of surprise often arises in comparisons.

**Listing 61-9.** *Mystery Program*

```cpp
#include <algorithm>
#include <iostream>
#include <iterator>
#include <ostream>
#include <vector>

template<class T>
void append(std::vector<T>& data, const T& value, int max_size)
{
  if (data.size() < max_size - 1)
    data.push_back(value);
}

int main()
{
  std::vector<int> data;
  append(data, 10, 3);
  append(data, 20, 2);
  append(data, 30, 1);
  append(data, 40, 0);
  append(data, 50, 0);
  std::copy(data.begin(), data.end(),
            std::ostream_iterator<int>(std::cout, " "));
  std::cout << '\n';
}
```

**Before you run the program, predict what Listing 61-9 will print.**

_____

_____

_____

_____

_____

**Try it. Were you correct?** _____ **Explain what the program does.**

_____

_____

_____

The program succeeds in appending 10 to data because the vector size is zero, which is less than 2. The next call to append, however, does nothing because the vector size is 1, and max_size - 1 is also 1. The next call fails for a similar reason. So why does the next call succeed in appending 40 to data? Because max_size is 0, you might think the comparison would be with -1, but -1 is signed, and data.size() is unsigned. Therefore the compiler converts -1 to unsigned, which is an implementation-defined conversion. On typical workstations, -1 converts to the largest unsigned integer, so the test succeeds.

The first moral of the story is to avoid expressions that mix signed and unsigned values. Your compiler might help you here by issuing warnings when you mix signed and unsigned values. A common source for unsigned values is from the size() member functions in the standard library, which all return an unsigned result. You can reduce the chances for surprises by using one of the standard typedefs for sizes, such as std::size_t (defined in <cstdlib>), which is an implementation-defined unsigned integer type. The standard containers all define a member type, size_type, to represent sizes and similar values for that container. Use these typedefs for your variables when you know you need to store sizes, indices, or counts.

"That's easy!" you say. "Just change the declaration of max_size to std::vector<T>::size_type, and problem solved!" Maybe you can avoid this kind of problem by sticking with the standard member typedefs, such as size_type and difference_type (Exploration 41). Take a gander at Listing 61-10 and see what you think.

**Listing 61-10.** _Another Mystery Program_

```
#include <algorithm>
#include <iostream>
#include <iterator>
#include <ostream>
#include <vector>

/** Return the index of a value in a range.
 * Look for the first occurrence of @p value in the range
 * [<tt>first</tt>,<tt>last</tt>), and return the zero-based
 * index or -1 if @p value is not found.
 * @param first The start of the range to search
```

```
 * @param last One past the end of the range to search
 * @param value The value to search for
 * @return [0, size), such that size == last-first, or -1
 */
template<class InputIter>
typename std::iterator_traits<InputIter>::difference_type
index_of(InputIter first, InputIter last,
        typename std::iterator_traits<InputIter>::value_type const& value)
{
   InputIter iter(std::find(first, last, value));
   if (iter == last)
      return -1;
   else
      return std::distance(first, iter);
}


/** Determine whether the first occurrence of a value in a container is
 * in the last position in the container.
 * @param container Any standard container
 * @param value The value to search for.
 * @return true if @p value is at the last position,
 *         or false if @p value is not found or at any other position.
 */
template<class T>
bool is_last(T const& container, typename T::value_type const& value)
{
    return index_of(container.begin(), container.end(), value) ==
           container.size() - 1;
}

int main()
{
   std::vector<int> data;
   if (is_last(data, 10))
      std::cout << "10 is the last item in data\n";
}
```

**Predict the output before you run the program in Listing 61-10.**

_____

**Try it. What do you actually get?**

_____

Can you spot the conceptual error that I committed? In a standard container, the difference_type typedef is always a signed integral type. Thus, index_of() always returns a signed value. I made the mistake of thinking that the signed value -1 would always be less than any unsigned value because they are always 0 or more. Thus, is_last() would not need to check for an empty container as a special case.

What I failed to take into account is that when a C++ expression mixes signed and unsigned values, the compiler converts the signed value to unsigned. Thus, the signed result from index_of becomes unsigned, and -1 becomes the largest possible unsigned value (on a typical two's complement system, such as most ordinary computers). If the container is empty, size() is zero, and size() - 1 (which the compiler interprets as size() - 1u) is also the largest possible unsigned integer.

If you are fortunate, your compiler issues a warning about comparing signed and unsigned values. That gives you a hint that something is wrong. **Fix the program. Compare your solution with Listing 61-11.**

**Listing 61-11.** *Fixing the Second Mystery Program*

```
#include <algorithm>
#include <iostream>
#include <iterator>
#include <ostream>
#include <vector>

/** Return the index of a value in a range.
 * Look for the first occurrence of @p value in the range
 * [<tt>first</tt>, <tt>last</tt>), and return the zero-based
 * index or -1 if @p value is not found.
 * @param first The start of the range to search
 * @param last One past the end of the range to search
 * @param value The value to search for
 * @return [0, size), such that size == last-first, or -1
 */
template<class InputIter>
typename std::iterator_traits<InputIter>::difference_type
index_of(InputIter first, InputIter last,
         typename std::iterator_traits<InputIter>::value_type const& value)
{
   InputIter iter(std::find(first, last, value));
   if (iter == last)
      return -1;
   else
      return std::distance(first, iter);
}

/** Determine whether the first occurrence of a value in a container is
 * in the last position in the container.
 * @param container Any standard container
 * @param value The value to search for.
 * @return true if @p value is at the last position,
 *          or false if @p value is not found or at any other position.
 */
```

```
template<class T>
bool is_last(T const& container, typename T::value_type const& value)
{
    typename T::difference_type
        pos(index_of(container.begin(), container.end(), value));
    return pos != -1 and pos == container.size() - 1;
}

int main()
{
    std::vector<int> data;
    if (is_last(data, 10))
        std::cout << "10 is the last item in data\n";
}
```

The second moral of the story is not to use unsigned types if you don't need to. Most of the time, signed types work just as well. Just because a type's range of legal values happens to be non-negative is not a reason to use an unsigned type. Doing so just complicates any code that must cooperate with the unsigned type.

---

■**Tip**   When using the standard library, make use of the typedefs and member typedefs that it provides. When you have control over the types, use signed types for all numeric types, including sizes, and reserve the unsigned types for bitmasks. And always be very, very careful every time you write an expression that uses an unsigned type with other integers.

---

# Overflow

Until now, I've told you to ignore arithmetic overflow. That's because it's a difficult topic. Strictly speaking, if an expression involving signed integers or floating-point numbers overflows, the results are undefined. In reality, your typical desktop system wraps integer overflow (so adding two positive numbers can yield a negative result). Overflow of floating-point numbers can yield infinity or the program may terminate.

If you explicitly cast a signed value to a type such that the value overflows the destination type, the results are not so dire. Instead of undefined behavior, the results are defined by the implementation. Most implementations simply discard the excess bits. Therefore, for maximum safety and portability, you should check for overflow. Use `numeric_limits` (Exploration 23) to learn the maximum or minimum value of a type.

Unsigned integers are different. The standard explicitly permits unsigned arithmetic to overflow. The result is to discard any extra high-order bits. Mathematically speaking, this means unsigned arithmetic is modulo $2^n$, where $n$ is the number of bits in the unsigned type.

# Introducing Bitfields

A *bitfield* is a way to partition an integer within a class into individual bits or masks of adjacent bits. Declare a bitfield using an unsigned integer type or `bool`, the field name, a colon, and the number of bits in the field. Listing 61-12 shows how you might store the I/O formatting flags using bitfields.

**Listing 61-12.** *Declaring Formatting Flags with Bitfields*

```
struct fmtflags {
    bool skipws_f :        1;
    bool boolalpha_f:      1;
    bool showpoint_f:      1;
    bool showbase_f:       1;
    bool showpos_f:        1;
    unsigned adjustfield_f: 2;
    unsigned floatfield_f:  2;

    static unsigned const left    = 0;
    static unsigned const right   = 1;
    static unsigned const internal = 2;

    static unsigned const fixed      = 1;
    static unsigned const scientific = 2;
};
```

Use a bitfield member the way you would use any other data member. For example, to set the `skipws` flag, use

```
flags.skipws_f = true;
```

and to clear the flag, use the following:

```
flags.skipws_f = false;
```

To select scientific notation, try the line that follows:

```
flags.floatfield_f = fmtflags::scientific;
```

As you can see, code that uses bitfields is easier to read and write than the equivalent code using shift and bitwise operators. That's what makes bitfields popular. On the other hand, it is hard to write functions such as `setf` and `unsetf`. It is hard to get or set multiple, non-adjacent bits at one time. That's why your library probably doesn't use bitfields to implement I/O formatting flags.

Another limitation is that you cannot take the address of a bitfield (with the & operator) because an individual bit is not directly addressable in the C++ memory model.

Nonetheless, the clarity that bitfields offer puts them at the top of the list when choosing an implementation. Sometimes, other factors knock them off the list, but you should always consider bitfields first. With bitfields, you don't need to be concerned with bitwise operators, shift operators, mixed-up operator precedence, and so on.

# Portability

The C++ standard leaves several details up to each implementation. In particular, the order of bits in a field is left up to the implementation. A bitfield cannot cross a word boundary, where the definition of a *word* is also left up to the implementation. Popular desktop and workstation computers often use 32 bits or 64 bits, but there is no guarantee that a word is the same size as an int. An unnamed bitfield of size zero tells the compiler to insert pad bits so the subsequent declaration aligns on a word boundary.

```
class demo {
  unsigned bit0 : 1;
  unsigned bit1 : 1;
  unsigned bit2 : 3;
  unsigned      : 0;
  unsigned word1: 2;
};
```

The size of a demo object depends on the implementation. Whether bit0 is the least or most significant bit of a demo's actual implementation also varies from one system to another. The number of pad bits between bit2 and word1 also depends on the implementation.

Most code does not need to know the layout of the bits in memory. On the other hand, if you are writing code that interprets the bits in a hardware control register, you need to know the order of bits, the exact nature of padding bits, and so on. But you probably aren't expecting to write highly portable code, anyway. In the most common case, when you are trying to express a compact set of individual set members or small bitmasks, bitfields are wonderful. They are easy to write and easy to read. They are limited, however, to a single word, often 32 bits. For larger bitfields, you need to use a class, such as std::bitset.

# The bitset Class Template

Sometimes, you need to store more bits than can fit in an integer. In that case, you can use the std::bitset class template, which implements a fixed-size string of bits of any size.

The std::bitset class template takes one template argument: the number of bits in the set. Use a bitset object the way you would any other value. It supports all the bitwise and shift operators, plus a few member functions for further convenience. Another nifty trick that bitset can perform is the subscript operator, which lets you access individual bits in the set as discrete objects. The right-most (least significant) bit is at index zero. Construct a bitset from an unsigned long (to set the least-significant bits of the bitset, initializing the remaining bits to zero) or from a string of '0' and '1' characters, as illustrated in Listing 61-13.

**Listing 61-13.** *Example of Using std::bitset*

```
#include <bitset>
#include <cstdlib>
#include <iostream>
#include <ostream>
#include <string>
```

```
/** Find the first 1 bit in a bitset, starting from the most significant bit.
 * @param bitset The bitset to examine
 * @return A value in the range [0, bitset.size()-1) or
 *         size_t(-1) if bitset.none() is true.
 */
template<std::size_t N>
std::size_t first(std::bitset<N> const& bitset)
{
    for (std::size_t i(bitset.size()); i-- != 0;)
      if (bitset.test(i))
          return i;
    return std::size_t(-1);
}

int main()
{
    std::bitset<50> lots_o_bits(std::string("10110111011110111110111111101111111"));
    std::cout << "bitset: " << lots_o_bits << '\n';
    std::cout << "first 1 bit: " << first(lots_o_bits) << '\n';
    std::cout << "count of 1 bits: " << lots_o_bits.count() << '\n';
    lots_o_bits[first(lots_o_bits)] = false;
    std::cout << "new first 1 bit: " << first(lots_o_bits) << '\n';
    lots_o_bits.flip();
    std::cout << "bitset: " << lots_o_bits << '\n';
    std::cout << "first 1 bit: " << first(lots_o_bits) << '\n';
}
```

In Exploration 23, I presented static_cast<> as a way to convert one integer to a different type. Listing 61-13 demonstrates another syntax for a static cast: std::size_t(-1). This syntax makes the type cast look like a constructor call, pretending std::size_t is a class. For a simple type conversion, this syntax is often easier to read than static_cast<>. I recommend using this syntax when converting literals; use static_cast<> for more complicated expressions.

Unlike working with bitfields, most of the behavior of bitset is completely portable. Thus, every implementation gives the same results when running the program in Listing 61-13. The following output displays those results:

```
bitset: 00000000000000001011011101111011111011111101111111
first 1 bit: 33
count of 1 bits: 28
new first 1 bit: 31
```

**Write a function template, find_pair, that takes two arguments: a bitset to search, and a bool value to compare.** The function searches for the first pair of adjacent bits that are equal to the second argument and returns the index of the most significant bit of the pair. **What should the function return if it cannot find a matching pair of bits? Write a simple test program, too.**

Compare your solution with mine, which is presented in Listing 61-14.

**Listing 61-14.** *The find_pair Function and Test Program*

```
#include <bitset>
#include <cassert>
#include <cstdlib>
#include <iostream>
#include <ostream>

template<std::size_t N>
std::size_t find_pair(std::bitset<N> const& bitset, bool value)
{
    if (bitset.size() >= 2)
        for (std::size_t i(bitset.size()); i-- != 1; )
            if (bitset[i] == value and bitset[i-1] == value)
                return i;
    return std::size_t(-1);
}

int main()
{
    std::size_t const not_found(-1);
    std::bitset<0> bs0;
    std::bitset<1> bs1;
    std::bitset<2> bs2;
    std::bitset<3> bs3;
    std::bitset<100> bs100;

    assert(find_pair(bs0, false) == not_found);
    assert(find_pair(bs0, true) == not_found);
    assert(find_pair(bs1, false) == not_found);
    assert(find_pair(bs1, true) == not_found);
    assert(find_pair(bs2, false) == 1);
    assert(find_pair(bs2, true) == not_found);
    bs2[0] = true;
    assert(find_pair(bs2, false) == not_found);
    assert(find_pair(bs2, true) == not_found);
    bs2.flip();
    assert(find_pair(bs2, false) == not_found);
    assert(find_pair(bs2, true) == not_found);
    bs2[0] = true;
    assert(find_pair(bs2, false) == not_found);
    assert(find_pair(bs2, true) == 1);
    assert(find_pair(bs3, false) == 2);
    assert(find_pair(bs3, true) == not_found);
    bs3[2].flip();
    assert(find_pair(bs3, false) == 1);
    assert(find_pair(bs3, true) == not_found);
    bs3[1].flip();
```

```
   assert(find_pair(bs3, false) == not_found);
   assert(find_pair(bs3, true) == 2);
   assert(find_pair(bs100, false) == 99);
   assert(find_pair(bs100, true) == not_found);
   bs100[50] = true;
   assert(find_pair(bs100, true) == not_found);
   bs100[51] = true;
   assert(find_pair(bs100, true) == 51);
}
```

Although bitset is not widely used, when you need it, it can be extremely helpful. The next Exploration covers a language feature that is much more widely used than bitset: enumerations.

■ ■ ■

# Enumerations

The final mechanism for defining types in C++ is the enum keyword, which is short for enumeration. This Exploration has two parts. The first part presents enumerations as you probably expect them to work; the second part presents how enumerations actually work. The differences may surprise you.

## Ideal Enumerations

An enumerated type is a user-defined type that defines a set of identifiers as the values of the type. Define an enumerated type with the enum keyword, followed by the type name, followed by the enumerated literals in curly braces. The following code shows some examples of enumerated types:

```
enum color { black, red, green, yellow, blue, magenta, cyan, white };
enum sign { negative, positive };
enum flags { boolalpha, showbase, showpoint, showpos, skipws };
```

An enum definition adds the names of all the enumerators to the same scope that gets the enum type name. It does not create its own scope, which surprises some people. Usually curly braces denote a scope, whether a local block, a namespace, a class, etc. In this case, the curly braces do not introduce a new scope, but simply delimit the enumerator names. Therefore, in a single scope, an identifier cannot be an element of more than one enumerated type. Thus, given the previous three enumerations, you could not also define the following enumeration:

```
enum primary { red, green, blue }; // error when color also defines red, etc.
```

Defining an enumerated type within a namespace or class definition is an easy way to avoid this kind of name conflict.

```
namespace color {
    enum t { black, red, green, yellow, blue, magenta, cyan, white };
}
namespace primary {
  enum t { red, green, blue };
}
color::t c(color::red);
primary::t p(primary::red);
```

Although some languages implement a mechanism for discovering the largest and smallest values of an enumeration, C++ does not.

The only value that you can assign to a variable of enumerated type is an expression of the same type, such as one of the literals of that type, another variable of the same type, or the result of a function that returns the enumerated type. In particular, you cannot assign an integer to an enumerated-type variable.

The compiler automatically converts enumerated-type values to integer values when it needs to. The first literal in a type definition has value zero; the next is one, and so on. For example, if you print an enumerated value green, what you actually see printed is 2.

```
color c(green);
std::cout << c << '\n';
```

Use the type name as a constructor name, passing an integer argument to convert that integer to the corresponding enumerated-type value.

```
color c;
c = color(3); // yellow
```

You can also use a static_cast, as shown in the following:

```
color c;
c = static_cast<color>(3); // yellow
```

There is no input operator for enumerations. If you want to be able to read an enumerated literal as a string, you need to implement your own mechanism to map strings to values. Even though C++ can print enumerated values by converting them to integers, the reverse is not automatic for input. You cannot read an integer into an enum-type variable. Instead, you can read an integer into an integer-type variable, check the value for validity, then convert the integer to the enumerated type, as described earlier.

The increment and decrement operators are not defined for enumerated types. A common language feature in other languages is the successor and predecessor operators for enumerated types. C++ does not offer these operators by default, but you are free to implement them yourself. You need to decide what to do at the limits of the type: throw an exception, stick at the end, or wrap back to the beginning.

Enumerated types have their uses, but in C++, they seem to be extremely limited. To understand why, you need to understand that this idealized view of enumerations is a lie. The next part of this Exploration reveals the truth.

# Enumerations As Bitmasks

An enumerated type defines an integer bitmask type, with a set of predefined mask values. Every enumerated type corresponds to one of the built-in primitives types; the exact type is implementation-defined.

You define an enumerated type with the enum keyword, the name of the enumerated type, and the literals in curly braces. A literal can be just a name, or it can be a name followed by an equal sign and constant integer value. A value expression can refer to enumerators that appear earlier in the same type. If you omit a value for a particular enumerator name, the compiler picks a value by adding one to the value of the preceding literal value. The implicit value of the first enumerator is zero. Thus,

```
enum color { black, red, green, yellow, blue, magenta, cyan, white };
```

and

```
enum color { black, red = 1, green = 2, blue = 4, yellow = red+green,
             magenta=red+blue, cyan=green+blue, white=red+green+blue };
```

mean exactly the same thing. Enumerator values do not need to be contiguous, adjacent, ordered, or complete. Duplicate values are permitted; duplicate names are not.

The compiler does not define the arithmetic operators for enumerated types, leaving you free to define these operators. The compiler can convert an enumerated value to its corresponding integer value, but to convert back, you must use an explicit type cast. Use the enumerated type name in the manner of a constructor with an integer argument, or use static_cast.

```
int i(yellow);
color c1( color(i + 1) );
color c2( static_cast<color>(i + 1) );
```

Suppose you define the following enumeration:

```
enum sample { low=4, high=256 };
```

The permissible values for an object of type sample are all values in the range [sample(0), sample(511)], which may strike you as a little odd. To understand how the compiler determines the permissible values, you need to remember that enumerated types are actually bitmask types. The permissible values are all the bitmask values that fit into a bitfield that can hold the largest and smallest bitmask values among the enumerators.

The first step to understanding the full range of permissible values is to determine the minimum size of the bitfield that can hold all the enumerators. For sample, this is nine bits (in order to hold $256_{10}$ or $100000000_2$). The minimum bitmask value is a bitmask of all zeros and the maximum is all ones: thus, the range of bitmasks is $000000000_2$ to $111111111_2$ or $0_{10}$ to $511_{10}$.

If any enumerator is negative, the same rules apply, but are more complicated because you need to consider the native representation of negative numbers (typically two's complement for most desktop and workstations, but it also can be signed-magnitude or ones' complement for specialized devices).

You can use an enumerated type for a bitfield (Exploration 61). It is your responsibility to ensure that the bitfield is large enough to store all the possible enumeration values, as demonstrated in the following:

```
class demo {
  color okay  : 3; // big enough
  color small : 2; // oops, not enough bits, but valid C++
};
```

The compiler will let you declare a bitfield that is too small; if you are fortunate, your compiler will warn you about the problem.

# Simulating Enumerations

Even though enumerations are grossly misnamed, you can implement an enumerated type with a C++ enum and a class. It just takes a little extra work. (Or a lot of extra work, depending on how fancy you want your simulation to be.) Override the increment and decrement operators to implement the successor and predecessor operations. You need to decide what to do at the limits—that is, if you take the successor of the last enumeration or the predecessor of the first. Do you stick at the limit, wrap to the other limit, or throw an exception?

If you want to be able to read and write the literal names instead of integers, this requires quite a bit of extra work, but work that helps complete the simulation.

## Enumerating Computer Languages

For example, let's define an enumeration of computer programming languages. Start with a short list. Once you see how the mechanism works, you can easily extend the list with additional languages.

Start by defining a class that will contain the actually enumerated type and associated information.

```
class language {
public:
    enum type { apl, c, cpp, forth, haskell, jovial, lisp };
    language(type value) : value_(value) {}
private:
    type value_;
};
```

Notice how the class name is the meaningful name. The enumeration itself has a place-holder name. In order to use the enumerated literals, you must qualify the literal names with the class name (e.g., language::c). This avoids conflicts with any other uses of c as a name.

The first thing to add are successor and predecessor operators, which we implement as member functions for the increment the decrement operators.

```
language& operator++() { value_ = type(value_ + 1); return *this; }
language operator++(int) { language tmp(*this); ++*this; return tmp; }
```

Because enumerated types do not allow increment and decrement operators, the pre-increment function must use a type cast. Implement the decrement operators similarly.

But what happens when you increment past the largest value or decrement prior to the smallest value? Let's add some error checking and throw an exception in these cases. Listing 62-1 shows the latest incarnation of the language class.

**Listing 62-1.** *The language Class with Error-Checked Successor Functions*

```
#include <stdexcept>

class language {
public:
    enum type { apl, low=apl, c, cpp, forth, haskell, jovial, lisp, high=lisp };
    language(type value) : value_(value) {}
```

```
   language& operator++() {
      if (value_ == high)
         throw std::overflow_error("language::operator++ overflow");
      value_ = type(value_ + 1);
      return *this;
   }
   language operator++(int) { language tmp(*this); ++*this; return tmp; }
private:
   type value_;
};
```

Notice the addition of high and low enumerators. Whenever you change the list of languages, you must take care to ensure that high and low are correct. **Implement the decrement operators; throw std::underflow_error when appropriate.**

## Comparing Languages

C++ lets you compare enumerated values using the relational operators because the compiler converts the values to integers and compares the integers. We can take advantage of this when implementing comparison operators for the language class. Because we are simulating an enumerated type, we have no reason to specify that lisp is greater than or less than forth. Thus, we should define the equality and inequality operators, but not the relational operators. Ideally, you should define comparison operators as free functions, but so far, we have not defined any way to discover the underlying enumerated value of a language object. Thus, the next task is to define a type conversion operator.

```
operator type() const { return value_; }
```

A member function that has the form operator, followed by a type, is a *type conversion* operator. It defines the means of converting an object of the class type to the target type. Note that the return type of the function is the target of the type conversion. The compiler calls the type conversion operator when you explicitly ask it to with static_cast<>,

```
language h(language::haskell);
language::type value( static_cast<language::type>(h) );
```

or when the compiler determines that an implicit conversion is allowed and necessary, such as the following:

```
language h(language::haskell);
language::type value( h );
```

Now implement the equality and inequality operators as free functions.

Implementing a default constructor is usually a good idea. **Which value should the default constructor use? _____ Implement the default constructor.** Note that the implicit copy constructor and copy assignment operator work just fine.

Without relational operators, however, you cannot use a language object as a key in a set or map. To do this, you should specialize the std::less template so it compares language objects by casting to the enumerated type, as shown in the following:

```
namespace std {
  template<>
  class less<language> {
  public:
    bool operator()(language a, language b) const {
      return language::type(a) < language::type(b);
    }
  };
}
```

## Assignment

Now that you can get a language::type value out of a language object, add an assignment operator that assigns a language::type value to a language object. Remember that C++ permits values in an enumeration that are not among the listed enumerated literals. In order to simulate a true enumerated type, we must not permit this. **Implement assignment of language::type that ensures the source value is in the range [low, high], and throws std::out_of_range if the value is out of range.**

Listing 62-2 shows the current language class and related functions.

**Listing 62-2.** *The Language Class with Comparison and Assignment*

```
class language {
public:
  enum type { apl, low=apl, c, cpp, forth, haskell, jovial, lisp, high=lisp };
  language() : value_(low) {}
  language(type value) : value_(value) {}

  language& operator=(language::type value) {
    if (value < low or value > high)
      throw std::out_of_range("language assignment out of range");
    value_ = value;
    return *this;
  }

  language& operator++() {
    if (value_ == high)
      throw std::overflow_error("language::operator++ overflow");
    value_ = type(value_ + 1);
    return *this;
  }
  language operator++(int) { language tmp(*this); ++*this; return tmp; }
  language& operator--() {
    if (value_ == low)
      throw std::underflow_error("language::operator-- underflow");
    value_ = type(value_ - 1);
    return *this;
```

```
  }
  language operator--(int) { language tmp(*this); --*this; return tmp; }

  operator type() const { return value_; }
private:
  type value_;
};

bool operator==(language a, language b)
{
  return static_cast<language::type>(a) == static_cast<language::type>(b);
}

bool operator!=(language a, language b)
{
  return not (a == b);
}
namespace std {
  template<>
  class less<language> {
  public:
    bool operator()(language a, language b) const {
      return language::type(a) < language::type(b);
    }
  };
}
```

## Strings and Languages

Before we can tackle I/O, we need to be able to map a string to a language and vice versa. This is difficult because C++ gives us no way to discover the literal names with any reflection or introspection mechanism. Instead, we need to duplicate information and hope we don't make any mistakes.

Assume that conversions to and from strings will occur frequently. **What data structure should you use to convert strings to language::type values?** _____ **What data structure should you use for the reverse conversion?** _____

If you have TR1 available, use an std::tr1::unordered_map to map strings to values and std::tr1::array to map values to strings; otherwise, use std::map and std::vector. To reduce the amount of redundant information in the program, write a helper function to populate both data structures simultaneously. **Implement the to_string() member function to return the language as a string, and a function, from_string(), to convert a string to a value. Throw std::invalid_argument if the string is not a valid language name. Implement a constructor that takes a string as an argument and calls from_string() to construct a language from the string. Write a function, void initialize(), that initializes the internal data structures.**

See Listing 62-3 for the string conversion code for the language class.

**Listing 62-3.** *The Language Class with String Conversion*

```cpp
#include <map>
#include <stdexcept>
#include <string>
#include <vector>

class language {
public:
    enum type { apl, low=apl, c, cpp, forth, haskell, jovial, lisp, high=lisp };
    language() : value_(low) {}
    language(type value) : value_(value) {}
    language(std::string const& str) : value_(from_string(str)) {}

    language& operator=(language::type value) {
        if (value < low or value > high)
            throw std::out_of_range("language assignment out of range");
        value_ = value;
        return *this;
    }

    language& operator++() {
        if (value_ == high)
            throw std::overflow_error("language::operator++ overflow");
        value_ = type(value_ + 1);
        return *this;
    }
    language operator++(int) { language tmp(*this); ++*this; return tmp; }
    language& operator--() {
        if (value_ == low)
            throw std::underflow_error("language::operator-- underflow");
        value_ = type(value_ - 1);
        return *this;
    }
    language operator--(int) { language tmp(*this); --*this; return tmp; }

    operator type() const { return value_; }

    std::string const& to_string() const { return to_string_.at(value_); }

    type from_string(std::string const& str) const {
        map::const_iterator iter(from_string_.find(str));
        if (iter == from_string_.end())
            throw std::invalid_argument("No such language: " + str);
        else
            return iter->second;
    }
```

```
   void initialize()
   {
      // pre-allocate the vector, so it's easier to fill
      to_string_.resize(high+1, std::string());
      store("apl", apl);
      store("c", c);
      store("cpp", cpp);
      store("forth", forth);
      store("haskell", haskell);
      store("jovial", jovial);
      store("lisp", lisp);
   }

private:
   typedef std::map<std::string, type> map;
   typedef std::vector<std::string> vector;

   type value_;

   void store(std::string const& str, type value)
   {
      from_string_[str] = value;
      to_string_.at(value) = str;
   }

   static map from_string_;
   static vector to_string_;
};
```

Recall from Exploration 38 that the static modifier on a data member instructs the compiler to create a single instance of the data member and share that single instance among all objects of that class and derived classes. The to_string_ and from_string_ members are static because you want to use a single, shared map to convert strings to language values and a single, shared vector to perform the opposite conversion.

Because the from_string, store, and initialize functions do not need to use any data members except the static data members, to_string_ and from_string_, you should make these functions static, too. A static function is one that does not need to be called for a specific object. Instead, you can call it as a free function, qualified with the class name, for example, language::initialize().

To declare a static member function, use the static keyword as a modifier on the return type. By convention, it is the first modifier (e.g., static void initialize()). See Listing 62-4 for this new incarnation of the *language.hpp* header.

**Listing 62-4.** *The Language Class with All Enhancements*

```
#ifndef LANGUAGE_HPP_
#define LANGUAGE_HPP_
#include <map>
```

```cpp
#include <stdexcept>
#include <string>
#include <vector>

class language {
public:
   enum type { apl, low=apl, c, cpp, forth, haskell, jovial, lisp, high=lisp };
   language() : value_(low) {}
   language(type value) : value_(value) {}
   language(std::string const& str) : value_(from_string(str)) {}

   language& operator=(language::type value) {
      if (value < low or value > high)
         throw std::out_of_range("language assignment out of range");
      value_ = value;
      return *this;
   }

   language& operator++() {
      if (value_ == high)
         throw std::overflow_error("language::operator++ overflow");
      value_ = type(value_ + 1);
      return *this;
   }
   language operator++(int) { language tmp(*this); ++*this; return tmp; }
   language& operator--() {
      if (value_ == low)
         throw std::underflow_error("language::operator-- underflow");
      value_ = type(value_ - 1);
      return *this;
   }
   language operator--(int) { language tmp(*this); --*this; return tmp; }

   operator type() const { return value_; }

   std::string const& to_string() const { return to_string_.at(value_); }

   static type from_string(std::string const& str) const {
      map::const_iterator iter(from_string_.find(str));
      if (iter == from_string_.end())
         throw std::invalid_argument("No such language: " + str);
      else
         return iter->second;
   }

   static void initialize()
   {
```

```
        // pre-allocate the vector, so it's easier to fill
        to_string_.resize(high+1, std::string());
        store("apl", apl);
        store("c", c);
        store("cpp", cpp);
        store("forth", forth);
        store("haskell", haskell);
        store("jovial", jovial);
        store("lisp", lisp);
    }

private:
    typedef std::map<std::string, type> map;
    typedef std::vector<std::string> vector;

    type value_;

    static void store(std::string const& str, type value)
    {
        from_string_[str] = value;
        to_string_.at(value) = str;
    }

    static map from_string_;
    static vector to_string_;
};

bool operator==(language a, language b)
{
    return static_cast<language::type>(a) == static_cast<language::type>(b);
}
bool operator==(language a, language::type b)
{
    return static_cast<language::type>(a) == b;
}
bool operator==(language::type a, language b)
{
    return a == static_cast<language::type>(b);
}

bool operator!=(language a, language b)
{
    return not (a == b);
}
bool operator!=(language a, language::type b)
{
    return not (a == b);
```

```
}
bool operator!=(language::type a, language b)
{
   return not (a == b);
}
namespace std {
  template<>
  class less<language> {
  public:
    bool operator()(language a, language b) const {
      return language::type(a) < language::type(b);
    }
  };
}


#endif // LANGUAGE_HPP_
```

---

**Note** The static keyword has multiple uses in C++. When used with a class member, it means that member is shared among all instances of the class and is not tied to any particular instance. It has an entirely different meaning outside of a class. If you use static on a free function or global object, it keeps that function or object private to the source file in which it is defined. As you learned in Exploration 50, an unnamed namespace does the same thing, so there is no need to use static this way in C++. I recommend not using static outside of a class, but you might read code that uses it, so you should know what it means.

---

## Initializing

The next task is to ensure that language::initialize() is called. The common idiom is to define an initialization class, call it initializer. Its constructor calls language::initialize(). Thus, constructing a single instance of initializer ensures that the language class is initialized. In *language.cpp*, define this instance in an unnamed namespace, as shown in Listing 62-5.

**Listing 62-5.** *The* language.cpp *File Initializes the Language Data Structures*

```
#include "language.hpp"

namespace {
   class initializer {
   public:
      initializer() { language::initialize(); }
   };
   initializer init;
}
```

Objects at namespace or global scope are constructed before `main()` begins or before the use of any function or object in the same file. Thus, the `init` object is constructed early, which calls `language::initialize()`, which in turn ensures the `language` data structures are properly initialized.

The one difficulty is when another global initializer needs to use `language`. C++ offers no convenient way to ensure that objects in one file are initialized before objects in another file. Within a single file, objects are initialized in the order of declaration, starting at the top of the file. Dealing with this issue is beyond the scope of this book. None of the examples in this book depend on the order of initialization across files. In fact, most programs don't face this problem. So we can return to the immediate problem: reading and writing `language` values.

## Reading and Writing Languages

Now that the hard work of converting to and from strings is done, it is time to use them for I/O. **Read a `language` by reading a string and mapping the string to a `language` value.** Use a try-catch statement to catch the exception that `language` throws for an unknown language, and set the `fail` bit for invalid input. **Write a `language` by mapping to a string and writing the string.** See Listing 62-6 for the I/O operators.

**Listing 62-6.** *Just the I/O Operators for a Language Object*

```
template<class C, class T>
std::basic_ostream<C, T>&
  operator<<(std::basic_ostream<C, T>& stream, language lang)
{
   stream << lang.to_string();
   return stream;
}

template<class C, class T>
std::basic_istream<C, T>&
  operator>>(std::basic_istream<C, T>& stream, language& lang)
{
   std::string str;
   stream >> str;
   try {
      lang = language(str);
   } catch (std::invalid_argument const&) {
      stream.setstate(stream.failbit);
   }
   return stream;
}
```

## Using the Simulated Enumeration

Now that you have the `language` class, let's make sure it's easy to use. **Write a program that asks the user for his or her favorite language.** Read the response as a `language` object. Note that the normal input stream catches any exceptions and turns them into input failures. Thus, test for invalid input by testing for std::cin.fail(). After a failure, call clear() to reset the state and ask again. Otherwise, obtain the successor language and suggest that the user try that language instead. If the user likes the highest value language, recommend the lowest.

Compare your solution with Listing 62-7.

**Listing 62-7.** *Program to Test the language Class*

```
#include <iostream>
#include <istream>
#include <ostream>

#include "language.hpp"

int main()
{
   language lang;
   while (true) {
      std::cout << "What is your favorite programming language? ";
      std::cin >> lang;
      if (std::cin.good())
      {
         if (lang == language::high)
            lang = language::low;
         else
            ++lang;
         std::cout << "Have you considered " << lang << "?\n";
         return 0;
      }
      if (std::cin.fail())
      {
         std::cout << "Unknown language. Please choose one of the following:\n";
         for (language x(language::low); x != language::high; ++x)
            std::cout << x << ' ';
         std::cout << language(language::high) << '\n';
         std::cin.clear();
      }
   }
}
```

Writing the language class involves a certain amount of ugliness. Once it is written, however, you have a powerful type at your disposal, and you can customize it, enhance it, and improve it in any way you wish. Watch an expert C++ programmer, and you will see someone who is adept at hiding ugliness inside classes that are beautiful and elegant from the outside.

# Revisiting Projects

Now that you know all about enumerations, consider how you could improve some previous projects. For example, in Exploration 33, we wrote a constructor for the point class that uses a bool to distinguish between Cartesian and polar coordinate systems. Because it is not obvious whether true means Cartesian or polar, a better solution is to use an enumerated type, such as the following:

```
enum coordinate_system { cartesian, polar };
```

Another example that can be improved with enumerations is the card class, from Listing 51-5. Instead of using int constants for the suits, use an enumeration. You can also use an enumeration for the rank. The enumeration needs to specify enumerators only for ace, jack, queen, and king. Choose appropriate values, and you can cast the integers 2 through 10 to the rank type for the other card ranks. Write your new, improved card class and compare it with my solution in Listing 62-8.

**Listing 62-8.** *Improving the card Class with Enumerations*

```
#ifndef CARD_HPP_
#define CARD_HPP_

#include <istream>
#include <ostream>

/// Represent a standard western playing card.
class card
{
public:
  enum suit { nosuit, diamonds, clubs, hearts, spades };
  enun rank { norank=0, jack = 11, queen, king, ace };

  card() : rank_(norank), suit_(nosuit) {}
  card(rank r, suit s) : rank_(r), suit_(s) {}

  void assign(rank r, suit s);
  suit get_suit() const { return suit_; }
  rank get_rank() const { return rank_; }
private:
  rank rank_;
  suit suit_;
};

bool operator==(card a, card b);
bool operator!=(card a, card b);
std::ostream& operator<<(std::ostream& out, card c);
std::istream& operator>>(std::istream& in, card& c);
```

```
/// In some games, Aces are high. In other Aces are low. Use different
/// comparison functors depending on the game.
bool acehigh_compare(card a, card b);
bool acelow_compare(card a, card b);

/// Generate successive playing cards, in a well-defined order,
/// namely, 2-10, J, Q, K, A. Diamonds first, then Clubs, Hearts, and Spades.
/// Roll-over and start at the beginning again after generating 52 cards.
class card_generator
{
public:
  card_generator();
  card operator()();
private:
  card card_;
};

#endif
```

What other projects can you improve with enumerations?

# Multiple Inheritance

Unlike some other object-oriented languages, C++ lets a class have more than one base class. This feature is known as *multiple inheritance*. Several recent languages permit a single base class, and introduce a variety of mechanisms for pseudo-inheritance, such as Java interfaces and Ruby mix-ins and modules. Multiple inheritance in C++ is a superset of all these other behaviors.

## Multiple Base Classes

Declare more than one base class by listing all the base classes in a comma-separated list. Each base class gets its own access specifier, as demonstrated in the following:

```
class derived : public base1, private base2, public base3 {
};
```

As with single inheritance, the derived class has access to all the non-private members of all of its base classes. The derived class constructor initializes all the base classes in order of declaration. If you need to pass arguments to any base class constructor do so in the initializer list. As with data members, the order of initializers does not matter—only the order of declaration matters, as illustrated in Listing 63-1.

**Listing 63-1.** *Demonstrating the Order of Initialization of Base Classes*

```
#include <iostream>
#include <ostream>
#include <string>

class visible {
public:
    visible(std::string const& msg) : msg_(msg) { std::cout << msg << '\n'; }
    std::string const& msg() const { return msg_; }
private:
    std::string msg_;
};
```

```cpp
class base1 : public visible {
public:
   base1(int x) : visible("base1 constructed"), value_(x) {}
   int value() const { return value_; }
private:
   int value_;
};

class base2 : public visible {
public:
   base2(std::string const& str) : visible("base2(" + str + ") constructed") {}
};

class base3 : public visible {
public:
   base3() : visible("base3 constructed") {}
   int value() const { return 42; }
};

class derived : public base1, public base2, public base3 {
public:
   derived(int i, std::string const& str) : base3(), base2(str), base1(i) {}
   int value() const { return base1::value() + base3::value(); }
   std::string msg() const
   {
      return base1::msg() + "\n" + base2::msg() + "\n" + base3::msg();
   }
};

int main()
{
   derived d(42, "example");
}
```

Your compiler may issue a warning when you compile the program, pointing out that the order of base classes in derived's initializer list does not match the order in which the initializers are called. Running the program shows that the order of the base classes controls the order of the constructors, as shown in the following output:

```
base1 constructed
base2(example) constructed
base3 constructed
```

Figure 63-1 illustrates the class hierarchy of Listing 63-1. Notice that each of the base1, base2, and base3 classes has its own copy of the visible base class. Don't be concerned now, but this point will arise later, so pay attention.

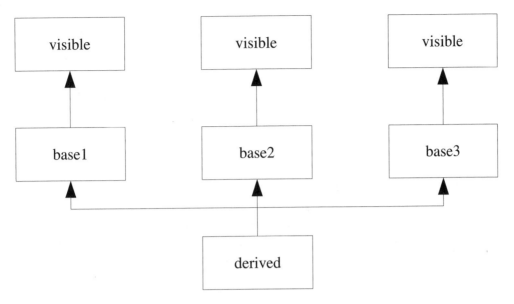

**Figure 63-1.** *UML diagram of classes in Listing 63-1*

If two or more base classes have a member with the same name, you need to indicate to the compiler which of them you mean if you want to access that particular member. Do this by qualifying the member name with the desired base class name when you access the member in the derived class. See the examples in the derived class in Listing 63-1. **Change the main() function to the following**:

```
int main()
{
   derived d(42, "example");
   std::cout << d.value() << '\n' << d.msg() << '\n';
}
```

**Predict the output from the new program:**

_____

_____

_____

_____

_____

_____

_____

Compare your results with the output I got:

```
base1 constructed
base2(example) constructed
base3 constructed
84
base1 constructed
base2(example) constructed
base3 constructed
```

# Virtual Base Classes

Sometimes, you don't want a separate copy of a common base class. Instead, you want a single instance of the common base class, and every class shares that one common instance. To share base classes, insert the `virtual` keyword when declaring the base class. The `virtual` keyword can come before or after the access specifier; convention is to list it first.

---

■**Note**  C++ overloads certain keywords, such as `static` and `virtual`. A virtual base class has no relationship with virtual functions. They just happen to use the same keyword.

---

Imagine changing the `visible` base class to be virtual when each of `base1`, `base2`, and `base3` derive from it. **Can you think of any difficulty that might arise?**

---

Notice that each of the classes that inherit from `visible` pass a different value to the constructor for `visible`. If you want to share a single instance of `visible`, you need to pick one value and stick with it. To enforce this rule, the compiler ignores all the initializers for a virtual base class except the one that it requires in the most-derived class (in this case, `derived`). Thus, to change `visible` to be virtual, not only must you change the declarations of `base1`, `base2`, and `base3`, but you must also change `derived`. When `derived` initializes `visible` it initializes the sole, shared instance of `visible`. **Try it.** Your modified program should look something like Listing 63-2.

**Listing 63-2.** *Changing the Inheritance of Visible to Virtual*

```cpp
#include <iostream>
#include <ostream>
#include <string>

class visible {
public:
    visible(std::string const& msg) : msg_(msg) { std::cout << msg << '\n'; }
    std::string const& msg() const { return msg_; }
private:
    std::string msg_;
};
```

```
class base1 : virtual public visible {
public:
  base1(int x) : visible("base1 constructed"), value_(x) {}
  int value() const { return value_; }
private:
  int value_;
};

class base2 : virtual public visible {
public:
  base2(std::string const& str) : visible("base2(" + str + ") constructed") {}
};

class base3 : virtual public visible {
public:
  base3() : visible("base3 constructed") {}
  int value() const { return 42; }
};

class derived : public base1, public base2, public base3 {
public:
  derived(int i, std::string const& str)
  : base3(), base2(str), base1(i), visible("derived")
  {}
  int value() const { return base1::value() + base3::value(); }
  std::string msg() const
  {
    return base1::msg() + "\n" + base2::msg() + "\n" + base3::msg();
  }
};

int main()
{
  derived d(42, "example");
  std::cout << d.value() << '\n' << d.msg() << '\n';
}
```

**Predict the output from Listing 63-2.**

_____

_____

_____

_____

_____

_____

Notice that the visible class is now initialized only once, and that the derived class is the one that initializes it. This example is unusual because I want to illustrate how virtual base classes work. Most virtual base classes define only a default constructor. This frees authors of derived classes from concerning themselves with passing arguments to the virtual base class constructor. Instead, every derived class invokes the default constructor; it doesn't matter which class is the most derived.

Figure 63-2 depicts the new class diagram, using virtual inheritance.

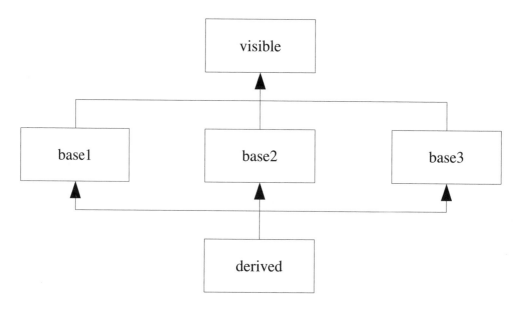

**Figure 63-2.** *Class diagram with virtual inheritance*

# Java-Like Interfaces

Programming with interfaces has some important advantages. Being able to separate interfaces from implementations makes it easy to change implementations without affecting other code. If you need to use interfaces, you can easily do so in C++.

C++ has no formal notion of interfaces, but it supports interface-based programming. The essence of an interface in Java and similar languages is that an interface has no data members, and the member functions have no implementations. Recall from Exploration 36 that such a function is called a *pure virtual function*. Thus, an interface is merely an ordinary class in which you do not define any data members and you declare all member functions as pure virtual.

For example, Java has the Hashable interface, which defines the hash and equalTo functions. Listing 63-3 shows the equivalent C++ class.

**Listing 63-3.** *The Hashable Interface in C++*

```cpp
class Hashable
{
public:
   virtual ~Hashable() = 0;
   virtual unsigned long hash() const = 0;
   virtual bool equalTo(Hashable const&) const = 0;
};
```

Any class that implements the Hashable interface must override all the member functions. For example, HashableString implements Hashable for a string, as shown in Listing 63-4.

**Listing 63-4.** *The HashableString Class*

```cpp
class HashableString : public Hashable
{
public:
   HashableString() : string_() {}
   ~HashableString();
   unsigned long hash() const;
   bool equalTo(Hashable const&) const;

   // Implement the entire interface of std::string ...
private:
   std::string string_;
};
```

Note that HashableString does *not* derive from std::string. Instead it encapsulates a string and delegates all string functions to the string_ object it holds.

The reason you cannot derive from std::string is the same reason Hashable contains a virtual destructor. Recall from Exploration 36 that any class with at least one virtual function should make its destructor virtual. Let me explain the reason.

To understand the problem, think about what would happen if HashableString derived from std::string. Suppose that somewhere else in the program is some code that frees strings (maybe a pool of common strings). This code stores strings as std::string pointers. If HashableString derives from std::string, this is fine. But when the pool object frees a string, it calls the std::string destructor. Because this destructor is not virtual, the HashableString destructor never runs, resulting in undefined behavior. Listing 63-5 illustrates this problem.

**Listing 63-5.** *Undefined Behavior Arises from HashableString That Derives from std::string*

```cpp
#include <iostream>
#include <istream>
#include <set>
#include <string>
#include "HashableString.hpp"
```

```cpp
class string_pool
{
public:
    string_pool() : pool_() {}
    ~string_pool() {
        while (not pool_.empty()) {
            std::string* ptr = *pool_.begin();
            pool_.erase(pool_.begin());
            delete ptr;
        }
    }
    std::string* add(std::string const& str) {
        std::string* ptr = new std::string(str);
        pool_.insert(ptr);
        return ptr;
    }
private:
    std::set<std::string*> pool_;
};

int main()
{
    string_pool pool;
    HashableString str;
    while (std::cin >> str)
    {
        std::cout << "hash of \"" << str << "\" = " << str.hash() << '\n';
        pool.add(str);
    }
}
```

On the other hand, if HashableString does not derive from std::string, how can the string pool manage these hashable strings? The short answer is that it cannot. The long answer is that thinking in terms of Java solutions does not work well in C++ because C++ offers a better solution to this kind of problem: templates.

# Interfaces vs. Templates

As you can see, C++ handily supports Java-style interfaces. There are times when Java-like interfaces are the correct C++ solution. There are other situations, however, when C++ offers superior solutions, such as templates.

Instead of writing a HashableString class, write a hash<> class template and specialize the template for any type that needs to be stored in a hash table. The primary template provides the default behavior; specialize hash<> for the std::string type. In this way, the string pool can easily store std::string pointers and destroy the string objects properly, and a hash table can compute hash values for strings (and anything else you need to store in the hash table). Listing 63-6 shows one way to write the hash<> class template and a specialization for std::string.

**Listing 63-6.** *The hash<> Class Template*

```
template<class T>
class hash
{
public:
   std::size_t operator()(T const& x) const
   {
     return reinterpret_cast<std::size_t>(&x);
   }
};

template<>
class hash<std::string>
{
public:
   std::size_t operator()(std::string const& str) const
   {
      std::size_t h(0);
      for (std::string::const_iterator i(str.begin()); i != str.end(); ++i)
         h = h << 1 | *i;
      return h;
   }
};
```

Now try using the hash<> class template to rewrite the string_pool class. Compare your solution with Listing 63-7.

**Listing 63-7.** *Rewriting string_pool to Use hash<>*

```
#include <iostream>
#include <istream>
#include "hash.hpp"
#include "string_pool.hpp"

int main()
{
   string_pool pool;
   std::string str;
   hash<std::string> hash;
   while (std::cin >> str)
   {
      std::cout << "hash of \"" << str << "\" = " << hash(str) << '\n';
      pool.add(str);
   }
}
```

Use the exact same `string_pool` class as you did in Listing 63-5. The program that uses the string pool is simple and clear and has the distinct advantage of being well-formed and correct.

# Mix-Ins

Another approach to multiple inheritance that you find in languages such as Ruby is the *mix-in*. A mix-in is a class that typically has no data members, although this is not a requirement in C++ (as it is in some languages). Usually, a C++ mix-in is a class template that defines some member functions that call upon the template arguments to provide input values for those functions.

For example, in Exploration 57 you saw a way to implement assignment in terms of a `swap` member function. This is a useful idiom, so why not capture it in a mix-in class so you can easily reuse it. The mix-in class is actually a class template that takes a single template argument: the derived class. The mix-in defines the assignment operator, using the `swap` function that the template argument provides.

Confused yet? You aren't alone. This is a common idiom in C++, but one that takes time before it becomes familiar and natural. Listing 63-8 helps to clarify how this kind of mix-in works.

**Listing 63-8.** *The assignment_mixin Class Template*

```
template<class T>
class assignment_mixin {
public:
    T& operator=(T rhs)
    {
        rhs.swap(static_cast<T&>(*this));
        return static_cast<T&>(*this);
    }
};
```

The trick is that instead of swapping *this, the mix-in class casts itself to a reference to the template argument, T. In this way, the mix-in never needs to know anything about the derived class. The only requirement is that the class, T, must be copyable (so it can be an argument to the assignment function) and have a `swap` member function.

In order to use the `assignment_mixin` class, derive your class from the `assignment_mixin` (as well as any other mix-ins you wish to use), using the derived class name as the template argument. Listing 63-9 shows an example of how a class uses mix-ins.

**Listing 63-9.** *Using mix-in Class Template*

```
class thing: public assignment_mixin<thing> {
public:
    thing() : value_() {}
    thing(std::string const& s) : value_(s) {}
    void swap(thing& other) { value_.swap(other.value_); }
private:
```

```
    std::string value_;
};

int main()
{
    thing one;
    thing two("two");
    one = two;
}
```

This C++ idiom is hard to comprehend at first, so let's break it down. First, consider the `assignment_mixin` class template. Like many other templates, it takes a single template parameter. It defines a single member function, which happens to be an overloaded assignment operator. There's nothing particularly special about `assignment_mixin`.

But `assignment_mixin` has one important property: the compiler can instantiate the template even if the template argument is an incomplete class. The compiler doesn't need to expand the assignment operator until it is used, and at that point, T must be complete. But for the class itself, T can be incomplete. If the mix-in class were to declare a data member of type T, then the compiler would require T be a complete type when the mix-in is instantiated because it would need to know the size of the mix-in.

In other words, you can use `assignment_mixin` as a base class, even if the template argument is an incomplete class.

When the compiler processes a class definition, immediately upon seeing the class name, it records that name in the current scope as an incomplete type. Thus, when `assignment_mixin<thing>` appears in the base class list, the compiler is able to instantiate the base class template using the incomplete type, `thing`, as the template argument.

By the time the compiler gets to the end of the class definition, `thing` becomes a complete type. After that, you will be able to use the assignment operator because when the compiler instantiates that template, it needs a complete type, and it has one.

# Friends to the Rescue

Mix-ins are a wonderful tool in C++. One difficulty, however, is that many operators should be implemented as free functions, not member functions. The trick is for a mix-in class to implement free functions. It turns out a mix-in class can indeed define a free function from within the class definition. This trick involves a new keyword, `friend`.

For example, recall from Exploration 28 how the `rational` class implements the relational operators in terms of two fundamental operators: `==` and `<`. This is a common pattern. Any type that can be compared with these two operators can follow the same pattern and implement all the relational operators. It seems perfectly reasonable to write a pair of mix-in class templates that implement the other comparison operators, based on these two. By using the `friend` modifier when defining the function, the mix-in class template defines a free function inside the class, as shown in Listing 63-10.

**Listing 63-10.** *The comparison_mixin and equality_mixin Class Templates*

```
template<class T>
class comparison_mixin
{
public:
    friend bool operator>(T const& lhs, T const& rhs) { return rhs < lhs; }
    friend bool operator>=(T const& lhs, T const& rhs) { return not (lhs < rhs); }
    friend bool operator<=(T const& lhs, T const& rhs) { return not (rhs < lhs); }
};
template<class T>
class equality_mixin
{
public:
    friend bool operator!=(T const& lhs, T const& rhs) { return not (lhs == rhs); }
};
```

Although this trick works fine, it abuses the `friend` keyword. The original purpose of `friend` is to give permission to a function or class to access the private members of another class. A class grants friendship, or access to its private members, by means of friend declarations. A friend declaration contains the `friend` keyword, followed by a class or function declaration. You must use the `class` or `struct` keyword when naming a friend class. The named function or all of the members of the named class can access all private and protected members of the class granting friendship, as illustrated in the following:

```
class secrets {
  friend int pal(secrets const&);
  int priv; // no one except pal() can access priv
};

int pal(secrets const& s) { return s.priv; }
```

When used in a mix-in, the fact that `friend` is meant to bypass access levels is irrelevant. The `comparison_mixin` class template has only public members, anyway. This trick is an unintended consequence of the definition of `friend`, but it is a highly useful unintended consequence.

**Write the < and == operators for the thing class. Then use the mix-ins to complete the suite of comparison functions.** Compare your result with Listing 63-11.

**Listing 63-11.** *The thing Class with All of Its Mix-Ins*

```
class thing: public assignment_mixin<thing>,
    public comparison_mixin<thing>,
    public equality_mixin<thing>
{
public:
    thing() : value_() {}
    thing(std::string const& s) : value_(s) {}
    void swap(thing& other) { value_.swap(other.value_); }
```

```
    std::string const& str() const { return value_; }
private:
    std::string value_;
};
bool operator==(thing const& lhs, thing const& rhs)
{
  return lhs.str() == rhs.str();
}

bool operator<( thing const& lhs, thing const& rhs)
{
  return lhs.str() < rhs.str();
}

int main()
{
    thing a, b("xyz"), c(b);
    assert(a == a);
    assert(a != b);
    assert(a <= b);
    assert(b >= c);
    assert(c > a);
    c = a;
    assert(a == c);
    assert(a != b);
    assert(c <= b);
}
```

Multiple inheritance even appears in the C++ standard library. You know about istream for input and ostream for output. The library also has iostream, so a single stream can perform input and output. As you might expect, iostream derives from istream and ostream. The only quirk has nothing to do with multiple inheritance: iostream is defined in the <istream> header. The <iostream> header defines the names std::cin, std::cout, etc. The header name is an accident of history.

The next Exploration continues your advanced study of class templates by looking at policies and traits.

## Protected Access Level

In addition to the private and public access levels, C++ offers the protected access level. A protected member is accessible only to the class itself and to derived classes. To all other would-be users, a protected member is off-limits, just like private members.

Most members are private or public. Use protected members only when you are designing a class hierarchy and you deliberately want derived classes to call a certain member function, but don't want anyone else to call it.

# EXPLORATION 64

████

# Traits and Policies

**A**lthough you may still be growing accustomed to templates, it's time to explore two common, related use patterns: traits and policies. Programming with traits and policies is probably a new style for you, but it is common in C++. As you will discover in this Exploration, this technique is extremely flexible and powerful. Traits and policies underlie much of the C++ standard library. This Exploration takes a look at some of the traits and policies in the standard library so you can learn how to take advantage of them. It then helps you take the first steps toward writing your own.

## Case Study: Iterators

Consider the humble iterator. Consider the `std::advance` function (Exploration 42). The advance function changes the position to which an iterator points. The advance function knows nothing about container types; it knows only about iterators. Yet somehow, it knows that if you try to advance a vector's iterator, it can do so simply by adding an integer to the iterator. But if you advance a list's iterator, the advance function must step the iterator one position at a time until it arrives at the desired destination. In other words, the advance function implements the optimal algorithm for changing the iterator's position. The only information available to the advance function must come from the iterators themselves, and the key piece of information is the iterator kind. In particular, only random access iterators permit rapid advancement via addition. All other iterators must follow the step-by-step approach. So how does advance know what kind of iterator it has?

In most OOP languages, an iterator would derive from a common base class, which would implement a virtual advance function. The advance algorithm would call that virtual function, and let normal object-oriented dispatching take care of the details. C++ certainly could take that approach, but it doesn't.

Instead, C++ uses a technique that does not require looking up a virtual function and making an extra function call. Instead, C++ uses a technique that does not force you to derive all iterators from a single base class. If you implement a new container, you get to pick the class hierarchy. C++ provides the std::iterator base class template, which you can use if you want, but you don't need to use it. Instead, the advance algorithm (and all other code that uses iterators) relies on a traits template.

*Traits* are attributes or properties of a type. In this case, an iterator's traits describe the iterator kind (random access, bidirectional, forward, input, or output), the type that the iterator points to, and so on. The author of an iterator class specializes the std::iterator_traits class template to define the traits of the new iterator class. Iterator traits make more sense with an example, so let's take a look at Listing 64-1, which shows one possible implementation of std::advance.

**Listing 64-1.** *One Possible Implementation of std::advance*

```
#include <iostream>
#include <iterator>
#include <ostream>
#include <string>

void trace(std::string const& msg)
{
   std::cout << msg << '\n';
}


// Default implementation: advance the slow way
template<class Kind>
class iterator_advancer
{
public:
   template<class InIter, class Distance>
   void operator()(InIter& iter, Distance distance)
   {
      trace("iterator_advancer<>");
      for ( ; distance != 0; --distance)
```

```
            ++iter;
      }
};

// Partial specialization for bi-directional iterators
template<>
class iterator_advancer<std::bidirectional_iterator_tag>
{
public:
   template<class BiDiIter, class Distance>
   void operator()(BiDiIter& iter, Distance distance)
   {
      trace("iterator_advancer<bidirectional_iterator_tag>");
      if (distance < 0)
         for ( ; distance != 0; ++distance)
            --iter;
      else
         for ( ; distance != 0; --distance)
            ++iter;
   }
};

template<class InIter, class Distance>
void my_advance(InIter& iter, Distance distance)
{
   iterator_advancer<typename std::iterator_traits<InIter>::iterator_category>()
      (iter, distance);
}
```

This code is not as difficult to understand as it appears. The `iterator_advancer` class template provides one function, the function call operator. The implementation advances an input iterator `distance` times. This implementation works for a non-negative `distance` with any kind of iterator.

Bi-directional iterators permit a negative value for `distance`. Partial template specialization permits a separate implementation of `iterator_advancer` just for bi-directional iterators. The specialization checks whether `distance` is negative; negative and non-negative values are handled differently.

---

■**Note** Remember from Exploration 50 that only classes can use partial specialization. That's why `iterator_advancer` is a class template with a function call operator instead of a function template. This idiom is common in C++. Another approach is to use function overloading, passing the iterator kind as an additional argument. The value is unimportant, so just pass a default-constructed object. I prefer partial specialization because it is more flexible, but feel free to use whichever technique you prefer.

---

Let's assemble the pieces. The my_advance function creates an instance of iterator_advancer and calls its function call operator, passing the iter and distance arguments. The magic is the std::iterator_traits class template. This class template has a few member typedefs, including iterator_category.

All bi-directional iterators must define the member typedef, iterator_category, as std::bidirectional_iterator_tag. Thus, when your program calls my_advance, and passes a bi-directional iterator (such as a std::list iterator) as the first argument, the my_advance function queries iterator_traits to discover the iterator_category. The compiler uses template specialization to decide which implementation of iterator_advancer to choose. The compiler then generates the code to call the correct function. The compiler takes care of all this magic— your program pays no runtime penalty.

Now try running the program in Listing 64-2 to see which iterator_advancer specialization is called in each situation.

**Listing 64-2.** *Example Program to Use the* my_advance *Function*

```
#include <fstream>
#include <iostream>
#include <istream>
#include <iterator>
#include <list>
#include <ostream>
#include <string>
#include <vector>

#include "advance.hpp" // the code from Listing 64-1

int main()
{
    std::vector<int> vector;
    vector.push_back(10);
    vector.push_back(20);
    vector.push_back(30);
    vector.push_back(40);
    std::list<int> list(vector.begin(), vector.end());
    std::vector<int>::iterator vector_iterator(vector.begin());
    std::list<int>::iterator list_iterator(list.begin());
    std::ifstream file("advance.hpp");
    std::istream_iterator<std::string> input_iterator(file);

    my_advance(input_iterator, 2);
    my_advance(list_iterator, 2);
    my_advance(vector_iterator, 2);
}
```

Notice any problems? **What kind of iterator does a vector use?** _____ **Which specialization does the compiler pick?** _____ The compiler does not follow class hierarchies when picking template specializations, so the fact that random_access_iterator_ tag derives from bidirectional_iterator_tag is irrelevant in this case. If you want to specialize iterator_advancer for random access iterators, you must provide another specialization, this time for random_access_iterator_tag. Remember from Exploration 42 that random access iterators permit arithmetic on iterators. Thus, you can advance an iterator rapidly by adding the distance. **Implement a partial specialization of iterator_advancer for random access iterators.**

Compare your solution with the snippet in Listing 64-3.

**Listing 64-3.** *Specializing iterator_advancer for Random Access Iterators*

```
// Partial specialization for random access iterators
template<>
class iterator_advancer<std::random_access_iterator_tag>
{
public:
   template<class RandomIter, class Distance>
   void operator()(RandomIter& iter, Distance distance)
   {
      trace("iterator_advancer<random_access_iterator_tag>");
      iter += distance;
   }
};
```

Now rerun the example program to see that the compiler picks the correct specialization.

A good optimizing compiler can take the my_advance function with the random-access specialization of iterator_advancer, and easily compile optimal code, turning a call to the my_advance function into a single addition, with no function-call overhead. In other words, the layers of complexity that traits and policies introduce do not necessarily equate to bloated code and poor runtime performance. The complexity is conceptual, and once you understand what the traits do and how they work, you can let them abstract away the underlying complexity. They will make your job easier.

## CONCEPTS, PART TWO

Concepts greatly simplify writing this style of code. Instead of using template specialization, you will be able to use concepts to state directly what you want to accomplish, as demonstrated in the following:

```
template<InputIterator Iterator>
void advance(Iterator& iterator, Iterator::difference_type n)
{
  for ( ; n != 0; ++n)
    ++iterator;
}
```

```
template<RandomAccessIterator Iterator>
void advance(Iterator& iterator, Iterator::difference_type n)
{
    iterator += n;
}
```

The compiler will use the iterator kind to invoke the correct advance function. Thus, you don't need to use template magic; the compiler does it for you when you overload advance using different concepts.

# Iterator Traits

The class template, iterator_traits (defined in <iterator>), is an example of a *traits* type. A traits type provides traits, or characteristics, of another type. In this case, iterator_traits informs you about several traits of an iterator exposed via typedefs:

- **difference_type:** A signed integer type that represents the difference between two iterators. If you have two iterators that point into the same container, the distance function returns the distance between them—that is, the number of positions that separate the iterators. If the iterators are bidirectional or random-access, the distance can be negative.

- **iterator_category:** The iterator kind, which must be one of the following types (also defined in <iterator>):

  - bidirectional_iterator_tag

  - forward_iterator_tag

  - input_iterator_tag

  - output_iterator_tag

  - random_access_iterator_tag

Some of the standard algorithms use template specialization and the iterator_category to provide optimal implementations for different kinds of iterators.

- **pointer:** A typedef that represents a pointer to a value.

- **reference:** A typedef that represents a reference to a value.

- **value_type:** The type of values to which the iterator refers.

**Can you think of another traits type in the standard library?** _____ The first one that I thought of is std::numeric_limits (Explorations 23 and 49). Another traits class that I've mentioned without explanation is std::char_traits (defined in <string>).

# Case Study: char_traits

As mentioned in the previous section, char_traits is another class template that implements traits, in this instance, of a character type (e.g., char or wchar_t). Let's take a look.

Among the difficulties in working with characters in C++ is the char type may be signed or unsigned. The size of a char relative to the size of an int varies from compiler to compiler. The range of valid character values also varies from one implementation to another, and can even change while a program is running. A time-honored convention is to use int to store a value that may be a char or a special value that marks end-of-file, but nothing in the standard supports this convention. You may need to use unsigned int or long.

In order to write portable code, you need a traits class to provide a typedef for the integer type to use, the value of the end-of-file marker, and so on. That's exactly what char_traits is for. When you use std::char_traits<char>::int_type, you know you can safely store any char value or the end-of-file marker (which is std::char_traits<char>::eof()).

The standard istream class has a get() function that returns an input character or the special end-of-file marker when there is no more input. The standard ostream class offers put(c) to write a character. **Use these functions with char_traits to write a function that copies its standard input to its standard output, one character at a time.** Call eof() to obtain the special end-of-file value and eq_int_type(a,b) to compare two integer representations of characters for equality. Both functions are static member functions of the char_traits template, which you must instantiate with the desired character type. Compare your solution with Listing 64-4.

**Listing 64-4.** *Using Character Traits When Copying Input to Output*

```
#include <iostream>
#include <istream>
#include <ostream>
#include <string>          // for char_traits

int main()
{
   typedef std::char_traits<char> char_traits; // for brevity and clarity
   char_traits::int_type c;
   while (c = std::cin.get(), not char_traits::eq_int_type(c, char_traits::eof()))
      std::cout.put(c);
}
```

First, notice the loop condition. Recall from Exploration 44 that the comma can separate two expressions; the first sub-expression is evaluated then the second. The result of the entire expression is the result of the second sub-expression. In this case, the first sub-expression assigns get() to c, and the second sub-expression calls eq_int_type, so the result of the loop condition is the return value from eq_int_type, testing whether the result of get, as stored in c, is equal to the end-of-file marker. Another way to write the loop condition is as follows:

```
not char_traits::eq_int_type(c = std::cin.get(), char_traits::eof())
```

I don't like to bury assignments in the middle of an expression, so I prefer to use the comma operator in this case. Other developers have a strong aversion to the comma operator.

They prefer the embedded assignment style. Another solution is to use a `for` loop instead of a `while` loop:

```
for (char_traits::int_type c = std::cin.get();
     not char_traits::eq_int_type(c, char_traits::eof());
     c = std::cin.get())
```

The for-loop solution has the advantage of limiting the scope of the variable, `c`. But it has the disadvantage of repeating the call to `std::cin.get()`. Any of these solutions is acceptable; pick a style and stick with it.

In this case, `char_traits` seems to make everything more complicated. After all, comparing two integers for equality is easier and clearer when using the `==` operator. On the other hand, using a member function gives the library-writer the opportunity for added logic, such as checking for invalid character values.

In theory, you could write a `char_traits` specialization that, for instance, implements case-insensitive comparison. In that case, the `eq()` (which compares two characters for equality) and `eq_int_type()` functions would certainly need extra logic. On the other hand, you learned in Exploration 18 that such a traits class cannot be written for many international character sets, at least not without knowing the locale.

In the real world, specializations of `char_traits` are rare.

The `char_traits` class template is interesting, nonetheless. A pure traits class template would implement only typedef members, static data members, and sometimes a member function that returns a constant, such as `char_traits::eof()`. Functions such as `eq_int_type()` are not traits, which describe a type. Instead they are policy functions. A policy class template contains member functions that specify behavior, or policies. The next section looks at policies.

# Policy-Based Programming

A *policy* is a class or class template that another class template can use to customize its behavior. In the standard library, the string and stream classes use the `char_traits` policy class template to obtain type-specific behavior for comparing characters, copying character arrays, and more. The standard library provides policy implementations for the `char` and `wchar_t` types.

Although the standard library provides and uses `char_traits`, it does not take full advantage of policy-based programming. Only in recent years has the C++ community come to embrace this style of programming, in large part due to the popularity of Andrei Alexandrescu's seminal work, *Modern C++ Design* (Addison-Wesley, 2001).

Suppose you are trying to write a high-performance server. After careful design, implementation, and testing, you discover that the performance of `std::string` introduces significant overhead. In your particular application, memory is abundant, but processor time is at a premium. Wouldn't it be nice to be able to flip a switch and change your `std::string` implementation from one that is optimized for space into one that is optimized for speed? Instead, you must write your own string replacement that meets your needs. In writing your own class, you end up rewriting the many member functions, such as `find_first_of`, that have nothing to do with your particular implementation, but are essentially the same for most string implementations. What a waste of time.

Imagine how simple your job would be if you had a string class template that took an extra template argument with which you could select a storage mechanism for the string, substituting memory-optimized or processor-optimized implementations according to your needs. That, in a nutshell, is what policy-based programming is all about.

A common implementation of std::string is to keep a small character array in the string object for small strings, and use dynamic memory allocation for larger strings. In order to conform to the C++ standard, these implementations cannot offer up a menu of policy template arguments that would let you pick the size of the character array. So let us free ourselves from this limitation, and write a class that implements all the members of the std::string class, but breaks the standard interface by adding a policy template argument. For the sake of simplicity, this book implements only a few functions. Completing the interface of std::string is left as an exercise for the reader. Listing 64-5 shows the new string class template and a few of its member functions. Take a look and you can see how it takes advantage of the Storage policy.

**Listing 64-5.** *The newstring Class Template*

```cpp
template<class Char, class Storage, class Traits>
class newstring {
public:
   typedef Char value_type;
   typedef std::size_t size_type;
   typedef typename Storage::iterator iterator;
   typedef typename Storage::const_iterator const_iterator;
   newstring() : storage_() {}
   newstring(Storage const& storage) : storage_(storage) {}
   newstring(newstring const& str) : storage_(str.storage_) {}
   newstring(Char const* ptr, size_type size) : storage_() {
      resize(size);
      std::copy(ptr, ptr + size, begin());
   }

   static const size_type npos = static_cast<size_type>(-1);

   newstring& operator=(newstring str) { swap(str); return *this; }
   newstring& operator=(std::string const& str) {
      return *this = newstring(str.data(), str.size());
   }
   void swap(newstring& str) { storage_.swap(str.storage_); }

   Char operator[](size_type i) const { return *(storage_.begin() + i); }
   Char& operator[](size_type i)       { return *(storage_.begin() + i); }

   void resize(size_type size, Char value = Char()) {
     storage_.resize(size, value);
   }
   void reserve(size_type size) { storage_.reserve(size); }
   size_type size() const       { return storage_.end() - storage_.begin(); }
   size_type max_size() const   { return storage_.max_size(); }
```

```
      Char const* c_str() const { return storage_.c_str(); }
      Char const* data() const  { return storage_.c_str(); }

      iterator begin()               { return storage_.begin(); }
      const_iterator begin() const { return storage_.begin(); }
      iterator end()                 { return storage_.end(); }
      const_iterator end() const   { return storage_.end(); }

      size_type find(newstring const& s, size_type pos = 0) const {
         pos = std::min(pos, size());
         const_iterator result( std::search(begin() + pos, end(),
                                 s.begin(), s.end(), Traits::eq) );
         if (result == end())
            return npos;
         else
            return result - begin();
      }

private:
   Storage storage_;
};

template<class Traits>
class newstringcmp
{
public:
   bool operator()(typename Traits::value_type a, typename Traits::value_type b)
   const
   {
      return Traits::cmp(a, b) < 0;
   }
};

template<class Char, class Storage1, class Storage2, class Traits>
bool operator <(newstring<Char, Storage1, Traits> const& a,
                newstring<Char, Storage2, Traits> const& b)
{
   return std::lexicographical_compare(a.begin(), a.end(), b.begin(), b.end(),
                                       newstringcmp<Traits>());
}

template<class Char, class Storage1, class Storage2, class Traits>
bool operator ==(newstring<Char, Storage1, Traits> const& a,
                 newstring<Char, Storage2, Traits> const& b)
{
   return std::equal(a.begin(), a.end(), b.begin(), b.end(), Traits::eq);
}
```

The newstring class relies on Traits for comparing characters and Storage for storing them. The Storage policy must provide iterators for accessing the characters themselves and a few basic member functions (data, max_size, reserve, resize, swap), and the newstring class provides the public interface, such as the assignment operator and search member functions.

Public comparison functions use standard algorithms and Traits for comparisons. Notice how the comparison functions require their two operands to have the same Traits (otherwise, how could the strings be compared in a meaningful way?) but allow different Storage. It doesn't matter how the strings store their contents if you want to know only whether two strings contain the same characters.

The next step is to write some storage policy templates. The storage policy is parameterized on the character type. The simplest Storage is vector_storage, which stores the string contents in a vector. In order to simplify the implementation of c_str, the vector stores a trailing null character. Listing 64-6 shows part of an implementation of vector_storage. You can complete the implementation on your own.

**Listing 64-6.** *The vector_storage Class Template*

```cpp
#include <vector>

template<class Char>
class vector_storage {
public:
   typedef std::size_t size_type;
   typedef Char value_type;
   typedef typename std::vector<Char>::iterator iterator;
   typedef typename std::vector<Char>::const_iterator const_iterator;

   vector_storage() : string_(1, Char()) {}

   void swap(vector_storage& storage) { string_.swap(storage.string_); }
   size_type max_size() const { return string_.max_size() - 1; }
   void reserve(size_type size) { string_.reserve(size + 1); }
   void resize(size_type newsize, value_type value) {
      // if the string grows, overwrite the null character, then resize
      if (newsize >= string_.size()) {
         string_[string_.size() - 1] = value;
         string_.resize(newsize + 1, value);
      }
      string_[string_.size() - 1] = Char();
   }
   Char const* c_str() const { return &string_[0]; }

   iterator begin()                { return string_.begin(); }
   const_iterator begin() const { return string_.begin(); }
   // Skip over the trailing null character at the end of the vector
   iterator end()                  { return string_.end() - 1; }
   const_iterator end() const    { return string_.end() - 1; }
```

```
private:
    std::vector<Char> string_;
};
```

The only difficulty in writing vector_storage is that the vector stores a trailing null byte, so the c_str function can return a valid C-style character array. Therefore, the end function has to adjust the iterator that it returns.

Another possibility for a storage policy is deque_storage, which is just like vector_storage, except it uses a deque. Because a deque does not stores its data in a single array, deque_storage does not need the added complexity of an extra null character, but it does need a new c_str function, which must allocate a single character array, copy the string into that array, and return a pointer to the array. It must therefore manage the memory for that array. **Write deque_storage**. Compare your result with mine, which can be seen in Listing 64-7.

**Listing 64-7.** *The deque_storage Class Template*

```
template<class Char>
class deque_storage {
public:
    typedef std::size_t size_type;
    typedef Char value_type;
    typedef typename std::deque<Char>::iterator iterator;
    typedef typename std::deque<Char>::const_iterator const_iterator;

    deque_storage() : string_() {}

    void swap(deque_storage& storage) { string_.swap(storage.string_); }
    size_type max_size() const        { return string_.max_size(); }
    void reserve(size_type size)      { string_.reserve(size); }
    void resize(size_type size, value_type value) { string_.resize(size, value); }
    Char const* c_str() const {
        data_.assign(begin(), end());
        data_.push_back(Char());
        return &data_[0];
    }

    iterator begin()                   { return string_.begin(); }
    const_iterator begin() const { return string_.begin(); }
    iterator end()                     { return string_.end(); }
    const_iterator end() const   { return string_.end(); }

private:
    std::deque<Char> string_;
    std::vector<Char> data_;
};
```

If no one ever calls the c_str function, the data_ vector is never created. On the other hand, the c_str function re-creates the vector every time it is called. The first improvement to make would be to re-create the data_ vector only if the string_ has changed since the last call to c_str. I leave this improvement as an exercise for you to do on your own.

Returning to the original problem—that of a high-performance server that makes heavy use of small strings—a policy to consider is array_storage. By replacing vector with a C-style array, you can eliminate all dynamic memory allocation, but at the cost of more memory usage if most strings are smaller than the array size, or array overflow if you have strings that exceed the array size. Thus, careful choice of array size is critical for success. **Write the array_storage class template so it takes the array size as a template argument.** One significant change is that the storage class template will need to keep track of the actual string size. See Listing 64-8 for one simple implementation of array_storage.

**Listing 64-8.** *The array_storage Class Template*

```cpp
#include <algorithm>
#include <cstdlib>
#include <stdexcept>

template<class Char, std::size_t MaxSize>
class array_storage {
public:
   typedef Char array_type[MaxSize];
   typedef std::size_t size_type;
   typedef Char value_type;
   typedef Char* iterator;
   typedef Char const* const_iterator;

   array_storage() : size_(0), string_() { string_[0] = Char(); }

   void swap(array_storage& storage) {
      // linear complexity
      std::swap_ranges(string_.begin(), string_.end(), storage.string_.begin());
      std::swap(size_, storage.size_);
   }
   size_type max_size() const { return MaxSize - 1; }
   void reserve(size_type size) {
     if (size > max_size()) throw std::length_error("reserve");
   }
   void resize(size_type newsize, value_type value) {
      if (newsize > max_size())
         throw std::length_error("resize");
      if (newsize > size_)
         std::fill(begin() + size_, begin() + newsize, value);
      size_ = newsize;
      string_[size_] = Char();
   }
   Char const* c_str() const { return &string_[0]; }
```

```
    iterator begin()               { return &string_[0]; }
    const_iterator begin() const { return &string_[0]; }
    iterator end()                 { return begin() + size_; }
    const_iterator end() const     { return begin() + size_; }

private:
    size_type size_;
    array_type string_;
};
```

If you have a TR1 or Boost array class template, you can take advantage of it for the array_
storage class template. The advantage being that you can use iterators instead of pointers, as
shown in Listing 64-9.

**Listing 64-9.** *The array_storage Class Template, Based on array<>*

```
#include <algorithm>
#include <cstdlib>
#include <stdexcept>
#include <array>

template<class Char, std::size_t MaxSize>
class array_storage {
public:
    typedef std::tr1::array<Char, MaxSize> array_type;
    typedef std::size_t size_type;
    typedef Char value_type;
    typedef typename array_type::iterator iterator;
    typedef typename array_type::const_iterator const_iterator;

    array_storage() : size_(0), string_() { string_[0] = Char(); }

    void swap(array_storage& storage) {
        string_.swap(storage.string_);
        std::swap(size_, storage.size_);
    }
    size_type max_size() const { return string_.max_size() - 1; }
    void reserve(size_type size) {
        if (size > max_size()) throw std::length_error("reserve");
    }
    void resize(size_type newsize, value_type value) {
        if (newsize > max_size())
            throw std::length_error("resize");
        if (newsize > size_)
            std::fill(begin() + size_, begin() + newsize, value);
        size_ = newsize;
        string_[size_] = Char();
    }
    Char const* c_str() const { return &string_[0]; }
```

```
    iterator begin()                 { return string_.begin(); }
    const_iterator begin() const { return string_.begin(); }
    iterator end()                   { return begin() + size_; }
    const_iterator end() const   { return begin() + size_; }

private:
    size_type size_;
    array_type string_;
};
```

One difficulty when writing new string classes is that you must write new I/O functions, too. Unfortunately, this takes a fair bit of work and a solid understanding of the stream class templates and stream buffers. A quick-and-dirty implementation, however, is to use a temporary std::string intermediary. On input, read into std::string and assign the string contents to a newstring. For output, copy newstring to std::string and write the std::string. For production code, you would want to avoid the extra copy of the string, but for now, it gets you up and running quickly. **Write input and output function templates for reading and writing newstring objects**. Compare your functions with Listing 64-10.

**Listing 64-10.** *Quick and Dirty I/O Functions for newstring*

```
template<class Char, class Storage, class Traits>
std::basic_istream<Char, Traits>&
    operator>>(std::basic_istream<Char, Traits>& stream,
              newstring<Char, Storage, Traits>& string)
{
    std::basic_string<Char, Traits> tmp;
    if (stream >> tmp)
        string = tmp;
    return stream;
}

template<class Char, class Storage, class Traits>
std::basic_ostream<Char, Traits>&
    operator<<(std::basic_ostream<Char, Traits>& stream,
              newstring<Char, Storage, Traits> const& string)
{
    std::basic_string<Char, Traits> tmp(string.begin(), string.end());
    stream << tmp;
    return stream;
}
```

As you know, the compiler finds your I/O operators by matching the type of the right-hand operand, newstring, with the type of the function parameter. In this simple case, you can easily see how the compiler performs the matching and finds the right function. Throw some namespaces into the mix, and add some type conversions, and everything gets a little bit more muddled. The next Exploration delves more closely into namespaces and the rules that the C++ compiler applies in order to find your overloaded function names (or not find them, and therefore how to fix that problem).

# EXPLORATION 65

■ ■ ■

# Names and Templates

For the simple programs in this book, the compiler never encounters difficulty looking up and finding names of objects, types, and functions. Real programs, however, are more complicated, and what seems simple and straightforward in principle turns out to be complex and tangled in reality. Templates are particularly challenging because they have two contexts: where your code defines the template and where the code instantiates the template. This Exploration helps you untangle the rules that the compiler uses to lookup names in a template.

## Problems with Qualified Names

Suppose you want to write an absolute value function for the rational type. (Remember rational? If not, refresh your memory in Exploration 47.) At first, it seems straightforward, and you may write something akin to Listing 65-1.

**Listing 65-1.** *Simple Overload of abs for rational Arguments*

```
namespace numeric {
  template<class T>
  rational<T> abs(rational<T> const& r)
  {
    return rational<T>(std::abs(r.numerator()), r.denominator());
  }
}
```

That works just fine if T is one of the built-in numeric types. The standard library overloads std::abs for int, long, float, double, and long double. For historical reasons, the integer overloads are declared in <cstdlib> and the floating-point overloads are in <cmath>, but you can handle that. The problem comes when the caller supplies some other, custom numeric type for T.

For the sake of argument, assume you have a class integer that implements arbitrary precision arithmetic. The implementation is beyond the scope of this book, but you can imagine what its interface may be like. Assume that it stores a packed vector of unsigned int to store the digits, plus a bool for the sign. Computing an absolute value is fast and easy because it involves nothing more than clearing the sign flag. Therefore, you want to overload abs for the integer type. Let's further assume that this new type is in the bigmath namespace, as shown in Listing 65-2.

**Listing 65-2.** *Hypothetical Arbitrary-Size Integer Class*

```
namespace bigmath
{
  class integer
  {
  public:
    integer() : negative_(false), digits_() {}
    integer(long value);
    void abs() { negative_ = false; }
  private:
    bool negative_;
    std::vector<unsigned int> digits_;
  };

  integer abs(integer const& i)
  {
    integer result(i);
    result.abs();
    return result;
  }
}
```

When you use rational<integer>, you get rational numbers with extremely large precision. **What do you think happens if you call abs on a rational<integer> object?**

_____

_____

_____

Remember that the compiler happily compiled the definition of the rational<> template. It doesn't realize that there's a problem until you try to instantiate rational<integer>. At first, the compiler instantiates only the function declarations. It's not until you actually call a function template or a member function of a class template that the compiler instantiates the definition. At that time, the compiler tries to compile a function definition that is equivalent to Listing 65-3.

**Listing 65-3.** *Equivalent Code to the Instantiation of abs(rational<integer>)*

```
rational<integer> abs(rational<integer> const& r)
{
  return rational<integer>(std::abs(r.numerator()), r.denominator());
}
```

Do you see the problem? The standard library does not define std::abs(bigmath::integer). The compiler reports an error and refuses to compile any code that calls the overloaded abs for rational<integer> arguments.

It would be nice if you could add overloads to the std namespace, the way you can add template specializations. But you can't. The standard disallows it.

The best solution is to change the rational implementation of abs and remove the std:: qualifier from std::abs. This change permits rational's abs implementation to be open to calling other implementations of abs, using argument-dependent lookup (Exploration 50). You must also make sure that the compiler searches the std namespace (with a *using* directive), to find abs for the built-in functions. Thus, your function may end up looking something like Listing 65-4.

**Listing 65-4.** *Rewriting abs to Take Advantage of a Using Declaration*

```
namespace numeric {
  template<class T>
  rational<T> abs(rational<T> const& r)
  {
    using namespace std;
    return rational<T>(abs(r.numerator()), r.denominator());
  }
}
```

Thus, in the case of rational<integer>, the compiler can find abs(integer) via ADL, and in the case of rational<int>, the compiler finds abs(int) in the std namespace.

As you learned in Exploration 50, some implementations put names such as std::abs in the global namespace, too. Thus, even without the *using* directive, Listing 65-4 may work just fine with your compiler and library, but to be fully portable to all implementations, you need the *using* directive.

---

■**Tip** The moral of this story is: when you write a function template, avoid namespace-qualified names because they interfere with argument-dependent name lookup.

---

# Problems with Unqualified Names

Now that you know to use unqualified names in a template, consider the program in Listing 65-5.

**Listing 65-5.** *Using an Unqualified Name in a Function Template*

```
1 #include <iostream>
2 #include <ostream>
3 #include <string>
4
5 class base
```

```
 6 {
 7 public:
 8   base(std::string const& x = std::string()) : label_(x) {}
 9   std::string label() const { return label_; }
10   void init(base const& b) { std::cout << "base::init(" << b.label() << ")\n"; }
11 private:
12   std::string label_;
13 };
14
15 template<class T>
16 class demo : T
17 {
18 public:
19   demo(T const& x) { init(x); }
20 };
21
22 template<class T>
23 void init(T const& x)
24 {
25   std::cout << "global init(" << x << ")\n";
26 }
27
28 int main()
29 {
30   demo<base> d1(base("d1"));
31   demo<std::string> d2("d2");
32 }
```

**Predict the output of the program in Listing 65-5.**

_____

_____

The program should produce the following output:

```
base::init(d1)
global init(d2)
```

The main program defines two demo objects. Notice how the demo class template uses the template argument as the base class name on line 16. The base class can be any class. In one case, the base class is base; in the other, it is std::string. The demo constructor calls init(). Because the function call is unqualified, the compiler starts by looking for this name in the demo class. When the compiler cannot find the name in demo, it searches the base class. However, when the compiler is on line 19, it doesn't know the base class and doesn't know what init() is. Consequently the compiler stops worrying about init, puts aside the demo constructor for now, and continues compiling the file.

At line 30, the compiler knows the base class, base, so when the compiler looks up init, it finds the function as a member of base, therefore the compiler instantiates the demo constructor so it calls base::init. On line 31, however, the base class is std::string, which does not provide init, so the compiler searches for a free function. It starts in the namespace that encloses the demo class, which happens to be the global namespace, which also happens to contain a definition of the init function. So the compiler instantiates the demo<std::string> constructor to call the global ::init function.

Now try an experiment. Move the global init function (lines 22–26) above line 15—that is, before the demo class template definition. **Predict the output from the program.**

Something different happened. The program no longer compiles because the compiler is trying to call the global init function in both cases, and init tries to print a base object, which has no overloaded output operator. **Add such an operator that prints the label_ member.** Your program should now look like Listing 65-6.

**Listing 65-6.** *Reordering Functions Affects Name Lookup in Function Templates*

```cpp
#include <iostream>
#include <ostream>
#include <string>

class base
{
public:
  base(std::string const& x = std::string()) : label_(x) {}
  std::string label() const { return label_; }
  void init(base const& b) { std::cout << "base::init(" << b.label() << ")\n"; }
private:
  std::string label_;
};

std::ostream& operator<<(std::ostream& out, base const& b)
{
  return out << b.label();
}

template<class T>
void init(T const& x)
{
  std::cout << "global init(" << x << ")\n";
}

template<class T>
class demo : T
{
```

```
public:
  demo(T const& x) { init(x); }
};

int main()
{
  demo<base> d1(base("d1"));
  demo<std::string> d2("d2");
}
```

As the compiler already informed you, it is trying to call the global `init` function for both `demo` instantiations. The reason is subtle. As I described earlier, when the compiler is first compiling the `demo` constructor, it looks up the `init` function in the `demo` class. It cannot find `init`, nor can it find a base class because it doesn't know what the base class will be when the template is instantiated. But the compiler can find `init` in the global namespace, so that will do. The compiler is able to finish the `demo` constructor, and it does so. When the `demo` class template is instantiated, the compiler has already compiled the constructor, so it never bothers to look for `base::init`.

In other words, by moving the declaration of `init` earlier in the file, you radically changed the way the compiler processes the definition of a function template. Briefly, if the compiler is able to resolve an unqualified name in a function template, it does so. If not, it saves the function and waits until the template is instantiated (if ever), and finishes compiling the function only when it knows the template arguments and uses the template arguments to look up the unqualified name.

Looking up names at two different times (when first parsing the template definition, and later when instantiating the template) is called *two-phase lookup*. It is a crucial, but subtle aspect of writing templates.

---

■**Note**  Two-phase lookup is hard for programmers to understand and harder for compiler-writers to implement. Only recently have many major compilers properly implemented two-phase lookup. Some C++ programmers are still using older compilers that get it wrong. As a result, you may write perfectly correct code, but have the compiler reject it. Alternatively, you may write ill-formed code, and have the compiler accept it and even work the way you intended. My recommendation is to keep your tools up-to-date.

---

Two-phase lookup applies only when the compiler cannot resolve a name because the name depends on a template argument. Such a name is said to be *dependent*. This means it depends on a template argument, directly or indirectly. Most template arguments are types, so dependent names are usually *type-dependent*.

So what if the compiler knows about the global `init` function, but you want to ensure that the compiler looks for the member function only? In this case, you *must* qualify the function name. The most common way to qualify such names is with `this->`, as shown in Listing 65-7.

**Listing 65-7.** *Qualifying Dependent Names*

```
#include <iostream>
#include <ostream>
#include <string>

class base
{
public:
  base(std::string const& x = std::string()) : label_(x) {}
  std::string label() const { return label_; }
  void init(base const& b)  { std::cout << "base::init(" << b.label() << ")\n"; }
private:
  std::string label_;
};

std::ostream& operator<<(std::ostream& out, base const& b)
{
  return out << b.label();
}

template<class T>
void init(T const& x)
{
  std::cout << "global init(" << x << ")\n";
}

template<class T>
class demo : T
{
public:
  demo(T const& x) { this->init(x); }
};

int main()
{
  demo<base> d1(base("d1"));
}
```

You already know another rule for working with dependent types. As you learned in Exploration 51, you must use the typename keyword before any dependent name of a type. The C++ syntax has some ambiguities if the parser does not know whether a name is an expression or a type. The compiler needs your help when dealing with dependent names because there is no way for the compiler to determine whether a name will be that of an expression or a type at the point of instantiation. You know what you require the name to be, so you need to help the compiler by using typename before types, and the compiler assumes other names are not types. Thus, typename is another way of qualifying a dependent name.

---

---

One difficulty when writing templates is that the compiler can easily become confused and issue error messages that are not helpful. The line number may be the point of instantiation, which doesn't help you find the source of the problem in the template definition. With practice and experience, you will become better at noticing certain patterns in the errors, and you will begin finding and fixing problems more easily. To help get you started, Listing 65-8 contains some errors related to names and templates. **With the compiler's help, find and fix the errors.**

**Listing 65-8.** *Fix the Mistakes*

```
 1 #include <algorithm>
 2 #include <cassert>
 3 #include <iostream>
 4 #include <istream>
 5 #include <iterator>
 6 #include <ostream>
 7 #include <set>
 8
 9 using namespace std;
10
11 int begin()
12 {
13    return 0;
14 }
15
16 template<class T>
17 void insert(T const& container, T::value_type const& value)
18 {
19    container.insert(value);
20 }
21
22 template<class T>
23 class wrapper : public T
24 {
25 public:
26    typedef T base;
27    typedef base::value_type value_type;
28    typedef base::iterator iterator;
29    typedef base::const_iterator const_iterator;
```

```
30
31    template<class Char, class Traits>
32    void load(std::basic_istream<Char, Traits>& stream) {
33       value_type x;
34       while(stream >> x)
35           insert(x);
36    }
37    template<class Char, class Traits>
38    void dump(std::basic_ostream<Char, Traits>& stream) {
39        copy(begin(), end(), ostream_iterator<value_type>(stream, "\n"));
40    }
41 };
42
43 int main()
44 {
45    wrapper<std::set<int> > data;
46    data.load(cin);
47    data.dump(cout);
48 }
```

The first error I get from my compiler is:

```
list6508.cxx:17: error: 'T::value_type' is not a type
```

**What is the problem?**

The problem is that T::value_type is a dependent name, so the compiler does not know what it is. You must tell the compiler that it is a type. Therefore, change line 17 to read as follows:

```
void insert(T const& container, typename T::value_type const& value)
```

Look for similar problems elsewhere and fix them, too. (Hint: see lines 27–29.)
The next error I get is the following:

```
list6509.cpp:39: error: there are no arguments to 'end' that depend on a template
 parameter, so a declaration of 'end' must be available
```

The end() function is a member function, so call it as this->end(). Line 35 has the same problem, but the compiler's message is completely different, as shown in the following:

```
list6509.cpp:35: error: no matching function for call to 'insert(int&)'
```

However, as demonstrated in the following output, the next problem is harder:

```
list6509.cpp:39: error: no matching function for call to 'copy(int,
 std::_Rb_tree_const_iterator<int>, std::ostream_iterator<int, char,
 std::char_traits<char> >)'
```

Most likely, you already fixed the problem by qualifying the call to begin(). The compiler issues this message because it finds the global begin() function and tries to use it, but that function return int, which is not an iterator, so the compiler cannot use the std::copy algorithm.

As you can see, the compiler's error messages are not always helpful. Sometimes, the same problem yields different messages in different contexts. Nonetheless, the compiler usually directs you to the source of the problem, and you can usually figure it out from there.

Regardless of how the compiler looks up a name, when it looks up a function name and finds more than one overloaded declaration for that name, it must resolve the overloading and pick the one, best match. The next Exploration examines the rules that govern this selection.

# EXPLORATION 66

▪▪▪

# Overloaded Functions

**E**xploration 22 introduced the notion of overloaded functions. Exploration 28 continued the journey with overloaded operators. Since then, we've managed to get by with a common-sense understanding of overloading. I would be remiss without delving deeper into this subject, so let's finish the story of overloading by examining the rules of overloaded functions in greater depth.

## Review of Overloaded Functions

Let's refresh the memory a bit. A function or operator name is *overloaded* when two or more function declarations declare the same name in the same scope. C++ imposes some restrictions on when you are allowed to overload a function name.

The primary restriction is that overloaded functions must have different argument lists. This means the number of arguments must be different, or the type of at least one argument must be different.

```
void print(int value);
void print(double value);        // valid overload: different argument type
void print(int value, int width); // valid overload: different number of arguments
```

You are not allowed to define two functions in the same scope when the functions differ only in the return type.

```
void print(int);
int print(int);  // illegal
```

Member functions can also differ by the presence or absence of the const qualifier.

```
class demo {
   void print();
   void print() const; // valid: const qualifier is different
};
```

A member function cannot be overloaded with a static member function in the same class.

```
class demo {
   void print();
   static void print(); // illegal
};
```

A key point is that overloading occurs within a single scope. Names in one scope have no influence or impact on names in another scope. Remember that a code block is a scope (Exploration 12), a class is a scope (Exploration 38), and a namespace is a scope (Exploration 50).

Thus, member functions in a base class are in that class's scope and do not impact overloading of names in a derived class, which has its own scope, separate and distinct from the base class's scope.

When you define a function in a derived class, it *hides* all functions with the same name in a base class or in an outer scope. This rule is a specific example of the general rule that a name in an inner scope hides names in outer scopes. Thus, any name in a derived class hides names in base classes and at namespace scope. Any name in a block hides names in outer blocks, and so on. The only way to call a hidden function from a derived class is to qualify the function name, as shown in Listing 66-1.

**Listing 66-1.** *Qualifying a Member Function with the base Class Name*

```
#include <iostream>
#include <ostream>

class base {
public:
   void print(int x) { std::cout << "int: " << x << '\n'; }
};
class derived : public base {
public:
   void print(double x) { std::cout << "double: " << x << '\n'; }
};
int main()
{
   derived d;
   d.print(3);           // prints double: 3
   d.print(3.0);         // prints double: 3
   d.base::print(3);     // prints int: 3
   d.base::print(3.0);   // prints int: 3
}
```

Sometimes, however, you want overloading to take into account functions in the derived class and the functions from the base class, too. The solution is to inject the base class name into the derived class scope. You do this with a *using* declaration (Exploration 50). **Modify Listing 66-1 so derived sees both print functions**. Change main so it calls d.print with an int argument and with a double argument, with no qualifying names. **What output do you expect?**

Try it and compare your result with that in Listing 66-2.

**Listing 66-2.** *Overloading Named with a* using *Declaration*

```
#include <iostream>
#include <ostream>

class base {
public:
   void print(int x) { std::cout << "int: " << x << '\n'; }
};
class derived : public base {
public:
   void print(double x) { std::cout << "double: " << x << '\n'; }
   using base::print;
};
int main()
{
   derived d;
   d.print(3);           // prints int: 3
   d.print(3.0);         // prints double: 3
}
```

A *using* declaration imports all the overloaded functions with that name. To see this, **add print(long) to the base class and a corresponding function call to** main. Now your example should look something like Listing 66-3.

**Listing 66-3.** *Adding a Base Class Overload*

```
#include <iostream>
#include <ostream>

class base {
public:
   void print(int x) { std::cout << "int: " << x << '\n'; }
   void print(long x) { std::cout << "long: " << x << '\n'; }
};
class derived : public base {
public:
   void print(double x) { std::cout << "double: " << x << '\n'; }
   using base::print;
};
int main()
{
   derived d;
   d.print(3);           // prints int: 3
   d.print(3.0);         // prints double: 3
   d.print(3L);          // prints long: 3
}
```

The overload rules usually work well. You can clearly see which print function the compiler selects for each function call in main. Sometimes, however, the rules get murkier.

For example, suppose you were to add the line d.print(3.0f); to main. **What do you expect the program to print?**

_____

The compiler promotes the float 3.0f to type double, and calls print(double), so the output is as follows:

```
double: 3
```

That was too easy. What about a short? **Try d.print(short(3)). What happens?**

_____

The compiler promotes the short to type int, and produces the following output:

```
int: 3
```

That was still too easy. Now try unsigned. **Add d.print(3u). What happens?**

_____

That doesn't work at all, does it? To understand what went wrong, you need a better understanding of how overloading works in C++, and that's what the rest of this Exploration is all about.

# Overload Resolution

When the compiler sees a function call, it must match up the function name with a particular function declaration. When the compiler has multiple declarations for a single name (that is, when the function is overloaded), the compiler must _resolve_ the overload to pick the right function. To resolve an overload, the compiler considers the arguments and their types, the types of the function parameters in the function declaration, and type conversions and promotions that are necessary to convert the argument types to match the parameter types. The detailed rules are complicated, so this Exploration presents a slightly simplified view of the C++ universe, but one that should work well for most situations that you are likely to encounter.

The first step to overload resolution is for the compiler to search scopes until it finds the scope that declares the function name using ordinary lookup, or multiple scopes that declare function when using argument-dependent lookup (Exploration 50).

The next step is to collect all the function declarations with the same name. These functions are called the _candidate functions_. The list of candidates is then examined to determine which functions are _viable_. To be viable, a function must have the right number of parameters, and the arguments must match the parameter types, or the compiler can implicitly convert each argument to the parameter type.

Finally, the viable candidates are examined to determine the best one—that is, the one with the closest match between argument types and parameter types. If the compiler can't decide because two or more functions are "best," it issues an error for an ambiguous overload.

If the best match is inaccessible because it is a private or protected member function, the compiler issues an error. Otherwise, it has a match, and so compiles the code to call the matching function. The following sections describe each of these steps in depth.

## Candidate Functions

The candidate functions are all the functions in the target scope with the same name. The compiler resolves overloaded operators using the same mechanism as overloaded functions, and the compiler also considers built-in operators as candidates.

   If the function call is in a class context (member function body or initial value of a static data member), the candidate functions can be member or non-member functions. The compiler does not prefer one kind to another, but treats member and non-member functions equivalently, albeit with some constraints on the object reference for member function calls.

   Initialization of a class instance follows the same overloading rules, using the class's constructors as the candidate functions. If the constructor of class C takes a single argument of class-type (call it A), additional candidate functions are type conversion operators (Exploration 62) of A and its ancestor classes that return a value or reference to C or a derived class.

   Listing 66-4 shows some examples of overloading and how C++ determines candidate functions.

**Listing 66-4.** *Determining Candidate Functions for Overload Resolution*

```
 1 #include <iostream>
 2 #include <ostream>
 3 #include <string>
 4
 5 void print(std::string const& str) { std::cout << str; }
 6 void print(int x)                   { std::cout << "int: " << x; }
 7 void print(double x)                { std::cout << "double: " << x; }
 8
 9 class base {
10 public:
11    void print(std::string const& str) const { ::print(str); ::print("\n"); }
12    void print(std::string const& s1, std::string const& s2)
13    {
14      print(s1); print(s2);
15    }
16 };
17
18 class convert : public base {
19 public:
20    convert()              { print("convert()"); }
21    convert(double)        { print("convert(double)"); }
22    operator int() const   { print("convert::operator int()"); return 42; }
23    operator float() const { print("convert::operator float()"); return 3.14159f; }
24 };
25
26 class demo : public base {
```

```
27 public:
28   demo(int)       { print("demo(int)"); }
29   demo(long)      { print("demo(long)"); }
30   demo(convert)   { print("demo(convert)"); }
31   demo(int, int)  { print("demo(int, int)"); }
32 };
33
34 class other {
35 public:
36   other()          { std::cout << "other::other()\n"; }
37   other(int,int) { std::cout << "other::other(int, int)\n"; }
38   operator convert() const
39   {
40     std::cout << "other::operator convert()\n"; return convert();
41   }
42 };
43
44 int operator+(demo const&, demo const&)
45 {
46   print("operator+(demo,demo)\n"); return 42;
47 }
48
49 int operator+(int, demo const&) { print("operator+(int,demo)\n"); return 42; }
50
51 int main()
52 {
53   other x;
54   demo d(x);
55   3L + d;
56   short s(2);
57   d + s;
58 }
```

The candidate functions for constructing d are the four demo constructors. The overloaded + operator also has three candidate functions: two user-defined and the built-in + operator. You can immediately see that the compiler cannot use the built-in + operator to add a demo object. That is an example of a function that is not viable. The next section explains how the compiler keeps only the viable candidate functions.

## Viable Functions

Once the compiler has its list of candidate functions, it examines the function call arguments and the candidate functions' parameters and decides which candidate functions are *viable*. A viable function is one for which the compiler can match up arguments with parameters, so that every parameter has an argument, and every argument is associated with a parameter.

Step one toward determining viability is matching each argument with a parameter. If any arguments are left over without parameters, that candidate function is not viable. If any parameters lack an argument, that candidate is not viable.

In order to normalize member and non-member candidate functions, the compiler treats the class as an implicit parameter for non-static member functions and considers the target object of a member function call as an implicit argument.

In addition to mere argument count, the compiler also ensures that it can convert each argument to the corresponding parameter type using its normal rules for type conversion. If the compiler cannot convert an argument to the parameter type, the function is not viable.

Of the four demo constructors in Listing 66-4, the two-argument form is not viable on line 54 because it has the wrong number of arguments. The int and long forms are not viable because the compiler cannot convert the other argument to either type. Thus, only one candidate is viable, so it is the one the compiler uses.

On line 55, the built-in + operator is not viable, but both user-defined forms are viable. The compiler must decide which one is better, as described in the next section.

## Best Viable Function

Once the compiler has narrowed the candidate list to only the viable candidates, it must pick the best viable function as the one to call. The compiler determines which candidate is best by checking how it must convert the arguments to the corresponding parameter types.

The compiler has several tools at its disposal to convert one type to another. Many of these you've seen earlier in the book, such as promoting arithmetic types (Exploration 23), converting a derived-class reference to a base-class reference (Exploration 37), or calling a type-conversion operator (Exploration 62). The compiler assembles a series of conversions into an implicit conversion sequence (ICS). An ICS is a sequence of small conversion steps that the compiler can apply to a function-call argument with the end result of converting the argument to the type of the corresponding function parameter.

An ICS may involve standard conversions or user-defined conversions. A *standard* conversion is inherent in the C++ language, such as arithmetic conversions. A *user-defined* conversion involves constructors and type conversion operators on class and enumerated types. A *standard ICS* is an ICS that contains only standard conversions. A *user-defined ICS* consists of a standard ICS, a single user-defined conversion, and another standard ICS.

For example, converting short to const int is a standard ICS with two steps: promoting short to int and adding the const qualifier. Line 11 of Listing 66-4 demonstrates a user-defined ICS. It begins with a standard ICS that converts an array of char to a char pointer, then a user-defined conversion, namely, the std::string constructor.

One exception is that invoking a copy constructor to copy identical source and destination type or derived-class source to a base-class type is a standard conversion, not user-defined conversion, even though the conversions invoke user-defined copy constructors.

The compiler needs to pick the best ICS of all the viable candidates. As part of this determination, it must be able to rank standard conversions within an ICS. The three ranks are, from best to worst: exact match, promotion, and conversion.

An *exact match* is when the argument type is the same as the parameter type. Examples of exact match conversions are:

- Changing only the qualification, e.g., the argument is type int and the parameter is const int
- Converting an array to a pointer (Exploration 59), e.g., char[10] to char*
- Converting an lvalue to an rvalue, e.g., int& to int

A *promotion* (Exploration 23) is an implicit conversion from a smaller arithmetic type (such as short) to a larger type (such as int).

All other implicit type conversions have *conversion* rank—for example, arithmetic conversions that discard information (such as long to int), and derived-class pointers to base-class pointers.

The rank of an ICS is the worst rank of all the conversions in the sequence. For example, converting short to const int involves an *exact match* conversion (const) and a *promotion* (short to int), so the rank for the ICS is *promotion*.

If one argument is an implicit object argument (for member function calls), the compiler ranks any conversions needed for it, too.

Now that you know how the compiler ranks standard conversions, you can see how it uses this information to compare ICSes. The compiler applies the following rules to determine which of two ICSes is better:

- A standard ICS is better than a user-defined ICS.

- An ICS with better rank is better than an ICS with a worse rank.

- An ICS that is a proper subset of another ICS is better.

- A user-defined ICS, ICS1, is better than another user-defined ICS, ICS2, if they have the same user conversion, and the second standard conversion in ICS1 is better than the second standard conversion of ICS2.

- Less restrictive types are better than more restrictive ones. This means an ICS with target type T1 is better than an ICS with target type T2 if T1 and T2 have the same base type, but T2 is const and T1 is not.

- A standard conversion sequence ICS1 is better than ICS2 if they have the same rank, but:

  - ICS1 converts a pointer to bool, or

  - ICS1 and ICS2 convert pointers to classes related by inheritance, and ICS1 is a "smaller" conversion. A smaller conversion is one that hops over fewer intermediate base classes. For example, if A derives from B and B from C, then converting B* to C* is better than converting A* to C*, and converting C* to void* is better than A* to void*.

If two conversion sequences are equally good, the compiler prefers a non-template function to a template function.

## CONVERSION TO BOOL

You know that the istream and ostream objects have an implicit conversion to bool that returns not fail(). They do not have a type conversion operator that returns bool. Instead, the type conversion operator returns void*, and the compiler implicitly converts the pointer to bool. As you can see in the overloading rules, the compiler prefers an ICS that converts a pointer to bool.

You should do the same for any class that you think should be usable as a condition. Implement a type conversion operator to void const*, and return a non-null pointer for true:

```
operator void const*() const {
  if (state_is_good())
    return this;
  else
    return 0;
}
```

Never write a type conversion operator to `bool`. The problem with such an operator is that it permits arithmetic on your object by implicitly converting `bool` to an `int`. A conversion to a pointer is safer and works just as well in a condition as a conversion to `bool`.

Thus, for each viable candidate, the compiler determines the sequence of conversions it needs to convert each argument to the desired parameter type. It then ranks these sequences and tries to find the best by comparing pairs of sequences. If it finds one viable candidate that is unequivocally better than all the others, that one is the best viable candidate and is the one the compiler uses. If the compiler cannot distinguish between two or more viable candidates at the top of the list, it reports an ambiguity error.

**What output do you expect from the program in Listing 66-4?**

_____

_____

_____

_____

_____

Most of the time, common-sense rules help you understand how C++ resolves overloading. Sometimes, however, you find the compiler reporting an ambiguity when you did not expect any. Other times, the compiler cannot find any viable candidates when you expected it to find at least one. The really bad cases are when you make a mistake and the compiler is able to find a unique best viable candidate anyway. Your tests fail, but when reading the code, you look in the wrong place because you expect the compiler to complain about bad code.

Sometimes, your compiler helps you by identifying the viable candidates that are tied for best viable candidate, or showing you candidate functions when none of them are viable. Sometimes, however, you might need to sit down with the rules and go over them carefully to figure out why the compiler isn't happy. To help you prepare for that day, Listing 66-5 presents some overloading errors. **See if you can find and fix the problems.**

**Listing 66-5.** *Fix the Overloading Errors*

```
#include <iostream>
#include <ostream>
#include <string>
```

```
void easy(long) {}
void easy(double) {}
void call_easy() {
    easy(42);
}

void pointer(double*) {}
void pointer(void*) {}
const int zero = 0;
void call_pointer() {
    pointer(&zero);
}

int add(int a) { return a; }
int add(int a, int b) { return a + b; }
int add(int a, int b, int c) { return a + b + c; }
int add(int a, int b, int c, int d) { return a + b + c + d; }
int add(int a, int b, int c, int d, int e) { return a + b + c + d + e; }
void call_add() {
    add(1, 2, 3L, 4.0);
}

void ref(int const&) {}
void ref(int) {}
void call_ref() {
    int x;
    ref(x);
}

class base {};
class derived : public base {};
class sibling : public base {};
class most_derived : public derived {};

void tree(derived&, sibling&) {}
void tree(most_derived&, base&) {}
void call_tree() {
    sibling s;
    most_derived md;
    tree(md, s);
}
```

The argument to easy() is an int, but the overloads are for long and double. Both conversions have conversion rank and neither one is better than the other, so the compiler issues an ambiguity error.

The problem with pointer() is that neither overload is viable. If zero were not const, the conversion to void* would be the sole viable candidate.

The add() function has all int parameters, but one argument is long and another is double. No problem, the compiler can convert long to int and double to int. You may not like the results, but it is able to do it, so it does. In other words, the problem here is that the compiler does not have a problem with this function. This isn't really an overloading problem, but you may not see it that way if you run into this problem at work.

Do you see the missing & in the second ref() function? The compiler considers both ref() functions to be equally good. If you declare the second to be ref(int&), it becomes the best viable candidate. The exact reason is that the type of x is int&, not int, that is, x is an int lvalue, an object that the program can modify. The subtle distinction has not been important before now, but with respect to overloading, the difference is crucial. The conversion from an lvalue to an rvalue has rank exact match, but it is a conversion step. The conversion from int& to int const& also has exact match. Faced with two candidates with one exact match conversion each, the compiler cannot decide which one is better. Changing int to int& removes the conversion step, and that function becomes the unambiguous best.

Both tree() functions require one conversion from derived-class reference to base-class reference, so the compiler cannot decide which one is better. The first call to tree requires a conversion of the first argument from most_derived& to derived&. The second call requires a conversion of the second argument from sibling& to base&.

# Default Arguments

Now that you think overloading is so frightfully complicated that you never want to overload a function, I will add yet another complexity. C++ lets you define a default argument for a parameter, which lets a function call omit the corresponding argument. You can define default arguments for any number of parameters, provided you begin with the right-most parameter and don't skip any. You can provide default arguments for every parameter, if you wish. Default arguments are often easy to understand. Read Listing 66-6 for an example.

**Listing 66-6.** *Default Arguments*

```cpp
#include <iostream>
#include <ostream>

int add(int x = 0, int y = 0)
{
  return x + y;
}

int main()
{
  std::cout << add() << '\n';
  std::cout << add(5) << '\n';
  std::cout << add(32, add(4, add(6))) << '\n';
}
```

**What does the program in Listing 66-6 print?**

_____

_____

_____

It's not hard to predict the results, which are shown in the following output:

```
0
5
42
```

Default arguments offer a shortcut in lieu of overloading. For example, instead of writing several constructors for the rational type, you can get by with one constructor and default arguments:

```
template<class T> class rational {
public:
  rational(T const& num = T(0), T const& den = T(1))
  : numerator_(num), denominator(den)
  {
    reduce();
  }
  ...omitted for brevity...
};
```

Our definition of a default constructor must change somewhat. Instead of being a constructor that declares no parameters, a default constructor is one that you can call with no arguments. This rational constructor meets that requirement.

As you may have guessed, default arguments complicate overload resolution. When the compiler searches for viable candidates, it checks every argument that explicitly appears in the function call, but does not check default argument types against their corresponding parameter types. As a result, you can run into ambiguous situations more easily with default arguments. For example, suppose you added the example rational constructor to the existing class template without deleting the old constructors. The following definitions would both result in ambiguity errors:

```
rational<int> zero;
rational<int> one(1);
```

Although you may not believe me, my intention was not to scare you away from overloading functions. Rarely will you have to delve into the subtleties of overloading. Most of the time, you can rely on common sense.

But sometimes, the compiler disagrees with your common sense. Knowing the compiler's rules can help you escape from a jam when the compiler complains about an ambiguous overload or other problems.

---

**■Tip** When you write overloaded functions, it shouldn't matter which exact function the compiler chooses. Be sure that every implementation of a particular function name has the same logical behavior. For example, when you use an output operator, `cout << x`, you just let the compiler pick the correct overload for `operator<<`, and you don't need to concern yourself with the detailed rules as laid out in this Exploration.

---

The next Exploration visits another aspect of C++ programming for which the rules can be complicated and scary: template metaprogramming.

# EXPLORATION 67

▪▪▪

# Metaprogramming

**S**imply put, metaprogramming is writing code that runs at compile time. This Exploration merely touches the surface of metaprogramming. If you want to learn more, see *Modern C++ Programming*, by Andrei Alexandrescu (Addison-Wesley, 2001) and *C++ Template Metaprogramming*, by David Abrahams and Aleksey Gurtovoy (Addison-Wesley, 2005).

## Compile-Time Programming

The simple definition of a metaprogram is code that runs at compile time. The compiler compiles and runs the metaprogram when it compiles the normal program. In C++, metaprograms are written using templates. Unfortunately, templates were not designed for compile-time programming, so the syntax is contorted and the semantics are limited. Nonetheless, metaprogramming is a useful technique for the advanced C++ programmer.

Many experienced C++ programmers will not approach metaprogramming out of fear of its complexities and difficulties. I don't blame them. It is a difficult subject, but one with rich rewards for those who dare to tackle it.

Another reason some accomplished C++ programmers avoid template metaprogramming is that it requires a different style of programming, namely functional programming. Or, put another way, the language has no variables in which to store the metaprogram's state—only functions. In a metaprogram, a template serves the role of the function.

This Exploration introduces the topic and lets you see what it's all about, but it doesn't teach you enough to run off and program a video game as a metaprogram.

## Template Specialization

The key to metaprogramming lies in template specialization. Although some metaprogramming examples are mere freak shows, other examples are seriously useful.

Recall the `fixed` class template from Exploration 49. That implementation of `fixed` relied on static constants `places` and `places10`, but only `places` could be initialized with a compile-time constant. The trick is to determine how to initialize `places10` with a compile-time constant. Somehow, you need to compute $10^{places}$ at compile time. It turns out you can do that with template metaprogramming. See Listing 67-1 for an excerpt of the `fixed` class template.

**Listing 67-1.** *Excerpt of the fixed Class Template*

```
template<class T, int N>
class fixed
{
public:
  typedef T value_type;
  static T const places = N;
  static T const places10 = power10<N>::value;

  fixed() : value_(0) {}
  fixed(value_type integer) : value_(integer * places10) {}

  value_type integer()  const { return value() / places10; }
  value_type fraction() const;
  value_type value()    const { return value_; }
private:
  value_type value_;
};

template<class T, int N>
typename fixed<T, N>::value_type fixed<T, N>::fraction()
const
{
  return std::abs(value()) % places10;
}
```

The interesting part is power10<N>::value. Clearly, power10 is a template, and the template argument is N. Somehow, this template raises 10 to the Nth power and uses it to initialize a compile-time constant data member, value.

Here's a hint: template metaprograming is a form of functional programming, so think in terms of recursion instead of iteration. Thus, the primary template for power10 is recursive, so power10<N>::value is equal to 10 times power10<N - 1>::value. That's not so hard, is it?

Every recursive algorithm must terminate. When computing a power, the base case is when the exponent is zero: $10^0$ is 1. Define the base case as an explicit specialization. It's that simple, as you can see in Listing 67-2.

**Listing 67-2.** *Simple Implementation of the power10 Class Template*

```
template<unsigned N>
struct power10
{
  enum t { value = 10 * power10<N - 1>::value };
};

template<>
struct power10<0>
```

```
{
  enum t { value = 1 };
};
```

Notice the use of enum to define value. One advantage of using enum instead of a static const data member is that enum does not require a separate definition of the data member. When using enum, be sure to provide a name for the enumerated type. Template type parameters must be named; you never know where you will want to use value. The name isn't important because its scope is limited to the power10 class template, so I just use t, for type.

**Write a program to test the power10 class template.** My test program is presented in Listing 67-3.

**Listing 67-3.** *Testing the power10 Class Template*

```
#include "power10.hpp"
#include "test.hpp"

int main()
{
  test(power10<0>::value == 1);
  test(power10<1>::value == 10);
  test(power10<2>::value == 100);
  test(power10<3>::value == 1000);
  test(power10<9>::value == 1000000000);
}
```

Template recursion can stress a compiler. The power10 template is unlikely to run into any limitations, but the compiler limits the recursion depth, and some metaprograms hit that limit all too easily. Any reduction in recursion depth can be helpful, possibly the difference between successful compilation and abandoning that compiler. **Can you see how to improve the power10 implementation?** _____ **If so, how?**

_____

_____

Instead of multiplying by 10 each time the template recurses, square the value and divide N by 2. Instead of a recursion depth of N, the depth becomes log N. In this particular case, the difference becomes important with large values of N on a 64-bit platform. If N is large enough, or with a different metaprogram, substituting an $O(\log N)$ algorithm for an $O(N)$ algorithm can be a huge win. Implementing the improved version of power10 requires partial template specialization.

# Partial Specialization

Template metaprogramming often requires partial specialization. As I discussed in the previous section, substituting an $O(\log N)$ algorithm for a $O(N)$ algorithm can sometimes make the difference between successful compilation and breaking a compiler.

The plan is to compute 10 raised to the Nth power: if N is even, square the result of power10<N / 2>::value. If N is odd, multiply power10<N - 1>::value by 10. Define the base case of power10<0>::value as 1. All you need to do is to figure out how to squeeze an if statement into a template specialization.

Hmm. Tricky, isn't it? Remember that template metaprogramming is all about specialization. Thus, conditions are also implemented using specialization.

Define an auxiliary template—call it power10_aux—that has two parameters: N and a bool parameter to indicate whether N is even. At first, the second parameter appears to be redundant. You can always determine whether a number is even, so the parameter offers no new information. This is true. What the second parameter offers is an opportunity for partial specialization. In this case, you need two templates, so arbitrarily pick the primary template to be even or odd. Let's say odd. Thus, the primary template computes the power of 10 for an odd number, and the partial specialization kicks in only when the second template argument is true, at which point it computes the power of 10 for an even number. Listing 67-4 shows the details.

**Listing 67-4.** *Computing a Power of 10 Efficiently*

```
template<int N>
struct power10; // forward declaration

template<int N>
struct square
{
  // A metaprogramming function to square a value.
  enum t { value = N * N };
};

template<int N, bool Even>
struct power10_aux
{
  // Primary template is for odd N (Even is false)
  enum t { value = 10 * power10<N - 1>::value };
};

template<int N>
struct power10_aux<N, true>
{
  // Specialization when N is even: square the value
  enum t { value = square<power10<N / 2>::value>::value };
};

template<int N>
struct power10
{
  enum t { value = power10_aux<N, N % 2 == 0>::value };
};
```

```
template<>
struct power10<0>
{
  enum t { value = 1 };
};
```

The first declaration is a forward declaration, which notifies the compiler that power10 is the name of a class template. Note that it is a declaration, not a definition. You need to supply the definition later, but by declaring the name early, you can use it in the power10_aux template.

The compiler needs a complete type when it instantiates the template, but not when you are defining the template. That's why power10_aux can refer to the value member of power10 even before power10 has been defined.

One difficulty I encountered when I first attempted metaprogramming was that I kept forgetting the ::value parts. I fell into the trap of thinking of power10 as a kind of compile-time "function." That's how we're using it, but it's not a real function. It's a class, and a class doesn't have a value. The only way to get a value out of a class is to declare a member: a compile-time constant data member or a member enumerated type. By convention, I always use the same name, value, so I can mix and match all my metaprogramming class templates without confusion.

Most programmers don't spend much time metaprogramming, but there are a number of situations when it can be extremely helpful, especially for library writers. For extra credit, complete the job started in Exploration 49. Your task is to finish converting the fixed class to a template with two parameters: a base type, and the number of places after the decimal point. Use the new power10 class template to help. This is actually quite a big job, with some subtle pitfalls. If you have difficulty, consult Listing 67-5, which shows the class definition and free function declarations. If you still have trouble, grab the entire *fixed.hpp* file from this book's web site.

**Listing 67-5.** *The fixed Class Template*

```
#ifndef FIXED_HPP_
#define FIXED_HPP_

#include <iomanip>
#include <istream>
#include <ostream>
#include <sstream>
#include <string>
#include <stdexcept>

#include "power10.hpp"

template<class T=long, int N=4>
class fixed
{
public:
  class fixed_error : std::runtime_error
  {
```

```
public:
  fixed_error(std::string const& arg) : runtime_error(arg) {}
};
typedef T value_type;                        ///< Type of the actual value
static int const places = N;                 ///< number of decimal places
static value_type const places10 = power10<N>::value;   ///< 10<sup>places</sup>

fixed();
fixed(value_type integer);
fixed(value_type integer, value_type fraction);
fixed(double value);
template<class U, int M>
fixed(fixed<U, M> const& rhs);

template<class U, int M>
fixed& operator=(fixed<U, M> rhs);

std::string as_string() const;
bool read(std::istream& strm);
/// Convert to some other type, especially floating point.
template<class U>
U convert() const;

/// Round off to the nearest integer.
value_type round() const;

/// Return the integer part (without rounding).
value_type integer() const;
/// Return the fraction part to @p M decimal places.
template<int M>
value_type fraction() const;
/// Return the fraction part to @p N (or @p places ) decimal places.
value_type fraction() const { return fraction<places>(); }

fixed& operator+=(fixed f);
fixed& operator-=(fixed f);
fixed& operator*=(fixed f);
fixed& operator/=(fixed f);

fixed& operator+=(T i);
fixed& operator-=(T i);
fixed& operator*=(T i);
fixed& operator/=(T i);

void negate();

fixed& operator++();
fixed operator++(int);
```

```
  fixed& operator--();
  fixed operator--(int);

  /// Return the internal value.
  value_type value();

private:
  value_type reduce(value_type frac);
  value_type make_value(value_type integer, value_type fraction);
  value_type value_;
};


/// Negate a fixed value
template<class T, int N>
fixed<T,N> operator-(fixed<T,N> a);

template<class T, int N>
std::istream& operator>>(std::istream& strm, fixed<T,N>& f);

/// Write a fixed value
template<class T, int N>
std::ostream& operator<<(std::ostream& strm, fixed<T,N> f);

/// Add fixed values
template<class T, int N> fixed<T,N> operator+(fixed<T,N> a, fixed<T,N> b);
template<class T, int N> fixed<T,N> operator+(fixed<T,N> a, T b);
template<class T, int N> fixed<T,N> operator+(T a, fixed<T,N> b);

/// Subtract fixed values
template<class T, int N> fixed<T,N> operator-(fixed<T,N> a, fixed<T,N> b);
template<class T, int N> fixed<T,N> operator-(fixed<T,N> a, T b);
template<class T, int N> fixed<T,N> operator-(T a, fixed<T,N> b);

/// Multiply fixed values
template<class T, int N> fixed<T,N> operator*(fixed<T,N> a, fixed<T,N> b);
template<class T, int N> fixed<T,N> operator*(fixed<T,N> a, T b);
template<class T, int N> fixed<T,N> operator*(T a, fixed<T,N> b);

/// Divide fixed values
template<class T, int N> fixed<T,N> operator/(fixed<T,N> a, fixed<T,N> b);
template<class T, int N> fixed<T,N> operator/(fixed<T,N> a, T b);
template<class T, int N> fixed<T,N> operator/(T a, fixed<T,N> b);

template<class T, int N> bool operator==(fixed<T,N> a, fixed<T,N> b);
template<class T, int N> bool operator==(fixed<T,N> a, T b);
template<class T, int N> bool operator==(T a, fixed<T,N> b);
template<class T, int N> bool operator!=(fixed<T,N> a, fixed<T,N> b);
```

```
template<class T, int N> bool operator!=(fixed<T,N> a, T b);
template<class T, int N> bool operator!=(T a, fixed<T,N> b);
template<class T, int N> bool operator<(fixed<T,N> a, fixed<T,N> b);
template<class T, int N> bool operator<(fixed<T,N> a, T b);
template<class T, int N> bool operator<(T a, fixed<T,N> b);
template<class T, int N> bool operator>(fixed<T,N> a, fixed<T,N> b);
template<class T, int N> bool operator>(fixed<T,N> a, T b);
template<class T, int N> bool operator>(T a, fixed<T,N> b);
template<class T, int N> bool operator<=(fixed<T,N> a, fixed<T,N> b);
template<class T, int N> bool operator<=(fixed<T,N> a, T b);
template<class T, int N> bool operator<=(T a, fixed<T,N> b);
template<class T, int N> bool operator>=(fixed<T,N> a, fixed<T,N> b);
template<class T, int N> bool operator>=(fixed<T,N> a, T b);
template<class T, int N> bool operator>=(T a, fixed<T,N> b);
```

```
#endif
```

One interesting aspect of metaprogramming with templates is that templates can operate on types as well as values. Using functional programming techniques, you can create lists of types and manipulate those lists in ways that LISP programmers would find astonishingly familiar.

In case you still think metaprogramming is primarily about parlor tricks, consider the homely vector and its insert member functions, which insert values into a vector (Exploration 51). One form of insert takes an unsigned integer count, n, and a value. The function inserts n copies of the value. Another form takes two iterators and copies all the values from that range into the vector. Both functions take an iterator argument; the values are inserted just before that iterator. As with any function that operates on iterators, the second form of insert is a template function, accepting any input iterator as an argument. The two functions are declared as follows:

```
void insert(iterator pos, size_type n, const value_type& value = value_type());
template<class InputIterator>
void insert(iterator pos, InputIterator first, InputIterator last);
```

Consider the following code:

```
std::vector<int> data;
data.insert(data.end(), 2, 10);
```

The compiler applies the usual rules of overloading. The type of 2 is int, but the first form of insert requires an unsigned integer as the first argument (the precise type is implementation-defined). The two arguments have the same type (int), which makes it a perfect match for the iterator form of insert.

Clearly, 2 and 10 are not input iterators. Rather than cause the compiler to fail in this case, the C++ standard requires the templatized insert function to interpret integer arguments as a count and a value. The second insert function behaves in the same manner as the first form of insert when its arguments are integers. In other words, the template form of insert has two distinct behaviors, depending on the template parameters. This is completely different from distinguishing between different kinds of iterators. How would you write a function that determines whether the type of its arguments are integral, and use a completely different implementation for integers than for iterators?

What you need is a little compile-time program that has a compile-time if statement to dispatch to two completely different functions. There are a variety of ways to solve this problem, and most involve template specialization and metaprogramming. Listing 67-6 gives you an idea of one approach to solving this problem.

**Listing 67-6.** *Using Metaprogramming to Implement vector's insert Function*

```
// is_integral<T>::type is true_type if T is an integral type, or false_type
// if T is any other type. A const type is the same as the base type.
class true_type {};
class false_type {};
template<class T>
struct is_integral {
   typedef false_type type;
};
template<> struct is_integral<int>          { typedef true_type type; };
template<> struct is_integral<char>         { typedef true_type type; };
template<> struct is_integral<unsigned int> { typedef true_type type; };
// etc. for all the built-in integral types

template<class T>
template<class InputIterator>
void vector<T>::do_insert(iterator pos, InputIterator first, InputIterator last,
                          false_type const&)
{
    // The real function is more complicated because it must handle exceptions
    // that might be thrown in the middle of copying. But you get the idea.
    for ( ; first != last; ++first)
        pos = insert(pos, *first);
}

template<class T>
template<class IntType>
void vector<T>::do_insert(iterator pos, IntType first, IntType last,
                          true_type const&)
{
    // Cast to an exact match to the other insert function.
    insert(pos, static_cast<size_type>(first),
           static_cast<value_type const&>(last));
}

template<class T>
template<class InputIterator>
void vector<T>::insert(iterator pos, InputIterator first, InputIterator last)
{
    do_insert(pos, first, last, is_integral<InputIterator>::type());
}
```

The is_integral class template is another example of a traits template (Exploration 64), this time revealing whether a type is an integral type. Partial specialization chooses the iterator form of insert or the integer form of insert, according to whether the type is integral. If you don't want to write your own is_integral template, use Boost, TR1, or the next language revision, which all contain a rich suite of type traits templates.

Here is one last exercise in template metaprogramming. See if you can wrap your head around metaprogramming and **write a class template, is_same, that takes two type parameters and declares an enum type with a single literal, value. The numeric value of value is equal to true if the two template parameters are the same type; otherwise it is false**. Think about how you can use partial specialization to help you solve the problem. My solution is displayed in Listing 67-7.

**Listing 67-7.** *Testing Two Types to See Whether They Are the Same*

```
#include <iostream>
#include <ostream>

template<class T, class U>
struct is_same {
   // Assume the types are different.
   enum t { value = false };
};

template<class T>
struct is_same<T, T> {
   // Partial specialization for when the types are the same
   enum t { value = true };
};

enum x { a };
enum y { b };

int main()
{
   std::cout << is_same<int, int>::value << '\n';
   std::cout << is_same<int, int&>::value << '\n';
   std::cout << is_same<int, unsigned>::value << '\n';
   std::cout << is_same<int, const int>::value << '\n';
   std::cout << is_same<x, y>::value << '\n';
   std::cout << is_same<int, signed>::value << '\n';
}
```

Don't worry if you don't get metaprogramming yet. It is an advanced topic, and a full understanding is beyond the scope of this book. I wanted to introduce the topic, however, because it is one of the highlights of programming in C++.

# EXPLORATION 68

■■■

# Project 4: Calculator

**N**ow is the time to apply everything you have learned in this book by writing a simple, textual calculator. If you type 1 + 2, for example, the calculator prints 3. This project can be as complicated as you wish or dare to make it. I recommend starting small and adding capability slowly and incrementally:

1. Start with a simple parser to read numbers and operators. If you are familiar with a parser generator, such as Bison or Antlr, go ahead and use it. If you are feeling adventurous, try learning about Spirit, which is part of the Boost project. Spirit makes use of C++ operator overloading to implement a BNF-like syntax for writing a parser in C++ without requiring additional tools. If you don't want to involve other tools or libraries, I recommend a simple, LISP-like syntax so you don't spend all your time on the parser. The code on this book's web site implements a simple, recursive-descent parser. Implement the basic arithmetic operators first: +, -, *, and /. Use double for all numbers. Do something helpful when dividing by zero.

2. Then add variables and the = operator. Initialize the calculator with some useful constants, such as pi.

3. The big leap forward is not to evaluate every expression when it is typed, but to create a parse tree. This requires some work on the parser, not to mention the addition of the parse-tree classes, that is, classes to represent expressions, variables, and values.

4. Given variables and parse trees, it is a smaller step to define functions and call user-defined functions.

5. Finally, add the ability to save functions to a file, and load them from a file. Now you can create libraries of useful functions.

6. If you are truly ambitious, try supporting multiple types. Use the pimpl idiom (Exploration 64) to define a number class and a number_impl class. Let the calculator use the number class, which frees it from the number_impl class. Implement derived classes for the types you want to support: integer, double, rational, etc.

As you can see, this kind of project can continue as long as you want it to. There will always be another feature to add. Just be sure to add features in small increments.

Similarly, your journey toward C++ expertise never ends. There will always be new surprises: waiting just around the corner, in the middle of your next project, with the next compiler upgrade. As I write this, the standardization committee is finishing work on the next version of the C++ language standard. After that will come the next language-revision cycle, and the next, and the next.

I wish you luck on your voyage, and I hope you enjoy the explorations to come.

# Index

# You Need the Companion eBook

**Your purchase of this book entitles you to buy the companion PDF-version eBook for only $10. Take the weightless companion with you anywhere.**

We believe this Apress title will prove so indispensable that you'll want to carry it with you everywhere, which is why we are offering the companion eBook (in PDF format) for $10 to customers who purchase this book now. Convenient and fully searchable, the PDF version of any content-rich, page-heavy Apress book makes a valuable addition to your programming library. You can easily find and copy code—or perform examples by quickly toggling between instructions and the application. Even simultaneously tackling a donut, diet soda, and complex code becomes simplified with hands-free eBooks!

Once you purchase your book, getting the $10 companion eBook is simple:

**❶** Visit **www.apress.com/promo/tendollars/**.

**❷** Complete a basic registration form to receive a randomly generated question about this title.

**❸** Answer the question correctly in 60 seconds, and you will receive a promotional code to redeem for the $10.00 eBook.

THE EXPERT'S VOICE™

2855 TELEGRAPH AVENUE | SUITE 600 | BERKELEY, CA 94705

**Offer valid through 6/22/09.**